An Introduction to Programming Using
Visual Basic®
Tenth Edition

David I. Schneider

University of Maryland

PEARSON

Boston Columbus Hoboken Indianapolis New York San Francisco
Amsterdam Cape Town Dubai London Madrid Milan Munich Paris Montreal Toronto
Delhi Mexico City São Paulo Sydney Hong Kong Seoul Singapore Taipei Tokyo

Vice President, Editorial Director, ECS: Marcia Horton
Executive Editor: Tracy Johnson
Editorial Assistant: Kristy Alaura
Vice President of Marketing: Christy Lesko
Director of Field Marketing: Tim Galligan
Product Marketing Manager: Bram Van Kempen
Field Marketing Manager: Demetrius Hall
Marketing Assistant: Jon Bryant
Director of Product Management: Erin Gregg
Team Lead, Program and Project Management:
    Scott Disanno
Program Manager: Carole Snyder
Senior Specialist, Program Planning and Support:
    Maura Zaldivar-Garcia

Cover Designer: Marta Samsel, Black Horse Designs
Manager, Rights and Permissions: Ben Ferrini
Project Manager, Rights and Permissions:
    Tamara Efsen, Aptara
Inventory Manager: Ann Lam
Cover Image: Justine Beckett/Alamy Stock Photo
Media Project Manager: Leslie Sumrall
Composition: SPi Global
Project Manager: Shylaja Gattupalli, SPi Global
Printer/Binder: RR Donnelley/Kendallville
Cover and Insert Printer: Phoenix Color/Hagerstown

Library of Congress Cataloging-in-Publication Data

Names: Schneider, David I., author.
Title: An introduction to programming using Visual Basic / David I.
    Schneider, University of Maryland.
Description: Tenth edition. | Boston : Pearson Education, [2017] | Includes
    bibliographical references and index.
Identifiers: LCCN 2016003346| ISBN 9780134542782 | ISBN 0134542789
Subjects: LCSH: BASIC (Computer program language) | Visual Basic.
Classification: LCC QA76.73.B3 S333633 2017 | DDC 005.26/8--dc23 LC record
available at http://lccn.loc.gov/2016003346

PEARSON

1   16

ISBN - 10: 0-13-454278-9
ISBN - 13: 978-0-13-454278-2

Attention Students

Installing Visual Studio

To complete the tutorials and programming problems in this book, you need to install Visual Studio 2015 on your computer.

We recommend that you download Visual Studio Community 2015 from the following Web site, and install it on your system:

www.visualstudio.com

Visual Studio Community 2015 is a free, full-featured development environment, and is a perfect companion for this textbook.

 NOTE: If you are working in your school's computer lab, there is a good chance that Microsoft Visual Studio has already been installed. If this is the case, your instructor will show you how to start Visual Studio.

Installing the Student Sample Program Files

The Student Sample Program files that accompany this book are available for download from the book's companion Web site at:

http://www.pearsonhighered.com/cs-resources

These files are required for many of the book's tutorials. Simply download the Student Sample Program files to a location on your hard drive where you can easily access them.

VideoNote

Guide to VideoNotes

www.pearsonhighered.com/cs-resources

Guide to Application Topics

Business and Economics

General Interest

Mathematics

Sports and Games

CONTENTS

Chapter 4 Decisions   113

Chapter 5 General Procedures   179

Chapter 6 Repetition   241

Chapter 7 Arrays   293

Chapter 8   Text Files   395

Chapter 9   Additional Controls and Objects   453

Chapter 10   Databases   513

Chapter 11 Object-Oriented Programming 551

Appendices 603

Answers 629

Index 695

PREFACE

Visual Basic has been a widely used programming language since its introduction in 1991. Its latest incarnation, Visual Basic 2015, brings continued refinement of the language. Visual Basic programmers are enthusiastically embracing the powerful capabilities of the language. Likewise, students learning their first programming language will find VB the ideal tool to understand the development of computer programs.

My objectives when writing this text were as follows:

1. *To develop focused chapters.* Rather than covering many topics superficially, I concentrate on important subjects and cover them thoroughly.

2. *To use examples and exercises with which students can relate, appreciate, and feel comfortable.* I frequently use real data. Examples do not have so many embellishments that students are distracted from the programming techniques illustrated.

3. *To produce compactly written text that students will find both readable and informative.* The main points of each topic are discussed first and then the peripheral details are presented as comments.

4. *To teach good programming practices that are in step with modern programming methodology.* Problem solving techniques and structured programming are discussed early and used throughout the book. The style follows object-oriented programming principles.

5. *To provide insights into the major applications of computers.*

What's New in the Tenth Edition

Among the changes in this edition, the following are the most significant.

1. ***Visual Basic Upgraded*** The version of Visual Basic has been upgraded from Visual Basic 2012 to Visual Basic 2015, and relevant new features of Visual Basic 2015 have been addressed.

2. ***Additional Exercises*** Sixty new exercises have been added, most of which are application exercises.

3. ***Updated Data*** The real-world data appearing in exercises, examples, and data files has been updated.

4. ***Decimal Data Type*** The Decimal data type has been introduced and used in all examples and exercises dealing with financial data.

5. ***Short-Circuit Evaluation*** AndAlso and OrElse are introduced for the evaluation of logical operators.

6. ***Windows 10*** The screen captures have been updated from Windows 8 to Windows 10 captures.

7. ***New Statements and Methods*** The Exit Sub and Exit Function statements and the string methods Remove and Replace are discussed.

Unique and Distinguishing Features

Exercises for Most Sections. Each section that teaches programming has an exercise set. The exercises both reinforce the understanding of the key ideas of the section and challenge the student to explore applications. Most of the exercise sets require the student to trace programs, find errors, and write programs. The answers to all the odd-numbered exercises in Chapters 2 through 7 and the short-answer odd-numbered exercises from Chapters 8, 9, 10, and 11 are given at the end of the text. A screen capture accompanies most programming answers.

Practice Problems. Practice Problems are carefully selected exercises located at the end of a section, just before the exercise set. Complete solutions are given following the exercise set. The practice problems often focus on points that are potentially confusing or are best appreciated after the student has thought about them. The reader should seriously attempt the practice problems and study their solutions before moving on to the exercises.

Programming Projects. Beginning with Chapter 3, every chapter contains programming projects. The programming projects not only reflect the variety of ways that computers are used in the business community, but also present some games and general-interest topics. The large number and range of difficulty of the programming projects provide the flexibility to adapt the course to the interests and abilities of the students. Some programming projects in later chapters can be assigned as end-of-the-semester projects.

Comments. Extensions and fine points of new topics are deferred to the "Comments" portion at the end of each section so that they will not interfere with the flow of the presentation.

Captions. Every example and applied exercise is labeled with a caption identifying its type of application.

Screen Captures. The output for most applied exercises and programming projects are shown in screen captures. This feature helps clarify the intent of the exercises.

Case Studies. Each of the three case studies focuses on an important programming application. The problems are analyzed and the programs are developed with top-down charts and pseudocode. The programs can be downloaded from the companion website at http://www.pearsonhighered.com/schneider.

Chapter Summaries. In Chapters 2 through 11, the key results are stated and the important terms are summarized at the end of the chapter.

"How To" Appendix. Appendix B provides a compact, step-by-step reference on how to carry out standard tasks in the Visual Basic and Windows environments.

Appendix on Debugging. The placing of the discussion of Visual Basic's sophisticated debugger in Appendix D allows the instructor flexibility in deciding when to cover this topic.

Guide to Application Topics. This section provides an index of programs that deal with various topics including Business, Mathematics, and Sports.

VideoNotes. Thirty VideoNotes are available at www.pearsonhighered.com/cs-resources. VideoNotes are Pearson's visual tool designed for teaching key programming concepts and techniques. VideoNote icons are placed in the margin of the text book to notify the reader when a topic is discussed in a video. Also, a Guide to Video Notes summarizing the different videos throughout the text is included.

Solution Manuals. The Student Solutions Manual contains the answer to every odd-numbered exercise. The Instructor Solutions Manual contains the answer to every exercise and programming project. Both solution manuals are in pdf format and can be downloaded from the Publisher's Web site.

Source Code. The programs for all examples and case studies can be downloaded from the Publisher's Web site.

How to Access Instructor and Student Resource Materials

Online Practice and Assessment with MyProgrammingLab™

MyProgrammingLab helps students fully grasp the logic, semantics, and syntax of programming. Through practice exercises and immediate, personalized feedback, MyProgrammingLab improves the programming competence of beginning students who often struggle with the basic concepts and paradigms of popular high-level programming languages.

A self-study and homework tool, the MyProgrammingLab course for Visual Basic consists of roughly two hundred small practice exercises covering introductory topics such as variables, calculations, decision statements, loops, procedures, arrays, and more. For students, the system automatically detects errors in the logic and syntax of their code submissions and offers targeted hints that enable students to figure out what went wrong—and why. For instructors, a comprehensive gradebook tracks correct and incorrect answers and stores the code inputted by students for review.

For a full demonstration, to see feedback from instructors and students, or to get started using MyProgrammingLab in your course, visit www.myprogramminglab.com.

Instructor Resources

The following protected instructor resource materials are available on the Publisher's Web site at www.pearsonhighered.com/cs-resources. For username and password information, please contact your local Pearson representative.

- Test Item File
- PowerPoint Lecture Slides
- Instructor Solutions Manual
- VideoNotes
- Programs for all examples, case studies, and answers to exercises and programming projects (Databases, text files, and picture files needed for the exercises are included in the Programs folder.)

Student Resources

Access to the Premium Website and VideoNotes tutorials is located at www. pearsonhighered.com/cs-resources. Students must use the access card located in the front of the book to register and access the online material. If there is no access card in the front of this textbook, students can purchase access by going to www.pearsonhighered. com/cs-resources and selecting "purchase access to premium content." Instructors must register on the site to access the material.

The following content is available through the Premium Web site:

- VideoNotes
- Student Solutions Manual
- Programs for examples and case studies (Databases, text files, and picture files needed for the exercises are included in the Programs folder.)

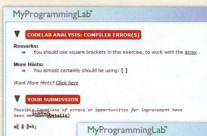

ACKNOWLEDGMENTS

Many talented instructors and programmers provided helpful comments and constructive suggestions during the many editions of this text and I am most grateful for their contributions. The current edition benefited greatly from the valuable comments of the following reviewers:

Milam Aiken, University of Mississippi
Geoffrey Campbell, Illinois State University
Sherrie Cannoy, North Carolina A&T State University
Joshua Cuneo, Georgia Gwinnett College
Jean Hendrix, University of Arkansas at Monticello
Colin Ikei, Long Beach City College
Ingyu Lee, Troy University
Pati Milligan, Baylor University
Mohammad Rob, University of Houston—Clear Lake
John Robinson, Rutgers University—Camden
Michael Zurad, University of Wisconsin—Parkside

Many people are involved in the successful publication of a book. I wish to thank the dedicated team at Pearson whose support and diligence made this textbook possible, especially Program Manager Carole Snyder and Team Lead Scott Disanno.

I am grateful to Kathy Liszka of the University of Akron for producing the VideoNotes that accompany the book. I would like to thank Kathy Liszka, Anne Bunner, and Howard Lerner for their excellent proofreading. The competence and graciousness of Shylaja Gattupalli at SPi Global made for a pleasant production process.

I extend special thanks to my editor Tracy Johnson. Her ideas and enthusiasm helped immensely with the preparation of the book.

David I. Schneider
dis@math.umd.edu

USING THIS BOOK FOR A SHORT OR CONDENSED COURSE

This book provides more than enough material for a complete semester course. For a course shorter than a semester in length, it will be necessary to bypass some sections. The following syllabus provides one possible way to present an abbreviated introduction to programming.

Chapter 1 An Introduction to Computers and Problem Solving

    1.1 An Introduction to Computing and Visual Basic

Chapter 2 Visual Basic, Controls, and Events

    2.1 An Introduction to Visual Basic 2015
    2.2 Visual Basic Controls
    2.3 Visual Basic Events

Chapter 3 Variables, Input, and Output

    3.1 Numbers
    3.2 Strings
    3.3 Input and Output

Chapter 4 Decisions

    4.1 Relational and Logical Operators
    4.2 If Blocks
    4.3 Select Case Blocks
    4.4 Input via User Selection

Chapter 5 General Procedures[1]

    5.1 Function Procedures
    5.2 Sub Procedures, Part I

Chapter 6 Repetition

    6.1 Do Loops
    6.2 For . . . Next Loops

Chapter 7 Arrays

    7.1 Creating and Accessing Arrays
    7.2 Using LINQ with Arrays

Chapter 8 Text Files[2]

    8.1 Managing Text Files
  or 8.2 StreamReaders, StreamWriters, Structured Exception Handling

---

[1] Passing by reference can be omitted or just mentioned briefly. In Chapters 6 through 11, ByRef is used only in Example 6 of Section 7.3 (Arrays of Structures) and in the Chapter 7 case study. In both of those programs, it is used to obtain input.

[2] Sections 8.1 and 8.2 are independent of each other.

1

An Introduction to Computers and Problem Solving

1.1 An Introduction to Computing and Visual Basic

An Introduction to Programming Using Visual Basic is about problem solving using computers. The programming language used is Visual Basic 2015 (hereafter shortened to Visual Basic), but the principles apply to most modern programming languages. Many of the examples and exercises illustrate how computers are used in the real world. Here are some questions that you may have about computers and programming.

Question: *How do we communicate with the computer?*

Answer: Many languages are used to communicate with the computer. At the lowest level, there is *machine language*, which is understood directly by the microprocessor but is difficult for humans to understand. Visual Basic is an example of a *high-level language*. It consists of instructions to which people can relate, such as Click, If, and Do. Some other well-known high-level languages are Java, C++, and Python.

Question: *How do we get computers to perform complicated tasks?*

Answer: Tasks are broken down into a sequence of instructions, called a *program*, that can be expressed in a computer language. Programs can range in size from two or three instructions to millions of instructions. The process of executing the instructions is called *running* the program.

Question: *What is a GUI?*

Answer: What the user views on the monitor and interacts with while a program is running is called the *user interface*. GUI (pronounced GOO-ee) stands for "graphical user interface". Both Windows and Visual Basic use a graphical user interface; that is, they employ objects such as windows, icons, and menus that can be manipulated by a mouse. Non-GUI-based programs use only text and are accessed solely via a keyboard.

Question: *What are the meanings of the terms "programmer" and "user"?*

Answer: A *programmer* (also called a *developer*) is a person who solves problems by writing programs on a computer. After analyzing the problem and developing a plan for solving it, the programmer writes and tests the program that instructs the computer how to carry out the plan. The program might be run many times, either by the programmer or by others. A *user* is any person who runs a program. While working through this text, you will function both as a programmer and as a user.

Question: *What is the meaning of the term "code"?*

Answer: The Visual Basic instructions that the programmer writes are called *code*. The process of writing a program is often called *coding*.

Question: *Are there certain characteristics that all programs have in common?*

Answer: Most programs do three things: take in data, manipulate data, and produce results. These operations are referred to as *input, processing,* and *output*. The input data might be held in the program, reside on a disk, or be provided by the user in response to requests made by the computer while the program is running. The processing of the input data occurs inside the computer and can take from a fraction of a second to many hours. The output data are displayed on a monitor, printed on a printer, or recorded on a disk. As a simple example, consider a program that computes sales tax. An item of input data is the cost of the thing purchased. The processing consists of multiplying the cost by the sales tax rate. The output data is the resulting product, the amount of sales tax to be paid.

Question: *Many programming languages, including Visual Basic, use a zero-based numbering system. What is a zero-based numbering system?*

Answer: In a zero-based numbering system, numbering begins with zero instead of one. For example, in the word "code", "c" would be the zeroth letter, "o" would be the first letter, and so on.

Question: *What are the meanings of the terms "hardware" and "software"?*

Answer: *Hardware* refers to the physical components of the computer, including all peripherals, the central processing unit, disk drives, and all mechanical and electrical devices. Programs are referred to as *software*.

Question: *How are problems solved with a program?*

Answer: Problems are solved by carefully reading them to determine what data are given and what outputs are requested. Then a step-by-step procedure is devised to process the given data and produce the requested output.

Question: *Are there any prerequisites to learning Visual Basic?*

Answer: You should be familiar with how folders (also called *directories*) and files are managed by Windows. Files reside on storage devices such as hard disks, USB flash drives, CDs, and DVDs. Traditionally, the primary storage devices for personal computers were hard disks and floppy disks. Therefore, the word *disk* is frequently used to refer to any storage device.

Question: *Will it matter whether Windows 7, Windows 8, or Windows 10 are used as the underlying operating system?*

Answer: Visual Basic runs fine with all three of these versions of Windows. However, the windows will vary slightly in appearance. Figure 1.1 shows the appearance of a typical window produced in Visual Basic with each of the three versions of Windows. The appearance of windows depends on the Windows product edition, the hardware on your system, and your own personal preferences. In this book, all screen captures have been done with the Windows 10 operating system.

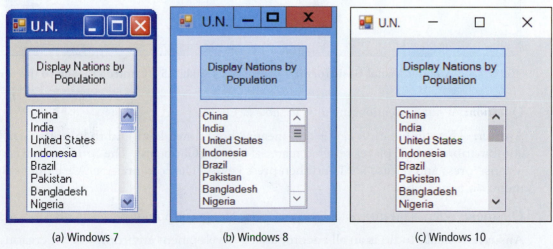

(a) Windows 7   (b) Windows 8   (c) Windows 10

FIGURE 1.1   Visual Basic windows.

Question: *What is an example of a program developed in this textbook?*

Answer: Figure 1.2 shows a program from Chapter 7 when it is first run. After the user types in a first name and clicks on the button, the names of the presidents who have that first name are displayed. Figure 1.3 shows the output.

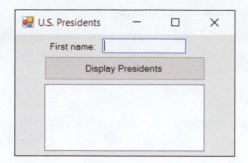

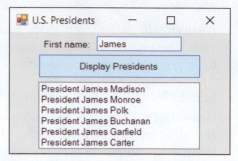

FIGURE 1.2 Window when program is first run.

FIGURE 1.3 Window after a name is entered and the button is clicked.

Question: *How does the programmer create the aforementioned program?*

Answer: The programmer begins with a blank window called a **form**. See Fig. 1.4. The programmer adds objects, called **controls**, to the form and sets properties for the controls. In Fig. 1.5, four controls have been placed on the form. The Text properties of the form, the label, and the button have been set to "U.S. Presidents", "First name:", and "Display Presidents". The Name property of the list box was set to "lstPres".

The code is written into a text-editing window called the **Code Editor**. The code tells the computer what to do after the button is clicked. The **program** includes the form (with its controls), the code, and a file containing the data.

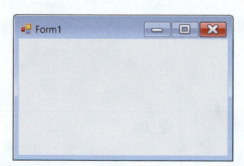

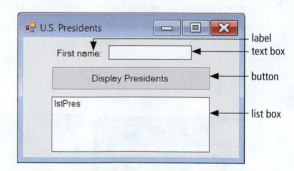

FIGURE 1.4 A blank Visual Basic form.

FIGURE 1.5 Controls added to the form.

Question: *What conventions are used to show keystrokes?*

Answer: The combination *key1+key2* means "hold down key1 and then press key2". The combination Ctrl+C places selected material into the Clipboard. The combination *key1/key2* means "press and release key1 and then press key2". The combination Alt/F opens the *File* menu on a menu bar.

Question: *What is the difference between Visual Studio and Visual Basic?*

Answer: Visual Studio is an all-encompassing development environment for creating websites and Windows applications. Visual Basic is a programming language that is part of Visual Studio.

Question: *How can the programs for the examples in this textbook be obtained?*

Answer: See the preface for information on how to download the programs from the Pearson website.

Question: *Are there any adjustments that should be made to Windows before using this textbook?*

Answer: Possibly. By default, Windows 7 and Windows 8 show only the base names of files. You should configure Windows to display the filename extensions for all known file types. (The details are presented in Appendix B in the "Configuring the Windows Environment" section.) Windows 10 shows the full file name by default.

Question: *Are there any adjustments that should be made to Visual Basic while using this textbook?*

Answer: Yes. Three adjustments are discussed in the textbook. In Section 2.2, a setting is specified that guarantees flexibility in naming, saving, and discarding programs. In Section 2.3, we specify the number of spaces that lines of code will be indented. In Section 3.2, we set some options that affect how rigorous we must be when declaring the data types of variables and using variables.

Question: *Where will new programs be saved?*

Answer: Before writing your first program, you should use File Explorer (with Windows 8 or 10) or Windows Explorer (with Windows 7) to create a separate folder to hold your programs. The first time you save a program, you will have to browse to that folder. Subsequent savings will use that folder as the default folder.

1.2   Program Development Cycle

We learned in Section 1.1 that hardware refers to the machinery in a computer system (such as the monitor, keyboard, and CPU) and software refers to a collection of instructions, called a **program**, that directs the hardware. Programs are written to solve problems or perform tasks on a computer. Programmers translate the solutions or tasks into a language the computer can understand. As we write programs, we must keep in mind that the computer will do only what we instruct it to do. Because of this, we must be very careful and thorough when writing our instructions. **Note:** Microsoft Visual Basic refers to a program as a **project**, **application**, or **solution**.

■ Performing a Task on the Computer

The first step in writing instructions to carry out a task is to determine what the **output** should be—that is, exactly what the task should produce. The second step is to identify the data, or **input**, necessary to obtain the output. The last step is to determine how to **process** the input to obtain the desired output—that is, to determine what formulas or ways of doing things should be used to obtain the output.

    This problem-solving approach is the same as that used to solve word problems in an algebra class. For example, consider the following algebra problem:

How fast is a car moving if it travels 50 miles in 2 hours?

The first step is to determine the type of answer requested. The answer should be a number giving the speed in miles per hour (the output). The information needed to obtain the answer is the distance and time the car has traveled (the input). The formula

$$\text{speed} = \text{distance/time}$$

is used to process the distance traveled and the time elapsed in order to determine the speed. That is,

$$speed = 50 \text{ miles}/2 \text{ hours}$$

$$= 25 \text{ miles/hours}$$

A graphical representation of this problem-solving process is shown in Fig. 1.6.

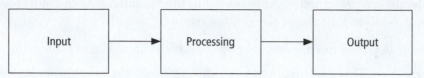

FIGURE 1.6   **The problem-solving process.**

We determine what we want as output, get the needed input, and process the input to produce the desired output.

In the chapters that follow, we discuss how to write programs to carry out the preceding operations. But first we look at the general process of writing programs.

■ Program Planning

A baking recipe provides a good example of a plan. The ingredients and the amounts are determined by what is to be baked. That is, the *output* determines the *input* and the *processing*. The recipe, or plan, reduces the number of mistakes you might make if you tried to bake with no plan at all. Although it's difficult to imagine an architect building a bridge or a factory without a detailed plan, many programmers (particularly students in their first programming course) try to write programs without first making a careful plan. The more complicated the problem, the more complex the plan may be. You will spend much less time working on a program if you devise a carefully thought out step-by-step plan and test it before actually writing the program.

Many programmers plan their programs using a sequence of steps, referred to as the **Software Development Life Cycle**. The following step-by-step process will enable you to use your time efficiently and help you design error-free programs that produce the desired output.

1. *Analyze:* Define the problem.

   Be sure you understand what the program should do—that is, what the output should be. Have a clear idea of what data (or input) are given and the relationship between the input and the desired output.

2. *Design:* Plan the solution to the problem.

   Find a logical sequence of precise steps that perform the task. Such a sequence of steps is called an **algorithm**. Every detail, including obvious steps, should appear in the algorithm. In the next section, we discuss three popular methods used to develop the logic plan: flowcharts, pseudocode, and hierarchy charts. These tools help the programmer break a problem into a sequence of small tasks the computer can perform to solve the problem. Planning also involves using representative data to test the logic of the algorithm by hand to ensure that it is correct.

3. *Design the interface:* Select the objects (text boxes, buttons, etc.).

   Determine how the input will be obtained and how the output will be displayed. Then create objects to receive the input and display the output. Also, create appropriate buttons and menus to allow the user to control the program.

4. *Code:* Translate the algorithm into a programming language.

Coding is the technical word for writing the program. During this stage, the program is written in Visual Basic and entered into the computer. The programmer uses the algorithm devised in Step 2 along with a knowledge of Visual Basic.

5. *Test and correct:* Locate and remove any errors in the program.

Testing is the process of finding errors in a program. (An error in a program is called a **bug** and testing and correcting is often referred to as **debugging**.) As the program is typed, Visual Basic points out certain kinds of program errors. Other kinds of errors will be detected by Visual Basic when the program is executed; however, many errors due to typing mistakes, flaws in the algorithm, or incorrect use of the Visual Basic language rules, can be uncovered and corrected only by careful detective work. An example of such an error would be using addition when multiplication was the proper operation.

6. *Complete the documentation:* Organize all the material that describes the program.

Documentation is intended to allow another person, or the programmer at a later date, to understand the program. Internal documentation (comments) consists of statements in the program that are not executed but point out the purposes of various parts of the program. Documentation might also consist of a detailed description of what the program does and how to use it (for instance, what type of input is expected). For commercial programs, documentation includes an instruction manual and on-line help. Other types of documentation are the flowchart, pseudocode, and hierarchy chart that were used to construct the program. Although documentation is listed as the last step in the program development cycle, it should take place as the program is being coded.

1.3   Programming Tools

This section discusses some specific algorithms and describes three tools used to convert algorithms into computer programs: flowcharts, pseudocode, and hierarchy charts.

You use algorithms every day to make decisions and perform tasks. For instance, whenever you mail a letter, you must decide how much postage to put on the envelope. One rule of thumb is to use one stamp for every five sheets of paper or fraction thereof. Suppose a friend asks you to determine the number of stamps to place on an envelope. The following algorithm will accomplish the task.

1. Request the number of sheets of paper; call it Sheets.   *(input)*

2. Divide Sheets by 5.   *(processing)*

3. If necessary, round the quotient up to a whole number; call it Stamps.   *(processing)*

4. Reply with the number Stamps.   *(output)*

The preceding algorithm takes the number of sheets (Sheets) as input, processes the data, and produces the number of stamps needed (Stamps) as output. We can test the algorithm for a letter with 16 sheets of paper.

1. Request the number of sheets of paper; Sheets = 16.

2. Dividing 5 into 16 gives 3.2.

3. Rounding 3.2 up to 4 gives Stamps = 4.

4. Reply with the answer, 4 stamps.

This problem-solving example can be illustrated by Fig. 1.7.

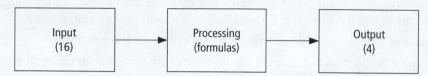

FIGURE 1.7   **The problem-solving process for the stamp problem.**

Of the program design tools available, three popular ones are the following:

Flowcharts: Graphically depict the logical steps to carry out a task and show how the steps relate to each other.

Pseudocode: Uses English-like phrases with some Visual Basic terms to outline the task.

Hierarchy charts: Show how the different parts of a program relate to each other.

◼ Flowcharts

A flowchart consists of special geometric symbols connected by arrows. Within each symbol is a phrase presenting the activity at that step. The shape of the symbol indicates the type of operation that is to occur. For instance, the parallelogram denotes input or output. The arrows connecting the symbols, called **flowlines**, show the progression in which the steps take place. Flowcharts should "flow" from the top of the page to the bottom. Although the symbols used in flowcharts are standardized, no standards exist for the amount of detail required within each symbol.

Symbol	Name	Meaning
→	*Flowline*	Used to connect symbols and indicate the flow of logic.
⬭	*Terminal*	Used to represent the beginning (Start) or the end (End) of a task.
▱	*Input/Output*	Used for input and output operations. The data to be input or output is described in the parallelogram.
▭	*Processing*	Used for arithmetic and data-manipulation operations. The instructions are listed inside the symbol.
◇	*Decision*	Used for any logic or comparison operations. Unlike the input/output and processing symbols, which have one entry and one exit flowline, the decision symbol has one entry and two exit paths. The path chosen depends on whether the answer to a question is "yes" or "no."
○	*Connector*	Used to join different flowlines.
⌐--	*Annotation*	Used to provide additional information about another flowchart symbol.

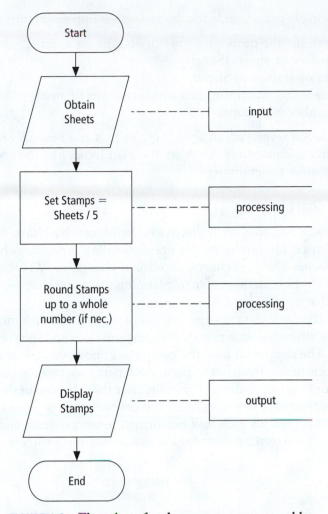

FIGURE 1.8 **Flowchart for the postage-stamp problem.**

The table of the flowchart symbols shown on the previous page has been adopted by the American National Standards Institute (ANSI). Figure 1.8 shows the flowchart for the postage-stamp problem.

The main advantage of using a flowchart to plan a task is that it provides a graphical representation of the task, thereby making the logic easier to follow. We can clearly see every step and how each is connected to the next. The major disadvantage is that when a program is very large, the flowcharts may continue for many pages, making them difficult to follow and modify.

■ Pseudocode

Pseudocode is an abbreviated plain English version of actual computer code (hence, *pseudocode*). The geometric symbols used in flowcharts are replaced by English-like statements that outline the process. As a result, pseudocode looks more like computer code than does a flowchart. Pseudocode allows the programmer to focus on the steps required to solve a problem rather than on how to use the computer language. The programmer can describe the algorithm in Visual Basic–like form without being restricted by the rules of Visual Basic. When the pseudocode is completed, it can be easily translated into the Visual Basic language.

The following is pseudocode for the postage-stamp problem:

Program: Determine the proper number of stamps for a letter.

Obtain the number of sheets (Sheets)	*(input)*
Set the number of stamps to Sheets / 5	*(processing)*
Round the number of stamps up to a whole number (if nec.)	*(processing)*
Display the number of stamps	*(output)*

Pseudocode has several advantages. It is compact and probably will not extend for many pages as flowcharts commonly do. Also, the plan looks like the code to be written and so is preferred by most programmers.

■ Hierarchy Chart

The last programming tool we'll discuss is the **hierarchy chart**, which shows the overall program structure. Hierarchy charts are also called structure charts, HIPO (Hierarchy plus Input-Process-Output) charts, top-down charts, or VTOC (Visual Table of Contents) charts. All these names refer to planning diagrams that are similar to a company's organization chart.

Hierarchy charts depict the organization of a program but omit the specific processing logic. They describe what each part of the program does and they show how the parts relate to each other. The details on how the parts work, however, are omitted. The chart is read from top to bottom and from left to right. Each part may be subdivided into a succession of subparts that branch out under it. Typically, after the activities in the succession of subparts are carried out, the part to the right of the original part is considered. A quick glance at the hierarchy chart reveals each task performed in the program and where it is performed. Figure 1.9 shows a hierarchy chart for the postage-stamp problem.

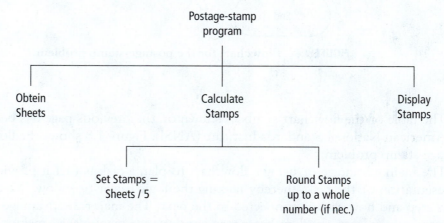

FIGURE 1.9 **Hierarchy chart for the postage-stamp problem.**

The main benefit of hierarchy charts is in the initial planning of a program. We break down the major parts of a program so we can see what must be done in general. From this point, we can then refine each part into more detailed plans using flowcharts or pseudocode. This process is called the **divide-and-conquer** method.

■ Decision Structure

The postage-stamp problem was solved by a series of instructions to read data, perform calculations, and display results. Each step was in a sequence; that is, we moved from one line to the next without skipping over any lines. This kind of structure is called a **sequence structure**. Many problems, however, require a decision to determine whether a series of instructions should be executed. If the answer to a question is "yes", then one group of instructions is

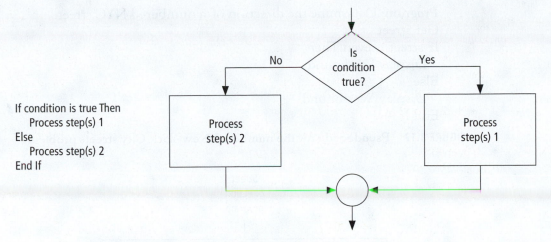

If condition is true Then
    Process step(s) 1
Else
    Process step(s) 2
End If

FIGURE 1.10 Pseudocode and flowchart for a decision structure.

executed. If the answer is "no", then another is executed. This structure is called a **decision structure**. Figure 1.10 contains the pseudocode and flowchart for a decision structure.

Sequence and decision structures are both used to solve the following problem.

■ Direction of Numbered NYC Streets Algorithm

Problem: Given a street number of a one-way street in New York City, decide the direction of the street, either eastbound or westbound.

Discussion: There is a simple rule to tell the direction of a one-way street in New York City: Even-numbered streets run eastbound.

Input: Street number.

Processing: Decide if the street number is divisible by 2.

Output: "Eastbound" or "Westbound".

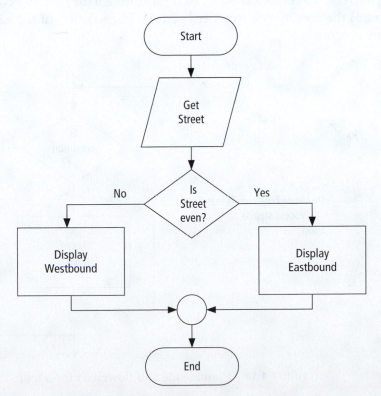

FIGURE 1.11 Flowchart for the numbered New York City streets problem.

```
Program: Determine the direction of a numbered NYC street.
Get street
If street is even Then
  Display Eastbound
Else
  Display Westbound
End If
```

FIGURE 1.12 **Pseudocode for the numbered New York City streets problem.**

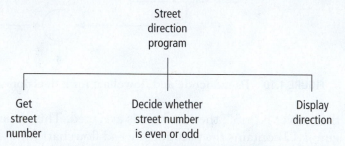

FIGURE 1.13 **Hierarchy chart for the numbered New York City streets problem.**

Figures 1.11 through 1.13 show the flowchart, pseudocode, and hierarchy chart for the numbered New York City streets problem.

Repetition Structure

A programming structure that executes instructions many times is called a **repetition structure** or a **loop structure.** Loop structures need a test (or condition) to tell when the loop should end. Without an exit condition, the loop would repeat endlessly (an infinite loop). One way to control the number of times a loop repeats (often referred to as the number of passes or iterations) is to check a condition before each pass through the loop and continue executing the loop as long as the condition is true. See Fig. 1.14. The solution of the next problem requires a repetition structure.

```
Do While condition is true
  Process step(s)
Loop
```

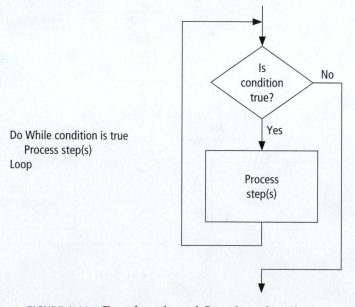

FIGURE 1.14 **Pseudocode and flowchart for a loop.**

◼ Class Average Algorithm

Problem: Calculate and report the average grade for a class.

Discussion: The average grade equals the sum of all grades divided by the number of students. We need a loop to read and then add (accumulate) the grades for each student in the class. Inside the loop, we also need to total (count) the number of students in the class. See Figs. 1.15 to 1.17.

Input: Student grades.

Processing: Find the sum of the grades; count the number of students; calculate average grade = sum of grades / number of students.

Output: Average grade.

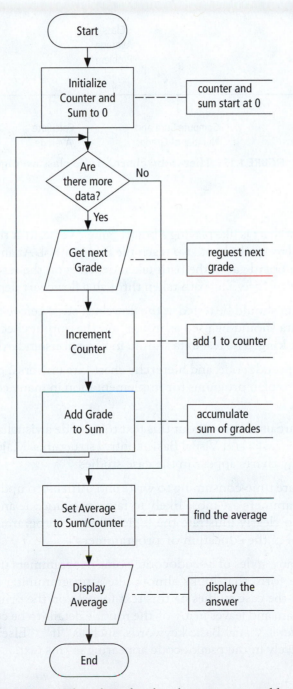

FIGURE 1.15 **Flowchart for the class average problem.**

Program: Calculate and report the average grade of a class.
Initialize Counter and Sum to 0
Do While there are more data
    Get the next Grade
    Increment the Counter
    Add the Grade to the Sum
Loop
Compute Average = Sum/Counter
Display Average

FIGURE 1.16   Pseudocode for the class average problem.

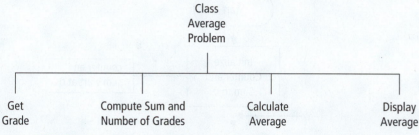

FIGURE 1.17   Hierarchy chart for the class average problem.

■ Comments

1. Tracing a flowchart is like playing a board game. We begin at the Start symbol and proceed from symbol to symbol until we reach the End symbol. At any time, we will be at just one symbol. In a board game, the path taken depends on the result of spinning a spinner or rolling a pair of dice. The path taken through a flowchart depends on the input.

2. The algorithm should be tested at the flowchart stage before being coded into a program. Different data should be used as input, and the output checked. This process is known as **desk checking**. The test data should include nonstandard data as well as typical data.

3. Flowcharts, pseudocode, and hierarchy charts are universal problem-solving tools. They can be used to plan programs for implementation in many computer languages, not just Visual Basic.

4. Flowcharts are used throughout this text to provide a visualization of the flow of certain programming tasks and Visual Basic control structures. Major examples of pseudocode and hierarchy charts appear in the case studies.

5. Flowcharts are time-consuming to write and difficult to update. For this reason, professional programmers are more likely to favor pseudocode and hierarchy charts. Because flowcharts so clearly illustrate the logical flow of programming techniques, they are a valuable tool in the education of programmers.

6. There are many styles of pseudocode. Some programmers use an outline form, whereas others use a form that looks almost like a programming language. The pseudocode appearing in the case studies of this text focuses on the primary tasks to be performed by the program and leaves many of the routine details to be completed during the coding process. Several Visual Basic keywords, such as "If", "Else", "Do", and "While", are used extensively in the pseudocode appearing in this text.

2

Visual Basic, Controls, and Events

2.1 An Introduction to Visual Basic 2015

Visual Basic 2015 is the latest generation of Visual Basic, a language used by many software developers. Visual Basic was designed to make user-friendly programs easier to develop. Prior to the creation of Visual Basic, developing a friendly user interface usually required a programmer to use a language such as C or C++, often requiring hundreds of lines of code just to get a window to appear on the screen. Now the same program can be created in much less time with fewer instructions.

■ Why Windows and Why Visual Basic?

What people call **graphical user interfaces**, or GUIs, have revolutionized the software industry. Instead of the confusing textual prompts that earlier users once saw, today's users are presented with such devices as icons, buttons, and drop-down lists that respond to mouse clicks. Accompanying the revolution in how programs look was a revolution in how they feel. Consider a program that requests information for a database. Figure 2.1 shows how a program written before the advent of GUIs got its information. The program requests the six pieces of data one at a time, with no opportunity to go back and alter previously entered information. Then the screen clears and the six inputs are again requested one at a time.

> Enter name (Enter EOD to terminate): <u>Mr. President</u>
> Enter Address: <u>1600 Pennsylvania Avenue</u>
> Enter City: <u>Washington</u>
> Enter State: <u>DC</u>
> Enter Zip code: <u>20500</u>
> Enter Phone Number: <u>202-456-1414</u>

FIGURE 2.1 Input screen of a pre-Visual Basic program to fill a database.

Figure 2.2 shows how an equivalent Visual Basic program gets its information. The boxes may be filled in any order. When the user clicks on a box with the mouse, the cursor moves to that box. The user can either type in new information or edit the existing information. When satisfied that all the information is correct, the user clicks on the *Write to Database* button. The boxes will clear, and the data for another person can be entered. After all names have been entered, the user clicks on the *Exit* button. In Fig. 2.1, the program is in control; in Fig. 2.2, the user is in control!

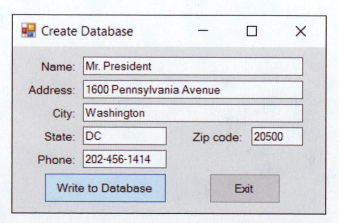

FIGURE 2.2 Input screen of a Visual Basic program to fill a database.

■ How You Develop a Visual Basic Program

A key element of planning a Visual Basic program is deciding what the user sees—in other words, designing the user interface. What data will he or she be entering? How large a window should the program use? Where will you place the buttons the user clicks on to activate actions in the program? Will the program have places to enter text (text boxes) and places to display output? What kind of warning boxes (message boxes) should the program use? In Visual Basic, the responsive objects a program designer places on windows are called *controls*. Two features make Visual Basic different from traditional programming tools:

1. You literally draw the user interface, much like using a paint program.

2. Perhaps more important, when you're done drawing the interface, the buttons, text boxes, and other objects that you have placed in a blank window will automatically recognize user actions such as mouse movements and button clicks. That is, the sequence of procedures executed in your program is controlled by "events" that the user initiates rather than by a predetermined sequence of procedures in your program.

In any case, only after you design the interface does anything like traditional programming occur. Objects in Visual Basic recognize events like mouse clicks. How the objects respond to them depends on the instructions you write. You always need to write instructions in order to make controls respond to events. This makes Visual Basic programming fundamentally different from traditional programming. Programs in traditional programming languages ran from the top down. For these programming languages, execution started from the first line and moved with the flow of the program to different parts as needed. A Visual Basic program works differently. Its core is a set of independent groups of instructions that are activated by the events they have been told to recognize. This event-driven methodology is a fundamental shift. The user decides the order in which things happen, not the programmer.

Most of the programming instructions in Visual Basic that tell your program how to respond to events like mouse clicks occur in what Visual Basic calls *event procedures*. Essentially, anything executable in a Visual Basic program either is in an event procedure or is used by an event procedure to help the procedure carry out its job. In fact, to stress that Visual Basic is fundamentally different from traditional programming languages, Microsoft uses the term *project* or *application*, rather than *program*, to refer to the combination of programming instructions and user interface that makes a Visual Basic program possible. Here is a summary of the steps you take to design a Visual Basic program:

1. Design the appearance of the window that the user sees.

2. Determine the events that the controls on the window should respond to.

3. Write the event procedures for those events.

Now here is what happens when the program is running:

1. Visual Basic monitors the controls in the window to detect any event that a control can recognize (mouse movements, clicks, keystrokes, and so on).

2. When Visual Basic detects an event, it examines the program to see if you've written an event procedure for that event.

3. If you have written an event procedure, Visual Basic executes the instructions that make up that event procedure and goes back to Step 1.

4. If you have not written an event procedure, Visual Basic ignores the event and goes back to Step 1.

These steps cycle continuously until the program ends. Usually, an event must happen before Visual Basic will do anything. Event-driven programs are more reactive than active—and that makes them more user friendly.

2.2   Visual Basic Controls

Visual Basic programs display a Windows-style screen (called a **form**) with boxes into which users type (and in which users edit) information and buttons that they click on to initiate actions. The boxes and buttons are referred to as **controls**. In this section, we examine forms and four of the most useful Visual Basic controls.

■ Starting a New Visual Basic Program

Each program is saved (as several files and subfolders) in its own folder. Before writing your first program, you should use File Explorer (with Windows 8 or 10) or Windows Explorer (with Windows 7) to create a folder to hold your programs.

The process for starting Visual Basic varies slightly with the version of Windows and the edition of Visual Studio installed on the computer. Some possible sequences of steps are shown below.

Windows 7 Click the Windows *Start* button, click *All Programs*, and then click on "Microsoft Visual Studio 2015."

Windows 8 and 8.1 Click the tile labeled "Visual Studio 2015." If there is no such tile, click on *Search* in the Charms bar, select the Apps category, type "Visual Studio" into the Search box in the upper-right part of the screen, and click on the rectangle labeled "Visual Studio 2015" that appears on the left side of the screen.

Windows 10 Click the Windows **Start** button, click *All apps,* and then click on *Visual Studio 2015*. Or, click on the tile labeled *Visual Studio 2015*.

Figure 2.3 shows the top part of the screen after Visual Basic is started. A Menu bar and a Toolbar are at the top of the screen. These two bars, with minor variations, are always

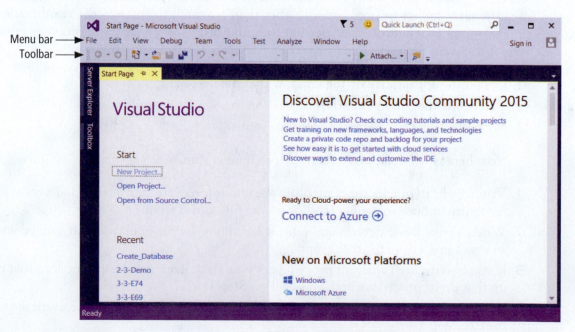

FIGURE 2.3   **Visual Basic opening screen.**

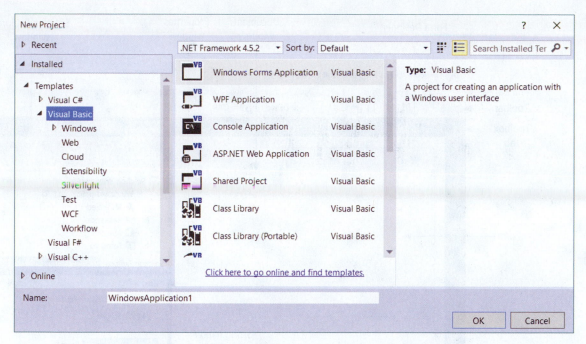

FIGURE 2.4   **The Visual Basic New Project dialog box.**

present while you are working with Visual Basic. The remainder of the screen is called the Start Page. Some tasks can be initiated from the Menu bar, the Toolbar, and the Start Page. We will usually initiate them from the Menu bar or the Toolbar.

The first item on the Menu bar is File. Click on File, hover over (or click on) *New*, and then click on *Project* to produce a New Project dialog box. (Alternately, press Alt/F/N/P or Ctrl+Shift+N.) Figure 2.4 shows a New Project dialog box produced by the Visual Basic Community 2015 edition. Your screen might look somewhat different than Fig. 2.4 even if you are using the Visual Basic Community 2015 edition.

Select *Visual Basic* in the *Templates* list on the left side of Fig. 2.4, and select *Windows Forms Application* in the center list. **Note:** The number of items in the center list will vary depending on the edition of Visual Studio you are using.

The name of the program, initially set to WindowsApplication1, can be specified at this time. Since we will have a chance to change it later, let's just use the name WindowsApplication1 for now. Click on the *OK* button to invoke the Visual Basic programming environment. See Fig. 2.5 on the next page. The Visual Basic programming environment is referred to as the **Integrated Development Environment** or **IDE**. The IDE contains the tools for writing, running, and debugging programs.

It is possible that your screen will look different than Fig. 2.5. The IDE is extremely configurable. Each window in Fig. 2.5 can have its location and size altered. New windows can be displayed in the IDE, and any window can be closed or hidden behind a tab. For instance, in Fig. 2.5 the Toolbox window is hidden behind a tab. The View menu is used to add additional windows to the IDE. If you would like your screen to look similar to Fig. 2.5, click on *Reset Windows Layout* in the Window menu, and then click on the *Yes* button.

The **Menu bar** of the IDE displays the menus of commands you use to work with Visual Basic. Some of the menus, like File, Edit, View, and Window, are common to most Windows applications. Others, such as Project, Debug, and Data, provide commands specific to programming in Visual Basic.

The **Toolbar** holds a collection of buttons that carry out standard operations when clicked. For example, you use the sixth button, which looks like two diskettes, to save the

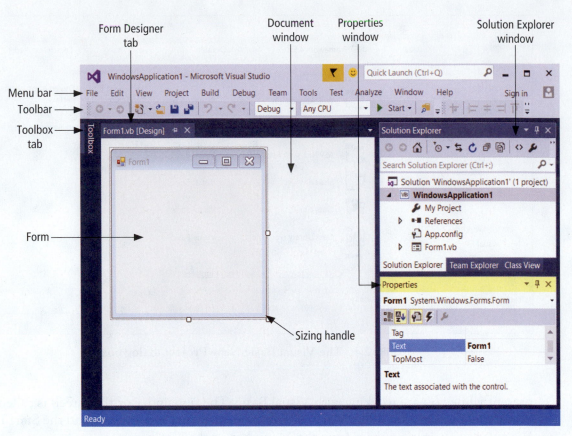

FIGURE 2.5 **The Visual Basic Integrated Development Environment in Form Designer mode.**

files associated with the current program. To reveal the purpose of a Toolbar button, hover the mouse pointer over it. The little information rectangle that pops up is called a **tooltip**.

The **Document window** currently holds the rectangular **Form window**, or **form** for short. (The Form window is also known as the **form designer window** or the **design window**.) The form becomes a Windows window when a program is executed. Most information displayed by the program appears on the form. The information usually is displayed in controls that the programmer has placed on the form. *Note:* You can change the size of the form by dragging one of its sizing handles.

The **Properties window** is used to change the initial appearance and behavior of objects on the form. Some (but not all) properties and appearances can be changed by code.

The **Solution Explorer** window displays the files associated with the program and provides access to the commands that pertain to them. (*Note:* If the Solution Explorer or the Properties window is not visible, click on it in the View menu.)

The **Toolbox** holds icons representing objects (called controls) that can be placed on the form. If your screen does not show the Toolbox, hover the mouse over the Toolbox tab at the left side of the screen. The Toolbox will come into view. Then click on the pushpin icon in the title bar at the top of the Toolbox to keep the Toolbox permanently displayed in the IDE. (*Note:* If there is no tab marked Toolbox, click on *Toolbox* in the View menu.)

The controls in the Toolbox are grouped into categories such as *All Windows Forms* and *Common Controls*. Figure 2.6 shows the Toolbox after the *Common Controls* group has been expanded. Most of the controls discussed in this text can be found in the list of common controls. (You can obtain a description of a control by hovering the mouse over the control.) The four controls discussed in this chapter are text boxes, labels, buttons, and list boxes. In order to see all the group names, collapse each of the groups.

Text boxes: Text boxes are used to get information from the user, referred to as **input**, or to display information produced by the program, referred to as **output**.

Labels: Labels are placed near text boxes to tell the user what type of information is displayed in the text boxes.

Buttons: The user clicks on a button to initiate an action.

List boxes: In the first part of this book, list boxes are used to display output. Later, they are used to make selections.

FIGURE 2.6 **The Toolbox's common controls.**

■ An Important Setting

The process of naming and saving programs can proceed in two different ways. In this book, we do not require that a program be given a name until it is saved. The following steps guarantee that Visual Basic will follow that practice.

1. Click on *Options* from the Tools menu to display an Options dialog box.

2. Click on the *Projects and Solutions* item in the left pane of the Options dialog box.

3. If the box labeled "Save new projects when created" is checked, uncheck it.

4. Click on the *OK* button.

5. Open the File menu in the Toolbar and click on *Close Solution*. **Note:** If a dialog box appears and asks you if you want to save or discard changes to the current project, click on the *Discard* button.

■ A Text Box Walkthrough

Place a text box on a form

1. Start a new Visual Basic program.

2. Double-click on the TextBox control () in the *Common Controls* group of the Toolbox.

   A rectangle with three small squares appears at the upper-left corner of the form. The square on the top of the text box, called the **Tasks button**, can be used to set the MultiLine property of the text box. The squares on the left and right sides of the text box are called **sizing handles**. See Fig. 2.7. An object showing its handles is said to be **selected**. A selected text box can have its width altered, location changed, and other properties modified. You alter the width of the text box by dragging one of its sizing handles.

FIGURE 2.7   Setting the Text property.

3. Move the mouse cursor to any point in the interior of the text box, hold down the left mouse button, and drag the text box to the center of the form.

4. Click anywhere on the form outside the rectangle to deselect the text box.

5. Click on the rectangle to reselect the text box.

6. Hover the mouse over the handle in the center of the right side of the text box until the cursor becomes a double-arrow, hold down the left mouse button, and move the mouse to the right.

   The text box is stretched to the right. Similarly, grabbing the handle on the left side and moving the mouse to the left stretches the text box to the left. You also can use the handles to make the text box smaller. Steps 2, 3, and 6 allow you to place a text box of any width anywhere on the form. **Note:** The text box should now be selected; that is, its sizing handles should be showing. If not, click anywhere inside the text box to select it.

7. Press the Delete key to remove the text box from the form.

   Step 8 gives an alternative way to place a text box of any width at any location on the form.

8. Click on the text box icon in the Toolbox, move the mouse pointer to any place on the form, hold down the left mouse button, drag the mouse on a diagonal, and release the mouse button to create a selected text box.

   You can now alter the width and location as before. **Note:** The text box should now be selected. If not, click anywhere inside the text box to select it.

Activate, move, and resize the Properties window

9. Press F4 to activate the Properties window.

   You also can activate the Properties window by clicking on it, clicking on *Properties Window* from the View menu, or right-clicking on the text box with the mouse button and selecting *Properties* from the context menu that appears. See Fig. 2.8. The first line of the Properties window (called the **Object box**) reads "TextBox1", etc.

TextBox1 is the current name of the text box. The third button in the row of buttons below the Object box, the *Properties* button (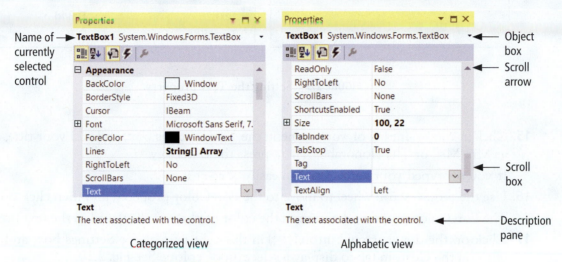), is normally highlighted. If not, click on it. The left column of the Properties window gives the available properties, and the right column gives the current settings of the properties. The first two buttons ( ) in the row of buttons below the Object box permit you to view the list of properties either grouped into categories or alphabetically. You can use the up- and down-arrow keys (or the scroll arrows, scroll box, or the mouse scroll wheel) to move through the list of properties.

FIGURE 2.8 **Text box Properties window.**

10. Click on the Properties window's title bar and drag the window to the center of the screen.

    The Properties window is said to be **floating** or **undocked**. Some people find a floating window easier to work with.

11. Drag the lower-right corner of the Properties window to change the size of the Properties window.

    An enlarged window will show more properties at once.

12. Hold down the Ctrl key and double-click on the title bar.

    The Properties window will return to its original docked location. We now will discuss four properties in this walkthrough.

Set four properties of the text box

Assume that the text box is selected and its Properties window activated.

Note 1: The third and fourth buttons below the Object box, the *Properties* button and the *Events* button, determine whether properties or events are displayed in the Properties window. Normally the *Properties* button is highlighted. If not, click on it.

Note 2: If the Description pane is not visible, right-click on the Properties window, then click on *Description*. The Description pane describes the currently highlighted property.

13. Move to the Text property with the up- and down-arrow keys (alternatively, scroll until the Text property is visible, and click on the property).

    The Text property, which determines the words displayed in the text box, is now high-lighted. Currently, there is no text displayed in the Text property's Settings box on its right.

14. Type your first name, and then press the Enter key or click on another property. Your name now appears in both the Settings box and the text box. See Fig. 2.9.

(a)   (b)

FIGURE 2.9 **Setting the Text property.**

15. Click at the beginning of your name in the Text Settings box, and add your title, such as Mr., Ms., or The Honorable. Then, press the Enter key.

If you mistyped your name, you can easily correct it now.

16. Use the mouse scroll wheel to move to the ForeColor property, and then click on it.

The ForeColor property determines the color of the text displayed in the text box.

17. Click on the down-arrow button (⌄) in the right part of the Settings box, and then click on the Custom tab to display a selection of colors. See Fig. 2.10.

FIGURE 2.10 **Setting the ForeColor property.**

18. Click on one of the colors, such as *blue* or *red*.

Notice the change in the color of your name.

19. Select the Font property with a single click of the mouse, and click on the ellipsis button (…) in the right part of its Settings box.

The Font dialog box in Fig. 2.11 is displayed. The three lists give the current name (Microsoft Sans Serif), current style (Regular), and current size (8 point) of the font. You can change any of these attributes by clicking on an item in its list or by typing into the box at the top of the list.

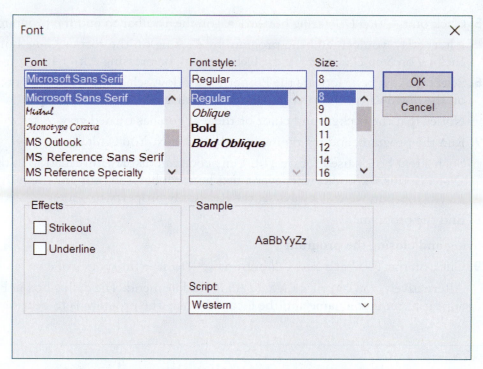

FIGURE 2.11 The Font dialog box.

20. Click on *Bold* in the *Font style* list, click on *12* in the *Size* list, and click on the OK button.

    Your name is now displayed in a larger bold font. The text box will expand so that it can accommodate the larger font.

21. Click on the text box and resize it to be about 3 inches wide.

    Visual Basic programs consist of three parts: interface, values of properties, and code. Our interface consists of a form with a single object—a text box. We have set a few properties for the text box—the text (namely, your name), the foreground color, the font style, and the font size. In Section 2.3, we discuss how to place code into a program. Visual Basic endows certain capabilities to programs that are independent of any code we write. We will now run the current program without adding any code and experience these capabilities.

Run and end the program

22. Click on the *Start* button (▶) on the Toolbar to run the program.

    Alternatively, you can press F5 to run the program or can click on *Start Debugging* in the Debug menu. After a brief delay, a copy of the form appears with your name highlighted.

23. Press the End key to move the cursor to the end of your name, type in your last name, and then keep typing.

    Eventually, the words will scroll to the left.

24. Press the Home key to return to the beginning of your name.

    The text box functions like a miniature word processor. You can place the cursor anywhere you like in order to add or delete text. You can drag the cursor across text to select a block, place a copy of the block in the Clipboard with Ctrl+C, and then duplicate it elsewhere with Ctrl+V.

25. Click on the *Stop Debugging* button (■) on the Toolbar to end the program.

Alternately, you can end the program by clicking on the form's *Close* button (✕), clicking on *Stop Debugging* in the Debug menu, or pressing Alt+F4.

26. Select the text box, activate the Properties window, select the ReadOnly property, click on the down-arrow button (⌄), and finally click on True.

Notice that the background color of the text box has turned gray.

27. Run the program, and try typing into the text box. You can't.

Such a text box is used for output. Only code can display information in the text box. (**Note:** In this textbook, whenever a text box will be used only for the purpose of displaying output, we will always set the ReadOnly property to True.)

28. End the program.

Saving and closing the program

29. Click on the Toolbar's *Save All* button (💾) to save the work done so far.

Alternatively, you can click on *Save All* in the File menu. The dialog box in Fig. 2.12 will appear to request a name and the location where the program is to be saved.

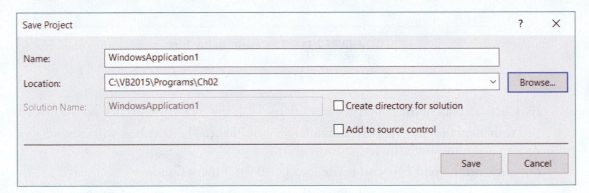

FIGURE 2.12 The Save Project dialog box.

30. Type a name for the program, such as "VBdemo".

Use Browse to locate a folder. (This folder will automatically be used the next time you click on the *Save All* button.) The files for the program will be saved in a subfolder of the selected folder.

Important: If the "Create directory for solution" check box is checked, then click on the check box to uncheck it.

31. Click on the *Save* button.

32. Click on *Close Solution* in the File menu.

In the next step we reload the program.

33. Hover over (or click on) *Open* in the File menu and then click on *Project/Solution* in the context menu that drops down. Navigate to the folder corresponding to the program you just saved, double-click on the folder, and double-click on the file with extension *sln*.

If you do not see the Form Designer for the program, double-click on Form1.vb in the Solution Explorer. The program now exists just as it did after Step 28. You can now modify the program and/or run it. (**Note:** You can also carry out the task in the first sentence by pressing Alt/F/O/P or Ctrl+Shift+O.)

34. Click on *Close Solution* in the File menu to close the program.

■ A Button Walkthrough

Place a button on a form

1. Click on the *New Project* button (icon) on the Toolbar and begin a new program.

2. Double-click on the Button control (🔘 Button) in the Toolbox to place a button on the form. The Button control is the second item in the *Common Controls* group of the Toolbox.

3. Drag the button to the center of the form.

4. Activate the Properties window, highlight the Text property, type "Please Push Me", and press the Enter key.

   The button is too small to accommodate the phrase. See Fig. 2.13.

(a)   (b)

FIGURE 2.13 **Setting the Text property.**

5. Click on the button to select it, and then drag the right-hand sizing handle to widen the button so that it can accommodate the phrase "Please Push Me" on one line.

   Alternately, you can drag the bottom sizing handle down and have the phrase displayed on two lines.

6. Run the program, and click on the button.

   The color of the button turns blue when the mouse hovers over it. In Section 2.3, we will write code that is executed when a button is clicked on.

7. End the program and select the button.

8. From the Properties window, edit the Text setting by inserting an ampersand (&) before the first letter *P*, and then press the Enter key.

   Notice that the first letter *P* on the button is now underlined. See Fig. 2.14. Pressing Alt+P while the program is running causes the same event to occur as does clicking the button. Here, *P* is referred to as the **access key** for the button. (The access key is always the character following the ampersand.)

(a)   (b)

FIGURE 2.14 **Designating P as an access key.**

9. Click on *Close Solution* in the File menu to close the program.

There is no need to save this program, so click on the *Discard* button.

■ A Label Walkthrough

1. Click on the *New Project* button on the Toolbar and begin a new program.

Feel free to keep the default name, such as WindowsApplication1.

2. Double-click on the Label control (**A** Label) in the Toolbox to place a label on the form.

3. Drag the label to the center of the form.

4. Activate the Properties window, highlight the Text property, type "Enter Your Phone Number:", and press the Enter key.

Such a label is placed next to a text box into which the user will type a phone number. Notice that the label widened to accommodate the text. This happened because the AutoSize property of the label is set to True by default.

5. Change the AutoSize property to False and press Enter.

Notice that the label now has eight sizing handles when selected.

6. Make the label narrower and longer until the words occupy two lines.

7. Activate the Properties window, and click on the down arrow to the right of the setting for the TextAlign property. Experiment by clicking on the various rectangles and observing their effects.

The combination of sizing and alignment permits you to design a label easily.

8. Run the program.

Nothing happens, even if you click on the label. Labels just sit there. The user cannot change what a label displays unless you write code to make the change.

9. End the program.

10. Click on *Close Solution* in the File menu to close the program.

There is no need to save this program, so click on the *Discard* button.

■ A List Box Walkthrough

1. Click on the *New Project* button on the Toolbar and begin a new program.

Feel free to keep the default name, such as WindowsApplication1.

2. Place a ListBox control (⊞ ListBox) on the form.

3. Press F4 to activate the Properties window and notice that the list box does not have a Text property.

The word ListBox1 that appears is actually the setting for the Name property.

4. Place a text box, a button, and a label on the form.

5. Click on the Object box just below the title bar of the Properties window.

The name of the form and the names of the four controls are displayed. If you click on one of the names, that object will become selected and its properties displayed in the Properties window.

6. Run the program.

Notice that the word ListBox1 has disappeared, but the words Button1 and Label1 are still visible. The list box is completely blank. In subsequent sections, we will write code to place information into the list box.

7. End the program.

8. Click on *Close Solution* in the File menu to close the program.

There is no need to save this program, so click on the *Discard* button.

■ The Name Property

The form and each control on it has a Name property. By default, the form is given the name Form1 and controls are given names such as TextBox1 and TextBox2. These names can (and should) be changed to descriptive ones that reflect the purpose of the form or control. Also, it is a good programming practice to have each name begin with a three-letter prefix that identifies the type of the object. See Table 2.1.

TABLE 2.1   **Some three-letter prefixes.**

Object	Prefix	Example
form	frm	frmPayroll
button	btn	btnComputeTotal
label	lbl	lblAddress
list box	lst	lstOutput
text box	txt	txtCity

The Solution Explorer window contains a file named Form1.vb that holds information about the form. Form1 is also the setting of the form's Name property in the Properties window. If you change the base name of the file Form1.vb, the setting of the Name property will automatically change to the new name. To make the change, right-click on Form1.vb in the Solution Explorer window, click on *Rename* in the context menu that appears, type in a new name (such as frmPayroll.vb), and press the Enter key. ***Important:*** Make sure that the new filename keeps the extension *vb*.

The name of a control placed on a form is changed from the control's Properties window. (The Name property is always the third property in the alphabetized list of properties.) Names of controls and forms must begin with a letter and can include numbers, letters, and underscore (_) characters, but cannot include punctuation marks or spaces.

The Name and Text properties of a button are both initially set to something like Button1. However, changing one of these properties does not affect the setting of the other properties, and similarly for the Name and Text properties of forms, text boxes, and labels. The Text property of a form specifies the words appearing in the form's title bar.

■ Fonts

The default font for controls is Microsoft Sans Serif. Courier New is another commonly used font. Courier New is a fixed-width font; that is, each character has the same width. With such a font, the letter i occupies the same space as the letter m. Fixed-width fonts are used with tables when information is to be aligned in columns.

■ Auto Hide

The Auto Hide feature allows you to make more room on the screen for the Document window by hiding windows (such as the Toolbox, Solution Explorer, and Properties windows). Let's illustrate the feature with a walkthrough using the Toolbox window.

1. If the Toolbox window is not visible, click on *Toolbox* in the Menu bar's View menu to see the window.

Auto Hide is enabled when the pushpin icon is horizontal (🔲). When the Auto Hide feature is enabled, the Toolbox window will move out of view when not needed.

2. If the pushpin icon is vertical ( ), then click on the icon to make it horizontal.

The Auto Hide feature is now enabled.

3. Press Ctrl+Alt+X to display the Toolbox, and then move the mouse cursor somewhere outside the Toolbox window and click the left mouse button.

The window becomes a tab captioned Toolbox on the left side of the screen.

4. Click on the tab.

The window comes into view and is ready for use. After you click outside the window, it will return back into the tab.

5. Click on the pushpin icon to make it vertical.

The Auto Hide feature is now *disabled*.

6. Click the mouse cursor somewhere outside the Toolbox window.

The Toolbox window stays fixed. **Note:** We recommend keeping Auto Hide disabled for the Toolbox, Solution Explorer, and Properties windows unless you are creating a program with a very large form and need extra space.

■ Positioning and Aligning Controls

Visual Basic provides several tools for positioning and aligning controls on a form. **Proximity lines** are short line segments that help you place controls a comfortable distance from each other and from the sides of the form. **Snap lines** are horizontal and vertical line segments that help you align controls. The Format menu is used to align controls, center controls horizontally and vertically in a form, and make a group of selected controls the same size.

A Positioning and Aligning Walkthrough

1. Begin a new program.

2. Place a button near the center of the form.

3. Drag the button toward the upper-right corner of the form until two short line segments appear. The line segments are called **proximity lines**. See Fig. 2.15(a). The button is now a comfortable distance from each of the two sides of the form.

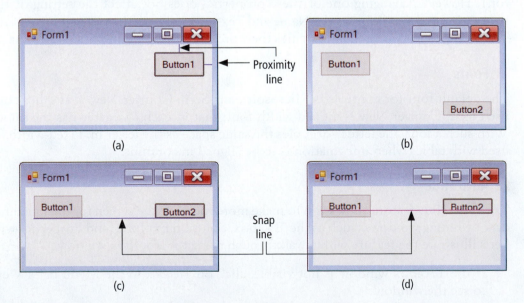

FIGURE 2.15   Positioning controls.

4. Place a second button below the first button and drag it upward until a proximity line appears between the two buttons.

   The buttons are now a comfortable distance apart.

5. Resize and position the two buttons as shown in Fig. 2.15(b).

6. Drag Button2 upward until a blue line appears along the bottoms of the two buttons.

   See Fig. 2.15(c). This blue line is called a **snap line**. The bottoms of the two buttons are now aligned.

7. Continue dragging Button2 upward until a purple snap line appears just underneath the words Button1 and Button2.

   See Fig. 2.15(d). The texts in the two buttons are now aligned. If we were to continue dragging Button2 upward, a blue snap line would tell us when the tops were aligned. Steps 8 and 9 present another way to align the tops of the controls.

8. Click on Button1 and then hold down the Ctrl key and click on Button2.

   After the mouse button is released, both buttons will be selected. **Note:** This process (called **selection of multiple controls**) can be repeated to select a group of any number of controls.

9. With the two buttons still selected, open the Format menu in the Menu bar, hover over *Align*, and click on *Tops*.

   The tops of the two buttons are now aligned. Precisely, Button1 (the first button selected) will stay fixed, and Button2 will move up so that its top is aligned with the top of Button1. The *Align* submenu also is used to align middles or corresponding sides of a group of selected controls. Some other useful submenus of the Format menu are as follows:

   Make Same Size: Equalize the width and/or height of the controls in a group of selected controls.

   Center in Form: Center a selected control either horizontally or vertically in a form.

   Vertical Spacing: Equalize the vertical spacing between a column of three or more selected controls.

   Horizontal Spacing: Equalize the horizontal spacing between a row of three or more selected controls.

10. With the two buttons still selected, open the Properties window and set the ForeColor property to blue.

    Notice that the ForeColor property has been altered for both buttons. Actually, any property that is common to every control in a group of selected multiple controls can be set simultaneously for the entire group of controls.

■ Multiple Controls

When a group of controls are selected with the Ctrl key, the first control selected (called the **dominant control** of the group) will have white sizing handles, while the other controls will have black sizing handles. All alignment and sizing statements initiated from the Format menu will keep the dominant control fixed and will align (or size) the other controls with respect to the dominant control. You can designate a different control to be the dominant control by clicking on it.

After multiple controls have been selected, they can be dragged, deleted, and have properties set as a group. The arrow keys also can be used to move and size multiple controls as a group.

A group of multiple controls also can be selected by clicking the mouse outside the controls, dragging it across the controls, and releasing it. The *Select All* command from the Edit menu (or the key combination Ctrl+A) causes all the controls on the form to be selected.

■ Setting Tab Order

At any time, only one control can receive user input through the keyboard. That control is said to have the *focus*. When a text box has the focus, there is a blinking cursor inside it.

Whenever the Tab key is pressed while a program is running, the focus moves from one control to another. The following walkthrough explains how to determine the order in which the focus moves and how that order can be changed.

1. Start a new program.

2. Place a button, a text box, and a list box on the form.

3. Run the program, and successively press the Tab key.

   Notice that the controls receive the focus in the order they were placed on the form.

4. End the program.

5. Click on *Tab Order* in the View menu.

   The screen appears as in Fig. 2.16(a). The controls are numbered from 0 to 2 in the order they were created. Each of the numbers is referred to as a **tab index**.

| (a) | (b) |

FIGURE 2.16   Tab order.

6. Click on the list box, then the text box, and finally the button.

   Notice that the tab indexes change as shown in Fig. 2.16(b).

7. Click again on *Tab Order* in the View menu to set the new tab order.

8. Run the program again, and successively press the Tab key.

   Notice that the controls receive the focus according to the new tab order.

9. End the program.

10. Add a label to the form, rerun the program, and successively press the Tab key.

    Notice that the label does not receive the focus. Whether or not a control can receive the focus is determined by the setting of its TabStop property. By default, the setting of the TabStop property is True for buttons, text boxes, and list boxes, and False for labels. In this book we always use these default settings. **Note:** Even though labels do not receive the focus while tabbing, they are still assigned a tab index.

■ Comments

1. While you are working on a program, the program resides in memory. Removing a program from memory is referred to as **closing** the program. A program is automatically closed when you begin a new program. Also, it can be closed directly with the *Close Solution* command from the File menu.

2. Three useful properties that have not been discussed are the following:

   (a) *BackColor:* This property specifies the background color for the form or a control.

(b) **Visible:** Setting the Visible property to False causes an object to disappear when the program is run. The object can be made to reappear with code.

(c) **Enabled:** Setting the Enabled property of a control to False restricts its use. It appears grayed and cannot receive the focus. Controls sometimes are disabled temporarily when they are not needed in the current state of the program.

3. Most properties can be set or altered with code as the program is running instead of being preset from the Properties window. For instance, a button can be made to disappear with a line such as `Button1.Visible = False`. The details are presented in Section 2.3.

4. If you inadvertently double-click on a form, a window containing text will appear. (The first line is Public Class Form1.) This is the Code Editor, which is discussed in the next section. To return to the Form Designer, click on the tab at the top of the Document window labeled "Form1.vb [Design]."

5. We have seen two ways to place a control onto a form. Another way is to just click on the control in the Toolbox and then drag the control from the Toolbox to the location in the form.

6. There is a small down-arrow button on the right side of the Text property setting box. When you click on that button, a rectangular box appears. The setting for the Text property can be typed into this box instead of into the Settings box. This method of specifying the setting is especially useful when you want a button to have a multi-line caption.

7. We recommend setting the StartPosition property of the form to CenterScreen. With this setting the form will appear in the center of the screen when the program is run.

8. Refer to the properties windows in Fig. 2.8. If you click on the button at the right side of the Properties window's Object box, a list showing all the controls on the form will drop down. You can then click on one of the controls to make it the selected control.

9. Exercises 35 through 47 develop additional techniques for manipulating and accessing controls placed on a form. We recommend that you work these exercises whether or not they are assigned by your instructor.

Practice Problems 2.2

1. What is the difference between the Text and the Name properties of a button?

2. The first two group names in the Toolbox are *All Windows Forms* and *Common Controls*. How many groups are there?

EXERCISES 2.2

1. Create a form with two buttons, run the program, and click on each button. What do you notice different about a button after it has been clicked?

2. While a program is running, a control is said to lose focus when the focus moves from that control to another control. Give three ways the user can cause a control to lose focus.

In Exercises 3 through 24, carry out the task.

3. Place "CHECKING ACCOUNT" in the title bar of a form.

4. Create a text box containing the words "PLAY IT, SAM" in blue letters.

5. Create a text box with a yellow background.

6. Create a text box named txtGreeting and containing the word "HELLO" in large italic letters.

7. Create a label containing the sentence "After all is said and done, more is said than done." The sentence should occupy three lines, and each line should be centered horizontally in the label.

8. Create a read-only text box containing the words "Visual Basic" in bold white letters on a red background.

9. Create a text box named txtLanguage containing the words "Visual Basic 2015" in Courier New font.

10. Create a yellow button named btnPush containing the word "PUSH".

11. Create a white button containing the word "PUSH" in large italic letters.

12. Create a button containing the word "PUSH" in bold letters with the letter P underlined.

13. Create a button containing the word "PUSH" with the letter H as the access key.

14. Create a label containing the word "ALIAS" in white on a blue background.

15. Create a label named lblAKA containing the centered italicized word "ALIAS".

16. Place "BALANCE SHEET" in the title bar of a form having a yellow background.

17. Create a label containing "VISUAL" on the first line and "BASIC" on the second line. Each word should be right-justified.

18. Create a form named frmHello whose title bar reads "Hello World".

19. Create a label containing the underlined word "PROGRAM" in italics.

20. Create a label containing the bold word "ALIAS" in the Courier New font.

21. Create a list box with a yellow background.

22. Create a list box that will be invisible when the program is run.

23. Create a form named frmYellow with a yellow background.

24. Create a button containing the bold underlined word "BUTTON".

In Exercises 25 through 30, create the form shown in the figure. (These exercises give you practice creating controls and assigning properties. The interfaces do not necessarily correspond to actual programs.)

25.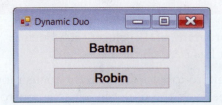

26.

27.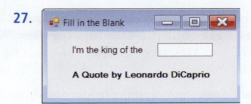

28.

29.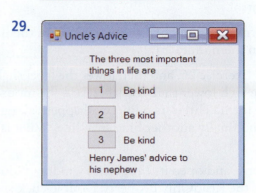

30.

31. Create a replica of your bank check on a form. Words common to all checks, such as "PAY TO THE ORDER OF", should be contained in labels. Items specific to your checks, such as your name at the top left, should be contained in text boxes. Make the check on the screen resemble your personal check as much as possible. *Note:* Omit the account number.

32. Create a replica of your campus ID on a form. Words that are on all student IDs, such as the name of the college, should be contained in labels. Information specific to your ID, such as your name and student ID number, should be contained in text boxes.

33. Consider the form shown in Exercise 25. Assume the *Batman* button was added to the form before the *Robin* button. What is the tab index of the *Robin* button?

34. Consider the form shown in Exercise 26. Assume the first control added to the form was the label. What is the tab index of the label?

The following hands-on exercises develop additional techniques for manipulating and accessing controls placed on a form.

35. Place a text box on a form and select the text box. What is the effect of pressing the various arrow keys?

36. Place a text box on a form and select the text box. What is the effect of pressing the various arrow keys while holding down the Shift key?

37. Repeat Exercise 36 for selected multiple controls.

38. Repeat Exercise 35 for selected multiple controls.

39. Place a label and a list box on a form and change their font sizes to 12 at the same time.

40. Place a button in the center of a form and select it. Hold down the Ctrl key and press an arrow key. Repeat this process for each of the other arrow keys. Describe what happens.

41. Place a label and a text box on a form with the label to the left of and above the text box. Select the label. Hold down the Ctrl key and press the down-arrow key twice. With the Ctrl key still pressed, press the right-arrow key. Describe what happens.

42. Place two buttons on a form with one button to the right of and below the other button. Select the lower button, hold down the Ctrl key, and press the left-arrow key. With the Ctrl key still pressed, press the up-arrow key. Describe the effect of pressing the two arrow keys.

43. Experiment with the *Align* command on the Format menu to determine the difference between the *center* and the *middle* of a control.

44. Place four large buttons vertically on a form. Use the Format menu to make them the same size and to make the spacing between them uniform.

45. Place a label and a text box on a form as in Exercise 26, and then lower the label slightly and lower the text box until it is about one inch lower than the label. Use the mouse to slowly raise the text box to the top of the form. Three snap lines will appear along the way: a blue snap line, a purple snap line, and finally another blue snap line. What is the significance of each snap line?

46. Place a text box on a form, select the text box, and open its Properties window. Double-click on the name (not the Settings box) of the ReadOnly property. Double-click again. What is the effect of double-clicking on a property whose possible settings are True and False?

47. Place a button on a form, select the button, and open its Properties window. Double-click on the name (not the Settings box) of the ForeColor property. Double-click repeatedly. Describe what is happening.

Solutions to Practice Problems 2.2

1. The text is the words appearing on the button, whereas the name is the designation used to refer to the button in code. Initially, they have the same value, such as Button1. However, each can be changed independently of the other.

2. The Toolbox in the Community Edition of Visual Basic contains 10 groups. Figure 2.17 shows the Toolbox after each group has been collapsed. **Note:** In some other editions of Visual Basic the Toolbox contains more groups.

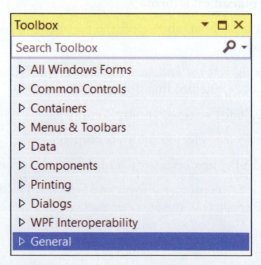

FIGURE 2.17   Toolbox group names.

2.3   Visual Basic Events

VideoNote
Event
Procedures

When a Visual Basic program runs, the form and its controls appear on the screen. Normally, nothing happens until the user takes an action, such as clicking a control or pressing a key. We call such an action an **event**. The programmer writes code that reacts to an event by performing certain tasks.

The three steps in creating a Visual Basic program are as follows:

1. Create the interface; that is, generate, position, and size the objects.
2. Set properties; that is, configure the appearance of the objects.
3. Write the code that executes when events occur.

Section 2.2 covered Steps 1 and 2. This section is devoted to Step 3. Code consists of statements that carry out tasks. Writing code in Visual Basic is assisted by an autocompletion system called **IntelliSense** that reduces the amount of memorization needed and helps prevent errors. In this section, we limit ourselves to statements that change properties of a control or the form while a program is running.

Properties of controls are changed in code with statements of the form

`controlName.property = setting`

where *controlName* is the name of the control, *property* is one of the properties of the control, and *setting* is a valid setting for that property. Such statements are called **assignment statements**. They assign values to properties. Here are three examples of assignment statements:

1. The statement

   `txtBox.Text = "Hello"`

   displays the word Hello in the text box.
2. The statement

   `btnButton.Visible = True`

   makes the button visible.
3. The statement

   `txtBox.ForeColor = Color.Red`

   sets the color of the characters in the text box named txtBox to red.

Most events are associated with controls. The event "click on btnButton" is different from the event "click on lstBox". These two events are specified as btnButton.Click and lstBox.Click. The statements to be executed when an event occurs are written in a block of code called an **event procedure** or **event handler**. The first line of an event procedure (called the **header**) has the form

`Private Sub` *`objectName_event`*`(sender `**`As`**` System.Object,`
        `e `**`As`**` System.EventArgs) `**`Handles`**` `*`objectName.event`*

Since we rarely make any use of the lengthy text inside the parentheses in this book, for the sake of readability we replace it with an ellipsis. However, it will automatically appear in our programs each time Visual Basic creates the header for an event procedure. The structure of an event procedure is

```
Private Sub objectName_event(...) Handles objectName.event
  statements
End Sub
```

where the three dots (that is, the ellipsis) represent

```
sender As System.Object, e As System.EventArgs
```

Words such as "Private," "As," "Sub," "Handles," and "End" have special meanings in Visual Basic and are referred to as **keywords** or **reserved words**. The Code Editor automatically capitalizes the first letter of a keyword and displays the word in blue. The word "Sub" in the first line signals the beginning of the procedure, and the first line identifies the object and the event occurring to that object. The last line signals the termination of the event procedure. The statements to be executed appear between these two lines. These statements are referred to as the **body** of the event procedure. (**Note:** The word "Private" indicates that the event procedure cannot be invoked by another form. This will not concern us until much later in the book. The expression following "Handles" identifies the object and the event happening to that object. The expression "**objectName_event**" is the default name of the procedure and can be changed if desired. In this book, we always use the default name. The word "Sub" is an abbreviation of *Subroutine*.) For instance, the event procedure

```
Private Sub btnButton_Click(...) Handles btnButton.Click
  txtBox.ForeColor = Color.Red
End Sub
```

changes the color of the words in the text box to red when the button is clicked. The clicking of the button is said to **raise** (or to **invoke**, **fire**, or **trigger**) the event, and the event procedure is said to **handle** the event.

■ An Event Procedure Walkthrough

The form in Fig. 2.18 which contains two text boxes and a button, will be used to demonstrate what event procedures are and how they are created. Three event procedures will be used to alter the appearance of a phrase appearing in a text box. The event procedures are named txtFirst_TextChanged, btnRed_Click, and txtFirst_Leave.

OBJECT	PROPERTY	SETTING
frmDemo	Text	Demo
txtFirst		
txtSecond		
btnRed	Text	Change Color to Red

FIGURE 2.18   **The interface for the event procedure walkthrough.**

1. Create the interface in Fig. 2.18 in the Form Designer. The Name properties of the form, text boxes, and button should be set as shown in the Object column. The Text property of the form should be set to Demo, and the Text property of the button should be set to Change Color to Red. No properties need be set for the text boxes.

2. Click the right mouse button anywhere on the Form Designer, and click on *View Code*. The Form Designer IDE is replaced by the **Code Editor** (also known as the *Code view* or the *Code window*). See Fig. 2.19.

Code Editor tab   Form Designer tab

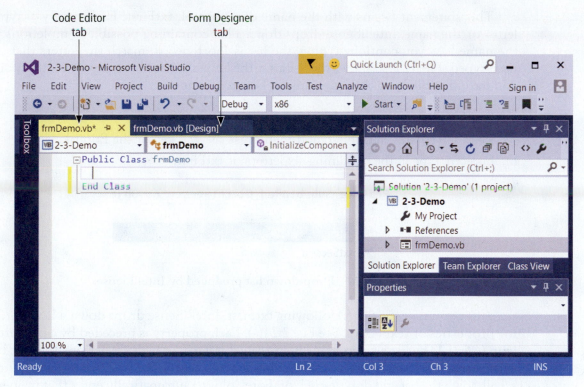

FIGURE 2.19 **The Visual Basic IDE in Code Editor mode.**

The tab labeled frmDemo.vb corresponds to the Code Editor. Click on the tab labeled frmDemo.vb [Design] when you want to return to the Form Designer. We will place our program code between the two lines shown.

Figure 2.19 shows that the Code Editor IDE has a Toolbox, Solution Explorer, and Properties window that support Auto Hide. The Solution Explorer window for the Code Editor functions exactly like the one for the Form Designer. The Code Editor's Toolbox has just one group, General, that is used to store code fragments that can be copied into a program when needed. The Code Editor's Properties window will not be used in this textbook.

3. Click on the tab labeled "frmDemo.vb [Design]" to return to the Form Designer. (You also can invoke the Form Designer by clicking on *Designer* in the View menu, or by right-clicking the Code Editor and clicking on *View Designer*.)

4. Double-click on the button. The Code Editor reappears, but now the following two lines of code have been added to it and the cursor is located on the blank line between them.

```
Private Sub btnRed_Click(...) Handles btnRed.Click

End Sub
```

The first line is the header for an event procedure named btnRed_Click. This procedure is invoked by the event btnRed.Click. That is, whenever the button is clicked, the code between the two lines just shown will be executed.

5. Type the line

```
txtFirst.ForeColor = Color.Red
```

at the cursor location.

This statement begins with the name of a control, txtFirst. Each time you type a letter of the name, IntelliSense drops down a list containing possible completions for the name.[1] As you continue typing, the list is shortened to match the letters that you have typed. Figure 2.20 shows the list after the letters *tx* have been typed. At this point, you have the following three options on how to continue:

i. Double-click on txtFirst in the list.

ii. Keep the cursor on txtFirst, and then press the Tab key or the Enter key.

iii. Directly type in the remaining six letters of txtFirst.

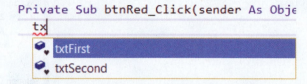

FIGURE 2.20 **Drop-down list produced by IntelliSense.**

After you type the dot (.) following txtFirst, IntelliSense drops down a list containing properties of text boxes. See Fig. 2.21(a). Each property is preceded by a properties icon (🔧). [The list also contains items called *methods*, which are actions the text box can perform. Methods are preceded by a method icon (🔾).] At this point, you can scroll down the list and double-click on ForeColor to automatically enter that property. See Fig. 2.21(b). Or, you can keep typing. After you have typed "For", the list shortens to the single word ForeColor. At that point, you can press the Tab key or the Enter key, or keep typing to obtain the word ForeColor.

After you type in the equal sign, IntelliSense drops down the list of colors shown in Fig. 2.22. You have the option of scrolling to Color.Red and double-clicking on it, or typing Color.Red into the statement.

6. Return to the Form Designer and double-click on the first text box. The Code Editor reappears, and the first and last lines of the event procedure txtFirst_TextChanged appear in it. This procedure is raised by the event txtFirst.TextChanged—that is, whenever there is a change in the text displayed in the text box txtFirst. Type the line that sets the Fore-Color property of txtFirst to blue. The event procedure will now appear as follows:

```
Private Sub txtFirst_TextChanged(...) Handles txtFirst.TextChanged
    txtFirst.ForeColor = Color.Blue
End Sub
```

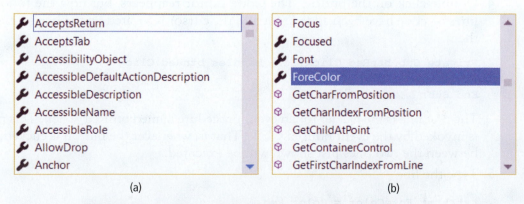

(a)   (b)

FIGURE 2.21 **Drop-down list produced by IntelliSense.**

---

[1] This feature of IntelliSense is referred to as Complete Word.

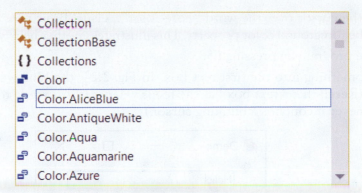

FIGURE 2.22 Drop-down list of colors produced by IntelliSense.

7. Return to the Form Designer and select txtFirst.

8. Click on the *Events* button ( ) in the toolbar near the top of the Properties window. The 63 events associated with text boxes are displayed, and the Description pane at the bottom of the window describes the currently selected event. (Don't be alarmed by the large number of events. Only a few events are used in this book.) Scroll to the Leave event. See Fig. 2.23.

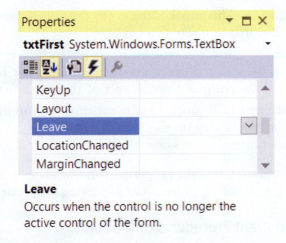

FIGURE 2.23 Events displayed in the Properties window.

9. Double-click on the Leave event. (The event txtFirst.Leave is raised when the focus is moved away from the text box.) The header and the last line of the event procedure txtFirst_Leave will be displayed. In this procedure, type the line that sets the ForeColor property of txtFirst to Black. The Code Editor will now look as follows:

```
Public Class frmDemo
  Private Sub btnRed_Click(...) Handles btnRed.Click
    txtFirst.ForeColor = Color.Red
  End Sub

  Private Sub txtFirst_Leave(...) Handles txtFirst.Leave
    txtFirst.ForeColor = Color.Black
  End Sub

  Private Sub txtFirst_TextChanged(...) Handles txtFirst.TextChanged
    txtFirst.ForeColor = Color.Blue
  End Sub
End Class
```

10. Hover the cursor over the word "ForeColor". Visual Basic now displays information about the foreground color property. This illustrates another help feature of Visual Basic.

11. Run the program by pressing F5.

12. Type something into the first text box. In Fig. 2.24, the blue word "Hello" has been typed. (Recall that a text box has the focus whenever it is ready to accept typing—that is, whenever it contains a blinking cursor.)

FIGURE 2.24 Text box containing input.

13. Click on the second text box. The contents of the first text box will become black. When the second text box was clicked, the first text box lost the focus; that is, the event Leave happened to txtFirst. Thus, the event procedure txtFirst_Leave was invoked, and the code inside the procedure was executed.

14. Click on the button. This invokes the event procedure btnRed_Click, which changes the color of the words in txtFirst to red.

15. Click on the first text box, and type the word "Friend" after the word "Hello". As soon as typing begins, the text in the text box is changed and the TextChanged event is raised. This event causes the color of the contents of the text box to become blue.

16. You can repeat Steps 12 through 15 as many times as you like. When you are finished, end the program by clicking on the *Stop Debugging* button on the Toolbar, clicking on the form's *Close* button, or pressing Alt+F4.

Note: After viewing events in the Properties window, click on the *Properties* button (🔲) to the left of the *Events* button to return to displaying properties in the Properties window.

■ Properties and Event Procedures of the Form

You can assign properties to the form itself in code. However, a statement such as

```
frmDemo.Text = "Demonstration"
```

will not work. The form is referred to by the keyword *Me*. Therefore, the proper statement is

```
Me.Text = "Demonstration"
```

To display a list of all the events associated with frmDemo, select the form in the Form Designer and then click on the *Events* button in the Properties window's toolbar.

■ The Header of an Event Procedure

As mentioned earlier, in the header for an event procedure such as

```
Private Sub btnOne_Click(...) Handles btnOne.Click
```

btnOne_Click is the name of the event procedure, and btnOne.Click identifies the event that invokes the procedure. The name can be changed at will. For instance, the header can be changed to

```
Private Sub ButtonPushed(...) Handles btnOne.Click
```

Also, an event procedure can handle more than one event. For instance, if the previous line is changed to

```
Private Sub ButtonPushed(...) Handles btnOne.Click, btnTwo.Click
```

the event procedure will be invoked if either btnOne or btnTwo is clicked.

We have been using ellipses (. . .) as place holders for the phrase

```
sender As System.Object, e As System.EventArgs
```

In Chapter 5, we will gain a better understanding of this type of phrase. Essentially, the word "sender" carries a reference to the object that raised the event, and the letter "e" carries some additional information that the sending object wants to communicate. We will make use of "sender" and/or "e" in Section 9.4 only when sending output to the printer. You can delete the entire phrase from any other type of program in this book and just leave the blank set of parentheses.

■ Opening a Program

Beginning with the next chapter, each example contains a program. These programs can be downloaded from the Pearson website for this book. See the discussion in the Preface for details. The process of loading a program stored on a disk into the Visual Basic environment is referred to as **opening** the program. Let's open the downloaded program 7-2-3 from Chapter 7. That program allows you to enter a first name, and then displays U.S. presidents having that first name.

1. From Visual Basic, hover over *Open* in the File menu and then click on *Project/Solution*. (An Open Project dialog box will appear.)

2. Navigate to the contents of the Ch07 subfolder downloaded from the website.

3. Double-click on 7-2-3.

4. Double-click on 7-2-3.sln.

5. If the Solution Explorer window is not visible, click on *Solution Explorer* in the View menu.

6. If the file frmPresident.vb is not visible in the Solution Explorer, click on the symbol to the left of 7-2-3 in the Solution Explorer in order to display the file.

7. Double-click on frmPresident.vb. The Form Designer for the program will be revealed and the Solution Explorer window will appear as in Fig. 2.25. (You can click on the *View Code* button to reveal the Code Editor. The *Show All Files* and *Refresh* buttons, which

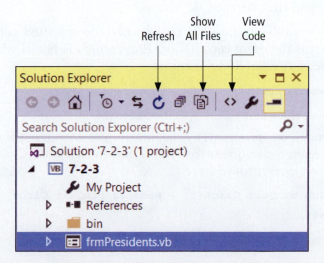

FIGURE 2.25 Solution Explorer window.

allow you to view all the files in a program's folder and to update certain files, will be used extensively beginning with Chapter 7.)

8. Press F5 to run the program.

9. Type in a name (such as James or William), and click the *Display Presidents* button. (See Fig. 2.26.) You can repeat this process as many times as desired.

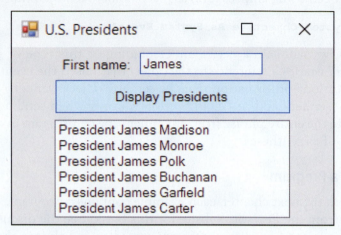

FIGURE 2.26 Possible output for program 7-2-3.

10. End the program.

The program just executed uses a text file named USPres.txt. To view the text file, open the folder *bin*, open the subfolder *Debug,* and click on USPres.txt. (If the *bin* folder is not visible, click on the *Show All Files* button. If USPres.txt is not listed in the *Debug* subfolder, click the *Refresh* button and reopen the folders. After reading Chapter 7, you will understand why text files are placed in the *Debug* subfolder of the *bin* folder.) The first line of the file gives the name of the first president; the second line gives the name of the second president, and so on. To close the text file, click on the *Close* button (❌) on the USPres.txt tab.

■ Comments

1. The Visual Basic editor automatically indents the statements inside procedures. In this book, we indent by two spaces. To instruct your editor to indent by two spaces, click on *Options* in the Tools menu to display an Options dialog box, expand the "Text Editor" item in the left pane, expand the "Basic" item, click on "Tabs", enter 2 into the "Indent size:" box, and click on the OK button.

2. The event *controlName.*Leave is raised when the specified control loses the focus. Its counterpart is the event *controlName.*Enter which is raised when the specified control gets the focus. A related statement is

`controlName.Focus()`

which moves the focus to the specified control.

3. We have ended our programs by clicking the *Stop Debugging* button or pressing Alt+F4. A more elegant technique is to create a button, call it btnQuit, with caption Quit and the following event procedure:

```
Private Sub btnQuit_Click(...) Handles btnQuit.Click
  Me.Close()
End Sub
```

4. For statements of the form

   object.**Text** = *setting*

   the expression for *setting* must be surrounded by quotation marks. (For instance, the statement might be lblName.Text = "Name:".) For properties where the proper setting is one of the words True or False, these words should *not* be surrounded by quotation marks.

5. Names of existing event procedures associated with an object are not automatically changed when you rename the object. You must change them yourself. However, the event that invokes the procedure (and all other references to the control) will change automatically. For example, suppose an event procedure is

   ```
   Private Sub btnOne_Click(...) Handles btnOne.Click
     btnOne.Text = "Push Me"
   End Sub
   ```

   and, in the Form Designer, you change the name of btnOne to btnTwo. Then, when you return to the Code Editor, the procedure will be

   ```
   Private Sub btnOne_Click(...) Handles btnTwo.Click
     btnTwo.Text = "Push Me"
   End Sub
   ```

6. The Code Editor has many features of a word processor. For instance, the operations cut, copy, paste, and find can be carried out from the Edit menu.

7. The Code Editor can detect certain types of errors. For instance, if you type

   ```
   txtFirst.Text = hello
   ```

   and then move away from the line, the automatic syntax checker will underline the word "hello" with a blue squiggle to indicate that something is wrong. When the mouse cursor is hovered over the underlined expression, the editor will display a message explaining what is wrong. If you try to run the program without correcting the error, the dialog box in Figure 2.27 will appear.

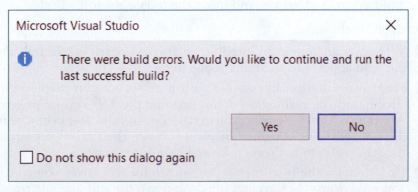

FIGURE 2.27 Error dialog box.

8. Each control has a favored event, called the **default event**, whose event procedure template can be generated from the Form Designer by double-clicking on the control. Table 2.2 on the next page shows some controls and their default events. The most common event appearing in this book is the Click event for a button. The TextChanged event for a text box was used in this section.

TABLE 2.2	**Some default events.**
Control	**Default Event**
form	Load
button	Click
label	Click
list box	SelectedIndexChanged
text box	TextChanged

The SelectedIndexChanged event for a list box is introduced in Section 4.4, and the Load event for a form is introduced in Section 7.1. The Click event for a label is never used in this book.

9. Font properties, such as the name, style, and size, are usually specified at design time. The setting of the properties can be displayed in code with statements such as

```
lstBox.Items.Add(txtBox.Font.Name)

lstBox.Items.Add(txtBox.Font.Bold)

lstBox.Items.Add(txtBox.Font.Size)
```

However, a font's name, style, and size properties cannot be altered in code with statements such as

```
txtBox.Font.Name = "Courier New"

txtBox.Font.Bold = True

txtBox.Font.Size = 16
```

10. When you make changes to a program, asterisks appear as superscripts on the tabs labeled "frmName.vb [design]" and "frmName.vb" to indicate that some part of the program is new. The asterisks disappear when the program is saved or run.

    Note: When a program has been saved to disk, all files for the program will be automatically updated on the disk whenever the program is saved or run.

11. You can easily change the size of the font used in the current program's Code Editor. Just hold down the Ctrl key and move the mouse's scroll wheel.

12. Notes on IntelliSense:

    (a) Whenever an item in an IntelliSense drop-down list is selected, a tooltip describing the item appears to the right of the item.

    (b) From the situation in Fig. 2.20, on page 40, we can display txtFirst by double-clicking on the highlighted item, pressing the Tab key, or pressing the Enter key. Another option is to press the period key. In this case, both the name txtFirst and the dot following it will be displayed. *Note:* The period key option works only if the selected item is always followed by a dot in code.

    (c) Occasionally, the IntelliSense drop-down list will cover some of your program. If you hold down the Ctrl key, the drop-down list will become transparent and allow you to see the covered-up code.

13. While working in the design window, you can obtain information about a control or a keyword by placing the cursor on it and pressing the F1 key. Visual Basic will connect to the Microsoft Website through your browser and display information about the selected item. This feature is called **context-sensitive help**.

Practice Problems 2.3

1. Describe the event that invokes the following event procedure

```
Private Sub btnCompute_Click(...) Handles txtBox.Leave
    txtBox.Text = "Hello world"
End Sub
```

2. Give a statement that will prevent the user from typing into txtBox.

EXERCISES 2.3

In Exercises 1 through 6, describe the contents of the text box after the button is clicked.

1.
```
Private Sub btnOutput_Click(...) Handles btnOutput.Click
    txtBox.Text = "Hello"
End Sub
```

2.
```
Private Sub btnOutput_Click(...) Handles btnOutput.Click
    txtBox.ForeColor = Color.Red
    txtBox.Text = "Hello"
End Sub
```

3.
```
Private Sub btnOutput_Click(...) Handles btnOutput.Click
    txtBox.BackColor = Color.Orange
    txtBox.Text = "Hello"
End Sub
```

4.
```
Private Sub btnOutput_Click(...) Handles btnOutput.Click
    txtBox.Text = "Goodbye"
    txtBox.Text = "Hello"
End Sub
```

5.
```
Private Sub btnOutput_Click(...) Handles btnOutput.Click
    txtBox.Text = "Hello"
    txtBox.Visible = False
End Sub
```

6.
```
Private Sub btnOutput_Click(...) Handles btnOutput.Click
    txtBox.BackColor = Color.Yellow
    txtBox.Text = "Hello"
End Sub
```

In Exercises 7 through 10, assume that the three objects on the form were created in the order txtFirst, txtSecond, and lblOne. Determine the output displayed in lblOne when the program is run and the Tab key is pressed. *Note:* Initially, txtFirst has the focus.

7.
```
Private Sub txtFirst_Leave(...) Handles txtFirst.Leave
    lblOne.ForeColor = Color.Green
    lblOne.Text = "Hello"
End Sub
```

8. ```
Private Sub txtFirst_Leave(...) Handles txtFirst.Leave
    lblOne.BackColor = Color.White
    lblOne.Text = "Hello"
End Sub
```

9. ```
Private Sub txtSecond_Enter(...) Handles txtSecond.Enter
    lblOne.BackColor = Color.Gold
    lblOne.Text = "Hello"
End Sub
```

10. ```
Private Sub txtSecond_Enter(...) Handles txtSecond.Enter
    lblOne.Visible = False
    lblOne.Text = "Hello"
End Sub
```

**In Exercises 11 through 16, determine the errors.**

11. ```
Private Sub btnOutput_Click(...) Handles btnOutput.Click
    Form1.Text = "Hello"
End Sub
```

12. ```
Private Sub btnOutput_Click(...) Handles btnOutput.Click
    txtBox.Text = Hello
End Sub
```

13. ```
Private Sub btnOutput_Click(...) Handles btnOutput.Click
    txtFirst.ForeColor = Red
End Sub
```

14. ```
Private Sub btnOutput_Click(...) Handles btnOutput.Click
    txtBox = "Hello"
End Sub
```

15. ```
Private Sub btnOutput_Click(...) Handles btnOutput.Click
    txtBox.Font.Size = 20
End Sub
```

16. ```
Private Sub btnOutput_Click(...) Handles btn1.Click, btn2.Click
    Me.Color = Color.Yellow
End Sub
```

**In Exercises 17 through 28, write a line (or lines) of code to carry out the task.**

17. Display "E.T. phone home." in lblTwo.

18. Display "Play it, Sam." in red in lblTwo.

19. Display "The stuff that dreams are made of." in red letters in txtBox.

20. Display "Life is like a box of chocolates." in txtBox with blue letters on a gold background.

21. Disable txtBox.

22. Change the words in the form's title bar to "Hello World."

23. Make lblTwo disappear.
```

24. Change the color of the letters in lblName to red.

25. Enable the disabled button btnOutcome.

26. Give the focus to btnCompute.

27. Give the focus to txtBoxTwo.

28. Change the background color of the form to White.

29. Describe the Enter event in your own words.

30. Describe the Leave event in your own words.

31. The label control has an event called DoubleClick that is raised by double-clicking the left mouse button. Write a simple program to test this event. Determine whether you can raise the DoubleClick event without also raising the Click event.

32. Write a simple program to demonstrate that a button's Click event is raised when you press the Enter key while the button has the focus.

In Exercises 33 through 38, the interface and initial properties are specified. Write a program to carry out the stated task.

33. When one of the three buttons is pressed, the words on the button are displayed in the text box with the stated alignment. *Note:* Rely on IntelliSense to provide you with the proper settings for the TextAlign property.

OBJECT	PROPERTY	SETTING
frmAlign	Text	Align Text
txtBox	ReadOnly	True
btnLeft	Text	Left Justify
btnCenter	Text	Center
btnRight	Text	Right Justify

34. When one of the buttons is pressed, the face changes to a smiling face [emoticon :-)] or a frowning face [emoticon :-( ].

OBJECT	PROPERTY	SETTING
frmFace	Text	Face
lblFace	Font Size	18
	Text	:-|
btnSmile	Text	Smile
btnFrown	Text	Frown

35. Pressing the buttons alters the background and foreground colors in the text box.

OBJECT	PROPERTY	SETTING
frmColors	Text	Colorful Text
lblBack	Text	Background
btnRed	Text	Red
btnBlue	Text	Blue
txtBox	Text	Beautiful Day
	TextAlign	Center
lblFore	Text	Foreground
btnWhite	Text	White
btnYellow	Text	Yellow

36. When one of the three text boxes receives the focus, its text becomes red. When it loses the focus, the text returns to black. The buttons set the alignment in the text boxes to Left or Right. ***Note:*** Rely on IntelliSense to provide you with the proper settings for the TextAlign property.

OBJECT	PROPERTY	SETTING
frm123	Text	1, 2, 3
txtOne	Text	One
txtTwo	Text	Two
txtThree	Text	Three
btnLeft	Text	Left
btnRight	Text	Right

37. When the user moves the focus to one of the three small text boxes at the bottom of the form, an appropriate saying is displayed in the large text box. Use the sayings "I like life, it's something to do."; "The future isn't what it used to be."; and "Tell the truth and run."

OBJECT	PROPERTY	SETTING
frmQuote	Text	Sayings
txtQuote	ReadOnly	True
txtLife	Text	Life
txtFuture	Text	Future
txtTruth	Text	Truth

38. The user can disable or enable the text box by clicking on the appropriate button. After the user clicks the *Enable* button, the text box should receive the focus.

OBJECT	PROPERTY	SETTING
frmTextBox	Text	Text Box
txtBox		
btnDisable	Text	Disable Text Box
btnEnable	Text	Enable Text Box

In Exercises 39 through 44, write a program to carry out the task.

39. The form contains four square buttons arranged in a rectangular array. Each button has the caption "Push Me". When the user clicks on a button, the button disappears and the other three become or remain visible. See Fig. 2.28.

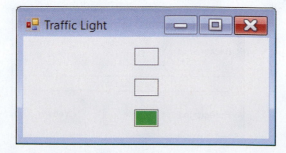

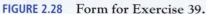

FIGURE 2.28   Form for Exercise 39.   **FIGURE 2.29   Form for Exercise 40.**

40. Simulate a traffic light with three small square text boxes placed vertically on a form. See Fig. 2.29. Initially, the bottom text box is solid green and the other text boxes are dark gray. When the Tab key is pressed, the middle text box turns yellow and the bottom text box turns dark gray. The next time Tab is pressed, the top text box turns red and the middle text box turns dark gray. Subsequent pressing of the Tab key cycles through the three colors. **Hint:** First place the bottom text box on the form, then the middle text box, and finally the top text box.

41. Use the same form and properties as in Exercise 34, with the captions for the buttons replaced with Vanish and Reappear. Clicking a button should produce the stated result.

FIGURE 2.30   Possible output of Exercise 41.

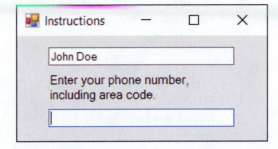

FIGURE 2.31   Possible output of Exercise 42.

42. A form contains two text boxes and one large label between them with no preset caption. When the first text box receives the focus, the label reads "Enter your full name." When the second text box receives the focus, the label reads "Enter your phone number, including area code." See Fig 2.31.

43. The form contains a single read-only text box and two buttons. When the user clicks on one of the buttons, the sentence "You just clicked on a button." is displayed in the text box. The program should consist of a single event procedure. See Fig 2.32.

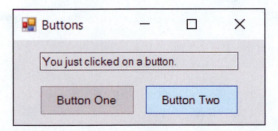

FIGURE 2.32   Possible output of Exercise 43.

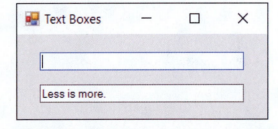

FIGURE 2.33   Possible output of Exercise 44.

44. The form contains two text boxes into which the user types information. When the user clicks on one of the text boxes, it becomes blank and its contents are displayed in the other text box. **Note:** A text box can be cleared with the statement `txtBox.Clear()` or the statement `txtBox.Text = ""`. See Fig 2.33.

Solutions to Practice Problems 2.3

1. The event is raised when txtBox loses the focus since txtBox.Leave is the event following the keyword Handles. The name of the event procedure, btnCompute_Click, can be anything; it plays no role in determining the action that raises the event.

2. Three possibilities are

```
txtBox.Enabled = False
txtBox.ReadOnly = True
txtBox.Visible = False
```

CHAPTER 2   SUMMARY

1. The Visual Basic Form Designer displays a *form* that can hold a collection of *controls* for which various attributes (called *properties*) can be set. Some examples of controls are text boxes, labels, buttons, and list boxes. Some useful properties are Text (sets the text displayed in a control), Name (used to give a meaningful name to a control), Font. Name (selects the name of the font used), Font.Size (sets the size of the text displayed), Font.Bold (displays boldface text), Font.Italic (displays italics text), BackColor (sets the background color), ForeColor (sets the color of the text), ReadOnly (determines whether text can be typed into a text box when the program is running), TextAlign (sets the type of alignment for the text in a control), Enabled (determines whether a control can respond to user interaction), and Visible (determines whether an object can be seen or is hidden).

2. An *event procedure* is invoked when something happens to a specified object. Some events are *object*.Click (*object* is clicked), *object*.TextChanged (a change occurred in the value of the object's Text property), *object*.Leave (*object* loses the focus), and *object*.Enter (*object* receives the focus). **Note:** The statement *object*.Focus() moves the focus to the specified object.

3. *IntelliSense* provides a host of features that help you write code.

4. *Tab order,* the order in which the user moves the focus from one control to another by pressing the Tab key while the program is running, can be set from the Properties window.

3

Variables, Input, and Output

53

3.1 Numbers

Much of the data processed by computers consist of numbers. In programming terms, numbers are called **numeric literals**. This section discusses the operations that are performed with numbers and the ways numbers are displayed.

■ Arithmetic Operations

The five standard arithmetic operations in Visual Basic are addition, subtraction, multiplication, division, and exponentiation. Addition, subtraction, and division are denoted in Visual Basic by the standard symbols $+$, $-$, and $/$, respectively. However, the notations for multiplication and exponentiation differ from the customary mathematical notations.

Mathematical Notation	Meaning	Visual Basic Notation
$a \cdot b$ or $a \times b$	a times b	$a * b$
a^r	a to the rth power	$a \wedge r$

One way to show a number on the screen is to display it in a list box. If n is a number, then the instruction

```
lstBox.Items.Add(n)
```

displays the number n as the last item in the list box. *Add* is called a **method**. (Generally, a method is a process that performs a task for a particular object.) If the parentheses contain a combination of numbers and arithmetic operations, the operations are carried out and then the *Add* method displays the result. Another important method is *Clear*. The statement

```
lstBox.Items.Clear()
```

removes all the items displayed in the list box.

 Example 1 **Arithmetic Operations** The following program applies each of the five arithmetic operations. Preceding the program are the form design and a table showing the names of the objects on the form and the altered settings, if any, for properties of these objects. This form design is also used in the discussion and examples in the remainder of this section.

The word "Run" in the phrasing [Run . . .] indicates that the *Start* button or F5 should be pressed to execute the program. Notice that in the output 3 / 2 is displayed in decimal form. Visual Basic never displays numbers as fractions. In the evaluation of $2*(3 + 4)$, the operation inside the parentheses is calculated first.

Note: All programs appearing in examples and case studies are provided on the companion website for this book. See the discussion in the Preface for details.

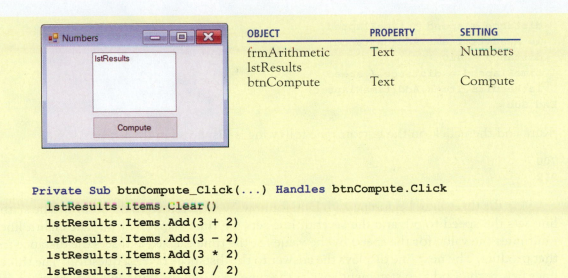

OBJECT	PROPERTY	SETTING
frmArithmetic	Text	Numbers
lstResults		
btnCompute	Text	Compute

```
Private Sub btnCompute_Click(...) Handles btnCompute.Click
    lstResults.Items.Clear()
    lstResults.Items.Add(3 + 2)
    lstResults.Items.Add(3 - 2)
    lstResults.Items.Add(3 * 2)
    lstResults.Items.Add(3 / 2)
    lstResults.Items.Add(3 ^ 2)
    lstResults.Items.Add(2 * (3 + 4))
End Sub
```

[Run, and then click on the button.]

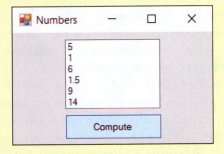

■ Variables

In mathematics problems, quantities are referred to by names. For instance, consider the following algebra problem: "If a car travels at 50 miles per hour, how far will it travel in 14 hours? Also, how many hours are required to travel 410 miles?" The solution to this problem uses the well-known formula

$$\text{distance} = \text{speed} \times \text{time elapsed}$$

Here's how this problem would be solved with a computer program:

```
Private Sub btnCompute_Click(...) Handles btnCompute.Click
    Dim speed As Double
    Dim timeElapsed As Double
    Dim distance As Double
    lstResults.Items.Clear()
    speed = 50
    timeElapsed = 14
```

```
    distance = speed * timeElapsed
    lstResults.Items.Add(distance)
    distance = 410
    timeElapsed = distance / speed
    lstResults.Items.Add(timeElapsed)
End Sub
```

[Run, and then click on the button. The following is displayed in the list box.]

```
700
8.2
```

Skip the three lines beginning with Dim for now. We will return to them soon. The sixth line sets the speed to 50, and the seventh line sets the time elapsed to 14. The eighth line multiplies the value for the speed by the value for the time elapsed and sets the distance to that product. The next line displays the answer to the distance-traveled question. The three lines before the End Sub statement answer the time-required question in a similar manner.

The names *speed*, *timeElapsed*, and *distance*, which hold values, are referred to as **variables**. Consider the variable *timeElapsed*. In the seventh line, its value was set to 14. In the eleventh line, its value was changed as the result of a computation. On the other hand, the variable *speed* had the same value, 50, throughout the program.

VideoNote

Numbers & Strings

A variable is an object used to store a value. The value assigned to the variable may change during the execution of the program. In Visual Basic, variable names must begin with a letter or an underscore, and can consist only of letters, digits, and underscores. (The shortest variable names consist of a single letter.) Visual Basic does not distinguish between uppercase and lowercase letters used in variable names. Some examples of variable names are *total*, *numberOfCars*, *taxRate_2016*, and *n*. As a convention, we write variable names in lowercase letters except for the first letters of each additional word (as in *gradeOnFirstExam*). This convention is called **camel casing**. Descriptive variable names such as *distance* and *timeElapsed* help others (and you at a later time) easily recall what the variable represents.

If *var* is a variable and *n* is a numeric literal, then the statement

var = n

assigns the number *n* to the variable *var*. Such a statement is another example of an assignment statement.

A variable is declared to be of a certain type depending on the sort of data that can be assigned to it. The most versatile type for holding numbers is called **Double**. A variable of type Double can hold whole, fractional, or mixed numbers between about $-1.8 \cdot 10^{308}$ and $1.8 \cdot 10^{308}$. Dim statements (also called **declaration statements**) declare the names and types of the variables to be used in the program. The second, third, and fourth lines of the preceding event procedure declare three variables of type Double and give them the names *speed*, *timeElapsed*, and *distance*. Variables must be declared before values can be assigned to them.

In general, a statement of the form

Dim *varName* As Double

declares a variable named *varName* to be of type Double. Actually, the Dim statement causes the computer to set aside a location in memory referenced by *varName*. You might think of the word *Dim* as meaning "make some space in memory for." The data type specifies the kind of value that will be placed into the space.

Since *varName* is a numeric variable, the Dim statement initially places the number zero in that memory location. (We say that zero is the **initial value** or **default value** of the variable.) Each subsequent assignment statement having *varName* to the left of the equal sign will change the value of the number.

The initial value can be set to a value other than zero. To specify a nonzero initial value, follow the declaration statement with an equal sign followed by the initial value. The statement

```
Dim varName As Double = 50
```

declares the specified variable as a variable of type Double and gives it the initial value 50.

The statement

```
lstBox.Items.Add(varName)
```

looks into this memory location for the current value of the variable and adds that value to the list box.

IntelliSense provides assistance with both declaration and assignment statements. Consider the pair of statements

```
Dim interestRate As Double
interestRate = 0.05
```

In the first statement, IntelliSense will suggest the word "As" after you type "Dim interestRate", and will suggest the word "Double" after you type "Dou". In the second statement, IntelliSense will suggest the word "interestRate" after you type "inte". Thus, IntelliSense both speeds up the writing of programs and helps protect against spelling errors.

A combination of literals, variables, and arithmetic operations that can be evaluated to yield a number is called a **numeric expression**. Expressions are evaluated by replacing each variable by its value and carrying out the arithmetic. Some examples of expressions are (2*distance) + 7, n + 1, and (a + b) / 3.

Example 2 **Evaluate Expressions** The following program displays the default value of a variable and the value of an expression:

```
Private Sub btnCompute_Click(...) Handles btnCompute.Click
  Dim a As Double
  Dim b As Double = 3
  lstResults.Items.Clear()
  lstResults.Items.Add(a)
  lstResults.Items.Add(b)
  a = 5
  lstResults.Items.Add(a * (2 + b))
End Sub
```

[Run, and then click on the button. The following is displayed in the list box.]

```
0
3
25
```

If *var* is a variable, then the assignment statement

var = expression

first evaluates the expression on the right and *then* assigns its value to the variable on the left. For instance, the event procedure in Example 2 can be written as

```
Private Sub btnCompute_Click(...) Handles btnCompute.Click
  Dim a As Double
  Dim b As Double = 3
  Dim c As Double
  lstResults.Items.Clear()
  lstResults.Items.Add(a)
  lstResults.Items.Add(b)
  a = 5
  c = a * (2 + b)
  lstResults.Items.Add(c)
End Sub
```

The expression a*(2 + b) is evaluated to 25, and then this value is assigned to the variable c.

■ Augmented Assignments

Because the expression on the right side of an assignment statement is evaluated *before* an assignment is made, a statement such as

var = var + 1

is meaningful. It first evaluates the expression on the right (that is, it adds 1 to the value of the variable *var*) and then assigns this sum to the variable *var*. The effect is to increase the value of the variable *var* by 1. In terms of memory locations, the statement retrieves the value of *var* from *var*'s memory location, uses it to compute *var* + 1, and then places the sum back into *var*'s memory location. This type of calculation is so common that Visual Basic provides a special operator to carry it out. The statement **var = var + 1** can be replaced with the statement

var += 1

In general, if *n* has a numeric value, then the statement

var += n

adds the value of *n* to the value of *var*. The operator += is said to perform an **augmented assignment**. Some other augmented assignment operators are −=, *=, /=, and ^=.

■ Mathematical Functions

There are several common operations that we often perform on numbers other than the standard arithmetic operations. For instance, we may take the square root of a number or round a number. These operations are performed by built-in functions. Functions associate with one or more values, called the *input*, a single value called the *output*. The function is said to **return** the output value. The three functions considered here have numeric input and output.

The function Math.Sqrt calculates the square root of a number. The function Int finds the greatest integer less than or equal to a number. Therefore, Int discards the decimal part of positive numbers. The value of Math.Round(n, r) is the number n rounded to r decimal places. The parameter r can be omitted. If so, n is rounded to a whole number. Some examples follow:

EXPRESSION	VALUE	EXPRESSION	VALUE	EXPRESSION	VALUE
Math.Sqrt(9)	3	Int(2.7)	2	Math.Round(2.7)	3
Math.Sqrt(0)	0	Int(3)	3	Math.Round(2.317, 2)	2.32
Math.Sqrt(6.25)	2.5	Int(−2.7)	−3	Math.Round(2.317, 1)	2.3

The terms inside the parentheses can be numbers (as shown), numeric variables, or numeric expressions. Expressions are first evaluated to produce the input.

Example 3 **Evaluate Mathematics Functions** The following program evaluates each of the functions for a specific input given by the value of the variable *n*:

```
Private Sub btnCompute_Click(...) Handles btnCompute.Click
  Dim n As Double
  Dim root As Double
  n = 6.76
  root = Math.Sqrt(n)
  lstResults.Items.Clear()
  lstResults.Items.Add(root)
  lstResults.Items.Add(Int(n))
  lstResults.Items.Add(Math.Round(n, 1))
End Sub
```

[Run, and then click on the *Compute* button. The following is displayed in the list box.]

```
2.6
6
6.8
```

Example 4 **Evaluate Mathematics Functions** The following program evaluates each of the preceding functions at an expression:

```
Private Sub btnCompute_Click(...) Handles btnCompute.Click
  Dim a As Double
  Dim b As Double
  a = 2
  b = 3
  lstResults.Items.Clear()
  lstResults.Items.Add(Math.Sqrt((5 * b) + 1))
  lstResults.Items.Add(Int((a ^ b) + 0.8))
  lstResults.Items.Add(Math.Round(a / b, 3))
End Sub
```

[Run, and then click on the button. The following is displayed in the list box.]

```
4
8
0.667
```

■ The Integer Data Type

In this text, we sometimes need to use variables of type **Integer**. An integer variable is declared with a statement of the form

```
Dim varName As Integer
```

and can be assigned only whole numbers from about −2 billion to 2 billion. Integer variables are commonly used for counting.

■ Two Other Integer Operators

In addition to the five arithmetic operators discussed at the beginning of this section, the *Mod* operator and the *integer division* operator (\ ) are also available in Visual Basic. Let m and n be positive whole numbers. When you use long division to divide m by n, you obtain an integer quotient and an integer remainder. In Visual Basic, the integer quotient is denoted $m \setminus n$ and the integer remainder is denoted m Mod n. For instance,

$$
\begin{array}{r}
4 \leftarrow 14 \setminus 3 \\
3\overline{)14} \\
\underline{12} \\
2 \leftarrow 14 \text{ Mod } 3
\end{array}
$$

Essentially, $m \setminus n$ divides two numbers and chops off the fraction part, and m Mod n is the remainder when m is divided by n. Some examples are as follows.

EXPRESSION	VALUE	EXPRESSION	VALUE
19 \ 5	3	19 Mod 5	4
10 \ 2	5	10 Mod 2	0
5 \ 7	0	5 Mod 7	5

Example 5   **Convert Lengths** The following program converts 41 inches to 3 feet and 5 inches:

```
Private Sub btnCompute_Click(...) Handles btnCompute.Click
  Dim totalInches As Integer
  Dim feet As Integer
  Dim inches As Integer
  totalInches = 41
  feet = totalInches \ 12
  inches = totalInches Mod 12
  lstResults.Items.Add(feet)
  lstResults.Items.Add(inches)
End Sub
```

[Run, and then click on the button. The following is displayed in the list box.]

```
3
5
```

Note: You can think of integer division as throwing away the fractional part of an ordinary division.

■ The Decimal Data Type

The Double data type provides the largest and smallest possible magnitudes for a number. However, the Double data type is subject to rounding errors. The rounding errors are slight and inconsequential except in applications that manipulate dollar amounts.

The **Decimal** data type uses a different format for storing numbers than the Double data type. The Decimal data type requires more memory space than the Double data type and limits the magnitude of numbers that can be handled. However, the Decimal data type is not subject to rounding errors. In this textbook, we use the Decimal data type for all financial calculations.

A Decimal variable is declared with a statement of the form

```
Dim varName As Decimal
```

and can be assigned numbers with up to 29 significant digits. For reasons that will be explained in the next section, when a literal number containing a decimal point is assigned to a variable of type Decimal, the letter *D* must be appended to the end of the literal number.

 Example 6 **Calculate a New Balance** The following program calculates the balance in a savings account after one year when $1,025.45 is deposited at 4% interest compounded annually:

```
Private Sub btnCalculate_Click(...) Handles btnCalculate.Click
  Dim balance As Decimal = 1025.45D
  Dim interestRate As Decimal = 0.04D
  balance = balance + (interestRate * balance)
  lstResult.Items.Add(Math.Round(balance, 2))
End Sub
```

[Run, and then click on the button. The following is displayed in the list box.]
```
1066.47
```

Multiple Declarations

Several variables of the same type can be declared with a single Dim statement. For instance, the two Dim statements in Example 4 can be replaced by the single statement

```
Dim a, b As Double
```

Two other types of multiple-declaration statement are

```
Dim a As Double, b As Integer, c As Decimal
Dim a As Double = 2, b As Integer = 5, c As Decimal = 1.5D
```

Parentheses, Order of Precedence

Parentheses should be used to clarify the meaning of a numeric expression. When there are insufficient parentheses, the arithmetic operations are performed in the following order of precedence:

1. terms inside parentheses (inner to outer)

2. exponentiation

3. multiplication, division (ordinary and integer), and modulus

4. addition and subtraction.

In the event of a tie, the leftmost operation is performed first. For instance, 8 / 2 * 3 is evaluated as (8 / 2) * 3.

A good programming practice is to use parentheses liberally so that you *never* have to remember the order of precedence. For instance, write (2 * 3) + 4 instead of 2 * 3 + 4 and write (2 ^ 3) + 4 instead of 2 ^ 3 + 4.

Parentheses cannot be used to indicate multiplication, as is commonly done in algebra. For instance, the expression $x(y + z)$ is not valid. It must be written as x * (y + z).

■ Three Kinds of Errors

Grammatical and punctuation errors are called **syntax errors**. Most syntax errors are spotted by the Code Editor when they are entered. The editor underlines the syntax error with a wavy blue line and displays a description of the error when the mouse cursor is hovered over the wavy line. Some incorrect statements and their errors are shown in Table 3.1.

TABLE 3.1	Three syntax errors.
Statement	**Reason for Error**
`lstBox.Itms.Add(3)`	The word "Items" is misspelled.
`lstBox.Items.Add(2 + )`	The number following the plus sign is missing.
`Dim m; n As Integer`	The semicolon should be a comma.

Errors that occur while a program is running are called **runtime errors** or **exceptions**. (Exceptions are said to be **thrown** by Visual Basic.) They usually occur because something outside the program does not behave as expected. For instance, if the file Data.txt is not in the root folder of the C drive, then a statement that refers to the file by the filespec "C:\Data.txt" will cause the program to stop executing and produce a message box with the title

`FileNotFoundException was unhandled.`

Also, a yellow arrow will appear at the left side of the line of code that caused the error. At that point, you should end the program.

A third type of error is called a **logic error**. Such an error occurs when a program does not perform the way it was intended. For instance, the statement

`average = firstNum + secondNum / 2`

is syntactically correct. However, an incorrect value will be generated, since the correct way to calculate the average is

`average = (firstNum + secondNum) / 2`

Logic errors are the most difficult type to find. Appendix D discusses debugging tools that can be used to detect and correct logic errors.

■ The Error List Window

Syntax errors are not only indicated in the Code Editor, but also are listed in the Error List window. **Note:** If the window is not visible, click on *Error List* in the View menu.

 Example 7 **Identify Errors** The following program contains errors. **Note:** Line 1 of the Code Editor contains the Public Class statement and line 2 is a blank line. Therefore, the Private Sub statement is in line 3 and the Dim statement is in line 4.

```
Private Sub btnCompute_Click(...) Handles btnCompute.Click
  Dim m; n As Double
  lstResults.Items.Add(5
  lstResults.Items.Add(a)
End Sub
```

[Run, click on the button, and click on the *No* button in the error dialog box that appears.]

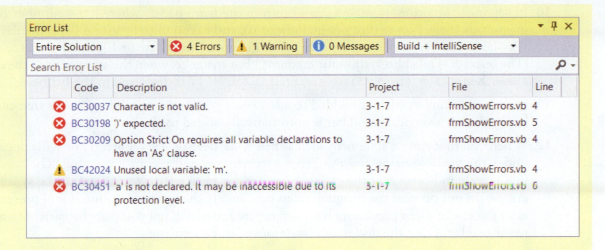

Note: If you double-click on one of the error lines in the Error List window, the Code Editor will appear with the cursor at the location of the error.

■ Comments

1. Declaring all variables at the beginning of each event procedure is considered good programming practice because it makes programs easier to read and helps prevent certain types of errors.

2. Keywords (reserved words) cannot be used as names of variables. For instance, the statements `Dim private As Double` and `Dim sub As Double` are not valid.

3. Names given to variables are sometimes referred to as *identifiers*.

4. In math courses, *literals* are referred to as *constants*. However, the word "constant" has a special meaning in programming languages.

5. Since a numeric expression is any combination of literals, variables, functions, and operators that can be evaluated to produce a number, a single literal or variable is a special case of an expression.

6. Numeric literals used in expressions or assigned to variables must not contain commas, dollar signs, or percent signs. Also, mixed numbers, such as 8 1/2, are not allowed.

7. Although requesting the square root of a negative number does not terminate the execution of the program, it can produce unexpected results. For instance, the statement

```
lstBox.Items.Add(Math.Sqrt(-1))
```

displays **NaN**. **Note:** NaN is an abbreviation for "Not a Number."

8. If the value of *numVar* is 0 and *numVar* has type Double, then the statements

```
numVarInv = 1 / numVar
lstBox.Items.Add(numVarInv)
lstBox.Items.Add(1 / numVarInv)
```

cause the following items to be displayed in the list box:

```
Infinity

0
```

9. When a number is halfway between two successive whole numbers (such as 1.5, 2.5, 3.5, and 4.5), the Round function rounds to the nearest even number. For instance, Math. Round (2.5) is 2 and Math.Round (3.5) is 4.

10. In scientific notation, numbers are written in the form $b \cdot 10^r$, where b is a number of magnitude from 1 up to (but not including) 10, and r is an integer. Visual Basic displays very large and very small numbers in **scientific notation**, where $b \cdot 10^r$ is written as bEr. (The letter E is an abbreviation for *exponent*.) For instance, when the statement `lstBox.Items.Add(123 * (10 ^ 15))` is executed, 1.23E + 17 is displayed in the list box.

11. If the total number of items added to a list box exceeds the number of items that can be displayed, a vertical scroll bar is automatically added to the list box.

12. When you first enter a statement such as `Dim n As Double`, a wavy green line will appear under the variable name and the Error List window will record a warning. The wavy line merely indicates that the variable has not yet been used. Warnings, unlike syntax errors, do not prevent the program from running. If the wavy green line is still present after the entire event procedure has been entered, this will tell you that the variable was never used and that the declaration statement can be removed.

13. Syntax errors prevent programs from starting; runtime and logic errors do not. A runtime error causes a program to stop executing and displays an error message. A logic error is a mistake that might cause incorrect output.

14. The rounding function can take the form Math.Round(n, r) or Math.Round(n). That is, the argument r is optional. Microsoft documentation denotes the optionality of the r argument by referring to the function as Math.Round($n[, r]$).

15. The functions discussed in this section are referred to as **built-in functions** since they are part of the Visual Basic language. Chapter 5 shows how we can create our own functions. Such functions are commonly referred to as *user-defined functions*. The term *user-defined* is a bit of a misnomer; such functions should really be called *programmer-defined functions*.

Practice Problems 3.1

1. Evaluate 2 + 3 * 4.

2. Explain the difference between the assignment statement

   ```
   var1 = var2
   ```

   and the assignment statement

   ```
   var2 = var1
   ```

3. Complete the table by filling in the value of each variable after each line is executed.

	a	b	c
`Private Sub btnEvaluate_Click(...) Handles btnEvaluate.Click`			
`Dim a, b, c As Double`	0	0	0
`a = 3`	3	0	0
`b = 4`	3	4	0
`c = a + b`			
`a = c * a`			
`lstResults.Items.Add(a - b)`			
`b = b * b`			
`End Sub`			

4. Write a statement that increases the value of the Double variable *var* by 5%.

In Exercises 1 through 6, evaluate the numeric expression without a computer, and then use Visual Basic to check your answer.

1. 3 * 4   **2.** 7 ^ 2
3. 1 / (2 ^ 3)   **4.** 3 + (4 * 5)
5. (5 − 3) * 4   **6.** 3 * ((−2) ^ 5)

In Exercises 7 through 12, evaluate the expression.

7. 7 \ 3   **8.** 14 Mod 4
9. 5 \ 5   **10.** 7 Mod 3
11. 14 \ 4   **12.** 5 Mod 5

In Exercises 13 through 18, determine whether the name is a valid variable name.

13. sales.2015   **14.** room&Board
15. fOrM_1040   **16.** 1040B
17. expenses?   **18.** INCOME 2015

In Exercises 19 through 24, evaluate the numeric expression where $a = 2, b = 3$ and $c = 4$.

19. (a * b) + c   **20.** a * (b + c)
21. (1 + b) * c   **22.** a ^ c
23. b ^ (c − a)   **24.** (c − a) ^ b

In Exercises 25 through 30, write lines of code to calculate and display the value of the expression.

25. $7 \cdot 8 + 5$ **26.** $(1 + 2 \cdot 9)^3$
27. 5.5% of 20   **28.** $15 − 3(2 + 3^4)$
29. 17(3 + 162)   **30.** $4\,1/2 − 3\,5/8$

In Exercises 31 and 32, complete the table by filling in the value of each variable after each line is executed.

31.

	X	Y
`Private Sub btnEvaluate_Click(...) Handles btnEvaluate.Click`		
`    Dim x, y As Double`		
`    x = 2`		
`    y = 3 * x`		
`    x = y + 5`		
`    lstResults.Items.Clear()`		
`    lstResults.Items.Add(x + 4)`		
`    y = y + 1`		
`End Sub`		

32.

	bal	inter	withDr
`Private Sub btnEvaluate_Click(...) Handles` `   btnEvaluate.Click`			
`Dim bal, inter, withDr As Decimal`			
`bal = 100`			
`inter = 0.05D`			
`withDr = 25`			
`bal += inter * bal`			
`bal = bal - withDr`			
`End Sub`			

In Exercises 33 through 40, determine the output displayed in the list box by the lines of code.

33.
```
Dim amount As Double
amount = 10
lstOutput.Items.Add(amount - 4)
```

34.
```
Dim a, b As Integer
a = 4
b = 5 * a
lstOutput.Items.Add(a + b)
```

35.
```
Dim n As Integer = 7
n += 1
lstOutput.Items.Add(1)
lstOutput.Items.Add(n)
lstOutput.Items.Add(n + 1)
```

36.
```
Dim num As Integer = 5
num = 2 * num
lstOutput.Items.Add(num)
```

37.
```
Dim a, b As Integer
lstOutput.Items.Add(a + 1)
a = 4
b = a * a
lstOutput.Items.Add(a * b)
```

38.
```
Dim tax As Double
tax = 200
tax = 25 + tax
lstOutput.Items.Add(tax)
```

39.
```
Dim totalMinutes, hours, minutes As Integer
totalMinutes = 135
hours = totalMinutes \ 60
minutes = totalMinutes Mod 60
lstResults.Items.Add(hours)
lstResults.Items.Add(minutes)
```

40.
```
Dim totalOunces, pounds, ounces As Integer
   totalOunces = 90
   pounds = totalOunces \ 16
   ounces = totalOunces Mod 16
   lstResults.Items.Add(pounds)
   lstResults.Items.Add(ounces)
```

In Exercises 41 through 46, identify the errors.

41.
```
Dim a, b, c As Double
   a = 2
   b = 3
   a + b = c
   lstOutput.Items.Add(c)
```

42.
```
Dim a, b, c, d As Double
   a = 2
   b = 3
   c = d = 4
   lstOutput.Items.Add(5((a + b) / (c + d))
```

43.
```
Dim balance, deposit As Decimal
   balance = 1,234D
   deposit = $100
   lstOutput.Items.Add(balance + deposit)
```

44.
```
Dim interest, balance As Decimal
   0.05D = interest
   balance = 800
   lstOutput.Items.Add(interest * balance)
```

45.
```
Dim 9W As Double
   9W = 2 * 9W
   lstOutput.Items.Add(9W)
```

46.
```
Dim n As Double = 1.2345
   lstOutput.Items.Add(Round(n, 2))
```

In Exercises 47 and 48, rewrite the code using one line.

47.
```
Dim quantity As Integer
   quantity = 12
```

48.
```
Dim m As Integer
   Dim n As Double
   m = 2
   n = 3
```

In Exercises 49 through 54, find the value of the given function.

49. Int(10.75)

50. Int(9 − 2)

51. Math.Sqrt(3 * 12)

52. Math.Sqrt(64)

53. Math.Round(3.1279, 3)

54. Math.Round(−2.6)

In Exercises 55 through 60, find the value of the given function where *a* and *b* are numeric variables of type Double, *a* = 5 and *b* = 3.

55. Int (−a/2) **56.** Math.Round(a / b) **57.** Math.Sqrt(a − 5)

58. Math.Sqrt(4 + a) **59.** Math.Round(a + .5) **60.** Int(b * 0.5)

In Exercises 61 through 66, rewrite the statements using augmented assignment operators. Assume that each variable is of type Double.

61. cost = cost + 5 **62.** sum = sum*2 **63.** cost = cost/6

64. sum = sum − 7 **65.** sum = sum ^ 2 **66.** sum = sum + 3

In Exercises 67 through 74, write an event procedure with the header `Private Sub btnCompute_Click(...) Handles btnCompute.Click`, and that has one line of code for each step. Lines that display data should use the given variable names.

67. Calculate Profit The following steps calculate a company's profit:

(a) Declare the variables *revenue*, *costs*, and *profit* as type Decimal.
(b) Assign the value 98456 to the variable *revenue*.
(c) Assign the value 45000 to the variable *costs*.
(d) Assign the difference between the values of the variables *revenue* and *costs* to the variable *profit*.
(e) Display the value of the variable *profit* in a list box.

68. Stock Purchase The following steps calculate the amount of a stock purchase:

(a) Declare the variables *costPerShare*, *numberOfShares*, and *amount* as type Decimal.
(b) Assign the value 25.625D to the variable *costPerShare*.
(c) Assign the value 400 to the variable *numberOfShares*.
(d) Assign the product of the values of *costPerShare* and *numberOfShares* to the variable *amount*.
(e) Display the value of the variable *amount* in a list box.

69. Discounted Price The following steps calculate the price of an item after a 30% reduction:

(a) Declare the variables *price*, *discountPercent*, and *markdown* as type Decimal.
(b) Assign the value 19.95D to the variable *price*.
(c) Assign the value 30 to the variable *discountPercent*.
(d) Assign the value of (*discountPercent* divided by 100) times *price* to the variable *markdown*.
(e) Decrease the value of *price* by the value of *markdown*.
(f) Display the value of *price* (rounded to two decimal places) in a list box.

70. Break-Even Point The following steps calculate a company's break-even point, the number of units of goods the company must manufacture and sell in order to break even:

(a) Declare the variables *fixedCosts*, *pricePerUnit*, and *costPerUnit* as type Decimal.
(b) Assign the value 5000 to the variable *fixedCosts*.
(c) Assign the value 8 to the variable *pricePerUnit*.
(d) Assign the value 6 to the variable *costPerUnit*.

(e) Assign the value of *fixedCosts* divided by (the difference of *pricePerUnit* and *costPerUnit*) to the variable *breakEvenPoint*.

(f) Display the value of the variable *breakEvenPoint* in a list box.

71. **Savings Account** The following steps calculate the balance after three years when $100 is deposited in a savings account at 5% interest compounded annually:

(a) Declare the variable *balance* as type Decimal.
(b) Assign the value 100 to the variable *balance*.
(c) Increase the variable *balance* by 5% of its value. (Write 5% as 0.05D.)
(d) Increase the variable *balance* by 5% of its value.
(e) Increase the variable *balance* by 5% of its value.
(f) Display the value of *balance* (rounded to two decimal places) in a list box.

72. **Savings Account** The following steps calculate the balance at the end of three years when $100 is deposited at the beginning of each year in a savings account at 5% interest compounded annually:

(a) Declare the variable *balance* as type Decimal.
(b) Assign the value 100 to the variable *balance*.
(c) Increase the value of variable *balance* by 5% of its value, and add 100. (5% = 0.05D)
(d) Increase the value of variable *balance* by 5% of its value, and add 100.
(e) Increase the value of variable *balance* by 5% of its value.
(f) Display the value of *balance* (rounded to two decimal places) in a list box.

73. **Percentage Markup** The *markup* of an item is the difference between its *selling price* and its *purchase price*. The *percentage markup* is the quotient *markup/purchase price* expressed as a percentage. The following steps calculate the percentage markup of an item.

(a) Declare the variable *purchasePrice* as type Decimal and assign it the value 215.50.
(b) Declare the variable *sellingPrice* as type Decimal and assign it the value 644.99.
(c) Declare the variable *markup* as type Decimal and assign it the difference of the selling price and the purchase price.
(d) Declare the variable *percentageMarkup* as type Decimal and assign it 100 times the quotient of the markup and the purchase price.
(e) Display the percentage markup in a list box.

74. **Profit Margin** The *markup* of an item is the difference between its *selling price* and its *purchase price*. The *profit margin* is the quotient *markup/selling price* expressed as a percentage. The following steps calculate the profit margin of an item.

(a) Declare the variable *purchasePrice* as type Decimal and assign it the value 215.50.
(b) Declare the variable *sellingPrice* as type Decimal and assign it the value 29.99.
(c) Declare the variable *markup* as type Decimal and assign it the difference of the selling price and the purchase price.
(d) Declare the variable *profitMargin* as type Decimal and assign it 100 times the quotient of the markup and the selling price.
(e) Display the profit margin in a list box.

In Exercises 75 through 86, write a program to solve the problem and display the answer in a list box. The program should use variables for each of the quantities.

75. Corn Production Suppose each acre of farmland produces 18 tons of corn. How many tons of corn can be grown on a 30-acre farm? See Fig. 3.1.

FIGURE 3.1 Outcome of Exercise 75.

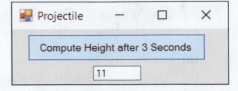

FIGURE 3.2 Outcome of Exercise 76.

76. Projectile Motion Suppose a ball is thrown straight up in the air with an initial velocity of 50 feet per second and an initial height of 5 feet. How high will the ball be after 3 seconds? See Fig. 3.2.

Note: The height after t seconds is given by the expression $-16t^2 + v_0 t + h_0$, where v_0 is the initial velocity and h_0 is the initial height.

77. Average Speed If a car left Washington, D.C., at 2 o'clock and arrived in New York at 7 o'clock, what was its average speed? **Note:** New York is 233 miles from Washington. See Fig. 3.3.

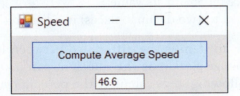

FIGURE 3.3 Outcome of Exercise 77.

FIGURE 3.4 Outcome of Exercise 78.

78. Gas Mileage A motorist wants to determine her gas mileage. At 23,352 miles (on the odometer) the tank is filled. At 23,695 miles the tank is filled again with 14 gallons. How many miles per gallon did the car average between the two fillings? See Fig. 3.4.

79. Water Usage A survey showed that Americans use an average of 1600 gallons of water per person per day, including industrial use. How many gallons of water are used each year in the United States? **Note:** The current population of the United States is about 315 million people. See Fig. 3.5.

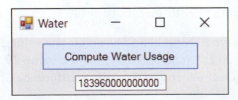

FIGURE 3.5 Outcome of Exercise 79.

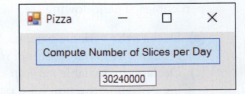

FIGURE 3.6 Outcome of Exercise 80.

80. Pizza Americans eat an average of 350 slices of pizza per second. How many slices of pizza do they eat per day? See Fig. 3.6.

81. Restaurants About 12% of the restaurants in the United States are pizzerias, and there are about 70,000 pizzerias in the United States. Estimate the total number of restaurants in the United States. See Fig. 3.7.

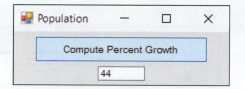

FIGURE 3.7 Outcome of Exercise 81. FIGURE 3.8 Outcome of Exercise 82.

82. Population Growth The population of the United States was about 281 million in 2000 and is predicted to be about 404 million in 2050. Approximate the percentage population growth in the United States during the first half of the 21st century. Round the percentage to the nearest whole number. See Fig. 3.8.

83. Convert Speeds On May 6, 1954, British runner Sir Roger Bannister became the first person to run the mile in less than 4 minutes. His average speed was 24.20 kilometers per hour. Write a program that converts kilometers per hour to miles per hour. See Fig. 3.9. **Note:** One kilometer is .6214 of a mile.

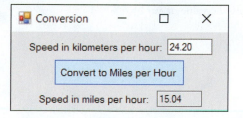

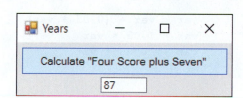

FIGURE 3.9 Outcome of Exercise 83. FIGURE 3.10 Outcome of Exercise 84.

84. Gettysburg Address The number 20 is called a *score*. Write a program to calculate the value of "four score plus seven." See Fig. 3.10.

85. Calories Estimate the number of calories in one cubic mile of chocolate ice cream. See Fig. 3.11. **Note:** There are 5280 feet in a mile and one cubic foot of chocolate ice cream contains about 48,600 calories.

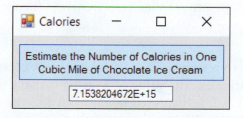

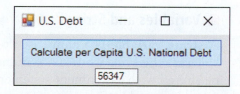

FIGURE 3.11 Outcome of Exercise 85. FIGURE 3.12 Outcome of Exercise 86.

86. U.S. National Debt Suppose the U.S. national debt is $1.82 \cdot 10^{13}$ dollars and the U.S. population is $3.23 \cdot 10^{8}$. Calculate the per capita U.S. national debt. Display the answer rounded to the nearest whole number. See Fig. 3.12.

Solutions to Practice Problems 3.1

1. 14. Multiplications are performed before additions. If the intent is for the addition to be performed first, the expression should be written (2 + 3) * 4.

2. The first assignment statement assigns the value of the variable *var2* to the variable *var1*, whereas the second assignment statement assigns *var1*'s value to *var2*.

3.

	a	b	c
`Private Sub btnEvaluate_Click(...) Handles` `  btnEvaluate.Click`			
`    Dim a, b, c As Double`	0	0	0
`    a = 3`	3	0	0
`    b = 4`	3	4	0
`    c = a + b`	3	4	7
`    a = c * a`	21	4	7
`    lstResults.Items.Add(a - b)`	21	4	7
`    b = b * b`	21	16	7
`End Sub`			

Each time an assignment statement is executed, only one variable (the variable to the left of the equal sign) has its value changed.

4. Each of the three following statements increases the value of *var* by 5%.

```
var = var + (0.05 * var)
var = 1.05 * var
var += 0.05 * var
```

3.2   Strings

The most common types of data processed by Visual Basic are numbers and strings. Sentences, phrases, words, letters of the alphabet, names, telephone numbers, addresses, and social security numbers are all examples of strings. Formally, a **string literal** is a sequence of characters that is treated as a single item. (The characters in our strings will be letters, digits, punctuation, and special symbols such as $, #, and %.) Double quotes are used to mark its beginning and end. String literals can be assigned to variables, displayed in text boxes and list boxes, and combined by an operation called concatenation (denoted by &).

■ Variables and Strings

A **string variable** is a name used to refer to a string. The allowable names of string variables are the same as those of numeric variables. The value of a string variable is assigned or altered with assignment statements and can be displayed in a list box like the value of a numeric variable. String variables are declared with statements of the form

```
Dim varName As String
```

 Example 1   **Display Output** The following program shows how assignment statements and the Add method are used with strings. The string variable *president* is assigned a value by the third line, and this value is displayed by the sixth line. The quotation marks surrounding each string literal mark the beginning and end of the string. They are not part of the literal and are not displayed by the Add method. (The form for this example contains a button and a list box.) **Note:** The Code Editor colors string literals red.

```
Private Sub btnDisplay_Click(...) Handles btnDisplay.Click
  Dim president As String
  president = "George Washington"
  lstOutput.Items.Clear()
  lstOutput.Items.Add("president")
  lstOutput.Items.Add(president)
End Sub
```

[Run, and then click on the button. The following is displayed in the list box.]

```
president
George Washington
```

If $x, y, \ldots, z$ are characters and *strVar* is a string variable, then the statement

```
strVar = "xy...z"
```

assigns the string literal $xy \ldots z$ to the variable and the statement

```
lstBox.Items.Add("xy...z")
```

or

```
lstBox.Items.Add(strVar)
```

displays the string $xy \ldots z$ in a list box. If *strVar2* is another string variable, then the statement

```
strVar2 = strVar
```

assigns the value of the variable *strVar* to the variable *strVar2*. (The value of *strVar* will remain the same.) String literals used in assignment or lstBox.Items.Add statements must be surrounded by quotation marks, but string variables are never surrounded by quotation marks.

■ Using Text Boxes for Input and Output

The content of a text box is always a string. Therefore, statements such as

```
strVar = txtBox.Text
```

and

```
txtBox.Text = strVar
```

can be used to assign the contents of the text box to the string variable *strVar* and vice versa.

Numbers typed into text boxes are stored as strings. Such strings must be converted to numeric values before they can be assigned to numeric variables or used in numeric expressions. The functions CDbl, CDec, and CInt convert strings representing numbers (such as "20") into numbers of type Double, Decimal, and Integer, respectively. Going in the other direction, the function CStr converts a number into a string representation of the number. Therefore, statements such as

```
dblVar = CDbl(txtBox.Text)
```

and

```
txtBox.Text = CStr(dblVar)
```

can be used to assign the contents of a text box to the double variable *dblVar* and vice versa. CDbl, CDec, CInt, and CStr, which stand for "convert to Double", "convert to Decimal", "convert to Integer", and "convert to String", are referred to as **data conversion** or **type-casting functions**.

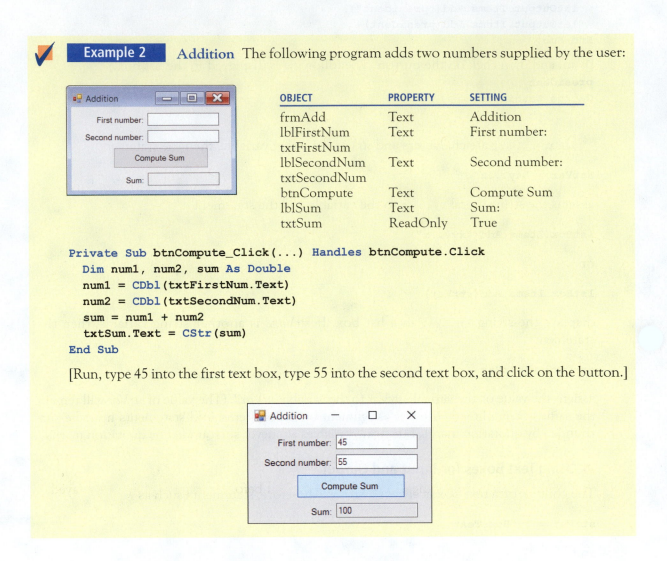

Example 2   **Addition**   The following program adds two numbers supplied by the user:

OBJECT	PROPERTY	SETTING
frmAdd	Text	Addition
lblFirstNum	Text	First number:
txtFirstNum		
lblSecondNum	Text	Second number:
txtSecondNum		
btnCompute	Text	Compute Sum
lblSum	Text	Sum:
txtSum	ReadOnly	True

```
Private Sub btnCompute_Click(...) Handles btnCompute.Click
  Dim num1, num2, sum As Double
  num1 = CDbl(txtFirstNum.Text)
  num2 = CDbl(txtSecondNum.Text)
  sum = num1 + num2
  txtSum.Text = CStr(sum)
End Sub
```

[Run, type 45 into the first text box, type 55 into the second text box, and click on the button.]

■ Option Explicit and Option Strict

Option Explicit and **Option Strict** affect how programs are written. Option Explicit requires that all variables be declared with Dim statements. The disabling of this option can lead to errors resulting from the misspelling of names of variables. Option Strict requires explicit conversions with typecasting functions in most cases where a value or variable of one type is assigned to a variable of another type. The absence of this option can lead to data loss. Having both Option Explicit and Option Strict enabled is considered good programming practice. In this book, we assume that both options are in effect.

Visual Basic provides a way to enforce Option Explicit and Option Strict for all programs you create. Click on *Options* in the Menu bar's Tools menu to open the Options dialog box. In the left pane, expand the Projects and Solutions entry. Then click on the subentry VB Defaults. Four default project settings will appear on the right. (See Fig. 3.13 on the next page.) If the settings for Option Explicit and Object Strict are not already set to On, change them to On. **Note:** Option Infer is discussed in Chapter 6.

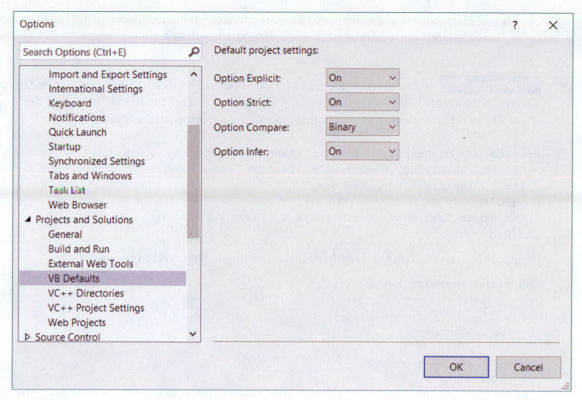

FIGURE 3.13   Option default project settings.

■ Concatenation

Two strings can be combined to form a new string consisting of the strings joined together. This operation is called **concatenation** and is represented by an ampersand (&). For instance, "good" & "bye" is "goodbye". (Concatenation can be thought of as *addition for strings*.) A combination of strings and ampersands that can be evaluated to form a string is called a **string expression**. When a string expression appears in an assignment statement or an Add method, the string expression is evaluated before being assigned or displayed.

Example 3   **Concatenate Strings**   The following program illustrates concatenation. (The form for this example contains a button and a text box.) Notice the space at the end of the string assigned to *quote1*. If that space was not present, then the statement that assigns a value to *quote* would have to be `quote = quote1 & " " & quote2` in order to achieve the same output.

```
Private Sub btnDisplay_Click(...) Handles btnDisplay.Click
  Dim quote1, quote2, quote As String
  quote1 = "The ballgame isn't over, "
  quote2 = "until it's over."
  quote = quote1 & quote2
  txtOutput.Text = quote & " Yogi Berra"
End Sub
```

[Run, and then click on the button. The following is displayed in the text box.]

```
The ball game isn't over, until it's over. Yogi Berra
```

Visual Basic also allows strings to be concatenated with numbers and allows numbers to be concatenated with numbers. In each case, the result is a string.

 Example 4   **Concatenate Strings and Numbers**   The following program concatenates a string with a number. Notice that a space was inserted after the word "has" and before the word "keys." (The form for this example contains a button and a text box.)

```
Private Sub btnDisplay_Click(...) Handles btnDisplay.Click
  Dim str As String, numOfKeys As Integer
  str = "The piano keyboard has "
  numOfKeys = 88
  txtOutput.Text = str & numOfKeys & " keys."
End Sub
```

[Run, and then click on the button. The following is displayed in the text box.]

```
The piano keyboard has 88 keys.
```

The statement

```
strVar = strVar & strVar2
```

will assign to *strVar* a new string that is the concatenation of *strVar* and *strVar2*. The same result can be accomplished with the statement

```
strVar &= strVar2
```

■ String Properties and Methods

We have seen that controls, such as text and list boxes, have properties and methods. A control placed on a form is an example of an object. A string is also an object, and, like a control, has both properties and methods that are specified by following the string with a period and the name of the property or method. The **Length** property gives the number of characters in a string. The **ToUpper** and **ToLower** methods produce a copy of a string in uppercase and lowercase characters. The **Trim** method deletes all leading and trailing spaces from a string. The **Substring** method extracts a sequence of consecutive characters from a string. The **IndexOf** method searches for the first occurrence of one string in another and gives the position at which the first occurrence is found.

If *str* is a string, then

```
str.Length
```

is the number of characters (including spaces and punctuation marks) in the string,

```
str.ToUpper
```

is the string with all its letters capitalized,

```
str.ToLower
```

is the string with all its letters in lowercase, and

```
str.Trim
```

is the string with all spaces removed from the front and back of the string. For instance,

EXPRESSION	VALUE	EXPRESSION	VALUE
"Visual".Length	6	"Visual".ToUpper	VISUAL
"123 Hike".Length	8	"123 Hike".ToLower	123 hike
"a" & " b ".Trim & "c"	abc		

■ Indices and Substrings

The **position** or **index** of a character in a string is identified with one of the numbers 0, 1, 2, 3, ... For instance, the first character of a string is said to have index 0, the second character is said to have index 1, and so on. Figure 3.14 shows the indices of the characters of the string "spam & eggs".

FIGURE 3.14   **Indices of the characters of the string "spam & eggs".**

A **substring** of a string is a sequence of consecutive characters from the string. For instance, consider the string "spam & eggs". The substrings "spa", "am", and "ggs" begin at positions 0, 2, and 8, respectively.

If *str* is a string, then

```
str.Substring(m, n)
```

is the substring of *str* consisting of *n* characters beginning with the character having index *m* of *str*. If the comma and the number *n* are omitted, then the substring starts at position *m* and continues until the end of *str*. The value of

```
str.IndexOf(str2)
```

is −1 if *str2* is not a substring of *str*; otherwise it is the beginning index of the first occurrence of *str2* in *str*. Some examples using these two methods are as follows:

EXPRESSION	VALUE	EXPRESSION	VALUE
"fantastic".Substring(0, 3)	"fan"	"fantastic".IndexOf("tas")	3
"fantastic".Substring(6, 2)	"ti"	"fantastic".IndexOf("a")	1
"fantastic".Substring(6)	"tic"	"fantastic".IndexOf("tn")	−1

The IndexOf method has a useful extension. The value of **str.IndexOf(str2, n)**, where *n* is an integer, is the index of the first occurrence of *str2* in *str* having index *n* or greater. For instance, the value of **"Mississippi".IndexOf("ss", 3)** is 5.

Like the numeric functions discussed before, string properties and methods also can be applied to variables and expressions.

  Example 5   **String Operations** The following program uses variables and expressions with the property and methods just discussed:

```
Private Sub btnEvaluate_Click(...) Handles btnEvaluate.Click
  Dim str1, str2, str3 As String
  str1 = "Quick as "
  str2 = "a wink"
  lstResults.Items.Clear()
```

```
lstResults.Items.Add(str1.Substring(0, 7))
lstResults.Items.Add(str1.IndexOf("c"))
lstResults.Items.Add(str1.Substring(0, 3))
lstResults.Items.Add((str1 & str2).Substring(6, 6))
lstResults.Items.Add((str1 & str2).ToUpper)
lstResults.Items.Add(str1.Trim & str2)
str3 = str2.Substring(str2.Length - 4)
lstResults.Items.Add("The average " & str3 & " lasts .1 second.")
End Sub
```

[Run, and then click on the button. The following is displayed in the list box.]

```
Quick a
3
Qui
as a w
QUICK AS A WINK
Quick asa wink
The average wink lasts .1 second.
```

Note: In Example 5, *c* is in the third position of *str1*, and there are three characters of *str1* to the left of *c*. In general, there are *n* characters to the left of the character in position *n*. This fact is used in Example 6.

Example 6 **Parse a Name** The following program parses a name. The fifth line locates the position, call it *n*, of the space separating the two names. The first name will contain *n* characters, and the last name will consist of all characters to the right of the *n*th character.

```
Private Sub btnAnalyze_Click(...) Handles btnAnalyze.Click
  Dim fullName, firstName, lastName As String
  Dim n As Integer
  fullName = txtName.Text
  n = fullName.IndexOf(" ")
  firstName = fullName.Substring(0, n)
  lastName = fullName.Substring(n + 1)
  lstResults.Items.Clear()
  lstResults.Items.Add("First name: " & firstName)
  lstResults.Items.Add("Your last name has " & lastName.Length & " letters.")
End Sub
```

[Run, type "Charles Babbage" into the text box, and then click on the button.]

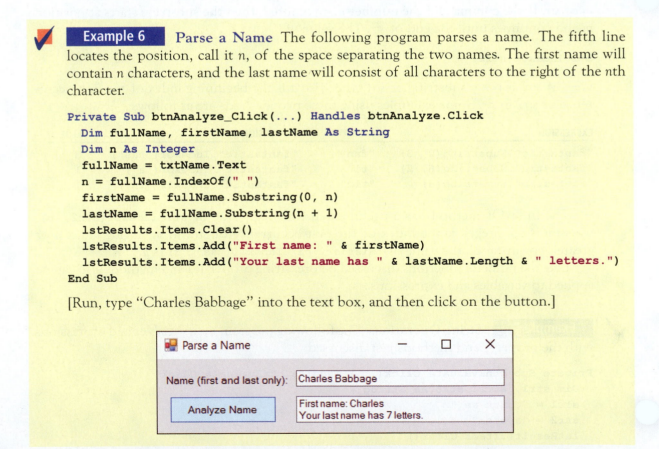

■ The Empty String

The string `""`, which contains no characters, is called the **empty string** or the **zero-length string**. It is different from `" "`, the string consisting of a single space.

The statement `lstBox.Items.Add("")` inserts a blank line into the list box. The contents of a text box can be cleared with either the statement

```
txtBox.Clear()
```

or the statement

```
txtBox.Text = ""
```

■ Initial Value of a String Variable

When a string variable is declared with a Dim statement, it has the keyword Nothing as its default value. To specify a different initial value, follow the declaration statement with an equal sign followed by the initial value. For instance, the statement

```
Dim pres As String = "Adams"
```

declares the variable *pres* to be of type String and assigns it the initial value "Adams".

An error occurs whenever an attempt is made to access a property or method for a string variable having the value Nothing or to display it in a list box. Therefore, unless a string variable is guaranteed to be assigned a value before being used, you should initialize it—even if you just assign the empty string to it.

■ Widening and Narrowing

The assignment of a value or variable of type Double to a variable of type Integer or Decimal is called **narrowing** because the possible values of an Integer and Decimal variable are a subset of the possible values of a Double variable. The assignment of a value or variable of type Decimal to a variable of type Integer is another example of narrowing. As there are more possible values of a variable of type Double than of type Integer or Decimal, assigning in the reverse direction is called **widening**. Option Strict requires the use of a typecasting function when narrowing, but allows widening without a typecasting function. Specifically, widening statements of the form

```
dblVar = intVar, decVar = intVar, and dblVar = decVar
```

are valid. However, narrowing statements of the form

```
intVar = dblVar, intVar = decVar, and decVar = dblVar
```

are not valid. They must be replaced with

```
intVar = CInt(dblVar), intVar = CInt(decVar), and decVar = CDec(dblVar)
```

Great care must be taken when computing with Integer variables. For instance, the value of an expression involving division or exponentiation has type Double and therefore cannot be assigned to an Integer variable without explicit conversion even if the value is a whole number. For instance, Option Strict makes each of the following two assignment statements invalid.

```
Dim m As Integer
m = 2 ^ 3
m = 6 / 2
```

In order to avoid such errors, we primarily use variables of type Integer for counting or identifying positions.

■ Data Types of Literals and Expressions

Visual Basic considers literal numbers written without a decimal point to have type Integer, and literal numbers written with a decimal point to have type Double. Only literal numbers with the suffix D are considered to have type Decimal.

The value of an expression involving exponentiation has type Double and therefore must be converted before it can be assigned to an Integer or Decimal variable. For instance, Option Strict makes the following statements invalid:

```
Dim m As Integer = 2 ^ 3
Dim n As Decimal = 2D ^ 3
```

They must be changed to the following statements:

```
Dim m As Integer = CInt(2 ^ 3)
Dim n As Decimal = CDec(2D ^ 3)
```

A quotient of two Decimal values or a quotient of a Decimal value and an Integer value has type Decimal. However, the quotient of two Integer values has type Double.

If one of the terms in a numeric expression has data type Double, then the value of the expression will have type Double. If one of the terms in a numeric expression has data type Decimal and there are no terms of type Double, then the value of the expression will have type Decimal. Table 3.2 gives some examples of the data types of expressions.

TABLE 3.2 Data types of expressions.

Expression	Data Type	Expression	Data Type
3D + 4.6 + 2.2D	Double	3 + 4D	Decimal
(6/2) + 5	Double	6D / 3D	Decimal
3.0 + 4D	Double	6D / 3	Decimal

■ Internal Documentation

Program documentation is the inclusion of comments that are meant to be read only by the programmer and the person maintaining the code. They specify the intent of the program, the purpose of the variables, and the tasks performed by individual portions of the program. To create a comment statement, begin the line with an apostrophe. Such a statement appears green on the screen and is completely ignored by Visual Basic when the program is executed. Comments are sometimes called *remarks*. A line of code can be documented by adding an apostrophe, followed by the desired information, after the end of the line. The *Comment Out* button (≣) and the *Uncomment* button (?≣) on the Toolbar can be used to comment and uncomment selected blocks of code.

Example 7 **Parse a Name** The following rewrite of Example 6 uses internal documentation. The first comment describes the entire program, the comment in line 5 gives the meaning of the variable, and the final comment describes the purpose of the three lines that follow it.

```
Private Sub btnAnalyze_Click(...) Handles btnAnalyze.Click
  'Determine a person's first name and the length of the second name
  Dim fullName, firstName, lastName As String
```

```
    Dim m As Integer
    Dim n As Integer    'location of the space separating the two names
    fullName = txtName.Text
    n = fullName.IndexOf(" ")
    firstName = fullName.Substring(0, n)
    lastName = fullName.Substring(n + 1)
    m = lastName.Length
    'Display the desired information in a list box
    lstResults.Items.Clear()
    lstResults.Items.Add("First name: " & firstName)
    lstResults.Items.Add("Your last name has " & m & " letters.")
End Sub
```

Some of the benefits of documentation are as follows:

1. Other people can easily understand the program.

2. You can understand the program when you read it later.

3. Long programs are easier to read because the purposes of individual pieces can be determined at a glance.

Good programming practice requires that programmers document their code while they are writing it. In fact, many software companies require a certain level of documentation before they release software and some judge a programmer's performance on how well their code is documented.

■ Line Continuation

Thousands of characters can be typed in a line of code. If you use a statement with more characters than can fit in the window, Visual Basic scrolls the Code Editor toward the right as needed. However, most programmers prefer having lines that are no longer than the width of the Code Editor. A long statement can be split across two or more lines by ending each line (except the last) with an underscore character (_) preceded by a space. For instance, the line

```
Dim quotation As String = "Good code is its own best documentation."
```

can be written as

```
Dim quotation As String = "Good code is its own " & _
                    "best documentation."
```

A feature called **implicit line continuation** allows underscore characters to be omitted from the end of a line that obviously has a continuation—for instance, a line that ends with an ampersand, an arithmetic operator, or a comma. We use this feature throughout this textbook. For example, the line above will be written

```
Dim quotation As String = "Good code is its own " &
                    "best documentation."
```

Line continuation, with or without an underscore character, cannot be used inside a pair of quotation marks. Whenever you want to display a literal string on two lines of the screen, you must first break it into two shorter strings joined with an ampersand. IntelliSense is reliable in letting you know if you have broken a line improperly.

Line continuation, with or without an underscore character, does not work with comment statements. Therefore, each line of a comment statement must begin with its own apostrophe.

VideoNote
Variable
Scope

■ Scope of a Variable

When a variable is declared in an event procedure with a Dim statement, a portion of memory is set aside to hold the value of the variable. As soon as the End Sub statement for the procedure is reached, the memory location is freed up; that is, the variable is discarded. The variable is said to be **local** to the procedure and to have **procedure scope**. In general, the **scope** of a variable is the portion of the program that can refer to it.

Visual Basic provides a way to make a variable recognized by every procedure in a form's code. Such a variable is called a **class-level variable** and is said to have **class scope**. The Dim statement for a class-level variable can be placed anywhere between the statements **Public Class *formName*** and **End Class**, provided that the Dim statement is not inside an event procedure. Normally, we place the Dim statement just after the **Public Class *formName*** statement. (We refer to this region as the **Declarations section** of the class.) When a class-level variable has its value changed by a procedure, the value persists even after the procedure has finished executing.

If an event procedure declares a local variable with the same name as a class-level variable, then the name refers to the local variable for code inside the procedure. To refer to the class-level variable inside the procedure, prefix the name with M*e* followed by a period.

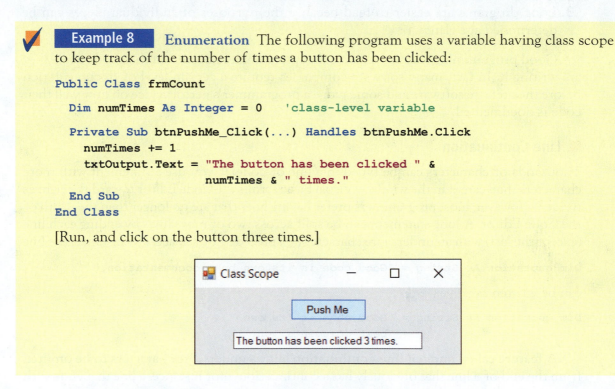

Example 8   **Enumeration** The following program uses a variable having class scope to keep track of the number of times a button has been clicked:

```
Public Class frmCount

  Dim numTimes As Integer = 0    'class-level variable

  Private Sub btnPushMe_Click(...) Handles btnPushMe.Click
    numTimes += 1
    txtOutput.Text = "The button has been clicked " &
                     numTimes & " times."
  End Sub
End Class
```

[Run, and click on the button three times.]

■ Auto Correction

The **Auto Correction** feature of IntelliSense suggests corrections when errors occur and allows you to select a correction to be applied to the code. When an invalid statement is entered, a wavy red error line appears under the incorrect part of the statement, and the Auto Correction feature is available for the error. When you hover the cursor over the wavy line, a small Error Correction icon (💡▾) appears along with a tinted rectangular box describing the error. Figures 3.15, 3.16, and 3.17 show how Auto Correction points out a type-conversion error and assists with the correction.

When you click on the down-arrow of the Error Correction icon (or the last line of the tinted box) in Fig. 3.15, a potential fix for the problem is displayed. See Fig. 3.16.

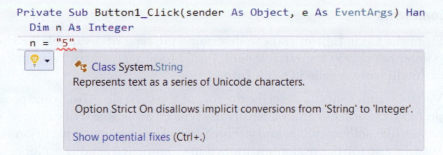

```
Private Sub Button1_Click(sender As Object, e As EventArgs) Han
    Dim n As Integer
    n = "5"
```

💡 ▾   🏷 Class System.String
Represents text as a series of Unicode characters.

Option Strict On disallows implicit conversions from 'String' to 'Integer'.

Show potential fixes (Ctrl+.)

FIGURE 3.15   Description-of-Error box.

```
Private Sub Button1_Click(sender As Object, e As EventArgs) Handles Button1.Click
    Dim n As Integer
    n = "5"
```

💡 ▾

| Insert Missing Cast | ▸ |

❌ BC30512 Option Strict On disallows implicit conversions from 'String' to 'Integer'.

...
```
Dim n As Integer
n = "5"
n = CInt("5")
```
...

Preview changes

FIGURE 3.16   Suggested-Change box.

When you click on *Preview changes*, a Preview Changes window (see Fig. 3.17) shows a corrected portion of the program. After you click on the *Apply* button, the recommended correction to the program will be carried out.

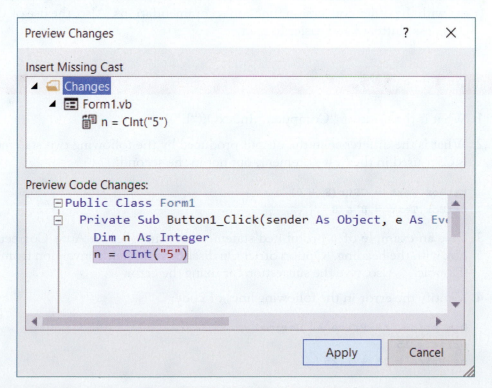

FIGURE 3.17   Description-of-Error box.

■ Comments

1. From the Code Editor, you can determine the type of a variable by letting the mouse pointer hover over the variable name until a tooltip giving the type appears. This feature of IntelliSense is called **Quick Info**.

2. Variable names should describe the role of the variable. Also, some programmers use a prefix, such as *dbl* or *str*, to identify the type of a variable. For example, they would use names like *dblInterestRate* and *strFirstName*. This naming convention is not needed in Visual Basic for the reason mentioned in Comment 1, and is no longer recommended by Microsoft.

3. Since a string expression is any combination of literals, variables, functions, methods, and operators that can be evaluated to produce a string, a single string literal or variable is a special case of an expression.

4. The functions CInt, CDec, and CDbl are user friendly. If the user types a number into a text box and precedes it with a dollar sign or inserts commas as separators, the values of CInt (txtBox.Text), CDec (txtBox.Text), and CDbl (txtBox.Text) will be the number with the dollar sign and/or commas removed.

5. The Trim method is useful when reading data from a text box. Sometimes users type spaces at the end of the input. Unless the spaces are removed, they can cause havoc elsewhere in the program.

6. When an incorrect or missing conversion to a number or date is detected by the Code Editor, Auto Correction recommends and implements the use of the CInt, CDec, CDbl, or CDate functions.

   When an incorrect or missing conversion to a string is detected by the Code Editor, Auto Correction recommends the function CType. For instance, the recommended correction for `txtBox.Text = 5` is `txtBox.Text = CType(5, String)`. However, we have decided to favor `txtBox.Text = CStr(5)` since the use of the CStr function is consistent with the other conversion function recommendations. Also, the use of CStr makes code less cluttered and easier to read.

Practice Problems 3.2

1. What is the value of "Computer".IndexOf("E")?

2. What is the difference in the output produced by the following two statements? Why is CStr used in the first statement, but not in the second?

   ```
   txtBox.Text = CStr(8 + 8)
   txtBox.Text = 8 & 8
   ```

3. Give an example of a prohibited statement that invokes an Auto Correction helper box with the heading "Option Strict On disallows implicit conversion from 'String' to 'Double'." Also, give the suggestion for fixing the error.

4. Identify the error in the following lines of code:

   ```
   Dim price, newPrice As Decimal
   price = 15
   newPrice = 15 + 1.25
   ```

In Exercises 1 through 28, determine the output displayed in the text box or list box by the lines of code.

1. `txtBox.Text = "Visual Basic"`

2. `lstBox.Items.Add("Hello")`

3.
```
Dim var As String
var = "Ernie"
lstBox.Items.Add(var)
```

4.
```
Dim var As String
var = "Bert"
txtBox.Text = var
```

5. `txtBox.Text = "f" & "lute"`

6. `lstBox.Items.Add("a" & "cute")`

7.
```
Dim var As Double
var = 123
txtBox.Text = CStr(var)
```

8.
```
Dim var As Double
var = 3
txtBox.Text = CStr(var + 5)
```

9. `txtBox.Text = "Your age is " & 21 & "."`

10. `txtBox.Text = "Fred has " & 2 & " children."`

11.
```
Dim r, b As String
r = "A ROSE"
b = " IS "
txtBox.Text = r & b & r & b & r
```

12.
```
Dim s As String, n As Integer
s = "trombones"
n = 76
txtBox.Text = n & " " & s
```

13.
```
Dim num As Double
txtBox.Text = "5"
num = 0.5 + CDbl(txtBox.Text)
txtBox.Text = CStr(num)
```

14.
```
Dim num As Integer = 2
txtBox.Text = CStr(num)
txtBox.Text = CStr(1 + CInt(txtBox.Text))
```

15.
```
txtBox.Text = "good"
txtBox.Text &= "bye"
```

16.
```
Dim var As String = "eight"
var &= "h"
txtBox.Text = var
```

17.
```
Dim var As String = "WALLA"
var &= var
txtBox.Text = var
```

18.
```
txtBox.Text = "mur"
txtBox.Text &= txtBox.Text
```

19. ```
lstBox.Items.Add("aBc".ToUpper)
lstBox.Items.Add("Wallless".IndexOf("lll"))
lstBox.Items.Add("five".Length)
lstBox.Items.Add(" 55 ".Trim & " mph")
lstBox.Items.Add("UNDERSTUDY".Substring(5, 3))
```

20. ```
lstBox.Items.Add("8 Ball".ToLower)
lstBox.Items.Add("colonel".IndexOf("k"))
lstBox.Items.Add("23.45".Length)
lstBox.Items.Add("revolutionary".Substring(1))
lstBox.Items.Add("whippersnapper".IndexOf("pp", 5))
```

21. ```
Dim a As Integer = 4
Dim b As Integer = 2
Dim c As String = "Municipality"
Dim d As String = "pal"
lstBox.Items.Add(c.Length)
lstBox.Items.Add(c.ToUpper)
lstBox.Items.Add(c.Substring(a, b) & c.Substring(5 * b))
lstBox.Items.Add(c.IndexOf(d))
```

22. ```
Dim m As Integer = 4
Dim n As Integer = 3
Dim s As String = "Microsoft"
Dim t As String = "soft"
lstOutput.Items.Add(s.Length)
lstOutput.Items.Add(s.ToLower)
lstOutput.Items.Add(s.Substring(m, n - 1))
lstOutput.Items.Add(s.IndexOf(t))
```

23. How many positions does a string of eight characters have?

24. What is the highest numbered position for a string of eight characters?

25. (True or False) If *n* is the length of *str*, then `str.Substring(n - 1)` is the string consisting of the last character of *str*.

26. (True or False) If *n* is the length of *str*, then `str.Substring(n - 2)` is the string consisting of the last two characters of *str*.

In Exercises 27 through 34, identify any errors.

27. ```
Dim phoneNumber As Double
phoneNumber = "234-5678"
txtBox.Text = "My phone number is " & phoneNumber
```

28. ```
Dim quote As String
quote = I came to Casablanca for the waters.
txtBox.Text = quote & ": " & "Bogart"
```

29. ```
Dim end As String
end = "happily ever after."
txtBox.Text = "They lived " & end
```

30. ```
Dim hiyo As String
hiyo = "Silver"
txtBox = "Hi-Yo " & hiYo
```

31. ```
Dim num As Double = 1234
txtBox.Text = CStr(num.IndexOf("2"))
```

32. ```
Dim num As Integer = 45
txtBox.Text = CStr(num.Length)
```

33.
```
Dim m As Decimal, n As Integer
   m = 2 ^ 3
   n = 4 / 2
```

34.
```
Dim m As Decimal, n As Integer
   m = 3.45
   n = 2.0 + 3.0
```

In Exercises 35 and 36, write an event procedure with the header `Private Sub btnDisplay_Click(...) Handles btnDisplay.Click`, and having one line for each step. Display each result by assigning it to the txtOutput.Text property. Lines that display data should use the given variable names.

35. **Inventor** The following steps give the name and birth year of a famous inventor:

   (a) Declare the variables *firstName*, *middleName*, and *lastName* as String. Declare the variable *yearOfBirth* as type Integer.
   (b) Assign "Thomas" to the variable *firstName*.
   (c) Assign "Alva" to the variable *middleName*.
   (d) Assign "Edison" to the variable *lastName*.
   (e) Assign 1847 to the variable *yearOfBirth*.
   (f) Display the inventor's full name followed by a comma and his year of birth.

36. **Price of Ketchup** The following steps compute the price of ketchup:

   (a) Declare the variable *item* as type String. Declare the variables *regularPrice* and *discount* as type Decimal.
   (b) Assign "ketchup" to the variable *item*.
   (c) Assign 1.80 to the variable *regularPrice*.
   (d) Assign .27 to the variable *discount*.
   (e) Assign to the variable *discountPrice* the expression 1.80*(1 − .27). (**Note:** The product is 1.53.)
   (f) Display the sentence "1.53 is the sale price of ketchup."

In Exercises 37 and 38, write a line of code to carry out the task. Specify where in the program the line of code should be placed.

37. Declare the variable *str* as a string variable visible to all parts of the program.

38. Declare the variable *str* as a string variable visible only to the btnTest_Click event procedure.

In Exercises 39 through 44, write a program to carry out the stated task.

39. **Distance from a Storm** If *n* is the number of seconds between lightning and thunder, the storm is *n*/5 miles away. Write a program that reads the number of seconds between lightning and thunder and reports the distance of the storm rounded to two decimal places. A sample run is shown in Fig. 3.18.

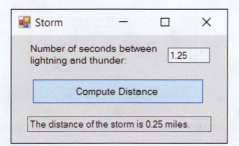

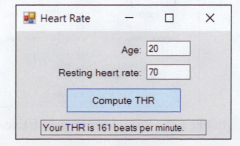

FIGURE 3.18 Possible outcome of Exercise 39. **FIGURE 3.19** Possible outcome of Exercise 40.

40. Training Heart Rate The American College of Sports Medicine recommends that you maintain your *training heart rate* during an aerobic workout. Your training heart rate is computed as $.7 * (220 - a) + .3 * r$, where a is your age and r is your resting heart rate (your pulse when you first awaken). Write a program to read a person's age and resting heart rate and display the training heart rate. (Determine *your* training heart rate.) A sample run is shown in Fig. 3.19 on the previous page.

41. Triathlon The number of calories burned per hour by cycling, running, and swimming are 200, 475, and 275, respectively. A person loses 1 pound of weight for each 3500 calories burned. Write code to read the number of hours spent at each activity and then display the number of pounds worked off. A sample run is shown in Fig. 3.20.

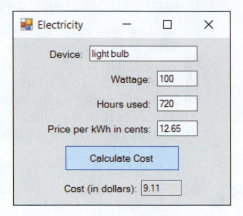

FIGURE 3.20 Possible outcome of Exercise 41.　　**FIGURE 3.21** Possible outcome of Exercise 42.

42. Cost of Electricity The cost of the electricity used by a device is given by the formula

$$\text{cost of electricity (in dollars)} = \frac{\text{wattage of device} \cdot \text{hours used} \cdot \text{cost per kWh in cents}}{100{,}000}$$

where kWh is an abbreviation for "kilowatt hour." The cost per kWh of electricity varies with locality. On April 1, 2015, the average cost of electricity for a residential customer in the United States was 12.65¢ per kWh. Write a program that allows the user to calculate the cost of operating an electrical device. Figure 3.21 calculates the cost of keeping a light bulb turned on for an entire month.

43. Add Times Write a program to add two times, where the times are given in hours and minutes. See Fig. 3.22. The program should use both integer division and the Mod operator.

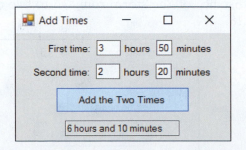

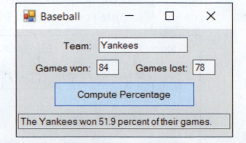

FIGURE 3.22 Possible outcome of Exercise 43.　　**FIGURE 3.23** Possible outcome of Exercise 44.

44. Baseball Write code to read the name of a baseball team, the number of games won, and the number of games lost, and display the name of the team and the percentage of games won. A sample run is shown in Fig. 3.23.

In the following exercises, write a program to carry out the task. The program should use variables for each of the quantities.

45. Income Request a company's annual revenue and expenses as input, and display the company's net income (revenue minus expenses). See Fig. 3.24.

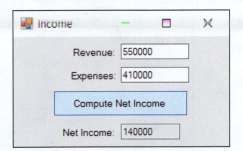

FIGURE 3.24 Possible outcome of Exercise 45.   **FIGURE 3.25** Possible outcome of Exercise 46.

46. Price-to-Earnings Ratio Request a company's earnings-per-share for the year and the price of one share of stock as input, and then display the company's price-to-earnings ratio (that is, price/earnings). See Fig. 3.25.

47. Car Speed The formula $s = \sqrt{24d}$ gives an estimate of the speed in miles per hour of a car that skidded d feet on dry concrete when the brakes were applied. Write a program that requests the distance skidded and then displays the estimated speed of the car. See Fig. 3.26.

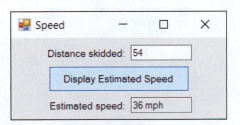

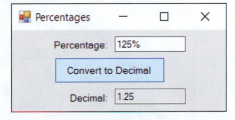

FIGURE 3.26 Possible outcome of Exercise 47.   **FIGURE 3.27** Possible outcome of Exercise 48.

48. Percentages Convert a percentage to a decimal. See Fig. 3.27.

49. Enumeration Write a program that contains a button and a read-only text box on the form, with the text box initially containing 100. Each time the button is clicked on, the number in the text box should decrease by 1. See Fig. 3.28.

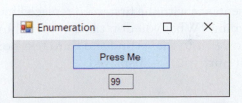

FIGURE 3.28 Possible outcome of Exercise 49.   **FIGURE 3.29** Possible outcome of Exercise 50.

50. Area Code Write a program that requests a (complete) phone number in a text box and then displays the area code in another text box when a button is clicked on. See Fig. 3.29.

51. Average Write a program that allows scores to be input one at a time, and then displays the average of the scores upon request. (See Fig. 3.30.) The user should type a score into the top text box and then click on the *Record* button. This process can be repeated as many times as desired. At any time the user should be able to click on the *Calculate* button to display the average of all the scores that were entered so far. **Note:** This program requires two class-level variables.

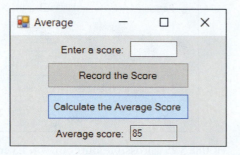

FIGURE 3.30 Possible outcome of Exercise 51.

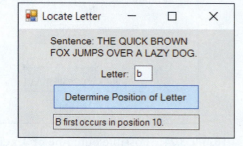

FIGURE 3.31 Possible outcome of Exercise 52.

52. Locate a Letter Write a program that requests a letter, converts it to uppercase, and gives its first position in the sentence "THE QUICK BROWN FOX JUMPS OVER A LAZY DOG." See Fig. 3.31.

53. Server's Tip Calculate the amount of a server's tip, given the amount of the bill and the percentage tip as input. See Fig. 3.32.

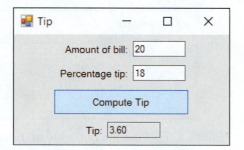

FIGURE 3.32 Possible outcome of Exercise 53.

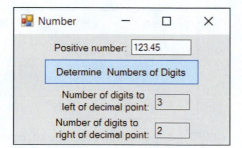

FIGURE 3.33 Possible outcome of Exercise 54.

54. Analyze a Number Write a program that requests a positive number containing a decimal point as input and then displays the number of digits to the left of the decimal point and the number of digits to the right of the decimal point. See Fig. 3.33.

55. Word Replacement Write a program that requests a sentence, a word in the sentence, and another word and then displays the sentence with the first word replaced by the second. In Fig. 3.34 the user responds by typing "What you don't know won't hurt you." into the first text box and "know" and "owe" into the second and third text boxes, and the message "What you don't owe won't hurt you." is displayed.

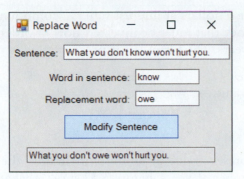

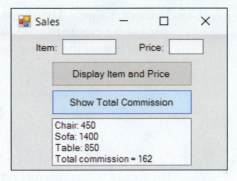

FIGURE 3.34 Possible outcome of Exercise 55.

FIGURE 3.35 Possible outcome of Exercise 56.

56. Sales Write a program that allows furniture sales (item and price) to be displayed in a list box one at a time, and then shows the total commission of the sales (6%) upon request. (See Fig. 3.35.) The user should type each item and price into the text boxes and then click the *Display* button. This process can be repeated as many times as desired. At any time the user should be able to click the *Show* button to display the total commission of all the sales that were entered. **Note:** This program requires a class-level variable.

57. Addition Add an event procedure to Example 2 so that txtSum will be cleared whenever either the first number or the second number is changed.

58. Future Value If *P* dollars (called the principal) is invested at *r*% interest compounded annually, then the future value of the investment after *n* years is given by the formula

$$\text{future value} = P\left(1 + \frac{r}{100}\right)^n$$

Write a program that calculates the balance of the investment after the user gives the principal, interest rate, and number of years. Figure 3.36 shows that $1000 invested at 5% interest will grow to $1,157.63 in 3 years.

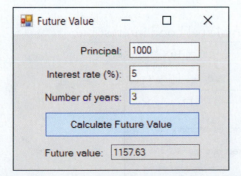

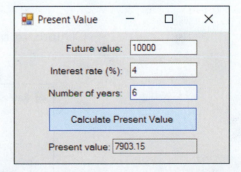

FIGURE 3.36 Possible outcome of Exercise 58.   FIGURE 3.37 Possible outcome of Exercise 59.

59. Present Value   The present value of F dollars at interest rate r% compounded annually for n years is the amount of money that must be invested now in order to have F dollars (called the future value) in n years. The formula for present value is

$$\text{present value} = \frac{F}{\left(1 + \dfrac{r}{100}\right)^n}$$

Write a program that calculates the present value of an investment after the user gives the future value, interest rate, and number of years. Figure 3.37 shows that at 4% interest, $7,903.15 must be invested now in order to have $10,000 after 6 years.

60. Convert Months   Write a program that allows the user to enter a whole number of months and then converts that amount of time to years and months. See Fig. 3.38. The program should use both integer division and the Mod operator.

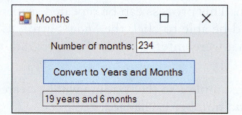

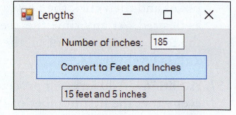

FIGURE 3.38   Possible outcome of Exercise 60.   **FIGURE 3.39**   Possible outcome of Exercise 61.

61. Convert Lengths   Write a program that allows the user to enter a whole number of inches and then converts that length to feet and inches. See Fig. 3.39. The program should use both integer division and the Mod operator.

62. Equivalent Interest Rates   Interest earned on municipal bonds from an investor's home state is not taxed, whereas interest earned on CDs *is* taxed. Therefore, in order for a CD to earn as much as a municipal bond, the CD must pay a higher interest rate. How much higher the interest rate must be depends on the investor's tax bracket. Write a program that allows the user to enter a tax bracket and a municipal bond interest rate and then finds the CD interest rate with the same yield. See Fig. 3.40. **Note:** If the tax bracket is expressed as a decimal, then

$$\text{CD interest rate} = \frac{\text{municipal bond interest rate}}{(1 - \text{tax bracket})}.$$

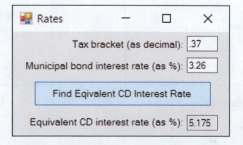

FIGURE 3.40   Possible outcome of Exercise 62.

1. −1. There is no uppercase letter *E* in the string "Computer". IndexOf distinguishes between uppercase and lowercase.

2. The first statement displays 16 in the text box, whereas the second statement displays 88. With Option Strict in effect, the first statement would not be valid if CStr were missing, since 8 + 8 is a number and txtBox.Text is a string. Visual Basic treats the second statement as if it were

   ```
   txtBox.Text = CStr(8) & CStr(8)
   ```

3. Some possibilities are

PROHIBITED STATEMENT	SUGGESTION FOR FIXING
`Dim x As Double = "23"`	Replace "23" with CDbl("23").
`dblVar = txtBox.Text`	Replace txtBox.Text with CDbl(txtBox.Text).
`dblVar = 2 & 3`	Replace 2 & 3 with CDbl(2 & 3).

4. In the third line, **15 + 1.25** has type Double and therefore cannot be assigned to a variable of type Decimal. The line should be replaced with either **newPrice = 15 + 1.25D** or **newPrice = CDec(15 + 1.25)**. *Note:* The second line is fine since **15** is of type Integer and an Integer value *can* be assigned to a Decimal variable.

3.3   Input and Output

■ Formatting Numeric Output

So far, we have relied on the CStr function to convert numbers into strings. The ToString method does the same job, and has the added feature that it allows numbers to be displayed in familiar formats. For instance, it allows a number to be displayed with thousands separators and a specified number of decimal places, allows an amount of money to be displayed with a dollar sign, and allows a percentage to be displayed with a percent symbol.

The value of

```
variableName.ToString(formatString)
```

where ***formatString*** might be **"N"** for a number, **"C"** for an amount of money (Currency), and "**P**" for a percent is a suitably formatted string representation of the value of the variable. The value is given rounded to two decimal places. The number of decimal places can be changed by following the letter with the number.

The variable in the aforementioned ToString expression can be replaced by a literal number or an expression involving literals. Expressions involving literals must be surrounded by parentheses. For clarity, we will surround all literals and expressions with parentheses. Table 3.3 gives some examples of the use of the ToString method.

TABLE 3.3   **Some formatted values.**

Expression	Value
`(12345.676).ToString("N")`	12,345.68
`(12345.676D).ToString("C")`	$12,345.68
`(0.185).ToString("P")`	18.50 %
`(1 + 0.5^3).ToString("N3")`	1.125
`(-1000D).ToString("C0")`	($1,000)
`(50/75).ToString("P4")`	66.6667 %

Notice that the currency format string **"C"** uses the accountant's convention of denoting negative amounts by surrounding them with parentheses.

■ **Dates as Input and Output**

So far, all input and output has been either numbers or strings. However, applications sometimes require dates as input and output. Visual Basic has a **Date** data type and a **Date** literal.

A variable of type Date is declared with a statement of the form

```
Dim varName As Date
```

Just as string literals are written surrounded by quotation marks, date literals are written surrounded by number signs. For instance, the statement

```
Dim dayOfIndependence As Date = #7/4/1776#
```

declares a date variable and assigns a value to it.

The function CDate converts a string to a date. For instance, the statement

```
Dim dt As Date = CDate(txtBox.Text)
```

assigns the contents of a text box to a variable of type Date.

Dates can be formatted with the ToString method. If *dateVar* is a variable of type Date, then the value of

```
dateVar.ToString("D")
```

is a string consisting of the date specified by *dateVar* with the day of the week and the month spelled out. For instance, the two lines of code

```
Dim dayOfIndependence As Date = #7/4/1776#
txtBox.Text = dayOfIndependence.ToString("D")
```

display Thursday, July 04, 1776 in the text box. **Note:** If **"D"** is replaced with **"d"**, 7/4/1776 will be displayed in the text box.

There are many functions involving dates. Several of them are listed in Table 3.4.

TABLE 3.4	Some date functions.
Function	**Output**
`Today`	current date (such as 7/14/2016)
`dt.Day`	1, 2, . . . , 31
`dt.Month`	1, 2, . . . , 12
`dt.Year`	such as 2016, 2017, etc.
`dt.ToString("dddd")`	Sunday, Monday, . . . , Saturday
`dt.ToString("MMMM")`	January, February, . . . , December
`DateDiff(DateInterval.Day, dt1, dt2)`	number of days between the two dates

Note: The way certain dates are formatted depends on the *Home location* setting in Windows. The examples in this book use the United States location setting and therefore the value of *Today* is displayed in the form mm/dd/yyyy. With the Italian location setting, for example, the value of *Today* is displayed in the form dd/mm/yyyy and days and months have names such as Martedi and Aprile.

AddYears is a useful method for working with dates. If *dt* is a variable of type Date, and *n* is an integer, then the value of **dt.AddYears(n)** is the value of *dt* advanced by *n* years. When *n* is negative, the value of *dt* is decreased. Two similar methods are AddDays and AddMonths.

`DateDiff(DateInterval.Year, d1, d2)` gives the number of years (sort of) between the two dates. It must be employed with care since it only uses the year parts of the two dates.

■ Using a Masked Text Box for Input

Problems can arise when the wrong type of data are entered as input into a text box. For instance, if the user replies to the request for an age by entering "twenty-one" into a text box, the program can easily crash. Sometimes this type of predicament can be avoided by using a masked text box for input. (In later chapters, we will consider other ways of ensuring the integrity of input.)

In the Toolbox, the icon for the MaskedTextBox control [⟨.⟩-   MaskedTextBox] consists of a pair of parentheses containing a period and followed by a hyphen. The most important property of a masked text box is the Mask property that is used to restrict the characters entered into the box. Also, the Mask property is used to show certain characters in the control—to give users a visual cue that they should be entering a phone number or a social security number, for example. Some possible settings for the Mask property are shown in Table 3.5. The first four settings can be selected from a list of specified options. The last three settings generalize to any number of digits, letters, or ampersands. If the Mask property is left blank, then the MaskedTextBox control is nearly identical to the TextBox control.

TABLE 3.5   Some settings for the Mask property.

Setting	Effect
000-00-0000	The user can enter a social security number.
000-0000	The user can enter a phone number (without an area code).
(000)000-0000	The user can enter a phone number (with an area code).
00/00/0000	The user can enter a date.
0000000	The user can enter a positive integer consisting of up to 7 digits.
LLLLL	The user can enter a string consisting of up to 5 letters.
&&&&&&&&	The user can enter a string consisting of up to 8 characters.

Suppose a form contains a masked text box whose Mask property has the setting 000-00-0000. When the program is run, the string "___-__-____" will appear in the masked text box. The user will be allowed to type a digit in place of each of the nine underscore characters. The hyphens cannot be altered, and no characters can be typed anywhere else in the masked text box.

At run time, the characters 0, L, and & in the setting for a Mask property are replaced by underscore characters that are place holders for digits, letters, and characters, respectively. (Spaces are also allowed. However, trailing spaces are dropped.) When the characters "–", "(", ")", or "/" appear in a setting for a Mask property, they appear as themselves in the masked text box and cannot be altered. There are some other mask settings, but these seven will suffice for our purposes.

Figure 3.41(a) shows a masked text box during design time. It looks like an ordinary text box. However, the *Tasks* button for the masked text box is used to set the Mask property rather than the Multiline property. Figure 3.41(b) on the next page shows the result of clicking on the *Tasks* button. Then, clicking on "Set Mask. . ." brings up the Input Mask dialog box shown in Figure 3.42. (This input dialog box is the same input dialog box that is invoked when you click on the ellipsis in the Mask property's Settings box.) You can use this input dialog box to select a commonly used value for the Mask property, or create your own customized mask in the Mask text box. To produce the settings 00/00/0000 and 000–00–0000, click on "Short date" and "Social security number", respectively. We use the prefix *mtb* for the names of masked text boxes.

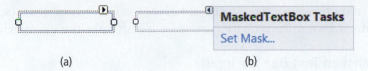

(a)   (b)

FIGURE 3.41   The Masked TextBox control.

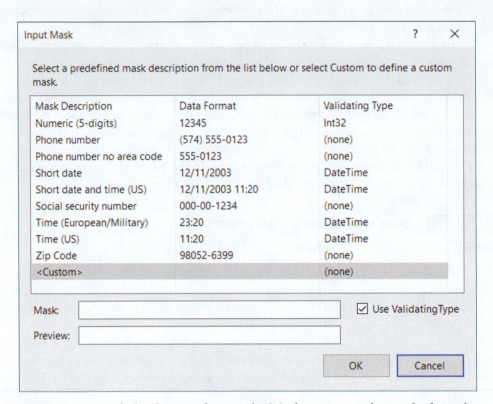

FIGURE 3.42   Input dialog box used to set the Mask property of a masked text box.

✔ **Example 1**   **Age in Days** The following program gives information pertaining to a date input by the user. The mask for the masked text box can be set by clicking on *Short date* in the Input Mask dialog box.

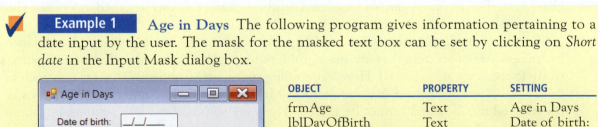

OBJECT	PROPERTY	SETTING
frmAge	Text	Age in Days
lblDayOfBirth	Text	Date of birth:
mtbDayOfBirth	Mask	00/00/0000
btnComputeOfBirth	Text	Compute Data
lblFullDateOfBirth	Text	Full birth date:
txtFullDateOfBirth	ReadOnly	True
lblToday	Text	Today's date:
txtToday	ReadOnly	True
lblAgeInDays	Text	Age in days:
txtAgeInDays	ReadOnly	True

```
Private Sub btnCompute_Click(...) Handles btnCompute.Click
  Dim dob As Date = CDate(mtbDayOfBirth.Text)
  txtFullDateOfBirth.Text = dob.ToString("D")
  txtToday.Text = Today.ToString("D")
  txtAgeInDays.Text = DateDiff(DateInterval.Day, dob, Today).ToString("N0")
End Sub
```

[Run, enter your birthday, and click on the button. One possible outcome is the following.]

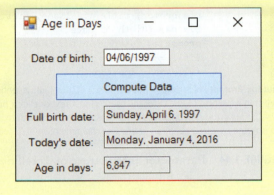

■ Getting Input from an Input Dialog Box

VideoNote
Input Boxes and Message Boxes

Normally, a text box is used to obtain input, where the type of information requested is specified in a label adjacent to the text box. Sometimes, we want just one piece of input and would rather not have a text box and label stay on the form permanently. The problem can be solved with an **input dialog box**. When a statement of the form

stringVar = InputBox(*prompt, title*)

is executed, an input dialog box similar to the one shown in Fig. 3.43 pops up on the screen. After the user types a response into the text box at the bottom of the dialog box and presses the Enter key (or clicks on the OK button), the response is assigned to the string variable. The *title* argument is optional and provides the text that appears in the title bar. The *prompt* argument is a string that tells the user what information to type into the text box.

When you type the opening parenthesis following the word InputBox, the Code Editor displays a line containing the general form of the InputBox statement. See Fig. 3.44. This feature of IntelliSense is called **Parameter Info**. Optional parameters are surrounded by square brackets. All the parameters in the general form of the InputBox statement are optional except for *prompt*.

The response typed into an input dialog box is treated as a single string value, no matter what is typed. (Quotation marks are not needed and, if included, are considered as part of the string.) Numeric data typed into an input dialog box should be converted to a number with CDbl or CInt before being assigned to a numeric variable or used in a calculation. Just as with a text box, the typed data must be literals. They cannot be variables or expressions. For instance, *num*, 1/2, and 2 + 3 are not acceptable.

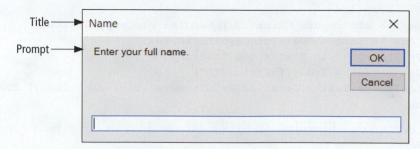

FIGURE 3.43 Sample input dialog box.

```
Dim prompt, title, fullName, firstName As String
Dim dayOfBirth As Date
prompt = "Enter your full name."
title = "Name"
fullName = InputBox(|)
```

Interaction.InputBox(**Prompt As String**, [Title As String = ""], [DefaultResponse As String = ""], [X
Displays a prompt in a dialog box, waits for the user to input text or click a button, and then retur
Prompt: *Required String expression displayed as the message in the dialog box. The maximum lengt*
carriage return character (Chr(13)), a line feed character (Chr(10)), or a carriage return/line

FIGURE 3.44 Parameter Info feature of IntelliSense.

✔ **Example 2**   **Age in Days** The following program uses two InputBox functions. Whenever an InputBox function is encountered in a program, an input dialog box appears, and execution stops until the user responds to the request. The function returns the value entered into the input dialog box.

```
Private Sub btnDisplay_Click(...) Handles btnDisplay.Click
  Dim prompt, title, fullName, firstName As String
  Dim dateOfBirth As Date
  prompt = "Enter your full name."
  title = "Name"
  fullName = InputBox(prompt, title)
  firstName = fullName.Substring(0, fullName.IndexOf(" "))
  prompt = "Enter your date of birth."
  title = "Birthday"
  dateOfBirth = CDate(InputBox(prompt, title))
  txtToday.Text = CStr(Today)
  txtOutput.Text = firstName & ", you are " &
    DateDiff(DateInterval.Day, dateOfBirth, Today).ToString("N0") & " days old."
End Sub
```

[Run, click on the button, enter *Emma Smith* into the first input dialog box, and enter *4/6/1994* into the second input dialog box.]

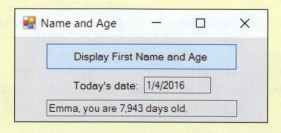

■ Using a Message Dialog Box for Output

Sometimes you want to grab the user's attention with a brief message such as "Correct" or "Nice try, but no cigar." You want this message to appear on the screen only until the user has read it. This task is easily accomplished with a **message dialog box** such as the one shown in Fig. 3.45.

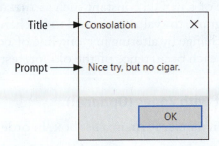

Title ⟶ Consolation
Prompt ⟶ Nice try, but no cigar.

FIGURE 3.45 **Sample message dialog box.**

When a statement of the form

```
MessageBox.Show(prompt, title)
```

is executed, where *prompt* and *title* are strings, a message dialog box appears with *prompt* displayed and title bar caption *title*, and stays on the screen until the user presses Enter, clicks on the *Close* button in the upper-right corner, or clicks OK. For instance, the statement

```
MessageBox.Show("Nice try, but no cigar.", "Consolation")
```

produces the output in Fig. 3.45. You can omit the value for the argument *title* and just execute **MessageBox.Show** (*prompt*). If you do, the title bar will be blank and the rest of the message dialog box will appear as before.

■ Named Constants

Often a program uses a special constant whose value does not change during program execution. Some examples might be the minimum wage, the sales tax rate, and the name of a master file. Programs are often made easier to understand and maintain if such a constant is given a name. Visual Basic has an object, called a **named constant**, that serves this purpose. A named constant is declared and used in a manner similar to a variable. The two main differences are that in the declaration of a named constant, Dim is replaced with Const, and the value of the named constant cannot be changed elsewhere in the program. Named constants can be thought of as read-only variables.

A named constant is declared and assigned a value with a statement of the form

```
Const CONSTANT_NAME As DataType = value
```

The standard convention is that the names be written in uppercase letters with words separated by underscore characters. Like a Dim statement, a Const statement can be placed in the Declarations section of a class (for class scope) or in a procedure (for procedure scope). Named constant declarations in procedures usually are placed near the beginning of the procedure. Some examples of named constant declarations are

```
Const INTEREST_RATE As Double = 0.04
Const PI As Double = 3.1416
Const BOOK_TITLE As String = "Programming with VB2015"
```

Examples of statements using these named constants are

```
interestEarned = INTEREST_RATE * CDbl(txtAmount.Text)
circumference = 2 * PI * radius
MessageBox.Show(BOOK_TITLE, "Title of Book")
```

Although the value of a named constant such as **INTEREST_RATE** will not change during the execution of a program, the value may need to be changed at a later time. The programmer can adjust to this change by altering just one line of code instead of searching through the entire program for each occurrence of the old interest rate.

■ Formatting Output with Zones (Optional)

Data can be displayed in tabular form in a list box. In order to have the items line up nicely in columns, you must

1. use a fixed-width font such as Courier New so that each character will have the same width.
2. divide the line into zones with a format string.

Figure 3.46 shows a line of a list box divided into zones of widths 15 characters, 10 characters, and 8 characters. The leftmost zone is referred to as zone 0, the next zone is zone 1, and so on. These zones are declared in a string with the statement

```
Dim fmtStr As String = "{0, 15}{1, 10}{2, 8}"
```

Note: The pairs of numbers are surrounded by curly brackets, not parentheses.

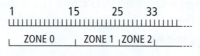

FIGURE 3.46 Zones.

If *data0*, *data1*, and *data2* are strings or numbers, the statement

```
lstOutput.Items.Add(String.Format(fmtStr, data0, data1, data2))
```

displays the pieces of data right justified into the zones. If any of the width numbers (such as 15, 10, or 8) is preceded with a minus sign, the data placed into the corresponding zone will be left justified.

 Example 3   The following program displays information about two colleges in the United States. *Note:* The endowments are in billions of dollars. The final column tells what fraction of the student body graduates.

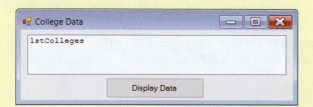

OBJECT	PROPERTY	SETTING
frmColleges	Text	College Data
lstColleges	Font	Courier New
btnDisplay	Text	Display Table

```
Private Sub btnDisplay_Click(...) Handles btnDisplay.Click
  Dim fmtStr As String = "{0,-10}{1,12}{2,14}{3,12}"
  lstColleges.Items.Clear()
  lstColleges.Items.Add(String.Format(fmtStr, "College",
                  "Enrollment", "Endowment", "Grad Rate"))
  lstColleges.Items.Add(String.Format(fmtStr, "Harvard", 10093, 32.3, 0.97))
  lstColleges.Items.Add(String.Format(fmtStr, "Yale", 12109, 20.8, 0.98))
End Sub
```

[Run, and click on the button.]

College Data   — ☐ ✕

College	Enrollment	Endowment	Grad Rate
Harvard	10093	32.3	0.97
Yale	12109	20.8	0.98

Display Data

There is no limit to the number of zones, and the zones can be of any widths. In addition, by placing a colon and formatting symbols after the width, you can instruct Visual Basic to specially format numeric data. (String data are not affected.) The most used formatting symbols consist of a letter (*N* for number, *C* for currency, or *P* for percent) followed by a digit specifying the number of decimal places. If there is no digit after the letter, two decimal places are displayed. Here are some examples of such formatting.

ZONE FORMAT TERM	NUMBER TO BE FORMATTED	NUMBER DISPLAYED
{1, 12: N3}	1234.5679	1,234.568
{1, 12: N0}	34.6	35
{1, 12: C1}	1234.567	$1,234.6
{1, 12: P}	0.569	56.90%

If the second line of the program in Example 1 is replaced with

```
Dim fmtStr As String = "{0,-10}{1,12:N0}{2,14:C}{3,12:P0}"
```

the output will be as follows.

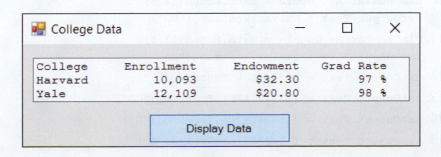

College Data   — ☐ ✕

College	Enrollment	Endowment	Grad Rate
Harvard	10,093	$32.30	97 %
Yale	12,109	$20.80	98 %

Display Data

The format strings considered so far consist of a sequence of pairs of curly brackets. We also can insert spaces between successive pairs of brackets. If so, the corresponding zones in the output will be separated by those spaces. The lines of code

```
Dim fmtStr As String = "{0, 5} {1, -5}" 'Two spaces after the
'                                         first right curly bracket
lstOutput.Items.Add("12345678901234567890")
lstOutput.Items.Add(String.Format(fmtStr, 1, 2))
```

produce the output

```
12345678901234567890
    1 2
```

Practice Problems 3.3

1. What is the difference between `(12.345).ToString` and `CStr(12.345)`?

2. What is the difference in the outcomes of the following two sets of code?

```
strVar = InputBox("How old are you?", "Age")
numVar = CDbl(strVar)
txtOutput.Text = numVar
```

```
numVar = CDbl(InputBox("How old are you?", "Age"))
txtOutput.Text = numVar
```

EXERCISES 3.3

In Exercises 1 through 56, determine the output produced by the lines of code.

1. `txtOutput.Text = (1234.56).ToString("N0")`

2. `txtOutput.Text = (-12.3456).ToString("N3")`

3. `txtOutput.Text = (1234).ToString("N1")`

4. `txtOutput.Text = (12345).ToString("N")`

5. `txtOutput.Text = (0.012).ToString("N1")`

6. `txtOutput.Text = (5 * (10 ^ -2)).ToString("N1")`

7. `txtOutput.Text = (-2 / 3).ToString("N")`

8. `Dim numVar As Double = Math.Round(1.2345, 1)`
   `txtOutput.Text = numVar.ToString("N")`

9. `Dim numVar As Double = Math.Round(12345.9)`
   `txtOutput.Text = numVar.ToString("N3")`

10. `Dim numVar As Double = Math.Round(12.5)`
    `txtOutput.Text = numVar.ToString("N0")`

11. `Dim numVar As Double = Math.Round(11.5)`
    `txtOutput.Text = numVar.ToString("N0")`

12. `txtOutput.Text = (1234.5D).ToString("C")`

13. `txtOutput.Text = (12345.67D).ToString("C0")`

14. `txtOutput.Text = (-1234567D).ToString("C")`

15. `txtOutput.Text = (-0.225D).ToString("C")`

16. `txtOutput.Text = (32 * (10 ^ -2)).ToString("C")`

17. `txtOutput.Text = (4D / 5D).ToString("C")`

18. `txtOutput.Text = (0.04D).ToString("C0")`

19. `txtOutput.Text = (0.075D).ToString("C")`

20. `txtOutput.Text = (-0.05D).ToString("C3")`

21. `txtOutput.Text = (1).ToString("P")`

22. `txtOutput.Text = (0.01).ToString("P")`

23. `txtOutput.Text = (2 / 3).ToString("P")`

24. `txtOutput.Text = (3 / 4).ToString("P1")`

25. `txtOutput.Text = "Pay to France " & (27267622D).ToString("C")`

26. `txtOutput.Text = "Manhattan was purchased for " & (24D).ToString("C")`

27.
```
Dim popUSover24 As Double = 177.6        'Million
Dim collegeGrads As Double = 45.5        'Million
'45.5/177.6 = 0.2561937
txtOutput.Text = (collegeGrads / popUSover24).ToString("P1") &
    " of the U.S. population 25+ years old are college graduates."
```

28.
```
Dim degrees As String = (1711500).ToString("N0")
txtOutput.Text = degrees & " degrees were conferred."
```

29.
```
txtOutput.Text = "The likelihood of Heads is " &
                (1 / 2).ToString("P0")
```

30. `txtOutput.Text = "Pi = " & (3.1415926536).ToString("N4")`

31. `txtOutput.Text = CStr(#10/23/2015#)`

32.
```
Dim dt As Date = #6/18/2017# 'Father's Day
txtOutput.Text = dt.ToString("D")
```

33.
```
Dim dt As Date = #11/24/2016# 'Thanksgiving Day
txtOutput.Text = dt.ToString("D")
```

34.
```
Dim dt As Date = #1/1/2000#
txtOutput.Text = CStr(dt.AddYears(15))
```

35.
```
Dim dt As Date = #9/29/2017#
txtOutput.Text = CStr(dt.AddDays(3))
```

36.
```
Dim dt As Date = #10/9/2015#
txtOutput.Text = CStr(dt.AddMonths(4))
```

37.
```
Dim dt As Date = #4/5/2017#
txtOutput.Text = CStr(dt.AddYears(2))
```

38.
```
Dim dt As Date = #10/1/2015#
txtOutput.Text = CStr(dt.AddDays(32))
```

39.
```
Dim dt1 As Date = #2/1/2016#    '2016 was a leap year
Dim dt2 As Date = dt1.AddMonths(1)
txtOutput.Text = CStr(DateDiff(DateInterval.Day, dt1, dt2))
```

40.
```
Dim dt1 As Date = #1/1/2016#    '2016 was a leap year
Dim dt2 As Date = #1/1/2017#
txtOutput.Text = CStr(DateDiff(DateInterval.Day, dt1, dt2))
```

41.
```
Dim dt1 As Date = Today
Dim dt2 As Date = dt1.AddDays(5)
txtOutput.Text = CStr(DateDiff(DateInterval.Day, dt1, dt2))
```

42. ```
Dim dt As Date = #1/2/2016#
txtOutput.Text = CStr(dt.Day)
```

43. ```
Dim dt As Date = #1/2/2016#
txtOutput.Text = CStr(dt.Month)
```

44. ```
Dim dt As Date = #1/2/2016#
txtOutput.Text = CStr(dt.Year)
```

45. ```
Dim dt As Date = #1/2/2016#
MessageBox.Show(CStr(dt.Day + dt.Year))
```

46. ```
Dim dt As Date = #1/2/2016#
MessageBox.Show("1, 2, " & CStr(dt.Day + dt.Month))
```

47. ```
Dim bet As Decimal     'amount bet at roulette
bet = CDec(InputBox("How much do you want to bet?", "Wager"))
txtOutput.Text = "You might win " & 36 * bet & " dollars."
```
    (Assume that the response is *10*.)

48. ```
Dim word As String
word = InputBox("Word to negate:", "Negatives")
txtOutput.Text = "un" & word
```
    (Assume that the response is *tied*.)

49. ```
Dim lastName, message, firstName As String
lastName = "Jones"
message = "What is your first name Mr. " & lastName & "?"
firstName = InputBox(message, "Name")
txtOutput.Text = "Hello " & firstName & " " & lastName
```
    (Assume that the response is *John*.)

50. ```
Dim intRate, doublingTime As Decimal 'interest rate, time to double
intRate = CDec(InputBox("Current interest rate?", "Interest"))
doublingTime = 72D / intRate
lstOutput.Items.Add("At the current interest rate, money will")
lstOutput.Items.Add("double in " & doublingTime & " years.")
```
    (Assume that the response is *4*.)

51. ```
Const SALES_TAX_RATE As Decimal = 0.06D
Dim price As Decimal = 100
Dim cost = (1 + SALES_TAX_RATE) * price
txtOutput.Text = cost.ToString("C")
```

52. ```
Const ESTATE_TAX_EXEMPTION As Double = 1000000
Const TAX_RATE As Decimal = 0.45D
Dim valueOfEstate As Decimal = 3000000
Dim tax As Double = TAX_RATE * (valueOfEstate - ESTATE_TAX_EXEMPTION)
txtOutput.Text = "You owe " & tax.ToString("C") & " in estate taxes."
```

In Exercises 53 through 56, determine the output produced by the lines of code where Courier New is the font setting for the list box.

53. ```
Dim fmtStr As String = "{0,-13}{1,-10}{2,-7:N0}"
lstOutput.Items.Add("12345678901234567890123456789 0")
lstOutput.Items.Add(String.Format(fmtStr, "Mountain", "Place", "Ht (ft)"))
lstOutput.Items.Add(String.Format(fmtStr, "K2", "Kashmir", 28250))
```

54.
```
Dim fmtStr As String = "{0,11} {1,-11}" 'Three spaces
lstOutput.Items.Add("12345678901234567890")
lstOutput.Items.Add(String.Format(fmtStr, "College", "Mascot"))
lstOutput.Items.Add(String.Format(fmtStr, "Univ. of MD", "Terrapins"))
lstOutput.Items.Add(String.Format(fmtStr, "Duke", "Blue Devils"))
```

55.
```
'Elements in a 150 Pound Person
Dim fmtStr As String = "{0,-7} {1,-7:N1} {2,-7:P1}" 'Two spaces
lstOutput.Items.Clear()
lstOutput.Items.Add("12345678901234567890")
lstOutput.Items.Add(String.Format(fmtStr, "Element", "Weight", "Percent"))
lstOutput.Items.Add(String.Format(fmtStr, "Oxygen", 97.5, 97.5 / 150))
lstOutput.Items.Add(String.Format(fmtStr, "Carbon", 27, 27 / 150))
```

56.
```
Dim fmtStr As String = "{0,10} {1,-10:C0}" 'Three spaces
lstOutput.Items.Clear()
lstOutput.Items.Add("12345678901234567890")
lstOutput.Items.Add(String.Format(fmtStr, "", "Tuition"))
lstOutput.Items.Add(String.Format(fmtStr, "College", "& Fees"))
lstOutput.Items.Add(String.Format(fmtStr, "Stanford", 42690))
lstOutput.Items.Add(String.Format(fmtStr, "Harvard", 42292))
```

In Exercises 57 through 64, identify any errors.

57.
```
Const n As Integer = 5
n += 1
txtOutput.Text = CStr(n)
```

58.
```
Const n As String = "abc"
n = n.ToUpper
txtOutput.Text = n
```

59.
```
Dim num As Double
num = InputBox("Pick a number from 1 to 10.")
txtOutput.Text = "Your number is " & num
```

60.
```
info = InputBox()
```

61.
```
Dim num As Double = (123456).ToString("N")
lstOutput.Items.Add(num)
```

62.
```
txtOutput.Text = ($1234).ToString("C")
```

63.
```
MessageBox("Olive Kitteridge", "Pulitzer Prize for Fiction")
```

64.
```
MessageBox.Show(1776, "Year of Independence")
```

In Exercises 65 through 70, give a setting for the Mask property of a masked text box used to input the stated information.

65. A number from 0 to 999.

66. A word of at most ten letters.

67. A Maryland license plate consisting of three letters followed by three digits. (*Example:* BHC365)

68. A license plate consisting of a digit followed by three letters and then three digits. (*Example:* 7BHC365)

69. An ISBN number. [Every book is identified by a ten-character International Standard Book Number (ISBN). The first nine characters are digits and the last character is either a digit or the letter X.] (*Example:* 0–32–108599–X)

70. A two-letter state abbreviation. (*Example:* CA)

In Exercises 71 and 72, write a statement to carry out the task.

71. Pop up a message dialog box with "Good Advice" in the title bar and the message "First solve the problem. Then write the code."

72. Pop up a message dialog box with "Taking Risks Proverb" in the title bar and the message "You can't steal second base and keep one foot on first."

In Exercises 73 and 74, write an event procedure with the header `Private Sub btnDisplay_Click(...)` Handles btnDisplay.Click, and having one, two, or three lines for each step. Lines that display data should use the given variable names.

73. Inflation The following steps calculate the percent increase in the cost of a typical grocery basket of goods:

(a) Declare the variables *begOfYearCost*, *endOfYearCost*, and *percentIncrease* as type Decimal.
(b) Assign 200 to the variable *begOfYearCost*.
(c) Request the cost at the end of the year with an input dialog box, and assign it to the variable *endOfYearCost*.
(d) Assign (*endOfYearCost* – *begOfYearCost*) / *begOfYearCost* to the variable *percentIncrease*.
(e) Display a sentence giving the percent increase for the year.

74. Walk-a-Thon The following steps calculate the amount of money earned in a walk-a-thon:

(a) Declare the variables *pledge* and *miles* as type Decimal.
(b) Request the amount pledged per mile from an input dialog box, and assign it to the variable *pledge*.
(c) Request the number of miles walked from an input dialog box, and assign it to the variable *miles*.
(d) Display a sentence giving the amount to be paid.

75. Reminder Design a form with two text boxes labeled "Name" and "Phone number". Then write an event procedure that shows a message dialog box stating "Be sure to include the area code!" when the second text box receives the focus. See Fig. 3.47.

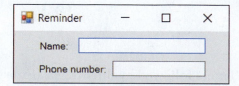

FIGURE 3.47 Form for Exercise 75.

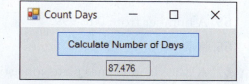

FIGURE 3.48 Possible outcome of Exercise 76.

76. Declaration of Independence   Write a program that calculates the number of days since the Declaration of Independence was ratified (7/4/1776). See Fig. 3.48.

77. Length of Year   Write a program that requests a year in a masked text box and then displays the number of days in the year. See Fig. 3.49. **Hint:** Use the AddYears method and the DateDiff function.

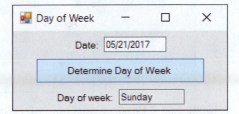

FIGURE 3.49   Possible outcome of Exercise 77.   **FIGURE 3.50**   Possible outcome of Exercise 78.

78. Day of Week   Write a program that requests a date in a masked text box, and then displays the day of the week (such as Sunday, Monday, . . .) for that date. See Fig. 3.50.

79. Day of Week   Write a program that requests a date as input and then displays the day of the week (such as Sunday, Monday, . . .) for that date ten years hence. See Fig. 3.51.

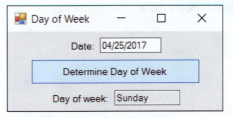

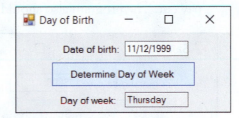

FIGURE 3.51   Possible outcome of Exercise 79.   **FIGURE 3.52**   Possible outcome of Exercise 80.

80. Day of Birth   Write a program that requests the user's date of birth and then displays the day of the week (such as Sunday, Monday) on which the user will have (or had) their 21st birthday. See Fig. 3.52.

81. Convert Date Formats   Dates in the U.S. are written in the format month/day/year, whereas dates in Europe are written in the format day/month/year. Write a program to convert a date from U.S. format to European format. See Fig. 3.53. Use the Day and Month methods for variables of type Date.

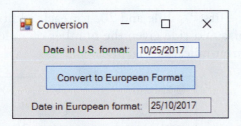

FIGURE 3.53   Possible outcome of Exercise 81.   **FIGURE 3.54**   Possible outcome of Exercise 82.

82. Valentine's Day   Write a program to determine the full date of Valentine's Day for a year input by the user. See Fig. 3.54. **Note:** Valentine's Day is always celebrated on the 14th of February.

83. Length of Month   Write a program that requests a month and a year as input and then displays the number of days in that month. *Hint:* Use the AddMonths method. See Fig. 3.55.

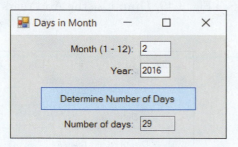

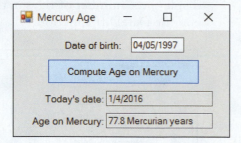

FIGURE 3.55   Possible outcome of Exercise 83.   **FIGURE 3.56**   Possible outcome of Exercise 84.

84. How Old Would You Be on Mercury?   The length of a Mercurian year is 88 Earth days. Write a program that requests your date of birth and computes your Mercurian age. See Fig. 3.56.

85. Change in Salary   A common misconception is that if you receive a 10% pay raise and later a 10% pay cut, your salary will be unchanged. Write a program that requests a salary as input and then calculates the salary after receiving a 10% pay raise followed by a 10% pay cut. The program also should calculate the percentage change in salary. See Fig. 3.57.

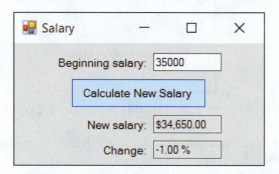

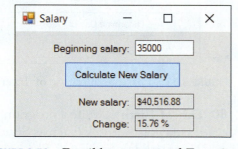

FIGURE 3.57   Possible outcome of Exercise 85.   **FIGURE 3.58**   Possible outcome of Exercise 86.

86. Change in Salary   A common misconception is that if you receive three successive 5% pay raises, then your original salary will have increased by 15%. Write a program that requests a salary as input and then calculates the salary after receiving three successive 5% pay raises. The program also should calculate the percentage change in salary. See Fig. 3.58.

87. Taxi Fare   If a taxi ride costs $1 for the first $1/4$ mile and 20¢ for each additional $1/4$ mile, write a program to find the cost of a taxi ride given the number of miles. **Note:** Assume that the meter clicks on the quarter-mile. See Fig. 3.59.

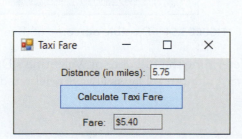

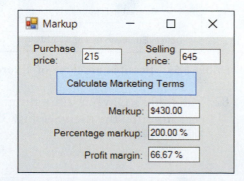

FIGURE 3.59   Possible outcome of Exercise 87.   **FIGURE 3.60**   Possible outcome of Exercise 88.

88. Marketing Terms The *markup* of an item is the difference between its *selling price* and its *purchase price*. Two other marketing terms are

$$\text{percentage markup} = \frac{\text{markup}}{\text{purchase price}} \quad and \quad \text{profit margin} = \frac{\text{markup}}{\text{selling price}}$$

where the quotients are expressed as percentages. Write a program that computes the markup, percentage markup, and profit margin of an item. See Fig. 3.60. Notice that when the purchase price is tripled, the percentage markup is 200%.

Solutions to Practice Problems 3.3

1. None. **Note:** The Auto Correction feature of IntelliSense seems to prefer the use of CStr. When the smart editor encounters a statement such as **txtBox. Text = 12.345**, it signals that a syntax error has occurred and recommends changing **12.345** to **CStr (12.345)**. The convention in this book is to use the ToString method whenever formatting is wanted and to otherwise use CStr.

2. The outcomes are identical. In this text, we primarily use the second style.

CHAPTER 3 SUMMARY

1. Three types of *literals* that can be stored and processed by Visual Basic are numbers, strings, and dates.

2. Many Visual Basic tasks are carried out by methods such as Clear (erases the contents of a text box or list box), Add (places an item into a list box), ToUpper (converts a string to uppercase), ToLower (converts a string to lowercase), Trim (removes leading and trailing spaces from a string), IndexOf (searches for a specified substring in a string and gives its position if found), and Substring (produces a sequence of consecutive characters from a string).

3. The *arithmetic operations* are +, −, *, /, ^, \, and Mod. The only string operation is &, concatenation. An *expression* is a combination of literals, variables, functions, and operations that can be evaluated.

4. A *variable* is a name used to refer to data. Variable names must begin with a letter or an underscore and may contain letters, digits, and underscores. Dim statements declare variables, specify the data types of the variables, and assign initial values to the variables. In this book, most variables have data types Double, Decimal, Integer, String, or Date.

5. Values are assigned to variables by *assignment statements*. The values appearing in assignment statements can be literals, variables, or expressions. String literals used in assignment statements must be surrounded by quotation marks. Date literals used in assignment statements must be surrounded by number signs.

6. *Comment statements* are used to explain formulas, state the purposes of variables, and articulate the purposes of various parts of a program.

7. *Option Explicit* requires that all variables be declared with Dim statements. *Option Strict* requires the use of conversion functions in certain situations.

8. The *Error List window* displays, and helps you find, errors in the code. The *Auto Correction* feature of IntelliSense suggests corrections when errors occur.

9. *Line continuation* is used to extend a Visual Basic statement over two or more lines.

10. The *scope* of a variable is the portion of the program in which the variable is visible and can be used. A variable declared inside an event procedure is said to have *procedure* scope and is visible only inside the procedure. A variable declared in the Declarations section of a class is said to have *class* scope and is visible throughout the entire program.

11. *Masked text boxes* help obtain correct input with a Mask property that limits the kind of data that can be typed into the text box.

12. The *Date* data type facilitates computations involving dates.

13. An *input dialog box* is a window that pops up and displays a message for the user to respond to in a text box. The response is assigned to a variable.

14. A *message dialog box* is a window that pops up to display a message to the user.

15. *Named constants* store values that cannot change during the execution of a program. They are declared with Const statements.

16. The following *functions* accept numbers, strings, or dates as input and return numbers or strings as output.

FUNCTION/METHOD	INPUT	OUTPUT
CDbl	string or number	number
CDec	string or number	number
CInt	string or number	number
CStr	string or number	string
ToString ("N")	number	string
ToString ("C")	number	string
ToString ("P")	number	string
ToString ("D")	date	string
ToString ("d")	date	string
DateDiff	date, date	number
InputBox	string, string	string
Int	number	number
Math.Round	number, number	number
Math.Sqrt	number	number

CHAPTER 3　PROGRAMMING PROJECTS

1. **Calculator**　Write a program that allows the user to specify two numbers and then adds, subtracts, or multiplies them when the user clicks on the appropriate button. The output should give the type of arithmetic performed and the result. See Fig. 3.61. **Note:** When one of the numbers in an input text box is changed, the output text box should be cleared.

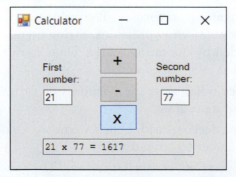

FIGURE 3.61　Possible outcome of Programming Project 1.

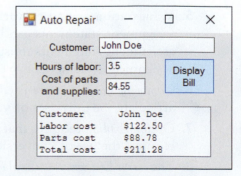

FIGURE 3.62　Possible outcome of Programming Project 2.

2. **Repair Bill**　Suppose automobile repair customers are billed at the rate of $35 per hour for labor. Also, suppose costs for parts and supplies are subject to a 5% sales tax. Write a program to display a simplified bill. The customer's name, the number of hours of labor, and the cost of parts and supplies should be entered into the program via text

boxes. When a button is clicked, the customer's name and the three costs should be displayed in a list box, as shown in Fig. 3.62.

3. **Change**   Write a program to make change for an amount of money from 0 through 99 cents input by the user. The output of the program should show the number of coins from each denomination used to make change. See Fig. 3.63.

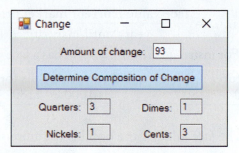

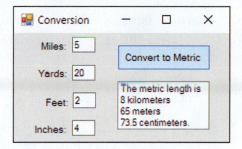

FIGURE 3.63   Possible outcome of Programming Project 3.

FIGURE 3.64   Possible outcome of Programming Project 4.

4. **Length Conversion**   Write a program to convert a U.S. Customary System length in miles, yards, feet, and inches to a Metric System length in kilometers, meters, and centimeters. A sample run is shown in Fig. 3.64. After the numbers of miles, yards, feet, and inches are read from the text boxes, the length should be converted entirely to inches and then divided by 39.37 to obtain the value in meters. The Int function should be used to break the total number of meters into a whole number of kilometers and meters. The number of centimeters should be displayed to one decimal place. The needed formulas are as follows:

$$\text{total inches} = 63360*\text{miles} + 36*\text{yards} + 12*\text{feet} + \text{inches}$$
$$\text{total meters} = \text{total inches}/39.37$$
$$\text{kilometers} = \text{Int}(\text{meters}/1000)$$

5. **Car Loan**   If A dollars are borrowed at $r\%$ interest compounded monthly to purchase a car with monthly payments for n years, then the monthly payment is given by the formula

$$\text{monthly payment} = \frac{i}{1 - (1 + i)^{-12n}} \cdot A,$$

where $i = \dfrac{r}{1200}$. Write a program that calculates the monthly payment after the user gives the amount of the loan, interest rate, and number of years. Figure 3.65 shows that monthly payments of $234.23 are required to pay off a 5-year loan of $12,000 at 6.4% interest.

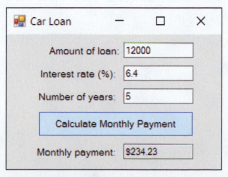

FIGURE 3.65   Possible outcome of Programming Project 5.

FIGURE 3.66   Possible outcome of Programming Project 6.

6. **Unit Price**   Write a program that requests the price and weight of an item in pounds and ounces, and then determines the price per ounce. See Fig. 3.66 on the previous page.

7. **Bond Yield**   One measure of a bond's performance is its *Yield To Maturity* (YTM). YTM values for government bonds are complex to calculate and are published in tables. However, they can be approximated with the simple formula $YTM = \dfrac{intr + a}{b}$, where *intr* is the interest earned per year, $a = \dfrac{\text{face value} - \text{current market price}}{\text{years until maturity}}$, and $b = \dfrac{\text{face value} + \text{current market price}}{2}$. For instance, suppose a bond has a face value of $1000, a coupon interest rate of 4%, matures in 15 years, and currently sells for $1180. Then $intr = .04 \cdot 1000 = 40$, $a = \dfrac{1000 - 1180}{15} = -12$, $b = \dfrac{1000 + 1180}{2} = 1090$, and $YTM = \dfrac{40 - 12}{1090} \approx 2.57\%$. **Note:** The *face value* of the bond is the amount it will be redeemed for when it matures, and the *coupon interest rate* is the interest rate stated on the bond. If a bond is purchased when it is first issued, then the YTM is the same as the coupon interest rate. Write a program that requests the face value, coupon interest rate, current market price, and years until maturity for a bond, and then calculates the bond's YTM. See Fig. 3.67.

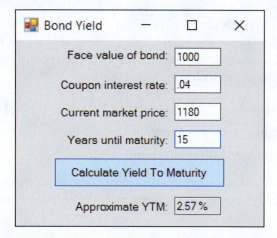

FIGURE 3.67   **Possible outcome of Programming Project 7.**

4

Decisions

4.1   Relational and Logical Operators

In Chapter 1, we discussed the two logical programming constructs *decision* and *repetition*. In order to make a decision we need to specify a condition that determines the course of action.

A **condition** is an expression involving relational operators (such as < and =) that is either true or false. Conditions also may incorporate logical operators (such as And, Or, and Not). ANSI values determine the order used to compare strings with the relational operators. Boolean variables and literals can assume the values True or False.

■ ANSI Values

Each of the 47 keys in the center typewriter portion of the keyboard can produce two characters, for a total of 94 characters. Adding 1 for the character produced by the space bar makes 95 characters. Associated with these characters are numbers ranging from 32 to 126. These values, called the ANSI (or ASCII) values of the characters, are given in Appendix A. Table 4.1 shows a few of them.

TABLE 4.1   A few ANSI values.

32 (space)	48 0	66 B	122 z
33 !	49 1	90 Z	123 {
34 "	57 9	97 a	125 }
35 #	65 A	98 b	126 ~

Most of the common fonts, such as Courier New, Microsoft San Serif, and Times New Roman, adhere to the ANSI standard, which assigns characters to the numbers from 0 to 255. Table 4.2 shows a few of the higher ANSI values.

TABLE 4.2   A few higher ANSI values.

162 ¢	177 ±	181 μ	190 $^3/_4$
169 ©	178 ^{2}	188 $^1/_4$	247 ÷
176 °	179 ^{3}	189 $^1/_2$	248 ϕ

If *n* is a number between 0 and 255, then

```
Chr(n)
```

is the string consisting of the character with ANSI value *n*. If *str* is any string, then

```
Asc(str)
```

is the ANSI value of the first character of *str*. For instance, the statement

```
txtBox.Text = Chr(65)
```

displays the letter A in the text box, and the statement

```
lstBox.Items.Add(Asc("Apple"))
```

displays the number 65 in the list box.

Concatenation can be used with Chr to obtain strings using the higher ANSI characters. For instance, with one of the fonts that conforms to the ANSI standard, the statement

```
txtBox.Text = 32 & Chr(176) & " Fahrenheit"
```

displays **32° Fahrenheit** in the text box.

The quotation-mark character (") can be placed into a string by using Chr(34). For example, after the statement

```
txtBox.Text = "George " & Chr(34) & "Babe" & Chr(34) & " Ruth"
```

is executed, the text box contains

```
George "Babe" Ruth
```

■ Relational Operators

The relational operator *less than* (<) can be applied to numbers, strings, and dates. The number a is said to be less than the number b if a lies to the left of b on the number line. For instance, $2 < 5$, $-5 < -2$, and $0 < 3.5$.

VideoNote
Relational
and Logical
Operators

The string a is said to be less than the string b if a precedes b when using the ANSI table to order their characters. For instance, "cat" < "dog", "cart" < "cat", and "cat" < "catalog". Digits precede uppercase letters, which precede lowercase letters. Two strings are compared (working from left to right), character by character, to determine which string should precede the other. Therefore, "9W" < "bat", "Dog" < "cat", and "Sales-99" < "Sales-retail". This type of ordering is called **lexicographical ordering**.

The date $d1$ is said to be less than the date $d2$ if $d1$ precedes $d2$ chronologically. For instance, #12/7/1941# < #6/6/1944#.

Table 4.3 shows the different relational operators and their meanings.

TABLE 4.3	**Relational operators.**		
Visual Basic Notation	**Numeric Meaning**	**String Meaning**	**Date Meaning**
=	equal to	identical to	same as
<>	not equal to	different from	different than
<	less than	precedes lexicographically	precedes chronologically
>	greater than	follows lexicographically	follows chronologically
<=	less than or equal to	precedes lexicographically or is identical to	precedes chronologically or is the same as
>=	greater than or equal to	follows lexicographically or is identical to	follows chronologically or is the same as

 Example 1   **Relational Operators** Determine whether each of the following conditions is true or false:

(a) $1 <= 1$

(b) $1 < 1$

(c) "car" < "cat"

(d) "Dog" < "dog"

(e) Today < Today.AddDays(1)

SOLUTION

(a) True. The notation <= means "less than *or* equal to." That is, the condition is true provided either of the two circumstances holds. The second one (equal to) holds.

(b) False. The notation $<$ means "strictly less than" and no number can be strictly less than itself.

(c) True. The characters of the strings are compared one at a time working from left to right. Because the first two characters match, the third character determine the order.

(d) True. Because uppercase letters precede lowercase letters in the ANSI table, the first character of "Dog" precedes the first character of "dog".

(e) True. Today precedes tomorrow chronologically.

Conditions also can involve variables, numeric operators, and functions. To determine whether a condition is true or false, first evaluate the numeric or string expressions and then decide if the resulting assertion is true or false.

 Example 2 **Relational Operators** Suppose the numeric variables *a* and *b* have values 4 and 3, and the string variables *c* and *d* have values "hello" and "bye". Are the following conditions true or false?

(a) $(a + b) < 2*a$

(b) $(c.Length - b) = (a/2)$

(c) $c < ("good" \& d)$

SOLUTION

(a) The value of a + b is 7 and the value of 2 * a is 8. Because $7 < 8$, the condition is true.

(b) True, because the value of c.Length − b is 2, the same as (a / 2).

(c) The condition "hello" $<$ "goodbye" is false, because "h" follows "g" in the ANSI table.

■ Logical Operators

Programming often requires more complex conditions than those considered so far. For instance, suppose we would like to state that the value of a numeric variable, *n*, is strictly between 2 and 5. The proper Visual Basic condition is

$$(2 < n) \text{ And } (n < 5)$$

This condition is a combination of the two conditions $2 < n$ and $n < 5$ with the logical operator And.

The three main logical operators are And, Or, and Not. Conditions that use these operators are called **compound conditions**. If *cond1* and *cond2* are conditions, then the compound condition

cond1 And cond2

is true if both *cond1* and *cond2* are true. Otherwise, it is false. The compound condition

cond1 Or cond2

is true if either *cond1* or *cond2* (or both) is true. Otherwise, it is false. The compound condition

Not cond1

is true if *cond1* is false, and is false if *cond1* is true.

Example 3   **Logical Operators**   Suppose the numeric variable *n* has value 4 and the string variable *answ* has value "Y". Determine whether each of the following conditions is true or false:

(a) (2 < n) And (n < 6)

(b) (2 < n) Or (n = 6)

(c) Not (n < 6)

(d) (answ = "Y") Or (answ = "y")

(e) (answ = "Y") And (answ = "y")

(f) Not (answ = "y")

(g) ((2 < n) And (n = 5 + 1)) Or (answ = "No")

(h) ((n = 2) And (n = 7)) Or (answ = "Y")

(i) (n = 2) And ((n = 7) Or (answ = "Y"))

SOLUTION

(a) True, because the conditions (2 < 4) and (4 < 6) are both true.

(b) True, because the condition (2 < 4) is true. The fact that the condition (4 = 6) is false does not affect the conclusion. The only requirement is that at least one of the two conditions be true.

(c) False, because (4 < 6) is true.

(d) True, because the first condition becomes ("Y" = "Y") when the value of *answ* is substituted for *answ*.

(e) False, because the second condition is false. Actually, this compound condition is false for any value of *answ*.

(f) True, because ("Y" = "y") is false.

(g) False. In this logical expression, the compound condition ((2 < n) and (n = 5 + 1)) and the simple condition (answ = "No") are joined by the logical operator Or. Because both of these conditions are false, the total condition is false.

(h) True, because the second Or clause is true.

(i) False. Comparing (h) and (i) shows the necessity of using parentheses to specify the intended grouping.

■ Boolean Data Type

A statement of the form

```
txtBox.Text = CStr(condition)
```

will display either True or False in the text box, depending on the condition. Any variable or expression that evaluates to either True or False is said to have a **Boolean data type**. The following lines of code display False in the text box:

```
Dim x As Integer = 5
txtBox.Text = CStr((3 + x) < 7)
```

A variable is declared to be of type Boolean with a statement of the form

```
Dim varName As Boolean
```

The following lines of code will display True in the text box:

```
Dim boolVar As Boolean
Dim x As Integer = 2
Dim y As Integer = 3
boolVar = x < y
txtBox.Text = CStr(boolVar)
```

The answer to part (i) of Example 3 can be confirmed to be False by executing the following lines of code:

```
Dim n as Integer = 4
Dim answ as String = "Y"
txtBox.Text = CStr((n = 2) And ((n = 7) Or (answ = "Y")))
```

■ Two Methods That Return Boolean Values

If *strVar* is a string variable, then the expression

```
strVar.Substring(strVar.length − 3) = "ing"
```

is true if and only if the value of *strVar* ends with *ing*. To generalize, if *strVar2* is another string variable, then the expression

```
strVar.SubString(strVar.length − strVar2.Length) = strVar2
```
(1)

is true if and only if the value of *strVar* ends with the value of *strVar2*.

The EndsWith method provides an alternate way to test for the end of a string. The value of

```
strVar.EndsWith(strVar2)
```
(2)

is True if and only if the value of *strVar* ends with the value of *strVar2*.

Expression (2) is preferable to expression (1) since it is more concise and readable. Code such as expression (2) is called **declarative code** (or **self-evident code**), since it clearly declares *what* you want to accomplish. Expression (1) shows *how* to accomplish the task but requires some analysis to figure out what is being achieved. One of our guiding programming principles is to write declarative code whenever possible. We prefer *what* to *how*.

The counterpart of the EndsWith method is the StartsWith method. The value of

```
strVar.StartsWith(strVar2)
```

is True if and only if the value of *strVar* begins with the value of *strVar2*.

■ A Boolean-Valued Function

The IsNumeric function is used to determine if a value input by the user, such as in a text box or input dialog box, can be used in numeric computations. The value of

```
IsNumeric(strVar)
```

is True if *strVar* can be converted to a number with CInt, CDec, or CDbl, and is False otherwise. For instance, `IsNumeric(strVar)` will be True when the value of *strVar* is "2345", "$123", or "5,677,890". The function value will be False when the value of *strVar* is "five" or "4 − 2".

■ Comments

1. A condition involving numeric variables is different from an algebraic identity. The assertion (a + b) < 2*a, considered in Example 2, is not a valid algebraic identity because it isn't true for all values of *a* and *b*. When encountered in a Visual Basic program, however, it will be considered true if it is correct for the current values of the variables.

2. Conditions evaluate to either True or False. These two values often are called the possible **truth values** of the condition.

3. A condition such as 2 < n < 5 should never be used, because Visual Basic will not evaluate it as intended. The correct condition is (2 < n) And (n < 5).

4. A common error is to replace the condition Not (n < m) by the condition (n > m). The correct replacement is (n >= m).

Practice Problems 4.1

1. Is the condition **"Hello " = "Hello"** true or false?

2. Explain why (27 > 9) is true, whereas ("27" > "9") is false.

3. Complete Table 4.4.

TABLE 4.4 Truth values of logical operators.

cond1	cond2	cond1 And cond2	cond1 Or cond2	Not cond2
True	True	True		
True	False		True	
False	True			False
False	False			

Exercises 4.1

In Exercises 1 through 6, determine the output displayed in the text box.

1. ```
txtBox.Text = Chr(104) & Chr(105)
```

2. ```
txtBox.Text = "C" & Chr(35)
```

3. ```
txtBox.Text = "The letter before G is " & Chr(Asc("G") - 1)
```

4. ```
txtBox.Text = Chr(Asc("B"))  'The ANSI value of B is 66
```

5. ```
Dim quote, person, qMark As String
quote = "We're all in this alone."
person = "Lily Tomlin"
qMark = Chr(34)
txtBox.Text = qMark & quote & qMark & " - " & person
```

6. ```
Dim letter As String
letter = "D"
txtBox.Text = letter & " is the " & (Asc(letter) - Asc("A") + 1) &
              "th letter of the alphabet."
```

In Exercises 7 through 18, determine whether the condition is true or false. Assume a = 2 and b = 3.

7. 3*a = 2*b

8. (5 − a)*b < 7

9. b <= 3

10. a^b = b^a

11. a^(5 − 2) > 7

12. 3E−02 < .01*a

13. (a < b) Or (b < a)

14. (a*a < b) Or Not (a*a < a)

15. Not ((a < b) And (a < (b + a)))

16. Not (a < b) Or Not (a < (b + a))

17. ((a = b) And (a*a < b*b)) Or ((b < a) And (2*a < b))

18. ((a = b) Or Not (b < a)) And ((a < b) Or (b = a + 1))

In Exercises 19 through 30, determine whether the condition is true or false.

19. "9W" <> "9w"

20. "Inspector" < "gadget"

21. "Car" < "Train"

22. "J" >= "J"

23. "99" > "ninety-nine"

24. "B" > "?"

25. ("Duck" < "pig") And ("pig" < "big")

26. "Duck" < "Duck" & "Duck"

27. Not (("B" = "b") Or ("Big" < "big"))

28. #7/4/1776# >= #7/4/1776#

29. #6/17/1775# <= #7/4/1776#

30. (7 < 34) And ("7" > "34")

In Exercises 31 through 38, determine whether or not the two conditions are equivalent— that is, whether they will both be true or false for any values of the variables appearing in them.

31. a <= b; (a < b) Or (a = b)

32. Not (a < b); a > b

33. (a = b) Or (a < b); a <> b

34. Not ((a = b) Or (a = c)); (a <> b) And (a <> c)

35. Not ((a = b) And (a = c)); (a <> b) Or (a <> c)

36. (a < b) And ((a > d) Or (a > e));
   ((a < b) And (a > d)) Or ((a < b) And (a > e))

37. (a < b + c) Or (a = b + c); Not ((a > b) Or (a > c))

38. Not (a >= b); (a <= b) And Not (a = b)

In Exercises 39 through 44, simplify the condition by writing an equivalent condition that does not include Not. (For example, Not(a <> b) is equivalent to a = b.)

39. Not (a > b)

40. Not ((a = b) Or (a = d))

41. Not ((a < b) And (c <> d))

42. Not (Not((a = b) Or (a > b)))

43. Not ((a <> "") And (a < b) And (a.Length < 5))

44. Not (a <= b)

45. Rework Exercise 19 by evaluating the Boolean expression in a program.

46. Rework Exercise 20 by evaluating the Boolean expression in a program.

47. Rework Exercise 21 by evaluating the Boolean expression in a program.

48. Rework Exercise 22 by evaluating the Boolean expression in a program.

In Exercises 49 through 60, determine whether True or False is displayed in the text box.

49. `txtBox.Text = CStr("Colonel".StartsWith("k"))`

50.
```
Dim str As String = "target"
txtBox.Text = CStr(str.StartsWith("t") And str.EndsWith("t"))
```

51.
```
Dim str As String = "ticket"
txtBox.Text = CStr(str.StartsWith("T") Or str.EndsWith("T"))
```

52.
```
Dim str1 As String = "target"
Dim str2 As String = "get"
txtBox.Text = CStr(str1.EndsWith(str2))
```

53.
```
Dim str1 As String = "Teapot"
Dim str2 As String = "Tea"
txtBox.Text = CStr(str1.StartsWith(str2))
```

54.
```
Dim str As String = "$1,234.56"
txtBox.Text = CStr(IsNumeric(str))
```

55.
```
Dim str As String = "10,000,000"
txtBox.Text = CStr(IsNumeric(str))
```

56.
```
Dim str As String = "10 million"
txtBox.Text = CStr(IsNumeric(str))
```

57.
```
Dim str As String = "2 + 3"
txtBox.Text = CStr(IsNumeric(str))
```

58.
```
Dim str As String = "10E+06"
txtBox.Text = CStr(IsNumeric(str))
```

59.
```
Dim str As String = "5E-12"
txtBox.Text = CStr(IsNumeric(str))
```

60. `txtBox.Text = CStr(IsNumeric("seven"))`

61. Position in the Alphabet Write a program that finds the location of a letter of the alphabet input by the user. See Fig. 4.1. [**Note:** Asc("A") has the value 65.]

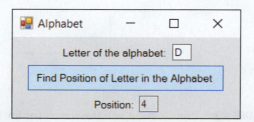

FIGURE 4.1 Possible outcome of Exercise 61.

1. False. The first string has six characters, whereas the second has five. Two strings must be 100% identical to be called equal.

2. When 27 and 9 are compared as strings, their first characters, 2 and 9, determine their order. Since 2 precedes 9 in the ANSI table, "27" < "9".

3.

cond1	cond2	cond1 And cond2	cond1 Or cond2	Not cond2
True	True	True	True	False
True	False	False	True	True
False	True	False	True	False
False	False	False	False	True

4.2   If Blocks

An **If block** allows a program to decide on a course of action based on whether a certain condition is true or false.

VideoNote
If Blocks

■ If Block

A block of the form:

```
If condition Then
   action 1
Else
   action 2
End If
```

causes the program to take *action 1* if *condition* is true and *action 2* if *condition* is false. Each action consists of one or more Visual Basic statements. After an action is taken, execution continues with the line after the End If. Figure 4.2 contains the pseudocode and flowchart for an If block.

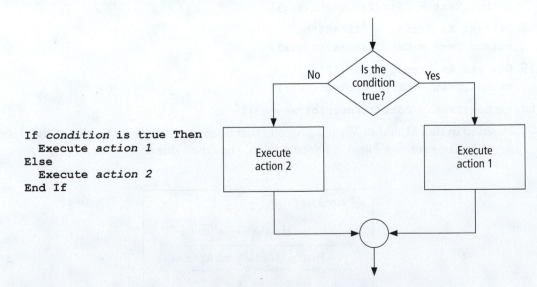

FIGURE 4.2   Pseudocode and flowchart for an If block.

Example 1   **Find Largest Value**   The following program finds the largest value for two numbers input by the user. The condition is

```
num1 > num2
```

and each action consists of a single assignment statement. With the inputs 3 and 7, the condition is false, and so the second action is taken.

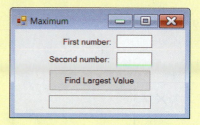

OBJECT	PROPERTY	SETTING
frmMaximum	Text	Maximum
lblFirstNum	Text	First number:
txtFirstNum		
lblSecondNum	Text	Second number:
txtSecondNum		
btnFindLargest	Text	Find Largest Value
txtResult	ReadOnly	True

```vb
Private Sub btnFindLargest_Click(...) Handles btnFindLargest.Click
  Dim num1, num2, largestValue As Double
  num1 = CDbl(txtFirstNum.Text)
  num2 = CDbl(txtSecondNum.Text)
  If num1 > num2 Then        'condition is (num1 > num2)
    largestValue = num1      'take this action if the condition is true
  Else
    largestValue = num2      'take this action if the condition is false
  End If
  txtResult.Text = "The largest value is " & largestValue & "."
End Sub
```

[Run, type 3 and 7 into the text boxes, and click on the button.]

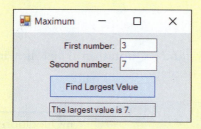

Note: The smart indenting feature of the Code Editor automatically indents the lines following the If and Else clauses of an If block.

 Example 2   **Volume of Ten-Gallon Hat**   The If block in the following program has a logical operator in its condition.

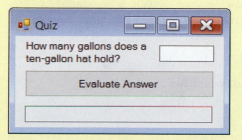

OBJECT	PROPERTY	SETTING
frmQuiz	Text	Quiz
lblQuestion	AutoSize	False
	Text	How many gallons does a ten-gallon hat hold?
txtAnswer		
btnEvaluate	Text	Evaluate Answer
txtSolution	ReadOnly	True

```
Private Sub btnEvaluate_Click(...) Handles btnEvaluate.Click
  Dim answer As Double
  answer = CDbl(txtAnswer.Text)
  If (answer >= 0.5) And (answer <= 1) Then
    txtSolution.Text = "Good, "
  Else
    txtSolution.Text = "No, "
  End If
  txtSolution.Text &= "it holds about 3/4 of a gallon."
End Sub
```

[Run, type 10 into the text box, and click on the button.]

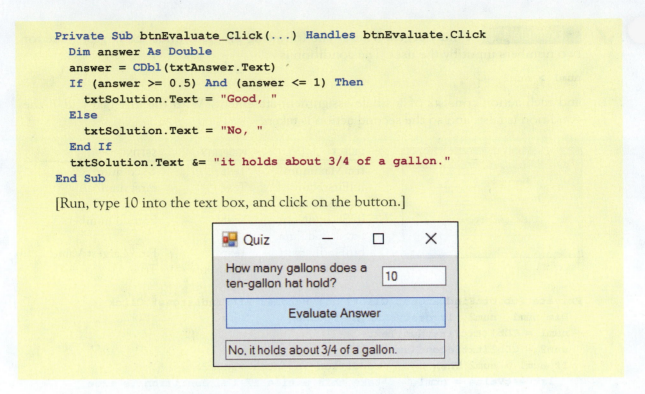

The Else part of an If block can be omitted. If so, when the condition is false no action occurs and execution continues with the line after the End If. This important type of If block appears in the next example.

✔ **Example 3** **Understand a Quotation** The following program offers assistance to the user before presenting a quotation.

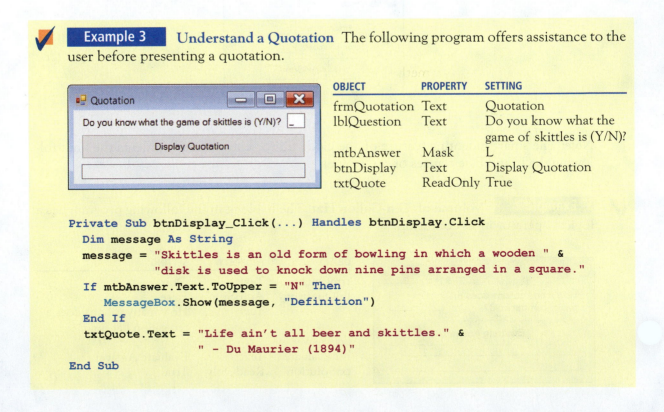

OBJECT	PROPERTY	SETTING
frmQuotation	Text	Quotation
lblQuestion	Text	Do you know what the game of skittles is (Y/N)?
mtbAnswer	Mask	L
btnDisplay	Text	Display Quotation
txtQuote	ReadOnly	True

```
Private Sub btnDisplay_Click(...) Handles btnDisplay.Click
  Dim message As String
  message = "Skittles is an old form of bowling in which a wooden " &
           "disk is used to knock down nine pins arranged in a square."
  If mtbAnswer.Text.ToUpper = "N" Then
    MessageBox.Show(message, "Definition")
  End If
  txtQuote.Text = "Life ain't all beer and skittles." &
                " - Du Maurier (1894)"
End Sub
```

[Run, type "N" into the masked text box, and click on the button.]

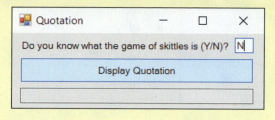

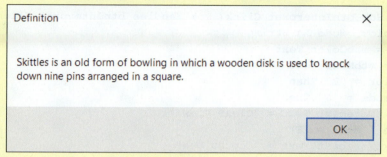

[Click on the OK button.]

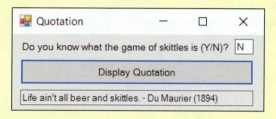

[Rerun the program, type "Y" into the masked text box, click on the button, and observe that the description of the game is skipped.]

Note: Logic errors are the most difficult errors to find. A common type of logic error is the omission of the ToUpper method in Example 3.

■ Nested If Blocks

An action part of an If block can consist of another If block. In this situation the If blocks are said to be **nested**. Examples 4 and 5 use nested If blocks.

  Example 4   **Interpret Beacon**   The color of the beacon light atop Boston's old John Hancock building forecasts the weather according to the following rhyme:

Steady blue, clear view.
Flashing blue, clouds due.
Steady red, rain ahead.
Flashing red, snow instead.

The following program requests a color (Blue or Red) and a mode (Steady or Flashing) as input and displays the weather forecast. Both actions associated with the main If block consist of If blocks.

OBJECT	PROPERTY	SETTING
frmWeather	Text	Weather
lblColor	Text	Color of the light (B or R):
mtbColor	Mask	L
lblMode	Text	Mode (S or F):
mtbMode	Mask	L
btnInterpret	Text	Interpret Beacon
txtForecast	ReadOnly	True

```
Private Sub btnInterpret_Click(...) Handles btnInterpret.Click
  Dim color, mode As String
  color = mtbColor.Text
  mode = mtbMode.Text
  If color = "B" Then
    If mode = "S" Then
      txtForecast.Text = "Clear View"
    Else    'mode = "F"
      txtForecast.Text = "Clouds Due"
    End If
  Else    'color = "R"
    If mode = "S" Then
      txtForecast.Text = "Rain Ahead"
    Else    'mode = "F"
      txtForecast.Text = "Snow Ahead"
    End If
  End If
End Sub
```

[Run, type *R* and *F* into the masked text boxes, and click on the button.]

 Example 5 **Evaluate Profit** The following program requests the costs and revenue for a company and displays the message "Break even" if the costs and revenue are equal; otherwise, it displays the profit or loss. The action following Else is another If block.

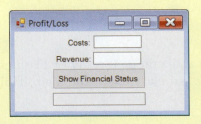

OBJECT	PROPERTY	SETTING
frmStatus	Text	Profit/Loss
lblCosts	Text	Costs:
txtCosts		
lblRev	Text	Revenue:
txtRev		
btnShow	Text	Show Financial Status
txtResult	ReadOnly	True

```
Private Sub btnShow_Click(...) Handles btnShow.Click
  Dim costs, revenue, profit, loss As Decimal
  costs = CDec(txtCosts.Text)
  revenue = CDec(txtRev.Text)
  If costs = revenue Then
    txtResult.Text = "Break even"
  Else
    If costs < revenue Then
      profit = revenue - costs
      txtResult.Text = "Profit is " & profit.ToString("C") & "."
    Else
      loss = costs - revenue
      txtResult.Text = "Loss is " & loss.ToString("C") & "."
    End If
  End If
End Sub
```

[Run, type 9500 and 8000 into the text boxes, and click on the button.]

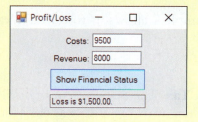

■ ElseIf Clauses

An extension of the If block allows for more than two possible alternatives with the inclusion of ElseIf clauses. A typical block of this type is

```
If condition 1 Then
  action 1
ElseIf condition 2 Then
  action 2
ElseIf condition 3 Then
  action 3
Else
  action 4
End If
```

Visual Basic searches for the first true condition, and carries out its associated action. If none of the conditions are true, then Else's action is carried out. Execution then continues with the statement following the End If statement. In general, an If block can contain any number of ElseIf clauses. As before, the Else clause is optional.

✔ **Example 6**   **Find Largest Value** The following program modifies Example 1 so that the program reports if the two values are equal.

```
Private Sub btnFindLargest_Click(...) Handles btnFindLargest.Click
  Dim num1, num2 As Double
  num1 = CDbl(txtFirstNum.Text)
  num2 = CDbl(txtSecondNum.Text)
  If (num1 > num2) Then
    txtResult.Text = "The largest value is " & num1
```

```
    ElseIf (num2 > num1) Then
      txtResult.Text = "The largest value is " & num2
    Else
      txtResult.Text = "The two values are equal."
    End If
End Sub
```

[Run, type 7 into both text boxes, and click on the button.]

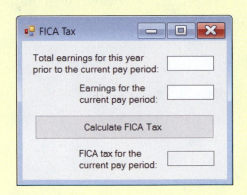

The If block in Example 7 allows us to calculate values that are not determined by a simple formula.

 Example 7   **FICA Tax** The Social Security or FICA tax has two components—the Social Security Benefits tax, which in 2015 was 6.2% on the first $118,500 of earnings for the year, and the Medicare tax, which was 1.45% of earnings plus 0.9% of earnings above $200,000 (for unmarried employees). The following program calculates a single employee's FICA withholding tax for the current pay period.

OBJECT	PROPERTY	SETTING
frmFICA	Text	FICA Tax
lblToDate	AutoSize	False
	Text	Total earnings for this year prior to the current pay period:
txtToDate		
lblCurrent	AutoSize	False
	Text	Earnings for the current pay period:
txtCurrent		
btnCalculate	Text	Calculate FICA Tax
lblTax	AutoSize	False
	Text	FICA tax for the current pay period:
txtTax	ReadOnly	True

```
Private Sub btnCalculate_Click(...) Handles btnCalculate.Click
  'Calculate social security benefits tax and medicare tax
  'for a single employee.
  Const WAGE_BASE As Decimal = 118500D   'There is no Social Security Benefits
  '                                       tax on income above this level.
  Const SOCIAL_SECURITY_RATE As Decimal = 0.062D
  Const MEDICARE_RATE As Decimal = 0.0145D
  Dim ytdEarnings, curEarnings, totalEarnings As Decimal
```

```
    Dim socialSecurityBenTax, medicareTax, ficaTax As Decimal
    ytdEarnings = CDec(txtToDate.Text)
    curEarnings = CDec(txtCurrent.Text)
    totalEarnings = ytdEarnings + curEarnings
    'Calculate the Social Security Benefits tax.
    If totalEarnings <= WAGE_BASE Then
      socialSecurityBenTax = SOCIAL_SECURITY_RATE * curEarnings
    ElseIf ytdEarnings < WAGE_BASE Then
      socialSecurityBenTax = SOCIAL_SECURITY_RATE * (WAGE_BASE - ytdEarnings)
    End If
    'Calculate the FICA tax.
    medicareTax = MEDICARE_RATE * curEarnings
    If ytdEarnings >= 200000D Then
      medicareTax += 0.009D * (totalEarnings - 200000D)
    End If
    ficaTax = socialSecurityBenTax + medicareTax
    txtTax.Text = ficaTax.ToString("C")
End Sub
```

[Run, type 12345.67 and 543.21 into the top two text boxes and click on the button.]

The following example illustrates the fact that when an If block contains ElseIf clauses, Visual Basic executes the action corresponding to the first condition that is satisfied and ignores all subsequent clauses—even if they also satisfy the condition.

✔ **Example 8**   **Graduation Honors** The following program assumes that the user will graduate (that is, has a GPA of 2 or more) and determines if the user will graduate with honors.

```
Private Sub btnDetermine_Click(...) Handles btnDetermine.Click
  Dim gpa As Double = CDbl(txtGPA.Text)
  Dim honors As String
  If gpa >= 3.9 Then
    honors = " summa cum laude."
  ElseIf gpa >= 3.6 Then
    honors = " magna cum laude."
  ElseIf gpa >= 3.3 Then
    honors = " cum laude."
  ElseIf gpa >= 2 Then
    honors = "."
  End If
  txtOutput.Text = "You graduated" & honors
End Sub
```

[Run, enter a grade point average between 2 and 4, and click on the button.]

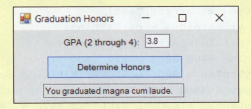

■ Condensed If Statements

When *boolExp* is a Boolean expression, a statement of the form

```
If boolExp = True Then
```

can be shortened to

```
If boolExp Then
```

Similarly, a statement of the form

```
If boolExp = False Then
```

can be shortened to

```
If Not boolExp Then
```

■ Input Validation with If Blocks

Suppose a program calls for the user to enter a number into a text box, and then the program uses the number in a calculation. If the user leaves the text box empty or enters an inappropriate number, the program will crash. The Boolean-valued function IsNumeric can be used to prevent this from happening.

 Example 9   **Input Validation**   The following program uses the function IsNumeric to guard against improper input.

OBJECT	PROPERTY	SETTING
frmAddition	Text	Addition
lblFirstNum	Text	First number:
txtFirstNum		
lblSecondNum	Text	Second number:
txtSecondNum		
btnAdd	Text	Add Numbers
lblSum	Text	Sum:
txtSum	ReadOnly	True

```
Private Sub btnAdd_Click(...) Handles btnAdd.Click
    If IsNumeric(txtFirstNum.Text) And IsNumeric(txtSecondNum.Text) Then
        txtSum.Text = CStr(CDbl(txtFirstNum.Text) + CDbl(txtSecondNum.Text))
    ElseIf Not IsNumeric(txtFirstNum.Text) Then
        If Not IsNumeric(txtSecondNum.Text) Then
```

```
      MessageBox.Show("Each text box is empty or has an improper entry.")
    Else
      MessageBox.Show("The first text box is empty or has an improper entry.")
    End If
  Else
    MessageBox.Show("The second text box is empty or has an improper entry.")
  End If
End Sub
```

[Run, leave the first text box empty, enter "two" into the second text box, and click on the button.]

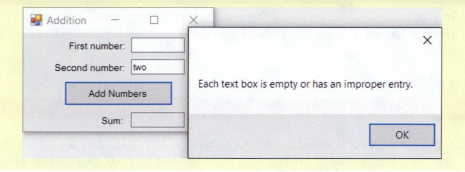

If blocks also can be used to guarantee that a number input by the user is in the proper range. For instance, when the user is asked to input an exam grade, a statement such as

```
If (grade >= 0) And (grade <= 100) Then
```

can be used to guarantee that the number input is between 0 and 100.

■ Short-Circuit Evaluation with AndAlso and OrElse

When Visual Basic encounters the compound condition *cond1* **And** *cond2*, it evaluates both cond1 and cond2 before deciding the truth value of the compound condition. However, if *cond1* is false, there is no need to evaluate *cond2*. The compound condition

cond1 **AndAlso** *cond2*

has the same truth value as *cond1* **And** *cond2*. However when AndAlso is used and *cond1* is false, Visual Basic recognizes that the compound condition is false and therefore does not bother to evaluate *cond2*.

The compound condition

cond1 **OrElse** *cond2*

has the same truth value as *cond1* **Or** *cond2*. However when OrElse is used and *cond1* is true, Visual Basic recognizes that the compound condition is true and does not bother to evaluate *cond2*.

The logical operators AndAlso and OrElse are said to **short-circuit** the evaluation of compound conditions. They sometimes shorten the execution of a program and make it more efficient. Such can be the case, for instance, when the evaluation of *cond2* is time-consuming.

■ Comments

1. Care should be taken to make If blocks easy to understand. For instance, the block on the left below is difficult to follow and should be replaced by the clearer block on the right.

```
If cond1 Then                    If cond1 And cond2 Then
  If cond2 Then                    action
    action                       End If
  End If
End If
```

2. In Appendix D, the section "Stepping through Programs Containing Decision Structures: Chapter 4" uses the Visual Basic debugging tools to trace the flow through an If block.

Practice Problems 4.2

1. Suppose the user is asked to input a number into txtNumber for which the square root is to be taken. Fill in the If block so that the lines of code that follow will display either the message "Number can't be negative." or the square root of the number.

```
Private Sub btnSqrt_Click(...) Handles btnSqrt.Click
  'Check reasonableness of data
  Dim num As Double
  num = CDbl(txtNumber.Text)
  If

  End If
End Sub
```

2. Improve the block

```
If a < b Then
  If c < 5 Then
    txtBox.Text = "hello"
  End If
End If
```

3. Rewrite the following lines of code so that it contains only one If block.

```
If number <> 0 Then
  If m = n / number Then
    MessageBox.Show("Success")
  End If
End If
```

4. Explain the following scenario.

A woman called her programmer husband at work and left the message "Stop by the grocery store and buy a quart of milk. If they have eggs, buy a dozen." Her husband came home with a dozen quarts of milk.

In Exercises 1 through 10, determine the output displayed in the text box when the button is clicked.

1.
```
Private Sub btnDisplay_Click(...) Handles btnDisplay.Click
    Dim num As Double = 4
    If num <= 9 Then
      txtOutput.Text = "Less than ten."
    Else
      If num = 4 Then
        txtOutput.Text = "Equal to four."
      End If
    End If
End Sub
```

2.
```
Private Sub btnDisplay_Click(...) Handles btnDisplay.Click
    Dim gpa As Double = 3.49
    txtOutput.Clear()
    If gpa >= 3.5 Then
      txtOutput.Text = "Honors "
    End If
    txtOutput.Text &= "Student"
End Sub
```

3.
```
Private Sub btnDisplay_Click(...) Handles btnDisplay.Click
    Dim change As Double = 356     'Amount of change in cents
    If change >= 100 Then
      txtOutput.Text = "Your change contains " &
                      Int(change / 100) & " dollars."
    Else
      txtOutput.Text = "Your change contains no dollars."
    End If
End Sub
```

4.
```
Private Sub btnDisplay_Click(...) Handles btnDisplay.Click
    'Determine the cost of a piece of cloth.
    Dim length, cost as Decimal
    length = CDec(InputBox("Enter length of cloth in yards."))
    If length < 1 Then
      cost = 3D 'cost in dollars
    Else
      cost = 3D + ((length - 1) * 2.5D)
    End If
    txtBox.Text = "Cost of cloth: " & cost.ToString("C")
End Sub
```

(Assume the response is 6.)

```
5. Private Sub btnDisplay_Click(...) Handles btnDisplay.Click
      Dim letter As String
      letter = InputBox("Enter A, B, or C.")
      letter = letter.ToUpper
      If letter = "A" Then
        txtOutput.Text = "A, my name is Alice."
      ElseIf letter = "B" Then
        txtOutput.Text = "To be, or not to be."
      ElseIf letter = "C" Then
        txtOutput.Text = "Oh, say, can you see."
      Else
        txtOutput.Text = "Not a valid letter."
      End If
    End Sub
```

(Assume the response is B.)

```
6. Private Sub btnDisplay_Click(...) Handles btnDisplay.Click
      Dim vowel As Boolean = False
      Dim ltr As String
      ltr = InputBox("Enter a letter.")
      ltr = ltr.ToUpper
      If (ltr = "A") Or (ltr = "E") Or (ltr = "I") Or
         (ltr = "O") Or (ltr = "U") Then
        vowel = True
      End If
      If vowel Then
        txtOutput.Text = ltr & " is a vowel."
      Else
        txtOutput.Text = ltr & " is not a vowel."
      End If
    End Sub
```

(Assume the response is a.)

```
7. Private Sub btnDisplay_Click(...) Handles btnDisplay.Click
      Dim a As Double = 5
      If (a > 2) And ((a = 3) Or (a < 7)) Then
        txtOutput.Text = "Hi"
      End If
    End Sub
```

```
8. Private Sub btnDisplay_Click(...) Handles btnDisplay.Click
      Dim num As Double = 5
      If num < 0 Then
        txtOutput.Text = "neg"
      Else
        If num = 0 Then
          txtOutput.Text = "zero"
        Else
          txtOutput.Text = "positive"
        End If
      End If
    End Sub
```

9.
```vb
Private Sub btnCompute_Click(...) Handles btnCompute.Click
    Dim msg As String = "You are old enough to vote"
    Dim dateOfBirth As Date = CDate(InputBox("Enter your date of birth."))
    If dateOfBirth.AddYears(18) <= Today Then
        txtOutput.Text = msg & "."
    Else
        txtOutput.Text = msg & " in " &
            DateDiff(DateInterval.Day, Today, dateOfBirth.AddYears(18)) &
            " days."
    End If
End Sub
```
(Assume that your 18th birthday is one week away.)

10.
```vb
Private Sub btnCompute_Click(...) Handles btnCompute.Click
    Dim dateOfBirth As Date = CDate(InputBox("Enter your date of birth."))
    Dim nicksDateOfBirth As Date = #9/16/1992#
    If dateOfBirth < nicksDateOfBirth Then
        txtOutput.Text = "You are older than Nick."
    ElseIf dateOfBirth = nicksDateOfBirth Then
        txtOutput.Text = "You are the exact same age as Nick."
    Else
        txtOutput.Text = "You are younger than Nick."
    End If
End Sub
```
(Assume that the response is *10/25/1992*.)

In Exercises 11 through 14, identify the errors, state the type of each error (syntax, runtime, or logic), and correct the block of code.

11.
```vb
Private Sub btnDisplay_Click(...) Handles btnDisplay.Click
    Dim num As Double = 0.5
    If (1 < num < 3) Then
        txtOutput.Text = "Number is between 1 and 3."
    End If
End Sub
```

12.
```vb
Private Sub btnDisplay_Click(...) Handles btnDisplay.Click
    Dim num As Double = 6
    If num > 5 And < 9 Then
        txtOutput.Text = "Yes"
    Else
        txtOutput.Text = "No"
    End If
End Sub
```

13.
```vb
Private Sub btnDisplay_Click(...) Handles btnDisplay.Click
    Dim major As String
    major = "Computer Science"
    If major = "Business" Or "Computer Science" Then
        txtOutput.Text = "Yes"
    End If
End Sub
```

14.
```
Private Sub btnDisplay_Click(...) Handles btnDisplay.Click
    'Toggle switch from on to off and from off to on.
    Dim switchOn As Boolean
    switchOn = CBool(InputBox("Enter True or False.", "The switch is on."))
    If switchOn Then
      switchOn = False
    End If
    If Not switchOn Then
      switchOn = True
    End If
    txtOutput.Text = CStr(switchOn)
End Sub
```

In Exercises 15 through 18, improve the code.

15.
```
If (a = 2) Then
    a = 3 + a
Else
    a = 5
End If
```

16.
```
If (j = 7) Then
    b = 1
Else
    If (j <> 7) Then
      b = 2
    End If
End If
```

17.
```
message = "Is Alaska bigger than Texas and California combined?"
answer = InputBox(message)
If (answer.Substring(0, 1) = "Y") Then
  answer = "YES"
End If
If (answer.Substring(0, 1) = "y") Then
  answer = "YES"
End If
If (answer = "YES") Then
  txtOutput.Text = "Correct"
Else
  txtOutput.Text = "Wrong"
End If
```

18.
```
message = "How tall (in feet) is the Statue of Liberty?"
feet = CDbl(InputBox(message))
If (feet <= 141) Then
  lstOutput.Items.Add("Nope")
End If
If (feet > 141) Then
    If (feet < 161) Then
      lstOutput.Items.Add("Close")
    Else
      lstOutput.Items.Add("Nope")
    End If
End If
lstOutput.Items.Add("The statue is 151 feet from base to torch.")
```

In Exercises 19 and 20, rewrite the lines of code so that it contains only one If block.

19.
```
If IsNumeric(txtBox.Text) Then
    If (CDbl(txtBox.Text) < 0) Then
        MessageBox.Show("negative")
    End If
End If
```

20.
```
If (str1 <> "") Then
    If m = (str2.Length / str1.Length) Then
        txtBox.Text = str1 & str2
    End If
End If
```

21. Restaurant Tip   Write a program to determine how much to tip the server in a restaurant. The tip should be 18% of the check, with a minimum of $1. See Fig. 4.3.

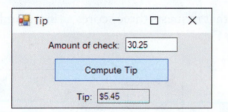

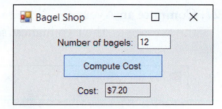

FIGURE 4.3   Possible outcome of Exercise 21.   **FIGURE 4.4**   Possible outcome of Exercise 22.

22. Cost of Bagels   A bagel shop charges 75 cents per bagel for orders of less than a half-dozen bagels and 60 cents per bagel for orders of a half-dozen or more. Write a program that requests the number of bagels ordered and displays the total cost. See Fig. 4.4.

23. Cost of Widgets   A store sells widgets at 25 cents each for small orders or at 20 cents each for orders of 100 or more. Write a program that requests the number of widgets ordered and displays the total cost. See Fig. 4.5.

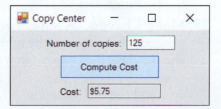

FIGURE 4.5   Possible outcome of Exercise 23.   **FIGURE 4.6**   Possible outcome of Exercise 24.

24. Cost of Copies   A copy center charges 5 cents per copy for the first 100 copies and 3 cents per copy for each additional copy. Write a program that requests the number of copies as input and displays the total cost. See Fig. 4.6.

25. Quiz   Write a quiz program to ask "Who was the first Ronald McDonald?" The program should display "Correct." if the answer is "Willard Scott" and "Nice try." for any other answer. See Fig. 4.7.

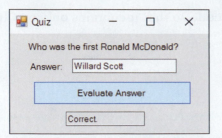

FIGURE 4.7 Possible outcome of Exercise 25.   **FIGURE 4.8** Possible outcome of Exercise 26.

26. **Overtime Pay**   Federal law requires that hourly employees be paid "time-and-a-half" for work in excess of 40 hours in a week. For example, if a person's hourly wage is $8 and they work 60 hours in a week, the person's gross pay should be

$$(40 \times 8) + (1.5 \times 8 \times (60 - 40)) = \$560$$

Write a program that requests as input the number of hours a person works in a given week and the person's hourly wage, and then displays the person's gross pay. See Fig. 4.8.

27. **Compute an Average**   Write a program that requests three scores as input and displays the average of the two highest scores. See Fig. 4.9.

FIGURE 4.9 Possible outcome of Exercise 27.   **FIGURE 4.10** Possible outcome of Exercise 28.

28. **Pig Latin**   Write a program that requests a word (in lowercase letters) as input and translates the word into Pig Latin. See Fig. 4.10. The rules for translating a word into Pig Latin are as follows:

    (a) If the word begins with a group of consonants, move them to the end of the word and add *ay*. For instance, *chip* becomes *ipchay*.

    (b) If the word begins with a vowel, add *way* to the end of the word. For instance, *else* becomes *elseway*.

29. **Make Change**   A supermarket sells apples for $2.50 per pound. Write a cashier's program that requests the number of pounds and the amount of cash tendered as input and displays the change from the transaction. If the cash is not enough, the message "I need $x.xx more." should be displayed, where $x.xx is the difference between the total cost and the cash. See Fig. 4.11.

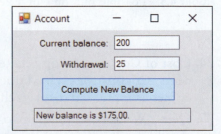

FIGURE 4.11 Possible outcome of Exercise 29.   **FIGURE 4.12** Possible outcome of Exercise 30.

30. **Savings Account**   Write a program to process a savings-account withdrawal. The program should request the current balance and the amount of the withdrawal as input and then display the new balance. If the withdrawal is greater than the original balance, the program should display "Withdrawal denied." If the new balance is less than $150, the message "Balance below $150" also should be displayed. See Fig. 4.12.

31. **Quit Button**   Suppose that a program has a button with the caption "Quit". Suppose also that the Name property of this button is btnQuit. Write a btnQuit_Click event procedure that gives the user a second chance before ending the program. The procedure should use an input dialog box to request that the user confirm that the program should be terminated, and then end the program only if the user responds in the affirmative.

32. **Leap Year**   The current calendar, called the Gregorian calendar, was introduced in 1582. Every year divisible by four was declared to be a leap year, with the exception of the years ending in 00 (that is, those divisible by 100) and not divisible by 400. For instance, the years 1600 and 2000 are leap years, but 1700, 1800, and 1900 are not. Write a program that requests a year as input and states whether it is a leap year. The program should not use any variables of type Date. See Fig. 4.13.

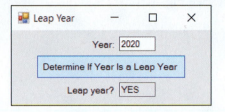

FIGURE 4.13   Possible outcome of Exercise 32.   FIGURE 4.14   Possible outcome of Exercise 33.

33. **Film Repartee**   Create a form with a text box and two buttons captioned Bogart and Raines. When Bogart is first pressed, the sentence "I came to Casablanca for the waters." is displayed in the text box. The next time Bogart is pressed, the sentence "I was misinformed." is displayed. When Raines is pressed, the sentence "But we're in the middle of the desert." is displayed. Run the program and then click Bogart, Raines, and Bogart to obtain a dialogue. See Fig. 4.14.

34. **Toggle Color**   Write a program that allows the user to use a button to toggle the color of the text in a text box between black and red. See Fig. 4.15.

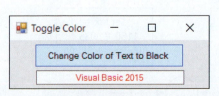

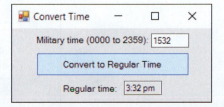

FIGURE 4.15   Possible outcome of Exercise 34.   FIGURE 4.16   Possible outcome of Exercise 35.

35. **Military Time**   In military time, hours are numbered from 00 to 23. Under this system, midnight is 00, 1 a.m. is 01, 1 p.m. is 13, and so on. Time in hours and minutes is given as a four-digit string with minutes following hours and given by two digits ranging from 00 to 59. For instance, military time 0022 corresponds to 12:22 a.m. regular time, and military time 1200 corresponds to noon regular time. Write a program that converts from military time to regular time. See Fig. 4.16.

36. **Highest Scores**   Write a program that reads a test score from a text box each time a button is clicked and then displays the two highest scores whenever a second button is clicked. Use two class-level variables to track the two highest scores. See Fig. 4.17.

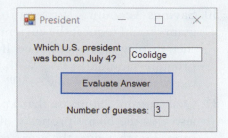

FIGURE 4.17 Possible outcome of Exercise 36. **FIGURE 4.18** Possible outcome of Exercise 37.

37. Quiz Write a program that allows the user ten tries to answer the question, "Which U.S. president was born on July 4?" After three incorrect guesses, the program should display the hint, "He once said, 'If you don't say anything, you won't be called upon to repeat it.'" in a message box. After seven incorrect guesses, the program should give the hint, "His nickname was 'Silent Cal.'" The number of guesses should be successively displayed in a text box. (See Fig. 4.18.) **Note:** Calvin Coolidge was born on July 4, 1872.

38. Income Tax The flowchart in Fig. 4.19 calculates a person's state income tax. Write a program corresponding to the flowchart. See Fig. 4.20.

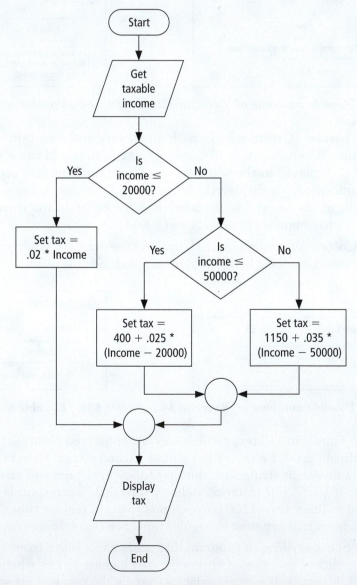

FIGURE 4.19 **Flowchart for Exercise 38.**

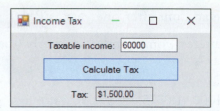

FIGURE 4.20   Possible outcome of Exercise 38.

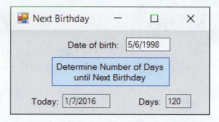

FIGURE 4.21   Possible outcome of Exercise 39.

39. Next Birthday   Write a program that requests your date of birth as input and then determines the number of days until your next birthday. See Fig. 4.21. (**Note:** The DateDiff function yields a value of type Double.)

40. Age   Write a program that requests your date of birth as input and tells whether or not you are 25 years old or older. If not, the program should tell you the number of days until you will have your 25th birthday. See Fig. 4.22. **Note:** `DateDiff(DateInterval.Year, d1, d2)` gives the number of years (sort of) between the two dates. It only uses the year parts of the two dates.

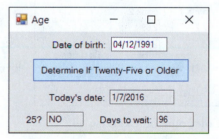

FIGURE 4.22   Possible outcome of Exercise 40.

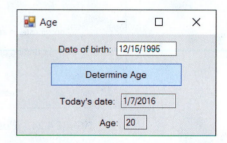

FIGURE 4.23   Possible outcome of Exercise 41.

41. Age   Write a program that requests your date of birth as input and tells your age. **Hint:** Use the DateDiff function with the DateInterval.Year option, and then use an If block to modify the result. See Fig. 4.23 and the note in Exercise 40.

42. Hide and Seek   Write a program to play "Hide and Seek" with the name of our programming language. When the button is clicked on, the name should disappear and the caption on the button should change to "Show Name of Language". The next time the button is clicked, the name should reappear and the caption should revert to "Hide Name of Language", and so on.

OBJECT	PROPERTY	SETTING
frmHideSeek	Text	Hide and Show
lblLanguage	Text	VB 2015
	Font.Size	26
btnDisplay	Text	Hide Name of Language

43. Leap Year   Rework Exercise 32 using a variable of type Date and the DateDiff function.

44. Interest Rates   Savings accounts state an interest rate and a compounding period. If the amount deposited is P, the stated interest rate is r, and interest is compounded m

times per year, then the balance in the account after one year is $P \cdot \left(1 + \dfrac{r}{m}\right)^m$. For instance, if $1000 is deposited at 3% interest compounded quarterly (that is, 4 times per year), then the balance after one year is

$$1000 \cdot \left(1 + \frac{.03}{4}\right)^4 = 1000 \cdot 1.0075^4 = \$1{,}030.34.$$

Interest rates with different compounding periods cannot be compared directly. The concept of APY (annual percentage yield) must be used to make the comparison. The APY for a stated interest rate r compounded m times per year is defined by

$$APY = \left(1 + \frac{r}{m}\right)^m - 1.$$

(The APY is the simple interest rate that yields the same amount of interest after one year as the compounded annual rate of interest.) Write a program to compare interest rates offered by two different banks and determine the most favorable interest rate. See Fig. 4.24.

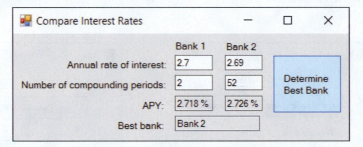

FIGURE 4.24 **Possible outcome of Exercise 44.**

45. Graduation Honors Rewrite the program in Example 8 without using ElseIf clauses. That is, the task should be carried out with a sequence of simple If blocks.

46. Graduation Honors Rewrite the program in Example 8 so that the GPA is validated to be between 2 and 4 before the If block is executed.

47. Largest Number Write a program that allows the user to enter three numbers into text boxes and then displays the largest of the three numbers. See Fig. 4.25.

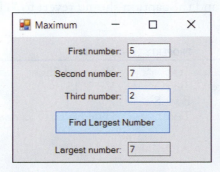

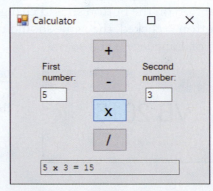

FIGURE 4.25 **Possible outcome of Exercise 47.**

FIGURE 4.26 **Possible outcome of Exercise 48.**

48. **Calculator** Write a program that allows the user to specify two numbers and then adds, subtracts, multiplies, or divides them when the user clicks on the appropriate button. The output should give the type of arithmetic performed and the result. See Fig. 4.26. **Note:** Whenever one of the numbers in an input text box is changed, the output text box should be cleared. Also, if the number 0 is entered into the second text box, the division button should be disabled.

49. **Buy Two, Get-One-Free Sale** A clothing store advertises "BUY 2 ITEMS AND THE 3RD IS FREE." What they mean is that if you buy three items, then the lowest cost item is free. Write a program that accepts the three costs as input and then calculates the total cost after dropping the lowest cost. See Fig. 4.27.

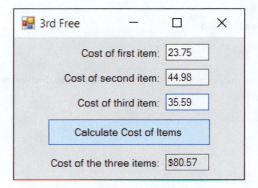

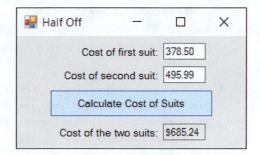

FIGURE 4.27 Possible outcome of Exercise 49. **FIGURE 4.28** Possible outcome of Exercise 50.

50. **Second Suit Half-Off Sale** A men's clothing store advertises that if you buy a suit, you can get a second suit at half-off. What they mean is that if you buy two suits, then the price of the lower-cost suit is reduced by 50%. Write a program that accepts the two costs as input and then calculates the total cost after halving the cost of the lowest price suit. See Fig. 4.28.

51. **Sort Three Numbers** Write a program that requests three different numbers as input and then displays the numbers in order. See Fig. 4.29.

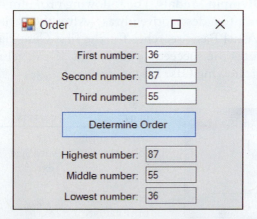

FIGURE 4.29 Possible outcome of Exercise 51.

1.
```
If (num < 0) Then
    MessageBox.Show("Number can't be negative.", "Input Error")
    txtNumber.Clear()
    txtNumber.Focus()
Else
    txtSquareRoot.Text = CStr(Math.Sqrt(num))
End If
```

2. The word "hello" will be displayed when (a < b) is true and (c < 5) is also true. That is, it will be displayed when both of these two conditions are true. The clearest way to write the block is
```
If (a < b) And (c < 5) Then
    txtBox.Text = "hello"
End If
```

3.
```
If number <> 0 AndAlso m = (n / number) Then
    MessageBox.Show("Success")
End If
```
Note: Had And been used in the first line (instead of AndAlso), the program would have crashed when the value of *number* was zero.

4. The husband interpreted his wife's request as follows.
```
Dim quartsOfMilk As Integer = 1
If (grocery store has eggs) Then
    quartsOfMilk = 12
End If
```

4.3   Select Case Blocks

A Select Case block is an efficient decision-making structure that simplifies choosing among several actions. It avoids complex If constructs. If blocks make decisions based on the truth value of a condition; Select Case choices are determined by the value of an expression called a **selector**. Each possible action is preceded by a clause of the form

Case *valueList*

where *valueList* itemizes the values of the selector for which the action should be taken.

 Example 1   **Olympic Medals** The following program converts the finishing position in an Olympic event into a descriptive phrase. After the variable *position* is assigned a value from txtPosition, Visual Basic searches for the first Case clause whose value list contains that value and executes the succeeding statement. If the value of *position* is greater than 5, then the statement following Case Else is executed.

OBJECT	PROPERTY	SETTING
frmOlympics	Text	Olympics
lblPosition	AutoSize	False
	Text	Finishing position (1, 2, 3, . . .):
txtPosition		
btnEvaluate	Text	Evaluate Position
txtOutcome	ReadOnly	True

```
Private Sub btnEvaluate_Click(...) Handles btnEvaluate.Click
  Dim position As Integer 'selector
  position = CInt(txtPosition.Text)
  Select Case position
    Case 1
      txtOutcome.Text = "Gold medalist"
    Case 2
      txtOutcome.Text = "Silver medalist"
    Case 3
      txtOutcome.Text = "Bronze medalist"
    Case 4, 5
      txtOutcome.Text = "You almost won a medal."
    Case Else
      txtOutcome.Text = "Nice try."
  End Select
End Sub
```

[Run, type 2 into the text box, and click on the button.]

Olympics — □ ✕

Finishing position
(1, 2, 3, . . .): `2`

Evaluate Position

Silver medalist

✔ **Example 2** **Olympic Medals** In the following variation of Example 1, the value lists specify ranges of values. The first value list provides another way to stipulate the numbers 1, 2, and 3. The second value list covers all numbers from 4 on.

```
Private Sub btnEvaluate_Click(...) Handles btnEvaluate.Click
  Dim position As Integer
  position = CInt(txtPosition.Text)
  Select Case position
    Case 1 To 3
      txtOutcome.Text = "Olympic medalist"
    Case Is >= 4
      txtOutcome.Text = "No medal this time."
  End Select
End Sub
```

[Run, type 2 into the text box, and click on the button.]

Olympics — □ ✕

Finishing position
(1, 2, 3, . . .): `2`

Evaluate Position

Olympic medalist

VideoNote
Select Case Blocks

■ General Form of a Select Case Block

A typical form of the Select Case block is

```
Select Case selector
  Case valueList 1
    action 1
  Case valueList 2
    action 2
  Case Else
    action of last resort
End Select
```

where Case Else (and its action) is optional, and each value list contains one or more of the following types of items:

1. a literal

2. a variable

3. an expression

4. an inequality sign preceded by Is and followed by a literal, variable, or expression

5. a range expressed in the form **a To b**, where *a* and *b* are literals, variables, or expressions

Two or more items appearing in the same value list must be separated by commas. Each action consists of one or more statements. After the selector is evaluated, Visual Basic looks for the first value-list item including the value of the selector and carries out its associated action. (If the value of the selector appears in two different value lists, only the action associated with the first value list will be carried out.) If there is a Case Else clause and the value of the selector does not appear in any of the value lists, then the action associated with the Case Else clause will be executed. In any event, execution of the program will continue with the statement following End Select.

Figure 4.30 on the next page contains the flowchart for a Select Case block. The pseudocode for a Select Case block is the same as for the equivalent If block.

 Example 3 Days in a Month The following program requests a month and a year, and then displays the number of days in that month. The program uses an If block nested inside a Select Case block. The If block determines whether the year is a leap year. (A year is a leap year if there are 366 days from January 1 of that year to January 1 of the next year.) The value lists come from the rhyme "Thirty days hath September."

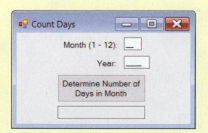

OBJECT	PROPERTY	SETTING
frmDays	Text	Count Days
lblMonth:	Text	Month (1–12):
mtbMonth	Mask	00
lblYear	Text	Year:
mtbYear	Mask	0000
btnDetermine	Text	Determine Number of Days in Month
txtOutput	ReadOnly	True

```
Private Sub btnDetermine_Click(...) Handles btnDetermine.Click
  Dim month As Integer = CInt(mtbMonth.Text)
  Dim yr As Integer = CInt(mtbYear.Text)
  Dim dt1, dt2 As Date
  Dim numberOfDays As Integer
```

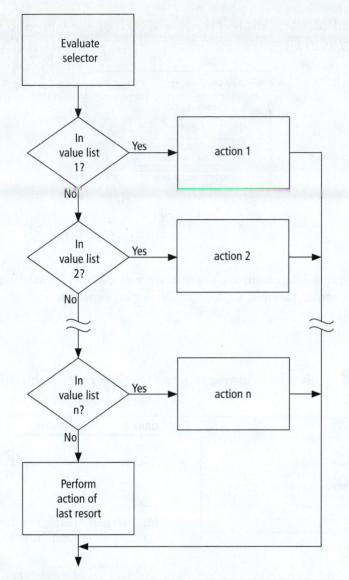

FIGURE 4.30 Flowchart for a Select Case block.

```
Select Case month
  Case 9, 4, 6, 11 'September, April, June, and November
    numberOfDays = 30
  Case 2 'February
    dt1 = CDate("1/1/" & yr)
    dt2 = d1.AddYears(1)
    If DateDiff(DateInterval.Day, dt1, dt2) = 366 Then
      numberOfDays = 29
    Else
      numberOfDays = 28
    End If
  Case Else 'all the rest
    numberOfDays = 31
End Select
txtOutput.Text = month & "/" & yr & " has " &
    numberOfDays & " days."
End Sub
```

[Run, enter 2 and 2016 into the text boxes, and click on the button to find the number of days in February 2016.]

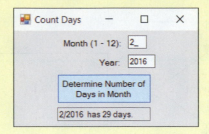

In the three preceding examples, the selector was a numeric variable; however, the selector also can be a string variable, a date variable, or an expression.

Example 4   **Quiz** The following program has the string variable *firstName* as a selector.

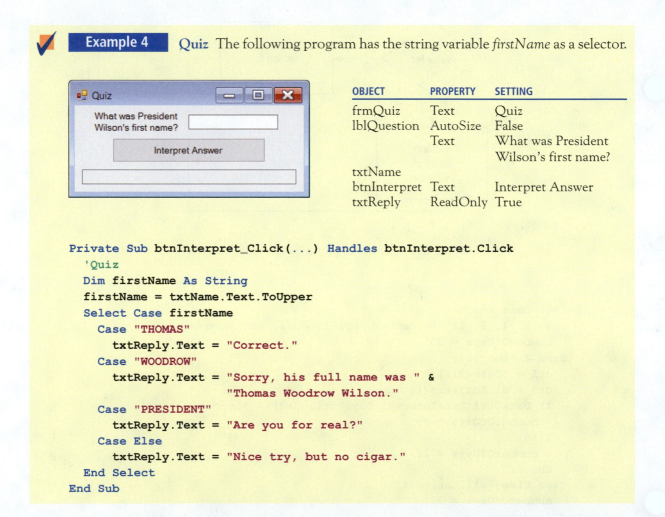

OBJECT	PROPERTY	SETTING
frmQuiz	Text	Quiz
lblQuestion	AutoSize	False
	Text	What was President Wilson's first name?
txtName		
btnInterpret	Text	Interpret Answer
txtReply	ReadOnly	True

```
Private Sub btnInterpret_Click(...) Handles btnInterpret.Click
  'Quiz
  Dim firstName As String
  firstName = txtName.Text.ToUpper
  Select Case firstName
    Case "THOMAS"
      txtReply.Text = "Correct."
    Case "WOODROW"
      txtReply.Text = "Sorry, his full name was " &
                      "Thomas Woodrow Wilson."
    Case "PRESIDENT"
      txtReply.Text = "Are you for real?"
    Case Else
      txtReply.Text = "Nice try, but no cigar."
  End Select
End Sub
```

[Run, type "Woodrow" into the text box, and click on the button.]

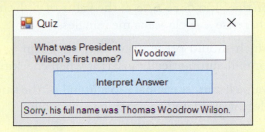

Example 5 **Analyze a Character** The following program has *anyString. Substring (0, 1)* as selector. In the sample run, only the first action was carried out, even though the value of the selector was in both of the first two value lists. Visual Basic stops looking as soon as it finds the value of the selector.

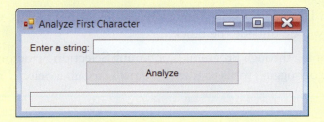

OBJECT	PROPERTY	SETTING
frmAnalyze	Text	Analyze First Character
lblEnter	Text	Enter a string:
txtString		
btnAnalyze	Text	Analyze
txtResult	ReadOnly	True

```
Private Sub btnAnalyze_Click(...) Handles btnAnalyze.Click
  'Analyze the first character of a string
  Dim anyString As String
  anyString = txtString.Text.ToUpper
  Select Case anyString.Substring(0, 1)
    Case "A", "E", "I", "O", "U"
      txtResult.Text = "The string begins with a vowel."
    Case "A" To "Z"
      txtResult.Text = "The string begins with a consonant."
    Case "0" To "9"
      txtResult.Text = "The string begins with a digit."
  End Select
End Sub
```

[Run, type a string into the text box, and click on the button.]

■ Comments

1. In a Case clause of the form **Case _b_ To _c_**, the value of _b_ should be less than or equal to the value of _c_. Otherwise, the clause is meaningless.

2. If the word **Is**, which should precede an inequality sign in a value list, is accidentally omitted, the editor will automatically insert it when checking the line.

3. The items in the value list must evaluate to a literal of the same type as the selector. For instance, if the selector evaluated to a string value, as in

```
Dim firstName As String
firstName = txtBox.Text
Select Case firstName
```

then the clause

```
Case firstName.Length
```

would be meaningless.

4. Any variable declared inside an If or Select Case block has **block scope**; that is, the variable cannot be referred to by code outside the block.

5. In Appendix D, the section "Stepping through Programs Containing Selection Structures: Chapter 4" uses the Visual Basic debugging tools to trace the flow through a Select Case block.

Practice Problems 4.3

1. Suppose the selector of a Select Case block is the numeric variable _num_. Determine whether the following Case clauses are valid.

   (a) `Case 1, 4, Is < 10`
   (b) `Case Is < 5, Is >= 5`
   (c) `Case num = 2` (where the selector _num_ is of type Double)

2. Do the following two programs always produce the same output for a whole-number grade from 0 to 100?

```
grade = CInt(txtBox.Text)          grade = CInt(txtBox.Text)
Select Case grade                  Select Case grade
  Case Is >= 90                      Case Is >= 90
    txtOutput.Text = "A"               txtOutput.Text = "A"
  Case Is >= 60                      Case 60 To 89
    txtOutput.Text = "Pass"            txtOutput.Text = "Pass"
  Case Else                          Case 0 To 59
    txtOutput.Text = "Fail"            txtOutput.Text = "Fail"
End Select                         End Select
```

In Exercises 1 through 6, for each of the responses shown in the parentheses, determine the output displayed in the text box when the button is clicked on.

1.
```
Private Sub btnDisplay_Click(...) Handles btnDisplay.Click
    Dim age, price As Double
    age = CDbl(InputBox("What is your age?"))
    Select Case age
      Case Is < 6
        price = 0
      Case 6 To 17
        price = 3.75
      Case Is >= 17
        price = 5
    End Select
    txtOutput.Text = "The price is " & price.ToString("C")
End Sub
```
(8.5, 17)

2.
```
Private Sub btnDisplay_Click(...) Handles btnDisplay.Click
    Dim num As Double
    num = CDbl(InputBox("Enter a number from 5 to 12"))
    Select Case num
      Case 5
        txtOutput.Text = "case 1"
      Case 5 To 7
        txtOutput.Text = "case 2"
      Case 7 To 12
        txtOutput.Text = "case 3"
    End Select
End Sub
```
(7, 5, 11.2)

3.
```
Private Sub btnDisplay_Click(...) Handles btnDisplay.Click
    Dim age As Integer
    age = CInt(InputBox("Enter age (in millions of years)"))
    Select Case age
      Case Is < 70
        txtOutput.Text = "Cenozoic Era"
      Case Is < 225
        txtOutput.Text = "Mesozoic Era"
      Case Is <= 600
        txtOutput.Text = "Paleozoic Era"
      Case Else
        txtOutput.Text = "?"
    End Select
End Sub
```
(100, 600, 700)

4.
```
Private Sub btnDisplay_Click(...) Handles btnDisplay.Click
    Dim pres As String
    pres = InputBox("Who was the youngest U.S. president?")
    Select Case pres.ToUpper
      Case "THEODORE ROOSEVELT", "TEDDY ROOSEVELT"
        txtOutput.Text = "Correct. He became president at age 42 " & 
                         "when President McKinley was assassinated."
      Case "JFK", "JOHN KENNEDY", "JOHN F. KENNEDY"
        txtOutput.Text = "Incorrect. At age 43, he was the youngest " & 
                         "person elected president."
      Case Else
        txtOutput.Text = "Nope"
    End Select
End Sub
```

(JFK, Teddy Roosevelt)

5.
```
Private Sub btnDisplay_Click(...) Handles btnDisplay.Click
    Dim message As String, a, b, c As Double
    message = "Analyzing solutions to the quadratic equation " & 
              "AX^2 + BX + C = 0. Enter the value for "
    a = CDbl(InputBox(message & "A"))
    b = CDbl(InputBox(message & "B"))
    c = CDbl(InputBox(message & "C"))
    Select Case (b ^ 2) - (4 * a * c)
      Case Is < 0
        txtOutput.Text = "The equation has no real solutions."
      Case 0
        txtOutput.Text = "The equation has exactly one solution."
      Case Is > 0
        txtOutput.Text = "The equation has two solutions."
    End Select
End Sub
```

(1,2,3; 1,5,1; 1,2,1)

6.
```
Private Sub btnDisplay_Click(...) Handles btnDisplay.Click
    Dim whatever As Double
    whatever = CDbl(InputBox("Enter a number:"))
    Select Case whatever
      Case Else
        txtOutput.Text = "Hi"
    End Select
End Sub
```

(7, −1)

In Exercises 7 through 12, identify the errors.

7.
```
Private Sub btnDisplay_Click(...) Handles btnDisplay.Click
    Dim num As Double = 2
    Select Case num
      txtOutput.Text = "Two"
    End Select
End Sub
```

8.
```
Private Sub btnDisplay_Click(...) Handles btnDisplay.Click
    Dim num1 As Double = 5
    Dim num2 As Double = 2
    Select Case num1
      Case 3 <= num1 <= 10
        txtOutput.Text = "between 3 and 10."
      Case num2 To 5; 4
        txtOutput.Text = "near 5."
    End Select
End Sub
```

9.
```
Private Sub btnDisplay_Click(...) Handles btnDisplay.Click
    Dim nom As String
    nom = InputBox("What is your name?")
    Select Case nom
      Case nom = "Bob"
        txtOutput.Text = "Hi, Bob."
      Case Else
    End Select
End Sub
```

10.
```
Private Sub btnDisplay_Click(...) Handles btnDisplay.Click
    Dim word As String = "hello"
    Select Case word.Substring(0,1)
      Case h
        txtOutput.Text = "begins with h."
    End Select
End Sub
```

11.
```
Private Sub btnDisplay_Click(...) Handles btnDisplay.Click
    Dim fruit As String = "Peach"
    Select Case fruit.ToUpper
      Case Is >= "Peach"
        txtOutput.Text = "Georgia"
      Case "ORANGE To PEACH"
        txtOutput.Text = "Ok"
    End Select
End Sub
```

12.
```
Private Sub btnDisplay_Click(...) Handles btnDisplay.Click
    Dim purchase As Double
    purchase = CDbl(InputBox("Quantity purchased?"))
    Select Case purchase
      Case purchase < 10000
        txtOutput.Text = "Five dollars per item."
      Case Is 10000 To 30000
        txtOutput.Text = "Four dollars per item."
      Case Is > 30000
        txtOutput.Text = "Three dollars per item."
    End Select
End Sub
```

In Exercises 13 through 18, suppose the selector of a Select Case block, *word*, evaluates to a String value. Determine whether the Case clause is valid.

13. `Case "un" & "til"`

14. `Case "hello", Is < "goodbye"`

15. `Case 0 To 9`

16. `Case word <> "No"`

17. `Case "abc".Substring(0, 1)`

18. `Case Is <> "No"`

In Exercises 19 through 22, rewrite the code using a Select Case block.

19.
```
If a = 1 Then
    txtOutput.Text = "one"
Else
  If a > 5 Then
    txtOutput.Text = "two"
  End If
End If
```

20.
```
If a = 1 Then
    lstOutput.Items.Add("lambs")
End If
If ((a <= 3) And (a < 4)) Then
  lstOutput.Items.Add("eat")
End If
If ((a = 5) Or (a > 7)) Then
  lstOutput.Items.Add("ivy")
End If
```

21.
```
If a > 5 Then
  If a = 2 Then
    txtOutput.Text = "yes"
  Else
    txtOutput.Text = "no"
  End If
Else
  If a = 2 Then
    txtOutput.Text = "maybe"
  End If
End If
```

22.
```
If a = 3 Then
  a = 1
End If
If a = 2 Then
  a = 3
End If
If a = 1 Then
  a = 2
End If
```

23. **Cloudiness Descriptors**   Table 4.5 gives the terms used by the National Weather Service to describe the degree of cloudiness. Write a program that requests the percentage of cloud cover as input and then displays the appropriate descriptor. See Fig. 4.31.

TABLE 4.5	Cloudiness descriptors.
Percentage of Cloud Cover	**Descriptor**
0–30	clear
31–70	partly cloudy
71–99	cloudy
100	overcast

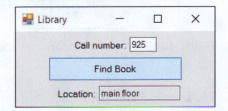

FIGUREF 4.31   Possible outcome of Exercise 23.   **FIGURE 4.32**   Possible outcome of Exercise 24.

24. **Library Books**   Table 4.6 shows the location of books in the library stacks according to their call numbers. Write a program that requests the call number of a book as input and displays the location of the book. See Fig. 4.32.

TABLE 4.6	Location of library books.	
	Call Numbers	**Location**
	100 to 199	basement
	200 to 500 and over 900	main floor
	501 to 900 except 700 to 750	upper floor
	700 to 750	archives

25. Areas   Figure 4.33 shows some geometric shapes and formulas for their areas. Write a program that requests the user to select one of the shapes, requests the appropriate lengths with input dialog boxes, and then gives the area of the figure. In Fig. 4.34, the numbers 4 and 5 were entered into the input dialog boxes.

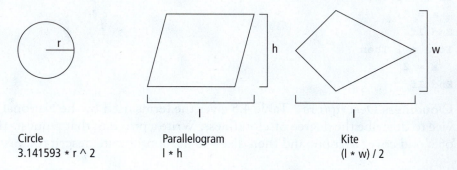

Circle
3.141593 * r ^ 2

Parallelogram
l * h

Kite
(l * w) / 2

FIGURE 4.33   Areas of geometric shapes.

FIGURE 4.34   Possible outcome of Exercise 25.   FIGURE 4.35   Possible outcome of Exercise 26.

26. Break-Even Analysis   Suppose a certain product sells for a dollars per unit. Then the revenue from selling x units of the product is ax dollars. If the cost of producing each unit of the product is b dollars and the company has overhead costs of c dollars, then the total cost of producing x units of the product is $bx + c$ dollars. (**Note: Revenue** is the amount of money received from the sale of the product. The values of a, b, and c are called the **marginal revenue**, **marginal cost**, and **fixed cost**, respectively. The break-even point is the value of x for which the revenue equals the total cost.) Write a program that requests the marginal revenue, marginal cost, fixed cost, and number of units of the product produced and sold (x) and then displays one of the following three outputs: Profit, Loss, or Break Even. See Fig. 4.35.

27. Grades   Write a program that requests an exam score and assigns a letter grade with the scale 90–100 (A), 80–89 (B), 70–79 (C), 60–69 (D), 0–59 (F). See Fig. 4.36.

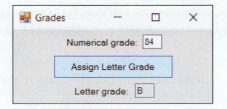

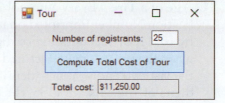

FIGURE 4.36   Possible outcome of Exercise 27.   **FIGURE 4.37**   Possible outcome of Exercise 28.

28. **Cost of a Tour**   A club contract with a tour company arranges a tour to New York City. The tour company requires that at least ten people register for the tour. The cost per person is $500. However, if more than 20 people register the cost per person will be reduced to $450. If more than 30 people register, the cost per person will be reduced to $400. Write a program that requests the number of registrants and calculates the total cost of the tour. Be sure to have the program check that the user entered a number into the top text box before clicking on the button. See Fig. 4.37.

29. **Rewards**   IRS informants are paid cash awards based on the value of the money recovered. If the information was specific enough to lead to a recovery, the informant receives 10% of the first $75,000, 5% of the next $25,000, and 1% of the remainder, up to a maximum award of $50,000. Write a program that requests the amount of the recovery as input and displays the award. See Fig. 4.38. **Note:** The source of this formula is *The Book of Inside Information*, Boardroom Books, 1993.

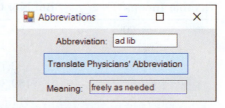

FIGURE 4.38   Possible outcome of Exercise 29.   **FIGURE 4.39**   Possible outcome of Exercise 30.

30. **Physicians' Abbreviations**   Table 4.7 contains the meanings of some abbreviations physicians often use for prescriptions. Write a program that requests an abbreviation and gives its meaning. The user should be informed if the meaning is not in the table. See Fig. 4.39.

TABLE 4.7   Physicians' abbreviations.

Abbreviation	Meaning
ac	before meals
ad lib	freely as needed
bid	twice daily
gtt	a drop
hs	at bedtime
qid	four times a day

31. **Age of a Tire** Every automobile tire manufactured since the year 2000 has a Tire Identification Number imprinted on its sidewall. The TIN consists of the letters DOT followed by 10, 11, or 12 letters and/or digits. The last four characters are digits identifying the date when the tire was manufactured. The first two of those ending digits identify the year and the last two ending digits identify the week during that year. For instance, if the last four digits of the TIN are 1135, the tire was manufactured during the 35th week of 2011. If the last four digits of the TIN are 0822, the tire was manufactured during the 22nd week of 2008. Write a program that allows the user to enter the last four digits of a Tire Identification Number and then tells when the tire was manufactured. See Fig. 4.40. **Note:** The number of the week should be displayed followed by "st", "nd", or "rd" as appropriate.

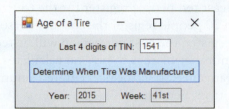

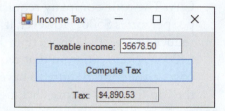

FIGURE 4.40 Possible outcome of Exercise 31. **FIGURE 4.41** Possible outcome of Exercise 32.

32. **Federal Income Tax** Table 4.8 gives the 2014 federal income tax rate schedule for single taxpayers. Write a program that requests taxable income in an input dialog box and calculates the federal income tax. See Fig. 4.41.

TABLE 4.8	2014 Federal income tax rates for single taxpayers.		
Taxable Income Over	**But Not Over**	**The Tax Is**	**Of Amount Over**
$0	$9,225	10%	$0
$9,225	$37,450	$922.50 + 15%	$9,225
$37,450	$90,750	$5,617.50 + 25%	$37,450
$90,750	$189,300	$22,687.50 + 28%	$90,750
$189,300	$411,500	$53,004.00 + 33%	$189,300
$411,500	$413,200	$135,795.00 + 35%	$411,500
$413,200		$144,620.00 + 39.6%	$413,200

33. **Consumer Options** Suppose an 18-oz bottle of shampoo normally sells for $9. Would you rather receive a bottle containing 50% more shampoo for the same price or a 35% price reduction for the 18-oz bottle? Write a program that determines the best option. See Fig. 4.42. **Note:** A recent study showed that most people prefer the 50% more option.

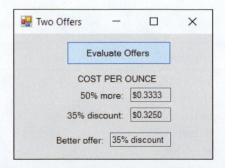

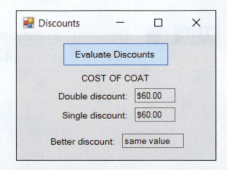

FIGURE 4.42 Possible outcome of Exercise 33. **FIGURE 4.43** Possible outcome of Exercise 34.

34. Consumer Options Suppose a coat originally costs $100 and is double-discounted; first by 20% and then by an additional 25%. Will the price be less than a single discount of 40%? Write a program that calculates the cost of the coat under each of the two discounts and determines the better discount. See Fig. 4.43. **Note:** Most people think that the double-discounted coat is cheaper.

35. U.S. Presidents Write a program that, given the last name of one of the six recent presidents beginning with Carter, displays his state and a colorful fact about him. (**Hint:** The program might need to request further information.) (**Note:** Carter: Georgia; The only soft drink served in the Carter White House was Coca-Cola. Reagan: California; His Secret Service code name was Rawhide. George H. W. Bush: Texas; He celebrated his 85th birthday by parachuting out of an airplane. Clinton: Arkansas; In college he did a good imitation of Elvis Presley. George W. Bush: Texas; He once owned the Texas Rangers baseball team. Obama: Illinois; He was the eighth left-handed president.) See Fig. 4.44.

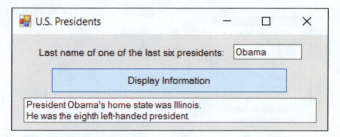

FIGURE 4.44 **Possible outcome of Exercise 35.**

36. Humor and Insults Write a program in which the user enters a number into a masked text box and then clicks on the appropriate button to have either one of three pieces of humor or one of three insults displayed in a text box below the buttons. If the number entered is not between 1 and 3, the masked text box should be cleared. (**Note:** Some possible bits of humor are "I can resist everything except temptation," "I just heard from Bill Bailey. He's not coming home," and "Adding people to a late software project makes it later." Some possible insults are "How much would you charge to haunt a house?" "I'll bet you have no more friends than an alarm clock," and "When your IQ rises to 30, sell.")

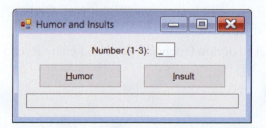

OBJECT	PROPERTY	SETTING
frmExercise36	Text	Humor and Insults
lblNumber	Text	Number (1–3):
mtbNumber	Mask	0
btnHumor	Text	Humor
btnInsult	Text	Insult
txtSentence	ReadOnly	True

Solutions to Practice Problems 4.3

1. (a) Valid. These items are redundant because 1 and 4 are just special cases of **Is < 10**. However, this makes no difference in Visual Basic.

(b) Valid. These items are complementary. However, Visual Basic looks at them one at a time until it finds an item containing the value of the selector. The action following this Case clause will always be carried out.

(c) Not valid. It should be **Case 2**.

2. Yes. However, the program on the right is clearer and therefore preferable.

4.4 Input via User Selection

Programs frequently ask the user to make selections from lists of options. In the questionnaire in Fig. 4.45, students can select their major from a list box, their year from a set of radio buttons, and their computer languages studied from a set of check boxes. After the selections have been made, the user clicks on the *Record Data* button to process the information. The set of radio buttons and set of check boxes are each contained in a group box control. The titles sunk into the tops of the group boxes are *Year* and *Languages Studied*. After selections are made from the three sets of choices, decision structures can be used to process the information. Let's consider the four types of controls in Fig. 4.45 one at a time.

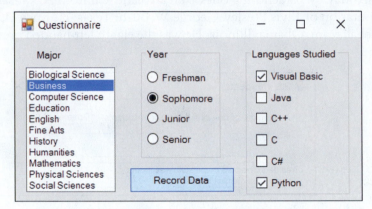

FIGURE 4.45 **Selection controls.**

VideoNote

Listboxes,
Radio
Buttons, and
Checkboxes for Input

■ Using a List Box for Input

The easiest way to populate a list box with items is to place the items into the list box's String Collection Editor at design time. When you click on the list box's *Tasks* button and then click on *Edit Items* (Fig. 4.46), the String Collection Editor appears. Figure 4.47 shows the String Collection Editor filled with the items from Fig. 4.45. Three ways to fill the String Collection Editor are as follows:

1. Type the items directly into the String Collection Editor.
2. Copy a list of items from any text editor (such as Notepad or Word) with Ctrl+C and paste the list into the String Collection Editor with Ctrl+V.
3. Copy a column of data from a spreadsheet program (such as Excel) and paste it into the String Collection Editor.

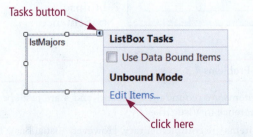

FIGURE 4.46 **Click on *Edit Items* to invoke the String Collection Editor.**

When the user clicks on an item at run time, that item is highlighted, and the value of lstBox.Text is that item represented as a string.

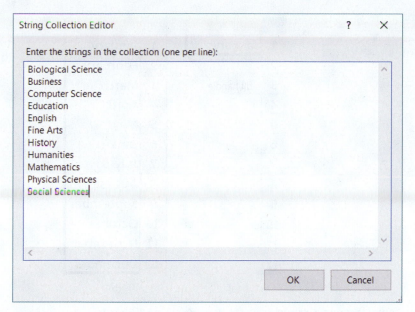

FIGURE 4.47 String Collection Editor.

Example 1 **Days in a Month** The following program uses a list of months. The months can be typed directly into the String Collection Editor. An alternate way to obtain the list of months is to generate it with Excel. To do so, type "January" into a cell of an Excel spreadsheet [see Fig. 4.48(a) on the next page], click on the cell, drag its fill handle down to create the other months [see Fig. 4.48(b)], and press Ctrl+C. Then the list of twelve months can be pasted into the String Collection Editor with Ctrl+V.

```
Private Sub btnDetermine_Click(...) Handles btnDetermine.Click
  Dim daysInMonth As String
  Select Case lstMonths.Text
    Case "September", "April", "June", "November"
      daysInMonth = "30"
    Case "February"
      daysInMonth = "28 or 29"
    Case Else
      daysInMonth = "31"
  End Select
  txtDays.Text = daysInMonth
End Sub
```

[Run, click on a month, and then click on the button.]

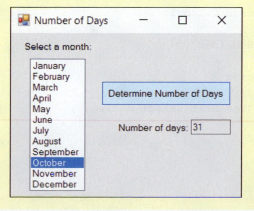

FIGURE 4.48   **Creating a list of months with Excel.**

Source: Excel 2016, Windows 10, Microsoft Corporation.

Each item in lstBox is identified by an index beginning with 0. The value of **lstBox. SelectedIndex** is the index number of the item currently highlighted in lstBox. If no item is highlighted, the value of Selectedindex is -1.

 Example 2   Movie Lines The following program presents a list of famous movie lines spoken by leading male actors. After the user makes a selection and clicks on the button, the actor is identified. The numbering of the lines allows the Select Case block to be simplified.

```
Private Sub btnDetermine_Click(...) Handles btnDetermine.Click
  Dim actor As String = ""
  If lstLines.SelectedIndex <> -1 Then
    Select Case lstLines.Text.Substring(0, 1)
      Case "1", "2"
        actor = "Marlon Brando"
      Case "3", "4"
        actor = "Humphrey Bogart"
      Case "5", "6"
        actor = "Harrison Ford"
      Case "7"
        actor = "Leonardo DiCaprio"
      Case "8"
        actor = "Roy Scheider"
    End Select
    txtActor.Text = actor
  Else
    MessageBox.Show ("You must select a line.")
  End If
End Sub
```

[Run, click on one of the lines in the list box, and then click on the button.]

When no item in a list box is highlighted, the value of lstBox.SelectedItem is *Nothing*. Also, the statement **lstBox.SelectedItem = Nothing** deselects any item that has been selected. By default, only one item at a time can be selected in a list box.

■ Group Box Control

Group boxes are passive objects that contain related sets of controls. In Fig. 4.45 on page 160, the group box titled *Year* contains four radio button controls and the group box titled *Languages Studied* contains six check boxes. Clusters of radio buttons are usually contained in group boxes. Actually, any set of controls can be placed into a group box for visual effect.

You rarely write event procedures for group boxes. When you move a group box, the controls inside it follow as a unit. Therefore, the controls are said to be **attached** to the group box. If you delete a group box, the attached controls will be deleted as well. To attach a control to a group box, just create the control any way you like and drag it inside the group box. The standard prefix for the name of a group box is *grp*. The title sunk into the top of a group box's border is set with the Text property.

A selected group box can be moved by pressing the arrow keys or by dragging the four-headed arrow (⊕) located near the upper-left corner of the group box. Also, the Format menu can be used to align, size, and center controls within a group box.

■ Using Radio Buttons for Input

Radio buttons allow the user to make a single choice from among several options. The term "radio button" comes from a reference to the first car radios, which had buttons that pressed in. Pressing one button would move the dial to a preset station and would raise any other button that was depressed.

Normally, a collection of several radio buttons is attached to a group box. Each button consists of a small circle accompanied by a caption that is set with the Text property. (As with ordinary buttons, an ampersand can be used to create an access key for a radio button.) When a circle or its accompanying caption is clicked, a solid dot appears in the circle and the button is said to be **selected**. At most one radio button in a group can be selected at any one time. Therefore, if one button is selected and another button in the group is clicked, the first button will be deselected. The standard prefix for the name of a radio button is *rad*. A single form can have several groups of radio buttons.

The Checked property of a radio button tells if the button is selected. The condition

radButton.Checked

is true when radButton is selected and false when radButton is not selected. The statement

radButton.Checked = True

selects radButton and deselects all other buttons in its group. The statement

radButton.Checked = False

deselects radButton and has no effect on the other buttons in its group.

 Example 3 **Admission Fee** The following program displays the admission fee for an event. After the user clicks on a radio button and clicks on the *Determine Fee* button, the fee is displayed in a text box. The Else clause in the If block handles the case where no selection was made.

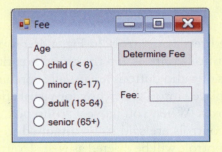

OBJECT	PROPERTY	SETTING
frmFee	Text	Fee
grpAge	Text	Age
radChild	Text	child (< 6)
radMinor	Text	minor (6-17)
radAdult	Text	adult (18-64)
radSenior	Text	senior (65+)
btnDetermine	Text	Determine Fee
lblFee	Text	Fee:
txtFee	ReadOnly	True

```
Private Sub btnDetermine_Click(...) Handles btnDetermine.Click
  If radChild.Checked Then
    txtFee.Text = (0).ToString("C")
  ElseIf radMinor.Checked Then
    txtFee.Text = (5).ToString("C")
  ElseIf radAdult.Checked Then
    txtFee.Text = (10).ToString("C")
  ElseIf radSenior.Checked Then
    txtFee.Text = (7.5).ToString("C")
  Else
    MessageBox.Show("You must make a selection.")
  End If
End Sub
```

[Run, click on a radio button, and click on the *Determine Fee* button.]

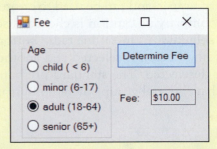

■ Using Check Boxes for Input

A **check box** is a small square and a caption (set with the Text property) that presents the user with a yes/no choice. The form in Fig. 4.45 on page 160 contains six check box controls. The Checked property of a check box has the value False when the square is empty and True when the square is checked. At run time, the user clicks on the square (or its accompanying caption) to toggle between the unchecked and checked states.

Example 4 **Cost of Benefits** The following program calculates the monthly cost of a company health plan. The user checks the desired plans, and then clicks on the button to calculate the total cost.

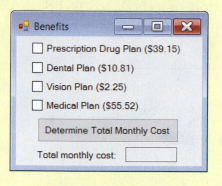

OBJECT	PROPERTY	SETTING
frmBenefits	Text	Benefits
chkDrug	Text	Prescription Drug Plan ($39.15)
chkDental	Text	Dental Plan ($10.81)
chkVision	Text	Vision Plan ($2.25)
chkMedical	Text	Medical Plan ($55.52)
btnDetermine	Text	Determine Total Monthly Cost
lblTotal	Text	Total monthly cost:
txtTotal	ReadOnly	True

```vb
Private Sub btnDetermine_Click(...) Handles btnDetermine.Click
  Dim sum As Decimal = 0
  If chkDrug.Checked Then
    sum += 39.15D
  End If
  If chkDental.Checked Then
    sum += 10.81D
  End If
  If chkVision.Checked Then
    sum += 2.25D
  End If
  If chkMedical.Checked Then
    sum += 55.52D
  End If
  txtTotal.Text = sum.ToString("C")
End Sub
```

[Run, select plans, and then click on the button.]

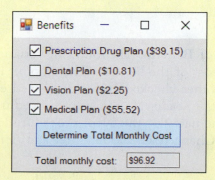

When a check box has the focus, the space bar can be used to check (or uncheck) the box. In addition, the state of a check box can be toggled from the keyboard without first setting the focus to the check box if you create an access key for the check box by including an ampersand in the Text property. (At run time, access keys appear underlined after the Alt key is pressed.) For instance, if the Text property for the Dental Plan in Example 4 is set as "&Dental Plan", then the user can check (or uncheck) the box by pressing Alt+D.

■ Events Raised by Selections

In most real-life programs, the user is asked to make selections from several different controls and then click on a button in order to process the information. Such is the case with the Visual Basic Font selection window shown in Fig. 4.49, where the OK button is clicked after the selections have been made. Sometimes, however, you would like to process information as soon as an item in a list box, a radio button, or a check box is clicked. Visual Basic provides event procedures for immediate processing.

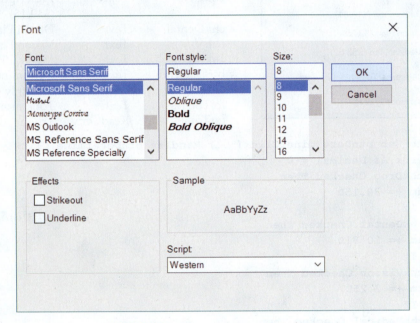

FIGURE 4.49 **Font selection window.**

When you click on an unselected item in a list box, the **SelectedIndexChanged event** is raised. When you click on an unselected radio button or a check box, the **CheckedChanged event** is raised. These events are the default events for their controls.

 Example 5 **Cost of Benefits** The following variation of Example 4 keeps a running total of the monthly cost of the benefits. The amount in the text box is increased each time a check box becomes checked and is decreased each time a check box becomes unchecked. To create the header for the event procedure we double-clicked on the first check box, changed the name of the event procedure from chkDrug_CheckedChanged to checkBox_CheckedChanged, and added three additional events following the keyword Handles.

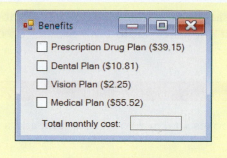

OBJECT	PROPERTY	SETTING
frmBenefits	Text	Benefits
chkDrug	Text	Prescription Drug Plan ($39.15)
chkDental	Text	Dental Plan ($10.81)
chkVision	Text	Vision Plan ($2.25)
chkMedical	Text	Medical Plan ($55.52)
lblTotal	Text	Total monthly cost:
txtTotal	ReadOnly	True

```
Private Sub checkBox_CheckedChanged(...) Handles _
                    chkDrug.CheckedChanged, chkDental.CheckedChanged,
                    chkVision.CheckedChanged, chkMedical.CheckedChanged
  Dim sum As Decimal
  If chkDrug.Checked Then
    sum += 39.15D
  End If
  If chkDental.Checked Then
    sum += 10.81D
  End If
  If chkVision.Checked Then
    sum += 2.25D
  End If
  If chkMedical.Checked Then
    sum += 55.52D
  End If
  txtTotal.Text = sum.ToString("C")
End Sub
```

■ Comments

1. Both list boxes and radio buttons can be used to select a single item from a list of options. As a rule of thumb, radio buttons should be used with short lists (at most seven options) and list boxes should be used with long lists.

2. When the user clicks on a checked check box, it becomes unchecked. Such is not the case with a radio button. A radio button can only be deselected with code or by selecting another radio button.

3. Figure 4.50 shows the form for Example 3 after you click on *Tab Order* in the View menu. The tab indexes of the objects inside the group box have an integer part that is the same as the index number of the group box and a decimal part that is numbered beginning with 0. **Note:** In the Properties window, the TabIndex settings for the radio buttons will be 1, 2, 3 and 4.

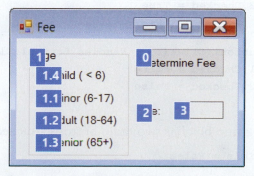

FIGURE 4.50   Tab Order.

4. A set of radio buttons on a form that are not inside a group box are treated as members of the same group. Therefore, if a form has just one set of radio buttons, they do not have to be placed in a group box.

Practice Problems 4.4

1. What is the difference between a set of check boxes attached to a group box and a set of radio buttons attached to a group box?

2. Suppose a form contains two sets of radio buttons. Why is it essential for the sets to be contained in separate group boxes? Do the same concerns apply to sets of check boxes?

3. Suppose a group box contains a set of radio buttons. Give two ways to guarantee that the user will select one of the radio buttons.

EXERCISES 4.4

In Exercises 1 through 8, determine the effect of setting the property to the value shown.

1. `GroupBox1.Text = "Income"`

2. `CheckBox1.Checked = True`

3. `CheckBox1.Checked = False`

4. `CheckBox1.Text = "&Vanilla"`

5. `RadioButton1.Checked = False`

6. `txtOutput.Text = lstBox.Text`

7. `RadioButton1.Text = "Clear &All"`

8. `RadioButton1.Checked = True`

In Exercises 9 through 12, write one or more lines of code to carry out the task.

9. Set the caption for RadioButton1 to Yes.

10. Clear the small rectangular box of CheckBox1.

11. Guarantee that CheckBox1 is checked.

12. Turn off RadioButton2.

In Exercises 13 and 14, determine the state of the two radio buttons after Button1 is clicked.

13.
```
Private Sub Button1_Click(...) Handles Button1.Click
    RadioButton1.Checked = True
    RadioButton2.Checked = True
End Sub
```

14.
```
Private Sub Button1_Click(...) Handles Button1.Click
    RadioButton1.Checked = False
    RadioButton2.Checked = False
End Sub
```

15. Suppose that a group box has two radio buttons attached to it. If the statement

```
GroupBox1.Visible = False
```

is executed, will the radio buttons also vanish? Test your answer.

16. Create a form with two group boxes, each having two radio buttons attached to it. Run the program and confirm that the two pairs of radio buttons operate independently of each other.

17. **Cost of a Computer** A computer dealer offers two basic computers, the Deluxe ($1000) and the Super ($1500). The customer can order any of the following additional options: upgraded video card ($200), internal modem plus Wi-Fi ($30), or 1 GB of added memory ($120). Write a program that calculates the cost of the computer system selected. See Fig. 4.51.

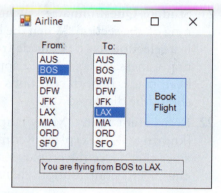

FIGURE 4.51 Possible outcome of Exercise 17.   **FIGURE 4.52** Possible outcome of Exercise 18.

18. **Airline Flights** Write a program to book an airline flight. See Fig. 4.52. If the same airport is selected from the two list boxes, the user should be informed immediately that the departure and arrival airports must be different. If no airport has been selected from one or both of the list boxes when the button is clicked, then the user should be told what information must be provided. Use message boxes to inform the user of such problems.

19. **Cast a Vote** Write a program that allows you to vote for one of two presidential candidates. See Fig. 4.53. When the *Cast Vote* button is clicked on, the text box should display your vote. In the event that neither radio button is selected, the sentence "You voted for neither." should appear in the text box.

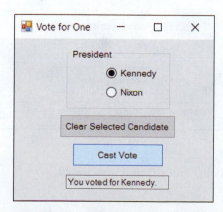

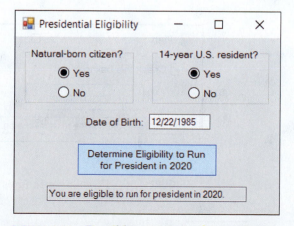

FIGURE 4.53 Possible outcome of Exercise 19.   **FIGURE 4.54** Possible outcome of Exercise 20.

20. **Presidential Eligibility** Article 02 Section 01 Clause 05, US Constitution of the United States, states that "No Person except a natural born Citizen, or a Citizen of the United States at the time of the Adoption of this Constitution, shall be eligible to the Office of President; neither shall any Person be eligible to that Office who shall not have attained to the Age of thirty five Years, and been fourteen Years a Resident within the United States." Write a program that determines if a person is eligible to run for president of the United States in 2016. (**Note:** A natural-born citizen is a person who is born within the jurisdiction of the U.S. government. A 2016 candidate for president must achieve age 35 by Inauguration Day, 1/20/2017.) See Fig. 4.54 on the previous page. **Hint:** Use the AddYears method.

21. **Student Questionnaire** Write a program that uses the form in Fig. 4.45 at the beginning of the section. When the button is clicked on, the program should first determine if a selection has been made from both the list box and the group of radio buttons. If not, a message box should appear telling the user which types of selections have not been made. If both selections have been made, the message "Information Processed" should be displayed.

22. **Retirement Plan** Many employers offer their employees a retirement benefit plan [known as a 401(k) plan]. Retirement benefit plans are usually beneficial to an employee, since they force the employee to save. In addition, employers often match part of the employee's contribution; therefore the employee receives free money.

    (a) Write a program that uses the form in Fig. 4.55(a) to ask an employee whether or not he or she would like to participate. When the program starts, the check box should be unchecked and the text box should be empty. If the employee clicks on the button without checking the check box, the statement "You have opted out of the retirement plan." should appear in the text box.

    (b) Write a program that uses the form in Fig. 4.55(b) to ask an employee whether or not he or she would like to participate. When the program starts, both radio buttons should be unchecked and the text box should be empty. If the employee clicks on the button without checking a radio button, the message "You must make a selection." should be displayed in a message box. Otherwise, one of the two statements appearing in the text boxes in Figs. 4.55 (a) and (b) should appear in the text box.

    Note: In part (a), opting out is the default option. A study[2] has shown that employees are more likely to opt-in for the retirement plan when the question is posed as in part (b).

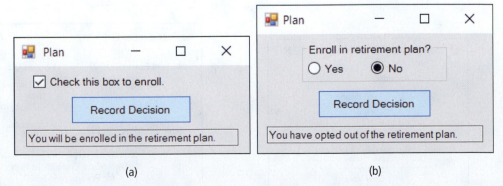

(a) (b)

FIGURE 4.55 Possible outcomes for parts (a) and (b) of Exercise 22.

[2]Gabriel D. Carroll, James J. Choi, David Laibson, Brigitte Madrian, and Andrew Metrick, *Optimal Defaults and Active Decisions*, NBER Working Paper no. 11074, 2005.

23. Form 1040 Figure 4.56 shows an item from the 2014 U.S. Individual Income Tax Return. Write a program whose form resembles item 39a. Initially the number in the large text box at the right should be zero, and should be increased by one each time an item is checked.

39a	Check if:	☐ **You** were born before January 2, 1950,	☐ **Blind.**	**Total boxes**	
		☐ **Spouse** was born before January 2, 1950,	☐ **Blind.**	checked ▶ 39a	

FIGURE 4.56 Item 39a from Form 1040 of the 2014 U.S. Individual Income Tax Return.

24. Select Colors Write a program to specify the foreground and background colors for a label containing the words "VISUAL BASIC". See Fig. 4.57. If the same color is selected from the two group boxes, the user should be informed immediately that the two colors must be different. If no color has been selected from one or both of the group boxes when the button is clicked, then the user should be told what information must be supplied. Use message boxes to inform the user of problems.

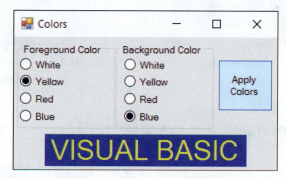

FIGURE 4.57 Possible outcome for Exercise 24.

25. Membership Fee The basic monthly cost of a membership in a sport and health club is $100 for adults and $75 for seniors. Available extras cost $25 each per month. Write a program that uses the form in Fig. 4.58 to calculate a member's monthly fee. Before calculating the fee, make sure that a membership category has been selected.

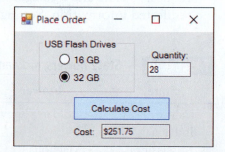

FIGURE 4.58 Possible outcome for Exercise 25. **FIGURE 4.59** Possible outcome for Exercise 26.

26. Cost of Flash Drives A company sells 16 GB flash drives for $5.99 each and 32 GB flash drives for $9.99 each. However, large-quantity orders of flash drives of the same type receive discounts. Orders of between 25 and 49 flash drives receive a 10% discount, orders of between 50 and 99 flash drives receive a 15% discount, and orders of 100 or more flash drives receive a 20% discount. Write a program that uses the type and quantity of flash drives ordered, and calculates the cost of the order. See Fig. 4.59.

27. **Age on Various Planets**   Table 4.9 shows the number of Earth days in each year of the first four planets in our solar system, and the number of Earth years in each year of the last four planets. For instance, the table says that one year on Mercury is 88 Earth days long. Write a program that asks you to select the name of a planet and your date of birth, and then gives today's date and your age on the selected planet. See Fig. 4.60.

FIGURE 4.60   Possible outcome for Exercise 27.

FIGURE 4.61   Possible outcome for Exercise 28.

TABLE 4.9	Duration of one year on each planet.		
Year	**Earth Days**	**Year**	**Earth Years**
Mercurian	88	Jovian	11.86
Venusian	224.7	Saturian	29.46
Earth	365.4	Uranian	84.07
Martian	687	Neptuian	164.8

28. **States**   Table 4.10 contains information about several states. Write a program that requests a state and a category (flower, nickname, and motto) as input and displays the requested information. See Fig 4.61.

TABLE 4.10	State flowers, nicknames, and mottoes.		
State	**Flower**	**Nickname**	**Motto**
California	Golden poppy	Golden State	Eureka
Indiana	Peony	Hoosier State	Crossroads of America
Mississippi	Magnolia	Magnolia State	By valor and arms
New York	Rose	Empire State	Ever upward

29. **Investment**   If $10,000 is invested at an annual interest r compounded n times per year, then the amount of the investment after 5 years will be $10000 \left(1 + \dfrac{r}{n}\right)^{5 \cdot n}$. Some possible values for r are .02, .025, and .03. Some possible values for n are 1, 2, and 4.

Write a program that allows the user to select interest rates and compounding periods from list boxes and calculates the amount after 5 years. See Fig. 4.62.

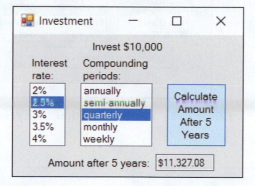

FIGURE 4.62 Possible outcome of Exercise 29.   **FIGURE 4.63** Possible outcome of Exercise 30.

30. Display Hello   Write a program using radio buttons that permits the user to display the word "Hello" in red, blue, or green, and in English, French (Bonjour), or Italian (Ciao). When the program begins, the Red and English radio button should appear selected. See Fig. 4.63. As soon as a different radio button is clicked on, the appropriate change should appear immediately.

31. Railroad Properties   One of the four railroad properties in Monopoly is not an actual railroad. Write a program that displays the names of the four properties in a list box and asks the user to click on the property that is not a railroad. The user should be informed if the selection is correct or not in a message box. See Fig. 4.64.

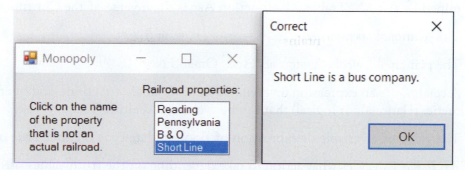

FIGURE 4.64 Possible outcome of Exercise 31.

32. Workplaces   Table 4.11 contains five people and their places of employment. Write a program that displays the people in one list box and the workplaces in another list box, with the names in the left list box in alphabetical order. The user should try to match a person with their workplace by selecting an item from each list. When they click on the button, they should be told whether or not they made a correct match. See Fig. 4.65 on the next page. If they do not make two selections, they should be instructed to do so by a message box.

TABLE 4.11	Place of employment.
Person	**Workplace**
Bruce Wayne	Wayne Enterprises
Clark Kent	Daily Planet
Peter Parker	Daily Bugle
Rick Blaine	Rick's American Cafe
Willie Wonka	Chocolate Factory

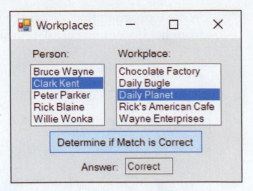

FIGURE 4.65 Possible outcome of Exercise 32.

Solutions to Practice Problems 4.4

1. With radio buttons, at most one button can be selected at any given time, whereas several check boxes can be checked simultaneously.

2. With two sets of radio buttons, you would like to make two selections. However, if the two sets are in the same group box, then at most one radio button can be selected at any time. Since several check boxes can be checked at any time, you needn't have this concern with check boxes. However, the two sets of check boxes are usually placed in separate group boxes to improve the visual effect.

3. Method 1: Make one of the radio buttons the default radio button; that is, set its Checked property to True at design time.

   Method 2: Place the code that refers to the radio buttons in an If block that displays a message when no radio button in the group box has been checked.

CHAPTER 4 SUMMARY

1. The function *Chr* associates a character with each number from 0 through 255 as determined by the ANSI table. The function Asc is the inverse of the Chr function.

2. The *relational operators* are $<$, $>$, $=$, $<>$, $<=$, and $>=$.

3. The principal *logical operators* are And, Or, and Not.

4. A *condition* is an expression involving literals, variables, functions, and operators (arithmetic, relational, or logical) that can be evaluated as either True or False.

5. The value of a variable or expression of Boolean data type is either True or False.

6. An *If block* decides what action to take depending on the truth values of one or more conditions. To allow several courses of action, the If, ElseIf, and Else parts of an If block can contain other If blocks.

7. When AndAlso and OrElse are used as operators, the evaluation of logical expressions proceeds from left to right and stops as soon as the truth value is determined.

8. A *Select Case block* selects from one of several actions depending on the value of an expression, called the *selector*. The entries in the *value lists* should have the same type as the selector.

9. *List boxes, radio buttons,* and *check boxes* provide an efficient way for a user to select among a set of possible options.

CHAPTER 4 PROGRAMMING PROJECTS

1. **Rental Cost** Table 4.12 gives the price schedule for Eddie's Equipment Rental. Full-day rentals cost one-and-a-half times half-day rentals. Write a program that displays Table 4.9 in a list box when an appropriate button is clicked on and displays a bill in another list box based on the item number and time period chosen by a customer. The bill should include a $30.00 deposit. A sample output is shown in Fig. 4.66.

TABLE 4.12	Price schedule for Eddie's Equipment Rental.		
Piece of Equipment		**Half-Day**	**Full-Day**
1. Rug cleaner		$16.00	$24.00
2. Lawn mower		$12.00	$18.00
3. Paint sprayer		$20.00	$30.00

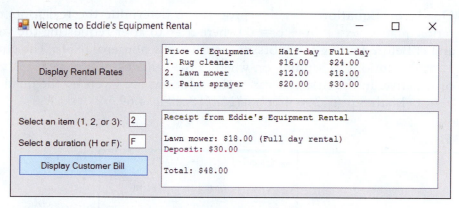

FIGURE 4.66 Possible output for Programming Project 1.

2. **Nutrition** The American Heart Association suggests that at most 30% of the calories in our diet come from fat. Although food labels give the number of calories and amount of fat per serving, they often do not give the percentage of calories from fat. This percentage can be calculated by multiplying the number of grams of fat in one serving by 9 and dividing that number by the total number of calories per serving. Write a program that requests the name, number of calories per serving, and the grams of fat per serving as input, and tells whether the food meets the American Heart Association recommendation. A sample run is shown in Fig. 4.67.

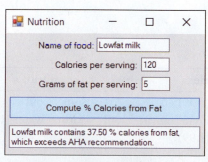

FIGURE 4.67 Possible outcome of Programming Project 2.

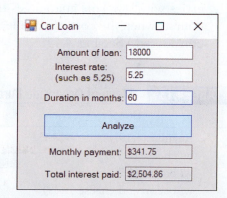

FIGURE 4.68 Possible outcome of Programming Project 3.

3. **Car Loan** Write a program to analyze a car loan. See Fig. 4.68. The user should enter the amount of the loan, the annual percentage rate of interest, and the duration of the loan in months. When the user clicks on the button, the information that was entered should be checked to make sure it is reasonable. If bad data have been supplied, the user should be so advised. Otherwise, the monthly payment and the total amount of interest paid should be displayed. The formula for the monthly payment is

$$\text{monthly payment} = \frac{p \cdot r}{1 - (1 + r)^{-n}}$$

where p is the amount of the loan, r is the monthly interest rate (annual rate divided by 12) given as a number between 0 (for 0%) and 1 (for 100%), and n is the duration of the loan in months. The formula for the total interest paid is

$$\text{total interest} = n \cdot [\text{monthly payment}] - p$$

4. **Quadratic Equation** Write a program to determine the real roots of the quadratic equation $ax^2 + bx + c = 0$ (where $a \neq 0$) after requesting the values of a, b, and c. Before finding the roots, ensure that a is nonzero. [**Note:** The equation has 2, 1, or 0 solutions depending on whether the value of $b^2 - 4*a*c$ is positive, zero, or negative. In the first two cases, the solutions are given by the quadratic formula $(-b \pm \text{Math.Sqrt}(b^2 - 4*a*c))/(2*a)$.] See Fig. 4.69.

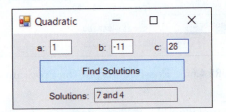

FIGURE 4.69 Possible outcome of Programming Project 4.

5. **Restaurant Menu** Write a program to place an order from the restaurant menu in Table 4.13. Use the form in Fig. 4.70, and write the program so that each group box is invisible and becomes visible only when its corresponding check box is checked. After the button is clicked, the cost of the meal should be calculated. (**Note:** The Checked property of the first radio button in each group box should be set to True in its Properties window. This guarantees that a selection is made in each visible group box. Of course, when the cost of the meal is calculated, only the visible group boxes should be considered.) See Fig. 4.71.

TABLE 4.13	Menu of Oceanside Burgers & Fries.	
Burgers	**Fries**	**Drinks**
Regular (4.19)	Small (2.39)	Soda (1.69)
w/ cheese (4.79)	Medium (3.09)	Bottled water (1.49)
w/ bacon (4.79)	Large (4.99)	
w/ bacon and cheese (5.39)		

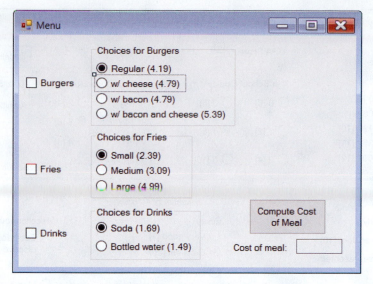

FIGURE 4.70   Form for Programming Project 5.

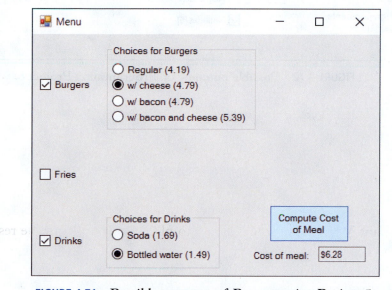

FIGURE 4.71   Possible outcome of Programming Project 5.

6. **College Admissions**   The admissions offices of colleges often rely on a point system. A point system similar to the one in Fig. 4.72 on the next page is used by a large state university. Write a program that allows an admissions officer to determine whether an applicant should be admitted. The numbers in brackets give the point count for each response. The GPA score entered into the text box at the top of the form should be from 2.0 to 4.0. The point value in the brackets to the right of the text box is 20 times the GPA and should appear automatically after the focus leaves the text box. A total of at most 40 points can be earned for the responses below the line. The program should calculate the total score and then admit an applicant whose score is at least 100.

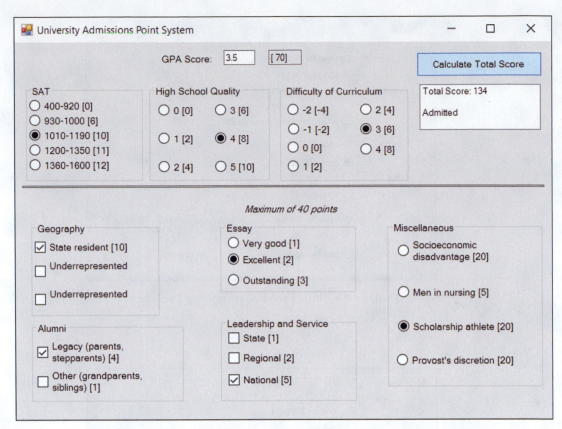

FIGURE 4.72   **Possible outcome of Programming Project 6.**

5

General Procedures

5.1 Function Procedures

Visual Basic has two devices, **Function procedures** and **Sub procedures**, that are used to break complex problems into small problems to be solved one at a time. To distinguish them from event procedures, Function and Sub procedures are referred to as **general procedures**. General procedures allow us to write and read a program in such a way that we first focus on the tasks and later on how to accomplish each task. They also eliminate repetitive code and sometimes can be reused in other programs.

In this section we show how Function procedures are defined and used. Sub procedures are presented in Sections 5.2 and 5.3.

Visual Basic has many built-in functions. In one respect, functions are like miniature programs. They receive input, they process the input, and they produce output. Some functions we encountered earlier are listed in Table 5.1.

TABLE 5.1   **Some Visual Basic built-in functions.**

Function	Example	Input	Output
Int	Int(2.6) is 2	number	number
Chr	Chr(65) is "A"	number	string
Asc	Asc("Apple") is 65	string	number
Math.Round	Math.Round(2.34, 1) is 2.3	number, number	number

Although the input can consist of several values, the output is always a single value. A function is said to **return** its output. For instance, in the first example of Table 5.1, we say that the Int function returns the value 2. The items inside the parentheses are called **arguments**. The first three functions in Table 5.1 have one argument and the fourth function has two arguments. Arguments can be literals (as in Table 5.1), variables, or expressions. Variables are the most common types of arguments. The following lines of code illustrate the use of variables and expressions as arguments for the Int function:

```
Dim num1 As Double = 2.6
Dim num2 As Double = Int(num1)          'variable as an argument

Dim num1 As Double = 1.3
Dim num2 As Double = Int(2 * num1)      'expression as an argument
```

The second line of code above is said to **call** the Int function and to **pass** the value of *num1* to the function.

In addition to using built-in functions, we can define functions of our own. These new functions, called **Function procedures** are used in the same way as built-in functions. Like built-in functions, Function procedures have a single output that can be of any data type. Function procedures are used in exactly the same way as built-in functions. Function procedures are defined by function blocks of the form

VideoNote

Function
Procedures

```
Function FunctionName(var1 As Type1, var2 As Type2,...) As ReturnDataType
   statement(s)
   Return expression
End Function
```

The first line of the procedure is called the **header**. The variables appearing in the header are called **parameters**. The header declares a parameter to be of a certain type and sets aside a portion of memory to hold its value. The scope of each parameter is limited to its function block, as is any variable declared inside the Function procedure.

Function names should indicate the role performed by the function and must conform to the rules for naming variables. By convention, function names begin with an uppercase letter. *ReturnDataType*, which specifies the type of the output, will be one of String, Integer, Decimal, Double, Date, Boolean, and so on. In the preceding general code, the Return statement specifies the output, which must be of type *ReturnDataType*. Function procedures can contain several Return statements, and must contain at least one.

Function procedures are typed directly into the Code Editor outside any other procedure. After you type the header and then press the Enter key, the editor automatically inserts the line "End Function" and a blank line separating the two lines of code. Also, the smart indenting feature of the Code Editor automatically indents all lines in the block of code between the header and "End Function" statements.

■ Functions Having One Parameter

The following two Function procedures have just one parameter. (Figure 5.1 identifies the different parts of the first function's header.)

```
Function FtoC(t As Double) As Double
  'Convert Fahrenheit temperature to Celsius
  Return (5 / 9) * (t - 32)
End Function

Function FirstName(fullName As String) As String
  'Extract the first name from a full name
  Dim firstSpace As Integer
  firstSpace = fullName.IndexOf(" ")
  Return fullName.Substring(0, firstSpace)
End Function
```

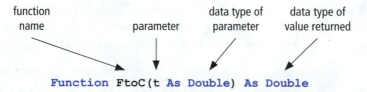

FIGURE 5.1   Header of the FtoC Function procedure.

 Example 1   **Temperature Conversion**   The following program uses the Function procedure FtoC. The fourth line of the btnConvert_Click event procedure, **celsiusTemp = FtoC(fahrenheitTemp)**, calls the function FtoC. The value of the argument *fahrenheitTemp* is assigned to the parameter *t* in the Function procedure header. (We say that the value of *fahrenheitTemp* is passed to the parameter *t*.) After the Function procedure does a calculation using the parameter *t*, the calculated value is the output of the function FtoC and is assigned to the variable *celsiusTemp*.

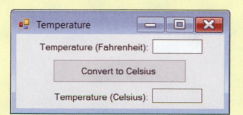

OBJECT	PROPERTY	SETTING
frmConvert	Text	Temperature
lblTempF	Text	Temperature (Fahrenheit):
txtTempF		
btnConvert	Text	Convert to Celsius
lblTempC	Text	Temperature (Celsius):
txtTempC	ReadOnly	True

```
Private Sub btnConvert_Click(...) Handles btnConvert.Click
  Dim fahrenheitTemp, celsiusTemp As Double
  fahrenheitTemp = CDbl(txtTempF.Text)
  celsiusTemp = FtoC(fahrenheitTemp)
  txtTempC.Text = CStr(celsiusTemp)
  'Note: The above four lines can be replaced with the single line
  'txtTempC.Text = CStr(FtoC(CDbl(txtTempF.Text)))
End Sub


Function FtoC(t As Double) As Double
  'Convert Fahrenheit temperature to Celsius
  Return Math.Round((5 / 9) * (t - 32), 2)
End Function
```

[Run, type 212 into the text box, and then click on the button.]

Example 2   **Parse a Name**   The following program uses the Function procedure First-Name. The fifth line of the btnDetermine_Click event procedure, **txtFirstName.Text = FirstName(fullName)**, passes the value of the argument *fullName* to the parameter *full-Name* in the Function procedure. Although the parameter in the Function procedure has the same name as the argument passed to it, they are different variables.

OBJECT	PROPERTY	SETTING
frmFirstName	Text	First Name
lblName	Text	Full name:
txtFullName		
btnDetermine	Text	Determine First Name
lblFirstName	Text	First name:
txtFirstName	ReadOnly	True

```
Private Sub btnDetermine_Click(...) Handles btnDetermine.Click
  'Determine a person's first name
  Dim fullName As String
  fullName = txtFullName.Text
  txtFirstName.Text = FirstName(fullName)
End Sub


Function FirstName(fullName As String) As String
  'Extract the first name from a full name
  Dim firstSpace As Integer
  firstSpace = fullName.IndexOf(" ")
  Return fullName.Substring(0, firstSpace)
End Function
```

[Run, type Franklin Delano Roosevelt into the text box, and then click on the button.]

Passing by Value

If the argument in a function call is a variable, the *value* of the argument variable (not the argument variable itself) is passed to a parameter variable. Therefore, if the Function procedure happens to change the value of the parameter variable, no change will occur in the argument variable. Such is the case even if the two variables have the same name. For instance, after the following program is run and the button is clicked on, the value 6 will appear in TextBox1 and the value 2 will appear in Textbox2. The two variables have the same name, but are different variables. This is analogous to the situation in which variables in two different event procedures have the same name, but separate identities. This method of passing information to a Function procedure is called **passing by value**.

```
Private Sub btnTriple_Click(...) Handles btnTriple.Click
  Dim num As Integer = 2
  TextBox1.Text = CStr(Triple(num))
  TextBox2.Text = CStr(num)
End Sub

Function Triple(num As Integer) As Integer
  num = 3 * num
  Return num
End Function
```

Restriction on Data Types

Consider the following statement and the related function procedure header:

```
Dim var1 as Type1 = FunctionName(arg)
Function FunctionName(par As parameterType) As ReturnDataType
```

The variables *arg* and *par* must have compatible data types, and *Type1* must be compatible with *ReturnDataType*. In this book, the data types of *arg* and *par* will usually be the same. (As an example of compatibility, Visual Basic allows a numerical argument to be passed to a numerical parameter whose data type is wider than the data type of the argument.) Code is easier to read when the same name is used for the argument and the parameter it is passed to.

Functions Having Several Parameters

The following two Function procedures have more than one parameter. In the second function, one-letter names have been used for the parameters so that the mathematical formulas will look familiar and be easy to read. However, since the names are not descriptive, the meanings of these parameters are spelled out in comment statements.

```
Function Pay(wage As Decimal, hrs As Decimal) As Decimal
  'Calculate weekly pay with time-and-a-half for overtime
  Dim amount As Decimal
  Select Case hrs
    Case Is <= 40
      amount = wage * hrs
    Case Is > 40
      amount = (wage * 40) + ((1.5D) * wage * (hrs - 40))
  End Select
  Return amount
End Function

Function FutureValue(p As Decimal, r As Decimal, m As Integer, t As Integer)
                As Decimal
  'Find the future value of a bank savings account
  'p  principal, the amount deposited
  'r  annual rate of interest in decimal form
  'm  number of times interest is compounded per year
  't  number of years
  Dim i As Decimal    'interest rate per period
  Dim n As Integer    'total number of times interest is compounded
  i = r / m
  n = m * t
  Return CDec(p * ((1 + i) ^ n))
End Function
```

When a function with several parameters is called, the values of the arguments (from left to right) are assigned to the parameters (from left to right). Therefore, there must be the same number of arguments as parameters, and each argument must have a type compatible with the corresponding parameter. In most cases, each argument will have the same data type as its corresponding parameter. For instance in a statement of the form

```
numVar = FutureValue(arg1, arg2, arg3, arg4)
```

arg1 and *arg2* will have types Integer or Decimal, and *arg3* and *arg4* will have type Integer.

 Example 3   **Earnings** The following program uses the Function procedure Pay. Here the arguments have different names than the corresponding parameters. As required, however, they have the same data types.

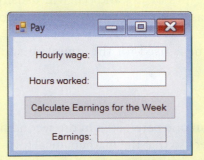

OBJECT	PROPERTY	SETTING
frmPay	Text	Pay
lblWage	Text	Hourly wage:
txtWage		
lblHours	Text	Hours worked:
txtHours		
btnCalculate	Text	Calculate Earnings for the Week
lblEarnings	Text	Earnings:
txtEarnings	ReadOnly	True

```
Private Sub btnCalculate_Click(...) Handles btnCalculate.Click
  'Calculate a person's weekly pay
  Dim hourlyWage, hoursWorked As Decimal
  hourlyWage = CDec(txtWage.Text)
  hoursWorked = CDec(txtHours.Text)
  txtEarnings.Text = (Pay(hourlyWage, hoursWorked)).ToString("C")
End Sub

Function Pay(wage As Decimal, hrs As Decimal) As Decimal
  'Calculate weekly pay with time-and-a-half for overtime
  Dim amount As Decimal
  Select Case hrs
    Case Is <= 40
      amount = wage * hrs
    Case Is > 40
      amount = (wage * 40) + ((1.5D) * wage * (hrs - 40))
  End Select
  Return amount
End Function
```

[Run, enter values into the top two text boxes, and click on the button.]

Pay

Hourly wage: 14.50

Hours worked: 45

Calculate Earnings for the Week

Earnings: $688.75

✔ **Example 4**   **Future Value of a Bank Deposit**   The following program uses the Function procedure FutureValue. The function computes the balance in a saving account given the amount deposited (p), the annual rate of interest (r), the number of times interest is compounded per year (m), and the number of years that interest accrues (t). The formula for the future value is

$$p\left(1 + \frac{r}{m}\right)^{mt}.$$

Bank

Amount of bank deposit:

Annual rate of interest:

Number of times interest
is compounded per year:

Number of years:

Compute Balance

Balance:

OBJECT	PROPERTY	SETTING
frmBank	Text	Bank
lblAmount	Text	Amount of bank deposit:
txtAmount		
lblRate	Text	Annual rate of interest:
txtRate		
lblNumComp	AutoSize	False
	Text	Number of times interest is compounded per year:
txtNumComp		
lblNumYrs	Text	Number of years:
txtNumYrs		
btnCompute	Text	Compute Balance
lblBalance	Text	Balance:
txtBalance	ReadOnly	True

```vb
Private Sub btnCompute_Click(...) Handles btnCompute.Click
  'Find the future value of a bank deposit
  Dim p As Decimal = CDec(txtAmount.Text)
  Dim r As Decimal = CDec(txtRate.Text)
  Dim m As Integer = CInt(txtNumComp.Text)
  Dim t As Integer = CInt(txtNumYrs.Text)
  Dim balance As Decimal = FutureValue(p, r, m, t)
  txtBalance.Text = balance.ToString("C")
End Sub

Function FutureValue(p As Decimal, r As Decimal, c As Integer, n As Integer)
                As Decimal
  'Find the future value of a bank savings account
  'p  principal, the amount deposited
  'r  annual rate of interest in decimal form
  'm  number of times interest is compounded per year
  't  number of years
  Dim i As Decimal     'interest rate per period
  Dim n As Integer     'total number of times interest is compounded
  i = r / m
  n = m * t
  Return CDec(p * ((1 + i) ^ n))
End Function
```

[Run, type 100, .04, 4, and 5 into the text boxes, and then click on the button.]

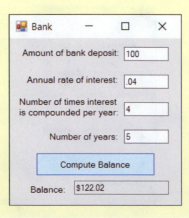

■ Boolean-Valued Functions

So far, the values returned by Function procedures have been numbers or strings. However, a Function procedure can also return a Boolean value—that is, True or False. The following program uses a Boolean-valued function and demonstrates an important feature of Function procedures: namely, a Function procedure can contain more than one Return statement. When the first Return statement is encountered, it determines the function value, and the execution of code in the function block terminates.

Example 5 **Vowel Words** The following program uses a Boolean-valued function to determine whether a word input by the user is a vowel word—that is, contains every vowel. Some examples of vowel words are "sequoia", "facetious", and "dialogue". The Function procedure IsVowelWord examines the word for vowels one at a time and terminates when a vowel is found to be missing.

```
Private Sub btnDetermine_Click(...) Handles btnDetermine.Click
  Dim word As String
  word = txtWord.Text.ToUpper
  If IsVowelWord(word) Then
    txtOutput.Text = word & " contains every vowel."
  Else
    txtOutput.Text = word & " does not contain every vowel."
  End If
End Sub

Function IsVowelWord(word As String) As Boolean
  If word.IndexOf("A") = -1 Then
    Return False
  End If
  If word.IndexOf("E") = -1 Then
    Return False
  End If
  If word.IndexOf("I") = -1 Then
    Return False
  End If
  If word.IndexOf("O") = -1 Then
    Return False
  End If
  If word.IndexOf("U") = -1 Then
    Return False
  End If
  Return True       'All vowels are present.
End Function
```

[Run, type a word into the top text box, and click on the button.]

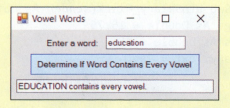

■ The Exit Function Statement

The Exit Function statement immediately exits the Function procedure in which it appears.

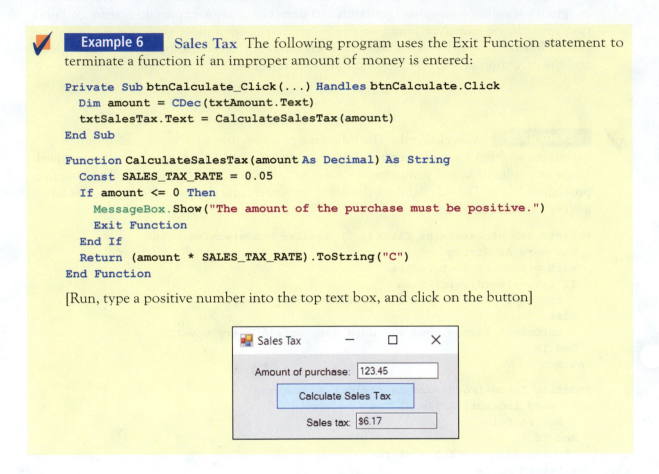

Example 6   **Sales Tax** The following program uses the Exit Function statement to terminate a function if an improper amount of money is entered:

```
Private Sub btnCalculate_Click(...) Handles btnCalculate.Click
  Dim amount = CDec(txtAmount.Text)
  txtSalesTax.Text = CalculateSalesTax(amount)
End Sub

Function CalculateSalesTax(amount As Decimal) As String
  Const SALES_TAX_RATE = 0.05
  If amount <= 0 Then
    MessageBox.Show("The amount of the purchase must be positive.")
    Exit Function
  End If
  Return (amount * SALES_TAX_RATE).ToString("C")
End Function
```

[Run, type a positive number into the top text box, and click on the button]

■ Comments

1. After a Function procedure has been defined, IntelliSense helps you call the function. Word Completion helps type the function's name, and Parameter Info displays the function's parameters. As soon as you type in the left parenthesis preceding the arguments, a Parameter Info banner appears giving information about the number, names, and types of the parameters required by the function. See Fig. 5.2. A syntax error occurs if the number of arguments in the calling statement is different from the number of parameters in the called Function procedure. Also, having an argument of a data type that cannot be assigned to the corresponding parameter is a syntax error. Parameter Info helps you prevent both of these kinds of syntax errors.

```
Private Sub btnSalary_Click(sender As Object, e As Even
    Dim wage As Double = 15.75
    Dim hrs As Double = 45
    txtSalary.Text = Pay(
```
Pay(**wage As Double**, hrs As Double) As String

FIGURE 5.2   The Parameter Info help feature.

2. In this text, Function procedure names begin with uppercase letters in order to distinguish them from variable names. Like variable names, however, they can be written with any combination of uppercase and lowercase letters.

3. Function procedures are not required to have any parameters. However, Function procedures without parameters are rarely used and do not appear in this text.

Practice Problems 5.1

1. Suppose a program contains the lines

```
Dim n As Double, x As String
lstOutput.Items.Add(Arc(n, x))
```

What types of inputs (numeric or string) and output does the function Arc have?

2. Determine the error in the following program.

```
Private Sub btnOutput_Click(...) Handles btnOutput.Click
    Dim num As Integer = 3
    Dim word As String = "Visual"
    MessageBox.Show("The third letter of the word is " &
                    FindLetter(word, num) & ".")
End Sub

Function FindLetter(num As Integer, word As String) As String
    Return word.Substring(num - 1, 1)
End Function
```

EXERCISES 5.1

In Exercises 1 through 10, determine the output displayed when the button is clicked.

1.
```
Private Sub btnConvert_Click(...) Handles btnConvert.Click
    'Convert Celsius to Fahrenheit
    Dim temp As Double = 15
    txtOutput.Text = CStr(CtoF(temp))
End Sub

Function CtoF(t As Double) As Double
    Return ((9 / 5) * t) + 32
End Function
```

2.
```
Private Sub btnDisplay_Click(...) Handles btnDisplay.Click
    Dim acres As Double 'number of acres in a parking lot
    acres = 5
    txtOutput.Text = "You can park about " & Cars(acres) & " cars."
End Sub

Function Cars(x As Double) As Double
    'Number of cars that can be parked on x acres
    Return 100 * x
End Function
```

3. ```
Private Sub btnDisplay_Click(...) Handles btnDisplay.Click
    Dim p As Double
    p = CDbl(txtPopGr.Text) 'population growth as a percent
    txtOutput.Text = "The population will double in " &
                     DoublingTime(p) & " years."
End Sub

Function DoublingTime(x As Double) As Double
    'Estimate time required for a population to double
    'at a growth rate of x percent
    Return 72 / x
End Function
```

(Assume the text box txtPopGr contains the number 3.)

4. ```
Private Sub btnDetermine_Click(...) Handles btnDetermine.Click
    Dim numOne, numTwo, numThree, numLowest As Double
    numOne = CDbl(txtOne.Text)
    numTwo = CDbl(txtTwo.Text)
    numThree = CDbl(txtThree.Text)
    numLowest = FindLowest(numOne, numTwo, numThree)
    txtLowest.Text = CStr(numLowest)
End Sub

Function FindLowest(x As Double, y As Double, z As Double) As Double
    'Find the lowest of three numbers denoted by x, y, and z
    Dim lowest As Double
    lowest = x
    If y < lowest Then
        lowest = y
    End If
    If z < lowest Then
        lowest = z
    End If
    Return lowest
End Function
```

(Assume the first three text boxes contain the numbers 7, 4, and 3.)

5. ```
Private Sub btnOutput_Click(...) Handles btnOutput.Click
    Dim num As Integer = 27
    If IsEven(num) Then
        MessageBox.Show(num & " is an even number.")
    Else
        MessageBox.Show(num & " is an odd number.")
    End If
End Sub

Function IsEven(n As Integer) As Boolean
    If n Mod 2 = 0 Then
        Return True
    Else
        Return False
```
```

```
    End If
  End Function
```

6.
```
Private Sub btnDisplay_Click(...) Handles btnDisplay.Click
  Dim dt As Date = #12/4/2016#
  txtOutput.Text = MonthAbbr(dt)
End Sub
```

```
Function MonthAbbr(dt As Date) As String
  Dim str As String = dt.ToString("D")
  Dim n As Integer = str.IndexOf(" ")
  Return str.Substring(n + 1, 3)
End Function
```

7.
```
Private Sub btnOutput_Click(...) Handles btnOutput.Click
  Dim taxableIncome As Decimal = 5000
  MessageBox.Show("Your state income tax is " &
              (StateTax(taxableIncome)).ToString("C") & ".")
End Sub
```

```
Function StateTax(income As Decimal) As Decimal
  'Calculate state tax for a single resident of Connecticut
  Select Case income
    Case Is <= 10000
      Return 0.03D * income
    Case Else
      Return 300 + (0.05D * (income - 10000))
  End Select
End Function
```

8.
```
Private Sub btnDisplay_Click(...) Handles btnDisplay.Click
  'Triple a number
  Dim num As Double = 5
  lstOutput.Items.Add(Triple(num))
  lstOutput.Items.Add(num)
End Sub
```

```
Function Triple(x As Double) As Double
  Dim num As Double = 3
  Return num * x
End Function
```

9.
```
Private Sub btnOutput_Click(...) Handles btnOutput.Click
  Dim word1 As String = "beauty"
  Dim word2 As String = "age"
  MessageBox.Show(First(word1, word2) & " before " & Last(word1, word2))
End Sub
```

```
Function First(w1 As String, w2 As String) As String
  If w1 < w2 Then
    Return w1
  Else
    Return w2
```

```
        End If
    End Function

    Function Last(w1 As String, w2 As String) As String
        If w1 > w2 Then
            Return w1
        Else
            Return w2
        End If
    End Function
```

10.
```
    Private Sub btnOutput_Click(...) Handles btnOutput.Click
        Dim num1 As Integer = 84
        Dim num2 As Integer = 96
        If IsAnA(num1, num2) Then
            MessageBox.Show("A average")
        Else
            MessageBox.Show("not an A average")
        End If
    End Sub

    Function IsAnA(n1 As Integer, n2 As Integer) As Boolean
        If ((n1 + n2) / 2) >= 89.5 Then
            Return True
        Else
            Return False
        End If
    End Function
```

In Exercises 11 and 12, identify the errors.

11.
```
    Private Sub btnDisplay_Click(...) Handles btnDisplay.Click
        'Select a greeting
        Dim answer As Integer
        answer = CInt(InputBox("Enter 1 or 2."))
        txtOutput.Text = CStr(Greeting(answer))
    End Sub

    Function Greeting(x As Integer) As Integer
        Return "hellohi ya".Substring(5 * (x − 1), 5)
    End Function
```

12.
```
    Private Sub btnDisplay_Click(...) Handles btnDisplay.Click
        Dim word As String
        word = InputBox("What is your favorite word?")
        txtOutput.Text = "When the word is written twice, " &
                        Twice(word) & " letters are used."
    End Sub

    Function Twice(w As String) As Integer
        'Compute twice the length of a string
        Dim len As Integer
        Return len = 2 * w.Length
    End Function
```

In Exercises 13 through 26, construct Function procedures to carry out the primary task(s) of the program.

13. **Area** To determine the number of square centimeters of tin needed to make a tin can, add the square of the radius of the bottom of the can to the product of the radius of the bottom and height of the can, and then multiply this sum by 6.283. Write a program that requests the radius and height of a tin can in centimeters as input and displays the number of square centimeters of tin required to make the can. See Fig. 5.3.

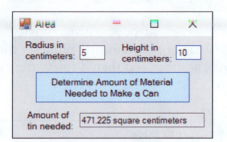

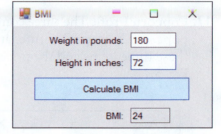

FIGURE 5.3 Possible outcome of Exercise 13.   **FIGURE 5.4** Possible outcome of Exercise 14.

14. **Body Mass Index** The federal government developed the body mass index (BMI) to determine ideal weights. Body mass index is calculated as 703 times the weight in pounds, divided by the square of the height in inches, and then rounded to the nearest whole number. Write a program that accepts a person's weight and height as input and gives the person's body mass index. See Fig. 5.4. **Note:** A BMI of 19 to 25 corresponds to a healthy weight.

15. **Hurricane** Table 5.2 gives the Saffir–Simpson scale for categorizing hurricanes. Write a program that requests a wind speed in miles/hour and displays the category of the storm. See Fig. 5.5.

TABLE 5.2	Rating of hurricanes.
Wind Speed (in mph)	**Rating**
74 to 95	Category One
96 to 110	Category Two
111 to 130	Category Three
131 to 155	Category Four
Over 155	Category Five

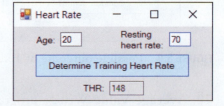

FIGURE 5.5 Possible outcome of Exercise 15.   **FIGURE 5.6** Possible outcome of Exercise 16.

16. Training Heart Rate In order for exercise to be beneficial to the cardiovascular system, the heart rate (number of heart beats per minute) must exceed a value called the *training heart rate*, THR. A person's THR can be calculated from his or her age and resting heart rate (pulse rate when first awakening) as follows:

(a) Calculate the maximum heart rate as 220 − age.

(b) Subtract the resting heart rate from the maximum heart rate.

(c) Multiply the result in step (b) by 60%, and then add the resting heart rate.

Write a program to request a person's age and resting heart rate as input and display his or her THR. See Fig. 5.6 on the previous page.

17. Popcorn Profit The three components for a serving of popcorn at a movie theater are popcorn, butter substitute, and a bucket. Write a program that requests the cost of these three items and the price of the serving as input and then displays the profit. See Fig. 5.7.

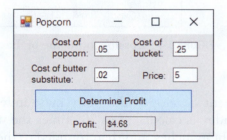

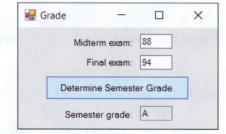

FIGURE 5.7   Possible outcome of Exercise 17.   **FIGURE 5.8   Possible outcome of Exercise 18.**

18. Semester Grade Write a program that requests the numeric grades on a midterm and a final exam and then uses a Function procedure to assign a semester grade (A, B, C, D, or F). The final exam should count twice as much as the midterm exam, the semester average should be rounded up to the nearest whole number, and the semester grade should be assigned by the following criteria: 90–100 (A), 80–89 (B) . . . . See Fig. 5.8. Use a function called Ceil that rounds noninteger numbers up to the next integer. The function Ceil can be defined by $\text{Ceil}(x) = -\text{Int}(-x)$.

19. Cost of Postage The original postage cost of airmail letters was 5 cents for the first ounce and 10 cents for each additional ounce. Write a program to compute the cost of a letter whose weight is given by the user in a text box. See Fig. 5.9. Use a function called Ceil that rounds noninteger numbers up to the next integer. The function Ceil can be defined by $\text{Ceil}(x) = -\text{Int}(-x)$.

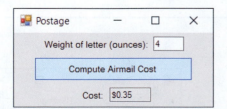

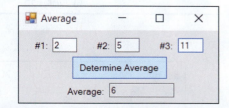

FIGURE 5.9   Possible outcome of Exercise 19.   **FIGURE 5.10   Possible outcome of Exercise 20.**

20. Average Value Write a program that requests three numbers as input and then determines the average of the three numbers. See Fig. 5.10.

21. **Maximum Value** Write a program that requests three numbers as input and then determines the largest of the three numbers. See Fig. 5.11.

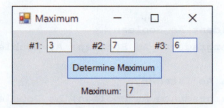
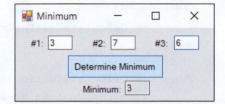

FIGURE 5.11   Possible outcome of Exercise 21.   FIGURE 5.12   Possible outcome of Exercise 22.

22. **Minimum Value** Write a program that requests three numbers as input and then determines the smallest of the three numbers. See Fig. 5.12.

23. **Address for a Letter** Write a program to request the name of a United States senator as input and display the address and salutation for a letter to the senator. See Fig. 5.13. Assume the name has two parts, and use a function to determine the senator's last name.

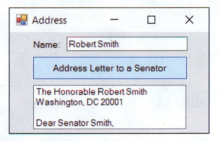
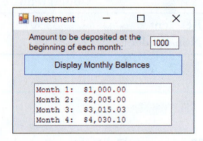

FIGURE 5.13   Possible outcome of Exercise 23.   FIGURE 5.14   Possible outcome of Exercise 24.

24. **Growth of an Investment** Suppose a fixed amount of money is deposited at the beginning of each month into an investment paying 6% interest compounded monthly. After each deposit is made, [new balance] = 1.005 * [previous balance one month ago] + [fixed amount]. Write a program that requests the fixed amount of the deposits as input and displays the balance after each of the first four deposits. See Fig. 5.14.

25. **Leap Year** Write a program that requests a year as input and then tells whether or not the year is a leap year. See Fig. 5.15. The program should use a Boolean-value function named IsLeapYear. *Hint:* Use the DateDiff function.

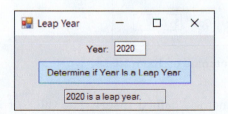
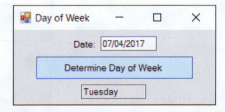

FIGURE 5.15   Possible outcome of Exercise 25.   FIGURE 5.16   Possible outcome of Exercise 26.

26. **Day of the Week** Write a program that requests a date as input and then gives the spelled-out day of the week for that date as output. See Fig. 5.16. The program should use a function with the following header.

```
Function DayOfWeek(dt As Date) As String
```

27. College Tuition Table 5.3 gives the cost per credit at a state university. Write a program that requests a student's resident status, standing, and number of credits taken, and then calculate the student's tuition. See Fig. 5.17. The program should use functions with headers

```
Function CalculateCostPerCredit(resident As Boolean,
                                undergraduate As Boolean) As Double
```
and
```
Function CalculateTuition(numCredits As Integer,
          resident As Boolean, undergraduate As Boolean) As Double
```

where, the second function calls the first function. Also, the program should check that the number of credits text box has a numeric entry before the calculation is made.

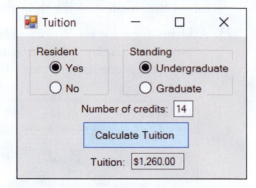

TABLE 5.3	Cost per credit.	
	Undergraduate	Graduate
Resident	$90	$110
Non-resident	$150	$180

FIGURE 5.17 Possible outcome of Exercise 27.

28. Camper Cabins A state park rents camper cabins to state residents for $65 per day for the first six days and then for $50 per day for any additional days. Non-residents pay $75 per day. Write a program that requests a camper's resident status and the number of days, and then calculates the cost of the rental. See Fig. 5.18. The program should use a function with a Boolean parameter *resident* and an Integer parameter *numDays* to calculate the cost.

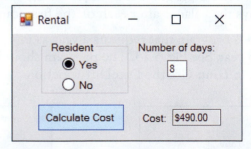

FIGURE 5.18 Possible outcome of Exercise 28.

29. Insert Method Visual Basic has a string method named **Insert**. The value of **strVar1.Insert(n, strVar2)** is ***strVar1*** with strVar2 inserted into it beginning at the nth position. For instance, if **strVar1 = "John Kennedy"** and **strVar2 = "F. "** then the value of **strVar1.Insert(5, strVar2)** is "John F. Kennedy". Write a function named *Embed* that performs the same task as the Insert method (without using the Insert method). For instance, the value of **Embed("John Kennedy", 5, "F. ")** should be "John F. Kennedy". The Embed function should use **Exit Function** to keep the program from crashing when the value of *n* is out of range.

30. Remove Method Visual Basic has a string method named **Remove**. The value of `strVar.Remove(n, m)` is strVar with *m* consecutive characters from it deleted beginning with the character in the *n*th position. For instance, if `strVar = "President"` then the value of `strVar.Remove(4, 2)` is "Present". Write a function named *Eliminate* that performs the same task as the Remove method (without using the Remove method). For instance, the value of `Eliminate("President", 4, 2)` should be "Present".

Solutions to Practice Problems 5.1

1. The parameter *n* is assigned a value of type Double and the parameter *x* is assigned a String value; therefore, the input consists of a number and a string. From the two lines shown here, there is no way to determine the type of the output. This can be determined only by looking at the definition of the function.

2. The two arguments in **FindLetter(word, num)** are in the wrong order. Since the two parameters in the header for the Function procedure have types Integer and String, in that order, the arguments must have the same types and order when the Function procedure is called. The function call should be **FindLetter(num, word)**. Visual Basic matches arguments to parameters based on their positions, not on their names.

5.2   Sub Procedures, Part I

Sub procedures are just Function procedures that don't return values. Sub procedures and Function procedures share the following features:

- Both are written as a separate block of code that can be called to perform a specific task.
- Both are used to break complex problems into small problems.
- Both are used to eliminate repetitive code.
- Both can be reused in other programs.
- Both make a program easier to read by separating it into logical units.
- Both have parameters that are declared in a header.

Sub procedures, however, do not return a value associated with their name. The most common uses of Sub procedures are to receive input, process input, or display output.

■ Defining and Calling Sub Procedures

The Sub procedures discussed in this section are defined by blocks of the form

```
Sub ProcedureName(par1 As Type1, par2 As Type2,..., parN As TypeN)
    statement(s)
End Sub
```

VideoNote
Sub
Procedures

The primary difference between Sub procedures and Function procedures is that Sub procedures perform tasks (such as displaying output) rather than return values. Like Function procedures, the names of Sub procedures must conform to the rules for naming variables. By convention, a Sub procedure's name begins with an uppercase letter and describes the procedure's purpose.

Sub procedures are called by statements of the form

```
ProcedureName(arg1, arg2, ..., argN)
```

When a Sub procedure is called, the value of each argument is assigned to the corresponding parameter, the statement(s) inside the procedure block is (are) carried out, and execution continues with the statement following the calling statement.

Here is an example of a Sub procedure.

```
Sub DisplaySum(num1 As Double, num2 As Double)
  Dim z As Double
  z = num1 + num2
  lstOutput.Items.Add(z)
End Sub
```

When a statement such as

```
DisplaySum(3, 4)
```

is executed, the number 3 is assigned to the parameter *num1*, the number 4 is assigned to the parameter *num2*, and the three statements inside the Sub procedure block are carried out. As a result, the number 7 is displayed in the list box. We say that the numbers 3 and 4 are **passed** to the Sub procedure. See Fig. 5.19.

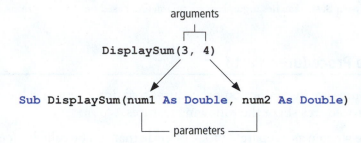

FIGURE 5.19   **Passing arguments to a Sub procedure.**

■ Variables and Expressions as Arguments

Just as with function calls, the arguments in Sub procedure calls can be literals (as in Fig. 5.19), variables, or expressions.

 Example 1   **Add Numbers**   The following program calls an expanded version of the Sub procedure DisplaySum three times. The first time the arguments are literals, the second time the arguments are variables, and the third time the arguments are expressions. In the second call of DisplaySum, the values of the variables are passed to the Sub procedure. In the third call, the expressions are evaluated and the resulting numbers are passed to the Sub procedure.

```
Private Sub btnAddNumbers_Click(...) Handles btnAddNumbers.Click
  DisplaySum(1, 2)
  Dim x As Double = 3
  Dim y As Double = 4
  DisplaySum(x, y)
  DisplaySum(2 * x, y + 5)
End Sub

Sub DisplaySum(num1 As Double, num2 As Double)
  Dim z As Double
  z = num1 + num2
  lstOutput.Items.Add("The sum of " & num1 & " and " & num2 &
                      " is " & z & ".")
End Sub
```

[Run, and click on the button.]

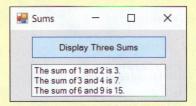

 Example 2 **Population Density** The following program passes a string and two numbers to a Sub procedure. When the Sub procedure is first called, the string parameter *state* is assigned the value "Hawaii", and the numeric parameters *pop* and *landArea* are assigned the values 1,420,000 and 6423, respectively. The Sub procedure then uses these parameters to carry out the task of calculating and displaying the population density of Hawaii. The second calling statement assigns different values to the parameters.

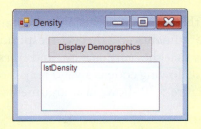

OBJECT	PROPERTY	SETTING
frmDensities	Text	Density
btnDisplay	Text	Display Demographics
lstDensity		

```
Private Sub btnDisplay_Click(...) Handles btnDisplay.Click
  'Calculate the population densities of states
  Dim state As String, pop, landArea As Double
  lstDensity.Items.Clear()
  state = "Hawaii"
  pop = 1420000
  landArea = 6423
  CalculateDensity(state, pop, landArea)
  lstDensity.Items.Add("")
  state = "Alaska"
  pop = 736732
  landArea = 570600
  CalculateDensity(state, pop, landArea)
End Sub

Sub CalculateDensity(state As String, pop As Double, landArea As Double)
  'The density (number of people per square mile)
  'will be displayed rounded to one decimal place.
  Dim density As Double
  density = pop / landArea
  lstDensity.Items.Add("The density of " & state & " is")
  lstDensity.Items.Add(density.ToString("N1") & " people per square mile.")
End Sub
```

[Run, and then click on the button.]

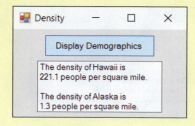

Notice that in the calling statement

```
CalculateDensity(state, pop, landArea)
```

the variable types have the order String, Double, and Double; the same types and order as in the Sub procedure header. This order is essential. For instance, the calling statement cannot be written as

```
CalculateDensity(pop, landArea, state)
```

In Example 2 the arguments and parameters have the same name. Using same names sometimes makes a program easier to read. However, arguments and their corresponding parameters often have different names. What matters is that the *order*, *number*, and *types* of the arguments and parameters match. For instance, the following code is a valid revision of the btnDisplay_Click event procedure in Example 2. (Figure 5.20 shows how arguments are passed to parameters with this code.)

```
Private Sub btnDisplay_Click(...) Handles btnDisplay.Click
    'Calculate the population densities of states.
    lstDensity.Items.Clear()
    Dim s As String, p As Double, a As Double
    s = "Hawaii"
    p = 1420000
    a = 6423
    CalculateDensity(s, p, a)
    lstDensity.Items.Add("")
    s = "Alaska"
    p = 736732
    a = 570600
    CalculateDensity(s, p, a)
End Sub
```

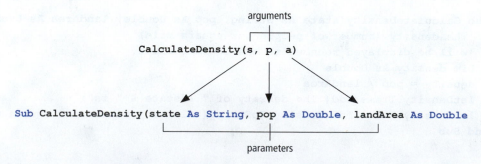

FIGURE 5.20   **Passing arguments to a Sub procedure.**

Sub Procedures Having No Parameters

Sub procedures, like Function procedures, are not required to have any parameters. A parameterless Sub procedure can be used to give instructions or provide a description of a program.

Example 3   Population Density   The following variation of Example 2 gives the population density of a single state. The parameterless Sub procedure DescribeTask gives an explanation of the program.

```
Private Sub btnDisplay_Click(...) Handles btnDisplay.Click
  DescribeTask()
  CalculateDensity("Hawaii", 1420000, 6423)
End Sub

Sub DescribeTask()
  lstOutput.Items.Clear()
  lstOutput.Items.Add("This program displays the")
  lstOutput.Items.Add("population density of the last state")
  lstOutput.Items.Add("to become part of the United States.")
End Sub

Sub CalculateDensity(state As String, pop As Double, landArea As Double)
  Dim density As Double
  density = pop / landArea
  lstOutput.Items.Add("")  'insert a blank line
  lstOutput.Items.Add("The population density of " & state & " is")
  lstOutput.Items.Add(density.ToString("N1") & " people per square mile.")
End Sub
```

[Run, and then click on the button.]

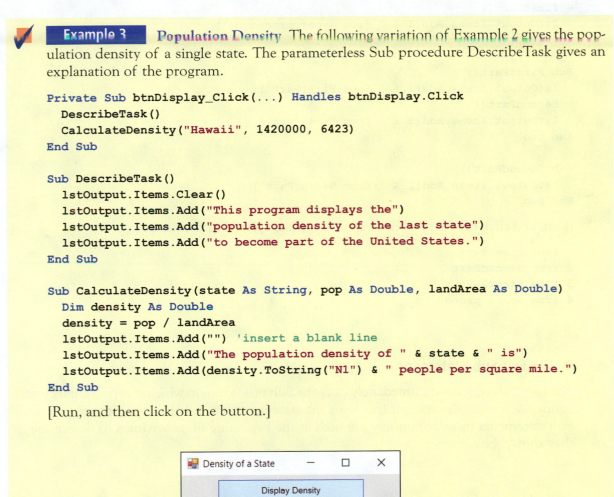

Sub Procedures Calling Other Sub Procedures

A Sub procedure can call another Sub procedure. If so, after the End Sub statement at the end of the called Sub procedure is reached, execution continues with the line in the calling Sub procedure following the calling statement.

Example 4   **Call Sub Procedures** In the following program, the Sub procedure First-Part calls the Sub procedure SecondPart. After the statements in SecondPart are executed, execution continues with the remaining statements in the Sub procedure FirstPart before returning to the event procedure. The form contains a button and a list box.

```vb
Private Sub btnDisplay_Click(...) Handles btnDisplay.Click
  'Demonstrate Sub procedure calling other Sub procedures
  FirstPart()
  lstOutput.Items.Add(4 & " from event procedure")
End Sub

Sub FirstPart()
  lstOutput.Items.Add(1 & " from FirstPart")
  SecondPart()
  lstOutput.Items.Add(3 & " from FirstPart")
End Sub

Sub SecondPart()
  lstOutput.Items.Add(2 & " from SecondPart")
End Sub
```

[Run, and click on the button. The following is displayed in the list box.]

```
1 from FirstPart
2 from SecondPart
3 from FirstPart
4 from event procedure
```

■ The Exit Sub Statement

The Exit Sub statement immediately exits the Sub procedure in which it appears. Execution continues with the statement following the statement that called the Sub procedure. Exit Sub statements most commonly are used at the beginning of procedures to determine if they should be executed.

 Example 5   **Demonstrate the use of Exit Sub** The following Sub procedure uses an Exit Sub statement to check the validity of an input value and determine if the main part of the procedure should be executed.

```vb
Sub AgeNextYear(age As Integer)
  If age < 0 Then
    MessageBox.Show("Age cannot be a negative number.")
    Exit Sub
  End If
  MessageBox.Show("Next year you will be " & (age + 1) & " years old.")
End Sub
```

■ **Comments**

1. Sub procedures allow programmers to focus on the main flow of a complex task and defer the details of implementation. Modern programs use them liberally. This method of program construction is known as **top-down** design. As a rule, a Sub procedure should perform only one task, or several closely related tasks, and should be kept relatively small.

2. The first line inside a Sub procedure is often a comment statement describing the task performed by the Sub procedure. If necessary, several comment statements should be used. Conventional programming practice also recommends that all variables used by the Sub procedure be listed in comment statements with their meanings. In this text, we give several examples of this practice, but adhere to it only when the variables are especially numerous or lack descriptive names.

3. In Section 5.1, we saw that Word Completion and Parameter Info help us write a function call. These IntelliSense features provide the same assistance for Sub procedure calls. (Of course, Word Completion and Parameter Info work only after the Sub procedure has been created.) See Fig. 5.21.

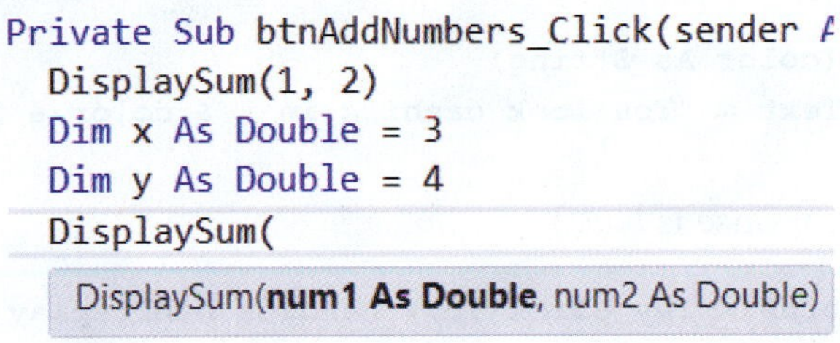

```
Private Sub btnAddNumbers_Click(sender A
    DisplaySum(1, 2)
    Dim x As Double = 3
    Dim y As Double = 4
    DisplaySum(

    DisplaySum(num1 As Double, num2 As Double)
```

FIGURE 5.21 The Parameter Info help feature.

Practice Problems 5.2

1. What is the difference between an event procedure and a Sub procedure?

2. What is wrong with the following code?

```
Private Sub btnDisplay_Click(...) Handles btnDisplay.Click
  Dim phone As String
  phone = mtbPhoneNum.Text
  AreaCode(phone)
End Sub


Sub AreaCode()
  txtOutput.Text = "Your area code is " & phone.Substring(0, 3)
End Sub
```

EXERCISES 5.2

In Exercises 1 through 20, determine the output displayed when the button is clicked.

1. ```
Private Sub btnDisplay_Click(...) Handles btnDisplay.Click
    Piano(88)
End Sub
```
```

```
     Sub Piano(num As Integer)
       txtOutput.Text = num & " keys on a piano"
     End Sub
```

2.
```
  Private Sub btnDisplay_Click(...) Handles btnDisplay.Click
    'Opening line of Moby Dick
    FirstLine("Ishmael")
  End Sub


  Sub FirstLine(name As String)
    'Display first line
    txtOutput.Text = "Call me " & name & "."
  End Sub
```

3.
```
  Private Sub btnDisplay_Click(...) Handles btnDisplay.Click
    Dim color As String
    color = InputBox("What is your favorite color?")
    Flattery(color)
  End Sub


  Sub Flattery(color As String)
    txtOutput.Text = "You look dashing in " & color & "."
  End Sub
```
(Assume the response is *blue*.)

4.
```
  Private Sub btnDisplay_Click(...) Handles btnDisplay.Click
    Dim num As Double = 144
    Gross(num)
  End Sub


  Sub Gross(amount As Double)
    txtOutput.Text = amount & " items in a gross"
  End Sub
```

5.
```
  Private Sub btnDisplay_Click(...) Handles btnDisplay.Click
    Dim hours As Double
    hours = 24
    Minutes(60 * hours)
  End Sub


  Sub Minutes(num As Double)
    txtOutput.Text = num & " minutes in a day"
  End Sub
```

6.
```
  Private Sub btnDisplay_Click(...) Handles btnDisplay.Click
    Dim states, senators As Double
    states = 50
    senators = 2
    Senate(states * senators)
  End Sub


  Sub Senate(num As Double)
    txtBox.Text = "The number of U.S. Senators is " & num
  End Sub
```

7.
```
Private Sub btnDisplay_Click(...) Handles btnDisplay.Click
  Question()
  Answer()
End Sub

Sub Answer()
  lstOutput.Items.Add("Because they were invented in the northern")
  lstOutput.Items.Add("hemisphere where sundials go clockwise.")
End Sub

Sub Question()
  lstOutput.Items.Add("Why do clocks run clockwise?")
  lstOutput.Items.Add("")
End Sub
```

8.
```
Private Sub btnDisplay_Click(...) Handles btnDisplay.Click
  Answer()
  Question()
End Sub

Sub Answer()
  lstOutput.Items.Add("The answer is 9W.")
  lstOutput.Items.Add("What is the question?")
End Sub

Sub Question()
  'Note: "Wagner" is pronounced "Vagner"
  lstOutput.Items.Add("Do you spell your name with a V,")
  lstOutput.Items.Add("Mr. Wagner?")
End Sub
```

9.
```
Private Sub btnDisplay_Click(...) Handles btnDisplay.Click
  'Beginning of Tale of Two Cities
  Times("best")
  Times("worst")
End Sub

Sub Times(word As String)
  'Display sentence
  lstOutput.Items.Add("It was the " & word & " of times.")
End Sub
```

10.
```
Private Sub btnDisplay_Click(...) Handles btnDisplay.Click
  'Sentence using number, thing, and place
  Sentence(168, "hour", "a week")
  Sentence(76, "trombone", "the big parade")
End Sub

Sub Sentence(num As Double, thing As String, where As String)
  lstOutput.Items.Add(num & " " & thing & "s in " & where)
End Sub
```

11.
```
Private Sub btnDisplay_Click(...) Handles btnDisplay.Click
  'The fates of Henry the Eighth's six wives
  CommonFates()
  lstOutput.Items.Add("died")
  CommonFates()
  lstOutput.Items.Add("survived")
End Sub


Sub CommonFates()
  'The most common fates
  lstOutput.Items.Add("divorced")
  lstOutput.Items.Add("beheaded")
End Sub
```

12.
```
Private Sub btndisplay_Click(...) Handles btndisplay.Click
  Dim pres, college As String
  pres = "Bush"
  college = "Yale"
  PresAlmaMater(pres, college)
  pres = "Obama"
  college = "Columbia"
  PresAlmaMater(pres, college)
End Sub


Sub PresAlmaMater(pres As String, college As String)
  lstOutput.Items.Add("President " & pres & " is a graduate of " &
                      college & ".")
End Sub
```

13.
```
Private Sub btnDisplay_Click(...) Handles btnDisplay.Click
  HowMany(24)
  lstOutput.Items.Add("a pie.")
End Sub


Sub HowMany(num As Integer)
  What(num)
  lstOutput.Items.Add("baked in")
End Sub


Sub What(num As Integer)
  lstOutput.Items.Add(num & " blackbirds")
End Sub
```

14.
```
Private Sub btnDisplay_Click(...) Handles btnDisplay.Click
  'Good advice to follow
  Advice()
End Sub


Sub Advice()
  lstOutput.Items.Add("Keep cool, but don't freeze.")
  Source()
End Sub
```

```
Sub Source()
    lstOutput.Items.Add("Source: A jar of mayonnaise.")
End Sub
```

15.
```
Private Sub btnDisplay_Click(...) Handles btnDisplay.Click
    Dim word As String, num As Integer
    word = "Visual Basic"
    num = 6
    FirstPart(word, num)
End Sub

Sub FirstPart(term As String, digit As Integer)
    txtOutput.Text = "The first " & digit & " letters are " &
                  term.Substring(0, digit) & "."
End Sub
```

16.
```
Private Sub btnDisplay_Click(...) Handles btnDisplay.Click
    Dim dt As Date = Today
    DisplayTypeOfDay(dt)
End Sub

Sub DisplayTypeOfDay(dt As Date)
    If IsWeekendDay(dt) Then
        txtOutput.Text = "Today is a weekend day."
    Else
        txtOutput.Text = "Today is a weekday."
    End If
End Sub

Function IsWeekendDay(dt As Date) As Boolean
    Dim jour As String = dt.ToString("D")
    If jour.StartsWith("Saturday") Or jour.StartsWith("Sunday") Then
        Return True
    Else
        Return False
    End If
End Function
```

17.
```
Private Sub btnDisplay_Click(...) Handles btnDisplay.Click
    Dim cost As Double = 250
    DisplayBill(cost, ShippingCost(cost))
End Sub

Function ShippingCost(costOfGoods As Double) As Double
    Select Case costOfGoods
        Case Is < 100
            Return 10
        Case Is < 500
            Return 15
        Case Else
            Return 20
    End Select
End Function
```

```
    Sub DisplayBill(cost As Double, addedCost As Double)
      lstOutput.Items.Add("Cost: " & cost.ToString("C"))
      lstOutput.Items.Add("Shipping cost: " & addedCost.ToString("C"))
      lstOutput.Items.Add("Total cost: " & (cost + addedCost).ToString("C"))
    End Sub
```

18.
```
    Private Sub btnDisplay_Click(...) Handles btnDisplay.Click
      Dim language As String = "Visual Basic"
      ShowWord(language)
    End Sub

    Sub ShowWord(word As String)
      If word.Length < 5 Then
        txtOutput.ForeColor = Color.Red
      Else
        txtOutput.ForeColor = Color.Blue
      End If
      txtOutput.Text = word
    End Sub
```

19.
```
    Private Sub btnDisplay_Click(...) Handles btnDisplay.Click
      Dim grade = CDbl(InputBox("What is your numeric grade?", "Grade"))
      ShowResult(grade)
    End Sub

    Sub ShowResult(grade As Double)
      If (grade < 0) Or (grade > 100) Then
        MessageBox.Show("Improper grade")
        Exit Sub
      End If
      If PassedExam(grade) Then
        txtOutput.Text = "You passed with a grade of " & grade & "."
      Else
        txtOutput.Text = "You failed the exam."
      End If
    End Sub

    Function PassedExam(grade As Double) As Boolean
      Select Case grade
        Case Is >= 60
          Return True
        Case Else
          Return False
      End Select
    End Function
```

    (Assume the response is 92.)

20.
```
    Private Sub btnDisplay_Click(...) Handles btnDisplay.Click
      Dim anyDate As Date
      anyDate = CDate(InputBox("Input a past date. (mm/dd/yyyy)"))
      ShowCentury(anyDate)
    End Sub
```

```
Sub ShowCentury(anyDate As Date)
  Select Case anyDate
    Case Is >= #1/1/2000#
      txtOutput.Text = "twenty-first century"
    Case Is >= #1/1/1900#
      txtOutput.Text = "twentieth century"
    Case Else
      txtOutput.Text = "prior to the twentieth century"
  End Select
End Sub
```

(Assume the response is 6/5/1955.)

In Exercises 21 through 24, find the errors.

21.
```
Private Sub btnDisplay_Click(...) Handles btnDisplay.Click
  Dim n As Integer = 5
  Alphabet()
End Sub

Sub Alphabet(n As Integer)
  txtOutput.Text = "abcdefghijklmnopqrstuvwxyz".Substring(0, n)
End Sub
```

22.
```
Private Sub btnDisplay_Click(...) Handles btnDisplay.Click
  Dim word As String, number As Double
  word = "seven"
  number = 7
  Display(word, number)
End Sub

Sub Display(num As Double, term As String)
  txtOutput.Text = num & " " & term
End Sub
```

23.
```
Private Sub btnDisplay_Click(...) Handles btnDisplay.Click
  Dim name As String
  name = InputBox("Name")
  Handles(name)
End Sub

Sub Handles(moniker As String)
  txtOutput.Text = "Your name is " & moniker
End Sub
```

24.
```
Private Sub btnDisplay_Click(...) Handles btnDisplay.Click
  Dim num As Integer = 2
  Tea(num)
End Sub

Sub Tea()
  txtOutput.Text = "Tea for " & num
End Sub
```

In Exercises 25 through 28, rewrite the program with the output performed by a call to a Sub procedure.

25.
```vb
Private Sub btnDisplay_Click(...) Handles btnDisplay.Click
    'Display a lucky number
    Dim num As Integer = 7
    txtOutput.Text = num & " is a lucky number."
End Sub
```

26.
```vb
Private Sub btnDisplay_Click(...) Handles btnDisplay.Click
    'Greet a friend
    Dim name As String = "Jack"
    txtOutput.Text = "Hi, " & name
End Sub
```

27.
```vb
Private Sub btnDisplay_Click(...) Handles btnDisplay.Click
    'Information about trees
    Dim tree As String, ht As Double
    tree = "redwood"
    ht = 362
    lstBox.Items.Add("The tallest " & tree &
                    " tree in the U.S. is " & ht & " feet.")
    tree = "pine"
    ht = 223
    lstBox.Items.Add("The tallest " & tree &
                    " tree in the U.S. is " & ht & " feet.")
End Sub
```

28.
```vb
Private Sub btnDisplay_Click(...) Handles btnDisplay.Click
    Dim city As String
    Dim householdIncome As Decimal 'median household income
    lstOutput.Items.Clear()
    city = "San Jose"
    householdIncome = 81349D
    lstOutput.Items.Add("In 2012, the median household income for " &
        city & " was " & householdIncome.ToString("C0") & ".")
    city = "Hartford"
    householdIncome = 28931D
    lstOutput.Items.Add("In 2012, the median household income for " &
        city & " was " & householdIncome.ToString("C0") & ".")
End Sub
```

In Exercises 29 through 32, write a program that displays the output shown. The last two lines of the output should be displayed by one or more Sub procedures using data passed by variables from an event procedure.

29.
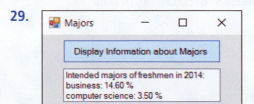

30.
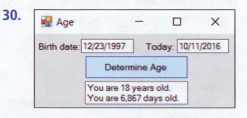

31.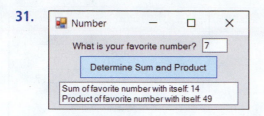

32.

33. Old McDonald Had a Farm Write a program to display three verses of "Old McDonald Had a Farm". The primary verse, with variables substituted for the animals and sounds, should be contained in a Sub procedure. The program should pass the following animal and sound pairs to the Sub procedure: lamb, baa; duck, quack; firefly, blink. The first verse of the output should be

```
Old McDonald had a farm. Eyi eyi oh.
And on his farm he had a lamb. Eyi eyi oh.
With a baa baa here, and a baa baa there.
Here a baa, there a baa, everywhere a baa baa.
Old McDonald had a farm. Eyi eyi oh.
```

34. Tipping Write a program to compute tips for services rendered. The program should request the person's occupation, the amount of the bill, and the percentage tip as input and pass this information to a Sub procedure to display the person and the tip. A sample run is shown in Fig. 5.22.

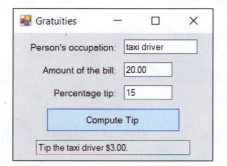
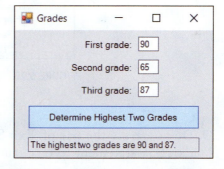

FIGURE 5.22 Possible outcome of Exercise 34.   **FIGURE 5.23** Possible outcome of Exercise 35.

35. Grades Write a program that requests three grades as input and then passes the three grades to a Sub procedure that determines and displays the highest two grades. See Fig. 5.23.

36. Semester Grade Write a program that requests a student's first name, last name, and the numeric grades on three exams, and then uses a Sub procedure to display the student's name and semester grade (A, B, C, D, or F). A Function procedure (called by the Sub procedure) should be used to calculate the semester grade. The lowest grade should be dropped, the semester average should be rounded to the nearest whole number, and the semester grade should be assigned using the following criteria: 90–100 (A), 80–89 (B), . . . See Fig. 5.24 on the next page.

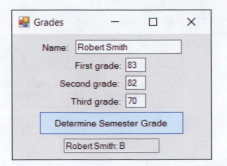

FIGURE 5.24 Possible outcome of Exercise 36.   **FIGURE 5.25** Possible outcome of Exercise 37.

37. **Alphabetize Two Words** Write a program that requests two words as input and then passes the words to a Sub procedure that displays the words in alphabetical order. See Fig. 5.25.

38. **Birthday Song** Write a program that requests a name and calls a Sub procedure to display the birthday song with the name inserted into the song. See Fig. 5.26.

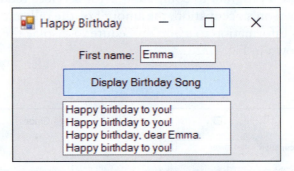

FIGURE 5.26 Possible outcome of Exercise 38.

39. **Demonstrate the use of Exit Sub** Rewrite the Sub procedure in Exercise 20 using an Exit Sub statement to terminate the Sub procedure when the date input is not in the past.

40. **Demonstrate the use of Exit Sub** In the following Sub procedure *numStr* is the (string) contents of a text box into which the user was requested to enter a number. Insert an If block containing an Exit Sub statement into the Sub procedure that will prevent the program from crashing when the contents of the text box is not a number. For example, the user might have entered "seven" into the text box, instead of 7.

```
Sub ShowParity(numString As String)
  txtOutput.Text = numString
  Select Case (CInt(numString) Mod 2)
    Case 0
      txtOutput.Text &= " rounds to an even number."
    Case 1, - 1
      txtOutput.Text &= " rounds to an odd number."
  End Select
End Sub
```

1. The header of an event procedure has parameters (such as *e* and "sender") that are provided automatically by Visual Basic, and the procedure is invoked when an event is raised. On the other hand, a Sub procedure is invoked by a line of code containing the name of the Sub procedure.

2. The statement **Sub AreaCode()** must be replaced by **Sub AreaCode(phone As String)**. Whenever a value is passed to a Sub procedure, the Sub statement must provide a parameter to receive the value.

5.3   Sub Procedures, Part II

In the previous section values were passed to Sub procedures. In this section we show how to pass values back from Sub procedures.

■ Passing by Value

In Section 5.1, all argument variables passed to parameter variables were passed by value. That is, they retained their original value after the function was called—regardless of what changes were made to the value of the parameter inside the Function procedure. Example 1 illustrates that argument variables are also passed by value to parameter variables of Sub procedures.

Example 1   **Pass by Value**   The following program illustrates the fact that changes to the value of a parameter have no effect on the value of the argument in the calling statement:

```
Private Sub btnDisplay_Click(...) Handles btnDisplay.Click
  'Illustrate that a change in value of a parameter
  'does not alter the value of the corresponding argument
  Dim amt As Double = 2
  lstResults.Items.Add(amt & " from event procedure")
  Triple(amt)
  lstResults.Items.Add(amt & " from event procedure")
End Sub

Sub Triple(num As Double)
  'Triple a number
  lstResults.Items.Add(num & " from Sub procedure")
  num = 3 * num
  lstResults.Items.Add(num & " from Sub procedure")
End Sub
```

[Run, and then click the button. The following is displayed in the list box.]

```
2 from event procedure
2 from Sub procedure
6 from Sub procedure
2 from event procedure
```

When a variable is passed by value, two memory locations are involved. Figure 5.27 shows the status of the memory locations as the program in Example 1 executes. At the time the Sub procedure is called, a temporary second memory location for the parameter is set aside for the Sub procedure's use and the value of the argument is copied into that location. After the completion of the Sub procedure, the temporary memory location is released, and the value in it is lost.

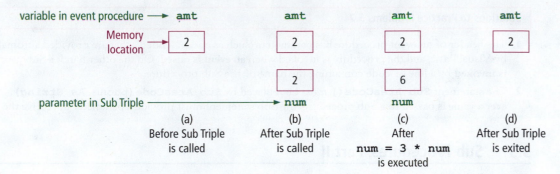

FIGURE 5.27 Passing a variable by value to a Sub procedure.

■ Passing by Reference

Another way to pass a variable to a Sub procedure is called "By Reference". In this case the parameter is preceded by the keyword ByRef. Suppose a variable, call it *arg*, appears as an argument in a procedure call, and its corresponding parameter in the Sub procedure's header, call it *par*, is preceded by ByRef. After the Sub procedure has been executed, *arg* will have whatever value *par* had in the Sub procedure.

In Example 1, if the header of the Sub procedure is changed to

```
Sub Triple(ByRef num As Double)
```

then the last number of the output in Example 1 will be 6. Although this feature may be surprising at first glance, it provides a means for passing values from a Sub procedure back to the place from which the Sub procedure was called. Different names may be used for an argument and its corresponding parameter, but only one memory location is involved. Initially, the btnDisplay_Click() event procedure allocates a memory location to hold the value of *amt* [Fig. 5.28(a)]. When the Sub procedure is called, the parameter *num* becomes the Sub procedure's name for this memory location [Fig. 5.28(b)]. When the value of *num* is tripled, the value in the memory location becomes 6 [Fig. 5.28(c)]. After the completion of the Sub procedure, the parameter name *num* is forgotten; however, its value lives on in *amt* [Fig. 5.28(d)]. The variable *amt* is said to be **passed by reference**.

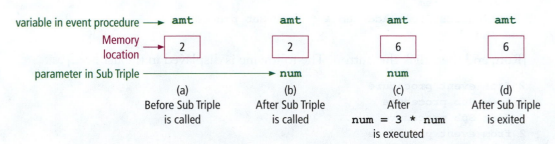

FIGURE 5.28 Passing a variable by reference to a Sub procedure.

Note: The Sub procedure Triple discussed above is solely for illustrative purposes and is not representative of the way Sub procedures are used in practice. Examples 2 and 3 show typical uses of Sub procedures.

Example 2   **Add Numbers** The following program uses a Sub procedure to acquire input. The variables *x* and *y* are not assigned values prior to the execution of the first procedure call. Therefore, before the procedure call is executed, they have the value 0. After the procedure call is executed, however, they have the values entered into the text boxes. These values then are passed by the second procedure call to the Sub procedure DisplaySum.

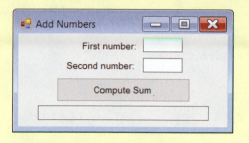

OBJECT	PROPERTY	SETTING
frmAdd	Text	Add Numbers
lblFirstNum	Text	First number:
txtFirstNum		
lblSecondNum	Text	Second number:
txtSecondNum		
btnCompute	Text	Compute Sum
txtResult	ReadOnly	True

```
Private Sub btnCompute_Click(...) Handles btnCompute.Click
  'This program requests two numbers and
  'displays the two numbers and their sum.
  Dim x, y As Double
  GetNumbers(x, y)
  DisplaySum(x, y)
End Sub

Sub GetNumbers(ByRef x As Double, ByRef y As Double)
  'Retrieve the two numbers from the text boxes
  x = CDbl(txtFirstNum.Text)
  y = CDbl(txtSecondNum.Text)
End Sub

Sub DisplaySum(num1 As Double, num2 As Double)
  'Display two numbers and their sum
  Dim sum As Double
  sum = num1 + num2
  txtResult.Text = "The sum of " & num1 & " and " &
                  num2 & " is " & sum & "."
End Sub
```

[Run, type 2 and 3 into the top two text boxes, and then click on the button.]

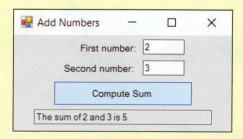

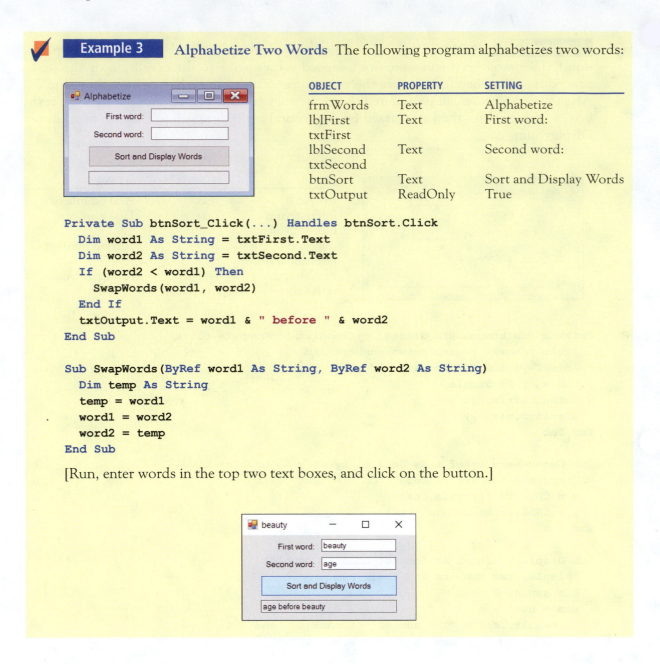

OBJECT	PROPERTY	SETTING
frmWords	Text	Alphabetize
lblFirst	Text	First word:
txtFirst		
lblSecond	Text	Second word:
txtSecond		
btnSort	Text	Sort and Display Words
txtOutput	ReadOnly	True

```vb
Private Sub btnSort_Click(...) Handles btnSort.Click
  Dim word1 As String = txtFirst.Text
  Dim word2 As String = txtSecond.Text
  If (word2 < word1) Then
    SwapWords(word1, word2)
  End If
  txtOutput.Text = word1 & " before " & word2
End Sub

Sub SwapWords(ByRef word1 As String, ByRef word2 As String)
  Dim temp As String
  temp = word1
  word1 = word2
  word2 = temp
End Sub
```

[Run, enter words in the top two text boxes, and click on the button.]

Sub Procedures That Return a Single Value

A Sub procedure having the ByRef keyword in its list of parameters can be thought of as returning values to the calling statement. In Examples 2 and 3, the Sub procedures returned two values to the event procedure. Sub procedures also can be used to return just a single value. However, good programming practice dictates that unless the Sub procedure does more that just return a single value, it should be replaced by a Function procedure. For instance, consider the following procedure call and Sub procedure combination where the Sub procedure returns a single value, namely the sum of two numbers:

```vb
CalculateSum(x, y, s)
```

```vb
Sub CalculateSum(num1 As Double, num2 As Double, ByRef sum As Double)
  'Add the values of num1 and num2
  sum = num1 + num2
End Sub
```

It should be replaced with the combination

```
s = CalculateSum(x, y)

Function CalculateSum(num1 As Double, num2 As Double) As Double
  Dim sum As Double
  sum = num1 + num2
  Return sum
End Function
```

■ Scope and Lifetime of Variables and Constants

The **scope** of a variable or constant is the portion of the program that can refer to it. For instance, a variable or constant declared inside an If or a Select Case block has **block scope** and cannot be accessed outside the block. When a variable or constant is declared inside a Function, Sub, or event procedure, but not within a block, the variable is visible to any code inside the procedure that follows the declaration. The variable is not visible outside the procedure. We can think of the variable as having block scope where the procedure is the block.

A variable or constant declared outside a procedure is said to have **class scope** and can be referred to by any procedure. A variable or constant declared in a procedure or block is called a **local variable** or a **local constant**. Good programming practice dictates that the scope of a variable or constant be as narrow as possible. For a variable, this reduces the number of places in which its value can be modified incorrectly or accidentally.

When a variable or constant is declared, a portion of memory is set aside to hold its value. For variables or constants having block scope, the memory is released when the block terminates. For other local variables or constants declared inside a general procedure, the memory is released when the procedure's End Function or End Sub statement is reached. The **lifetime** of the variable or constant is the period during which it remains in memory.

Example 4   **Scope of Variables** The following program illustrates the fact that variables are local to the part of the program in which they reside. The variable *x* in the event procedure and the variable *x* in the Sub procedure are treated as different variables. Visual Basic handles them as if their names were separate, such as xbtnDisplay_Click and xTrivial. Also, each time the Sub procedure is called, the value of variable *x* inside the Sub procedure is reset to 0.

```
Private Sub btnDisplay_Click(...) Handles btnDisplay.Click
  'Demonstrate the local nature of variables
  Dim x As Double = 2
  lstResults.Items.Add(x & " : event procedure")
  Trivial()
  lstResults.Items.Add(x & " : event procedure")
  Trivial()
  lstResults.Items.Add(x & " : event procedure")
End Sub
```

```
Sub Trivial()
  Dim x As Double
  lstResults.Items.Add(x & " : Sub procedure")
  x = 3
  lstResults.Items.Add(x & " : Sub procedure")
End Sub
```

[Run, and then click on the button.]

```
Scope Demo        —   □   ✕

       Display Results

  2 : event procedure
  0 : Sub procedure
  3 : Sub procedure
  2 : event procedure
  0 : Sub procedure
  3 : Sub procedure
  2 : event procedure
```

VideoNote

Debugging Functions and Sub Procedures

■ Debugging

Programs with Sub procedures are easier to debug. Each Sub procedure can be checked individually before being placed into the program.

In Appendix D, the section "Stepping through a Program Containing a General Procedure: Chapter 5" uses the Visual Basic debugger to trace the flow through a program and observe the interplay between arguments and parameters.

■ Comments

1. In this textbook, passing by reference is used primarily to acquire input.

2. When an argument that is a literal, a named constant, or an expression is passed to a procedure, there is no difference between passing it by reference and passing it by value. Only a variable argument can possibly have its value changed by a Sub procedure.

Practice Problems 5.3

1. In Example 3, change the header of the Sub procedure to

```
Sub SwapWords(ByRef word1 As String, word2 As String)
```

and determine the output when the input is *beauty* and *age*.

2. When the following program is entered, Visual Basic will display a wavy green line under the argument *state* in the fourth line. However, there is no wavy line under the argument *pop*. What do you think the reason is for Visual Basic's concern?

```
Private Sub btnDisplay_Click(...) Handles btnDisplay.Click
  Dim state As String
  Dim pop As Double
  InputData(state, pop)
  txtOutput.Text = state & " has population " & pop.ToString("N0")
End Sub
```

```
Sub InputData(ByRef state As String, ByRef pop As Double)
  state = "California"
  pop = 34888000
End Sub
```

EXERCISES 5.3

In Exercises 1 through 10, determine the output displayed when the button is clicked on.

1.
```
Private Sub btnDisplay_Click(...) Handles btnDisplay.Click
  Dim name As String = ""
  Dim yob As Integer
  GetVita(name, yob)
  txtOutput.Text = name & " was born in the year " & yob & "."
End Sub

Sub GetVita(ByRef name As String, ByRef yob As Integer)
  name = "Gabriel"
  yob = 1980 'year of birth
End Sub
```

2.
```
Private Sub btnDisplay_Click(...) Handles btnDisplay.Click
  Dim country As String = ""
  Dim pop As Double
  GetFacts(country, pop)
  txtOutput.Text = "The population of " & country & " is about " &
                   pop.ToString("N0") & "."
End Sub

Sub GetFacts(ByRef country As String, ByRef pop As Double)
  country = "the United States"
  pop = 315000000 'population
End Sub
```

3.
```
Private Sub btnDisplay_Click(...) Handles btnDisplay.Click
  Dim state As String = ""
  Dim flower As String = ""
  GetFacts(state, flower)
  txtOutput.Text = "The state flower of " & state &
                   " is the " & flower & "."
End Sub

Sub GetFacts(ByRef place As String, ByRef plant As String)
  place = "Alaska"
  plant = "Forget Me Not"
End Sub
```

4.
```
Private Sub btnDisplay_Click(...) Handles btnDisplay.Click
  Dim film As String = ""
  Dim year As Integer
  GetFacts(film, year)
  txtOutput.Text = film & " won the award in " & year & "."
End Sub
```

```
Sub GetFacts(ByRef movie As String, ByRef yr As Integer)
  movie = "The Artist"
  yr = 2012
End Sub
```

5.
```
Private Sub btnDisplay_Click(...) Handles btnDisplay.Click
  Dim word As String = ""
  Dim num As Integer
  GetFacts(word, num)
  txtOutput.Text = "The first " & num & " letters of " & word &
                   " are " & BegOfWord(word, num) & "."
End Sub

Sub GetFacts(ByRef w As String, ByRef n As Integer)
  w = InputBox("Enter a word:")
  n = CInt(InputBox("Enter a number less than the length of the word:"))
End Sub

Function BegOfWord(word As String, num As Integer) As String
  Return word.Substring(0, num)
End Function
```

(Assume the two responses are *EDUCATION* and *3*.)

6.
```
Private Sub btnDisplay_Click(...) Handles btnDisplay.Click
  Dim price, markdown, salesTax, finalCost As Decimal
  InputData(price, markdown, salesTax)
  finalCost = CostOfItem(price, markdown, salesTax)
  DisplayOutput(price, finalCost)
End Sub

Sub InputData(ByRef price As Decimal, ByRef markdown As Decimal,
            ByRef salesTax As Decimal)
  price = CDec(InputBox("Price of item:"))
  markdown = CDec(InputBox("Percentage discount:"))
  salesTax = CDec(InputBox("Percentage state sales tax:"))
End Sub

Function CostOfItem(pr As Decimal, md As Decimel,
                   st As Decimal) As Decimal
  Dim reducedPrice, cost As Decimal
  reducedPrice = pr - ((md / 100) * pr)
  cost = reducedPrice + ((st / 100) * reducedPrice)
  Return cost
End Function

Sub DisplayOutput(amount As Decimal, customerCost As Decimal)
  lstOutput.Items.Add("Original Price: " & amount.ToString("C"))
  lstOutput.Items.Add("Cost: " & customerCost.ToString("C"))
End Sub
```

(Assume the three responses are *125*, *20*, and *6*.)

7.
```
Private Sub btnDisplay_Click(...) Handles btnDisplay.Click
    Dim a, b, s, d As Integer
    InputData(a, b)
    Combine(a, b, s, d)
    DisplayResults(s, d)
End Sub

Sub InputData(ByRef num1 As Integer, ByRef num2 As Integer)
    num1 = 3
    num2 = 1
End Sub

Sub Combine(x As Integer, y As Integer, ByRef sum As Integer,
            ByRef difference As Integer)
    sum = x + y
    difference = x - y
End Sub

Sub DisplayResults(s As Integer, d As Integer)
    lstOutput.Items.Add("sum = " & s)
    lstOutput.Items.Add("difference = " & d)
End Sub
```

8.
```
Private Sub btnCalculate_Click(...) Handles btnCalculate.Click
    Dim wholesaleCost, salePrice, percentCommission,
        salesTax, profit As Decimal
    InputData(wholesaleCost, salePrice, percentCommission)
    CalculateSomeValues(wholesaleCost, salePrice, percentCommission,
                        salesTax, profit)
    DisplayData(salesTax, profit)
End Sub

Sub InputData(ByRef wholesaleCost As Decimal, ByRef salePrice As Decimal,
              ByRef percentCommission As Decimal)
    wholesaleCost = 100
    salePrice = 300
    percentCommission = 5
End Sub

Sub CalculateSomeValues(wholesaleCost As Decimal,
        salePrice As Decimal, percentCommission As Decimal,
        ByRef salesTax As Decimal, ByRef profit As Decimal)
    salesTax = 0.06D * salePrice
    profit = salePrice - wholesaleCost -
             salePrice * (percentCommission / 100)
End Sub

Sub DisplayData(salesTax As Decimal, profit As Decimal)
    lstOutput.Items.Add("sales tax: " & salesTax.ToString("C"))
    lstOutput.Items.Add("profit: " & profit.ToString("C"))
End Sub
```

9. **Pay Raise** Write a pay-raise program that requests a person's first name, last name, and current annual salary, and then displays the person's salary for next year. People earning less than $40,000 will receive a 5% raise, and those earning $40,000 or more will receive a raise of $2,000 plus 2% of the amount over $40,000. Use Sub procedures for input and output, and a Function procedure to calculate the new salary. See Fig. 5.29.

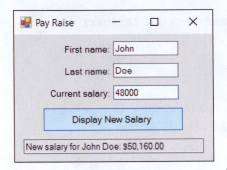

FIGURE 5.29   Outcome of Exercise 9.

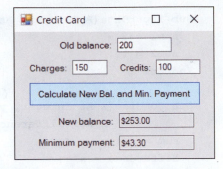

FIGURE 5.30   Possible outcome of Exercise 10.

10. **Credit Card Payment** Write a program to calculate the balance and minimum payment for a credit card statement. See Fig. 5.30. The program should use the event procedure shown in Fig. 5.31. The finance charge is 1.5% of the old balance. If the new balance is $20 or less, the minimum payment should be the entire new balance. Otherwise, the minimum payment should be $20 plus 10% of the amount of the new balance above $20.

```
Private Sub btnCalculate_Click(...) Handles btnCalculate.Click
    Dim oldBalance, charges, credits, newBalance, minPayment As Decimal
    InputData(oldBalance, charges, credits)
    CalculateNewValues(oldBalance, charges, credits, newBalance, minPayment)
    DisplayData(newBalance, minPayment)
End Sub
```

FIGURE 5.31   Event procedure for Exercise 10.

11. **Mortgage Calculations** Write a program to calculate three monthly values associated with a mortgage. See Fig. 5.33 on the next page. The program should use the event procedure shown in Fig. 5.32. The interest paid each month is the monthly rate of interest (annual Rate of Interest / 12) applied to the balance at the beginning of the month. Each month the reduction of principal equals the monthly payment minus the interest paid. At any time, the balance of the mortgage is the amount still owed; that is, the amount required to pay off the mortgage. The end of month balance is calculated as [beginning of month balance] − [reduction of principal].

```
Private Sub btnCalculate_Click(...) Handles btnCalculate.Click
    Dim annualRateOfInterest, monthlyPayment, begBalance As Decimal
    Dim intForMonth, redOfPrincipal, endBalance As Decimal
    InputData(annualRateOfInterest, monthlyPayment, begBalance)
    Calculate(annualRateOfInterest, monthlyPayment, begBalance,
            intForMonth, redOfPrincipal, endBalance)
    DisplayData(intForMonth, redOfPrincipal, endBalance)
End Sub
```

FIGURE 5.32   Event procedure for Exercise 11.

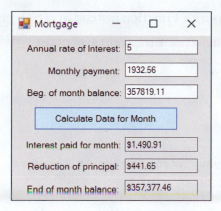

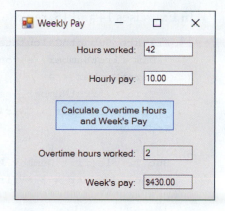

FIGURE 5.33 Possible outcome of Exercise 11.   **FIGURE 5.34** Outcome of Exercise 12.

12. **Earnings** Write a program to determine a person's weekly pay, where they receive time-and-a-half for overtime work beyond forty hours. See Fig. 5.34. The program should use the event procedure shown in Fig. 5.35.

```
Private Sub btnCalculate_Click(...) Handles btnCalculate.Click
  Dim hours, payPerHour, overtimeHours, pay As Decimal
  InputData(hours, payPerHour)
  CalculateValues(hours, payPerHour, overtimeHours, pay)
  DisplayData(overtimeHours, pay)
End Sub
```

FIGURE 5.35 Event procedure for Exercise 12.

13. **Sort Three Numbers** Write a program that requests three different numbers as input and then displays the numbers in order. Use a Procedure named Sort to which the three values are passed ByRef and use a "Swap" procedure similar to the one in Example 3. See Fig. 5.36.

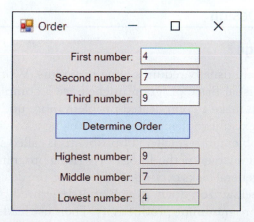

FIGURE 5.36 Possible outcome of Exercise 13.

In Exercises 14 and 15, rewrite the program using a Function instead of a Sub procedure.

14.
```
Private Sub btnCalculate_Click(...) Handles btnCalculate.Click
    Dim firstNumber, secondNumber As Integer
    firstNumber = 4
    Triple(firstNumber, secondNumber)
    txtResult.Text = CStr(secondNumber)
End Sub

Sub Triple(firstNumber As Integer, ByRef secondNumber As Integer)
    secondNumber = 3 * firstNumber
End Sub
```

15.
```
Private Sub btnCalculate_Click(...) Handles btnCalculate.Click
    Dim price, salesTaxRate, cost As Decimal
    price = 29.95D
    salesTaxRate = 0.05D
    FindCost(price, salesTaxRate, cost)
    txtResult.Text = cost.ToString("C")
End Sub

Sub FindCost(price As Decimal, salesTaxRate As Decimal, ByRef cost As Decimal)
    cost = price * (1 + salesTaxRate)
End Sub
```

Solutions to Practice Problems 5.3

1. `age before age`

2. Since *state* is a string variable, its default value is the keyword Nothing. The assignment of Nothing to an argument makes Visual Basic nervous. Therefore, to keep Visual Basic happy, we will assign the empty string to String variables that are passed to procedures. That is, we will change the first line inside the event procedure to **Dim state As String = ""**.

    Since the default value of the numeric variable *pop* is 0, Visual Basic has no issue with passing that value to a Sub procedure.

5.4   Program Design

■ Top-Down Design

Full-featured software usually requires large programs. Writing the code for an event procedure in such a Visual Basic program might pose a complicated problem. One method programmers use to make a complicated problem more understandable is to divide it into smaller, less complex subproblems. Repeatedly using a "divide-and-conquer" approach to break up a large problem into smaller subproblems is called **stepwise refinement**. Stepwise refinement is part of a larger methodology of writing programs known as **top-down design**, in which the more general tasks occur near the top of the design and tasks representing their refinement occur below. Top-down design and structured programming emerged as techniques to enhance programming productivity. Their use leads to programs that are easier to read and maintain. They also produce programs containing fewer initial errors, with these errors being easier to find and correct. When such programs are later modified, there is a much smaller likelihood of introducing new errors.

The goal of top-down design is to break a problem into individual subtasks that can easily be transcribed into pseudocode, flowcharts, or a program. Any subtasks that remain too complex are broken down further. The process of refining subtasks continues until the smallest subtasks can be coded directly. Each stage of refinement adds a more complete specification of what tasks must be performed. The main idea in top-down design is to go from the general to the specific. This process of dividing and organizing a problem into tasks can be pictured using a hierarchy chart. When using top-down design, certain criteria should be met:

1. The design should be easily readable and emphasize small subtask size.
2. Tasks proceed from general to specific as you read down the chart.
3. The subtasks, as much as possible, should be single-minded. That is, they should perform only a single well-defined task.
4. Subtasks should be independent of each other as much as possible, and any relationships among subtasks should be specified.

The following example illustrates this process.

 Example 1   Figure 5.37 is the beginning of a hierarchy chart for a program that gives information about a car loan. The inputs are the amount of the loan, the duration (in years), and the interest rate. The output consists of the monthly payment and the amount of interest paid for the first month. In the broadest sense, the program calls for obtaining the input, making calculations, and displaying the output.

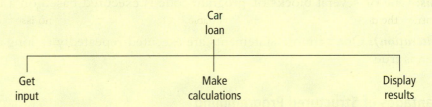

FIGURE 5.37   **Beginning of a hierarchy chart for the car loan program.**

Each task can be refined into more specific subtasks. (See Fig. 5.38 on the next page for the final hierarchy chart.) Most of the subtasks in the third row are straightforward and do not require further refinement. For instance, the first month's interest is calculated by multiplying the amount of the loan by one-twelfth of the annual rate of interest. The most complicated subtask, the computation of the monthly payment, has been broken down further. This task is carried out by applying a standard formula found in finance books; however, the formula requires the number of payments.

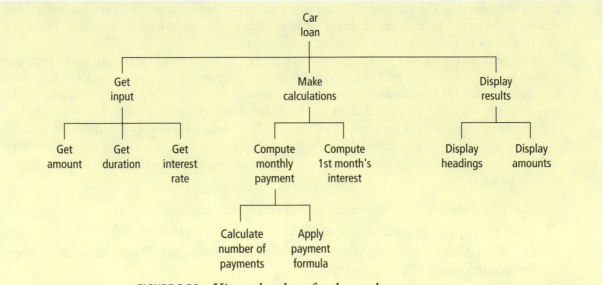

FIGURE 5.38 **Hierarchy chart for the car loan program.**

It is clear from the hierarchy chart that the top tasks manipulate the subtasks beneath them. While the higher-level tasks control the flow of the program, the lower-level tasks do the actual work. By designing the top tasks first, we can delay specific processing decisions.

■ Structured Programming

A program is said to be **structured** if it meets modern standards of program design. Although there is no formal definition of the term structured program, computer scientists agree that such programs should have top-down design and use only the three types of logical structures discussed in Chapter 1: sequences, decisions, and loops.

Sequences: Statements are executed one after another.

Decisions: One of several blocks of program code is executed based on a test for some condition.

Loops (iteration): One or more statements are executed repeatedly as long as a specified condition is true.

■ Advantages of Structured Programming

The goal of structured programming is to create correct programs that are easy to write, debug, understand, and change. Let us now take a closer look at the way structured design, contributes to attaining these goals.

1. *Easy to write.*

   Structured design increases the programmer's productivity by allowing the programmer to look at the big picture first and focus on the details later. During the actual coding, the programmer works with a manageable chunk of the program and does not have to think about an entire complex program. Several programmers can work on a single large program, each taking responsibility for a specific task.

   Studies have shown that structured programs require significantly less time to write than unstructured programs.

Often, procedures written for one program can be reused in other programs requiring the same task. Not only is time saved in writing a program, but reliability is enhanced, because reused procedures will already be tested and debugged. A procedure that can be used in many programs is said to be **reusable**.

2. *Easy to debug.*

Because each procedure is specialized to perform just one task or several related tasks, a procedure can be checked individually to determine its reliability. A dummy program, called a **driver**, is set up to test the procedure. The driver contains the minimum definitions needed to call the procedure to be tested. For instance, if the procedure to be tested is a function, the driver program assigns diverse values to the arguments and then examines the corresponding function return values. The arguments should contain both typical and special-case values.

The program can be tested and debugged as it is being designed with a technique known as **stub programming**. In this technique, the key event procedures and perhaps some of the smaller procedures are coded first. Dummy procedures, or stubs, are written for the remaining procedures. Initially, a stub procedure might consist of a message box to indicate that the procedure has been called, and thereby confirm that the procedure was called at the right time. Later, a stub might simply display values passed to it in order to confirm not only that the procedure was called, but also that it received the correct values from the calling procedure. A stub also can assign new values to one or more of its parameters to simulate either input or computation. This provides greater control of the conditions being tested. The stub procedure is always simpler than the actual procedure it represents. Although the stub program is only a skeleton of the final program, the program's structure can still be debugged and tested. (The stub program consists of some coded procedures and the stub procedures.)

Old-fashioned unstructured programs consist of a linear sequence of instructions that are not grouped for specific tasks. The logic of such a program is cluttered with details and therefore difficult to follow. Needed tasks are easily left out and crucial details easily neglected. Tricky parts of the program cannot be isolated and examined. Bugs are difficult to locate because they might be present in any part of the program.

3. *Easy to understand.*

The interconnections of the procedures reveal the structured design of the program.

The meaningful procedure names, along with relevant comments, identify the tasks performed by the procedures.

The meaningful variable names help the programmer recall the purpose of each variable.

4. *Easy to change.*

Because a structured program is self-documenting, it can easily be deciphered by another programmer.

Modifying a structured program often amounts to inserting or altering a few procedures rather than revising an entire complex program. The programmer does not even have to look at most of the program. This is in sharp contrast to the situation with unstructured programs, where one must understand the entire logic of the program before any changes can be made with confidence.

■ Object-Oriented Programming

An object is an encapsulation of data and code that operates on the data. Like controls, objects have properties, respond to methods, and raise events. The most effective type of programming for complex problems is called **object-oriented** design. An object-oriented program can be viewed as a collection of cooperating objects. Many modern programmers use a blend of traditional structured programming along with object-oriented design.

Visual Basic .NET was the first version of Visual Basic that was truly object oriented; in fact, every element such as a control or a string is actually an object. This book illustrates the building blocks of Visual Basic in the early chapters and then puts them together using object-oriented techniques in Chapter 11.

■ A Relevant Quote

We end this section with a few paragraphs from *Dirk Gently's Holistic Detective Agency*, by Douglas Adams, Published by Simon & Schuster, © 1987:

> "What really is the point of trying to teach anything to anybody?"
>
> This question seemed to provoke a murmur of sympathetic approval from up and down the table.
>
> Richard continued, "What I mean is that if you really want to understand something, the best way is to try and explain it to someone else. That forces you to sort it out in your own mind. And the more slow and dim-witted your pupil, the more you have to break things down into more and more simple ideas. And that's really the essence of programming. By the time you've sorted out a complicated idea into little steps that even a stupid machine can deal with, you've certainly learned something about it yourself. The teacher usually learns more than the pupil. Isn't that true?"

5.5 A Case Study: Weekly Payroll

This case study processes a weekly payroll using the 2015 Employer's Tax Guide. Table 5.4 shows typical data used by a company's payroll office. (**Note:** A withholding allowance is sometimes referred to as an *exemption*.) These data are processed to produce the information in Table 5.5 that is supplied to each employee along with his or her paycheck. The program should request the data from Table 5.4 for an individual as input and produce output similar to that in Table 5.5.

TABLE 5.4   **Employee data.**

Name	Hourly Wage	Hours Worked	Withholding Allowances	Marital Status	Previous Year-to-Date Earnings
Al Clark	$45.50	38	4	Married	$88,600.00
Ann Miller	$44.00	35	3	Married	$68,200.00
John Smith	$17.95	50	1	Single	$30,604.75
Sue Taylor	$25.50	43	2	Single	$36,295.50

TABLE 5.5   **Payroll information.**

Name	Current Earnings	Yr.-to-Date Earnings	FICA Tax	Income Tax Wh.	Check Amount
Al Clark	$1,729.00	$90,329.00	$132.27	$176.71	$1,426.02

The items in Table 5.5 should be calculated as follows:

Current Earnings: hourly wage times hours worked (with time-and-a-half after 40 hours)

Year-to-Date Earnings: previous year-to-date earnings plus current earnings

FICA Tax: The Social Security or FICA tax has two components—the Social Security Benefits tax, which in 2015 was 6.2% on the first $118,500 of earnings for the year, and the Medicare tax, which was 1.45% of earnings plus 0.9% of earnings above $200,000 for single employees ($250,000 for married employees).

Federal Income Tax Withheld: subtract $76.90 from the current earnings for each withholding allowance and use Table 5.6 or Table 5.7, depending on marital status

Check Amount: [current earnings] − [FICA taxes] − [income tax withheld]

TABLE 5.6   2015 federal income tax withheld for a single person paid weekly.

Adjusted Weekly Income	Income Tax Withheld
$0 to $44	$0
Over $44 to $222	10% of amount over $44
Over $222 to $764	$17.80 + 15% of amount over $222
Over $764 to $1,789	$99.10 + 25% of amount over $764
Over $1,789 to $3,685	$355.35 + 28% of amount over $1,789
Over $3,685 to $7,958	$886.23 + 33% of amount over $3,685
Over $7,958 to $7,990	$2,296.32 + 35% of amount over $7,958
Over $7,990	$2,307.52 + 39.6% of amount over $7,990

TABLE 5.7   2015 federal income tax withheld for a married person paid weekly.

Adjusted Weekly Income	Income Tax Withheld
$0 to $165	$0
Over $165 to $520	10% of amount over $165
Over $520 to $1,606	$35.50 + 15% of amount over $520
Over $1,606 to $3,073	$198.40 + 25% of amount over $1,606
Over $3,073 to $4,597	$565.15 + 28% of amount over $3,073
Over $4,597 to $8,079	$991.87 + 33% of amount over $4,597
Over $8,079 to $9,105	$2,140.32 + 35% of amount over $8,079
Over $9,105	$2,500.03 + 39.6% of amount over $9,105

■ Designing the Weekly Payroll Program

After the data for an employee from Table 5.4 have been input, the program must compute the five amounts appearing in Table 5.5 and then display the payroll information. These five computations form the basic tasks of the program:

1. Compute current earnings.
2. Compute year-to-date earnings.
3. Compute FICA tax.
4. Compute federal income tax withheld.
5. Compute paycheck amount (that is, take-home pay).

Tasks 1, 2, 3, and 5 are fairly simple. Each involves applying a formula to given data. (For instance, if hours worked are at most 40, then [current earnings] = [hourly wage] times [hours worked].) Thus, we won't break down these tasks any further. Task 4 is more complicated, so we continue to divide it into smaller subtasks.

4. *Compute federal income tax withheld.* First, the employee's pay is adjusted for withholding allowances, and then the amount of income tax to be withheld is computed. The computation of the income tax withheld differs for married and single individuals. Task 4 is, therefore, divided into the following subtasks:

4.1 Compute pay adjusted by withholding allowances.

4.2 Compute income tax withheld for single employee.

4.3 Compute income tax withheld for married employee.

The hierarchy chart in Fig. 5.39 shows the stepwise refinement of the problem.

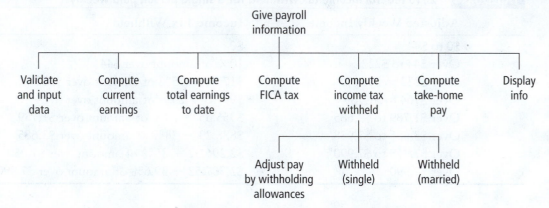

FIGURE 5.39 **Hierarchy chart for the weekly payroll program.**

■ Pseudocode for the Display Payroll Event Procedure

VALIDATE data (Function DataOK)
INPUT employee data (Sub procedure InputData)
COMPUTE CURRENT GROSS PAY (Function Gross_Pay)
COMPUTE TOTAL EARNINGS TO DATE (Function Total_Pay)
COMPUTE FICA TAX (Function FICA_Tax)
COMPUTE INCOME TAX WITHHELD (Function Fed_Tax)
    Adjust pay for withholding allowances
    If employee is single Then
        COMPUTE INCOME TAX WITHHELD (Function TaxSingle)
    Else
        COMPUTE INCOME TAX WITHHELD (Function TaxMarried)
    End If
COMPUTE PAYCHECK AMOUNT (Function Net_Check)
DISPLAY PAYROLL INFORMATION (Sub procedure ShowPayroll)

■ Writing the Weekly Payroll Program

The btnDisplay_Click event procedure calls a sequence of seven procedures. Table 5.8 shows the tasks and the procedures that perform the tasks.

TABLE 5.8 **Tasks and their procedures.**

Task	Procedure
0. Validate and input employee data	DataOK, InputData
1. Compute current earnings.	Gross_Pay
2. Compute year-to-date earnings.	Total_Pay
3. Compute FICA tax.	FICA_Tax

Task	Procedure
4. Compute federal income tax withheld.	Fed_Tax
4.1 Compute adjusted pay.	Fed_Tax
4.2 Compute amount withheld for single employee.	TaxSingle
4.3 Compute amount withheld for married employee.	TaxMarried
5. Compute paycheck amount.	Net_Check
6. Display payroll information.	ShowPayroll

■ The Program and the User Interface

Figure 5.40 and Table 5.9 define the user interface for the Weekly Payroll Program. Figure 5.41 shows a sample output.

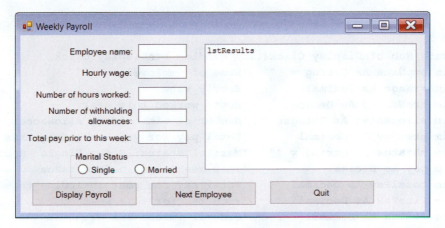

FIGURE 5.40   **Form for weekly payroll program.**

TABLE 5.9   **Objects and initial properties for the weekly payroll program.**

Object	Property	Setting
frmPayroll	Text	Weekly Payroll
lblName	Text	Employee name:
txtName		
lblWage	Text	Hourly wage:
txtWage		
lblHours	Text	Number of hours worked:
txtHours		
lblAllowances	AutoSize	False
	Text	Number of withholding allowances:
txtAllowances		
lblPriorPay	Text	Total pay prior to this week:
txtPriorPay		
grpMarital	Text	Marital Status:
radSingle	Text	Single
radMarried	Text	Married
btnDisplay	Text	Display Payroll
btnNext	Text	Next Employee
btnQuit	Text	Quit
lstResults	Font	Courier New

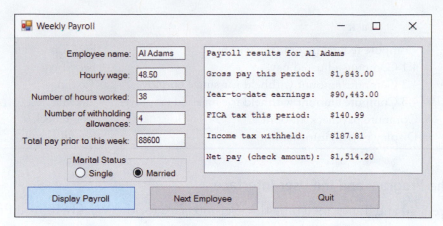

FIGURE 5.41 Sample output of weekly payroll problem.

```
Private Sub btnDisplay_Click(...) Handles btnDisplay.Click
  Dim empName As String = ""     'Name of employee
  Dim hrWage As Decimal          'Hourly wage
  Dim hrsWorked As Decimal       'Hours worked this week
  Dim allowances As Integer      'Number of withholding allowances for employee
  Dim prevPay As Decimal         'Total pay for year excluding this week
  Dim mStatus As String = ""     'Marital status: S for Single; M for Married
  Dim pay As Decimal             'This week's pay before taxes
  Dim totalPay As Decimal        'Total pay for year including this week
  Dim ficaTax As Decimal         'FICA tax for this week
  Dim fedTax As Decimal          'Federal income tax withheld this week
  Dim check As Decimal           'Paycheck this week (take-home pay)
  'Verify and obtain data, compute payroll, display results
  If Not DataOK() Then
    Dim msg As String = "At least one piece of requested data is missing" &
                        " or is provided improperly."
    MessageBox.Show(msg)
  Else
    InputData(empName, hrWage, hrsWorked, allowances, prevPay, mStatus) 'Task 0
    pay = Gross_Pay(hrWage, hrsWorked)                                   'Task 1
    totalPay = Total_Pay(prevPay, pay)                                   'Task 2
    ficaTax = FICA_Tax(pay, prevPay, totalPay, mStatus)                  'Task 3
    fedTax = Fed_Tax(pay, allowances, mStatus)                          'Task 4
    check = Net_Check(pay, ficaTax, fedTax)                              'Task 5
    ShowPayroll(empName, pay, totalPay, ficaTax, fedTax, check)          'Task 6
  End If
End Sub


Private Sub btnNext_Click(...) Handles btnNext.Click
  'Clear all text boxes and radio buttons for next employee's data
  txtName.Clear()
  txtWage.Clear()
  txtHours.Clear()
  txtAllowances.Clear()
  txtPriorPay.Clear()
  radSingle.Checked = False
  radMarried.Checked = False
```

```vb
    lstResults.Items.Clear()
    txtName.Focus()
  End Sub

  Private Sub btnQuit_Click(...) Handles btnQuit.Click
    Me.Close()
  End Sub

  Function DataOK() As Boolean
    'Task 0: Validate data
    If (txtName.Text = "") Or (Not IsNumeric(txtWage.Text)) Or
      (Not IsNumeric(txtHours.Text)) Or (Not IsNumeric(txtAllowances.Text)) Or
      (Not IsNumeric(txtPriorPay.Text)) Or
      ((Not radSingle.Checked) And (Not radMarried.Checked)) Then
      Return False
    Else
      Return True
    End If
  End Function

  Sub InputData(ByRef empName As String, ByRef hrWage As Decimal,
              ByRef hrsWorked As Decimal, ByRef allowances As Integer,
              ByRef prevPay As Decimal, ByRef mStatus As String)
    'Task 0: Validate data
    empName = txtName.Text
    hrWage = CDec(txtWage.Text)
    hrsWorked = CDec(txtHours.Text)
    allowances = CInt(txtAllowances.Text)
    prevPay = CDec(txtPriorPay.Text)
    If radMarried.Checked Then
      mStatus = "M"
    Else
      mStatus = "S"
    End If
  End Sub

  Function Gross_Pay(hrWage As Decimal, hrsWorked As Decimal) As Decimal
    'Task 1: Compute weekly pay before taxes
    If hrsWorked <= 40 Then
      Return hrsWorked * hrWage
    Else
      Return 40 * hrWage + (hrsWorked - 40) * 1.5D * hrWage
    End If
  End Function

  Function Total_Pay(prevPay As Decimal, pay As Decimal) As Decimal
    'Task 2: Compute total pay before taxes
    Return prevPay + pay
  End Function

  Function FICA_Tax(pay As Decimal, prevPay As Decimal, totalPay As Decimal,
                  mStatus As String) As Decimal
    'Task 3: Compute social security and medicare tax
    'Calculate social security benefits tax and medicare tax
    'for a single employee.
```

```vbnet
        Const WAGE_BASE As Decimal = 118500D 'There is no Social Security Benefits
        '                                     tax on income above this level.
        Const SOCIAL_SECURITY_RATE As Decimal = 0.062D
        Const MEDICARE_RATE As Decimal = 0.0145D
        Dim medicareIncreaseBase As Decimal
        If mStatus = "S" Then
          medicareIncreaseBase = 200000
        Else
          medicareIncreaseBase = 250000
        End If
        Dim socialSecurityBenTax, medicareTax, ficaTax As Decimal
        'Calculate the Social Security Benefits tax.
        If totalPay <= WAGE_BASE Then
          socialSecurityBenTax = SOCIAL_SECURITY_RATE * pay
        ElseIf prevPay < WAGE_BASE Then
          socialSecurityBenTax = SOCIAL_SECURITY_RATE * (WAGE_BASE - prevPay)
        End If
        'Calculate the FICA tax.
        medicareTax = MEDICARE_RATE * pay
        If prevPay >= medicareIncreaseBase Then
          medicareTax += 0.009D * (totalPay - 200000D)
        End If
        ficaTax = socialSecurityBenTax + medicareTax
        Return Math.Round(ficaTax, 2)
    End Function

    Function Fed_Tax(pay As Decimal, allowances As Integer, mStatus As String) As cimal
        'Task 4.1: Compute federal income tax withheld rounded to 2 decimal places
        Dim adjPay As Decimal
        Dim tax As Decimal  'unrounded federal tax withheld
        Const WITHHOLDING_EXEMPTION As Decimal = 76.9D
        adjPay = pay - (WITHHOLDING_EXEMPTION * allowances)
        If adjPay < 0 Then
          adjPay = 0
        End If
        If mStatus = "S" Then
          tax = TaxSingle(adjPay) 'Task 4.2
        Else
          tax = TaxMarried(adjPay) 'Task 4.3
        End If
        Return Math.Round(tax, 2) 'round to nearest cent
    End Function

    Function TaxSingle(adjPay As Decimal) As Decimal
        'Task 4.2: Compute federal tax withheld for single person
        Select Case adjPay
          Case 0 To 44
            Return 0
          Case 44 To 222
            Return (0.1D * (adjPay - 44))
          Case 222 To 764
            Return 17.8D + 0.15D * (adjPay - 222)
          Case 764 To 1789
            Return 99.1D + 0.25D * (adjPay - 764)
          Case 1789 To 3685
```

```vb
        Return 355.35D + 0.28D * (adjPay - 1789)
      Case 3685 To 7958
        Return 886.23D + 0.33D * (adjPay - 3685)
      Case 7958 To 7990
        Return 2296.32D + 0.35D * (adjPay - 3685)
      Case Is > 7958
        Return 2307.52D + 0.396D * (adjPay - 7958)
    End Select
  End Function


  Function TaxMarried(adjPay As Decimal) As Decimal
    'Task 4.3: Compute federal tax withheld for married person
    Select Case adjPay
    Case 0 To 165
      Return 0
    Case 165 To 520
      Return 0.1D * (adjPay - 165)
    Case 520 To 1606
      Return 35.5D + 0.15D * (adjPay - 520)
    Case 1606 To 3073
      Return 198.4D + 0.25D * (adjPay - 1606)
    Case 3073 To 4597
      Return 565.15D + 0.28D * (adjPay - 3073)
    Case 4597 To 8079
      Return 991.87D + 0.33D * (adjPay - 4597)
    Case 8079 To 9105
      Return 2140.32D + 0.35D * (adjPay - 8079)
    Case Is > 9105
      Return 2500.03D + 0.396D * (adjPay - 9105)
    End Select
  End Function


  Function Net_Check(pay As Decimal, ficaTax As Decimal, fedTax As Decimal) As Decimal
    'Task 5: Compute amount of money paid to employee
    Return pay - ficaTax - fedTax
  End Function


  Sub ShowPayroll(empName As String, pay As Decimal,
                  totalPay As Decimal, ficaTax As Decimal,
                  fedTax As Decimal, check As Decimal)
    'Task 6: Display results of payroll computations
    lstResults.Items.Clear()
    lstResults.Items.Add("Payroll results for " & empName)
    lstResults.Items.Add("")
    lstResults.Items.Add("Gross pay this period:" & " " & pay.ToString("C"))
    lstResults.Items.Add("")
    lstResults.Items.Add("Year-to-date earnings:" & "   " & totalPay.ToString("C"))
    lstResults.Items.Add("")
    lstResults.Items.Add("FICA tax this period:" & "  " & ficaTax.ToString("C"))
    lstResults.Items.Add("")
    lstResults.Items.Add("Income tax withheld:" & "   " & fedTax.ToString("C"))
    lstResults.Items.Add("")
    lstResults.Items.Add("Net pay (check amount):" & " " & check.ToString("C"))
  End Sub
```

■ Comments

1. In the function FICA_Tax, care has been taken to avoid computing Social Security benefits tax on income in excess of $118,500 per year. The logic of the program makes sure an employee whose income for the year crosses the $118,500 threshold during a given week is taxed only on the difference between $118,500 and their previous year-to-date earnings.

2. The two functions TaxMarried and TaxSingle use Select Case blocks to incorporate the tax brackets given in Tables 5.6 and 5.7 for the amount of federal income tax withheld. The upper limit of each Case clause is the same as the lower limit of the next Case clause. This ensures that fractional values for *adjPay*, such as 44.50 in the TaxSingle function, will be properly treated as part of the higher salary range.

CHAPTER 5 SUMMARY

1. A *general procedure* is a portion of a program that is accessed by event procedures or other general procedures. The two types of general procedures are *Function procedures* and *Sub procedures*.

2. *Function procedures* are defined in blocks beginning with Function headers and ending with End Function statements. A function is executed by a reference in an expression and returns a value.

3. *Sub procedures* are defined in blocks beginning with Sub headers and ending with End Sub statements. A Sub procedure is executed (called) by a statement consisting of the name of the procedure along with arguments.

4. In any procedure, the *arguments* appearing in the calling statement match the *parameters* of the Sub or Function statement in number, type, and order. They need not have the same names.

5. The *lifetime* of a variable or constant is the period during which it remains in memory. (The value of the variable might change over its lifetime, but it always holds some value.)

6. The *scope* of a variable or constant is the portion of the program that can refer to it. A variable or constant declared in a block can be referred to only inside the block. A variable or constant declared inside a procedure, but not inside a block, is said to have *procedure scope*. It can be referred to anywhere inside the procedure, and nowhere else.

7. *Structured programming* uses top-down design to refine large problems into smaller sub-problems. Programs are coded using the three logical structures of sequences, decisions, and loops.

CHAPTER 5 PROGRAMMING PROJECTS

1. **Grade Point Average**   Write a program to calculate a student's GPA. See Fig. 5.42. The user should enter the grade (A, B, C, D, or F) and the number of credit hours for a course, and then click on the *Record This Course* button. The user should then repeat

this process for all his or her courses. After all the courses have been recorded, the user should click on the *Calculate GPA* button. A Function procedure should be used to calculate the quality points for a course.

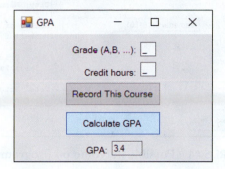

FIGURE 5.42 Possible outcome of Programming Project 1.

2. **Restaurant Bill** A fast-food vendor sells pizza slices ($1.75), fries ($2.00), and soft drinks ($1.25). Write a program to compute a customer's bill. The program should request the quantity of each item ordered in a Sub procedure, calculate the total cost with a Function procedure, and use a Sub procedure to display an itemized bill. A sample output is shown in Fig. 5.43.

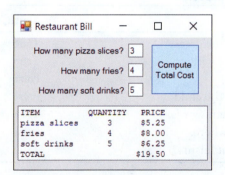

FIGURE 5.43 Possible outcome of Programming Project 2.

3. **Furniture Order** A furniture manufacturer makes two types of furniture—chairs and sofas. The price per chair is $350, the price per sofa is $925, and the sales tax rate is 5%. Write a program to create an invoice form for an order. See Fig. 5.44 on the next page. After the data on the left side of Fig. 5.44 are entered, the user can display an invoice in a list box by clicking the *Process Order* button. The user can click on the *Clear Order Form* button to clear all text boxes and the list box, and can click on the *Quit* button to exit the program. The invoice number consists of the capitalized first two letters of the customer's last name, followed by the last four digits of the zip code. The customer name is input with the last name first, followed by a comma, a space, and the first name. However, the name is displayed in the invoice in the proper order. The generation of the invoice number and the reordering of the first and last names should be carried out by Function procedures.

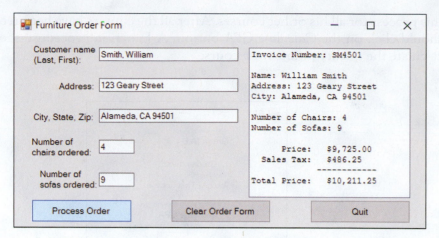

FIGURE 5.44   Possible outcome of Programming Project 3.

4. **Proverbs**   Table 5.10 contains seven proverbs and their truth values. Write a program that presents these proverbs one at a time and asks the user to evaluate them as true or false. The program should then tell the user how many questions were answered correctly and display one of the following evaluations: Perfect (all correct), Excellent (5 or 6 correct), You might consider taking Psychology 101 (less than 5 correct).

TABLE 5.10   Seven proverbs.

Proverb	Truth Value
The squeaky wheel gets the grease.	True
Giving is better than receivings.	True
Opposites attract.	False
Spare the rod and spoil the child.	False
Actions speak louder than words.	True
Flattery will get you nowhere.	False
Marry in haste, repent at leisure.	True

5. **Game**   Write a program that allows the user to challenge the computer to a game of Pick-Up Sticks. Here is how the game is played. The user chooses the number of matchsticks (from 5 to 40) to place in a pile. Then, the computer chooses who will go first. At each turn, the contestant can remove one, two, or three matchsticks from the pile. The contestant who removes the last matchstick loses. See Fig. 5.45.

FIGURE 5.45   Possible outcome of Programming Project 5.

The computer should make the user always select from a pile where the number of matchsticks has a remainder of 1 when divided by 4. For instance, if the user initially chooses a number of matchsticks that has a remainder of 1 when divided by 4, then the computer should have the user go first. Otherwise, the computer should go first and remove the proper number of matchsticks. [**Note:** The remainder when *n* is divided by 4 is (*n* Mod 4).] After writing the program, play a few games with the computer and observe that the computer always wins.

6. **Loan Calculator**   The most common types of loans are mortgage loans, which are used to finance the purchase of a house, and car loans. A loan consists of four components—amount, interest rate, duration, and periodic payment. The purpose of this programming project is to calculate the value of any one of the components given the values of the other three components.

   We will assume that the duration is in months, that interest (given as a percent) is compounded monthly, and that payments are made monthly. Currently home mortgages typically have an interest rate of about 4% and a duration of 30 years (360 months). Car loans typically have an interest rate of about 6% and a duration of between 3 and 5 years (36 to 60 months).

   Four built-in Visual Basic financial functions that perform loan calculations are as follows:

   Pmt(interest rate / 1200, duration, –amount) gives the monthly payment

   1200 * Rate(duration, monthly payment, –amount) gives the stated interest rate

   PV(interest rate / 1200, duration, –monthly payment) gives the amount of the loan

   NPer(interest rate / 1200, monthly payment, –amount) gives the duration of the loan in months

   Write a program in which the user specifies a value to calculate, enters the three other values, and clicks on the Calculate Value button. See Fig. 5.16. Before any calculations are made, the program should use a Function procedure to validate that a radio button is selected and that the values entered into the three text boxes corresponding to unselected radio buttons are valid.

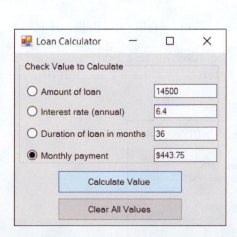

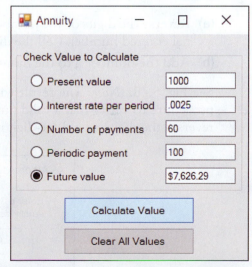

FIGURE 5.46   Possible outcome of Programming Project 6.

FIGURE 5.47   Possible outcome of Programming Project 7.

7. Annuity Calculator   If $1000 is deposited into a bank at an interest rate of 3% compounded monthly and $100 is added to the account at the end of each month, then the balance in the account after 5 years will be $7,626.29. This type of investment is called an *annuity*. The initial deposit ($1000) is called the present value, final balance ($7,626.29) is called the future value, the number of periodic payments will be 60 (= 5 · 12), the interest rate per period will be .25% (= 3%/12), and the periodic payment will be $100.

An annuity is described by the values of five components—present value, interest rate per period, number of periodic payments, amount of each periodic payment, and the future value. The purpose of this programming project is to calculate the value of any one of the components given the values of the other four components. The five built-in Visual Basic financial functions that perform annuity calculations are as follows:

PV(interest rate, number of payments, payment, –future value) gives the initial deposit

Rate(number of payments, –payment, –present value, future value) gives the interest rate per period

NPer(interest rate, –payment, –present value, future value) gives the number of periodic payments

Pmt(interest rate, number of payments, –present value, future value) gives the periodic payment

FV(interest rate, number of payments, –payment, –present value) gives the future value

Note: Money paid into the bank by the depositor is given a negative value in the functions above.

Write a program in which the user specifies a value to calculate, enters the four other values, and clicks on the Calculate Value button. See Fig. 5.47 on the previous page. Before any calculations are made, the program should use a Function procedure to validate that a radio button is checked and that the values entered into the four text boxes corresponding to unchecked radio buttons are valid.

8. An Interesting Numerical Algorithm   Write a program that asks the user to enter a three-digit number in which the digits are in decreasing order. (Two examples are 973 and 742.) Display the result of the following calculations:

(a) Reverse the digits of the number, then subtract the reversed number from the original entered number. Call the difference n.

(b) Add the number n to the number obtained by reversing the digits of n.

See Fig. 5.48. (*Note:* The result will always be 1089.) Use a Boolean-valued Function procedure to verify that a valid number is entered, and use a Function procedure that reverses the digits of a three-digit number.

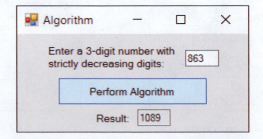

FIGURE 5.48   Output of Programming Project 8.

6

Repetition

6.1 Do Loops

A **loop,** one of the most important structures in programming, is used to repeat a sequence of statements a number of times. During each repetition, or **pass,** the statements act upon variables whose values are changing.

The **Do loop** repeats a sequence of statements either as long as or until a certain condition is true. A Do statement precedes the sequence of statements, and a Loop statement follows the sequence of statements. The condition, preceded by either the word "While" or the word "Until", follows the word "Do" or the word "Loop".

■ Pretest Form of a Do Loop

When Visual Basic encounters a Do loop of the form

```
Do While condition
    statement(s)
Loop
```

it first checks the truth value of *condition*. If *condition* is false, then the statements inside the loop are not executed, and the program continues with the line after the statement Loop. If *condition* is true, then the statements inside the loop are executed. When the statement Loop is encountered, the entire process is repeated, beginning with the testing of *condition* in the Do While statement. In other words, the statements inside the loop are repeatedly executed as long as (that is, while) the condition is true. Figure 6.1 contains the pseudocode and flowchart for this loop.

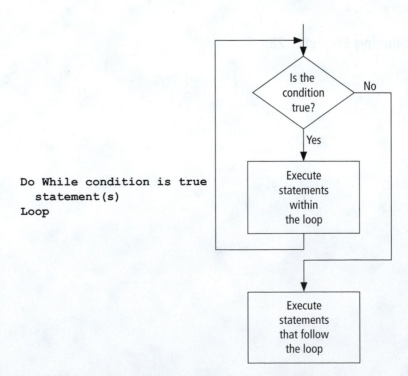

```
Do While condition is true
    statement(s)
Loop
```

FIGURE 6.1 **Pseudocode and flowchart for a Do loop with the condition tested at the top.**

Example 1 **Numbers** The following program, in which the condition in the Do loop is "num <= 7", displays the numbers from 1 through 7. (After the Do loop terminates, the value of *num* will be 8.)

```
Private Sub btnDisplay_Click(...) Handles btnDisplay.Click
  'Display the numbers from 1 to 7
  Dim num As Integer = 1
  Do While num <= 7
    lstNumbers.Items.Add(num)
    num += 1      'add 1 to the value of num
  Loop
End Sub
```

[Run, and click on the button. The following is displayed in the list box.]

```
1
2
3
4
5
6
7
```

Do loops can be used to ensure that a proper response is received from the InputBox function.

 Example 2 **Movie Quotations** The following program requires the user to enter a number from 1 through 3. The Do loop repeats the request until the user gives a proper response.

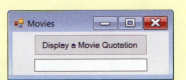

OBJECT	PROPERTY	SETTING
frmMovie	Text	Movies
btnDisplay	Text	Display a Movie Quotation
txtQuotation	ReadOnly	True

```
Private Sub btnDisplay_Click(...) Handles btnDisplay.Click
  Dim response As Integer = 0, quotation As String = ""
  Do While (response < 1) Or (response > 3)
    response = CInt(InputBox("Enter a number from 1 to 3."))
  Loop
  Select Case response
    Case 1
      quotation = "Plastics."
    Case 2
      quotation = "Rosebud."
    Case 3
      quotation = "That's all folks."
  End Select
  txtQuotation.Text = quotation
End Sub
```

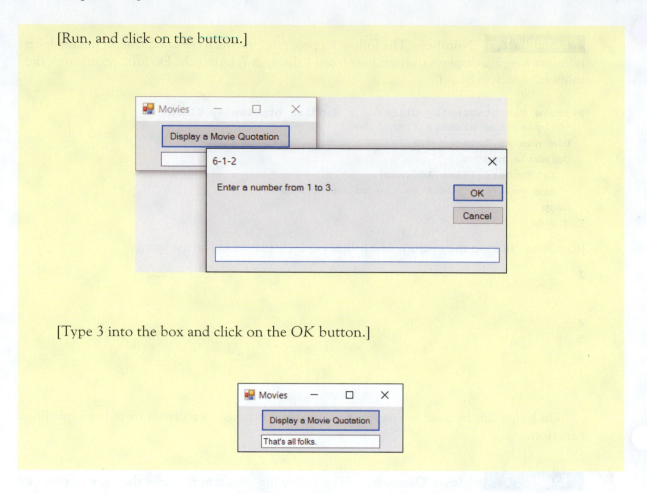

[Run, and click on the button.]

[Type 3 into the box and click on the OK button.]

In the next example, a Do loop is used to process data input by the user.

✓ **Example 3** **Average of Numbers** The following program finds the average of a sequence of nonnegative numbers entered by the user from input dialog boxes. The user should type in the number −1 to indicate the end of data entry. Since the first input dialog box appears before the loop is entered, there is the possibility that the entire loop will be skipped.

```
Private Sub btnCompute_Click(...) Handles btnCompute.Click
  Dim num As Double = 0
  Dim count As Integer = 0
  Dim sum As Double = 0
  Dim prompt As String = "Enter a nonnegative number. " &
                         "Enter -1 to terminate entering numbers."
  num = CDbl(InputBox(prompt))
  Do While num <> -1
    count += 1
    sum += num
    num = CDbl(InputBox(prompt))
  Loop
```

```
If count > 0 Then
    MessageBox.Show("Average: " & sum / count)
Else
    MessageBox.Show("No nonnegative numbers were entered.")
End If
End Sub
```

[Run, click on the button, and respond to the requests for input with 80, 90, and −1. The following is displayed in the message box.]

```
Average: 85
```

In Example 3, the variable *count* is called a **counter variable**, the variable *sum* is called an **accumulator variable**, the number −1 is called a **sentinel value**, and the loop is referred to as having **sentinel-controlled repetition**.

■ Posttest Form of a Do Loop

In Examples 1, 2, and 3 the condition was checked at the top of the loop—that is, before the statements were executed. Alternatively, the condition can be checked at the bottom of the loop when the Loop statement is reached. When Visual Basic encounters a Do loop of the form

```
Do
    statement(s)
Loop Until condition
```

it executes the statements inside the loop and then checks the truth value of *condition*. If *condition* is true, then the program continues with the line after the Loop statement. If *condition* is false, then the entire process is repeated beginning with the Do statement. In other words, the statements inside the loop are executed once and then are repeatedly executed *until* the condition is true. Figure 6.2 shows the pseudocode and flowchart for this type of Do loop.

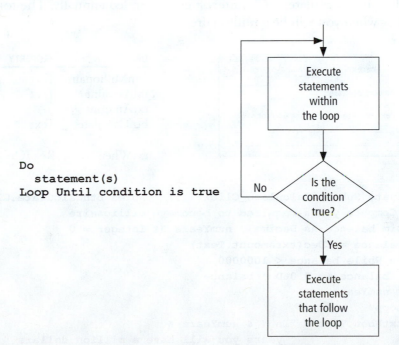

```
Do
    statement(s)
Loop Until condition is true
```

FIGURE 6.2 **Pseudocode and flowchart for a Do loop with the condition tested at the bottom.**

Example 4 Movie Quotations The following program is equivalent to Example 2, except that the condition is tested at the bottom of the loop.

```
Private Sub btnDisplay_Click(...) Handles btnDisplay.Click
  Dim response As Integer, quotation As String = ""
  Do
    response = CInt(InputBox("Enter a number from 1 to 3."))
  Loop Until (response >= 1) And (response <= 3)
  Select Case response
    Case 1
      quotation = "Plastics."
    Case 2
      quotation = "Rosebud."
    Case 3
      quotation = "That's all folks."
  End Select
  txtQuotation.Text = quotation
End Sub
```

■ A Financial Calculation

Do loops allow us to calculate useful quantities for which we might not know a simple formula. The calculation in Example 5 is easily carried out with a Do loop, whereas deriving a mathematical calculation requires knowledge of logarithms.

 Example 5 Compound Interest Suppose you deposit money into a savings account and let it accumulate at 6% interest compounded annually. The following program determines when you will be a millionaire.

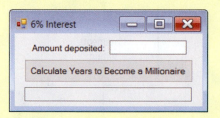

OBJECT	PROPERTY	SETTING
frmMillionaire	Text	6% Interest
lblAmount	Text	Amount deposited:
txtAmount		
btnCalculate	Text	Calculate Years to Become a Millionaire
txtWhen	ReadOnly	True

```
Private Sub btnCalculate_Click(...) Handles btnCalculate.Click
  'Compute years required to become a millionaire
  Dim balance As Decimal, numYears As Integer = 0
  balance = CDec(txtAmount.Text)
  Do While balance < 1000000
    balance += 0.06D * balance
    numYears += 1
  Loop
  txtWhen.Text = "In " & numYears &
                 " years you will have a million dollars."
End Sub
```

[Run, type 100000 into the text box, and click on the button.]

■ Comments

1. Avoid infinite loops—that is, loops that never end. The following loop is infinite because the condition "balance < 1000" will always be true. This logic error can be avoided by initializing *intRate* with a value greater than 0.

```
Private Sub btnButton_Click(...) Handles btnButton.Click
  'An infinite loop
  Dim balance As Double = 100, intRate As Double
  Do While balance < 1000
    balance = (1 + intRate) * balance
  Loop
  txtBalance.Text = balance.ToString("C")
End Sub
```

   Important: While an infinite loop is executing, the program can be terminated by clicking on the *Stop Debugging* button on the Toolbar.

2. Visual Basic provides a way to break out of a Do loop before the loop condition is met. When the statement **Exit Do** is encountered in the body of a loop, execution jumps immediately to the statement following the Loop statement.

3. A variable declared inside a Do loop has block scope; that is, the variable cannot be referred to by code outside the loop.

4. Visual Basic allows the use of the words "While" and "Until" at either the top or bottom of a Do loop. For instance, the fourth line in the program in Example 1 can be replaced with

```
Do Until num > 7
```

   and the fifth line of the program in Example 4 can be replaced with

```
Loop While (response < 1) Or (response > 3)
```

Practice Problems 6.1

1. How do you decide whether a condition should be checked at the top of a loop or at the bottom?

2. Change the following code segment so that the loop will execute at least once.

```
Do While answer.ToUpper = "Y"
  answer = InputBox("Do you want to continue? (Y or N)")
Loop
```

In Exercises 1 through 6, determine the output displayed when the button is clicked on.

1.
```
Private Sub btnDisplay_Click(...) Handles btnDisplay.Click
    Dim num As Integer = 3
    Do While num < 15
      num += 5
    Loop
    txtOutput.Text = CStr(num)
End Sub
```

2.
```
Private Sub btnDisplay_Click(...) Handles btnDisplay.Click
    Dim num As Integer = 3
    Do
      num = 2 * num
    Loop Until num > 15
    txtOutput.Text = CStr(num)
End Sub
```

3.
```
Private Sub btnDisplay_Click(...) Handles btnDisplay.Click
    Dim total As Double = 0
    Dim num As Integer = 1
    Do While num < 5
      total += num
      num += 1
    Loop
    txtOutput.Text = CStr(total)
End Sub
```

4.
```
Private Sub btnDisplay_Click(...) Handles btnDisplay.Click
    Dim total As Double = 0
    Dim num As Integer = 1
    Do
      total += num
      num += 1
    Loop Until num >= 5
    txtOutput.Text = CStr(total)
End Sub
```

5.
```
Private Sub btnCompute_Click(...) Handles btnCompute.Click
    Dim num As Double = 0
    Dim max As Double = -1
    Dim prompt As String = "Enter a nonnegative number. " &
                           "Enter -1 to terminate entering numbers."
    num = CDbl(InputBox(prompt))
    Do While num >= 0
      If num > max Then
```

```
        max = num
      End If
      num = CDbl(InputBox(prompt))
   Loop
   If max <> -1 Then
      MessageBox.Show("Maximum number: " & max)
   Else
      MessageBox.Show("No numbers were entered.")
   End If
End Sub
```

(Assume that the responses are 4, 7, 3, and −1.)

6.
```
Private Sub btnDisplay_Click(...) Handles btnDisplay.Click
   Dim numTries As Integer = 0
   Dim yr As Integer
   Dim msg As String = "In what year did the Beatles invade the U.S.?"
   Do
      numTries += 1
      yr = CInt(InputBox(msg, "Try #" & numTries))
      Select Case yr
        Case 1964
          MessageBox.Show("They appeared on the Ed Sullivan show in " &
                        "February 1964." & " You answered the question " &
                        "correctly in " & numTries & " tries.", "Correct")
        Case Is < 1964
          MessageBox.Show("Later than " & yr & ".")
        Case Is > 1964
          MessageBox.Show("Earlier than " & yr & ".")
      End Select
   Loop Until (yr = 1964) Or (numTries = 7)
   If yr <> 1964 Then
      MessageBox.Show("Your 7 tries are up, the answer is 1964.", "Sorry")
   End If
End Sub
```

(Assume that the responses are 1950, 1970, and 1964.)

In Exercises 7 through 10, identify the errors.

7.
```
Private Sub btnDisplay_Click(...) Handles btnDisplay.Click
   Dim q As Double = 1
   Do While q > 0
      q = 3 * q - 1
      lstOutput.Items.Add(q)
   Loop
End Sub
```

8.
```
Private Sub btnDisplay_Click(...) Handles btnDisplay.Click
    'Display the numbers from 1 to 5
    Dim num As Integer
    Do While num <> 6
      num = 1
      lstOutput.Items.Add(num)
      num += 1
    Loop
  End Sub
```

9.
```
Private Sub btnDisplay_Click(...) Handles btnDisplay.Click
    'Repeat until a yes response is given
    Dim answer As String = "N"
    Loop
      answer = InputBox("Did you chop down the cherry tree (Y/N)?")
    Do Until (answer.ToUpper = "Y")
  End Sub
```

10.
```
Private Sub btnDisplay_Click(...) Handles btnDisplay.Click
    'Repeat as long as desired
    Dim n As Integer = 0, answer As String = ""
    Do
      n += 1
      lstOutput.Items.Add(n)
      answer = InputBox("Do you want to continue (Y/N)?")
    Until answer.ToUpper = "N"
  End Sub
```

In Exercises 11 through 20, replace each phrase containing "Until" with an equivalent phrase containing "While", and vice versa. For instance, the phrase (Until sum $=$ 100) would be replaced by (While sum $<>$ 100).

11. `Until num < 7`

12. `Until name = "Bob"`

13. `While response = "Y"`

14. `While total = 10`

15. `While name <> ""`

16. `Until balance >= 100`

17. `While (a > 1) And (a < 3)`

18. `Until (ans = "") Or (n = 0)`

19. `Until Not(n = 0)`

20. `While (ans = "Y") And (n < 7)`

In Exercises 21 and 22, write simpler and clearer code that performs the same task as the given code.

21.
```
Private Sub btnDisplay_Click(...) Handles btnDisplay.Click
    Dim name As String
    name = InputBox("Enter a name:")
    lstOutput.Items.Add(name)
    name = InputBox("Enter a name:")
    lstOutput.Items.Add(name)
    name = InputBox("Enter a name:")
    lstOutput.Items.Add(name)
End Sub
```

22.
```
Private Sub btnDisplay_Click(...) Handles btnDisplay.Click
    Dim loopNum As Integer = 0, answer As String = ""
    Do
        If loopNum >= 1 Then
            answer = InputBox("Do you want to continue (Y/N)?")
            answer = answer.ToUpper
        Else
            answer = "Y"
        End If
        If (answer = "Y") Or (loopNum = 0) Then
            loopNum += 1
            txtOutput.Text = CStr(loopNum)
        End If
    Loop Until (answer <> "Y")
End Sub
```

23. **Temperature Conversions**   Write a program that displays a Celsius-to-Fahrenheit conversion table in a list box. Entries in the table should range from 10 to 40 degrees Celsius in increments of 5 degrees. See Fig. 6.3. **Note:** The formula $f = (9/5 * c) + 32$ converts Celsius to Fahrenheit.

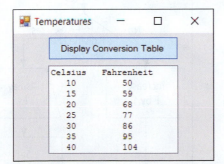

FIGURE 6.3   Outcome of Exercise 23.

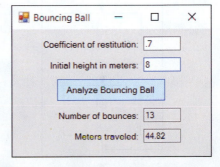

FIGURE 6.4   Possible outcome of Exercise 24.

24. **Bouncing Ball**   The *coefficient of restitution* of a ball, a number between 0 and 1, specifies how much energy is conserved when the ball hits a rigid surface. A coefficient of .9, for instance, means a bouncing ball will rise to 90% of its previous height after each bounce. Write a program to input a coefficient of restitution and an initial height in meters, and report how many times a ball bounces when dropped from its initial height

before it rises to a height of less than 10 centimeters. Also report the total distance traveled by the ball before that point. See Fig. 6.4 on the previous page. The coefficients of restitution of a tennis ball, basketball, super ball, and softball are .7, .75, .9, and .3, respectively.

25. Range of Numbers   Write a program that finds the range of a sequence of nonnegative numbers entered by the user from input dialog boxes. (The *range* is the difference between the largest and the smallest numbers in the sequence.) The user should be told to type in the number −1 to indicate that the entire sequence has been entered.

26. Smallest Number   Write a program that finds the smallest number in a sequence of nonnegative numbers entered by the user from input dialog boxes. The user should be told to type in the number −1 to indicate that the entire sequence has been entered.

In Exercises 27 and 28, write a program corresponding to the flowchart.

27. Greatest Common Divisor   The flowchart in Fig. 6.5 finds the greatest common divisor (the largest integer that divides both) of two positive integers input by the user. See Fig. 6.7.

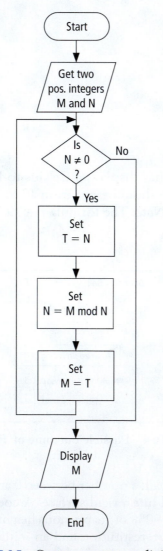

FIGURE 6.5   **Greatest common divisor.**

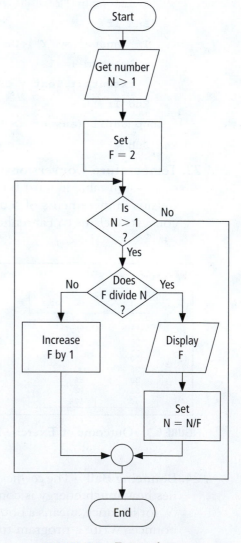

FIGURE 6.6   **Prime factors.**

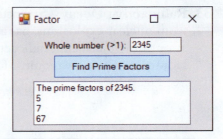

FIGURE 6.7   Possible outcome of Exercise 27.

FIGURE 6.8   Possible outcome of Exercise 28.

28. **Factorization**   The flowchart in Fig. 6.6 requests a whole number greater than 1 as input and factors it into a product of prime numbers. **Note:** A number is *prime* if its only factors are 1 and itself. See Fig. 6.8.

29. **First Tuesday**   Write a program that requests a month and year as input and then determines the date of the first Tuesday of that month. See Fig. 6.9.

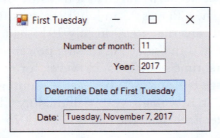

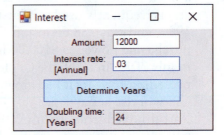

FIGURE 6.9   Possible outcome of Exercise 29.

FIGURE 6.10   Possible outcome of Exercise 30.

30. **Compound Interest**   Illustrate the growth of money in a savings account. When the user clicks the button, values for Amount and Interest Rate are obtained from text boxes and used to calculate the number of years until the money doubles. See Fig. 6.10. **Note:** The balance at the end of each year is $(1 + r)$ times the previous balance, where r is the annual rate of interest in decimal form.

In Exercises 31 through 38, write a program to answer the question.

31. **Age**   A person born in 1980 can claim, "I will be x years old in the year x squared." What is the value of x? See Fig. 6.11

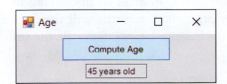

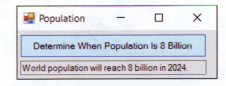

FIGURE 6.11   Outcome of Exercise 31.

FIGURE 6.12   Outcome of Exercise 32.

32. **Population Growth**   The world population reached 7 billion people on October 21, 2011, and was growing at the rate of 1.1% each year. Assuming that the population will continue to grow at the same rate, approximately when will the population reach 8 billion? See Fig. 6.12.

33. Radioactive Decay Strontium-90, a radioactive element that is part of the fallout from nuclear explosions, has a half-life of 28 years. This means that a given quantity of strontium-90 will emit radioactive particles and decay to one-half its mass every 28 years. How many years are required for 100 grams of strontium-90 to decay to less than 1 gram? See Fig. 6.13.

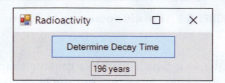

FIGURE 6.13   Outcome of Exercise 33.

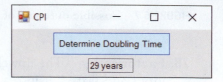

FIGURE 6.14   Outcome of Exercise 34.

34. Consumer Price Index The *consumer price index (CPI)* indicates the average price of a fixed basket of goods and services. It is customarily taken as a measure of inflation and is frequently used to adjust pensions. The CPI was 9.9 in July 1913, was 100 in July 1983, and was 238.65 in July 2015. This means that $9.90 in July 1913 had the same purchasing power as $100.00 in July 1983, and the same purchasing power as $238.65 in July 2015. In 2009, the CPI fell for the first time since 1955. However, for most of the preceding 15 years it had grown at an average rate of 2.5 % per year. Assuming that the CPI will rise at 2.5% per year in the future, in how many years will the July CPI have at least doubled from its July 2015 level? **Note:** Each year, the CPI will be 1.025 times the CPI for the previous year. See Fig. 6.14.

35. Loan When you borrow money to buy a house or a car, the loan is paid off with a sequence of equal monthly payments with a stated annual interest rate compounded monthly. The amount borrowed is called the *principal*. If the annual interest rate is 6% (or .06), then the monthly interest rate is .06/12 = .005. At any time, the *balance* of the loan is the amount still owed. The balance at the end of each month is calculated as the balance at the end of the previous month, plus the interest due on that balance, and minus the monthly payment. For instance, with an annual interest rate of 6%,

$$[\text{new balance}] = [\text{previous balance}] + .005 \cdot [\text{previous balance}] - [\text{monthly payment}]$$
$$= 1.005 \cdot [\text{previous balance}] - [\text{monthly payment}].$$

Suppose you borrow $15,000 to buy a new car at 6% interest compounded monthly and your monthly payment is $290.00. After how many months will the car be half paid off? That is, after how many months will the balance be less than half the principal? See Fig. 6.15.

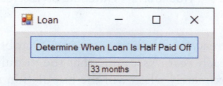

FIGURE 6.15   Outcome of Exercise 35.

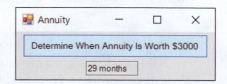

FIGURE 6.16   Outcome of Exercise 36.

36. **Annuity**   An *annuity* is a sequence of equal periodic payments. One type of annuity, called a *savings plan*, consists of monthly payments into a savings account in order to generate money for a future purchase. Suppose you decide to deposit $100 at the end of each month into a savings account paying 3% interest compounded monthly. The monthly interest rate will be .03/12 or .0025, and the balance in the account at the end of each month will be computed as

    [balance at end of month] = (1.0025)·[balance at end of previous month] + 100.

    After how many months will there be more than $3000 in the account? See Fig. 6.16.

37. **Annuity**   An *annuity* is a sequence of equal periodic payments. For one type of annuity, a large amount of money is deposited into a bank account and then a fixed amount is withdrawn each month. Suppose you deposit $10,000 into such an account paying 3.6% interest compounded monthly, and then withdraw $600 at the end of each month. The monthly interest rate will be .036/12 or .003, and the balance in the account at the end of each month will be computed as

    [balance at end of month] = (1.003)·[balance at end of previous month] − 600.

    After how many months will the account contain less than $600, and what will be the amount in the account at that time? See Fig. 6.17.

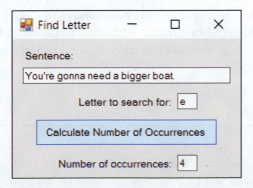

FIGURE 6.17   Outcome of Exercise 37.

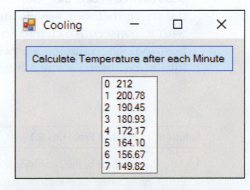

FIGURE 6.18   Possible outcome of Exercise 38.

38. **Annuity**   Redo Exercise 37 with the amount of money deposited being input by the user. See Fig. 6.18.

39. **Occurrences of a Letter**   Write a program that requests a sentence and a letter as input and then counts the number of times the letter (either upper- or lower-case) appears in the sentence. See Fig. 6.19.

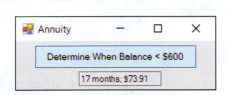

FIGURE 6.19   Possible outcome of Exercise 39.

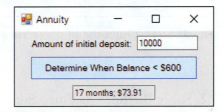

FIGURE 6.20   Outcome of Exercise 40.

40. **Cooling** *Newton's Law of Cooling* states that when a hot liquid is placed in a cool room, each minute the decrease in the temperature is approximately proportional to the differences between the liquid's temperature and the room's temperature. That is, there is a constant *k* such that each minute the temperature loss is $k \cdot$ (liquid's temperature − room's temperature). Suppose a cup of 212°F coffee is placed in a 70°F room and that $k = .079$. Write a program that determines the number of minutes required for the coffee to cool to below 150°F, and display the temperature at the end of each minute. See Fig. 6.20 on the previous page.

41. **Population Growth** In 2016 China's population was about 1.37 billion and growing at the rate of .66% per year. In 2016 India's population was about 1.31 billion and growing at the rate of 1.3% per year. Assuming the population growth rates stay constant, write a program to determine when India's population will surpass China's population. See Fig. 6.21.

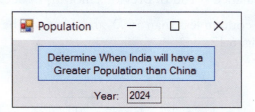

FIGURE 6.21 Outcome of Exercise 41.

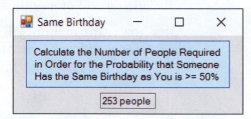

FIGURE 6.22 Outcome of Exercise 42.

42. **Same Birthday as You** Suppose you are in a large-lecture class with *n* other students. Write a program to determine how large *n* must be so that the probability that someone has the same birthday as you is greater than 50%. See Fig. 6.22. **Note:** Forgetting about leap years and so assuming 365 days in a year, the probability that no one has the same birthday as you is $\left(\dfrac{364}{365}\right)^n$.

43. **Replace Method** Visual Basic has a string method named **Replace**. The value of **strVar.Replace(strVar1, strVar2)** is *strVar* with each occurrence of the substring *strVar1* replaced with *strVar2*. For instance, if **strVar = "tat-tat-tat"** then the value of **strVar.Replace("tat", "cha")** is "cha-cha-cha". Write a function named *Substitute* that performs the same task as the *Replace* method. For instance, the value of **Substitute("tat-tat-tat", "tat", "cha")** should be "cha-cha-cha". Feel free to use the string methods **Remove** and **Insert**. The value of **strVar.Remove(n, m)** is *strVar* with *m* consecutive characters from it deleted beginning with the character in the *n*th position. The value of **strVar1.Insert(n, strVar2)** is *strVar1* with *strVar2* inserted into it, beginning at the *n*th position.

Solutions to Practice Problems 6.1

1. As a rule of thumb, the condition is checked at the bottom if the loop should be executed at least once.

2. Either precede the loop with the statement **answer = "Y"**, or change the first line to **Do** and replace the Loop statement with **Loop Until answer <> "Y"**.

6.2   For . . . Next Loops

When we know exactly how many times a loop should be executed, a special type of loop, called a **For . . . Next loop**, can be used. For . . . Next loops are easy to read and write and they have features that make them ideal for certain common tasks. The following code uses a For . . . Next loop to display a table:

```
Private Sub btnDisplayTable_Click(...) Handles btnDisplayTable.Click
  'Display a table of the first 5 numbers and their squares
  'Assume the font for lstTable is Courier New
  For i As Integer = 1 To 5
    lstTable.Items.Add(i & "   " & i ^ 2)
  Next
End Sub
```

[Run, and click on the button. The following is displayed in the list box.]

```
1   1
2   4
3   9
4   16
5   25
```

A similar program written with a Do loop is as follows.

```
Private Sub btnDisplayTable_Click(...) Handles btnDisplayTable.Click
  'Display a table of the first 5 numbers and their squares
  Dim i As Integer
  i = 1
  Do While i <= 5
    lstTable.Items.Add(i & "   " & i ^ 2)
    i += 1      'add 1 to i
  Loop
End Sub
```

■ General Form of a For . . . Next Loop

VideoNote

For . . . Next Loops

In general, a portion of a program of the form in Fig. 6.23 constitutes of For . . . Next loop.

```
initial value ──────┐
counter variable ───┤    For i As numDataType = m To n  ◄──────── terminating value
                         statement(s)                   ◄──────── body
                    Next
```

FIGURE 6.23   For . . . Next loop.

The pair of statements For and Next cause the statements between them to be repeated a specified number of times. The For statement declares a numeric variable, called the **counter variable**, that is initialized and then automatically changes after each pass through the loop. Also, the For statement gives the range of values this variable will assume. The Next statement increments the counter variable. If $m \leq n$, then i is assigned the values $m, m + 1, \ldots, n$ in order, and the body is executed once for each of these values. If $m > n$, then the body is skipped and execution continues with the statement after the Next statement.

When program execution reaches a For . . . Next loop, such as the one shown previously, the For statement assigns to the counter variable i the **initial value** m and checks to see whether i is greater than the **terminating value** n. If so, then execution jumps to the line following the Next statement. If $i <= n$, the statements inside the loop are executed. Then, the Next statement increases the value of i by 1 and checks this new value to see if it exceeds n. If not, the entire process is repeated until the value of i exceeds n. When this happens, the program moves to the line following the loop. Figure 6.24 contains the pseudocode and flowchart of a For . . . Next loop.

The counter variable can be any numeric variable. The most common single-letter names are i, j, and k; however, if appropriate, the name should suggest the meaning of the counter variable.

The counter variable, and any variable declared inside a For . . . Next loop, has **block scope**; that is, the variable cannot be referred to by code outside the loop.

```
For i As numDataType = m to n
    statement(s)
Next
```

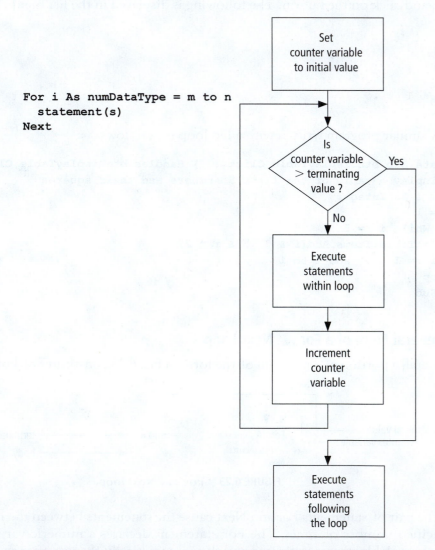

FIGURE 6.24 **Pseudocode and flowchart of a For . . . Next loop.**

A counter variable also can be declared with a Dim statement outside the For . . . Next loop. For instance, the following program produces the same output as the program shown at the beginning of this section.

```
Private Sub btnDisplay_Click(...) Handles btnDisplay.Click
  'Display a table of the first 5 numbers and their squares
  'Assume the font for lstTable is Courier New
  Dim i As Integer
  For i = 1 To 5
    lstTable.Items.Add(i & "   " & i ^ 2)
  Next
End Sub
```

In this case, the variable *i* does not have block scope, and therefore it violates the principle that the scope of a variable should be as small as possible. In this book, we never declare a counter variable outside a For . . . Next loop.

Example 1   **Population Growth** Suppose the population of a city is 300,000 in the year 2015 and is growing at the rate of 3% per year. The following program displays a table showing the population each year until 2019.

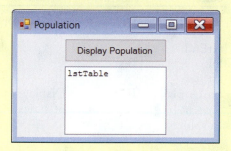

OBJECT	PROPERTY	SETTING
frmPopulation	Text	Population
btnDisplay	Text	Display Population
lstTable	Font	Courier New

```
Private Sub btnDisplay_Click(...) Handles btnDisplay.Click
  'Display population from 2015 to 2019
  Dim pop As Double = 300000
  For yr As Integer = 2015 To 2019
    lstTable.Items.Add(yr & "    " & pop.ToString("N0")
    pop += 0.03 * pop
  Next
End Sub
```

[Run, and click on the button.]

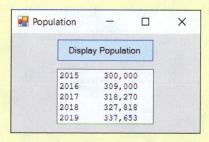

The initial and terminating values can be literals, variables, or expressions. For instance, the For statement in the preceding program can be replaced by

```
Dim firstYr As Integer = 2015
Dim lastYr As Integer = 2019
For yr As Integer = firstYr To lastYr
```

■ Step Keyword

In Example 1, the counter variable was increased by 1 after each pass through the loop. A variation of the For statement allows any number to be used as the increment. The statement

```
For i As numDataType = m To n Step s
```

instructs the Next statement to add s to the counter variable instead of 1. The numbers m, n, and s do not have to be whole numbers. The number s is called the **step value** of the loop. *Note 1:* If the counter variable will assume values that are not whole numbers, then the variable must be of type Decimal or Double. *Note 2:* The counter variable is also called the **index**.

 Example 2   **Index Values** The following program displays the values of the index of a For . . . Next loop for terminating and step values input by the user.

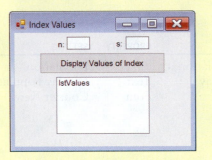

OBJECT	PROPERTY	SETTING
frmIndex	Text	Index Values
lblN	Text	n:
txtEnd		
lblS	Text	s:
txtStep		
btnDisplay	Text	Display Values of Index
lstValues		

```
Private Sub btnDisplay_Click(...) Handles btnDisplay.Click
  'Display values of index ranging from 0 to n Step s
  Dim n, s As Decimal
  n = CDec(txtEnd.Text)
  s = CDec(txtStep.Text)
  lstValues.Items.Clear()
  For index As Decimal = 0 To n Step s
    lstValues.Items.Add(index)
  Next
End Sub
```

[Run, type 3.2 and .6 into the text boxes, and click on the button.]

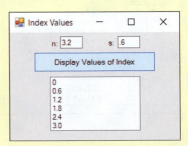

In the examples considered so far, the counter variable was successively increased until it reached the terminating value. However, if a negative step value is used and the initial value is greater than the terminating value, then the counter value is decreased until reaching the terminating value. In other words, the loop counts backward.

Example 3 **Reverse Letters** The following program accepts a word as input and displays it backward:

OBJECT	PROPERTY	SETTING
frmBackward	Text	Write Backward
lblWord	Text	Enter word:
txtWord		
btnReverse	Text	Reverse Letters
txtBackward	ReadOnly	True

```
Private Sub btnReverse_Click(...) Handles btnReverse.Click
   txtBackward.Text = Reverse(txtWord.Text)
End Sub

Function Reverse(info As String) As String
  Dim m As Integer, temp As String = ""
  m = info.Length
  For j As Integer = m - 1 To 0 Step -1
    temp &= info.Substring(j, 1)
  Next
  Return temp
End Function
```

[Run, type "SUEZ" into the text box, and click on the button.]

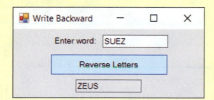

Note: The initial and terminating values of a For . . . Next loop can be expressions. For instance, the third and fourth lines of the function in Example 3 can be consolidated to

```
For j As Integer = (info.Length - 1) To 0 Step -1
```

■ Nested For . . . Next Loops

The body of a For . . . Next loop can contain any sequence of Visual Basic statements. In particular, it can contain another For . . . Next loop. However, the second loop must be completely contained inside the first loop and must have a different counter variable. Such a configuration is called **nested For . . . Next loops**.

Example 4 **Multiplication Table** The following program displays a multiplication table for the integers from 1 to 3. Here *j* denotes the left factors of the products, and *k* denotes the right factors. Each factor takes on a value from 1 to 3. The values are assigned to *j* in the outer loop (lines 4–11) and to *k* in the inner loop (lines 6–9). Initially, *j* is assigned the value 1, and then the inner loop is traversed three times to produce the first row of products. At the end of these three passes, the value of *j* will still be 1, and the first execution of the inner

loop will be complete. Following this, the statement Next increments the value of *j* to 2. The statement beginning "For *k*" is then executed. It resets the value of *k* to 1. The second row of products is displayed during the next three executions of the inner loop, and so on.

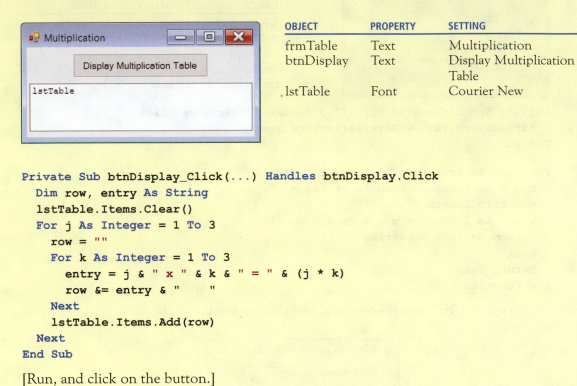

OBJECT	PROPERTY	SETTING
frmTable	Text	Multiplication
btnDisplay	Text	Display Multiplication Table
lstTable	Font	Courier New

```
Private Sub btnDisplay_Click(...) Handles btnDisplay.Click
  Dim row, entry As String
  lstTable.Items.Clear()
  For j As Integer = 1 To 3
    row = ""
    For k As Integer = 1 To 3
      entry = j & " x " & k & " = " & (j * k)
      row &= entry & "      "
    Next
    lstTable.Items.Add(row)
  Next
End Sub
```

[Run, and click on the button.]

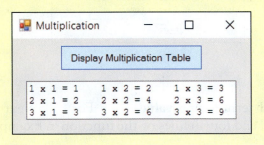

■ Local Type Inference

Local type inference (also referred to as *implicit typing*) allows you to declare and initialize a local variable without explicitly stating its type with an As clause. Local type inference is enabled if Option Infer is set to On in the VB Defaults dialog box shown in Figure 3.13 of Section 3.2. (It is enabled by default.)

Some examples of the use of local type inference are as follows:

Standard Declaration	Local Type Inference Equivalent
Dim count As Integer = 5	Dim count = 5
Dim rate As Decimal = 0.05D	Dim rate = 0.05D
Dim rate as Double = 0.05	Dim rate = 0.05
Dim name As String = "Fred"	Dim name = "Fred"
Dim d as Date = #6/4/2012#	Dim d = #6/4/2012#
For i As Integer = 1 To 3	For i = 1 To 3
For i As Double = 1 To 3 Step 0.5	For i = 1 To 3 Step 0.5
For i As Decimal = 1 To 3 Step 0.5D	For i = 1 To 3 Step 0.5D

With local type inference, the type of a local variable is determined by the values following the equal sign. If the values are all whole numbers (written without a decimal point) and in the range of values for Integers, then the variable is declared to be of type Integer. If any of the values are numeric literals containing a decimal point (and not followed by the letter *D*) or are outside the range of values for Integers, then the variable is declared to be of type Double. If the value is surrounded in quotes, then it is declared to be of type String. If the value is a date literal, then the variable is declared to be of type Date. **Note:** This feature *does not* apply to variables having class scope.

The following walkthrough (which assumes that Option Infer is On) demonstrates how local type inference works in a For . . . Next loop.

1. Create a new program consisting of a form having a button (btnConfirm) and a list box (lstBox).

2. Enter the following code:

```
Private Sub btnConfirm_Click(...) Handles btnConfirm.Click
  For i = 1 To 5 Step 2
    lstBox.Items.Add(i)
  Next
End Sub
```

3. In the Code Editor, hover the mouse pointer over the variable *i*. (The tooltip `Dim i As Integer` appears to confirm that the variable *i* has indeed been declared as type Integer.)

4. In the header of the For . . . Next loop, change the 2 to 2D and again hover the pointer over the letter *i*. (This time the tooltip reads `Dim i As Decimal`.)

Local type inference was added to Visual Basic in 2010 and is used extensively by LINQ (Language INtegrated Query), an innovative language feature that unifies the manipulation of diverse collections of data. LINQ is introduced in Chapter 7 of this book and is used extensively from then on. By necessity, we rely on local type inference when using LINQ. Although we do not use local type inference in the declaration of ordinary variables, you may feel free to do so if you prefer and your instructor permits.

Local type inference is also known as **duck typing**. This name comes from the well-known quote, "If it walks like a duck, and quacks like a duck, then it is a duck."

■ Comments

1. For and Next statements must be paired. If one is missing, the syntax checker will complain with a wavy blue line and a message such as "A 'For' must be paired with a 'Next'."

2. Consider a loop beginning with For $i = m$ To n Step s. The loop will be executed exactly once if m equals n no matter what value s has. The loop will not be executed at all if m is greater than n and s is positive, or if m is less than n and s is negative.

3. The value of the counter variable should not be altered within the body of the loop; doing so might cause the loop to repeat indefinitely or have an unpredictable number of repetitions.

4. The use of step values of type Double in For . . . Next loops can result in unexpected outcomes. For instance, if you change the data types in Example 2 to Double, the fourth number displayed will be 1.7999999999999998. All step values appearing in this book have data type Integer or Decimal.

5. Visual Basic provides a way to abort an iteration in a For . . . Next loop. When the statement **Continue For** is encountered in the body of the loop, execution immediately jumps to the Next statement. An analogous statement **Continue Do** is available for Do loops. Typically, Continue For and Continue Do statements appear inside conditional structures such as If blocks.

6. Visual Basic provides a way to back out of a For . . . Next loop. When the statement **Exit For** is encountered in the body of the loop, execution jumps immediately to the statement following the Next statement.

7. Counter variables and variables declared inside For . . . Next loops have block scope; that is, they cannot be referred to by code outside the loops.

8. Any type of loop can be nested inside another loop. For example, For . . . Next loops can be nested inside Do loops and vice versa. Also, Do loops can be nested inside other Do loops.

Practice Problems 6.2

1. Why won't the following lines of code work as intended?

```
For i As Integer = 15 To 1
    lstBox.Items.AddItem(i)
Next
```

2. When is a For . . . Next loop more appropriate than a Do loop?

EXERCISES 6.2

In Exercises 1 through 10, determine the output displayed in the list box when the button is clicked.

1.
```
Private Sub btnDisplay_Click(...) Handles btnDisplay.Click
    For i As Integer = 1 To 4
        lstBox.Items.Add("Pass #" & i)
    Next
End Sub
```

2.
```
Private Sub btnDisplay_Click(...) Handles btnDisplay.Click
    For i As Integer = 3 To 6
        lstBox.Items.Add(2 * i)
    Next
End Sub
```

3.
```
Private Sub btnDisplay_Click(...) Handles btnDisplay.Click
    For j As Integer = 2 To 8 Step 2
        lstBox.Items.Add(j)
    Next
    lstBox.Items.Add("Who do we appreciate?")
End Sub
```

4.
```
Private Sub btnDisplay_Click(...) Handles btnDisplay.Click
    For countdown As Integer = 10 To 1 Step -1
        lstBox.Items.Add(countdown)
    Next
    lstBox.Items.Add("blastoff")
End Sub
```

5.
```
Private Sub btnDisplay_Click(...) Handles btnDisplay.Click
    Dim num As Integer = 5
    For i As Integer = num To (2 * num - 3)
        lstBox.Items.Add(i)
    Next
End Sub
```

6.
```vb
Private Sub btnDisplay_Click(...) Handles btnDisplay.Click
    For i As Integer = -9 To -1 Step 3
        lstBox.Items.Add(i)
    Next
End Sub
```

7.
```vb
Private Sub btnDisplay_Click(...) Handles btnDisplay.Click
    'Chr(149) is a large dot
    Dim stringOfDots As String = ""
    For i As Integer = 1 To 10
        stringOfDots &= Chr(149)
    Next
    txtBox.Text = stringOfDots
End Sub
```

8.
```vb
Private Sub btnDisplay_Click(...) Handles btnDisplay.Click
    Dim n As Integer = 3
    Dim total As Integer = 0
    For i As Integer = 1 To n
        total += i
    Next
    txtBox.Text = CStr(total)
End Sub
```

9.
```vb
Private Sub btnDisplay_Click(...) Handles btnDisplay.Click
    'Note: Chr(65) is A and Chr(90) is Z
    Dim sentence, letter As String
    Dim numCaps As Integer = 0
    sentence = "The United States of America"
    For i As Integer = 0 To (sentence.Length - 1)
        letter = sentence.Substring(i, 1)
        If (Asc(letter) >= 65) And (Asc(letter) <= 90) Then
            numCaps += 1
        End If
    Next
    txtBox.Text = CStr(numCaps)
End Sub
```

10.
```vb
Private Sub btnDisplay_Click(...) Handles btnDisplay.Click
    Dim word As String = "courage"
    Dim letter As String = ""
    Dim numVowels As Integer = 0
    For i As Integer = 0 To (word.Length - 1)
        letter = word.Substring(i, 1)
        If IsVowel(letter) Then
            numVowels += 1
        End If
    Next
    txtBox.Text = CStr(numVowels)
End Sub
```

```
Function IsVowel(letter As String) As Boolean
  letter = letter.ToUpper
  If (letter = "A") Or (letter = "E") Or (letter = "I") Or
     (letter = "O") Or (letter = "U") Then
    Return True
  Else
    Return False
  End If
End Function
```

In Exercises 11 through 14, identify the errors.

11.
```
Private Sub btnDisplay_Click(...) Handles btnDisplay.Click

  For j As Integer = 1 To 25 Step -1
    lstBox.Items.Add(j)
  Next
End Sub
```

12.
```
Private Sub btnDisplay_Click(...) Handles btnDisplay.Click

  For i As Integer = 1 To 3
    lstBox.Items.Add(i & " " & 2 ^ i)
End Sub
```

13.
```
Private Sub btnDisplay_Click(...) Handles btnDisplay.Click

    'Display all numbers from 0 through 20 except for 13
    For i As Integer = 20 To 0
      If i = 13 Then
        i = 12
      End If
      lstBox.Items.Add(i)
    Next
End Sub
```

14.
```
Private Sub btnDisplay_Click(...) Handles btnDisplay.Click

    For j As Integer = 1 To 4 Step 0.5
      lstBox.Items.Add(j)
    Next
End Sub
```

In Exercises 15 and 16, rewrite the program using a For . . . Next loop.

15.
```
Private Sub btnDisplay_Click(...) Handles btnDisplay.Click

    Dim num As Integer = 1
    Do While num <= 9
      lstBox.Items.Add(num)
      num += 2 'add 2 to value of num
    Loop
End Sub
```

16.
```
Private Sub btnDisplay_Click(...) Handles btnDisplay.Click

    lstBox.Items.Add("hello")
    lstBox.Items.Add("hello")
    lstBox.Items.Add("hello")
    lstBox.Items.Add("hello")
End Sub
```

In Exercises 17 through 37, write a program containing a For . . . Next loop to carry out the stated task.

17. **Radioactive Decay** Cobalt-60, a radioactive form of cobalt used in cancer therapy, decays over a period of time. Each year, 12% of the amount present at the beginning of the year will have decayed. If a container of cobalt-60 initially contains 10 grams, determine the amount remaining after five years. See Fig. 6.25.

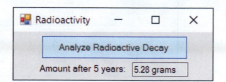

FIGURE 6.25   Outcome of Exercise 17.

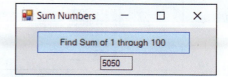

FIGURE 6.26   Outcome of Exercise 18.

18. **Sum of Numbers** Find the sum of the first one hundred positive integers. See Fig. 6.26.

19. **Average of Numbers** Find the average of five numbers obtained from the user with input dialog boxes.

20. **Largest Number** Find the largest of five numbers obtained from the user with input dialog boxes. See Fig. 6.27.

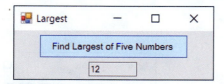

FIGURE 6.27   Possible outcome of Exercise 20.

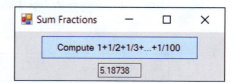

FIGURE 6.28   Outcome of Exercise 21.

21. **Sum of Fractions** Find the value of $1 + 1/2 + 1/3 + 1/4 + \cdots + 1/100$. See Fig. 6.28.

22. **String of Dots** Ask the user to input a positive integer (call it n) and then display a string of n large dots. See Fig. 6.29. **Note:** Chr(149) is a large dot.

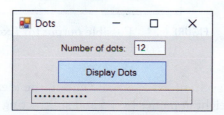

FIGURE 6.29   Possible outcome of Exercise 22.

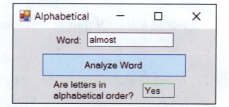

FIGURE 6.30   Possible outcome of Exercise 23.

23. **Alphabetical Order** Accept a word as input and determine if its letters are in alphabetical order. See Fig. 6.30. **Note:** Some words whose letters are in alphabetical order are "forty", "glory", "adept", and "bijoux".

24. Automobile Depreciation A rule of thumb states that cars in personal use depreciate by 15% each year. Suppose a new car is purchased for $20,000. Produce a table showing the value of the car at the end of each of the next five years. See Fig. 6.31.

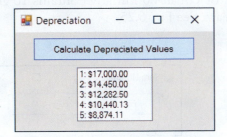

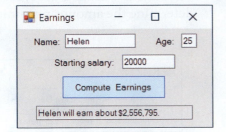

FIGURE 6.31 Outcome of Exercise 24. FIGURE 6.32 Possible outcome of Exercise 25.

25. Lifetime Earnings Estimate how much a young worker will earn before retiring at age 66. Request the worker's name, age, and starting salary as input. Assume the worker receives a 5% raise each year. See Fig. 6.32.

26. Simple versus Compound Interest When $1000 is invested at 5% simple interest, the amount grows by $50 each year. When money is invested at 5% interest compounded annually, the amount at the end of each year is 1.05 times the amount at the beginning of that year. Display the amounts for 9 years for a $1000 investment at 5% simple and compound interest. See Fig. 6.33.

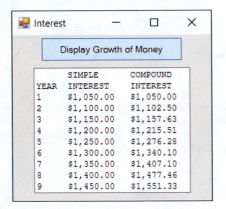

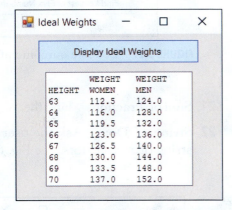

FIGURE 6.33 Output of Exercise 26. FIGURE 6.34 Possible output for Exercise 27.

27. Ideal Weight According to researchers at Stanford Medical School, the ideal weight for a woman is found by multiplying her height in inches by 3.5 and subtracting 108. The ideal weight for a man is found by multiplying his height in inches by 4 and subtracting 128. Request a lower and upper bound for heights and then produce a table giving the ideal weights for women and men in that height range. Figure 6.34 shows the output displayed in the list box when a lower bound of 63 and an upper bound of 70 are specified.

28. Sibilants Request a sentence, and then determine the number of sibilants (that is, letters S or Z) in the sentence. Carry out the counting with a Function procedure. See Fig. 6.35 on the next page.

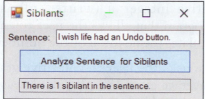

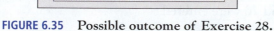

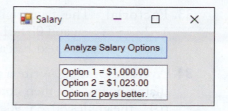

FIGURE 6.35 Possible outcome of Exercise 28.	FIGURE 6.36 Outcome of Exercise 29.

29. Salary Options   You are offered two salary options for ten days of work. Option 1: $100 per day. Option 2: $1 the first day, $2 the second day, $4 the third day, and so on, with the amount doubling each day. Determine which option pays better. See Fig. 6.36.

30. Car Loan   Consider the car loan discussed in Exercise 35 of Section 6.1. The loan will be paid off after five years. Assume that the car was purchased at the beginning of January 2016, and display the balance at the end of each year for five years. See Fig. 6.37. *Note:* The last payment will be slightly less than the other payments, since otherwise the final balance would be a negative amount.

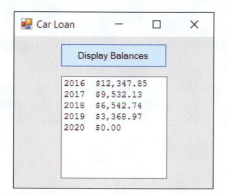

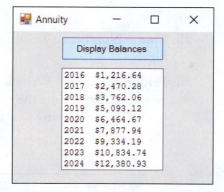

FIGURE 6.37 Outcome of Exercise 30.	FIGURE 6.38 Outcome of Exercise 31.

31. Annuity   Refer to the annuity discussed in Exercise 36 of Section 6.1. Assume that the first deposit is made at the end of January 2016, and display the balances in the account at the end of each year from 2016 to 2024. See Fig. 6.38.

32. Qwerty Word   The keyboard in use on nearly all computers is known as the Qwerty keyboard, since the letters in the top letter line read QWERTYUIOP. A word is called a Qwerty word if all its letters appear on the top letter line of the keyboard. Some examples are *typewriter*, *repertoire*, and *treetop*. Accept a word as input and determine whether or not it is a Qwerty word. Use a Boolean-valued function named IsQwerty that accepts a word as input. See Fig. 6.39.

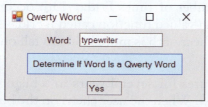

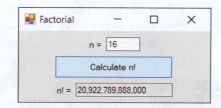

FIGURE 6.39 Possible outcome of Exercise 32.	FIGURE 6.40 Possible outcome of Exercise 33.

33. Factorial The factorial of a positive integer *n* (written n!) is the product 1·2·3·...·n and 0! = 1. Write a program that allows the user to enter a nonnegative integer into a text box and then calculates the factorial of the number. See Fig. 6.40.

34. Average Grade Write a program that asks the user to enter five grades into input dialog boxes, and then computes the average after dropping the lowest grade. In Fig. 6.41, the grades 80, 85, 90, 85, and 70 were entered.

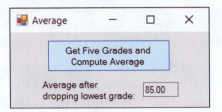

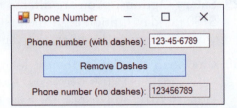

FIGURE 6.41   Possible outcome of Exercise 34.

FIGURE 6.42   Possible outcome of Exercise 35.

35. Phone Number Write a program that removes the dashes from a phone number. See Fig. 6.42.

36. Friday the 13th Write a program that lets the user enter a year into a masked text box and then counts the number of times Friday 13th occurs during that year. See Fig. 6.43. Use a Boolean-valued function called IsFriday with one parameter of type Date.

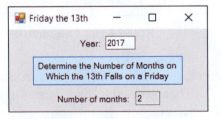

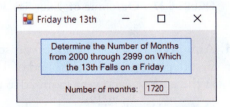

FIGURE 6.43   Possible outcome of Exercise 36.

FIGURE 6.44   Outcome of Exercise 37.

37. Friday the 13th Consider the 12,000 months during the one thousand years from 2000 through 2999. Since the 13th of each month can occur on any of the 7 days of the week, we would expect Friday 13th to occur 12,000/7 ≈ 1714 times during those years. Write a program that counts the number of times Friday 13th occurs during that time period. See Fig. 6.44. Use a Boolean-valued function called IsFriday with one parameter of type Date. **Note:** The 13th of the month is more likely to fall on a Friday than on any other day of the week.

38. Histogram Display a company's sales figures for several years in a histogram and calculate the average yearly sales. See Fig. 6.45. When the user clicks on the button, the amount of sales for each year should be obtained from the user with input dialog boxes. **Note:** Chr(149) is a large dot.

FIGURE 6.45 Possible outcome of Exercise 38.

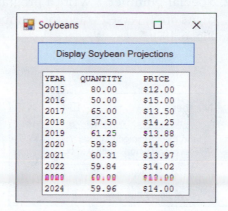

FIGURE 6.46 Outcome of Exercise 39.

39. Supply and Demand Each year's level of production and price (per bushel) for most agricultural products affects the level of production and price for the following year. Suppose the soybean crop in a country was 80 million bushels in 2015 and

$$\text{[price each year]} = 20 - .1 * \text{[quantity that year]}$$
$$\text{[quantity each year]} = 5 * \text{[price from the preceding year]} - 10,$$

where quantity is measured in units of millions of bushels. Generate a table to show the quantity and price from 2015 until 2024. See Fig. 6.46.

40. Quasi-Palindrome A word is said to be a *quasi-palindrome* if when you move the first letter to the end of the word and then read the new word backward, you get the original word. Some examples are *dresser*, *banana*, *potato*, and *uneven*. Write a program that requests a word as input and determines if it is a quasi-palindrome. See Fig. 6.47.

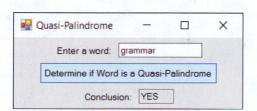

FIGURE 6.47 Possible outcome of Exercise 40.

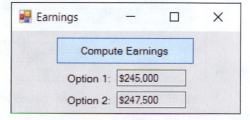

FIGURE 6.48 Outcome of Exercise 41.

41. Salary Options Suppose you are given the following two salary options:

> Option 1: $20,000 per year, with a raise of $1000 at the end of each year
> Option 2: $10,000 per half-year, with a raise of $250 per half-year at the end of each half-year

Write a program to calculate the amount you would receive for the next ten years under each option to determine the best choice. See Fig. 6.48. (Many people are surprised at the answer.)

42. Special Number Write a program to find the four-digit number, call it *abcd*, whose digits are reversed when the number is multiplied by 4. That is, 4 × *abcd* = *dcba*. See Fig. 6.49.

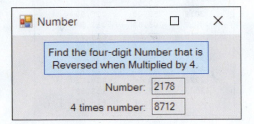

FIGURE 6.49 Outcome of Exercise 42.

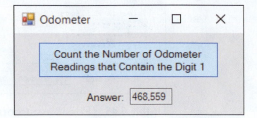

FIGURE 6.50 Outcome of Exercise 43.

43. Odometer Readings The numbers appearing on a car's odometer range from 000000 to 999999. Write a program to determine the number of readings that contain the digit 1. See Fig. 6.50.

44. Digit Sum Write a program to calculate the sum of the digits in the integers from 1 to a million. See Fig. 6.51.

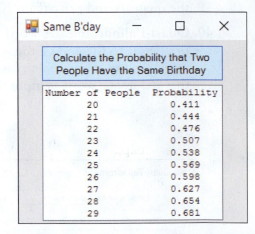

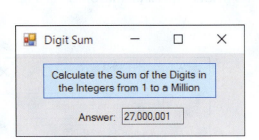

FIGURE 6.51 Outcome of Exercise 44.

FIGURE 6.52 Outcome of Exercise 45.

45. Same Birthday In a group of *r* people, the probability that at least two people have the same birthday is

$$1 - \left(\frac{n}{n} \times \frac{n-1}{n} \times \frac{n-2}{n} \times \cdots \times \frac{n-(r-1)}{n} \right)$$

where *n* is the number of days in the year. Write a program that calculates the probabilities for *r* = 20 through 29. Use *n* = 365. See Fig. 6.52.

46. Analyze a Sentence   Write a program that counts the number of words and letters in a sentence input by the user. See Fig. 6.53. Use functions to perform the calculations. *Note:* Assume that the number of words is one more than the number of spaces.

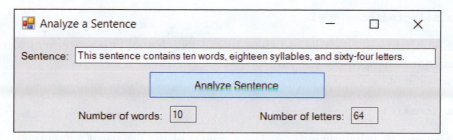

FIGURE 6.53   Possible outcome of Exercise 46.

Solutions to Practice Problems 6.2

1. The loop will never be entered because 15 is greater than 1. The intended first line might have been

```
For i As Integer = 15 To 1 Step -1
```
or
```
For i As Integer = 1 To 15
```

2. If the exact number of times the loop will be executed is known before entering the loop, then a For . . . Next loop should be used. Otherwise, a Do loop is more appropriate.

6.3   List Boxes and Loops

In previous sections we used list boxes to display output and to facilitate selection. In this section we explore some additional features of list boxes and use loops to analyze data in list boxes.

■ Some Properties, Methods, and Events of List Boxes

The value of

VideoNote

List Boxes and Loops

```
lstBox.Items.Count
```

is the number of items currently in the list box. Each item in lstBox is identified by an **index number** ranging from 0 through lstBox.Items.Count − 1. For instance, if the list box contains 10 items, then the first item has index 0, the second item has index 1, . . . and the last item has index 9. In general, the nth item in a list box has index $n − 1$.

During run time, the user can highlight an item in a list box by clicking on the item with the mouse or by moving to it with the up- and down-arrow keys when the list box has the focus. The SelectedIndexChanged event occurs each time an item of a list box is clicked on or each time an arrow key is used to change the highlighted item. It is the default event for list box controls.

The value of

```
lstBox.SelectedIndex
```

is the index number of the item currently highlighted in lstBox. If no item is highlighted, the value of SelectedIndex is −1. The statement

```
lstBox.SelectedIndex = -1
```

will unhighlight any highlighted item in the list. *Note:* This statement also raises the SelectedIndexChanged event.

The value of

```
lstBox.Items(n)
```

is the item of lstBox having index *n*. The elements of the list are of a data type called Object. A value of any type may be added to the list. However, typecasting must take place whenever an element of the list is assigned to a variable or is concatenated with another variable or literal. For instance, the statement

```
txtBox.Text = CStr(lstBox.Items(0))
```

displays the first item of lstBox in a text box.

The value of

```
lstBox.Text
```

is the currently highlighted item of lstBox converted to a string.

The Sorted property is perhaps the most interesting list box property. When it is set to True (at either design time or run time), items will automatically be displayed in lexicographical (i.e., ANSI) order. The default value of the Sorted property is False.

After the SelectedIndexChanged event, the two most important events for list boxes are the Click and DoubleClick events. However, if a program contains procedures for both of these events and the user double-clicks on the list box, only the Click event will be raised.

The items in a list box are usually all strings or all numbers. When the items are all strings, we use loops to search for items and to extract information. When the items are all numbers, we use loops to perform calculations.

■ List Boxes Populated with Strings

Example 1   **U.S. States**   The following program uses two list boxes, named lstStates and lstLastTen. We assume that the String Collection Editor of lstStates contains the names of the 50 U.S. states in the order they joined the union. The program displays the last 10 states to join the union beginning with the most recent. *Note:* If *n* is the number of items in lstStates, then the last item in lstStates has index $n - 1$.

```vb
Private Sub btnDisplay_Click(...) Handles btnDisplay.Click
  Dim n As Integer = lstStates.Items.Count
  For i As Integer = (n - 1) To (n - 10) Step -1
    lstLastTen.Items.Add(lstStates.Items(i))
  Next
End Sub
```

[Run, and click on the button.]

When a list is searched, we often use a Boolean variable called a **flag** to tell us whether or not the sought-after item has been found. The value of the flag is set to False initially and then is changed to True if and when the sought-after item is found.

 Example 2   **U.S. States** The following program uses a list box named lstStates whose String Collection Editor contains the names of the 50 U.S. states in the order they joined the union. The program also uses a masked text box with Mask "LL". After the user enters two letters into the masked text box, the program uses a Do loop to search the list box for a state beginning with those letters. The Do loop terminates when the first state beginning with those letters is found or when the last item in the list box has been examined. If a state is found, the program reports its full name and the order in which it joined the union. If there is no state beginning with the pair of letters, the program so reports.

```
Private Sub btnSearch_Click(...) Handles btnSearch.Click
  Dim letters As String = mtbFirstTwoLetters.Text.ToUpper
  Dim foundFlag As Boolean = False    'indicates whether state has been found
  Dim i As Integer = -1    'index of the state currently considered
  Do Until (foundFlag) Or (i = lstStates.Items.Count -1)
    i += 1
    If CStr(lstStates.Items(i)).ToUpper.StartsWith(letters) Then
      foundFlag = True
    End If
  Loop
  If foundFlag Then
    txtOutput.Text = CStr(lstStates.Items(i)) & " is state #" & (i + 1) & "."
  Else
    txtOutput.Text = "No state begins with " & mtbFirstTwo.Text & "."
  End If
End Sub
```

[Run, enter two letters into the masked text box, and click on the button.]

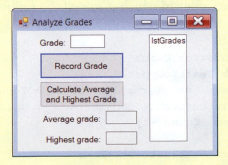

■ List Boxes Populated with Numbers

 Example 3   **Grades**   The following program evaluates exam grades. The user inserts a grade into the list box by typing it into the txtGrade text box and then clicking on the *Record* button. After all the grades have been entered, the user clicks on the *Calculate* button to determine the average grade and the highest grade for the exam. The average grade is calculated as [sum of grades] / [number of grades]. The variable *sum* adds up the grades during a loop through the grades. The number of grades is just the number of items in the list box. The variable *maxGrade* starts out set to 0. It is then adjusted during each pass through the loop. **Note:** To prevent the program from crashing, the btnCalculate_Click event procedure checks that the list box contains at least one item.

OBJECT	PROPERTY	SETTING
frmGrades	Text	Analyze Grades
lblGrade	Text	Grade:
txtGrade		
btnRecord	Text	Record Grade
btnCalculate	Text	Calculate Average and Highest Grade
lblAverage	Text	Average grade:
txtAverage	ReadOnly	True
lblHighest	Text	Highest grade:
txtHighest	ReadOnly	True
lstGrades		

```
Private Sub btnRecord_Click(...) Handles btnRecord.Click
  lstGrades.Items.Add(txtGrade.Text)
  txtGrade.Clear()
  txtGrade.Focus()
End Sub
```

```
Private Sub btnCalculate_Click(...) Handles btnCalculate.Click
  Dim sum As Double = 0
  Dim maxGrade As Double = 0
  If lstGrades.Items.Count > 0 Then  'condition is true if list box is nonempty
    For i As Integer = 0 To lstGrades.Items.Count -1
      sum += CDbl(lstGrades.Items(i))
      If CDbl(lstGrades.Items(i)) > maxGrade Then
        maxGrade = CDbl(lstGrades.Items(i))
      End If
    Next
    txtAverage.Text = (sum / lstGrades.Items.Count).ToString("N")
    txtHighest.Text = CStr(maxGrade)
  Else
    MessageBox.Show("You must first enter some grades.")
  End If
End Sub
```

[Run, enter some grades, and then click on the *Calculate* button.]

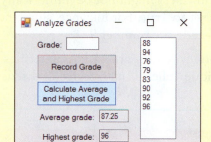

Note: In Example 3, the average grade and the highest grade could have been calculated without the grades being stored in a list box. Some calculations, however, such as the standard deviation, do require the grades to be stored.

■ Searching an Ordered List

When the items in a list of strings are in alphabetical order, the search can be shortened. For instance, if you are searching an ordered list of words for one that begins with the letter *D*, you can certainly stop the search when you reach words beginning with *E*. Consider Example 2. Whenever the pair of letters entered into the masked text box were not the first two letters of a state, the entire list was searched. Such searches can be shortened considerably if the states are first ordered.

  Example 4   **U.S. States** The following program has the same controls and settings as Example 2, except that the Sorted property of the list box is set to True. The program begins by looking at the items one at a time until it locates a state whose name exceeds the sought-after letters alphabetically. If the last state looked at doesn't begin with the sought-after letters, we can assume that no state in the list does.

```
Private Sub btnSearch_Click(...) Handles btnSearch.Click
  Dim letters As String = mtbFirstTwoLetters.Text.ToUpper
  Dim i As Integer = 0      'index of the state currently considered
  Do Until (CStr(lstStates.Items(i)).ToUpper > letters) Or
            (i = lstStates.Items.Count - 1)
    i += 1
  Loop
  If CStr(lstStates.Items(i)).ToUpper.StartsWith(letters) Then
    txtOutput.Text = CStr(lstStates.Items(i)) & " begins with " &
                      mtbFirstTwoLetters.Text & "."
  Else
    txtOutput.Text = "No state begins with " & mtbFirstTwoLetters.Text & "."
  End If
End Sub
```

■ Comments

1. A list box containing numbers might not be numerically in increasing order even when the Sorted property is set to True. For instance, since the ANSI table determines order, the number 88 will precede the number 9.

2. Example 4 presents one way to search a list of strings that are in alphabetical order. A more efficient technique, called a *binary search*, is discussed in Programming Project 11.

Practice Problems 6.3

1. Write a program that displays a message box telling you whether a SelectedIndex-Changed event was caused by the pressing of an arrow key or was caused by clicking on an item.

2. Consider Example 3. Why couldn't the maximum grade be calculated with the following code?

```
lstGrades.Sorted = True
maxGrade = CDbl(lstGrades.Items(lstGrades.Items.Count - 1))
```

EXERCISES 6.3

In Exercises 1 through 6, assume that lstBox is as shown below. Determine the contents of the text box after the code is executed.

```
Bach
Beethoven
Chopin
Mozart
Tchaikovsky
```

1. `txtOutput.Text = lstBox.Text`

2. `txtOutput.Text = CStr(lstBox.Items(2))`

3. `txtOutput.Text = CStr(lstBox.Items(lstBox.Items.Count - 1))`

4. `txtOutput.Text = CStr(lstBox.Items(lstBox.SelectedIndex))`

5. `txtOutput.Text = CStr(lstBox.SelectedIndex)`

6.
```
Dim total As Integer = 0
For n As Integer = 0 To (lstBox.Items.Count - 1)
  If CStr(lstBox.Items(n)).Length = 6 Then
    total += 1
  End If
Next
txtOutput.Text = CStr(total)
```

In Exercises 7 through 12, assume that lstBox is as shown below. Determine the contents of the text box after the code is executed.

7. `txtOutput.Text = CStr(lstBox.Items(0))`

8. `txtOutput.Text = lstBox.Text`

9. `txtOutput.Text = CStr(lstBox.Items(lstBox.SelectedIndex))`

10. `txtOutput.Text = CStr(lstBox.SelectedIndex)`

11.
```
Dim num As Integer = 0
For n As Integer = 0 To (lstBox.Items.Count - 1)
  num += CInt(lstBox.Items(n))
Next
txtOutput.Text = CStr(num)
```

12.
```
Dim min As Double = 100
For n As Integer = 0 To (lstBox.Items.Count - 1)
  If CDbl(lstBox.Items(n)) < min Then
    min = CDbl(lstBox.Items(n))
  End If
Next
txtOutput.Text = CStr(min)
```

In Exercises 13 through 18, fill the String Collection Editor of lstBox at design time with the winners of the 102 Rose Bowl games that have been played.[1] The first three items in the list box will be Michigan, Washington State, and Oregon. Some colleges appear many times in the list. Write a program that performs the indicated task.

13. Rose Bowl Count the number of times USC has won the Rose Bowl. See Fig. 6.54.

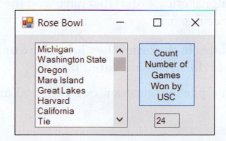
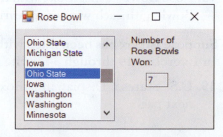

FIGURE 6.54 Outcome of Exercise 13.　　**FIGURE 6.55** Possible outcome of Exercise 14.

[1]The file Rosebowl.txt (found in the folder Programs\Ch06\Text_Files_for_Exercises) contains the names of the Rose Bowl winners (up through 2016) in the order the games were played. Copy the contents of the text file and Paste them into the String Collection Editor of lstBox.

14. **Rose Bowl**   After the user clicks on the name of a college in lstBox, count the number of times the college has won the Rose Bowl. See Fig. 6.55.

15. **Rose Bowl**   Determine if a college input by the user in a text box has won the Rose Bowl. Set the Sorted property of lstBox to False. The procedure should terminate the search if and when the college is found. See Fig. 6.56.

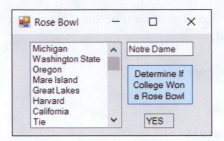

FIGURE 6.56   Possible outcome of Exercise 15.

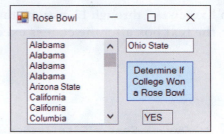

FIGURE 6.57   Possible outcome of Exercise 16.

16. **Rose Bowl**   Determine if a college input by the user in a text box has won the Rose Bowl. Set the Sorted property of lstBox to True. The procedure should terminate the search as soon as possible. See Fig. 6.57.

17. **Rose Bowl**   Fill lstBox2 with the entries of lstBox, but in reverse order. See Fig. 6.58.

FIGURE 6.58   Outcome of Exercise 17.

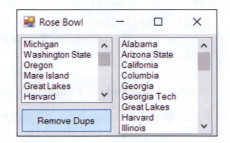

FIGURE 6.59   Outcome of Exercise 18.

18. **Rose Bowl**   Fill lstBox2 with the colleges (in alphabetical order) that have won the Rose Bowl, with each winner appearing just once. See Fig. 6.59.

Suppose lstBox has been filled with the 50 U.S. states in the order they joined the union.[2] In Exercises 19 through 34, write a program to perform the indicated task.

19. **U.S. States**   Display in lstBox2 the states in alphabetical order. See Fig. 6.60 on the next page.

---

[2]The file States.txt (found in the folder Programs\Ch06\Text_Files_for_Exercises) contains the names of the states in the order they joined the union.

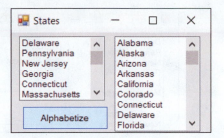

FIGURE 6.60   Outcome of Exercise 19.

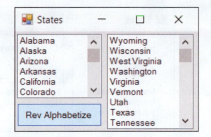

FIGURE 6.61   Outcome of Exercise 20.

20. U.S. States   Display in lstBox2 the states in reverse alphabetical order. See Fig. 6.61.

21. U.S. States   Display in lstBox2 the states whose names (including spaces) are seven letters long. See Fig. 6.62.

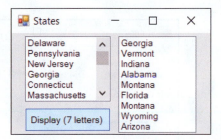

FIGURE 6.62   Outcome of Exercise 21.

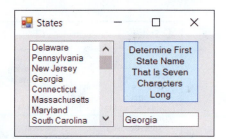

FIGURE 6.63   Outcome of Exercise 22.

22. U.S. States   Determine the first state in lstBox whose name is seven letters long. The program should terminate the search as soon as the state is found. See Fig. 6.63.

23. U.S. States   Determine the first state in lstBox whose name begins with "New". The program should terminate the search as soon as the state is found. See Fig. 6.64.

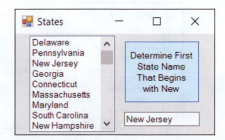

FIGURE 6.64   Outcome of Exercise 23.

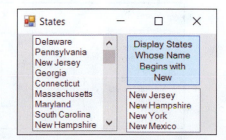

FIGURE 6.65   Outcome of Exercise 24.

24. U.S. States   Display in lstBox2 the states whose names begin with "New". See Fig. 6.65.

25. U.S. States   Determine the length of the longest state name, and display in lstBox2 the states having that length. See Fig. 6.66.

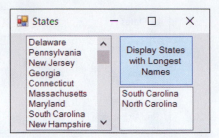

FIGURE 6.66 Outcome of Exercise 25.

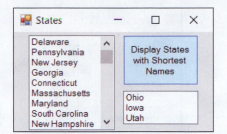

FIGURE 6.67 Outcome of Exercise 26.

26. **U.S. States** Determine the length of the shortest state name, and display in lstBox2 the states having that length. See Fig. 6.67.

27. **U.S. States** Display in lstBox2 the states whose names have four letters that are vowels. The program should call a Function procedure NumberOfVowels that counts the number of letters in a string that are vowels. See Fig. 6.68.

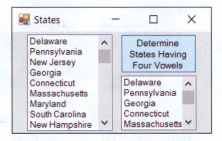

FIGURE 6.68 Outcome of Exercise 27.

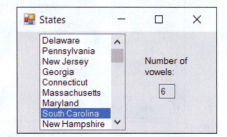

FIGURE 6.69 Outcome of Exercise 28.

28. **U.S. States** After the user clicks on a state, determine the number of letters in the state's name that are vowels. See Fig. 6.69.

29. **U.S. States** Determine the maximum number of letters that are vowels for the names of the 50 states. The program should call a Function procedure NumberOfVowels that counts the number of letters in a string that are vowels. See Fig. 6.70.

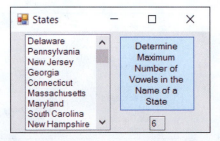

FIGURE 6.70 Outcome of Exercise 29.

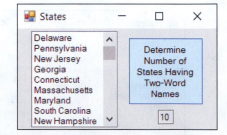

FIGURE 6.71 Outcome of Exercise 30.

30. **U.S. States** Determine the number of states whose name consists of two words. See Fig. 6.71.

31. **U.S. States** Display the name of the first state to join the union. See Fig. 6.72 on the next page.

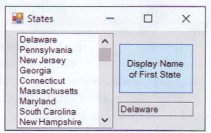

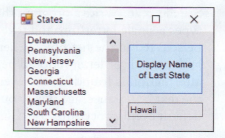

FIGURE 6.72   Outcome of Exercise 31.   **FIGURE 6.73**   Outcome of Exercise 32.

32. U.S. States   Display the name of the last state to join the union. See Fig. 6.73.

33. U.S. States   Display the name of the fifth state to join the union. See Fig. 6.74.

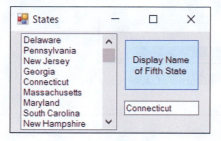

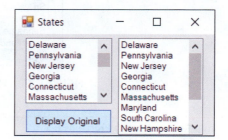

FIGURE 6.74   Outcome of Exercise 33.   **FIGURE 6.75**   Outcome of Exercise 34.

34. U.S. States   Display in lstBox2 the names of the original thirteen states. See Fig. 6.75.

35. Grades   Alter Example 3 so that the btnCalculate_Click event procedure calculates the lowest grade instead of the highest grade.

36. Standard Deviation   The **standard deviation** measures the spread or dispersal of a set of numbers about the mean. Formally, if $x_1, x_2, x_3, \ldots, x_n$ is a collection of n numbers with average value m, then

$$\text{standard deviation} = \sqrt{\frac{(x_1 - m)^2 + (x_2 - m)^2 + (x_3 - m)^2 + \cdots + (x_n - m)^2}{n}}.$$

Extend Example 3 so that the btnCalculate_Click event procedure also calculates the standard deviation of the grades.

37. Range   The **range** of a set of numbers is the difference between the highest and the lowest numbers. Modify Example 3 so that the btnCalculate_Click procedure calculates the range of the grades instead of the highest grade.

38. Grades   Alter Example 3 so that the btnCalculate_Click event procedure calculates the number of above-average grades instead of the maximum grade.

39. U.S. States   Rewrite Example 4 so that the btnSearch_Click event procedure starts at the last item and searches backward.

40. Locate Nations   Create a form containing a label, a text box, and a list box. The file Nations.txt (found in the folder Programs\Ch06\Text Files for Exercises) contains the names of the 193 members of the United Nations in alphabetical order. Copy the contents of the text file and paste them into the String Collection Editor of the list box.

See Fig. 6.76. Write a program that facilitates locating a nation in the list. When the user types a single letter into the text box, the first nation beginning with that letter should be selected in the list box. When the second letter is typed, the first nation beginning with the pair of letters should be selected. The process should continue until the sought after nation is found. In the event that there is no nation beginning with the letters in the text box, a message box should appear so as to inform the user. *Hint:* The text box's default event procedure, *TextChanged*, should be used in the program.

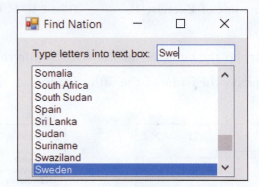

FIGURE 6.76   Possible outcome of Exercise 40.

Solutions to Practice Problems 6.3

```
1. Dim clickFlag As Boolean
   Private Sub lstBox_Click(...) Handles lstBox.Click
      clickFlag = True
   End Sub
   Private Sub lstBox_SelectedIndexChanged(...) Handles _
                     lstBox.SelectedIndexChanged
      Dim msg As String = "The SelectedIndexChanged event was caused by "
      If clickFlag Then
         MessageBox.Show(msg & "clicking on an item of the list box.")
      Else
         MessageBox.Show(msg & "pressing an arrow key.")
      End If
      clickFlag = False
   End Sub
```

2. The ordering in the list box is determined by the ANSI table (where the items are treated as strings), not the numerical value. Therefore the last item in the list box might not have the greatest numerical value.

CHAPTER 6   SUMMARY

1. A *Do loop* repeatedly executes a block of statements either as long as or until a certain condition is true. The condition can be checked either at the top of the loop or at the bottom.

2. A *For . . . Next loop* repeats a block of statements a fixed number of times. The *counter variable* assumes an initial value and increases it by one after each pass through the loop until it reaches the terminating value. Alternative increment values can be specified with the Step keyword.

3. Visual Basic uses *local type inference* to infer the data types of variables and constants having procedure or block scope that are declared without an As clause by looking at the data type of the initialization expression.

4. The items in a list box are assigned *index numbers* ranging from 0 to [number of items minus 1]. Loops can use the index numbers to extract information from list boxes.

5. A *flag* is a Boolean variable used to indicate whether a certain event has occurred or a certain situation exists.

CHAPTER 6   PROGRAMMING PROJECTS

1. **Caffeine Absorption**   After caffeine is absorbed into the body, 13% is eliminated from the body each hour. Assume a person drinks an 8-oz cup of brewed coffee containing 130 mg of caffeine, and the caffeine is absorbed immediately into the body. Write a program to calculate the following values. See Fig. 6.77.

   (a) The number of hours required until 65 mg (one-half the original amount) remain in the body.

   (b) The amount of caffeine in the body 24 hours after the person drinks the coffee.

   (c) Suppose the person drinks a cup of coffee at 7 a.m. and then drinks a cup of coffee at the end of each hour until 7 a.m. the next day. How much caffeine will be in the body at the end of the 24 hours?

2. **Rule of 72**   This rule is used to approximate the time required for prices to double due to inflation. If the inflation rate is r%, then the Rule of 72 estimates that prices will double in $72/r$ years. For instance, at an inflation rate of 6%, prices double in about 72/6 or 12 years. Write a program to test the accuracy of this rule. For each interest rate from 1% to 20%, the program should display the rounded value of $72/r$ and the actual number of years required for prices to double at an r% inflation rate. (Assume prices increase at the end of each year.) See Fig. 6.78.

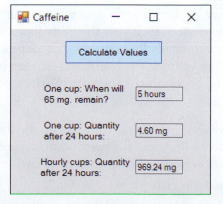

FIGURE 6.77   Outcome of Programming Project 1.

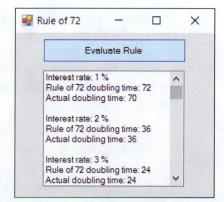

FIGURE 6.78   Outcome of Programming Project 2.

3. Projectile Motion Write a program to provide information on the height of a ball thrown straight up into the air. The program should request as input the initial height, *h* feet, and the initial velocity, *v* feet per second. The height of the ball (in feet) after *t* seconds is given by the formula $h + vt - 16t^2$ feet. The four options to be provided by buttons are as follows:

(a) Determine the maximum height of the ball. **Note:** The ball will reach its maximum height after $v/32$ seconds.

(b) Determine approximately when the ball will hit the ground. **Hint:** Calculate the height after every .1 second and determine when the height is no longer a positive number.

(c) Display a table showing the height of the ball every quarter second for five seconds or until it hits the ground. See Fig. 6.79.

(d) Quit.

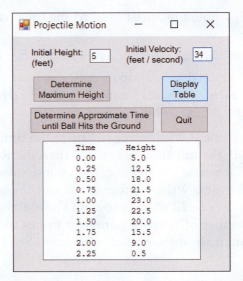

FIGURE 6.79 Possible outcome of Programming Project 3.

4. Depreciation For tax purposes an item may be depreciated over a period of several years, *n*. With the *straight-line* method of depreciation, each year the item depreciates by (1/*n*)th of its original value. With the *double-declining-balance* method of depreciation, each year the item depreciates by (2/*n*)ths of its value at the beginning of that year. (In the final year it is depreciated by its value at the beginning of the year.) Write a program that performs the following tasks:

(a) Request a description of the item, the year of purchase, the cost of the item, the number of years to be depreciated (estimated life), and the method of depreciation. The method of depreciation should be chosen by clicking on one of two buttons.

(b) Display a year-by-year description of the depreciation. See Fig. 6.80.

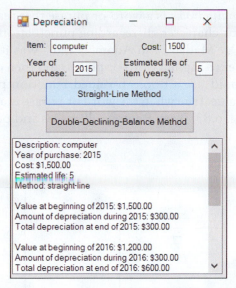

FIGURE 6.80   Possible outcome of Programming Project 4.

5. **Alphabetical Order**   The following words have three consecutive letters that are also consecutive letters in the alphabet: THI**RST**Y, A**FGH**ANISTAN, S**TU**DENT. Write a program that accepts a word as input and determines whether or not it has three consecutive letters that are consecutive letters in the alphabet. The program should use a Boolean-valued function named IsTripleConsecutive that accepts an entire word as input. *Hint:* Use the Asc function. See Fig. 6.81.

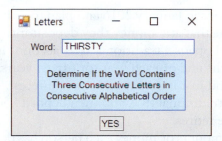

FIGURE 6.81   Possible outcome of Programming Project 5.

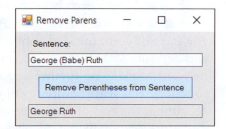

FIGURE 6.82   Possible outcome of Programming Project 6.

6. **Parentheses**   Write a program that uses a flag and does the following:

   (a) Ask the user to input a sentence containing parentheses. *Note:* The closing parenthesis should not directly precede the period.

   (b) Display the sentence with the parentheses and their contents removed. See Fig. 6.82.

7. Palindrome A *palindrome* is a word or phrase that reads the same forward and backward, character for character, disregarding punctuation, case, and spaces. Some examples are "racecar", "Madam, I'm Adam"., and "Was it a cat I saw?". Write a program that allows the user to input a word or phrase and then determines if it is a palindrome. The program should use a Boolean-valued Function procedure named IsPalindrome that returns the value True when the word or phrase is a palindrome and the value False otherwise. See Fig. 6.83. **Note:** Remove all spaces and punctuation before analyzing the word or phrase.

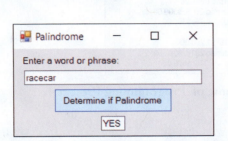

FIGURE 6.83   Possible outcome of Programming Project 7.

FIGURE 6.84   Outcome of Programming Project 8.

8. Individual Retirement Accounts Money earned in an ordinary savings account is subject to federal, state, and local income taxes. However, a special type of retirement savings account, called a **traditional individual retirement account** (traditional IRA), allows these taxes to be deferred until after retirement. IRAs are highly touted by financial planners. The purpose of this programming project is to show the value of starting an IRA early.

Earl and Larry each begin full-time jobs in January 2016 and plan to retire in January 2064 after working for 48 years. Assume that any money they deposit into IRAs earns 4% interest compounded annually. Earl opens a traditional IRA account immediately and deposits $5000 into his account at the end of each year for fifteen years. After that, he plans to make no further deposits and just let the money earn interest. Larry plans to wait fifteen years before opening his traditional IRA and then deposit $5000 into the account at the end of each year until he retires.

Write a program that calculates the amounts of money each person has deposited into his account and the amount of money in each account upon retirement. See Fig. 6.84.

9. Error Detection Suppose, you type a 14-digit credit card number into a Web site, but mistype one of the digits or inadvertently interchange two adjacent digits. The website will perform a validation check that always detects the first type of error and nearly always detects the second type of error. The validation check is as follows and will be illustrated with the credit card number 58667936100244.

(a) Consider the 1st, 3rd, 5th, 7th, 9th, 11th, and 13th digits of the credit card number (in this case, 5, 6, 7, 3, 1, 0, 4). Double each number. In this case, the results are: 10, 12, 14, 6, 2, 0, 8. If any product is a two-digit number, subtract 9. In this case, the results are: 1, 3, 5, 6, 2, 0, 8. Sum the resultant digits (in this case, the sum is 25).

(b) Sum together the remaining seven digits from the credit card number. That is, the 2nd, 4th, 6th, 8th, 10th, 12th, and 14th digits. With the credit card number above, we obtain $8 + 6 + 9 + 6 + 0 + 2 + 4 = 35$.

(c) Add together the two sums. If the result is a multiple of 10, then accept the credit card number. Otherwise, reject it. We accept the credit card number above since $25 + 35 = 60$, a multiple of 10.

Write a program that performs data validation on a credit card number. See Fig. 6.85.

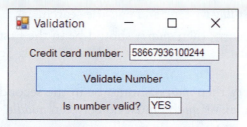

FIGURE 6.85 **Possible outcome of Programming Project 9.**

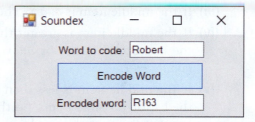

FIGURE 6.86 **Possible outcome of Programming Project 10.**

10. **Soundex System**   Soundex is a system that encodes a word into a letter followed by three digtis that roughly describe how the word sounds. That is, similar sounding words have similar four-character codes. For instance, the words *carrot* and *caret* are both coded as *C123*. A slight variation of the Soundex coding algorithm is as follows:

   1. Retain the first letter.

   2. For the remaining letters, delete all occurrences of *a, e, i, o, u, h, y,* and *w*.

   3. Replace the letters that remain with numbers so that

   (a) *b, f, p,* and *v* become 1

   (b) *c, g, j,* k, *q, s, x,* and *z* become 2

   (c) *d* and *t* both become 3

   (d) *l* (that is, el) becomes 4

   (e) *m* and *n* become 5

   (f) *r* becomes 6

   4. If the result contains two adjacent identical digits, eliminate the second of them.

   5. Keep only the first four characters of what you have left. If you have fewer than four, then add zeros on the end to make the string have length four.

Write a program that carries out the algorithm. See Fig. 6.86.

11. **Binary Search**   An especially efficient technique for searching an ordered list of items is called a *binary search*. A binary search looks for a value by first determining in which half of the list it resides. The other half of the list is then ignored, and the retained half is temporarily regarded as the entire list. The process is repeated until the item is found or the entire list has been considered. Use the algorithm and flowchart for a binary search shown below to rewrite the btnSearch_Click event procedure from Example 4 of Section 6.3.

Figure 6.87 shows a partial flowchart for a binary search. (The sought-after value is denoted by *quarry*. The Boolean variable *flag* keeps track of whether or not *quarry* has been found.) The algorithm for a binary search of the items in an ordered list box is as follows:

(i) At each stage, denote the index of the first item in the retained list by *first* and the index of the last item by *last*. Initially, set the value of *first* to 0, set the value of *last* to one less than the number of items in the list, and set the value of *flag* to False.

(ii) Look at the middle item of the current list—the item having index *middle* = CInt((*first* + *last*) / 2).

(iii) If the middle item is *quarry*, then set *flag* to True and end the search.

(iv) If the middle item is greater than *quarry*, then *quarry* should be in the first half of the list. So the index of *quarry* must lie between *first* and *middle* − 1. Set *last* to *middle* − 1.

(v) If the middle item is less than *quarry*, then *quarry* should be in the second half of the list of possible items. So the index of *quarry* must lie between *middle* + 1 and *last*. Set *first* to *middle* + 1.

(vi) Repeat steps (ii) through (v) until *quarry* is found or until the halving process uses up the entire list. (When the entire list has been used up, *first* > *last*.) In the second case, *quarry* was not in the original list.

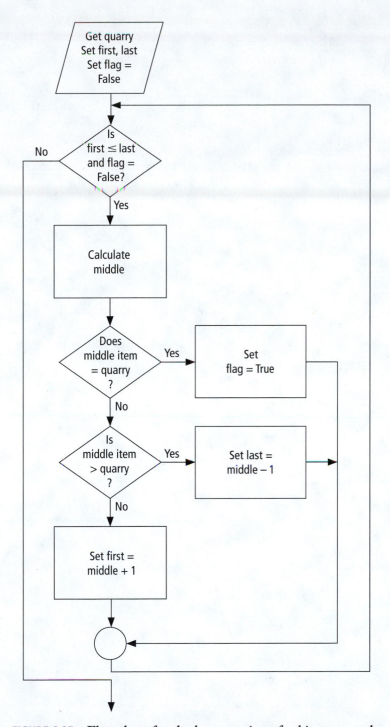

FIGURE 6.87   **Flowchart for the loop portion of a binary search.**

7

Arrays

7.1 Creating and Using Arrays

A variable (or simple variable) is a name to which Visual Basic can assign a single value. An **array variable** is an indexed list of simple variables of the same type, to and from which Visual Basic can efficiently assign and access a list of values.

Consider the following situation: Suppose you want to evaluate the exam grades for 30 students. Not only do you want to calculate the average score, but you also want to display the names of the students whose grades are above average. You might run the program outlined below. **Note:** Visual Basic uses zero-based numberings—that is, numberings beginning with 0 instead of 1. (We saw this practice in Chapter 3, where the numbering of the positions in a string began with 0.) Therefore we will number the 30 student names and grades from 0 through 29 instead of from 1 through 30.

```
Private Sub btnDisplay_Click(...) Handles btnDisplay.Click
  Dim student0 As String, grade0 As Double
  Dim student1 As String, grade1 As Double
    .
    .
    .
  Dim student29 As String, grade29 As Double
  'Analyze exam grades
  Dim promptName As String = "Enter name of student #"
  Dim promptGrade As String = "Enter grade for student #"
  student0 = InputBox(promptName & 0, "Name")
  grade0 = CDbl(InputBox(promptGrade & 0, "Grade"))
  student1 = InputBox(promptName & 1, "Name")
  grade1 = CDbl(InputBox(promptGrade & 1, "Grade"))
    .
    .
    .
  student29 = InputBox(promptName & 29, "Name")
  grade29 = CDbl(InputBox(promptGrade & 29, "Grade"))
  'Calculate the average grade.
    .
    .
    .
  'Display the names of students with above-average grades.
    .
    .
    .
End Sub
```

This program is going to be uncomfortably long. What's most frustrating is that the 30 Dim statements and 30 pairs of statements obtaining input are very similar and look as if they should be condensed into a loop. A shorthand notation for the many related variables would be welcome. It would be nice if we could just write

```
For i As Integer = 0 To 29
  studenti = InputBox(promptName & i, "Name")
  gradei = CDbl(InputBox(promptGrade & i, "Grade"))
Next
```

Of course, this will not work. Visual Basic will treat *studenti* and *gradei* as two variables and keep reassigning new values to them. At the end of the loop, they will have the values of the thirtieth student.

■ Declaring an Array Variable

Visual Basic provides a data structure called an **array** that lets us do what we tried to accomplish in the loop above. The variable names, similar to those in the loop, will be

```
students(0), students(1), students(2), students(3), ..., students(29)
```

and

```
grades(0), grades(1), grades(2), grades(3), ..., grades(29)
```

We refer to these collections of variables as the array variables *students* and *grades*. The numbers inside the parentheses of the array variables are called **subscripts** or **indexes**, and each individual variable is called a **subscripted variable** or **element**. For instance, *students*(3) is the fourth element of the array *students*, and *grades*(20) is the twenty-first element of the array *grades*. The elements of an array are located in successive memory locations. Figure 7.1 shows the memory locations for the array *grades*.

grades(0)	grades(1)	grades(2)		grades(29)
grades			. . .	

FIGURE 7.1   The array *grades*.

Names of array variables follow the same naming conventions as simple variables. If *arrayName* is the name of an array variable and *n* is a literal, variable, or expression of type Integer, then the declaration statement

VideoNote

Declaring and Using Arrays

```
Dim arrayName(n) As DataType
```

reserves space in memory to hold the values of type *DataType* of the subscripted variables *arrayName*(0), *arrayName*(1), *arrayName*(2), . . . , *arrayName*(n). The value of *n* is called the **upper bound** of the array. The number of elements in the array, *n* + 1, is called the **size** of the array. The subscripted variables will all have the same data type—namely, the type specified by *DataType*. For instance, they could all be variables of type String or all be variables of type Double. In particular, the statements

```
Dim students(29) As String
Dim grades(29) As Double
```

declare the 30-element arrays needed for the preceding program.

Values can be assigned to individual subscripted variables with assignment statements and displayed in text boxes and list boxes just like values of ordinary variables. The default initial value of each subscripted variable is the same as with an ordinary variable—that is, the keyword Nothing for String types, 0 for numeric types, and #1/1/0001# for Date types. The statement

```
Dim grades(29) As Double
```

sets aside a portion of memory for the array *grades* and assigns the default value 0 to each element.

grades(0)	grades(1)	grades(2)		grades(29)
grades			. . .	
	0	0	0	. . .	0

The statements

```
grades(0) = 87
grades(1) = 92
```

assign values to the first two elements of the array.

	grades(0)	grades(1)	grades(2)		grades(29)
grades	87	92	0	. . .	0

The statements

```
For i As Integer = 0 To 2
  lstBox.Items.Add(grades(i))
Next
```

then produce the following output in the list box:

```
87
92
0
```

As with an ordinary variable, an array variable declared in the Declarations section of the class has class scope. That is, it will be available to all procedures in the program, and any values assigned to it in a procedure will persist after the procedure terminates. Array variables declared inside a procedure are local to that procedure and cease to exist when the procedure is exited.

 Example 1 **Super Bowl Winners** The following program creates a string array consisting of the names of the first four Super Bowl winners. Figure 7.2 shows the array created by the program.

	teamNames(0)	teamNames(1)	teamNames(2)	teamNames(3)
teamNames	Packers	Packers	Jets	Chiefs

FIGURE 7.2 The array *teamNames* of Example 1.

OBJECT	PROPERTY	SETTING
frmBowl	Text	Super Bowl
lblNumber	Text	Number from 1 to 4:
mtbNumber	Mask	0
btnWhoWon	Text	Who Won?
lblWinner	Text	Winning team:
txtWinner	ReadOnly	True

```
Private Sub btnWhoWon_Click(...) Handles btnWhoWon.Click
  Dim teamNames(3) As String
  Dim n As Integer
  'Place Super Bowl Winners into the array
```

```
teamNames(0) = "Packers"
teamNames(1) = "Packers"
teamNames(2) = "Jets"
teamNames(3) = "Chiefs"
'Access array
n = CInt(mtbNumber.Text)
txtWinner.Text = teamNames(n - 1)
End Sub
```

[Run, type 2 into the masked text box, and click on the button.]

```
Super Bowl                    —    □    ✕

Number from 1 to 4: 2      Who Won?

            Winning team:  Packers
```

■ The Load Event Procedure

In Example 1, the array *teamNames* was assigned values in the btnWhoWon_Click event procedure. Every time the button is clicked, the values are reassigned to the array. This approach can be inefficient, especially in programs with large arrays, where the task of the program (in Example 1, looking up a fact) may be repeated numerous times for different user input. When, as in Example 1, the data to be placed in an array are known at the time the program begins to run, a more efficient location for the statements that fill the array is in the form's Load event procedure. A form's Load event occurs just before the form is displayed to the user. It is the default event for the form. The header for the Load event procedure is

```
Private Sub frmName_Load(...) Handles MyBase.Load
```

The keyword MyBase is similar to the Me keyword and refers to the form. Example 2 uses the frmBowl_Load procedure to improve Example 1.

✔ **Example 2**   **Super Bowl Winners** The following variation of Example 1 makes *teamNames* a class-level array and assigns values to the elements of the array in the event procedure frmBowl_Load.

```
Dim teamNames(3) As String

Private Sub frmBowl_Load(...) Handles MyBase.Load
  'Place Super Bowl Winners into the array
  teamNames(0) = "Packers"
  teamNames(1) = "Packers"
  teamNames(2) = "Jets"
  teamNames(3) = "Chiefs"
End Sub

Private Sub btnWhoWon_Click(...) Handles btnWhoWon.Click
  Dim n As Integer
  n = CInt(mtbNumber.Text)
  txtWinner.Text = teamNames(n - 1)
End Sub
```

■ Implicit Array Sizing and Initialization

Like ordinary variables, array variables can be assigned initial values when they are declared. A statement of the form

```
Dim arrayName() As DataType = {value0, value1, value2, ..., valueN}
```

declares an array having upper bound N and assigns *value0* to *arrayName*(0), *value1* to *arrayName*(1), *value2* to *arrayName*(2), . . . , and *valueN* to *arrayName*(N). For instance, in Example 2, the Dim statement and frmBowl_Load event procedure can be replaced by the single line

```
Dim teamNames() As String = {"Packers", "Packers", "Jets", "Chiefs"}
```

Note 1: If Option Infer is enabled and the statement above appeared inside a procedure, it could be shortened to

```
Dim teamNames = {"Packers", "Packers", "Jets", "Chiefs"}
```

Note 2: You cannot use a list of values in braces to fill an array if an upper bound has been specified for the array. For instance, the following line of code is not valid:

```
Dim teamNames(3) As String = {"Packers", "Packers", "Jets", "Chiefs"}
```

■ Text Files

The two methods we have used to fill an array are fine for small arrays. However, in practice arrays can be quite large. One way to fill a large array is to use a simple data file known as a **text file**. Text files can be created, viewed, and modified with sophisticated word processors such as Word, or with elementary word processors such as the Windows accessories WordPad and Notepad. They differ from files normally created with Word in that they have no formatting (such as line spacing and font style). They are pure text and nothing else—hence the name *text file*. For instance, a text file that could be used to fill the array in Example 1 would look as follows:

```
Packers
Packers
Jets
Chiefs
```

The text files needed for exercises in this book have been created for you and are in the material you downloaded from the companion website. They are contained in a subfolder (named Text_Files_for_Exercises) of the appropriate chapter folder. Each text file ends with the extension *txt*.

The Visual Basic IDE provides simple ways to create and edit text files. The details can be found in the "Manage Text Files" section of Appendix B. Chapter 8 shows how to create text files programmatically.

A statement of the form

```
Dim strArrayName() As String = IO.File.ReadAllLines(filespec)
```

where *filespec* refers to a text file, declares a string array whose size equals the number of lines in the file, and fills it with the contents of the file. A numeric array can be filled with a text file by first filling a temporary string array with the file and then using a loop, along with CInt, CDec, or CDbl, to transfer the numbers into the numeric array. (See Example 3.) **Note:** In Section 7.2, we present a way to fill a numeric array with the contents of a numeric text file without using a loop.

The Solution Explorer window has the name of the program as its first line. If only a few entries appear in the Solution Explorer, you can click on the *Show All Files* button ( ) at the top of the Solution Explorer window to display all the files and subfolders. One subfolder is named *bin*. The folder *bin* has a subfolder named *Debug*. If the *filespec* above consists only of a filename (that is, if no path is given), Visual Basic will look for the file in the *Debug* subfolder of the program's *bin* folder. **Throughout this book, we assume that every text file used by a program is located in the program's *bin\Debug* folder.** Every program downloaded from the companion website has this feature.

When you write a program that uses one of the text files from a Text_Files_for_Exercises folder, you can use File Explorer or Windows Explorer to place a copy of the text file into the program's *bin\Debug* folder. Alternatively, you can click on the name of the program near the top of the Solution Explorer window, select the *Add Existing Item* command from the Project menu, specify All Files (*.*), navigate to the text file, and double-click on the file. The text file will appear in the Solution Explorer window and can be moved to the *bin\Debug* folder with Cut and Paste.

■ Array Methods

Both numeric and string arrays have the Count, Max, Min, First, and Last methods.[1] The value of *arrayName*.Count is the size of the array, *arrayName*.Max is the highest value (alphabetically or numerically), *arrayName*.Min is the lowest value, *arrayName*.First is the first element of the array, and *arrayName*.Last is the last element. **Note:** The upper bound of the array is *arrayName*.Count − 1. Table 7.1 shows some values with the array from Example 1.

TABLE 7.1   Some values from Example 1.

Expression	Value
teamNames.Count	4
teamNames.Max	Packers
teamNames.Min	Chiefs
teamNames.First	Packers
teamNames.Last	Chiefs

When working with numeric arrays, we often also want to calculate the average and total values for the elements. The average value is given by *arrayName*.Average and the total value by *arrayName*.Sum. The program that follows illustrates the use of array methods for a numeric array.

Example 3   **U.S. Presidents** The file AgesAtInaugural.txt gives the ages at inauguration of the first 44 U.S. presidents. The first four lines contain the data 57, 61, 57, 57—the ages of Washington, Adams, Jefferson, and Madison at their inaugurations. (To see the contents of the file in a text editor, locate the file in the *bin\Debug* folder of the Solution Explorer and double-click on the file. You can remove the text editor by clicking the × symbol on its tab.)

```
Private Sub btnDisplay_Click(...) Handles btnDisplay.Click
  Dim ages(43) As Integer
  Dim temp() As String = IO.File.ReadAllLines("AgesAtInaugural.txt")
  For i As Integer = 0 To 43
    ages(i) = CInt(temp(i))
```

---

[1]The property Length can be used instead of the Count method. We favor Count, since it also can be used with LINQ queries.

```
  Next
  lstValues.Items.Add("Obama: " & ages(ages.Count - 1))
  lstValues.Items.Add("Washington: " & ages.First)
  lstValues.Items.Add("Obama: " & ages.Last)
  lstValues.Items.Add("Oldest age: " & ages.Max)
  lstValues.Items.Add("Youngest age: " & ages.Min)
  lstValues.Items.Add("Average age: " & (ages.Average).ToString("N"))
  lstValues.Items.Add("Average age: " & (ages.Sum / ages.Count).ToString("N"))
End Sub
```

[Run, and click on the button.]

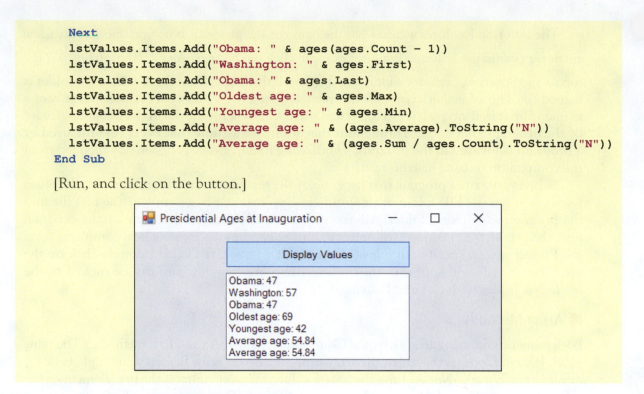

■ Calculating an Array Value with a Loop

Some of the values in Table 7.1 above also can be calculated with loops. The following example shows how the value returned by the Max method can be calculated with a For . . . Next loop. Some other values returned by methods are calculated with loops in the exercise set.

  Example 4 **U.S. Presidents** Consider the array consisting of the ages at inauguration of the last nine presidents. To find the maximum age, we temporarily take the age of the first of the nine presidents as the maximum and then adjust the maximum, if required, after looking at each successive age.

```
Private Sub btnCalculate_Click(...) Handles btnCalculate.Click
  'Calculate the maximum age at inauguration for the last 9 presidents
  Dim ages() As Integer = {55, 56, 61, 52, 69, 64, 46, 54, 47}
  Dim max As Integer = ages(0)
  For i As Integer = 1 To (Count to ages.Count - 1)
    If ages(i) > max Then
      max = ages(i)
    End If
  Next
  txtOutput.Text = "The greatest age is " & max & "."
End Sub
```

[Run, and click on the button. The following is displayed in the text box.]

```
The greatest age is 69.
```

■ The ReDim Statement

After an array has been declared, its upper bound (but not its type) can be changed to m with a procedure-level statement of the form

```
ReDim arrayName(m)
```

where *arrayName* is the name of the already declared array and *m* is an Integer literal, variable, or expression. *Note:* Since the type cannot be changed, there is no need for an "As *DataType*" clause at the end of a ReDim statement.

Visual Basic allows you to declare an array without specifying an upper bound with a statement of the form

```
Dim arrayName() As DataType
```

Later, the size of the array can be specified with a ReDim statement. (No values can be assigned to the elements of the array until a size is specified.)

The ReDim statement has one shortcoming: It releases the memory location of the array and creates a new array with the same name, thereby losing all of the original array's contents. That is, it resets all string values to Nothing and resets all numeric values to 0. This situation can be remedied by following ReDim with the keyword Preserve. The general form of a ReDim Preserve statement is

```
ReDim Preserve arrayName(m)
```

Of course, if you make an array smaller than it was, data at the end of the array will be lost.

Example 5   **Super Bowl Winners** The following program reads the names of the winners of the first 49 Super Bowl games from a text file and places them into an array. The user can type a team's name into a text box and then display the numbers of the Super Bowl games won by that team. The user has the option of adding winners of subsequent games to the array of winners. The program uses the file SBWinners.txt, whose lines contain the names of the winners in order. That is, the first four lines of the file contain the names Packers, Packers, Jets, and Chiefs.

```vb
Dim teamNames() As String
Dim numGames As Integer

Private Sub frmBowl_Load(...) Handles MyBase.Load
  teamNames = IO.File.ReadAllLines("SBWinners.txt")
  numGames = teamNames.Count
  'Note: "Me" refers to the form
  Me.Text = "First " & numGames & " Super Bowls"
  'Specify the caption of the Add Winner button
  btnAddWinner.Text = "Add Winner of Game " & (numGames + 1)
End Sub

Private Sub btnDisplay_Click(...) Handles btnDisplay.Click
  'Display the numbers of the games won by the team in the text box
  Dim noWinsFlag As Boolean = True    'flag to detect if any wins
  lstGamesWon.Items.Clear()
  For i As Integer = 0 To numGames - 1
    If teamNames(i).ToUpper = txtName.Text.ToUpper Then
      lstGamesWon.Items.Add(i + 1)
      noWinsFlag = False
    End If
  Next
  If noWinsFlag Then
    lstGamesWon.Items.Add("No Games Won")
  End If
End Sub
```

```
Private Sub btnAddWinner_Click(...) Handles btnAddWinner.Click
    'Add winner of next Super Bowl to the array
    Dim prompt As String
    'Add one more element to the array
    ReDim Preserve teamNames(numGames)
    numGames += 1
    'Request the name of the next winner
    prompt = "Enter winner of game #" & numGames & "."
    teamNames(numGames - 1) = InputBox(prompt, "Super Bowl")
    'Update the title bar of the form and the caption of the button
    Me.Text = "First" & numGames & "Super Bowls"
    btnAddWinner.Text = "Add Winner of Game " & (numGames + 1)
End Sub
```

[Run, type "Steelers" into the text box, and click on the *Display* button. Then feel free to add subsequent winners. Your additions will be taken into account when you next click the *Display* button.]

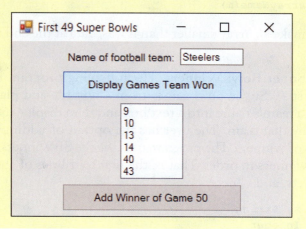

■ For Each Loops

VideoNote
For Each
Loops

Consider Example 3. The entire sequence of ages can be displayed in the list box with the following statements:

```
For i As Integer = 0 To 43
    lstValues.Items.Add(ages(i))
Next
```

The first line of the For . . . Next loop also could have been written as

```
For i As Integer = 0 To ages.Count - 1
```

In the two For statements, the lower bound and upper bound are given. Another type of loop, called a **For Each loop**, iterates through all the elements of the array in order with no mention whatsoever of the two bounds. The following block of code has the same output as the For . . . Next loop above.

```
For Each age As Integer In ages
    lstValues.Items.Add(age)
Next
```

In general, a block of the form

```
For Each variableName As DataType In arrayName
  statement(s)
Next
```

where *DataType* is the data type of the array, declares the looping variable *variableName* to be of that type, and executes the statement(s) once for each element of the array. That is, during each iteration of the loop, Visual Basic sets the variable to an element in the array and executes the statement(s). When all the elements in the array have been assigned to the variable, the For Each loop terminates and the statement following the Next statement is executed. *Note:* When you use local type inference (allowed when Option Infer is set to On), you can omit the *As DataType* clause.

Although For Each loops are less complicated to write than For . . . Next loops, they have a major limitation: They cannot alter the values of elements in an array.

■ Functions That Return Arrays

A Function procedure with a header of the form

```
Function FunctionName(var1 As Type1, var2 As Type2, ...) As DataType()
```

returns an array of type *DataType* as its value. The empty set of parentheses following *DataType* tells us that the Function procedure will return an array instead of just a single value.

✔ **Example 6** **Average Grade** The following program calculates the average of several grades. The number of grades and the grades themselves are input by the user via input dialog boxes. The Function procedure GetGrades returns an array containing the grades.

```
Private Sub btnGet_Click(...) Handles btnGet.Click
  Dim numGrades As Integer = CInt(InputBox("Number of grades: ", "Grades"))
  txtAverage.Text = CStr(GetGrades(numGrades).Average)
End Sub


Function GetGrades(numGrades As Integer) As Double()
  Dim grades(numGrades - 1) As Double
  For i As Integer = 1 To numGrades
    grades(i - 1) = CDbl(InputBox("Grade #" & i & ": ", "Get Grade"))
  Next
  Return grades
End Function
```

[Run, enter *3* as the number of grades, and then enter the grades *80, 85,* and *90.*]

```
Determine Average Grade        —    □    ×

      ┌──────────────────────────────────┐
      │  Get Grades and Calculate Average │
      └──────────────────────────────────┘

            Average:  85
```

Searching for an Element in an Array

In Example 5, a loop was used to find the indices of the elements having a value specified by the user. Visual Basic has a specific method for locating elements in an array. Let *numVar* be an integer variable and *value* be a literal or expression of the same type as the elements of *arrayName*. Then a statement of the form

```
numVar = Array.IndexOf(arrayName, value)
```

assigns to *numVar* the index of the first occurrence of the requested value in *arrayName*. If the value is not found, then −1 is assigned to *numVar*.

 Example 7   **U.S. States** The file States.txt contains the 50 U.S. states in the order in which they joined the union. The first four lines of the file are as follows:

```
Delaware
Pennsylvania
New Jersey
Georgia
```

The following program requests the name of a state and then tells the order in which it joined the union:

```vb
Dim states() As String = IO.File.ReadAllLines("States.txt")

Private Sub btnDetermine_Click(...) Handles btnDetermine.Click
  Dim n As Integer, state As String
  state = txtState.Text
  n = Array.IndexOf(states, state)
  If n <> -1 Then
    txtOutput.Text = state & " was state number " & n + 1 & "."
  Else
    MessageBox.Show("Re-enter a state name.", "Error")
    txtState.Clear()
    txtState.Focus()
  End If
End Sub
```

[Run, type a state into the top text box, and click on the button.]

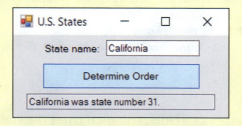

If a value occurs more than once in an array, an extension of the method above will locate subsequent occurrences. A statement of the form

```
numVar = Array.IndexOf(arrayName, value, startIndex)
```

where *startIndex* is an integer literal or expression, looks only at elements having index *startIndex* or greater, and assigns to *numVar* the index of the first occurrence of the requested value. If the value is not found, then −1 is assigned to *numVar*.

■ Copying an Array

If *arrayOne* and *arrayTwo* have been declared with the same data type, then the statement

```
arrayTwo = arrayOne
```

makes *arrayTwo* reference the same array as *arrayOne*. It will have the same size and contain the same data. This statement must be used with care, however, since after it is executed, *arrayOne* and *arrayTwo* will share the same portion of memory. Therefore, a change in the value of an element in one of the arrays will affect the other array.

One way to make a copy of an array that does not share the same memory location is illustrated by the following code:

```
'Assume arrayOne and arrayTwo have the same data type and size
For i As Integer = 0 To arrayOne.Count - 1
  arrayTwo(i) = arrayOne(i)
Next
```

■ Split Method and Join Function

The **Split method** provides another way to assign values to an array. The following code creates the array of Example 1:

```
Dim teamNames() As String
Dim line As String = "Packers,Packers,Jets,Chiefs"
teamNames = line.Split(","c)
```

In general, if *strArray* is a string array and the string variable *strVar* has been assigned a string of the form "*value0,value1,value2, . . . ,valueN*"; then a statement of the form

```
strArray = strVar.Split(","c)
```

resizes *strArray* to an array with upper bound N having *strArray*(0) = *value0*, *strArray*(1) = *value1*, . . . , *strArray*(N) = *valueN*. That is, the first element of the array contains the text preceding the first comma, the second element the text between the first and second commas, . . . , and the last element the text following the last comma. The comma character is called the **delimiter** for the statement above, and the letter *c* specifies that the comma has data type Character instead of String. Any character can be used as a delimiter. (The two most common delimiters are the comma character and the space character.) The Split method will play a vital role in Section 7.3.

 Example 8 **Parse a Name** The following program determines a person's first and last names. The space character is used as the delimiter for the Split method. Each element of the array contains one part of the person's full name.

OBJECT	PROPERTY	SETTING
frmName	Text	Name
lblFull	Text	Full name:
txtFull		
btnExtract	Text	Extract First and Last Names
lblFirst	Text	First name:
txtFirst	ReadOnly	True
lblLast	Text	Last name:
txtLast	ReadOnly	True

```
Private Sub btnExtract_Click(...) Handles btnExtract.Click
  Dim fullName As String = txtFull.Text
  Dim parsedName() As String = fullName.Split(" "c)
  txtFirst.Text = parsedName.First
  txtLast.Text = parsedName.Last
End Sub
```

[Run, enter a full name, and click on the button.]

| Name | — | □ | ✕ |

Full name: William Howard Taft

Extract First and Last Names

First name: William

Last name: Taft

The reverse of the Split method is the **Join function**, which returns a string value consisting of the elements of an array concatenated together and separated by a specified delimiter. For instance, the code

```
Dim greatLakes() As String =
            {"Huron", "Ontario", "Michigan", "Erie", "Superior"}
Dim lakes As String
lakes = Join(greatLakes, ","c)
txtOutput.Text = lakes
```

uses a comma as the delimiter and produces the output

```
Huron,Ontario,Michigan,Erie,Superior
```

■ Passing an Array to a Procedure

An array declared in a procedure is local to that procedure and is not available to other procedures. However, such an array can be passed to another procedure. The argument in the calling statement consists of the name of the array. The corresponding parameter in the header for the procedure must consist of an array name followed by an empty set of parentheses.

✔ **Example 9** **U.S. Presidents** The following variation of Example 4 calculates the maximum value with a Function procedure. Notice that the parameter in the function header is written **ages() As Integer**, not **ages As Integer**, and the function call is written **Maximum(ages)**, not **Maximum(ages())**.

```
Private Sub btnCalculate_Click(...) Handles btnCalculate.Click
  'Calculate the greatest age at inauguration for the last 9 presidents
  Dim ages() As Integer = {55, 56, 61, 52, 69, 64, 46, 54, 47}
  txtOutput.Text = "The greatest age is " & Maximum(ages) & "."
End Sub
```

```
Function Maximum(ages() As Integer) As Integer
  Dim max As Integer = ages(0)
  For i As Integer = 1 To (ages.Count - 1)
    If ages(i) > max Then
      max = ages(i)
    End If
  Next
  Return max
End Function
```

[Run, and click on the button. The following is displayed in the text box.]

The greatest age is 69.

Entire arrays are always passed by reference. That is, any changes to elements of an array passed to a procedure persist after the procedure terminates. However, an individual element of an array can be actually passed by value.

  Example 10   **Passing to Procedures** The following program demonstrates the results of passing an array and its elements to procedures in various ways:

```
Private Sub btnDisplay_Click(...) Handles btnDisplay.Click
  Dim ar() As Integer = {1, 2, 3}
  Triple(ar)
  For i As Integer = 0 To 2
    lstOutput.Items.Add(ar(i))
  Next
  Quadruple(ar(0))
  lstOutput.Items.Add(ar(0))
End Sub

Sub Triple(ar() As Integer)
  For i As Integer = 0 To 2
    ar(i) = 3 * ar(i)
  Next
End Sub

Sub Quadruple(num As Integer)
  num = 4 * num
  lstOutput.Items.Add(num)
End Sub
```

[Run, and click on the button. The following numbers are displayed in a column in the list box.]

```
3, 6, 9, 12, 3
```

■ Comments

1. Using a negative subscript or a subscript greater than the upper bound of an array is not allowed. For instance, at run time the two lines of code in Fig. 7.3 on the next page produce an exception dialog box.

```
Dim trees() As String = {"Redwood", "Sequoia", "Spruce"}
lstBox.Text = trees(5)
```

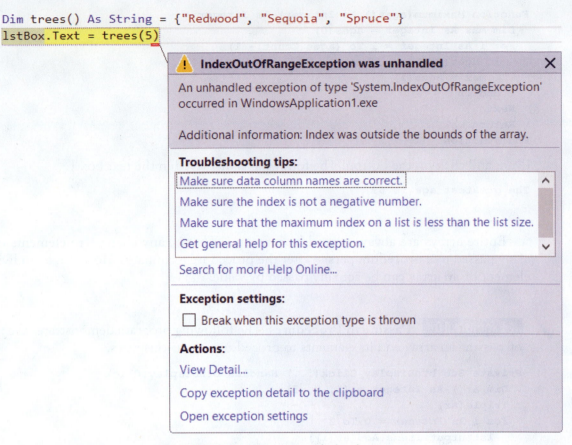

FIGURE 7.3   Exception dialog box.

2. The statements **Continue For** and **Exit For** can be used in For Each loops in much the same way they are used in For . . . Next loops. Also, a variable declared inside a For Each loop has block scope; that is, the variable cannot be referred to by code outside the loop.

3. After you double-click on the name of a text file and place it into the text editor, you can alter the file's contents and save the altered file. To save the altered file, right-click on the file name in the text editor's tab and click on "Save bin\Debug*fileName*."

Practice Problems 7.1

1. Give four ways to fill an array with the names of the three musketeers—Athos, Porthos, and Aramis.

2. Write two lines of code that add the name of the fourth musketeer, D'Artagnan, to the array filled in Problem 1.

3. Determine the output displayed when the button is clicked.

```
Private Sub btnDisplay_Click(...) Handles btnDisplay.Click
  Dim numWords As Integer
  Dim line As String = "This sentence contains five words."
  Dim words() As String = line.Split(" "c)
  numWords = words.Count
  txtOutput.Text = CStr(numWords)
End Sub
```

1. What is the size of an array whose upper bound is 100?

2. What is the upper bound of an array whose size is 100?

In Exercises 3 through 18, determine the output displayed when the button is clicked.

3.
```
Private Sub btnDisplay_Click(...) Handles btnDisplay.Click
    Dim n As Integer = 2
    Dim spoons(n) As String
    spoons(0) = "soup"
    spoons(1) = "dessert"
    spoons(2) = "coffee"
    txtOutput.Text = "Have a " & spoons(n - 1) & " spoon."
End Sub
```

4.
```
Private Sub btnDisplay_Click(...) Handles btnDisplay.Click
    'I'm looking over a four leaf clover.
    Dim leaves(3) As String
    leaves(0) = "sunshine"
    leaves(1) = "rain"
    leaves(2) = "the roses that bloom in the lane"
    leaves(3) = "somebody I adore"
    For i As Integer = 0 To 3
        lstOutput.Items.Add("Leaf " & (i + 1) & ": " & leaves(i))
    Next
End Sub
```

5.
```
Private Sub btnDisplay_Click(...) Handles btnDisplay.Click
    Dim colors(120) As String
    colors(0) = "Atomic Tangerine"
    colors(100) = "Tan"
    If colors(0).IndexOf(colors(100)) = -1 Then
        txtOutput.Text = "No"
    Else
        txtOutput.Text = "Yes"
    End If
End Sub
```

6.
```
Private Sub btnDisplay_Click(...) Handles btnDisplay.Click
    Dim years(1) As Integer
    years(0) = 1776
    years(1) = Now.Year 'current year as Integer
    txtOutput.Text = "Age of United States: " & (years(1) - years(0))
End Sub
```

7.
```
Private Sub btnDisplay_Click(...) Handles btnDisplay.Click
    Dim primes() As Integer = {2, 3, 5, 7, 11}
    lstOutput.Items.Add(primes(2) + primes(3))
End Sub
```

8.
```
Private Sub btnDisplay_Click(...) Handles btnDisplay.Click
    Dim pres() As String = {"Grant", "Lincoln", "Adams", "Kennedy"}
    txtOutput.Text = pres(3).Substring(0, 3)
End Sub
```

9.
```
Dim bands() As String = {"soloist", "duet", "trio", "quartet"}

Private Sub btnDisplay_Click(...) Handles btnDisplay.Click
    Dim num As Integer
    ReDim Preserve bands(9)
    bands(4) = "quintet"
    bands(5) = "sextet"
    bands(6) = InputBox("What do you call a group of 7 musicians?")
    num = CInt(InputBox("How many musicians are in your group?"))
    txtOutput.Text = "You have a " & bands(num - 1) & "."
End Sub
```

(Assume the first response is *septet* and the second response is *3*.)

10.
```
Private Sub btnDisplay_Click(...) Handles btnDisplay.Click
    'Compare the values of two chess pieces
    Dim chess() As String = {"king", "queen", ""}
    chess(2) = "rook"
    ReDim Preserve chess(6)
    chess(3) = "bishop"
    txtOutput.Text = "A " & chess(2) & " is worth more than a " & chess(3)
End Sub
```

11.
```
Dim grades(3) As Double

Private Sub frmGrades_Load(...) Handles MyBase.Load
    grades(0) = 80
    grades(1) = 90
End Sub

Private Sub btnDisplay_Click(...) Handles btnDisplay.Click
    Dim average As Double
    grades(2) = 70
    grades(3) = 80
    average = (grades(0) + grades(1) + grades(2) + grades(3)) / 4
    txtOutput.Text = "Your average is " & average
End Sub
```

12.
```
Dim names(3) As String

Private Sub frmNames_Load(...) Handles MyBase.Load
    names(0) = "Al"
    names(1) = "Gore"
    names(2) = "Vidal"
    names(3) = "Sassoon"
End Sub
```

```vbnet
Private Sub btnDisplay_Click(...) Handles btnDisplay.Click
    For i As Integer = 0 To 2
        lstOutput.Items.Add(names(i) & " " & names(i + 1))
    Next
End Sub
```

13.
```vbnet
Private Sub btnDisplay_Click(...) Handles btnDisplay.Click
    Dim line As String = "2012,Artist,The"
    Dim films() As String = line.Split(","c)
    txtOutput.Text = films(2) & " " & films(1) & " won in " & films(0)
End Sub
```

14.
```vbnet
Private Sub btnDisplay_Click(...) Handles btnDisplay.Click
    Dim line As String = "2,7,11,13,3"
    Dim nums() As String = line.Split(","c)
    txtOutput.Text = CStr(CInt(nums(4)) * CInt(nums(2)))
End Sub
```

15.
```vbnet
Private Sub btnDisplay_Click(...) Handles btnDisplay.Click
    Dim words() As String = {"one", "two", "three"}
    txtOutput.Text = Join(words, ","c)
End Sub
```

16.
```vbnet
Private Sub btnDisplay_Click(...) Handles btnDisplay.Click
    Dim nums() As Integer = {1, 2, 3}
    Dim temp(2) As String
    For i As Integer = 0 To 2
        temp(i) = CStr(nums(i))
    Next
    txtOutput.Text = Join(temp, ","c)
End Sub
```

17.
```vbnet
Private Sub btnDisplay_Click(...) Handles btnDisplay.Click
    Dim nums() As Integer = {3, 5, 8, 10, 21}
    Dim total As Integer = 0
    For Each num As Integer In nums
        If (num Mod 2 = 0) Then    '(num Mod 2) = 0 when num is even
            total += 1
        End If
    Next
    txtOutput.Text = total & " even numbers"
End Sub
```

18.
```vbnet
Private Sub btnDisplay_Click(...) Handles btnDisplay.Click
    Dim words() As String = {"When", "in", "the", "course",
                             "of", "human", "events"}
    Dim flag As Boolean = False
    For Each word As String In words
        If (word.Length = 5) Then
            flag = True
        End If
    Next
```

```
    If flag Then
      txtOutput.Text = "at least one five-letter word"
    Else
      txtOutput.Text = "no five-letter word"
    End If
End Sub
```

In Exercises 19 through 22, assume the five lines of the file Dates.txt contain the numbers 1492, 1776, 1812, 1929, and 1941 and the file is in the program's *bin\Debug* folder.

19.
```
Private Sub btnDisplay_Click(...) Handles btnDisplay.Click
    Dim dates() As String = IO.File.ReadAllLines("Dates.txt")
    txtOutput.Text = "Pearl Harbor: " & dates(4)
End Sub
```

20.
```
Private Sub btnDisplay_Click(...) Handles btnDisplay.Click
    Dim dates() As String = IO.File.ReadAllLines("Dates.txt")
    txtOutput.Text = "Bicentennial Year: " & (CInt(dates(1)) + 200)
End Sub
```

21.
```
Private Sub btnDisplay_Click(...) Handles btnDisplay.Click
    Dim dates() As String = IO.File.ReadAllLines("Dates.txt")
    Dim flag As Boolean = False
    For Each yr As String In dates
      If (CInt(yr) >= 1800) And (CInt(yr) <= 1899) Then
        flag = True
      End If
    Next
    If flag Then
      txtOutput.Text = "contains a 19th-century date"
    Else
      txtOutput.Text = "does not contain a 19th-century date"
    End If
End Sub
```

22.
```
Private Sub btnDisplay_Click(...) Handles btnDisplay.Click
    Dim dates() As String = IO.File.ReadAllLines("Dates.txt")
    Dim total As Integer = 0
    For Each yr As String In dates
      If (CInt(yr) >= 1900) Then
        total += 1
      End If
    Next
    txtOutput.Text = total & " 20th-century dates"
End Sub
```

23.
```
Private Sub btnDisplay_Click(...) Handles btnDisplay.Click
    Dim words() As String = {"We", "the", "People", "of", "the",
              "United", "States", "in", "Order", "to", "form",
              "a", "more", "perfect", "Union"}
    txtOutput.Text = BeginWithVowel(words) & " words begin with a vowel"
End Sub
```

```vb
Function BeginWithVowel(words() As String) As Integer
  Dim total As Integer = 0
  For Each word As String In words
    word = word.ToUpper
    If word.StartsWith("A") Or word.StartsWith("E") Or
      word.StartsWith("I") Or word.StartsWith("O") Or
      word.StartsWith("U") Then
      total += 1
    End If
  Next
  Return total
End Function
```

24.
```vb
Private Sub btnDisplay_Click(...) Handles btnDisplay.Click
  Dim grades() As Integer = {85, 95, 90}
  grades = CurveGrades(grades)
  For Each grade As Integer In grades
    lstOutput.Items.Add(grade)
  Next
End Sub

Function CurveGrades(scores() As Integer) As Integer()
  For i As Integer = 0 To (scores.Count - 1)
    scores(i) = scores(i) + 7
    If scores(i) > 100 Then
      scores(i) = 100
    End If
  Next
  Return scores
End Function
```

25.
```vb
Private Sub btnDisplay_Click(...) Handles btnDisplay.Click
  Dim nums() As Integer = {2, 6, 4}
  nums = Reverse(nums)
  For Each num As Integer In nums
    lstOutput.Items.Add(num)
  Next
End Sub

Function Reverse(nums() As Integer) As Integer()
  Dim n = nums.Count - 1        'upper bound of array
  Dim temp(n) As Integer
  For i As Integer = 0 To n
    temp(i) = nums(n - i)
  Next
  Return temp
End Function
```

26.
```vb
Private Sub btnDisplay_Click(...) Handles btnDisplay.Click
  Dim speech() As String = {"Four", "score", "and",
                            "seven", "years", "ago"}
  speech = UpperCase(speech)
  txtOutput.Text = speech(3)
End Sub
```

```
Function UpperCase(words() As String) As String()
  Dim n As Integer = words.Count - 1
  Dim temp(n) As String
  For i As Integer = 0 To n
    temp(i) = words(i).ToUpper
  Next
  Return temp
End Function
```

27. The array declared with the statement

```
Dim lakes() As String = {"Huron", "Ontario", "Michigan", "Erie",
                         "Superior"}
```

contains the names of the five Great Lakes. Evaluate and interpret each of the following:

(a) `lakes.Max`   (b) `lakes.Min`
(c) `lakes.First`   (d) `lakes.Last`
(e) `lakes.Count`   (f) `lakes(1)`
(g) `Array.IndexOf(lakes, "Erie")`

28. The array declared with the statement

```
Dim lakeAreas() As Integer = {23000, 8000, 22000, 10000, 32000}
```

contains the surface areas (in square miles) of the five Great Lakes. Evaluate and interpret each of the following:

(a) `lakeAreas.Max`   (b) `lakeAreas.Min`
(c) `lakeAreas.First`   (d) `lakeAreas.Last`
(e) `lakeAreas.Count`   (f) `lakeAreas.Sum`
(g) `lakeAreas.Average`   (h) `lakeAreas(2)`
(i) `Array.IndexOf(lakeAreas, 8000)`

29. The array declared with the statement

```
Dim statePops() As Double = {3.6, 6.7, 1.3, 1.1, 0.6, 1.3}
```

contains the populations (in millions) of the six New England states. Evaluate and interpret each of the following:

(a) `statePops.Max`   (b) `statePops.Min`
(c) `statePops.First`   (d) `statePops.Last`
(e) `statePops.Count`   (f) `statePops(3)`
(g) `Array.IndexOf(statePops, 1.1)`

30. The array declared with the statement

```
Dim statesNE() As String = {"Connecticut", "Massachusetts",
        "New Hampshire", "Rhode Island", "Vermont", "Maine"}
```

contains the names of the six New England states listed in the order in which they became part of the United States. Evaluate and interpret each of the following:

(a) `statesNE.Max`   (b) `statesNE.Min`
(c) `statesNE.First`   (d) `statesNE.Last`
(e) `statesNE.Count`   (f) `statesNE(0)`
(g) `Array.IndexOf(statesNE, "Maine")`

31. Suppose the array *states* has been filled with the names of the fifty states in the order in which they became part of the United States. Write code to display each of the following states in a list box:

    (a) the first state to join the union
    (b) the original thirteen states
    (c) the most recent state to join
    (d) the order number for Ohio
    (e) the second state to join the union
    (f) the twentieth state to join the union
    (g) the last ten states to join the union

32. Suppose the array *pres* has been filled with the names of the first 44 U.S. presidents in the order in which they served. Write code to display each of the following in a list box.

    (a) the first president
    (b) the first six presidents
    (c) the most recent president
    (d) the number for "James Monroe"
    (e) the second president
    (f) the tenth president
    (g) the last five presidents

Assume the array *nums* contains a list of positive integers. In Exercises 33 through 38, write a Function procedure that calculates the stated value with a For Each loop.

33. the sum of the numbers in the array

34. the average of the numbers in the array

35. the largest even number in the array (If there are no even numbers in the array, the Function procedure should return 0.)

36. the smallest number in the array

37. the number of two-digit numbers in the array

38. the number of even numbers in the array

In Exercises 39 through 42, identify the errors.

39. ```
Dim nums(3) As Integer = {1, 2, 3, 4}
```

40. ```
Dim nums(10) As Integer
nums(nums.Count) = 7
```

41. ```
Dim nums() As Integer = {1, 2, 3}
'Display 101 + 102 + 103
For Each num As Integer In nums
  num += 100
Next
MessageBox.Show(CStr(nums.Sum))
```

42. ```
Dim nums() As Integer = IO.File.ReadAllLines("Numbers.txt")
```

43. Write a single line of code that displays the number of words in a sentence, where the string variable *line* holds the sentence.

44. Write a single line of code that displays the number of names in the file Names.txt.

45. **Sum of Numbers** The file Numbers.txt contains a list of integers. Write a program that displays the number of integers in the file and their sum. See Fig. 7.4 on the next page.

46. **U.S. States** The file SomeStates.txt contains a list of some U.S. states. Write a program to determine if the states are in alphabetical order. See Fig. 7.5 on the next page.

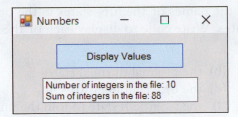

FIGURE 7.4   Outcome of Exercise 45.

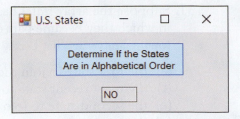

FIGURE 7.5   Outcome of Exercise 46.

47. Duplicate Names   The file Names2.txt contains a list of names in alphabetical order. Write a program to find and display those entries that are repeated in the file. When a name is found to be repeated, display it only once. See Fig. 7.6.

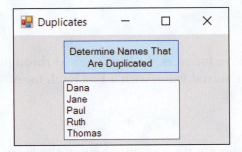

FIGURE 7.6   Outcome of Exercise 47.

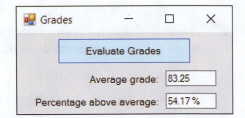

FIGURE 7.7   Outcome of Exercise 48.

48. Average Grade   Suppose the file Final.txt contains student grades on a final exam. Write a program that displays the average grade on the exam and the percentage of grades that are above average. See Fig. 7.7.

49. Sum of Numbers   Write a Function procedure to calculate the sum of the entries with odd subscripts in an integer array.

50. Compare Arrays   Write a Boolean-valued Function procedure AreSame to compare two integer arrays and determine whether they have the same size and hold identical values—that is, whether $a(i) = b(i)$ for all i.

51. Shakespearean Sonnet   The file Sonnet.txt contains Shakespeare's Sonnet 18. Each entry in the file contains a line of the sonnet. Write a program that reports the average number of words in a line and the total number of words in the sonnet. See Fig. 7.8.

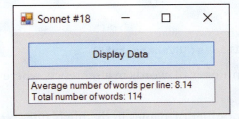

FIGURE 7.8   Outcome of Exercise 51.

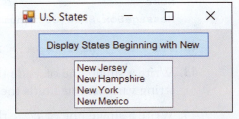

FIGURE 7.9   Outcome of Exercise 52.

52. U.S. States   The file States.txt contains the names of the 50 U.S. states. Write a program that creates an array consisting of the states beginning with "New". The program also should display the names of these states in a list box. See Fig. 7.9.

53. Sort Eggs Table 7.2 shows the different grades of eggs and the minimum weight required for each classification. Write a program that processes the text file Eggs.txt containing a list of the weights of a sample of eggs. The program should report the number of eggs in each grade and the weight of the lightest and heaviest egg in the sample. Figure 7.10 shows the output of the program. **Note:** Eggs weighing less than 1.5 ounces cannot be sold in supermarkets and therefore should not be counted.

TABLE 7.2 **Grades of eggs.**

Grade	Minimum Weight (in ounces)
Jumbo	2.5
Extra Large	2.25
Large	2
Medium	1.75
Small	1.5

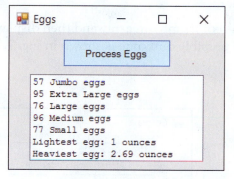

FIGURE 7.10 Outcome of Exercise 53.

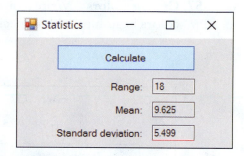

FIGURE 7.11 Outcome of Exercise 54.

54. Compile Statistics Statisticians use the concepts of range, mean, and standard deviation to describe a collection of numerical data. The **range** is the difference between the largest and smallest numbers in the collection. The **mean** is the average of the numbers, and the **standard deviation** measures the spread or dispersal of the numbers about the mean. Formally, if $x_1, x_2, x_3, \ldots, x_n$ is a collection of numbers, then

$$\text{mean} = \frac{x_1 + x_2 + x_3 + \cdots + x_n}{n} \qquad \text{(denote the mean by } m\text{)}$$

$$\text{standard deviation} = \sqrt{\frac{(x_1 - m)^2 + (x_2 - m)^2 + (x_3 - m)^2 + \cdots + (x_n - m)^2}{n}}$$

Write a program to calculate the range, mean, and standard deviation for the numbers in the file Data.txt. See Fig. 7.11.

55. Frequency of Digits The file Digits.txt contains a list of digits, all between 0 and 9. Write a program that displays the frequency of each digit. See Fig. 7.12 on the next page.

56. U.S. Presidents The file USPres.txt contains the names of the first 44 U.S. presidents in the order in which they served. Write a program that places the names in an array and displays all presidents for a requested range of numbers. Figure 7.13 on the next page shows one possible outcome. (John Tyler was the tenth president, James Polk was the eleventh president, and so on.)

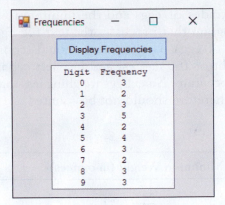

FIGURE 7.12   Outcome of Exercise 55.

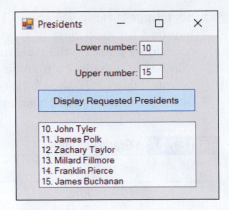

FIGURE 7.13   Possible outcome of Exercise 56.

Exercises 57 through 60 should use the file Colors.txt that contains the names of the colors of Crayola® crayons in alphabetical order.

57. Crayon Colors   Write a program to read the colors into an array and then display the colors beginning with a specified letter. One possible outcome is shown in Fig. 7.14.

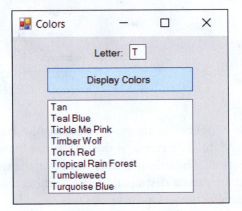

FIGURE 7.14   Possible outcome of Exercise 57.

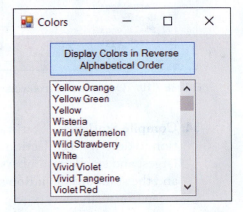

FIGURE 7.15   Outcome of Exercise 58.

58. Crayon Colors   Write a program that displays the colors in reverse alphabetical order. See Fig. 7.15.

59. Crayon Colors   Redo Exercise 57 with the letter passed to a Function procedure that returns a smaller array containing just the colors beginning with the specified letter.

60. Crayon Colors   Write a program that requests a color as input in a text box and then determines whether or not the color is in the text file. The program should use the Boolean-valued Function procedure IsCrayola that returns the value True if the color in the text box is a Crayola color. See Fig. 7.16.

61. U.S. Presidents   The file AgesAtInaugural.txt gives the ages at inauguration of the first 44 U.S. presidents. Write a program that calculates the number of presidents who were younger than 50 years old at their inaugurations. See Fig. 7.17.

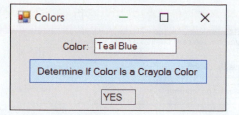

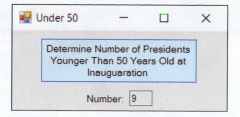

FIGURE 7.16 Possible outcome of Exercise 60.

FIGURE 7.17 Outcome of Exercise 61.

62. Analyze Scores   The file Scores.txt contains scores between 1 and 49. Write a program that uses these scores to create an array *frequencies* as follows:

frequencies(0) = # of scores < 10
frequencies(1) = # of scores with 10 ≤ score < 20
frequencies(2) = # of scores with 20 ≤ score < 30
frequencies(3) = # of scores with 30 ≤ score < 40
frequencies(4) = # of scores with 40 ≤ score < 50

The program should then display the results in tabular form, as shown in Fig. 7.18.

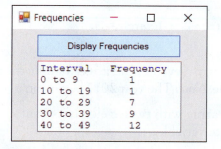

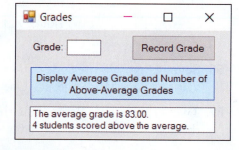

FIGURE 7.18 Outcome of Exercise 62.

FIGURE 7.19 Possible outcome of Exercise 63.

63. Average Grade   Write a program to display the average grade and the number of above-average grades on an exam. Each time the user clicks a *Record Grade* button, a grade should be read from a text box. The current average grade and the number of above-average grades should be displayed in a list box whenever the user clicks on a *Display Average* button. (Assume that the class has at most 100 students.) Use a Function procedure to count the number of above-average grades. See Fig. 7.19.

In Exercises 64 and 65, execute the statement sentence = sentence.Replace(",", "") **to remove all commas in** *sentence,* **and then remove other punctuation marks similarly. After that, use the space character as a delimiter for the Split method.**

64. Word Palindrome   A *word palindrome* is a sentence that reads the same, word by word, backward and forward (ignoring punctuation and capitalization). An example is "I am, therefore, am I?" Write a program that requests a sentence and then determines whether the sentence is a word palindrome. The program should place the words of the sentence in an array and use a Function procedure to determine whether the sentence is a word palindrome. See Fig. 7.20 on the next page.

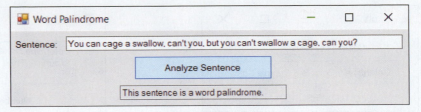

FIGURE 7.20 Possible outcome of Exercise 64.

65. **Chain-Link Sentence** A sentence is called a *chain-link* sentence if the last two letters of each word are the same as the first two letters of the next word—for instance, "The head administrator organized education on online networks." Write a program that accepts a sentence as input and determines whether it is a chain-link sentence. See Fig. 7.21. Assume that the only punctuation marks in the interior of the sentence are commas, colons, or semicolons.

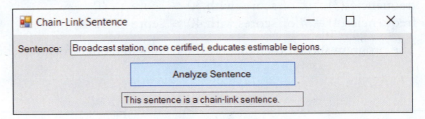

FIGURE 7.21 Possible outcome of Exercise 65.

66. **Seven Days** Write code that creates an array with seven elements containing the abbreviations Sun, Mon, Tue, etc. Use a date variable. **Note:** The year 2017 begins on a Sunday.

67. **Twelve Months** Write code that creates an array with twelve elements containing the abbreviations Jan, Feb, Mar, etc. Use a date variable.

Solutions to Practice Problems 7.1

1. *First:*
```
Dim names(2) As String
    names(0) = "Athos"
    names(1) = "Porthos"
    names(2) = "Aramis"
```

Second:
```
Dim names() As String = {"Athos", "Porthos", "Aramis"}
```

Third:
```
Dim line As String = "Athos,Porthos,Aramis"
Dim names() As String = line.Split(","c)
```

Fourth: Assume the text file Names.txt has the three names in three lines and is located in the *bin\Debug* folder of the program. Then execute the following line of code:
```
Dim names() As String = IO.File.ReadAllLines("Names.txt")
```

2.
```
ReDim Preserve names(3)       'resize the array
names(3) = "D'Artagnan"       'assign value to last element
```

3. 5

7.2   Using LINQ with Arrays

LINQ (Language-INtegrated Query), a recent exciting and powerful innovation in Visual Basic, provides a standardized way to retrieve information from data sources. In this book we use LINQ with arrays, text files, XML documents, and databases. Before LINQ you often had to write complex loops that specified *how* to retrieve information from a data source. With LINQ you simply state *what* you want to achieve and let Visual Basic do the heavy lifting. ***Important:*** Option Infer must be set to On in order to use LINQ. (See Comment 1 at the end of this section.)

■ LINQ Queries

VideoNote
LINQ

A LINQ *query* for an array is declarative (that is, self-evident) code that describes *what* you want to retrieve from the array. A statement of the form

```
Dim queryName = From var In arrayName Where [condition on var] Select var
```

is called a LINQ query. The variable *var* takes on the values of elements in the array much like the looping variable in a For Each loop. The statement declares a variable *queryName* and assigns it a sequence consisting of the elements of the array that satisfy the condition on *var*. The phrases "**From var In** *arrayName*", "**Where** [*condition on var*]", and "**Select** *var*" are called **query clauses**. The keywords From, Where, and Select are called **query operators**, *var* is called a **range variable**, and *arrayName* is called the **source data**. The entire expression to the right of the equal sign is called a **query expression**.

The LINQ query above is usually written in the style

```
Dim queryName = From var In arrayName
                Where [condition on var]
                Select var
```

As soon as you type the first line, the Code Editor will know that you are declaring a query and will treat each press of the Enter key as signaling a line continuation. However, after you type the last clause of the query, you can press Ctrl+Shift+Enter to tell the Code Editor that the query declaration is complete. (Alternately, you can press the Enter key twice to complete entry of the query.)

 Example 1   **U.S. States**   The file States.txt contains the 50 U.S. states in the order in which they joined the union. The following program first displays the states with five-letter names and then displays the states beginning with "New". Each query expression returns a sequence of states that is displayed with a For Each loop.

```
Private Sub btnDisplay_Click(...) Handles btnDisplay.Click
  Dim states() As String = IO.File.ReadAllLines("States.txt")
  Dim stateQuery1 = From state In states
                    Where state.Length = 5
                    Select state
  For Each state As String In stateQuery1
    lstStates.Items.Add(state)
  Next
```

```
        lstStates.Items.Add("")
      Dim stateQuery2 = From state In states
                        Where state.StartsWith("New")
                        Select state
      For Each state As String In stateQuery2
        lstStates.Items.Add(state)
      Next
    End Sub
```

[Run, and click on the button.]

The array methods Count, Max, Min, First, and Last apply to all sequences returned by LINQ queries, and the array methods Average and Sum apply to numeric sequences. Also, the successive elements in the sequence can be referred to by indices ranging from 0 to *queryName*.Count − 1. For instance, in Example 1, the values of **stateQuery1(0)**, **stateQuery1(1)**, and **stateQuery1(2)** are Maine, Texas, and Idaho.

✔ **Example 2**   **Display Numbers** The following program displays values associated with numeric sequences returned by LINQ queries. *Note:* The integer *n* is even if *n* Mod 2 is 0.

```
Private Sub btnDisplay_Click(...) Handles btnDisplay.Click
  Dim nums() As Integer = {5, 12, 8, 7, 11}
  Dim numQuery1 = From num In nums
                  Where num > 7
                  Select num
  For Each num As Integer In numQuery1
    lstBox.Items.Add(num)
  Next
  lstBox.Items.Add("Largest number: " & numQuery1.Max)
  lstBox.Items.Add("Second number: " & numQuery1(1))
  lstBox.Items.Add("Sum of numbers: " & numQuery1.Sum)
  lstBox.Items.Add("")
  Dim numQuery2 = From num In nums
                  Where num Mod 2 = 0
                  Select num
  lstBox.Items.Add("Number of even numbers: " & numQuery2.Count)
  lstBox.Items.Add("Average of even numbers: " & numQuery2.Average)
  lstBox.Items.Add("Last even number: " & numQuery2.Last)
End Sub
```

[Run, and click on the button.]

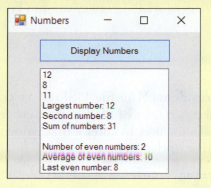

The variable in the Select clause can be replaced by an expression involving the variable. For instance, if the clause **Select num** in *numQuery1* of Example 2 were replaced by

```
Select num * num
```

then the first three lines in the list box would be 144, 64, and 121. Also, Where clauses and Select clauses are optional. When the Where clause is missing, all values in the source data are included. A missing Select clause produces the same effect as the clause **Select** *var*. In this textbook. we always include a Select clause.

■ The Distinct Operator

The sequence created with a LINQ query might contain duplicate elements. Duplicates can be eliminated by adding the Distinct operator to the query. For instance, using the array *teamNames* from Example 5 of the previous section, the lines of code

```
Dim teamQuery = From team In teamNames
                Select team
                Distinct
For Each team As String In teamQuery
  lstGamesWon.Items.Add(team)
Next
```

display the names of the teams that have won a Super Bowl, with each team listed once.

■ The ToArray Method

The sequence returned by a LINQ query has many of the features of an array. Its main limitation is that its values cannot be altered with assignment statements. However, the sequence can be converted to an array with the ToArray method. For instance, using the array *teamNames* from Example 5 of the previous section, the lines of code

```
Dim teamQuery = From team In teamNames
                Select team
                Distinct
Dim uniqueWinners() As String = teamQuery.ToArray
```

create the array named *uniqueWinners* containing the names of the teams that have won the Super Bowl, with each team appearing just once as an element of the array.

■ Use of Function Procedures in Queries

The Where and Select clauses of a LINQ query can use Function procedures, as illustrated in the next example.

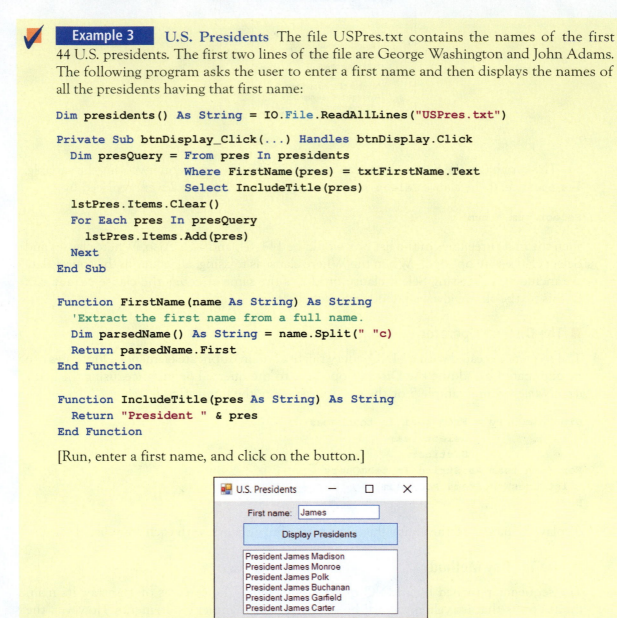

Example 3 **U.S. Presidents** The file USPres.txt contains the names of the first 44 U.S. presidents. The first two lines of the file are George Washington and John Adams. The following program asks the user to enter a first name and then displays the names of all the presidents having that first name:

```
Dim presidents() As String = IO.File.ReadAllLines("USPres.txt")

Private Sub btnDisplay_Click(...) Handles btnDisplay.Click
  Dim presQuery = From pres In presidents
                  Where FirstName(pres) = txtFirstName.Text
                  Select IncludeTitle(pres)
  lstPres.Items.Clear()
  For Each pres In presQuery
    lstPres.Items.Add(pres)
  Next
End Sub

Function FirstName(name As String) As String
  'Extract the first name from a full name.
  Dim parsedName() As String = name.Split(" "c)
  Return parsedName.First
End Function

Function IncludeTitle(pres As String) As String
  Return "President " & pres
End Function
```

[Run, enter a first name, and click on the button.]

U.S. Presidents

First name: James

Display Presidents

President James Madison
President James Monroe
President James Polk
President James Buchanan
President James Garfield
President James Carter

■ The Let Operator

The Let operator, which gives a name to an expression, makes queries easier to read. For instance, the query in Example 3 can be written as

```
Dim presQuery = From pres In presidents
                Where FirstName(pres) = txtFirstName.Text
                Let formalName = IncludeTitle(pres)
                Select formalName
```

■ The Order By Operator

An array or query result is said to be **ordered** if its values are in either ascending or descending order. With ascending order, the value of each element is less than or equal to the value of the next element. That is,

$$[\text{each element}] \leq [\text{next element}].$$

For string values, the ANSI table is used to evaluate the "less than or equal to" condition.

Putting elements in alphabetical or numeric order (either ascending or descending) is referred to as **sorting**. There are many algorithms for sorting arrays. The most efficient ones use complex nested loops and are tricky to program. However, LINQ provides the Order By query operator that spares us from having to code complicated sorting algorithms. The simplest form of an Order By clause is

```
Order By [expression] Direction
```

where *Direction* is one of the keywords Ascending or Descending, and the expression involves range and/or Let variables.

 Example 4   **Sort Numbers** The following program sorts an array of numbers in ascending order. *Note:* If the word Ascending is replaced by Descending, the array will be sorted in descending order.

```
Private Sub btnSort_Click(...) Handles btnSort.Click
  Dim nums() As Integer = {3, 6, 4, 1}
  Dim numQuery = From num In nums
                 Order By num Ascending
                 Select num
  For Each n As Integer In numQuery
    lstOutput.Items.Add(n)
  Next
End Sub
```

[Run, and click on the button.]

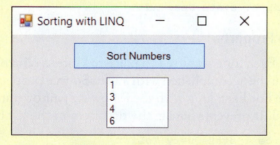

The Order By operator is quite flexible and can order arrays in ways other than just alphabetical or numeric order. Secondary criteria for ordering can be specified by listing two or more criteria separated by commas. In general, an Order By clause of the form

```
Order By expression1 Direction1, expression2 Direction2, ...
```

primarily sorts by expression1 and Direction1, secondarily by expression2 and Direction 2, and so on. For instance, an Order By clause such as

```
Order By lastName Ascending, firstName Ascending
```

can be used to alphabetize a sequence of full names. When two people have the same last name, their first names will be used to determine whose full name comes first.

✔ **Example 5** **Sort States** The following program uses the file States.txt considered in Example 1 and sorts the states by the length of their names in ascending order. States with names of the same length are sorted by their names in reverse alphabetical order.

```
Private Sub btnDisplay_Click(...) Handles btnDisplay.Click
  Dim states() As String = IO.File.ReadAllLines("States.txt")
  Dim stateQuery = From state In states
                   Order By state.Length Ascending, state Descending
                   Select state
  For Each state As String In stateQuery
    lstStates.Items.Add(state)
  Next
End Sub
```

[Run, and click on the button.]

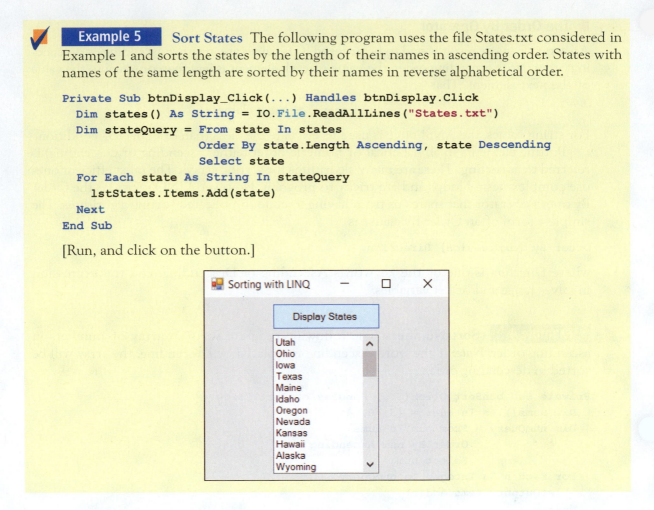

Note: In an Order By clause, the default direction is *Ascending.* For instance, the fourth line of Example 5 could have been written

```
Order By state.Length, state Descending
```

■ The DataSource Property

In Example 5 , a For Each loop was used to place the values returned by the query into a list box. The task also can be accomplished with a DataSource property. To use the DataSource property, replace the For Each loop with the following pair of statements. **Note:** The second statement is optional. It prevents having the first item in the list box selected at startup.

```
lstStates.DataSource = stateQuery.ToList
lstStates.SelectedItem = Nothing
```

The DataSource property also can be used to display the contents of an array directly into a list box with a statement of the form

```
lstBox.DataSource = arrayName
```

Note: If a SelectedIndexChanged event procedure has been defined for a list box, then execution of the DataSource property will raise the SelectedIndexChanged event.

■ Binary Search

A large array in ascending order is most efficiently searched with a **binary search**. The BinarySearch method looks for a value in the array by first determining in which half of the array it lies. The other half is then ignored, and the search is narrowed to the retained half.

The process is repeated until the item is found or the entire list has been considered. A statement of the form

```
numVar = Array.BinarySearch(arrayName, value)
```

assigns to *numVar* the index of an occurrence of the requested value in *arrayName*. If the value is not found, then a negative number is assigned to *numVar*.

■ Comments

1. The Option Infer setting can be made the default setting for all of your Visual Basic programs or can be made the setting for a single program.

   (a) If a value for Option Infer is set in the Option default project setting window shown in Fig. 3.1 of Section 3.2, then that setting will be the default setting for all new programs.

   (b) To override the default setting for an individual program, enter the statement **Option Infer On** or **Option Infer Off** at the top of the Code Window. Alternately, right-click on the program name at the top of Solution Explorer, click on Properties, click on the Compile tab, and change the value for "Option infer".

2. LINQ Where operators are said to *filter* data, and Select operators are said to *project* data.

3. Visual Basic has a built-in routine for sorting arrays. A statement of the form

   ```
   Array.Sort(arrayName)
   ```

   sorts the array in ascending order. This method is useful for simple sorting where the more advanced capabilities of LINQ are not needed. **Note:** A statement of the form **Array.Reverse(arrayName)** then sorts the array in descending order.

4. Visual Basic provides IntelliSense support for LINQ queries.

Practice Problems 7.2

1. Write a program that uses a LINQ query to calculate the sum of the numbers in the file Numbers.txt.

2. The file USPres.txt contains the full names of the first 44 U.S. presidents. The following program finds the full name of the president whose last name is "Eisenhower". Since there is only one such president, a text box (rather than a list box) is sufficient to display the output.

   ```
   Private Sub btnFind_Click(...) Handles btnFind.Click
     Dim presidents() As String = IO.File.ReadAllLines("USPres.txt")
     Dim query = From pres In presidents
                 Where pres.EndsWith("Eisenhower")
                 Select pres
     txtFullName.Text = query.First
   End Sub
   ```

   (a) Since the value of query consists of just one name, why can't the sixth line be replaced with **txtFullName.Text = query**?

   (b) What expressions, other than **query.First**, can be used for the right side of the sixth line that would yield the same result?

In Exercises 1 through 18, determine the output displayed when the button is clicked.

1.
```
Private Sub btnDisplay_Click(...) Handles btnDisplay.Click
    Dim nums() As Integer = {5, 7, 2, 3}
    Dim numQuery = From num In nums
                   Where num > 4
                   Select num
    For Each num As Integer In numQuery
        lstOutput.Items.Add(num)
    Next
End Sub
```

2.
```
Private Sub btnDisplay_Click(...) Handles btnDisplay.Click
    Dim words() As String = {"Houston", "we", "have", "a", "problem"}
    Dim wordQuery = From word In words
                    Where word.ToUpper.StartsWith("H")
                    Select word
    For Each word As String In wordQuery
        lstOutput.Items.Add(word)
    Next
End Sub
```

3.
```
Private Sub btnDisplay_Click(...) Handles btnDisplay.Click
    Dim line As String = "I'm going to make him an offer he can't refuse"
    Dim words() As String = line.Split(" "c)
    Dim wordQuery = From word In words
                    Where word.Length = 5
                    Select word
    lstOutput.DataSource = wordQuery.ToList
    lstOutput.SelectedItem = Nothing
End Sub
```

4.
```
Private Sub btnDisplay_Click(...) Handles btnDisplay.Click
    Dim line As String = "1492,1776,1812,1929,1941"
    Dim dates() As String = line.Split(","c)
    Dim dateQuery = From yr In dates
                    Where CInt(yr) < 1800
                    Select yr
    lstOutput.DataSource = dateQuery.ToList
    lstOutput.SelectedItem = Nothing
End Sub
```

5.
```
Private Sub btnDisplay_Click(...) Handles btnDisplay.Click
    Dim line As String = "If,you,fail,to,plan,then,you,plan,to,fail"
    Dim words() As String = line.Split(","c)
    Dim wordQuery = From word In words
                    Select word
                    Distinct
    txtOutput.Text = CStr(wordQuery.Count)
End Sub
```

6.
```
Private Sub btnDisplay_Click(...) Handles btnDisplay.Click
    Dim nums() As Integer = {2, 3, 4, 3, 2}
    Dim numQuery = From num In nums
                   Select num
                   Distinct
    txtOutput.Text = CStr(numQuery.Sum)
End Sub
```

7.
```
Private Sub btnDisplay_Click(...) Handles btnDisplay.Click
    Dim nums() As Integer = {2, 3, 4, 3, 2}
    Dim numQuery = From num In nums
                   Select num + 100
                   Distinct
    txtOutput.Text = CStr(numQuery.Average)
End Sub
```

8.
```
Private Sub btnDisplay_Click(...) Handles btnDisplay.Click
    Dim words() As String = {"racecar", "motor", "kayak", "civics"}
    Dim wordQuery = From word In words
                    Where IsPalindrome(word)
                    Select word.ToUpper
    For Each word As String In wordQuery
        lstOutput.Items.Add(word)
    Next
End Sub

Function IsPalindrome(word As String) As Boolean
    'A palindrome is a word that reads the same forward and backward.
    Dim n As Integer = word.Length
    For i As Integer = 0 To (n - 1) \ 2
        If word.Substring(i, 1) <> word.Substring(n - i - 1, 1) Then
            Return False
        End If
    Next
    Return True
End Function
```

9.
```
Private Sub btnDisplay_Click(...) Handles btnDisplay.Click
    'The first four lines of Numbers.txt contain the numbers 2, 6, 7, and 8.
    Dim numbers() as String = IO.File.ReadAllLines("Numbers.txt")
    Dim query = From num In numbers
                Select CInt(num)
    lstOutput.Items.Add(query(0) + query(1))
End Sub
```

10.
```
Private Sub btnDisplay_Click(...) Handles btnDisplay.Click
    'The first four lines of Words.txt contain scale, top, up, and low.
    Dim words() As String = IO.File.ReadAllLines("Words.txt")
    Dim query = From word In words
                Select word
    txtOutput.Text = query(2) & query(0)
End Sub
```

11.
```
Private Sub btnDisplay_Click(...) Handles btnDisplay.Click
    Dim grades() As Integer = {66, 68, 72, 76, 90, 92, 93, 94, 95}
    Dim query = From grade In grades
                Let newGrade = CurveGrade(grade)
                Where newGrade = 100
                Select newGrade
    txtOutput.Text = query.Count & " students have a grade of 100"
End Sub

Function CurveGrade(grade As Integer) As Integer
  grade += 7
  If grade > 100 Then
    grade = 100
  End If
  Return grade
End Function
```

12.
```
Private Sub btnDisplay_Click(...) Handles btnDisplay.Click
    Dim words() As String = {"rated", "savory", "able", "just"}
    Dim query = From word In words
                Let opposite = ("un" & word).ToUpper
                Select opposite
    txtOutput.Text = query.Max
End Sub
```

13.
```
Private Sub btnDisplay_Click(...) Handles btnDisplay.Click
    Dim nums() As Integer = {12, 5, 7, 10, 3, 15, 4}
    Dim query = From num In nums
                Where num > 10
                Order By num Descending
                Select num
    lstOutput.DataSource = query.ToList
    lstOutput.SelectedItem = Nothing
End Sub
```

14.
```
Private Sub btnDisplay_Click(...) Handles btnDisplay.Click
    Dim words() As String = {"When", "in", "the", "course",
                             "of", "human", "events"}
    Dim query = From word In words
                Order By word.Length
                Select word.Length
    Dim greatestLength As Integer = query.Last
    Dim query2 = From word In words
                 Where word.Length = greatestLength
                 Order By word Descending
                 Select word
    lstOutput.DataSource = query2.ToList
    lstOutput.SelectedItem = Nothing
End Sub
```

15.
```
Private Sub btnDisplay_Click(...) Handles btnDisplay.Click
    Dim grades() As Integer = {60, 70, 90, 80}
    Dim query = From grade In grades
                Order By grade Descending
                Select grade
    grades = query.ToArray
    ReDim Preserve grades(grades.Count - 2) 'drop lowest grade
    Dim str As String = "The average after dropping the lowest grade is "
    txtOutput.Text = str & grades.Average
End Sub
```

16.
```
Private Sub btnDisplay_Click(...) Handles btnDisplay.Click
    Dim golfers(2) As String 'top 3 golfers in tournament
    golfers(0) = "Funk,65,69,69,75"     'total = 278
    golfers(1) = "Ramaro,67,69,65,73"   'total = 274
    golfers(2) = "McNulty,68,70,73,68"  'total = 279
    Dim query = From golfer In golfers
                Let data = golfer.Split(","c)
                Let name = data(0)
                Let score = CInt(data(1)) + CInt(data(2)) +
                            CInt(data(3)) + CInt(data(4))
                Let result = score & "   " & name
                Order By score Ascending
                Select result
    For Each result As String In query
        lstOutput.Items.Add(result)
    Next
End Sub
```

17.
```
Private Sub btnDisplay_Click(...) Handles btnDisplay.Click
    Dim smallPrimes() As Integer = {2, 3, 5, 7, 11, 13, 17, 19, 23,
                                    29, 31, 37, 41, 43, 47, 53, 59,
                                    61, 67, 71, 73, 79, 83, 89, 97}
    Dim n As Integer = CInt(InputBox("Enter a number less than 100:"))
    If Array.BinarySearch(smallPrimes, n) < 0 Then
        txtOutput.Text = n & " is not a prime number"
    Else
        txtOutput.Text = n & " is a prime number"
    End If
End Sub
```
(Assume the response is *37*.)

18.
```
Private Sub btnDisplay_Click(...) Handles btnDisplay.Click
    Dim statesNE() As String = {"Connecticut", "Maine", "Massachusetts",
                                "New Hampshire", "Rhode Island", "Vermont"}
    Dim state As String = InputBox("Enter a state:")
    If Array.BinarySearch(statesNE, state) < 0 Then
        txtOutput.Text = state & " is not in New England."
    Else
        txtOutput.Text = state & " is in New England."
    End If
End Sub
```
(Assume the response is *New York*.)

Use LINQ to carry out the primary tasks of the programs in the remaining exercises of this section. In Exercises 19 through 24, redo the exercises from Section 7.1 using LINQ queries.

19. Exercise 17 of Section 7.1   **20.** Exercise 18 of Section 7.1

21. Exercise 21 of Section 7.1   **22.** Exercise 22 of Section 7.1

23. Exercise 25 of Section 7.1   **24.** Exercise 26 of Section 7.1

In Exercises 25 through 28, use the file SBWinners.txt that lists the winners of the first 49 Super Bowls.

25. Super Bowl Winners   Write a program that displays the teams (in alphabetical order) who have won a Super Bowl. Each team should appear only once. See Fig. 7.22.

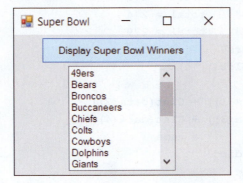

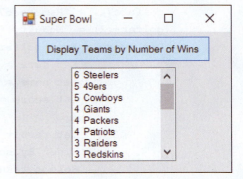

FIGURE 7.22   Outcome of Exercise 25.   **FIGURE 7.23**   Outcome of Exercise 26.

26. Super Bowl Winners   Write a program that displays a list of Super Bowl winners ordered by the number of games won. See Fig. 7.23.

27. Super Bowl Winners   Write a program that displays in a text box the number of games won by the team specified. See Fig. 7.24.

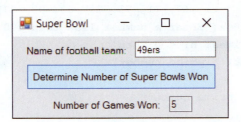

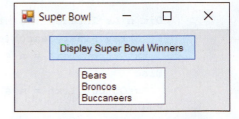

FIGURE 7.24   Possible outcome of Exercise 27.   **FIGURE 7.25**   Outcome of Exercise 28.

28. Super Bowl Winners   Write a program that displays the teams (in alphabetical order) who have won a Super Bowl and whose name begins with the letter B. Each team should appear only once. See Fig. 7.25.

29. Anagrams   An *anagram* of a word or phrase is another word or phrase that uses the same letters with the same frequency. Punctuation marks, case, and spaces are ignored. Write a program that requests two words (no punctuation) as input and determines if they are anagrams of each other. See Fig. 7.26.

30. Average Grade   The file Final.txt contains student grades on a final exam. Write a program using LINQ that displays the average grade on the exam and the percentage of grades that are above average. See Fig. 7.27.

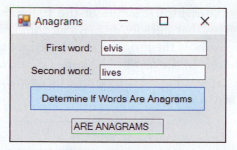

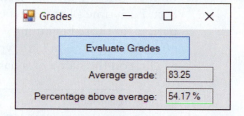

FIGURE 7.26 Possible outcome of Exercise 29.   FIGURE 7.27 Outcome of Exercise 30.

31. **Average Grade** Write a program that requests five grades from input dialog boxes and then calculates the average after dropping the two lowest grades. See Fig. 7.28.

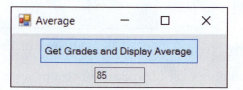

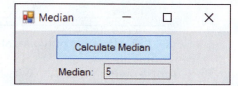

FIGURE 7.28 Possible outcome of Exercise 31.   FIGURE 7.29 Possible outcome of Exercise 32.

32. **Median** The **median** of an ordered set of measurements is a number separating the lower half from the upper half. If the number of measurements is odd, the median is the middle measurement. If the number of measurements is even, the median is the average of the two middle measurements. Write a program that requests a number *n* and a set of *n* measurements as input and then displays the median of the measurements. See Fig. 7.29.

33. **Original U.S. States** The file States.txt contains the 50 U.S. states in the order in which they joined the union. Write a program to display the original 13 states in alphabetical order. See Fig. 7.30.

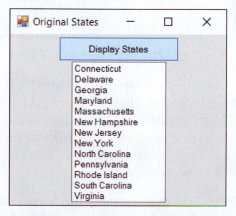

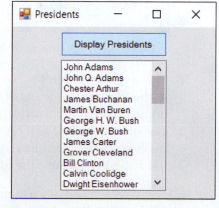

FIGURE 7.30 Outcome of Exercise 33.   FIGURE 7.31 Outcome of Exercise 34.

34. **U.S. Presidents** The file USPres.txt contains the names of the first 44 presidents in the order in which they served. The first two lines contain the names George Washington and John Adams. Write a program that displays the presidents ordered by their last name. See Fig. 7.31.

35. United Nations The file Nations.txt contains the names of the 193 member nations of the United Nations. Write a program that initially displays all the nations in a list box. Each time a letter is typed into a text box, the program should reduce the displayed nations to those beginning with the letters in the text box. Figure 7.32 shows the status after the letters "*Ma*" are typed into the text box. At any time, the user should be able to click on the name of a nation to have it appear in the text box.

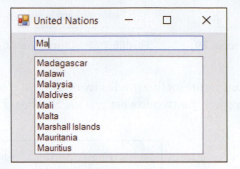

FIGURE 7.32 Possible outcome of Exercise 35.   **FIGURE 7.33** Outcome of Exercise 36.

36. Count Vowels The file Words.txt contains a list of words. Write a program that displays the words in a list box sorted by the number of different vowels (*A, E, I, O,* and *U*) in the word. When two words have the same number of different vowels, they should be ordered first by their length (descending) and then alphabetically. The display should show both the word and the number of different vowels in the word. See Fig. 7.33.

37. Sorting Numbers The left-hand list box in Fig. 7.34 has its sorted property set to True. Notice that the numbers are ordered according to the ANSI table. Write a program that places the numbers into the right-hand list box in proper numeric order. *Hint:* The **Array.Sort(arrayName)** statement takes data type into account when it sorts.

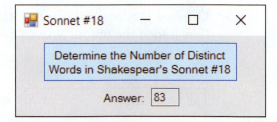

FIGURE 7.34 Outcome of Exercise 37.   **FIGURE 7.35** Outcome of Exercise 38.

38. Shakespeare Sonnet The file Sonnet.txt contains Shakespeare's Sonnet 18. Each entry in the file contains a line of the sonnet. Write a program that determines the number of unique words in the sonnet. See Fig. 7.35. **Note:** Be sure to strip all punctuation from the end of each word. You might find it easiest to first place all the words into an invisible list box, then create an array containing them, and then throw them into an array and use LINQ to create a list of the words with no repetitions.

In Exercises 39 and 40, use the file StatesBFNC.txt that contains the name, state bird, state flower, nickname, and capital of each state in the United States. (This file will also be used in four exercises in Section 8.2.) The states are listed in alphabetical order. The first three lines of the file are

```
Alabama,Yellowhammer,Camellia,Cotton State,Montgomery
Alaska,Willow ptarmigan,Forget-me-not,The Last Frontier,Juneau
Arizona,Cactus wren,Saguaro cactus,Grand Canyon State,Phoenix
```

39. State Flowers Write a program using the file StatesBFNC.txt that displays the state flowers in a list box and the number of different state flowers. Each flower should appear once in the list box and the flowers should be ordered by the lengths of their names. See Fig. 7.36.

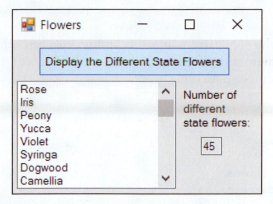

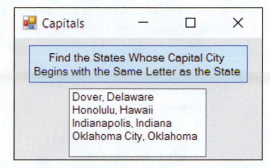

FIGURE 7.36 Outcome of Exercise 39.　　**FIGURE 7.37** Outcome of Exercise 40.

40. State Capitals Write a program using the file StatesBFNC.txt that displays the states (and their capitals) for which the names of the state and its capital begin with the same letter. See Fig. 7.37.

Solutions to Practice Problems 7.2

```
1. Private Sub btnDisplay_Click(...) Handles btnDisplay.Click
      Dim numbers() As String = IO.File.ReadAllLines("Numbers.txt")
      Dim query = From num In numbers
                  Select CDbl(num)
      MessageBox.Show(CStr(query.Sum), "Total")
   End Sub
```

2. **(a)** A text box can be filled only with a string. The value returned by a query is a *sequence* type that contains one string element. Only that element, not the sequence itself, can be assigned to the text property of the text box.

   (b) `query(0)`, `query.Last`, `query.Max`, `query.Min`

7.3 Arrays of Structures

Often we work with several pieces of related data. For instance, four related pieces of data about a country are *name*, *continent*, *population*, and *area*. Suppose we are considering such data for the 193 countries in the United Nations. In the early days of programming, the way to work with such information was to put it into four parallel arrays—one array of type String for names, a second array of type String for continents, a third array of type Double for populations, and a fourth array of type Double for areas. The modern way of dealing with such information is to place it into a single array of a composite data type that you define called a **structure**.

■ Structures

A structure contains variables of (possibly) different types, which are known as **members**. A structure is defined in the Declarations section of the class by a block of the form

```
Structure StructureName
  Dim memberName1 As MemberType1
  Dim memberName2 As MemberType2
       .
       .
End Structure
```

where *StructureName* is the name of the structure you are defining, *memberName1* and *memberName2* are the names of the members of the structure, and *MemberType1* and *MemberType2* are the corresponding member data types.

Some examples of structures are

```
Structure Nation
  Dim name As String
  Dim continent As String
  Dim population As Double    'in millions
  Dim area As Double          'in square miles
End Structure

Structure Employee
  Dim name As String
  Dim dateHired As Date
  Dim hourlyWage As Decimal
End Structure

Structure College
  Dim name As String
  Dim state As String         'state abbreviation
  Dim yearFounded As Integer
End Structure
```

Structure variables are declared with Dim statements just like ordinary variables. For instance, the statement

```
Dim country As Nation
```

declares a variable of data type Nation.

Dot notation is used to refer to an individual member of a structure variable. For instance, the set of statements

```
country.name = "China"
country.continent = "Asia"
country.population = 1355.7
country.area = 3696100
```

assigns values to the members of the variable *country* declared above. After these assignment statements are executed, the statement

```
txtOutput.Text = country.continent
```

will display the string "Asia" in a text box, and the statement

```
txtOutput.Text = CStr(1000000 * country.population / country.area)
```

will display the population density of China in a text box.

Although structures are always defined in the Declarations section of the class, structure variables can be declared anywhere in a program. Just like ordinary variables, they have class, procedure, or block scope depending on where they are declared.

Example 1 **China Facts** The following program uses the Split method to assign values to the members of a structure variable. This technique will play a vital role when values are assigned from text files to an array of structures. **Note:** Since the population member of the structure Nation is given in millions, the value has to be multiplied by one million when used in a calculation.

```
Structure Nation
  Dim name As String
  Dim continent As String
  Dim population As Double    'in millions
  Dim area As Double          'in square miles
End Structure

Dim country As Nation         'class-level variable

Private Sub frmCountry_Load(...) Handles MyBase.Load
  'Assign values to country's member variables
  Dim line As String = "China,Asia,1355.7,3696100"
  Dim data() As String = line.Split(","c)
  country.name = data(0)
  country.continent = data(1)
  country.population = CDbl(data(2))
  country.area = CDbl(data(3))
End Sub

Private Sub btnDisplay_Click(...) Handles btnDisplay.Click
  'Display data in text boxes
  txtName.Text = country.name
  txtContinent.Text = country.continent
  txtPop.Text = (1000000 * country.population).ToString("N0")
  txtArea.Text = (country.area).ToString("N0") & " square miles"
  txtDensity.Text = (1000000 * country.population / country.area).ToString("N") &
                    " people per square mile"
End Sub
```

[Run, and click on the button.]

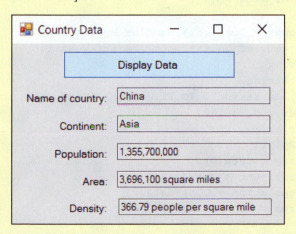

■ Arrays of Structures

Since a structure is a data type, an array can be declared with a structure as its data type. For instance, the statement

```
Dim nations(192) As Nation
```

declares *nations* to be an array of 193 elements, where each element has data type Nation. For each index *i*, *nations(i)* will be a variable of type Nation, and the values of its members will be *nations(i).name*, *nations(i).continent*, *nations(i).population*, and *nations(i).area*. Filling this 193-element array requires pieces of data. This amount of data is best supplied by a text file. The optimum design for this text file is to have 193 lines of text, each consisting of 4 pieces of data delimited by commas. The next example uses the file UN.txt that gives data about the 193 members of the United Nations with the countries listed in alphabetical order. Some lines of the file are

```
Canada,North America,34.8,3855000
France,Europe,66.3,211209
New Zealand,Australia/Oceania,4.4,103738
Nigeria,Africa,177.2,356669
Pakistan,Asia,196.2,310403
Peru,South America,30.1,496226
```

Each line of this text file is called a **record** and each record is said to contain four **fields**—a name field, a continent field, a population field, and an area field. The text file is said to use a **CSV format**. (CSV stands for "Comma Separated Values.")

Example 2   **United Nations** The following program uses the text file UN.txt to fill an array of structures and then uses the array to display the names of the countries in the continent selected by the user. The program uses two list boxes. Assume the String Collection Editor for lstContinents has been filled at design time with the names of the seven continents. The countries in the selected continent are displayed in lstCountries.

```
Structure Nation
  Dim name As String
  Dim continent As String
  Dim population As Double    'in millions
  Dim area As Double          'in square miles
End Structure

Dim nations(192) As Nation

Private Sub frmCountry_Load(...) Handles MyBase.Load
  'Place the contents of UN.txt into the array nations.
  Dim line As String
  Dim data(3) As String
  Dim countries() As String = IO.File.ReadAllLines("UN.txt")
  For i As Integer = 0 To 192
    line = countries(i)
    data = line.Split(","c)
    nations(i).name = data(0)
    nations(i).continent = data(1)
    nations(i).population = CDbl(data(2))
    nations(i).area = CDbl(data(3))
  Next
End Sub

Private Sub lstContinents_SelectedIndexChanged(...) Handles _
                         lstContinents.SelectedIndexChanged
  Dim selectedContinent As String = lstContinents.Text
```

```
    lstCountries.Items.Clear()
    If selectedContinent = "Antarctica" Then
      MessageBox.Show("There are no countries in Antarctica.")
    Else
      For i As Integer = 0 To 192
        If nations(i).continent = selectedContinent Then
          lstCountries.Items.Add(nations(i).name)
        End If
      Next
    End If
End Sub
```

[Run, and click on the name of a continent.]

Display Countries by Continent	— □ ✕
Click on the name of a continent:	Albania
	Andorra
Africa	Austria
Antarctica	Belarus
Asia	Belgium
Australia/Oceania	Bosnia and Herzegovina
Europe	Bulgaria
North America	Croatia
South America	Czech Republic
	Denmark

Queries can be used with arrays of structures in much the same way they are used with ordinary arrays.

Example 3   United Nations In the following variation of Example 2, the countries are displayed in descending order by their areas. LINQ is used both to filter the countries and to sort them by area. The query returns a sequence of names of countries.

```
Structure Nation
  Dim name As String
  Dim continent As String
  Dim population As Double    'in millions
  Dim area As Double          'in square miles
End Structure

  Dim nations(192) As Nation

Private Sub frmCountry_Load(...) Handles MyBase.Load
  Dim line As String
  Dim data(3) As String
  Dim countries() As String = IO.File.ReadAllLines("UN.txt")
  For i As Integer = 0 To 192
    line = countries(i)
    data = line.Split(","c)
    nations(i).name = data(0)
    nations(i).continent = data(1)
    nations(i).population = CDbl(data(2))
    nations(i).area = CDbl(data(3))
  Next
End Sub
```

```
Private Sub lstContinents_SelectedIndexChanged(...) Handles _
                          lstContinents.SelectedIndexChanged
  Dim selectedContinent As String = lstContinents.Text
  Dim query = From country In nations
              Where country.continent = selectedContinent
              Order By country.area Descending
              Select country.name
  lstCountries.Items.Clear()
  If selectedContinent = "Antarctica" Then
    MessageBox.Show("There are no countries in Antarctica.")
  Else
    For Each countryName As String In query
      lstCountries.Items.Add(countryName)
    Next
  End If
End Sub
```

[Run, and click on the name of a continent.]

So far, LINQ Select clauses have contained a single item. However, Select clauses can contain multiple items. In that case the query returns a sequence of structures.

The next example uses the file Colleges.txt that contains data (name, state, and year founded) about colleges founded before 1800. The first four lines of the file are

```
Harvard U.,MA,1636
William and Mary,VA,1693
Yale U.,CT,1701
U. of Pennsylvania,PA,1740
```

✓ **Example 4**   **Earliest Colleges**   The following program displays colleges alphabetically ordered (along with their year founded) that are in the state specified in a masked text box. In this program we do not assume that the number of colleges in the text file is known in advance. Also, the Select clause returns a sequence of values whose data type is a structure having two members—a name member and a yearFounded member.

```
Structure College
  Dim name As String
  Dim state As String          'state abbreviation
  Dim yearFounded As Integer
End Structure
```

```vb
Dim colleges() As College

Private Sub frmColleges_Load(...) Handles MyBase.Load
  'Place the data for each college into the array schools.
  Dim schools() As String = IO.File.ReadAllLines("Colleges.txt")
  Dim n As Integer = schools.Count - 1
  ReDim colleges(n)
  Dim line As String    'holds data for a single college
  Dim data(2) As String
  For i As Integer = 0 To n
    line = schools(i)
    data = line.Split(","c)
    colleges(i).name = data(0)
    colleges(i).state = data(1)
    colleges(i).yearFounded = CInt(data(2))
  Next
End Sub

Private Sub btnDisplay_Click(...) Handles btnDisplay.Click
  Dim query = From col In colleges
              Where col.state = mtbState.Text.ToUpper
              Order By col.name Ascending
              Select col.name, col.yearFounded
  lstColleges.Items.Clear()
  For Each institution In query
    lstColleges.Items.Add(institution.name & " " & institution.yearFounded)
  Next
End Sub
```

[Run, type a state abbreviation into the masked text box, and click on the button.]

```
┌─────────────────────────────────────────┐
│ 🖳 Earliest Colleges    —    □    ×       │
├─────────────────────────────────────────┤
│         State: [PA]                      │
│      ┌───────────────────────────┐       │
│      │      Display Colleges      │       │
│      └───────────────────────────┘       │
│      ┌───────────────────────────┐       │
│      │ Dickinson College 1773     │       │
│      │ Moravian College 1742      │       │
│      │ U. of Pennsylvania 1740    │       │
│      │ U. of Pittsburgh 1787      │       │
│      │ Wash. & Jefferson 1781     │       │
│      └───────────────────────────┘       │
└─────────────────────────────────────────┘
```

In the program above, the query returned a sequence of values whose data type is a structure having two members. (The number of members was determined by the number of items in the Select clause.) The new structure type has no declared name, and thus it is said to have an **anonymous type**. Local type inference (provided by having Option Infer set to On) spares us from having to know the names of anonymous data types.

■ The DataGridView Control

In Section 7.2, the DataSource property was used to display (as a list) the values returned by a query having a single item in its Select clause. The DataSource property also can be used to display (as a table) the structure values returned by a query having two or more expressions in its Select clause. Instead of a list box, the values are displayed in a DataGridView control. (The DataGridView control is found in the Toolbox's *All Windows Forms* and *Data* groups. The standard prefix for the name of a DataGridView control is *dgv*.)

If the Select clause of a query contains two or more items, then a pair of statements of the form

```
dgvOutput.DataSource = queryName.ToList
dgvOutput.CurrentCell = Nothing
```

displays the values returned by the query in the DataGridView control dgvOutput. (**Note:** The second statement is optional. It prevents having a shaded cell in the table.) For instance, consider the program in the previous example. If the list box is replaced by the DataGridView control dgvColleges, the statement `lstColleges.Items.Clear()` is deleted, and the For Each loop is replaced by the statements

```
dgvColleges.DataSource = query.ToList
dgvColleges.CurrentCell = Nothing
```

then the outcome will be as shown in Fig. 7.38.

The blank column at the left side of the DataGridView control can be removed by setting the RowHeadersVisible property of the DataGridView control to False at design time. By default, the column headers contain the member names from the query's Select clause. The column headers can be customized with the HeaderText property. Figure 7.39 results when the RowHeadersVisible property is set to False and the following two lines of code are added to the btnDisplay_Click event procedure:

```
dgvColleges.Columns("name").HeaderText = "College"
dgvColleges.Columns("yearFounded").HeaderText = "Year Founded"
```

Note: In this textbook, the heights of the DataGridView controls have been carefully sized to exactly fit the data. There is no need for you to strive for such precision when working the exercises. Also, the AutoSizeColumnsMode property of DataGridView controls are always set to Fill so that column widths will be automatically adjusted either to fill the control or to fit cell contents.

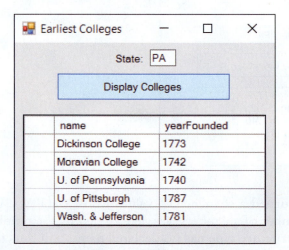

FIGURE 7.38 Use of a DataGridView in Example 4.

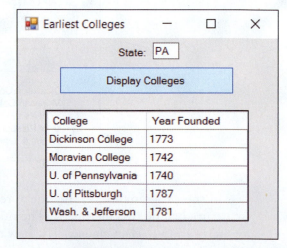

FIGURE 7.39 Customizing the headers in Example 4.

Searching an Array of Structures

Often one member (or pair of members) serves to uniquely identify each element in an array of structures. Such a member (or pair of members) is called a **key**. In Example 4, the *name* member is a key for the array of College structures. Often an array of structures is searched with a LINQ query for the sole element having a specific key value. If so, the query returns a sequence consisting of a single item, and a method such as the First method is used to display the value in a text box.

✔ **Example 5**   **Earliest Colleges** The following program provides information about a college selected from a list box by the user. (**Note:** In this program, the method First can be replaced by other methods, such as Last, Max, or Min.)

```
Structure College
  Dim name As String
  Dim state As String
  Dim yearFounded As Integer
End Structure

Dim colleges() As College

Private Sub frmColleges_Load(...) Handles MyBase.Load
  Dim schools() As String = IO.File.ReadAllLines("Colleges.txt")
  Dim n = schools.Count - 1
  ReDim colleges(n)
  Dim line As String    'holds data for a single college
  Dim data(2) As String
  For i As Integer = 0 To n
    line = schools(i)
    data = line.Split(","c)
    colleges(i).name = data(0)
    colleges(i).state = data(1)
    colleges(i).yearFounded = CInt(data(2))
  Next
  Dim query = From institution In colleges
              Order By institution.name
              Select institution
  For Each institution In query
    lstColleges.Items.Add(institution.name)
  Next
End Sub

Private Sub lstColleges_SelectedIndexChanged(...) Handles _
            lstColleges.SelectedIndexChanged
  Dim query = From institution In colleges
              Where institution.name = lstColleges.Text
              Select institution
  txtState.Text = query.First.state
  txtYear.Text = CStr(query.First.yearFounded)
End Sub
```

[Run, and click on a college.]

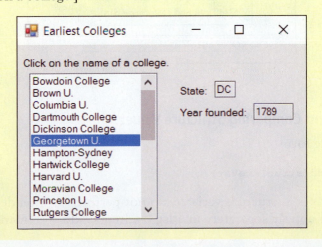

Using General Procedures with Structures

Variables whose type is a structure can be passed to Sub procedures and returned by Function procedures in the same way as variables of other data types.

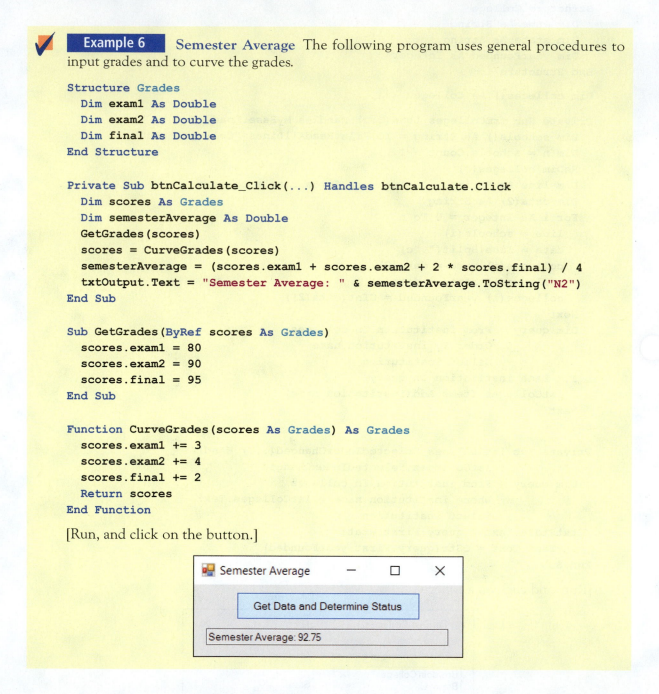

Example 6   **Semester Average** The following program uses general procedures to input grades and to curve the grades.

```
Structure Grades
  Dim exam1 As Double
  Dim exam2 As Double
  Dim final As Double
End Structure

Private Sub btnCalculate_Click(...) Handles btnCalculate.Click
  Dim scores As Grades
  Dim semesterAverage As Double
  GetGrades(scores)
  scores = CurveGrades(scores)
  semesterAverage = (scores.exam1 + scores.exam2 + 2 * scores.final) / 4
  txtOutput.Text = "Semester Average: " & semesterAverage.ToString("N2")
End Sub

Sub GetGrades(ByRef scores As Grades)
  scores.exam1 = 80
  scores.exam2 = 90
  scores.final = 95
End Sub

Function CurveGrades(scores As Grades) As Grades
  scores.exam1 += 3
  scores.exam2 += 4
  scores.final += 2
  Return scores
End Function
```

[Run, and click on the button.]

Semester Average

Get Data and Determine Status

Semester Average: 92.75

Displaying and Comparing Structure Values

Statements of the form

`lstBox.Items.Add(structureVar)`

where *structureVar* is a structure variable, do not perform as intended. Each member of a structure should appear separately in a lstBox.Items.Add statement. Also, comparisons involving structures using the relational operators <, >, =, <>, <=, and >= are valid only with individual members of the structures, not with the structures themselves.

◼ Complex Structures (Optional)

So far, the members of structures have had elementary types, such as String or Integer. However, the type for a member can be another structure or an array. When a member is given an array type, the defining Dim statement must not specify the upper bound; this task must be left to a ReDim statement. Example 7 demonstrates the use of both of these nonelementary types of members.

Example 7 **Graduation Status** The following program totals a person's college credits and determines whether that person has enough credits for graduation. ***Notes:*** The structure variable *person* is local to the btnGet_Click event procedure. In the fifth line of the procedure, `person.name.firstName` should be thought of as `(person.name).firstName`.

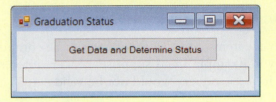

OBJECT	PROPERTY	SETTING
frmStatus	Text	Graduation Status
btnGet	Text	Get Data and Determine Status
txtResult	ReadOnly	True

```vb
Structure FullName
  Dim firstName As String
  Dim lastName As String
End Structure


Structure Student
  Dim name As FullName
  Dim credits() As Integer
End Structure


Private Sub btnGet_Click(...) Handles btnGet.Click
  Dim numYears As Integer
  Dim person As Student
  txtResult.Clear()
  person.name.firstName = InputBox("First Name:")
  person.name.lastName = InputBox("Last Name:")
  numYears = CInt(InputBox("Number of years completed:"))
  ReDim person.credits(numYears - 1)
  For i As Integer = 0 To (numYears - 1)
    person.credits(i) = CInt(InputBox("Credits in year " & i + 1))
  Next
  DetermineStatus(person)
End Sub


Sub DetermineStatus(person As Student)
  Dim query = From num In person.credits
              Select num
  Dim total As Integer = query.Sum
```

```
  If (total >= 120) Then
    txtResult.Text = person.name.firstName & " " &
             person.name.lastName & " has enough credits to graduate."
  Else
    txtResult.Text = person.name.firstName & " " &
                person.name.lastName & " needs " &
                (120 - total) & " more credits to graduate."
  End If
End Sub
```

[Run, click on the button, and respond to requests for input with *Miranda, Smith, 3, 34, 33, 34.*]

| Graduation Status | — | □ | × |

Get Data and Determine Status

Miranda Smith needs 19 more credits to graduate.

■ Comments

1. When a Select clause contains two or more items, none of the items can be computed values. For instance, consider the query in Example 3 and suppose we were interested in the age of each college in 2017. The following query would not be valid:

```
Dim collegeQuery = From col In colleges
                   Where col.state = mtbState.Text.ToUpper
                   Order By col.name Ascending
                   Select col.name, 2017 - col.yearFounded
```

Instead, the query must be written

```
Dim collegeQuery = From col In colleges
                   Where col.state = mtbState.Text.ToUpper
                   Order By col.name Ascending
                   Let age = 2017 - col.yearFounded
                   Select col.name, age
```

2. You can resize the width of a column of a DataGridView control while the program is running. Just position the mouse pointer on one of the vertical lines in the column header (the cursor becomes a horizontal two-headed arrow), click the mouse, and drag the vertical line.

3. CSV files can be converted to Excel spreadsheets and vice versa. For instance, consider the CSV file UN.txt. If you open it in Excel, you will obtain a spreadsheet with 193 lines and 4 columns. Figure 7.40 shows the first four lines of the spreadsheet.

	A	B	C	D
1	Afghanistan	Asia	31.8	251772
2	Albania	Europe	3	11100
3	Algeria	Africa	38.3	919595
4	Andorra	Europe	0.085	181

FIGURE 7.40 **Spreadsheet Created from UN.txt.**

Source: Excel 2016, Windows 10, Microsoft Corporation.

Conversely, a spreadsheet you create or download from the Internet can be converted to a CSV file. After clicking on "Save As" from the FILE menu, choose "CSV (Comma delimited)(*.csv)" in the "Save as type" dropdown box.

Practice Problems 7.3

1. Find the errors in the following event procedure:

```
Sub btnDisplay_Click(...) Handles btnDisplay.Click
   Structure Team
      Dim school As String
      Dim mascot As String
   End Structure

   Team.school = "Rice"
   Team.mascot = "Owls"
   txtOutput.Text = Team.school & " " & Team.mascot
End Sub
```

2. Correct the code in Practice Problem 1.

EXERCISES 7.3

In Exercises 1 through 10, determine the output displayed when the button is clicked.

1.
```
Structure Rectangle
   Dim length As Integer
   Dim width As Integer
End Structure

Private Sub btnDisplay_Click(...) Handles btnDisplay.Click
   Dim footballField As Rectangle
   footballField.length = 120    'yards
   footballField.width = 160     'yards
   Dim area As Integer = footballField.length * footballField.width
   txtOutput.Text = "The area of a football field is " & area &
                 " square yards."
End Sub
```

2.
```
Structure College
   Dim name As String
   Dim state As String
   Dim yearFounded As Integer
End Structure

Private Sub btnDisplay_Click(...) Handles btnDisplay.Click
   Dim school As College
   school.name = "USC"
   school.state = "CA"
   school.yearFounded = 1880
   'Now.Year is the current year
   Dim age As Integer = Now.Year - school.yearFounded
   txtOutput.Text = school.name & " is " & age & " years old."
End Sub
```

3.
```
Structure College
   Dim name As String
   Dim state As String
   Dim yearFounded As Integer
End Structure
```

```
      Private Sub btnDisplay_Click(...) Handles btnDisplay.Click
        Dim school As College
        Dim line As String = "Duke,NC,1838"
        Dim data() As String = line.Split(","c)
        school.name = data(0)
        school.state = data(1)
        school.yearFounded = CInt(data(2))
        txtOutput.Text = school.name & " was founded in " & school.state &
                        " in " & school.yearFounded & "."
      End Sub
```

4. ```
   Structure College
     Dim name As String
     Dim state As String
     Dim yearFounded As Integer
   End Structure

   Private Sub btnDisplay_Click(...) Handles btnDisplay.Click
     Dim school As College
     Dim data() As String = {"Stanford", "CA", "1885"}
     school.name = data(0)
     school.state = data(1)
     school.yearFounded = CInt(data(2))
     txtOutput.Text = school.name & " was founded in " & school.state &
                     " in " & school.yearFounded & "."
   End Sub
   ```

5. ```
   Structure Appearance
     Dim height As Double
     Dim weight As Double
   End Structure

   Private Sub btnDisplay_Click(...) Handles btnDisplay.Click
     Dim person1, person2 As Appearance
     person1.height = 72
     person1.weight = 170
     person2.height = 12 * 6
     If person1.height = person2.height Then
       lstOutput.Items.Add("heights are same")
     End If
     person2 = person1
     lstOutput.Items.Add(person2.weight)
   End Sub
   ```

6. ```
   Structure Employee
     Dim name As String
     Dim hoursWorked As Double
     Dim hourlyWage As Double
     Dim eligibleForBonus As Boolean
   End Structure

   Dim worker As Employee

   Private Sub frmWages_Load(...) Handles Me.Load
     worker.name = "John Q. Public"
     worker.hoursWorked = 40
   ```
   ```

```
    worker.hourlyWage = 25
    worker.eligibleForBonus = True
  End Sub

  Private Sub btnDetermine_Click(...) Handles btnDetermine.Click
    Dim wage As Double
    wage = worker.hoursWorked * worker.hourlyWage
    If worker.eligibleForBonus Then
      wage = wage + (0.1 * wage)
    End If
    MessageBox.Show("Wage for " & worker.name & ": " & wage.ToString("C"))
  End Sub
```

7.
```
Structure TestData
  Dim name As String
  Dim score As Double
End Structure

Dim students() As String = IO.File.ReadAllLines("Scores.txt")

Private Sub btnDisplay_Click(...) Handles btnDisplay.Click
  Dim student As TestData
  For i As Integer = 0 To (students.Count - 1)
    student = GetScore(i)
    DisplayScore(student)
  Next
End Sub


Function GetScore(i As Integer) As TestData
  Dim student As TestData
  Dim line As String = students(i)
  Dim data() As String = line.Split(","c)
  student.name = data(0)
  student.score = CDbl(data(1))
  Return student
End Function

Sub DisplayScore(student As TestData)
  lstOutput.Items.Add(student.name & ": " & student.score)
End Sub
```

(Assume that the three lines of the file Scores.txt contain the following data: Joe,88; Moe,90; Roe,95.)

8.
```
Structure Employee
  Dim name As String
  Dim dateHired As Date
  Dim hasDependents As Boolean
End Structure

Private Sub btnDisplay_Click(...) Handles btnDisplay.Click
  Dim worker As Employee
  worker.name = "John Jones"
  worker.dateHired = #9/20/2016#
  worker.hasDependents = True
  If DateDiff(DateInterval.Day, worker.dateHired, Today) < 180 Then
```

```
              MessageBox.Show("Not eligible to participate in the health plan.")
          Else
              MessageBox.Show("The monthly cost of your health plan is " &
                          HealthPlanCost(worker.hasDependents) & ".")
          End If
      End Sub


      Function HealthPlanCost(hasDependents As Boolean) As String
          If hasDependents Then
              Return (75).ToString("C")
          Else
              Return (50).ToString("C")
          End If
      End Function
```

(Assume that today is 1/1/2017.)

9.
```
  Structure Address
      Dim street As String
      Dim city As String
      Dim state As String
  End Structure


  Structure Citizen
      Dim name As String
      Dim dayOfBirth As Date
      Dim residence As Address
  End Structure


  Private Sub btnDisplay_Click(...) Handles btnDisplay.Click
      Dim person As Citizen
      person.name = "Mr. President"
      person.dayOfBirth = #8/4/1961#
      person.residence.street = "1600 Pennsylvania Avenue"
      person.residence.city = "Washington"
      person.residence.state = "DC"
      txtOutput.Text = person.name & " lives in " &
              person.residence.city & ", " & person.residence.state
  End Sub
```

10.
```
  Structure TaxData
      Dim socSecNum As String
      Dim numWithAllow As Integer 'number of withholding allowances
      Dim maritalStatus As String
      Dim hourlyWage As Double
  End Structure


  Structure Employee
      Dim name As String
      Dim hrsWorked As Double
      Dim taxInfo As TaxData
  End Structure
```

```
Private Sub btnDisplay_Click(...) Handles btnDisplay.Click
   Dim worker As Employee
   worker.name = "Hannah Jones"
   worker.hrsWorked = 40
   worker.taxInfo.hourlyWage = 20
   txtOutput.Text = worker.name & " earned " &
       (worker.hrsWorked * worker.taxInfo.hourlyWage).ToString("C")
End Sub
```

In Exercises 11 through 13, determine the errors.

11.
```
Structure Nobel
   Dim peace As String
   Dim yr As Integer
End Structure


Private Sub btnDisplay_Click(...) Handles btnDisplay.Click
   Dim prize As Nobel
   peace = "Martti Ahtisaari"
   yr = 2008
   txtOutput.Text = peace & " won the " & yr & " Nobel Peace Prize."
End Sub
```

12.
```
Structure Vitamins
   Dim a As Double
   Dim c As Double
End Structure


Private Sub btnDisplay_Click(...) Handles btnDisplay.Click
   Dim minimum As Vitamins
   minimum.c = 60
   minimum.a = 5000
   lstOutput.Items.Add(minimum)
End Sub
```

13.
```
Structure BallGame
   Dim hits As Integer
   Dim runs As Integer
End Structure


Private Sub btnDisplay_Click(...) Handles btnDisplay.Click
   Dim game1, game2 As BallGame
   game1.hits = 15
   game1.runs = 8
   game2.hits = 17
   game2.runs = 10
   If game1 > game2 Then
     txtOutput.Text = "The first game was better."
   Else
     txtOutput.Text = "The second game was at least as good."
   End If
End Sub
```

14. Write lines of code as instructed in Steps (a) through (e) to fill in the missing lines in the following program:

```
Structure Appearance
    Dim height As Double 'inches
    Dim weight As Double 'pounds
End Structure

Structure Person
    Dim name As String
    Dim stats As Appearance
End Structure

Private Sub btnDisplay_Click(...) Handles btnDisplay.Click
    Dim person1, person2 As Person
    (missing lines)
End Sub
```

(a) Give *person1* the name Michael.
(b) Set Michael's height and weight to 71 and 190, respectively.
(c) Give *person2* the name Jacob.
(d) Set Jacob's height and weight to 70 and 175, respectively.
(e) If one person is both taller and heavier than the other, display a sentence of the form "[name of bigger person] is bigger than [name of smaller person]."

In Exercises 15 through 18 describe the output that results from clicking on the button. The programs use the file Cities.txt that contains information about the 25 largest cities in the United States. Each record of the file has four fields—*name, state, population in 2000* (in 100,000s), and *population in 2010* (in 100,000s). The first four lines in the file are as follows:

```
New York,NY,80.1,82.7
Los Angeles,CA,36.9,38.84
Chicago,IL,29.0,28.7
Houston,TX,19.5,22.4
```

Assume that each program contains the following code:

```
Structure City
    Dim name As String
    Dim state As String
    Dim pop2000 As Double
    Dim pop2010 As Double
End Structure

Dim cities() As City

Private Sub frmCities_Load(...) Handles Me.Load
    'Place the data for each city into the array cities.
    Dim cityRecords() As String = IO.File.ReadAllLines("Cities.txt")
    'Use the array cityRecords to populate the array cities.
    Dim n = cityRecords.Count - 1
    ReDim cities(n)
    Dim line As String    'holds data for a single city
```

```
      Dim data(3) As String
      For i As Integer = 0 To n
        line = cityRecords(i)
        data = line.Split(","c)
        cities(i).name = data(0)
        cities(i).state = data(1)
        cities(i).pop2000 = CDbl(data(2))
        cities(i).pop2010 = CDbl(data(3))
      Next
    End Sub
```

15.
```
    Private Sub btnDisplay_Click(...) Handles btnDisplay.Click
      Dim query = From cty In cities
                  Where cty.state = "TX"
                  Order By cty.pop2010 Descending
                  Select cty.name, cty.pop2010
      For Each cty In query
        lstOutput.Items.Add(cty.name & "   " &
                        (100000 * cty.pop2010).ToString("N0"))
      Next
    End Sub
```

16.
```
    Private Sub btnDisplay_Click(...) Handles btnDisplay.Click
      Dim query = From cty In cities
                  Where cty.state = "TX"
                  Let growth = (cty.pop2010 - cty.pop2000) / cty.pop2000
                  Order By growth Descending
                  Select cty.name, cty.state, growth
      For Each cty In query
        lstOutput.Items.Add(cty.name & ",  " & cty.state)
      Next
      lstOutput.Items.Add("Greatest growth: " &
                        (query.First.growth).ToString("P"))
    End Sub
```

17.
```
    Private Sub btnDisplay_Click(...) Handles btnDisplay.Click
      Dim query = From cty In cities
                  Let increase = cty.pop2010 - cty.pop2000
                  Where cty.name = "Phoenix"
                  Select increase
      txtOutput.Text = (100000 * query.First).ToString("N0")
    End Sub
```

18.
```
    Private Sub btnDisplay_Click(...) Handles btnDisplay.Click
      Dim query = From cty In cities
                  Order By cty.pop2010 Descending
                  Select cty.pop2010
      Dim pops() As Double = query.ToArray
      ReDim Preserve pops(9)
      txtOutput.Text = (100000 * pops.Sum).ToString("N0")
    End Sub
```

In Exercises 19 through 22 use the file USStates.txt that consists of 50 records and four fields. Each field gives a piece of information about a state—*name, abbreviation, land area* (in square miles), *population in the year 2015*. The records are ordered by the states' date of entry into the union. The first four lines of the file are

```
Delaware,DE,1954,941875
Pennsylvania,PA,44817,12856989
New Jersey,NJ,7417,8969545
Georgia,GA,57906,10206445
Connecticut,CT,4845,3620979
```

19. **U.S. States** Write a program that accepts a state's abbreviation as input and displays the state's name and its area. See Fig. 7.41.

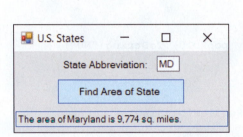

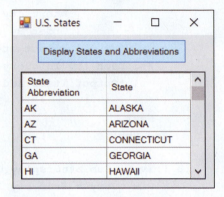

FIGURE 7.41 Possible outcome of Exercise 19.

FIGURE 7.42 Outcome of Exercise 20.

20. **U.S. States** Write a program that displays the names of the states whose abbreviations are different than the first two letters of their name. Both the abbreviations and the states should be displayed. See Fig. 7.42.

21. **U.S. States** Write a program that displays the names of the states sorted by their population densities in descending order. Next to each name should be the state's population density. See Fig. 7.43.

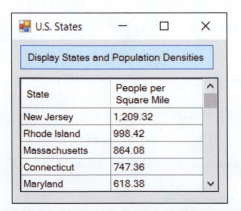

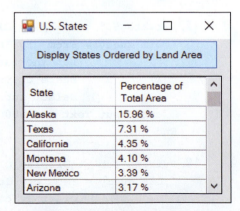

FIGURE 7.43 Outcome of Exercise 21.

FIGURE 7.44 Outcome of Exercise 22.

22. **U.S. States** Write a program that displays the names of the states ordered by land area. Next to each name should be the percentage of the total U.S. land area in that state. See Fig. 7.44.

In Exercises 23 through 26 use the file Baseball.txt that contains data about the performance of major league baseball players during the 2015 regular season. (Only the top 141 hitters with at least 440 at bats are included in the file.) Each record of the file contains four fields—*name, team, atBats,* and *hits*. Some lines of the file are as follows:

```
Josh Donaldson,Blue Jays,620,184
Buster Posey,Giants,557,177
Brian McCann,Yankees,465,108
```

23. **Baseball** Write a program using the file Baseball.txt that requests a team as input from a list and displays the players from that team. The players should be sorted in decreasing order by the number of hits they had during the season. The output should display each player's full name and number of hits. See Fig. 7.45.

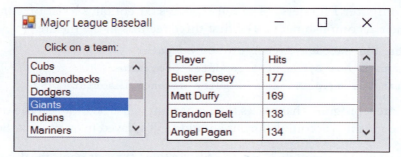

FIGURE 7.45 Possible outcome of Exercise 23.

24. **Baseball** Write a program using the file Baseball.txt that displays the names of the teams sorted alphabetically. See Fig. 7.46.

FIGURE 7.46 Outcome of Exercise 24.

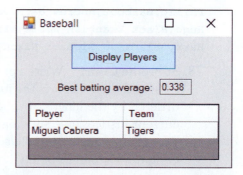

FIGURE 7.47 Outcome of Exercise 25.

25. **Baseball** Write a program that displays the highest batting average and the player (or players) having the highest batting average. The output also should display each player's team. See Fig. 7.47.

26. **Baseball** Write a program that requests a team as input and displays the players from that team. The players should be sorted alphabetically by their last names. Players having the same last name should be ordered secondarily by their first names. (**Note:** The Split method can be used to extract first and last names from a person's full name. For instance, the value of `"Babe Ruth".Split(" "c).Last` is `Ruth`.) The output should display each player's full name and batting average. See Fig. 7.48 on the next page.

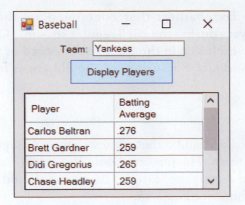

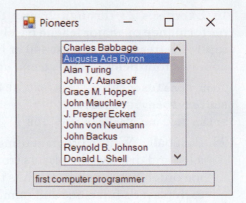

FIGURE 7.48 Possible outcome of Exercise 26.   **FIGURE 7.49** Possible outcome of Exercise 27.

27. **Computer Pioneers**   The file Pioneers.txt contains a list of computer pioneers and their accomplishments. The first three records in the file are

```
Charles Babbage,father of the computer
Augusta Ada Byron,first computer programmer
Alan Turing,prominent computer science theorist
```

Write a program that places the names into a list box. When the user clicks on a name, the person's accomplishment should be displayed in a text box. See Fig. 7.49.

In Exercises 28 through 31 use the file Justices.txt that contains data about the Supreme Court justices, past and present as of January 2016. Each record of the file contains six fields—*first name, last name, appointing president, the state from which they were appointed, year appointed,* and *the year they left the court.* (For current justices, the last field is set to 0.) The first five lines of the file are as follows:

```
Samuel,Alito,George W. Bush,NJ,2006,0
Henry,Baldwin,Andrew Jackson,PA,1830,1844
Philip,Barbour,Andrew Jackson,VA,1836,1841
Hugo,Black,Franklin Roosevelt,AL,1937,1971
Harry,Blackman,Richard Nixon,MN,1970,1994
```

28. **Supreme Court**   Write a program that requests the name of a president as input from a list and then displays the justices appointed by that president. The justices should be ordered by the length of time they served on the court in descending order. (**Note:** For current justices, use **Now.Year - yrAppointed** as their time of service. Otherwise, use **yrLeft - yrAppointed**.) Use the file USPres.txt to fill the presidents list box. That file contains the names of the presidents in the order they served. See Fig. 7.50.

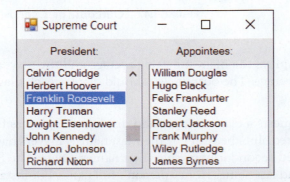

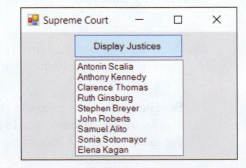

FIGURE 7.50 Possible outcome of Exercise 28.   **FIGURE 7.51** Outcome of Exercise 29.

29. **Supreme Court**   Write a program that displays the current justices ordered by the year they joined the Supreme Court. See Fig. 7.51.

30. Supreme Court Write a program that displays the composition of the Supreme Court at the beginning of 1980. The justices should be ordered by the year they were appointed, and the names of the appointing presidents should be displayed. See Fig. 7.52.

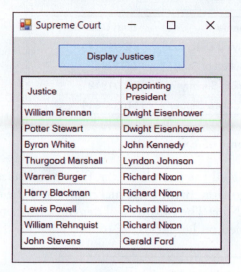

FIGURE 7.52 Outcome of Exercise 30.

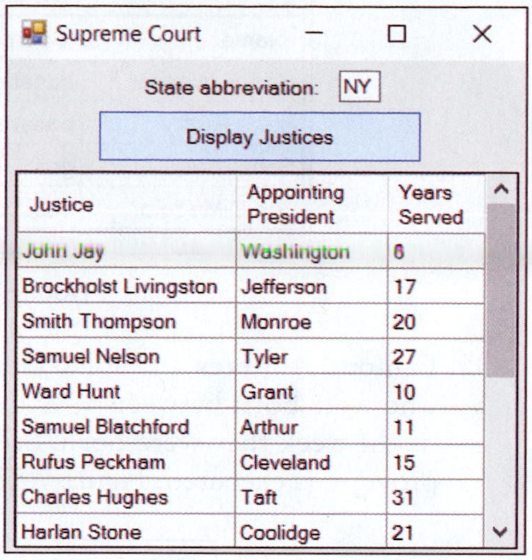

FIGURE 7.53 Possible outcome of Exercise 31.

31. Supreme Court Write a program that requests a state abbreviation as input and displays the justices appointed from that state. The justices should be ordered by their year appointed. The output should also display the last name of the appointing president and the length of time served. (*Note:* For current justices, use **Now.Year - yrAppointed** as their time of service. Otherwise, use **yrLeft - yrAppointed**.) Also, the program should inform the user if no justices have been appointed from the requested state. See Fig. 7.53.

The file SportsStars.txt contains the names of some famous athletes, their sports, nicknames, and birthdays. Use this file in Exercises 32 through 37. The first four lines of the file are

```
Alex Rodriguez,baseball,A-Rod,7/27/1975
Babe Ruth,baseball,The Sultan of Swat,2/6/1895
Clyde Dexter,basketball,The Glide,6/22/1962
Fred Couples,golf,Boom Boom,10/3/1959
```

32. Famous Athletes Display a list of the people in the file SportsStars.txt born on a Sunday. (*Hint:* Use **ToString("D")**.) See Fig. 7.54.

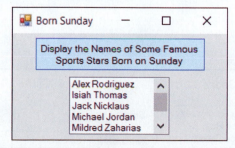

FIGURE 7.54 Outcome of Exercise 32.

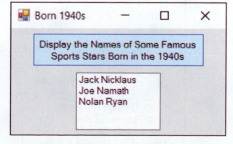

FIGURE 7.55 Outcome of Exercise 33.

33. Famous Athletes Display a list of the people in the file SportsStars.txt born during the 1940s. See Fig. 7.55.

34. Famous Athletes Display a table showing all the people in the file SportsStars.txt along with their sports, nicknames and birth dates. The people should be ordered by their birth dates in ascending order. See Fig. 7.56 on the next page.

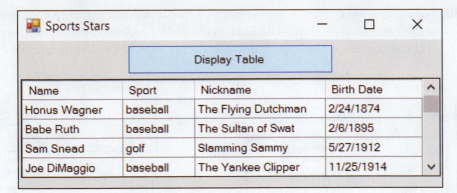

FIGURE 7.56   Outcome of Exercise 34.

35. Famous Athletes   Display a table showing all the people in the file SportsStars.txt who were born between 50 and 60 years ago along with their nicknames and the days of the week they were born. See Fig. 7.57. *Note:* The output will depend on when the program is executed. Figure 7.57 was obtained on January 1, 2016.

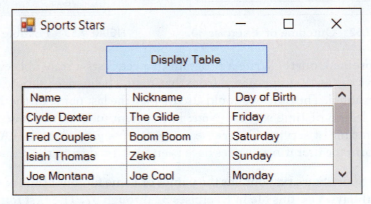

FIGURE 7.57   Outcome of Exercise 35.

36. Famous Athletes   See Fig. 7.58. Write a program that allows the user to select one of four sports and then displays the athletes who play that sport. Include the nickname of each of the athletes.

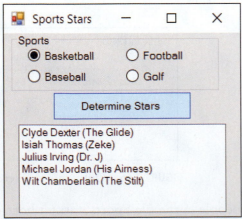

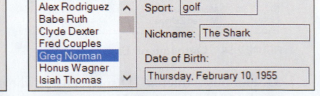

FIGURE 7.58   Possible outcome of Exercise 36.   **FIGURE 7.59**   Possible Outcome of Exercise 37.

37. Famous Athletes   See Fig. 7.59. Write a program that displays the names of all the athletes in SportsStars.txt and provides information on the athlete who is clicked on.

38. Presidential Colleges This exercise uses the file PresColl.txt that contains the names and undergraduate colleges attended by each of the first 44 U.S. presidents. The presidents are listed in the order they served. The first three lines of the file are

```
George Washington,No college
John Adams,Harvard
Thomas Jefferson,William and Mary
```

Write a program that fills a list box with the colleges (in alphabetical order) attended by U.S. presidents and then displays the presidents who attended that college when the user clicks on a college in the list box. See Fig. 7.60.

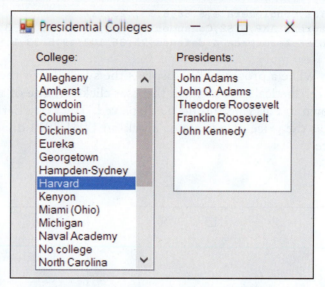

FIGURE 7.60 Possible outcome of Exercise 38.

In Exercises 39 and 40, use the file Oscars.txt that contains the names and genres of each film that won an Oscar for best picture of 1928 through 2014. The films are listed in the order they received the award. The first three lines of the file are

```
Wings,silent
The Broadway Melody,musical
All Quiet on the Western Front,war
```

39. Academy Awards Write a program that fills a list box with the different film genres and then displays the Oscar-winning films of a genre when the user clicks on the genre in the list box. See Fig. 7.61.

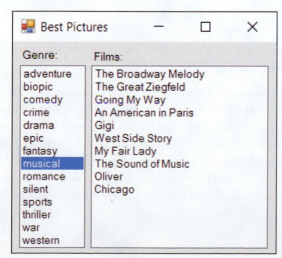

FIGURE 7.61 Possible outcome of Exercise 39.   **FIGURE 7.62** Possible outcome of Exercise 40.

40. Academy Awards Write a program that requests a year from 1928 through 2014 and then displays the name and genre of that year's best picture winner. See Fig. 7.62 on the previous page.

In Exercises 41 through 44, use the file DOW2014.txt that contains the name, symbol, exchange, industry, price at the end of trading on 12/31/2013, price at the end of trading on 12/31/2014, 2014 earnings per share, and the dividend paid in 2014 for each of the 30 stocks in the Dow Jones Industrial Average. (*Note:* The data for Visa has been revised to reflect a 4 for 1 stock split.) The first three lines of the file are

```
Alcoa,AA,NYSE,Conglomerate,8.68,8.33,.23,.12
American Express,AXP,NYSE,Consumer finance,57.48,78.04,3.96,.92
Boeing,BA,NYSE,Aerospace & defense,75.36,102.49,5.33,1.94
```

41. DOW Write a program that displays the symbols for the 30 DOW stocks in a list box in alphabetical order. When the user clicks on one of the symbols, the information shown in Fig. 7.63 should be displayed. The Price/Earnings ratio should be calculated as the price of a share of stock on 12/31/2014 divided by the 2014 earnings per share.

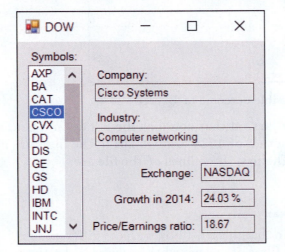

FIGURE 7.63 Possible outcome of Exercise 41.

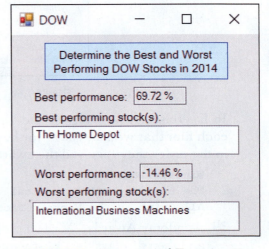

FIGURE 7.64 Outcome of Exercise 42.

42. DOW Write a program that determines the best and worst performing stock(s) in 2014 with regards to percentage growth. See Fig. 7.64.

43. Dogs of the DOW A simple investment strategy known as "Dogs of the DOW" has performed well in many years. An investor employing this strategy maintains a portfolio of 10 DOW stocks. At the beginning of each year, the portfolio is readjusted so that it contains equal amounts of money invested in the 10 stocks having the highest dividend yields. The dividend yield is the ratio of the dividend paid in a given year (that is, 2014) to the share price at the end of the year. Write a program to determine the 10 stocks that should be in the portfolio at the beginning of 2015. See Fig. 7.65.

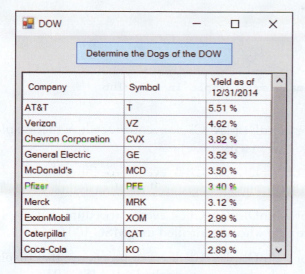

FIGURE 7.65 Outcome of Exercise 43.

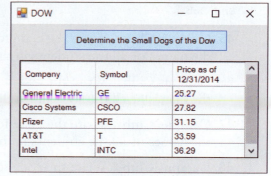

FIGURE 7.66 Outcome of Exercise 44.

44. **Small Dogs of the DOW** An investment strategy known as "Small Dogs of the DOW" has also performed well in many years. An investor employing this strategy maintains a portfolio of the 5 lowest-priced DOW stocks. The portfolio is readjusted at the beginning of each year. Write a program to determine the 5 stocks that should be in the portfolio at the beginning of 2015. See Fig. 7.66.

A campus club has 10 members. The following program stores information about the students into an array of structures. Each structure contains the student's name and a list of the courses the student is currently taking. Exercises 45 through 48 request that an additional event procedure be written for this program.

```
Structure Student
  Dim name As String
  Dim courses() As String
End Structure


Dim club(9) As Student    'holds all students in the club


Private Sub frmStudents_Load(...) Handles MyBase.Load
  Dim pupil As Student
  pupil.name = "Juan Santana"
  ReDim pupil.courses(2)
  pupil.courses(0) = "CMSC 100"
  pupil.courses(1) = "PHIL 200"
  pupil.courses(2) = "ENGL 120"
  club(0) = pupil
  pupil.name = "Mary Carlson"
  ReDim pupil.courses(3)
  pupil.courses(0) = "BIOL 110"
  pupil.courses(1) = "PHIL 200"
  pupil.courses(2) = "CMSC 100"
  pupil.courses(3) = "MATH 220"
  club(1) = pupil
  pupil.name = "George Hu"
```

```
      ReDim pupil.courses(2)
      pupil.courses(0) = "MATH 220"
      pupil.courses(1) = "PSYC 100"
      pupil.courses(2) = "ENGL 200"
      club(2) = pupil
      'Enter names and courses for remaining 7 people in the club
  End Sub
```

45. Campus Club   Write the code for a btnDisplay_Click event procedure that displays the names of all the students in the club in a list box.

46. Campus Club   Write the code for a btnDisplay_Click event procedure that displays the names of all the students in the club who are registered for three courses.

47. Campus Club   Write the code for a btnDisplay_Click event procedure that displays the names of all the students in the club who are enrolled in CMSC 100.

48. Campus Club   Write the code for a btnDisplay_Click event procedure that displays the names of all the students in the club who are *not* enrolled in CMSC 100.

Solutions to Practice Problems 7.3

1. The event procedure contains two errors. First, the definition of a structure cannot be inside a procedure; it must be typed into the Declarations section of the class. Second, the statements **Team.school = "Rice"** and **Team.mascot = "Owls"** are not valid. "Team" should be replaced by a variable of type Team that has previously been declared.

2.
```
Structure Team
    Dim school As String
    Dim mascot As String
End Structure

Private Sub btnDisplay_Click(...) Handles btnDisplay.Click
    Dim squad As Team
    squad.school = "Rice"
    squad.mascot = "Owls"
    txtOutput.Text = squad.school & " " & squad.mascot
End Sub
```

7.4   Two-Dimensional Arrays

Each array discussed so far held a list of items. Such an array is called a **one-dimensional** or **single-subscripted** array. An array also can hold the contents of a table with several rows and columns. Such an array is called a **two-dimensional, double-subscripted,** or **rectangular** array. Two tables follow. Table 7.3 gives the road mileage between certain cities. The numerical data consists of four rows and four columns. Table 7.4 shows the leading universities in three graduate-school programs. The array of colleges has three rows and five columns.

TABLE 7.3   Road mileage between selected U.S. cities.

	Chicago	Los Angeles	New York	Philadelphia
Chicago	0	2054	802	738
Los Angeles	2054	0	2786	2706
New York	802	2786	0	100
Philadelphia	738	2706	100	0

TABLE 7.4	Rankings of U.S. university graduate-school programs.				
	1	2	3	4	5
Education	Johns Hopkins	Harvard	Stanford	Vanderbilt	U of Wisconsin
Engineering	MIT	Stanford	UC Berk	C. Mellon	Cal Tech
Law	Yale	Harvard	Stanford	Columbia	U of Chicago

Source: Data from U.S. News and World Report, 2012, http://www.usnews.com/rankings.

Two-dimensional array variables store the contents of tables. They have the same types of names as other array variables. The only difference is that they have two subscripts, each with its own upper bound. The first upper bound is determined by the number of rows in the table, and the second upper bound is determined by the number of columns.

■ Declaring a Two-Dimensional Array Variable

The statement

```
Dim arrayName(m, n) As DataType
```

declares an array of type *DataType* corresponding to a table with rows labeled from 0 to *m* and columns labeled from 0 to *n*. The entry in the *j*th row, *k*th column is *arrayName(j, k)*. For instance, the data in Table 7.3 can be stored in an array named *rm*. The statement

```
Dim rm(3, 3) As Double
```

will declare the array. Each element of the array has the form *rm*(row, column). The values of the elements of the array are

rm(0, 0) = 0	rm(0, 1) = 2054	rm(0, 2) = 802	rm(0, 3) = 738
rm(1, 0) = 2054	rm(1, 1) = 0	rm(1, 2) = 2786	rm(1, 3) = 2706
rm(2, 0) = 802	rm(2, 1) = 2786	rm(2, 2) = 0	rm(2, 3) = 100
rm(3, 0) = 738	rm(3, 1) = 2706	rm(3, 2) = 100	rm(3, 3) = 0

The data in Table 7.4 can be stored in a two-dimensional string array named *univ*. The appropriate array is declared with the statement

```
Dim univ(2, 4) As String
```

Some of the entries of the array are

$$univ(0, 0) = \text{“Johns Hopkins”}$$
$$univ(1, 2) = \text{“UC Berk”}$$
$$univ(2, 3) = \text{“Columbia”}$$

■ Implicit Array Sizing and Initialization

A two-dimensional array can be declared and initialized at the same time with a statement of the form

```
Dim arrayName(,) As DataType = {{ROW0}, {ROW1}, ..., {ROWm}}
```

where ROW0 consists of the entries in the top row of the corresponding table delimited by commas, ROW1 consists of the entries in the next row of the corresponding table delimited by commas, and so on.

✔ **Example 1**   **Distances** The following program stores and accesses the data from Table 7.3:

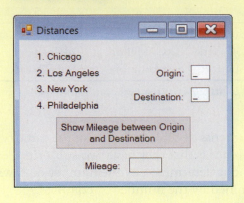

OBJECT	PROPERTY	SETTING
frmDistances	Text	Distances
lblCh	Text	1. Chicago
lblLA	Text	2. Los Angeles
lblNY	Text	3. New York
lblPh	Text	4. Philadelphia
lblOrig	Text	Origin:
mtbOrig	Mask	0
lblDest	Text	Destination:
mtbDest	Mask	0
btnShow	Text	Show Mileage between Origin and Destination
lblMiles	Text	Mileage:
txtMiles	ReadOnly	True

```
Dim rm(,) As Double = {{0, 2054, 802, 738},
                       {2054, 0, 2786, 2706},
                       {802, 2786, 0, 100},
                       {738, 2706, 100, 0}}

Private Sub btnShow_Click(...) Handles btnShow.Click
  'Determine road mileage between cities
  Dim row, col As Integer
  row = CInt(mtbOrig.Text)
  col = CInt(mtbDest.Text)
  If (row >= 1 And row <= 4) And (col >= 1 And col <= 4) Then
    txtMiles.Text = CStr(rm(row - 1, col - 1))
  Else
    MessageBox.Show("Origin and Destination must be numbers from 1 to 4",
              "Error")
  End If
End Sub
```

[Run, type 3 into the Origin box, type 1 into the Destination box, and click on the button.]

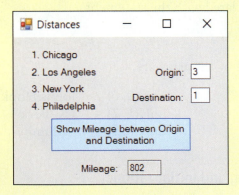

■ **The ReDim Statement**

A previously declared array can be resized with

```
ReDim arrayName(r, c)
```

which loses the current contents, or with

```
ReDim Preserve arrayName(r, c)
```

which keeps the current values. However, when the keyword Preserve is used, only the second dimension can be resized. The upper bound of the first dimension of the array is given by **arrayName.GetUpperBound(0)**, and the upper bound of the second dimension is given by **arrayName.GetUpperBound(1)**.

So far, two-dimensional arrays have been used only to store data for convenient lookup. In the next example, an array is used to make a valuable computation.

Example 2   **Nutritional Analysis** The Center for Science in the Public Interest publishes *The Nutrition Scorebook*, a highly respected rating of foods. The top two foods in each of five categories are shown in Table 7.5 along with some information on their composition. The following program computes the nutritional content of a meal. The table is read into three arrays—a one-dimensional array *foods* for the names of the ten foods, a one-dimensional array *nutrients* for the names of the five nutrients, and a two-dimensional array *nutTable* to hold the numbers from the table. [The value of *nutTable*(k, i) is the amount of the *i*th nutrient in the *k*th food.] The arrays *foods* and *nutrients* are filled from the files Foods.txt and Nutrients.txt, whose first three lines are as follows:

Foods.txt	Nutrients.txt
cups of spinach	calories
medium sweet potatoes	protein (grams)
8 oz servings of yogurt	fat (grams)

TABLE 7.5   **Composition of 10 top-rated foods.**

	Calories	Protein (grams)	Fat (grams)	Vit A (IU)	Calcium (mg)
Spinach (1 cup)	23	3	0.3	8100	93
Sweet potato (1 med.)	160	2	1	9230	46
Yogurt (8 oz)	230	10	3	120	343
Skim milk (1 cup)	85	8	0	500	302
Whole wheat bread (1 slice)	65	3	1	0	24
Brown rice (1 cup)	178	3.8	0.9	0	18
Watermelon (1 wedge)	110	2	1	2510	30
Papaya (1 lg.)	156	2.4	0.4	7000	80
Tuna in water (1 lb)	575	126.8	3.6	0	73
Lobster (1 med.)	405	28.8	26.6	984	190

The array *nutTable* is filled with elements hard-coded into the program.

The program uses an array of structures named *nutFacts* of type NutFact and having five elements (one for each nutrient). The structure NutFact has two members: the first member holding the name of a nutrient and the second holding the total amount of that nutrient in the meal.

The program is written in the input-processing-output format. The input Sub procedure GetAmounts loops through 10 input dialog boxes that request the quantities of each food and places them into a one-dimensional array named *servings*. The processing Function procedure ProcessData uses the array *servings*, along with the arrays *nutrients* and *nutTable*, to fill the array of structures *nutFacts*. Finally, the output Sub procedure ShowData uses the array *nutFacts* to display the nutritional content of the meal into a DataGridView control.

```vb
Structure NutFact
  Dim nutrient As String      'name of one of the five nutrients
  Dim amount As Double        'amount of the nutrient in the meal
End Structure

Private Sub btnDetermine_Click(...) Handles btnDetermine.Click
  Dim servings(9) As Double
  Dim nutFacts(4) As NutFact            'This array of structures has an
  '                                      element for each nutrient.
  GetAmounts(servings)                  'input
  nutFacts = ProcessData(servings)      'processing
  ShowData(nutFacts)                    'output
End Sub

Sub GetAmounts(ByRef servings() As Double)
  Dim foods() As String = IO.File.ReadAllLines("Foods.txt")
  'Get the number of servings of each food.
  For i As Integer = 0 To 9
    servings(i) = CDbl(InputBox("How many servings of " & foods(i)))
  Next
End Sub

Function ProcessData(servings() As Double) As NutFact()
  Dim nutrients() As String = IO.File.ReadAllLines("Nutrients.txt")
  Dim nutTable(,) As Double = {{23, 3, 0.3, 8100, 93},
                               {160, 2, 1, 9230, 46},
                               {230, 10, 3, 120, 343},
                               {85, 8, 0, 500, 302},
                               {65, 3, 1, 0, 24},
                               {178, 3.8, 0.9, 0, 18},
                               {110, 2, 1, 2510, 30},
                               {156, 2.4, 0.4, 7000, 80},
                               {575, 126.8, 3.6, 0, 73},
                               {405, 28.8, 26.6, 984, 190}}
  Dim nutritionFacts(4) As NutFact    'This array of structures has an
  '                                    element for each nutrient.
  For i As Integer = 0 To 4
    nutritionFacts(i).nutrient = nutrients(i)   'Place the name of a nutrient
    '                                            into an array element.
    'The next five lines calculate the total amount of the nutrient
    'in the meal and place it into the array element.
    Dim sum As Double = 0
    For k As Integer = 0 To 9
      sum += servings(k) * nutTable(k, i)
    Next
    nutritionFacts(i).amount = sum    'Place the amount of the nutrient into
    '                                  the array element.
  Next
  Return nutritionFacts
End Function
```

```
Sub ShowData(nutFacts() As NutFact)
  'Create a query and use it to place the data from the array
  'of structures into a DataGridView control.
  Dim query = From element In nutFacts
              Let Nutrient = element.nutrient
              Let Amount = (element.amount).ToString("N")
              Select Nutrient, Amount
  dgvOutput.DataSource = query.ToList
  dgvOutput.CurrentCell = Nothing
End Sub
```

[Run, click on the button, and enter the following menu: .5 cup of spinach, 1 medium sweet potato, 2 slices of whole wheat bread, .25 of a large papaya, and 1 medium lobster.]

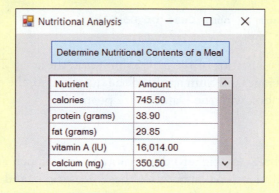

Filling a Two-Dimensional Array with a Text File

Text files used to fill two-dimensional arrays are similar to those used to fill arrays of structures. Each line of the text file corresponds to a row of the table, with the entries for each row separated by commas. For instance, the array *mileage* discussed earlier can be filled with the text file Distances.txt consisting of the following four lines:

```
0,2054,802,738
2054,0,2786,2706
802,2786,0,100
738,2706,100,0
```

The following code creates and fills the array *mileage:*

```
Dim mileage(3, 3) As Double
Dim rowOfNums() As String = IO.File.ReadAllLines("Distances.txt")
Dim line As String
Dim data() As String
For i As Integer = 0 To mileage.GetUpperBound(0)
  line = rowOfNums(i)
  data = line.Split(","c)
  For j As Integer = 0 To mileage.GetUpperBound(1)
    mileage(i, j) = CDbl(data(j))
  Next
Next
```

Note: These eleven lines of code, with slight modifications, are needed in many of the exercises. You can store this block of code (or any frequently used fragment of code) for later use by highlighting it and dragging it from the Code Editor into the Toolbox. To reuse the code, just drag it back from the Toolbox to the Code Editor. A copy of the code will remain in the Toolbox for further use. Alternately, you can click on the location in the Code Editor where you want the code to be inserted, and then double-click on the code in the Toolbox. We recommend that you place these lines of code in a program, highlight them, and drag them into the Toolbox. Then you can drag them out whenever you need them.

■ Using LINQ with Two-Dimensional Arrays

Although LINQ is not as useful with two-dimensional as it is with one-dimensional arrays, it is sometimes helpful. However, LINQ needs a Cast method to convert the two-dimensional array to a source data consisting of a one-dimensional array. Suppose *nums* is a two-dimensional array of type Double and having *m* rows and *n* columns. Then the code

```
Dim query = From num In nums.Cast(Of Double)()
            Select num
```

produces a sequence consisting of the $m \cdot n$ numbers in the array. The methods Count, Max, Min, First, Last, Average, and Sum apply to the query. Also, the sequence of numbers can be displayed in a list box with the DataSource property.

■ Comments

1. We can define three- (or higher-) dimensional arrays much as we do two-dimensional arrays. A three-dimensional array uses three subscripts, and the assignment of values requires a triple-nested loop. As an example, a meteorologist might use a three-dimensional array to record temperatures for various dates, times, and elevations. The array might be declared with the statement

   ```
   Dim temps(30, 23, 14) As Double
   ```

2. A ReDim statement cannot change the number of dimensions of an array. For instance, it cannot change a one-dimensional into a two-dimensional array.

Practice Problems 7.4

1. Consider the road-mileage program in Example 1. How can it be modified so the actual names of the cities can be supplied by the user?

2. In what types of problems are two-dimensional arrays superior to arrays of structures?

EXERCISES 7.4

In Exercises 1 through 16, assume the array *nums* is of type Double and has been filled with the contents of Table 7.6.

TABLE 7.6

7	3	1	0
2	5	9	8
0	6	4	10

In Exercises 1 through 12, determine or describe the output of the code.

1. ```
lstOutput.Items.Add(nums(0, 2))
```

2. ```
lstOutput.Items.Add(nums(2, 1))
```

3. ```
lstOutput.Items.Add(nums.GetUpperBound(1))
```

4. ```
lstOutput.Items.Add(nums.GetUpperBound(0))
```

5. ```
Dim total As Double = 0
For Each num In nums
  total += num
Next
lstOutput.Items.Add(total)
```

6. ```
Dim total As Double = 0
For c As Integer = 0 To nums.GetUpperBound(1)
  total += nums(2, c)
Next
lstOutput.Items.Add(total)
```

7. ```
Dim total As Double = 0
For r As Integer = 0 To nums.GetUpperBound(0)
  total += nums(r, 2)
Next
lstOutput.Items.Add(total)
```

8. ```
Dim total As Double = 0
For r As Integer = 0 To nums.GetUpperBound(0)
  For c As Integer = 0 To nums.GetUpperBound(1)
    total += nums(r, c)
  Next
Next
lstOutput.Items.Add(total)
```

9. ```
Dim query = From num In nums.Cast(Of Double)()
            Where (num > 8)
            Select num
lstOutput.Items.Add(query.Count)
```

10. ```
Dim query = From num In nums.Cast(Of Double)()
            Select num
lstOutput.Items.Add(query.Max)
```

11. ```
Dim query = From num In nums.Cast(Of Double)()
            Select num
lstOutput.Items.Add(query.Sum)
```

12. ```
Dim query = From num In nums.Cast(Of Double)()
            Where (num Mod 2 = 0)
            Order By num
            Select num / 2
            Distinct
For Each n As Double In query
  lstOutput.Items.Add(n)
Next
```

13. Write code that creates a new array whose entries are twice the entries of *nums*.

14. Write code that uses a For Each loop to find the average of the numbers in *nums*.

15. Write code that finds the sum of the even numbers in *nums* two ways: first with a For Each loop and then with a LINQ query.

16. Write code that finds the average of the odd numbers in *nums* two ways: first with a For Each loop and then with LINQ.

In Exercises 17 and 18, determine the output of the code.

17.
```
Dim nums(1, 2) As Double
Dim rowOfNums() As String = IO.File.ReadAllLines("Digits.txt")
Dim line As String
Dim data() As String
For i As Integer = 0 To nums.GetUpperBound(0)
  line = rowOfNums(i)
  data = line.Split(","c)
  For j As Integer = 0 To nums.GetUpperBound(1)
    nums(i, j) = CDbl(data(j))
  Next
Next
lstOutput.Items.Add(nums(0, 1) + nums(1, 0))
```

(Assume the two lines of the file Digits.txt are **9,7,6** and **5,4,3**.)

18.
```
Dim names(2, 1) As String
Dim rowOfNames() As String = IO.File.ReadAllLines("People.txt")
Dim line As String
Dim data() As String
For i As Integer = 0 To names.GetUpperBound(0)
  line = rowOfNames(i)
  data = line.Split(","c)
  For j As Integer = 0 To names.GetUpperBound(1)
    names(i, j) = data(j)
  Next
Next
lstOutput.Items.Add(names(2, 1) & " " & names(1, 1))
```

(Assume the three lines of the file People.txt are **Felix,Ungar**; **Oscar,Madison**; and **Henry,James**.)

In Exercises 19 through 29, write a program to perform the stated task.

19. Inventory   A company has two stores (1 and 2), and each store sells three items (1, 2, and 3). The following tables give the inventory at the beginning of the day and the amount of each item sold during that day.

		Beginning Inventory				Sales for Day		
		ITEM				**ITEM**		
		1	2	3		1	2	3
Store	1	25	64	23	Store 1	7	45	11
	2	30	82	19	2	4	24	8

(a) Record the values of each table in an array.

(b) Adjust the values in the first array to hold the inventories at the end of the day and display these new inventories.

(c) Calculate and display the number of items in each store at the end of the day. See Fig. 7.67.

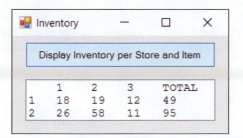

FIGURE 7.67   Outcome of Exercise 19.

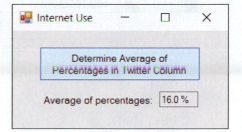

FIGURE 7.68   Outcome of Exercise 20.

20. Computer Uses   Table 7.7 gives the results of a survey on the use of social networking sites among adult Internet users. Each entry shows the percentage of respondents from the age category that use the computer for the indicated purpose.

(a) Place the data from the table in an array. (Use Internet.txt.)

(b) Determine the average of the percentages in the Twitter column. See Fig. 7.68.

TABLE 7.7	Use of social networking sites among adult internet users: 2013.				
Age	Facebook	Twitter	Instagram	Pinterest	LinkedIn
18–29	84	31	37	27	15
30–49	79	19	18	24	27
50–64	60	9	6	14	24
65 and older	45	5	1	9	13

Source: Data from "Table 1161 - Social Media: Use of Social Networking Sites Among Adult Internet Users: 2013" in ProQuest Statistical Abstract of the United States: 2015.

21. University Rankings   Consider Table 7.4 on page 363, the rankings of three graduate-school programs. Write a program that places the data into an array, allows the name of a university to be input, and displays the categories in which it appears. Of course, a university might appear more than once or not at all. (Use Ranking.txt.) See Fig. 7.69.

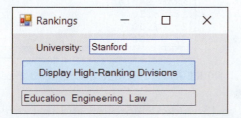

FIGURE 7.69   Possible outcome of Exercise 21.

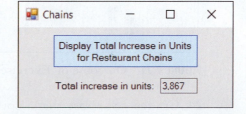

FIGURE 7.70   Outcome of Exercise 22.

22. Restaurants Table 7.8 gives the 2012 and 2014 number of units in the U.S. for the top five restaurant chains.

(a) Place the data into a two-dimensional array. (Use Restaurants.txt.)

(b) Display the number that gives the total increase in the number of units for these five restaurant chains. See Fig. 7.70 on the previous page.

TABLE 7.8 **Top restaurant chains in U.S.**

	Number of Units in 2012	Number of Units in 2014
1. Subway	25,549	27,205
2. McDonalds	14,157	14,350
3. Starbucks	11,128	12,107
4. Dunkin Donuts	7,306	8,082
5. Pizza Hut	7,600	7,863

Source: Data from the "Top 10 Restaurant Chains" in QSR Magazine, October 2012, http://www.qsrmagazine.com/reports/top-50-sorted-rank.

23. Golf Scores The scores for the top four golfers at the 2015 PGA Championship are shown in Table 7.9.

(a) Place the data into an array. (Use Golf.txt.)

(b) Display the total score for each player and the average score for each round. See Fig. 7.71.

TABLE 7.9 **2015 PGA Championship.**

Round	1	2	3	4
Jason Day	68	67	66	67
Jordan Spieth	71	67	65	68
Branden Grace	71	69	64	69
Justin Rose	69	67	68	70

FIGURE 7.71 Outcome of Exercise 23.

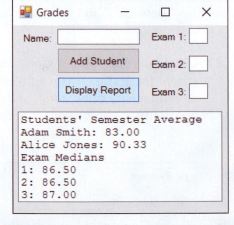

FIGURE 7.72 Possible outcome of Exercise 24.

24. Grades Suppose that a course has up to 15 students enrolled and that three exams are given during the semester. Write a program that accepts each student's name and grades as input, places the names in a one-dimensional array, and places the grades in a two-dimensional array. The program should then display each student's name and semester average. Also, the program should display the median for each exam. (For an odd number of grades, the median is the middle grade after the grades have been ordered. For an even number of grades, it is the average of the two middle grades.) See Fig. 7.72.

25. **Precipitation** Table 7.10 gives the monthly precipitation for a typical Nebraska city during a five-year period. Write a program that reads the table from a text file into an array and then displays the output shown in Fig. 7.73. (Use Months.txt and Rain.txt.)

TABLE 7.10 | **Monthly precipitation (in inches) for a typical Nebraska city.**

	Jan.	Feb.	Mar.	Apr.	May	June	July	Aug.	Sept.	Oct.	Nov.	Dec.
1986	0.88	1.11	2.01	3.64	6.44	5.58	4.23	4.34	4.00	2.05	1.48	0.77
1987	0.76	0.94	2.09	3.29	4.68	3.52	3.52	4.82	3.72	2.21	1.24	0.80
1988	0.67	0.80	1.75	2.70	4.01	3.88	3.72	3.78	3.55	1.88	1.21	0.61
1989	0.82	0.80	1.99	3.05	4.19	4.44	3.98	4.57	3.43	2.32	1.61	0.75
1990	0.72	0.90	1.71	2.02	2.33	2.98	2.65	2.99	2.55	1.99	1.05	0.92

FIGURE 7.73 Outcome of Exercise 25.

26. **Daily Sales** A company has three stores (1, 2, and 3), and each store sells five items (1, 2, 3, 4, and 5). The following tables give the number of items sold by each store and category on a particular day, and the cost of each item.

(a) Place the data from the left-hand table in a two-dimensional array and the data from the right-hand table in a one-dimensional array.

(b) Calculate and display the total dollar amount of sales for each store and for the entire company. See Fig. 7.74 on the next page.

Number of Items Sold during Day

			ITEM					ITEM	COST PER ITEM
		1	2	3	4	5		1	$12.00
	1	25	64	23	45	14		2	$17.95
Store	2	12	82	19	34	63		3	$95.00
	3	54	22	17	43	35		4	$86.50
								5	$78.00

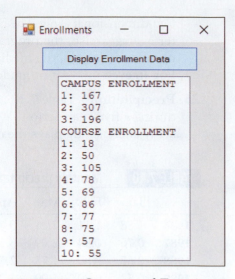

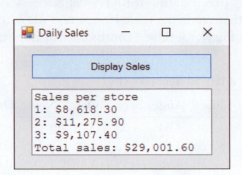

FIGURE 7.74 Outcome of Exercise 26.

FIGURE 7.75 Outcome of Exercise 27.

27. **Enrollments** A university offers 10 courses at each of three campuses. The number of students enrolled in each course is presented in Table 7.11. Display the total number of course enrollments on each campus and the total number of students taking each course. See Fig. 7.75. (Use Students.txt.)

TABLE 7.11   Number of students enrolled in courses.

		Course									
		1	2	3	4	5	6	7	8	9	10
	1	5	15	22	21	12	25	16	11	17	23
Campus	2	11	23	51	25	32	35	32	52	25	21
	3	2	12	32	32	25	26	29	12	15	11

28. **Federal Pay** Table 7.12 contains part of the pay schedule for federal employees in Washington, DC. Table 7.13 gives the number of employees in each classification in a certain division. Place the data from the two tables into arrays and compute the amount of money this division pays for salaries during the year. (Use GS-Pay.txt and GS-Employees.txt.)

TABLE 7.12   2015 pay schedule for federal white-collar workers.

Step	1	2	3	4
GS–1	18,161	18,768	19,372	19,973
GS–2	20,419	20,905	21,581	22,153
GS–3	22,279	23,022	23,765	24,508
GS–4	25,011	25,845	26,679	27,513
GS–5	27,982	28,915	29,848	30,781
GS–6	31,192	32,232	33,272	34,312
GS–7	34,662	35,817	36,972	38,127

TABLE 7.13   **Number of employees in each category.**

	1	2	3	4
GS–1	0	0	2	1
GS–2	2	3	0	1
GS–3	4	2	5	7
GS–4	12	13	8	3
GS–5	4	5	0	1
GS–6	6	2	4	3
GS–7	8	1	9	2

29. **Magic Squares**   A square array of numbers is called a *magic square* if the sums of each row, each column, and each diagonal are equal. Figure 7.76 shows an example of a magic square. Write a program that requests the number of rows of the array, call it n, and the n^2 entries of the array as input, and then determines if the array is a magic square. *Hint:* If at any time one of the sums is not equal to the sum of the numbers in the first row, then the search is complete.

$$\begin{pmatrix} 4 & 9 & 2 \\ 3 & 5 & 7 \\ 8 & 1 & 6 \end{pmatrix}$$

FIGURE 7.76   A magic square.

Solutions to Practice Problems 7.4

1. Replace the masked text boxes with ordinary text boxes to hold city names. The function FindCityNum can be used to determine the subscript associated with each city. This function and the modified event procedure btnShow_Click are as follows:

```
Function FindCityNum(city As String) As Integer
  Select Case city.ToUpper
    Case "CHICAGO"
      Return 1
    Case "LOS ANGELES"
      Return 2
    Case "NEW YORK"
      Return 3
    Case "PHILADELPHIA"
      Return 4
    Case Else
      Return 0
  End Select
End Function

Private Sub btnShow_Click(...) Handles btnShow.Click
  Dim orig, dest As String
  Dim row, col As Integer 'determine road mileage between cities
  orig = txtOrig.Text
  dest = txtDest.Text
  row = FindCityNum(orig)
  col = FindCityNum(dest)
  If (row <> 0) And (col <> 0) Then
    txtMiles.Text = CStr(rm(row - 1, col - 1))
  Else
    MessageBox.Show("Incorrect Origin and/or Destination", "Error")
  End If
End Sub
```

2. Both arrays of structures and two-dimensional arrays are used to hold related data. If some of the data are numeric and some are string, then structures must be used because all entries of a two-dimensional array must be of the same type. Arrays of structures should also be used if the data will be sorted. Two-dimensional arrays are best suited to tabular data.

7.5   A Case Study: Analyze a Loan

This case study develops a program to analyze a loan. Assume the loan is to be repaid in equal monthly payments and interest is compounded monthly. The program should request the amount (principal) of the loan, the annual rate of interest, and the number of years over which the loan is to be repaid. The five options to be provided by buttons are as follows:

1. Calculate the monthly payment. The formula is

$$[\text{monthly payment}] = \frac{p \cdot r}{1 - (1 + r)^{-n}}$$

where p is the principal of the loan, r is the monthly interest rate (annual rate divided by 12) given as a number between 0 (for 0 percent) and 1 (for 100 percent), and n is the number of months over which the loan is to be repaid. When a payment computed in this manner results in fractions of a cent, the value should be rounded up to the next nearest cent. This corrected payment can be achieved using the formula

[corrected payment] = `Math.Round(originalPayment + 0.005, 2)`

2. Display an amortization schedule—that is, a table showing for each month the amount of interest paid, the amount of principal repaid, and the balance on the loan at the end of the month. At any time, the balance of the loan is the amount of money that must be paid in order to retire the loan. The monthly payment consists of two parts—interest on the balance and repayment of part of the principal. Each month

$$[\text{interest payment}] = r * [\text{balance at beginning of month}]$$
$$[\text{amount of principal repaid}] = [\text{monthly payment}] - [\text{interest payment}]$$
$$[\text{new balance}] = [\text{balance at beginning of month}] -$$
$$[\text{amount of principal repaid}]$$

3. Calculate the interest paid during a calendar year. (This amount is deductible when itemizing deductions on a federal income tax return.) The user should specify the number of the payment made in January of that year. For instance, if the first payment was made in September 2016, then the payment made in January 2017 would be payment number 5.

4. Show the effect of changes in the interest rate. Display a table giving the monthly payment for each interest rate from 1% below to 1% above the specified annual rate in steps of one-eighth of 1%.

5. Quit.

■ The User Interface

Figure 7.77 shows a possible form design and Table 7.14 gives the initial settings for the form and its controls. Figures 7.78 , 7.79, 7.80, and 7.81 show possible outputs of the program for each task available through the buttons.

■ Designing the Analyze-a-Loan Program

Every routine uses data from the three text boxes. Therefore, we create a Sub procedure to read the contents of the text boxes and convert the contents into a usable form. Two of the routines display extensive tables in a DataGridView control. The simplest way to

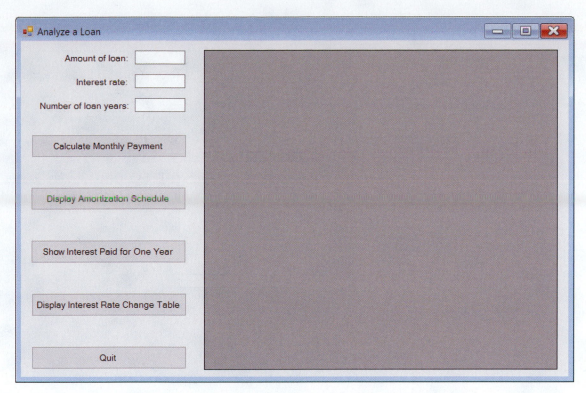

FIGURE 7.77   Template for the Analyze-a-Loan program.

TABLE 7.14	Objects and initial properties for the Analyze-a-Loan program.	
Object	**Property**	**Setting**
frmLoan	Text	Analyze a Loan
lblPrincipal	Text	Amount of loan:
txtPrincipal		
lblYearlyRate	Text	Interest rate:
txtYearlyRate		
lblNumYears	Text	Number of loan years:
txtNumYears		
btnPayment	Text	Calculate Monthly Payment
btnAmort	Text	Display Amortization Schedule
btnShow	Text	Show Interest Paid for One Year
btnRateTable	Text	Display Interest Rate Change Table
btnQuit	Text	Quit
dgvOutput	RowHeaderVisible	False

fill a table is to use an array of structures and a LINQ query. We will need two types of structures—one (named Month) to hold the amortization data for a month and the other (named EffectOfRate) to hold monthly payments for different interest rates. Since the array of Month structures is needed by two routines, we use a Function procedure to fill it so we won't have to duplicate the lengthy code. Since the value of the monthly payment is needed several times, we include a Function procedure called Payment.

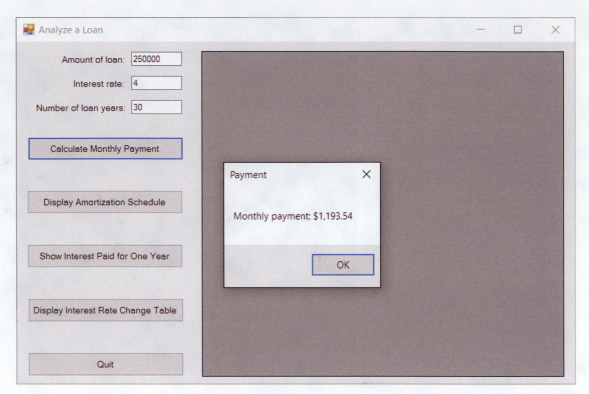

FIGURE 7.78 Monthly payment for a loan.

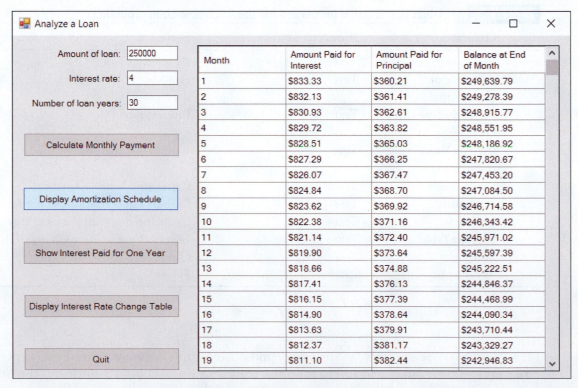

FIGURE 7.79 Amortization schedule for a loan.

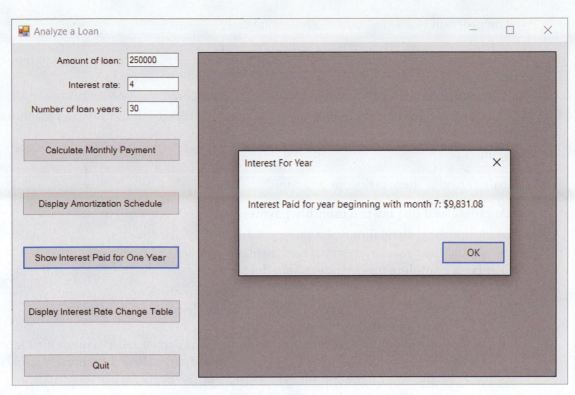

FIGURE 7.80   **Interest paid during one year.**

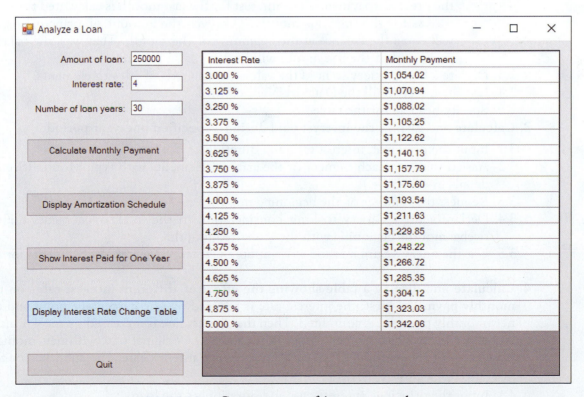

FIGURE 7.81   **Consequences of interest rate change.**

The program is divided into the following tasks:

1. Calculate and display the monthly payment.
2. Calculate and display a complete amortization schedule.
3. Calculate and display the interest paid during a specified one-year period.
4. Calculate and display a table showing the effect of different interest rates on the monthly payment.
5. Quit.

Let's consider these tasks one at a time.

1. **Calculate and display the monthly payment.**
   1.1 Input the principal, interest rate, and duration of the loan.
   1.2 Apply the function Payment and display its value.
2. **Display a complete amortization schedule.**
   2.1 Input the principal, interest rate, and duration of the loan.
   2.2 Assign values to each element of the array of elements with type Month.
      2.2.1 Determine the monthly payment.
      2.2.2 For each month, determine the apportionment of the payment into interest payment and amount of principal repaid, and then determine the balance at the end of the month. The balance at the beginning of each month is the same as the balance at the end of the previous month, except for the first month where the beginning balance is the principal. These values are calculated with the three formulas presented earlier, with the exception of the last month. Due to rounding, the last monthly payment will be slightly less than the previous payments. The interest for the last month is calculated the same way as for the previous months. However, the amount of principal repaid will equal the balance at the beginning of the month. That way, the balance at the end of the last month will be 0.
   2.3 Declare a LINQ query to hold the values in the array of Month elements.
   2.4 Use the query to fill the DataGridView control.
   2.5 Specify headers for the table.
3. **Calculate and display the interest paid during a specified one-year period.**
   3.1 Input the principal, interest rate, and duration of the loan.
   3.2 Assign values to each element of the array of elements with type Month. (See the details in 2.2 above.)
   3.3 Request the number of the beginning month.
   3.4 Declare a LINQ query to limit consideration to the interest payments for the twelve months beginning with the requested month.
   3.5 Use the query's Sum method to compute the total of the interest payments for the year.
4. **Calculate and display a table showing the effect of different interest rates on the monthly payment.** First, the interest rate is reduced by one percentage point and the new monthly payment is computed. Then the interest rate is increased by regular increments until it reaches one percentage point above the original rate, with new monthly payment amounts computed for each intermediate interest rate. The subtasks for this task are then as follows:
   4.1 Input the principal, interest rate, and duration of the loan.
   4.2 Assign values to each element of the array of elements with type EffectOfRate.

4.2.1 Reduce the interest rate from the text box by 1%.

4.2.2 Calculate the new monthly payment and place the interest rate and payment into an element of the array of type EffectOfRate.

4.2.3 Increase the interest rate by 1/8 of 1%.

4.2.4 Repeat until the interest rate is 1% percent above the interest rate in the text box.

4.3 Declare a LINQ query to hold the values in the array of EffectOfRate elements.

4.4 Use the query to fill the DataGridView control.

4.5 Specify headers for the table.

5. Quit. End the program.

The hierarchy chart in Figure 7.82 shows the stepwise refinement for second, third, and fourth tasks.

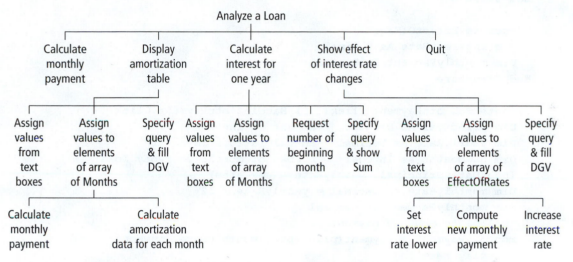

FIGURE 7.82 Hierarchy chart for the Analyze-a-Loan program.

■ Pseudocode for the Analyze-a-Loan Program

Calculate Monthly Payment button:

    INPUT LOAN DATA (Sub procedure InputData)
    COMPUTE MONTHLY PAYMENT (Function Payment)
    DISPLAY MONTHLY PAYMENT

Display Amortization Schedule button:

    INPUT LOAN DATA (Sub procedure InputData)
    ASSIGN VALUES TO EACH MONTH IN ARRAY OF MONTHS (Sub procedure GenerateMonthsArray)
    DEFINE QUERY TO HOLD DATA FROM ARRAY OF MONTHS
    DISPLAY AMORTIZATION SCHEDULE

Show Interest Paid in One Year button:

    INPUT THE NUMBER OF THE BEGINNING MONTH
    INPUT LOAN DATA (Sub procedure InputData)
    ASSIGN VALUES TO EACH MONTH IN ARRAY OF MONTHS (Sub procedure GenerateMonthsArray)
    DEFINE QUERY TO HOLD RELEVANT DATA FROM ARRAY OF MONTHS
    EVALUATE SUM OF QUERY AND DISPLAY

Display Interest Rate Change Table button:

    INPUT LOAN DATA (Sub procedure InputData)
    ASSIGN VALUES TO EACH INTEREST RATE IN ARRAY OF EffectOfRates
    DEFINE QUERY TO HOLD RELEVANT DATA FROM ARRAY OF EffectOfRates
    DISPLAY INTEREST RATE CHANGE TABLE

■ The Analyze-a-Loan Program

```vb
Structure Month
  Dim number As Integer
  Dim interestPaid As Decimal
  Dim principalPaid As Decimal
  Dim endBalance As Decimal
End Structure

Structure EffectOfRate
  Dim interestRate As Decimal
  Dim monthlyPayment As Decimal
End Structure

Private Sub btnPayment_Click(...) Handles btnPayment.Click
  Dim principal As Decimal     'amount of the loan
  Dim yearlyRate As Decimal    'annual rate of interest
  Dim numMonths As Integer     'number of months to repay loan
  InputData(principal, yearlyRate, numMonths)
  Dim monthlyRate As Decimal = yearlyRate / 12
  Dim monthlyPayment As Decimal
  'Calculate monthly payment
  monthlyPayment = Payment(principal, monthlyRate, numMonths)
  'Display results
  MessageBox.Show("Monthly payment: " & monthlyPayment.ToString("C"),
            "Payment")
End Sub

Private Sub btnAmort_Click(...) Handles btnAmort.Click
  Dim principal As Decimal     'amount of the loan
  Dim yearlyRate As Decimal    'annual rate of interest
  Dim numMonths As Integer     'number of months to repay loan
  InputData(principal, yearlyRate, numMonths)
  Dim months(numMonths - 1) As Month
  Dim monthlyRate As Decimal = yearlyRate / 12
  Dim monthlyPayment As Decimal = Payment(principal, monthlyRate, numMonths)
  months = GenerateMonthsArray(principal, monthlyRate, numMonths)
  Dim query = From mnth In months
            Let num = mnth.number
            Let interest = (mnth.interestPaid).ToString("C")
            Let prin = (mnth.principalPaid).ToString("C")
            Let bal = (mnth.endBalance).ToString("C")
            Select num, interest, prin, bal
  dgvResults.DataSource = query.ToList
  dgvResults.CurrentCell = Nothing
  dgvResults.Columns("num").HeaderText = "Month"
  dgvResults.Columns("interest").HeaderText = "Amount Paid for Interest"
  dgvResults.Columns("prin").HeaderText = "Amount Paid for Principal"
  dgvResults.Columns("bal").HeaderText = "Balance at End of Month"
End Sub
```

```vb
Private Sub btnShow_Click(...) Handles btnShow.Click
  Dim principal As Decimal   'amount of loan
  Dim yearlyRate As Decimal  'annual rate of interest
  Dim numMonths As Integer   'number of months to repay loan
  InputData(principal, yearlyRate, numMonths)
  Dim months(numMonths - 1) As Month
  Dim monthlyRate As Decimal = yearlyRate / 12
  Dim monthlyPayment As Decimal = Payment(principal, monthlyRate, numMonths)
  months = GenerateMonthsArray(principal, monthlyRate, numMonths)
  Dim beginningMonth As Integer = CInt(InputBox("Enter beginning month: "))
  Dim query = From month In months
              Where (month.number >= beginningMonth) And
                    (month.number < beginningMonth + 12)
              Select month.interestPaid
  MessageBox.Show("Interest paid for year beginning with month " &
                  beginningMonth & ": " & (query.Sum).ToString("C"),
                  "Interest For Year")
End Sub


Private Sub btnRateTable_Click(...) Handles btnRateTable.Click
  Dim principal As Decimal   'amount of loan
  Dim yearlyRate As Decimal  'annual rate of interest
  Dim numMonths As Integer   'number of months to repay loan
  InputData(principal, yearlyRate, numMonths)
  Dim rates(16) As EffectOfRate
  Dim monthlyRate As Decimal = yearlyRate / 12
  'Fill rates array
  For i As Integer = 0 To 16
    rates(i).interestRate = (yearlyRate - 0.01D) + i * 0.00125D
    rates(i).monthlyPayment = Payment(principal,
                              rates(i).interestRate / 12, numMonths)
  Next
  Dim query = From rate In rates
              Let annualRate = (rate.interestRate).ToString("P3")
              Let monthlyPayment = (rate.monthlyPayment).ToString("C")
              Select annualRate, monthlyPayment
  dgvResults.DataSource = query.ToList
  dgvResults.CurrentCell = Nothing
  dgvResults.Columns("annualRate").HeaderText = "Interest Rate"
  dgvResults.Columns("monthlyPayment").HeaderText = "Monthly Payment"
End Sub


Private Sub btnQuit_Click(...) Handles btnQuit.Click
  Me.Close()
End Sub


Sub InputData(ByRef principal As Decimal,
              ByRef yearlyRate As Decimal, ByRef numMonths As Integer)
  'Input loan amount, yearly rate of interest, and duration
  Dim percentageRate As Decimal, numYears As Integer
  principal = CDec(txtPrincipal.Text)
  percentageRate = CDec(txtYearlyRate.Text)
  yearlyRate = percentageRate / 100   'convert interest rate to decimal form
  numYears = CInt(txtNumYears.Text)
  numMonths = numYears * 12            'duration of loan in months
End Sub
```

```
Function Payment(principal As Decimal, monthlyRate As Decimal, numMonths As
                 Integer) As Decimal
  Dim estimate As Decimal              'estimate of monthly payment
  estimate = CDec(principal * monthlyRate / (1 - (1 + monthlyRate) ^ (-numMonths)))
  'Round the payment up if there are fractions of a cent
  If estimate = Math.Round(estimate, 2) Then
    Return estimate
  Else
    Return Math.Round(estimate + 0.005, 2)
  End If
End Function

Function GenerateMonthsArray(principal As Decimal, monthlyRate As Decimal,
                            numMonths As Integer) As Month()
  Dim months(numMonths - 1) As Month
  'Fill the months array
  Dim monthlyPayment As Decimal = Payment(principal, monthlyRate, numMonths)
  'Assign values for first month
  months(0).number = 1
  months(0).interestPaid = monthlyRate * principal
  months(0).principalPaid = monthlyPayment - months(0).interestPaid
  months(0).endBalance = principal - months(0).principalPaid
  'Assign values for interior months
  For i As Integer = 1 To numMonths - 2
    months(i).number = i + 1
    months(i).interestPaid = monthlyRate * months(i - 1).endBalance
    months(i).principalPaid = monthlyPayment - months(i).interestPaid
    months(i).endBalance = months(i - 1).endBalance - months(i).principalPaid
  Next
  'Assign values for last month
  months(numMonths - 1).number = numMonths
  months(numMonths - 1).interestPaid = monthlyRate *
                                    months(numMonths - 2).endBalance
  months(numMonths - 1).principalPaid = months(numMonths - 2).endBalance
  months(numMonths - 1).endBalance = 0
  Return months
End Function
```

CHAPTER 7   SUMMARY

1. For programming purposes, lists of data are most efficiently processed if stored in an *array*. An array is declared with a *Dim* statement, which also can specify its *size* and initial values. The size of an already declared array can be specified or changed with a *ReDim* or *ReDim Preserve* statement. The methods *Count*, *First*, *Last*, *Max*, and *Min* return the size of the array, first element, last element, largest element, and smallest element, respectively. For numeric arrays, the methods *Average* and *Sum* return the average and total of the numbers in the array.

2. The *IO.File.ReadAllLines* method returns a string array containing the contents of a file.

3. The *Split* method converts a line consisting of strings separated by a delimiter (usually a comma or a blank space) to a string array. The *Join* function is its inverse.

4. A *For Each loop* repeats a group of statements for each element in an array.

5. *LINQ* is a powerful Microsoft technology that provides a standardized way to set criteria for information retrieval from data sources, including arrays. Operators such as *From, Where, Distinct, Order By, Let,* and *Select* are used to create a *query expression* that can retrieve a list of information from the data source. When each element of the list is a single value, the *ToArray* method converts the list to an array. LINQ provides an easy way to sort the contents of an array.

6. The *DataSource* property can be used to display the sequence returned by a query. If the Select clause contains a single expression, a statement of the form

```
lstOutput.DataSource = query.ToList
```

displays the sequence in a list box. If the select clause contains two or more expressions, a statement of the form

```
dgvOutput.DataSource = query.ToList
```

displays the information returned by the query as a table in a DataGridView control.

7. The *binary search* method provides an efficient way to look for an element of an ordered array.

8. A *structure* is a composite programmer-designed data type with a fixed number of members, each of which can be of any data type. LINQ can be used to sort and search structures and to create new structures of *anonymous* data types.

9. A table can be effectively stored and accessed in a *two-dimensional array*.

CHAPTER 7   PROGRAMMING PROJECTS

1. **Unit Conversions**   Table 7.15 contains some lengths in terms of feet. Write a program that displays the nine different units of measure; requests the unit to convert from, the unit to convert to, and the quantity to be converted; and then displays the converted quantity. A typical outcome is shown in Fig. 7.83.

TABLE 7.15	Equivalent lengths.	
1 inch = .0833 foot	1 rod = 16.5 feet
1 yard = 3 feet	1 furlong = 660 feet
1 meter = 3.28155 feet	1 kilometer = 3281.5 feet
1 fathom = 6 feet	1 mile = 5280 feet

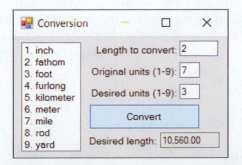

FIGURE 7.83   Possible outcome of Programming Project 1.

2. **ISBN Validator** Every book is identified by a ten-character International Standard Book Number (ISBN), which is usually printed on the back cover of the book. The first nine characters are digits and the last character is either a digit or the letter X (which stands for ten). Three examples of ISBNs are 0–13–030657–6, 0–32–108599–X, and 0–471–58719–2. The hyphens separate the characters into four blocks. The first block usually consists of a single digit and identifies the language (0 for English, 2 for French, 3 for German, etc.). The second block identifies the publisher (for example, 13 for Prentice Hall, 32 for Addison-Wesley-Longman, and 471 for Wiley). The third block is the number the publisher has chosen for the book. The fourth block, which always consists of a single character called the *check digit*, is used to test for errors. Let's refer to the ten characters of the ISBN as d_1, d_2, d_3, d_4, d_5, d_6, d_7, d_8, d_9, and d_{10}. The check digit is chosen so that the sum

$$10 \cdot d_1 + 9 \cdot d_2 + 8 \cdot d_3 + 7 \cdot d_4 + 6 \cdot d_5 + 5 \cdot d_6 + 4 \cdot d_7 + 3 \cdot d_8 + 2 \cdot d_9 + 1 \cdot d_{10} \quad (*)$$

is a multiple of 11. (**Note:** A number is a multiple of 11 if it is exactly divisible by 11.) If the last character of the ISBN is an X, then in the sum (*), d_{10} is replaced with 10. For example, with the ISBN 0–32–108599–X, the sum would be

$$10 \cdot 0 + 9 \cdot 3 + 8 \cdot 2 + 7 \cdot 1 + 6 \cdot 0 + 5 \cdot 8 + 4 \cdot 5$$
$$+ 3 \cdot 9 + 2 \cdot 9 + 1 \cdot 10 = 165$$

Since 165/11 is 15, the sum is a multiple of 11. This checking scheme will detect every single-digit and transposition-of-adjacent-digits error. That is, if while copying an IBSN number you miscopy a single character or transpose two adjacent characters, then the sum (*) will no longer be a multiple of 11.

Write a program to accept an ISBN type number (including the hyphens) as input, calculate the sum (*), and tell if it is a valid ISBN. See Fig. 7.84. (**Hint:** The number n is divisible by 11 if n Mod 11 is 0.) Before calculating the sum, the program should check that each of the first nine characters is a digit and that the last character is either a digit or an X.

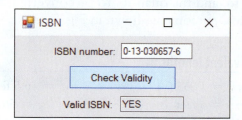

FIGURE 7.84 Possible outcome of Programming Project 2.

3. **Curve Grades** Statisticians use the concepts of **mean** and **standard deviation** to describe a collection of numbers. The mean is the average value of the numbers, and the standard deviation measures the spread or dispersal of the numbers about the mean. Formally, if x_1, x_2, x_3, ..., x_n, is a collection of numbers, then the mean is

$$m = \frac{x_1 + x_2 + x_3 + \cdots + x_n}{n}$$

and the standard deviation is

$$s = \sqrt{\frac{(x_1 - m)^2 + (x_2 - m)^2 + (x_3 - m)^2 + \cdots + (x_n - m)^2}{n}}$$

The file Scores.txt contains exam scores. The first four lines of the file hold the numbers 59, 60, 65, and 75. Write a program to calculate the mean and standard deviation of the exam scores, assign letter grades to each exam score, ES, as follows, and then display a list of the exam scores along with their corresponding grades, as shown in Fig. 7.85.

$$ES \geq m + 1.5s \qquad\qquad A$$

$$m + .5s \leq ES < m + 1.5s \quad B$$

$$m - .5s \leq ES < m + .5s \quad\; C$$

$$m - 1.5s \leq ES < m - .5s \quad D$$

$$ES < m - 1.5s \qquad\qquad F$$

For instance, if m were 70 and s were 12, then grades of 88 or above would receive A's, grades between 76 and 87 would receive B's, and so on. A process of this type is referred to as *curving grades*.

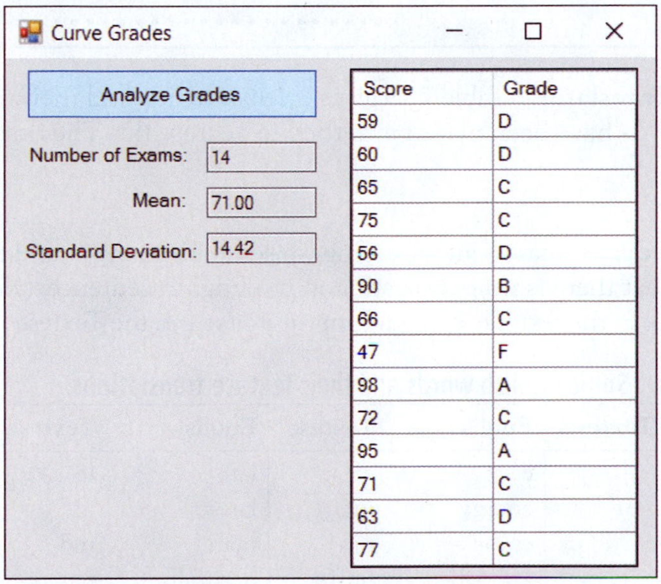

Curve Grades		Score	Grade
Analyze Grades		59	D
		60	D
Number of Exams: 14		65	C
Mean: 71.00		75	C
		56	D
Standard Deviation: 14.42		90	B
		66	C
		47	F
		98	A
		72	C
		95	A
		71	C
		63	D
		77	C

FIGURE 7.85   Outcome of Programming Project 3.

4. **Bachelor Degrees**   Table 7.16 shows the number of bachelor degrees conferred in 1981 and 2013 in certain fields of study. Tables 7.17 and 7.18 show the percentage change and a histogram of 2013 levels, respectively. Write a program that allows the user to display any one of these tables as an option and to quit as a fourth option. (Use Degrees.txt.) Table 7.16 is ordered alphabetically by field of study, Table 7.17 is ordered by decreasing percentages, and Table 7.18 is ordered by increasing number of degrees. **Note:** Chr(149) is a large dot.

TABLE 7.16   **Bachelor degrees conferred in certain fields.**

Field of Study	1981	2013
Business	200,521	360,823
Computer and info. science	15,121	50,962
Education	108,074	104,647
Engineering	63,642	85,980
Social sciences and history	100,513	177,778

Source: National Center for Education Statistics.

TABLE 7.17   Percentage change in bachelor degrees conferred.

Field of Study	% Change (1981–2013)
Computer and info. science	237.0 %
Business	79.9 %
Social sciences and history	76.9 %
Engineering	35.1 %
Education	−3.2 %

TABLE 7.18   Bachelor degrees conferred in 2013 in certain fields.

Field of Study	
Computer and info. science	• • • • • 50,962
Engineering	• • • • • • • • • 85,980
Education	• • • • • • • • • • 104,647
Social sciences and history	• • • • • • • • • • • • • • • • 177,778
Business	• 360,823

5. **Textese Translator**   Table 7.19 gives English words and their translations into Textese. These words have been placed into the file Textese.txt. The first two lines of the file are

```
adieu,+u
anyone,ne1
```

Write a program that requests an English sentence as input and translates it into Textese. Assume that there is no punctuation in the English sentence. (**Note:** If a word in the sentence is not in the text file, it should appear as itself in the Textese translation.) See Fig. 7.86.

TABLE 7.19   Some English words and their Textese translations.

English	Textese	English	Textese	English	Textese	English	Textese
adieu	+u	easy	ez	late	l8	text	txt
anyone	ne1	energy	nrg	later	l8r	thanks	thx
are	r	enjoy	njoy	mate	m8	to	2
ate	8	enough	nuff	naturally	natch	today	2day
band	b&	everyone	every1	oh	o	tomorrow	2mro
be	b	excellent	xlnt	okay	k	tonight	2nite
before	b4	favorite	fav	one	1	too	2
busy	bz	for	4	please	plz	wait	w8
computer	puter	forever	4ever	see	c	why	y
create	cr8	forget	4get	seriously	srsly	won	1
cutie	qt	great	gr8	skate	sk8	wonderful	1drfl
definitely	def	hate	h8	skater	sk8r	you	u
deviate	dv8	in	n	someone	sum1	your	ur

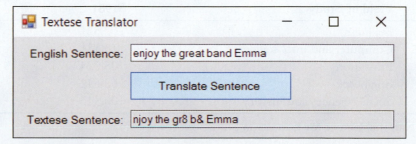

FIGURE 7.86   Possible outcome of Programming Project 5.

6. Soccer League   Each team in a six-team soccer league played each other team once. Table 7.20 shows the winners. Write a program to

(a) Place the team names in an array of structures that also holds the number of wins.

(b) Place the data from Table 7.20 in a two-dimensional array.

(c) Place the number of games won by each team in the array of structures.

(d) Display a listing of the teams giving each team's name and number of games won. The list should be in decreasing order by the number of wins. See Fig. 7.87

TABLE 7.20   **Soccer league winners.**

	Jazz	Jets	Owls	Rams	Cubs	Zips
Jazz	—	Jazz	Jazz	Rams	Cubs	Jazz
Jets	Jazz	—	Jets	Jets	Cubs	Zips
Owls	Jazz	Jets	—	Rams	Owls	Owls
Rams	Rams	Jets	Rams	—	Rams	Rams
Cubs	Cubs	Cubs	Owls	Rams	—	Cubs
Zips	Jazz	Zips	Owls	Rams	Cubs	—

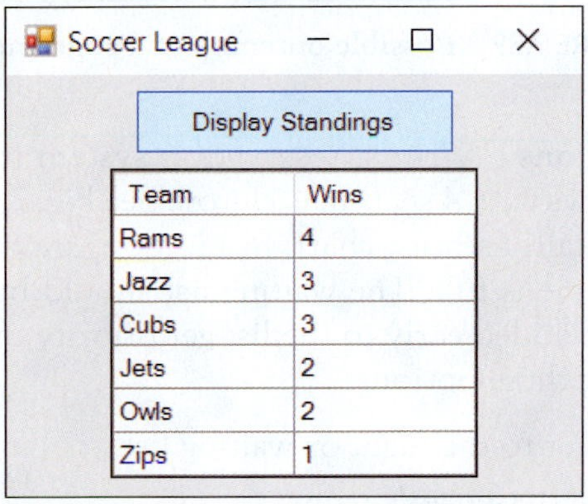

FIGURE 7.87   Outcome of Programming Project 6.

7. Poker   A poker hand can be stored in a two-dimensional array. The statement

```
Dim hand(3, 12) As Integer
```

declares an array with 52 elements, where the first subscript ranges over the four suits and the second subscript ranges over the thirteen ranks. A poker hand is specified by placing 1's in the elements corresponding to the cards in the hand. See Figure 7.88.

	A	2	3	4	5	6	7	8	9	10	J	Q	K
Club ♣	0	0	0	0	0	0	0	0	1	0	0	0	0
Diamond ♦	1	0	0	0	0	0	0	0	0	0	0	0	0
Heart ♥	1	0	0	0	0	0	0	0	0	0	0	1	0
Spade ♠	0	0	0	0	1	0	0	0	0	0	0	0	0

FIGURE 7.88   Array for the poker hand A ♥ A ♦ 5 ♠ 9 ♣ Q ♥.

Write a program that requests the five cards as input from the user, creates the related array, and passes the array to procedures to determine the type of the hand: flush (all cards have the same suit), straight (cards have consecutive ranks—ace can come either before 2 or after King), straight flush, four-of-a-kind, full house (three cards of one rank , two cards of another rank), three-of-a-kind, two pairs, one pair, or none of the above. See Fig. 7.89.

FIGURE 7.89   **Possible outcome of Programming Project 7.**

8. **Airline Reservations**   Write a reservation system for an airline flight. Assume the airplane has 10 rows with 4 seats in each row. See Fig. 7.90. Use a two-dimensional array of strings to maintain a seating chart. In addition, create an array to be used as a waiting list in case the plane is full. The waiting list should be "first come, first served"; that is, people who are added early to the list get priority over those added later. Allow the user the following three options:

(a) Add a passenger to the flight or waiting list.

   1. Request the passenger's name.

   2. Display a chart of the seats in the airplane in tabular form.

   3. If seats are available, let the passenger choose a seat. Add the passenger to the seating chart.

   4. If no seats are available, place the passenger on the waiting list.

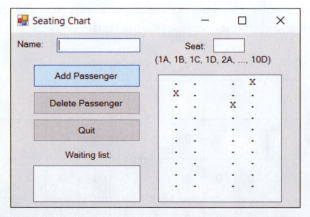

FIGURE 7.90   **Possible outcome of Programming Project 8.**

(b) Remove a passenger from the flight.

    1. Request the passenger's name.

    2. Search the seating chart for the passenger's name and delete it.

    3. If the waiting list is empty, update the array so the seat is available.

    4. If the waiting list is not empty, remove the first person from the list, and give him or her the newly vacated seat.

(c) Quit.

9. Game of Life The Game of Life was invented by John H. Conway to model some natural laws for birth, death, and survival. Consider a checkerboard consisting of an n–by–n array of squares. Each square can contain one individual (denoted by 1) or be empty (denoted by –). Figure 7.91(a) shows a 6–by–6 board with four of the squares occupied. The future of each individual depends on the number of his neighbors. After each period of time, called a *generation*, certain individuals will survive, others will die due to either loneliness or overcrowding, and new individuals will be born. Each non-border square has eight neighboring squares. After each generation, the status of the squares changes as follows:

(a) An individual *survives* if there are two or three individuals in neighboring squares.

(b) An individual *dies* if he has more than three individuals or less than two in neighboring squares.

(c) A new individual *is born* into each empty square that has exactly three individuals as neighbors.

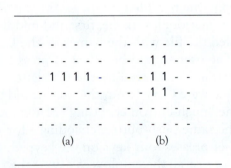

       (a)   (b)

FIGURE 7.91   **Two generations.**

Figure 7.91(b) shows the status after one generation. Write a program to do the following:

    1. Declare a two-dimensional array of size n by n, where n is input by the user, to hold the status of each square in the current generation. To specify the initial configuration, have the user input each row as a string of length n, and break the row into 1's or dashes with the Substring method.

    2. Declare a two-dimensional array of size n by n to hold the status of each square in the next generation. Compute the status for each square and produce the display in Figure 7.91(b). **Note:** The generation changes all at once. Only current cells are used to determine which cells will contain individuals in the next generation.

    3. Assign the next-generation values to the current generation and repeat as often as desired.

4. Display the individuals in each generation. (*Hint:* The hardest part of the program is determining the number of neighbors a cell has. In general, you must check a 3-by-3 square around the cell in question. Exceptions must be made when the cell is on the edge of the array. Don't forget that a cell is not a neighbor of itself.)

Test the program with the initial configuration shown in Figure 7.92. It is known as the figure-eight configuration and repeats after eight generations.

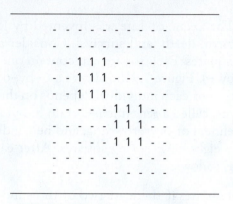

FIGURE 7.92 **The figure eight.**

10. Directory Assistance Have you ever tried to call someone at a place of business and been told to enter letters of the person's name on your telephone's keypad in order to connect to his or her extension? Write a program to simulate this type of directory assistance. Suppose the names and telephone extensions of all the employees of a company are contained in the text file Employees.txt. Each set of three lines of the file has three pieces of information: last name, first and middle name(s), and telephone extension. (We have filled the file with the names of the U.S. presidents so that the names will be familiar.) The user should be asked to press buttons for the first three letters of the person's last name followed by the first letter of the first name. For instance, if the person's name were Gary Land, the user would type in 5264. The number 5264 is referred to as the "push-button encoding" of the name. **Note:** People with different names can have the same push-button encoding—for instance, Herb James and Gary Land. After the user presses four keys on the keypad, the program should display the names and extensions of all the employees having the specified push-button encoding. See Fig. 7.93.

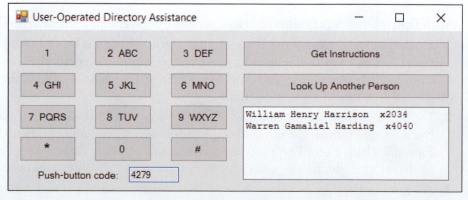

FIGURE 7.93 **Possible outcome of Programming Project 10.**

11. **Fuel Economy**   A fuel-economy study was carried out for five models of cars. Each car was driven 100 miles, and then the model of the car and the number of gallons used were placed in a line of the file Mileage.txt. Table 7.21 shows the data for the entries of the file. Write a program to display the models and their average miles per gallon in decreasing order with respect to mileage. See Fig. 7.94. The program should utilize an array of structures with upper bound 4, where each structure has three members. The first member should record the name of each model of car. The second member should record the number of test vehicles for each model. The third member should record the total number of gallons used by that model. [**Hint:** Two Function procedures that are helpful have the headers `Function NumCars(make As String) As Integer` and `Function NumGals(make As String) As Double`. *NumCars* calculates the number of cars of the specified model in the table, and *NumGals* calculates the number of gallons used by the model. Both Function procedures are easily coded with LINQ queries.]

TABLE 7.21	Gallons of gasoline used in 100 miles of driving.				
Model	Gal	Model	Gal	Model	Gal
Prius	2.1	Accord	4.1	Accord	4.3
Camry	4.1	Camry	3.8	Prius	2.3
Sebring	4.2	Camry	3.9	Camry	4.2
Mustang	5.3	Mustang	5.2	Accord	4.4

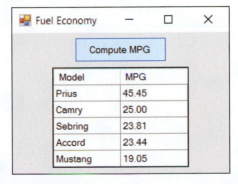

FIGURE 7.94   Outcome of Programming Project 11.

12. **Verbalize a Number**   Write a program that allows the user to enter a positive whole number no greater than 999 septillion (including commas) and then verbalizes the number. See Fig. 7.95.

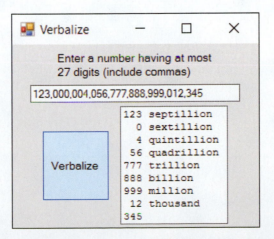

FIGURE 7.95   Possible outcome of Programming Project 12.

8

Text Files

8.1   Managing Text Files

This section presents efficient ways to sort, search, reorganize, combine, and retrieve information from text files. The section begins with some preliminaries. You can skip them if you have read Section 7.3.

■ Preliminaries

The text files considered in Sections 7.1 and 7.2 have a single piece of data per line. For instance, each line of the file States.txt contains the name of a state, and each line of the file USPres.txt contains the name of a president. Another type of text file, called a CSV formatted file, has several items of data on each line with the items separated by commas. (CSV stands for *Comma Separated Values.*) An example is the file USStates.txt, where each line contains four items for each state—*name, abbreviation, land area* (in square miles), and *population in the year 2015.* The first four lines of the file are

```
Delaware,DE,1954,941875
Pennsylvania,PA,44817,12856989
New Jersey,NJ,7417,8969545
Georgia,GA,57906,10206445
Connecticut,CT,4845,3620979
```

Each line of the file is called a **record**, and each of the four categories of data is a **field**. That is, each record consists of four fields—a name field, an abbreviation field, an area field, and a population field.

The Split method is used to access the fields of CSV formatted files. For instance, if the string variable *line* holds the first record of USStates.txt, the value of `line.Split(",")(0)` is Delaware, the value of `line.Split(",")(1)` is DE, the value of `CInt(line.Split(",")(2))` is the number 1954, and the value of `CInt(line.Split(",")(3))` is the number 941875.

The following code can be used to create a LINQ query holding the contents of the file USStates.txt:

```
Dim states() As String = IO.File.ReadAllLines("USStates.txt")
Dim query = From line In states
            Let data = line.Split(",")
            Let name = data(0)
            Let abbr = data(1)
            Let area = CInt(data(2))
            Let pop = CInt(data(3))
            Select name, abbr, area, pop
```

After this code is executed, *query* will be a sequence of elements, each element consisting of four components. If the variable *state* is assigned one of the elements, then the four components associated with *state* are denoted *state.name, state.abbr, state.area,* and *state.pop.* For instance, the following code fills a list box with the names of the states:

```
For Each state As String In query
  lstBox.Items.Add(state.name)
Next
```

The Select clause in the query above contains four items. A Select clause can contain any number of items. When a Select clause contains just one item, the sequence returned by the query can be displayed in a list box. If a Select clause of a query contains two or more items, all the values returned by the query can be displayed in a table by using a DataGridView control. (The DataGridView control is found in the Toolbox's *All Windows Forms* and

Data groups.) The standard prefix for the name of a DataGridView control is *dgv*. With the query above, the statements

```
dgvStates.DataSource = query.ToList
dgvStates.CurrentCell = Nothing
```

display the values returned by the query in the grid shown in Fig. 8.1. (**Note:** The second statement is optional. It prevents having a shaded cell in the grid.) Visual Basic automatically generates the column headings.

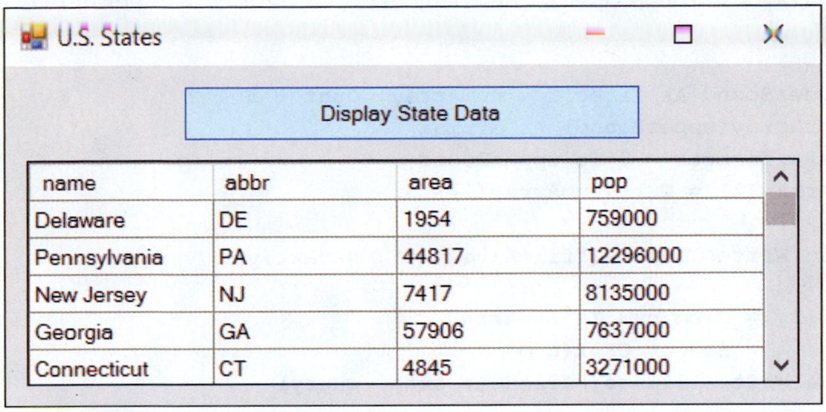

FIGURE 8.1   Displaying a table in a DataGridView control.

A blank column at the left side of the DataGridView control was avoided by setting the RowHeadersVisible property of the control to False. The column headers in the Data-GridView control can be customized with code that sets the HeaderText property. Figure 8.2 results when the RowHeadersVisible property is set to False at design time and the following four lines of code are added to the two lines of code above:

```
dgvStates.Columns("name").HeaderText = "State"
dgvStates.Columns("abbr").HeaderText = "State Abbreviation"
dgvStates.Columns("area").HeaderText = "Land Area"
dgvStates.Columns("pop").HeaderText = "Population"
```

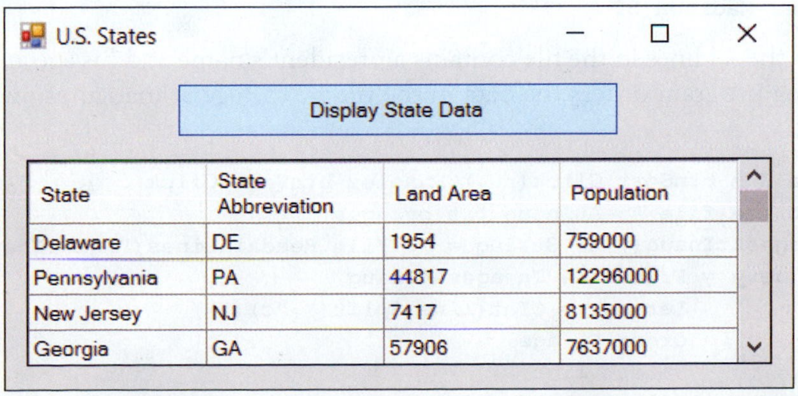

FIGURE 8.2   States table with modified headers.

Note: The DataGridView controls appearing in this textbook have been carefully sized to exactly fit the data. There is no need for you to strive for such precision when working the exercises.

■ WriteAllLines Method

In Chapter 7 we copied the contents of files into arrays with the ReadAllLines method. We can reverse the process with the WriteAllLines method. The following line of code creates a new text file and copies the contents of a string array (or a LINQ query that returns string values) into the file, placing one element on each line:

```
IO.File.WriteAllLines("fileName.txt", strArrayOrQueryName)
```

A simple numeric array can be copied into a text file by first converting the array to a string array and then copying the string array into a file using either of the following two sets of code:

```
Dim upperBound As Integer = numArray.Count − 1
Dim strArray(upperBound) As String
For i As Integer = 0 To upperBound
  strArray(i) = CStr(numArray(i))
Next
IO.File.WriteAllLines("fileName.txt", strArray)

Dim query = From num In numArray
            Select CStr(num)
IO.File.WriteAllLines("fileName.txt", query)
```

Note: If the WriteAllLines method references an existing file, then the file will be overwritten.

■ Sorting the Data in a Text File

Any text file can easily be sorted with a LINQ query.

 Example 1   **U.S. Presidents** The first four lines of the file AgeAtInaug.txt are

```
George Washington,57
John Adams,61
Thomas Jefferson,57
James Madison,57
```

Each of the 44 lines in the file contains a president's name and his age at inauguration. The following program orders the data in the file by the age at inauguration and creates a new sorted file:

```
Private Sub btnSort_Click(...) Handles btnSort.Click
  'Sort the file AgeAtInaug.txt by ages
  Dim agesAtInaug() As String = IO.File.ReadAllLines("AgeAtInaug.txt")
  Dim query = From line In agesAtInaug
              Let age = CInt(line.Split(","c)(1))
              Order By age
              Select line
  IO.File.WriteAllLines("Sorted.txt", query)
End Sub
```

[Run, click on the button, and terminate the program. Then click on the *Refresh* button in the Solution Explorer window, click on the *View All Files* button, and double-click on the new text file Sorted.txt in the *bin\Debug* subfolder. The first seven lines of the file are as follows.]

```
Theodore Roosevelt,42
John Kennedy,43
Ulysses Grant,46
Bill Clinton,46
Grover Cleveland,47
Barack Obama,47
Franklin Pierce,48
```

 Example 2   **U.S. Presidents** The following variation of Example 1 displays the data in the file AgeAtInaug.txt in a table ordered by the ages at inauguration:

```
Private Sub btnSort_Click(...) Handles btnSort.Click
  'Sort the file AgeAtInaug.txt by ages
  Dim agesAtInaug() As String = IO.File.ReadAllLines("AgeAtInaug.txt")
  Dim query = From line In agesAtInaug
              Let name = line.Split(","c)(0)
              Let age = CInt(line.Split(","c)(1))
              Order By age
              Select name, age
  dgvOutput.DataSource = query.ToList
  dgvOutput.CurrentCell = Nothing
End Sub
```

[Run, and click on the button.]

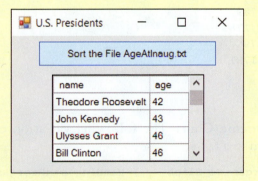

Reorganizing the Data in a CSV Text File

LINQ can retrieve specific data from a file and use it to create a new file containing those data.

 Example 3   **Supreme Court** The first four lines of the file Justices.txt are

```
Samuel,Alito,George W. Bush,NJ,2006,0
Henry,Baldwin,Andrew Jackson,PA,1830,1844
Philip,Barbour,Andrew Jackson,VA,1836,1841
Hugo,Black,Franklin Roosevelt,AL,1937,1971
```

Each line of the file contains the following information about a Supreme Court justice: first name, last name, appointing president, state from which they were appointed, year appointed, and year they left the court. (For current justices, the last field is set to 0.) The following program creates a new file, where each line is the full name of a justice and the year they were appointed. The justices are sorted by the year appointed in ascending order. Justices appointed during the same year are sorted by their first name in ascending order.

```
Private Sub btnReorganize_Click(...) Handles btnReorganize.Click
  'Take data from a file. Sort and restructure the data,
  'and write it to a new file.
  Dim justices() As String = IO.File.ReadAllLines("Justices.txt")
  Dim query = From line In justices
            Let data = line.Split(","c)
            Let firstName = data(0)
            Let lastName = data(1)
            Let yrAppointed = CInt(data(4))
            Order By yrAppointed, firstName
            Let newLine = firstName & " " & lastName & "," & yrAppointed
            Select newLine
  IO.File.WriteAllLines("NewFile.txt", query)
End Sub
```

[Run, click on the button, and terminate the program. Then click on the *Refresh* button in the Solution Explorer window, click on the *View All Files* button, and double-click the new text file in the *bin\Debug* subfolder. The first seven lines of the file are as follows.]

```
James Wilson,1789
John Blair,1789
John Jay,1789
John Rutledge,1789
William Cushing,1789
James Iredell,1790
Thomas Johnson,1791
```

 Example 4 **Supreme Court** The following variation of Example 3 displays the requested information in a table:

```
Private Sub btnReorganize_Click(...) Handles btnReorganize.Click
  'Take data from a text file. Sort and restructure the data,
  'and display it in a table.
  Dim justices() As String = IO.File.ReadAllLines("Justices.txt")
  Dim query = From line In justices
            Let data = line.Split(","c)
            Let firstName = data(0)
            Let lastName = data(1)
            Let yrAppointed = CInt(data(4))
            Let fullName = firstName & " " & lastName
            Order By yrAppointed, firstName
            Select fullName, yrAppointed
  dgvOutput.DataSource = query.ToList
  dgvOutput.CurrentCell = Nothing
End Sub
```

[Run, and click on the button.]

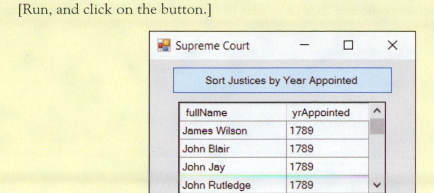

Set Operations

Often we want to create a new text file from two existing text files. For instance, we might want to merge the two files (with or without duplications). Or, we might want to update one file by deleting the items that also appear in the other file. Or, we might want the new file to contain the items that appear in both of the existing files. The three steps we will use to carry out such operations are as follows:

1. Use the ReadAllLines method to fill two arrays with the contents of the two existing text files.

2. Apply a set operation such as Concat, Union, Intersect, or Except to the arrays or to LINQ queries derived from the arrays.

3. Use the WriteAllLines method to write the resulting array into a new text file.

   If *array1* and *array2* are string arrays, then

array1.Concat(array2).ToArray is an array containing the elements of *array1* with *array2* appended, possibly with duplications.

array1.Union(array2).ToArray is an array containing the elements of *array1* with *array2* appended, without duplications.

array1.Intersect(array2).ToArray is an array containing the elements that are in both *array1* and *array2*.

array1.Except(array2).ToArray is an array containing the elements of *array1* with the elements of *array2* removed.

Note: When one of the four operations above is used as the second parameter of a WriteAll-Lines method, the ToArray method can be omitted.

   These four set operations are demonstrated with two simple files in Example 5 and then with more complex files in Example 6.

Example 5   **Set Operations**   The contents of two files are as follows:

File1.txt	File2.txt
Alpha	Bravo
Bravo	Delta
Charlie	

The following program combines these two files in four ways. Figure 8.3 shows the form for the program.

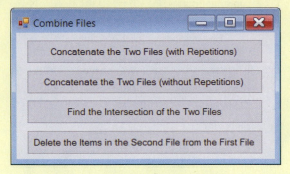

FIGURE 8.3   Form for Example 5.

```
Dim firstSet() As String = IO.File.ReadAllLines("File1.txt")
Dim secondSet() As String = IO.File.ReadAllLines("File2.txt")

Private Sub btnConcat_Click(...) Handles btnConcat.Click
  IO.File.WriteAllLines("Concat.txt", firstSet.Concat(secondSet))
End Sub

Private Sub btnUnion_Click(...) Handles btnUnion.Click
  IO.File.WriteAllLines("Union.txt", firstSet.Union(secondSet))
End Sub

Private Sub btnIntersect_Click(...) Handles btnIntersect.Click
  IO.File.WriteAllLines("Intersect.txt", firstSet.Intersect(secondSet))
End Sub

Private Sub btnExcept_Click(...) Handles btnExcept.Click
  IO.File.WriteAllLines("Except.txt", firstSet.Except(secondSet))
End Sub
```

[Run, click on each button, and terminate the program. Then click on the *Refresh* button in the Solution Explorer window, click on the *View All Files* button, and look at the new text files in the *bin\Debug* subfolder.]

The file Concat.txt contains the five words Alpha, Bravo, Charlie, Bravo, and Delta.
The file Union.txt contains the four words Alpha, Bravo, Charlie, and Delta.
The file Intersect.txt contains the single word Bravo.
The file Except.txt contains the two words Alpha and Charlie.

In the four set operations, one or both of the arrays can be replaced with LINQ queries. This allows the programmer to order, filter, and project the data before combining files.

 Example 6   **U.S. Presidents** The following program demonstrates the set operations with the two files Justices.txt and USPres.txt. The file USPres.txt is a single-field text file containing the names of the first 44 presidents. The first four lines of USPres.txt contain the names George Washington, John Adams, Thomas Jefferson, and James Madison. **Note:** The file Justices.txt shows all Supreme Court appointments as of January 1, 2016.

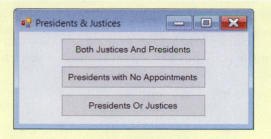

OBJECT	PROPERTY	SETTING
frmPnJ	Text	Presidents & Justices
btnBoth	Text	Both Justices And Presidents
btnNo	Text	Presidents with No Appointments
btnOr	Text	Presidents Or Justices

```
Dim justices() As String = IO.File.ReadAllLines("Justices.txt")
Dim presidents() As String = IO.File.ReadAllLines("USPres.txt")

Private Sub btnBoth_Click(...) Handles btnBoth.Click
  'Display justices who were also presidents
  Dim queryJustices = From line In justices
                      Let firstName = line.Split(","c)(0)
                      Let lastName = line.Split(","c)(1)
                      Let fullName = firstName & " " & lastName
                      Select fullName
  IO.File.WriteAllLines("Both.txt", queryJustices.Intersect(presidents))
End Sub


Private Sub btnNoAppointments_Click(...) Handles btnNoAppointments.Click
  'Display presidents who made no Supreme Court appointments
  Dim queryAppointers = From line In justices
                        Let president = line.Split(","c)(2)
                        Select president
  Dim queryNoAppoint = From pres In presidents.Except(queryAppointers)
                       Order By pres
                       Select pres
  IO.File.WriteAllLines("NoAppointments.txt", queryNoAppoint)
End Sub


Private Sub btnOr_Click(...) Handles btnOr.Click
  'Display a combined list of presidents and justices
  Dim queryJustices = From line In justices
                      Let firstName = line.Split(","c)(0)
                      Let lastName = line.Split(","c)(1)
                      Let fullName = firstName & " " & lastName
                      Select fullName
  Dim queryEither = From person In presidents.Union(queryJustices)
                    Order By person
                    Select person
  IO.File.WriteAllLines("PresOrJustice.txt", queryEither)
End Sub
```

[Run, click on each button, and terminate the program. Then click on the *Refresh* button in the Solution Explorer window, click on the *View All Files* button, and look at the new text files in the *bin\Debug* subfolder.]

The file Both.txt contains the single name "William Taft".
The file NoAppointments.txt contains the names of four presidents.
The file PresOrJustice.txt contains 155 names.

■ Searching a CSV Text File

In Section 7.3 we searched files having several fields by loading the data into arrays of structures and searching the arrays. The next example provides a more direct way of searching for data—no structure is used.

 Example 7   **U.S. States** Each record of the file USStates.txt contains a name field, an abbreviation field, an area field, and a population field. The first two records of the file are

```
Delaware,DE,1954,941875
Pennsylvania,PA,44817,12856989
```

The following program looks up the name of the state whose abbreviation is given. **Note:** The method First is required in the line **txtName.Text = query.First** because query is a sequence—namely, a sequence of one item.

```
Dim states() As String = IO.File.ReadAllLines("USStates.txt")

Private Sub btnFind_Click(...) Handles btnFind.Click
  'Note: mtbAbbr has the mask LL
  Dim query = From line In states
              Let name = line.Split(","c)(0)
              Let abbreviation = line.Split(","c)(1)
              Where abbreviation = mtbAbbr.Text.ToUpper
              Select name
  If query.Count = 1 Then
    txtName.Text = query.First
  Else
    Dim str As String = " is not a valid state abbreviation."
    MessageBox.Show(mtbAbbr.Text.ToUpper & str, "Error")
    mtbAbbr.Clear()
    mtbAbbr.Focus()
  End If
End Sub
```

[Run, enter a state abbreviation into the masked text box, and click on the button.]

 Example 8   **U.S. States** The following program searches the file USStates.txt for the states having population density less than 9.5 people per square mile and displays the names of the states and their population densities ordered by their population densities (in ascending order) in a table.

```
Private Sub btnSearch_Click(...) Handles btnSearch.Click
  Dim states() As String = IO.File.ReadAllLines("USStates.txt")
  Dim query = From line In states
              Let data = line.Split(","c)
              Let name = data(0)
              Let popDensity = CDbl(data(3)) / CDbl(data(2))
              Let formattedDensity = popDensity.ToString("N")
              Where popDensity < 9.5
              Order By popDensity Ascending
              Select name, formattedDensity
  dgvOutput.DataSource = query.ToList
  dgvOutput.CurrentCell = Nothing
  dgvOutput.Columns("name").HeaderText = "State"
  dgvOutput.Columns("formattedDensity").HeaderText = "Population Density"
End Sub
```

[Run, and click on the button.]

U.S. States		
Search the File USStates.txt		

State	Population Density
Alaska	1.33
Wyoming	5.99
Montana	6.98

■ The OpenFileDialog Control

Windows applications, such as Word, Excel, and Notepad, all provide the same standard Open dialog box to help you specify the file you want to open. Figure 8.4 on the next page shows an Open dialog box that could be used with Notepad to open a text file. The same Open dialog box, with all its functionality, is available to Visual Basic programs courtesy of the OpenFileDialog control.

The OpenFileDialog control is in the *Dialogs* group of the Toolbox. When you double-click on the icon in the Toolbox, the control will appear in the component tray below the Form Designer with the default name OpenFileDialog1. (We will not change the name, since the default name completely describes the control's function.) The only property we will set for the control is the Filter property, which determines the text that appears in the combo box above the *Open* button and the types of files that will be displayed in the dialog box. The simplest setting has the form

text for combo box | * *.ext*

where *ext* is a two-, three-, or four-letter extension describing the types of files to display. For our purposes, the most used setting for the Filter property will be

Text Documents (*.txt)|*.txt

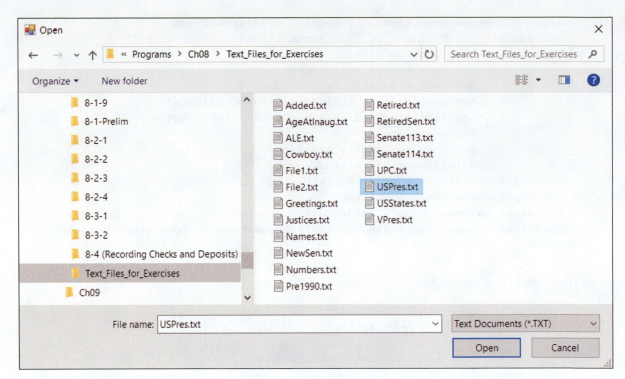

FIGURE 8.4 An Open dialog box.

The statement

```
OpenFileDialog1.ShowDialog()
```

displays the Open dialog box. After a file has been selected and the *Open* button pressed, the value of

```
OpenFileDialog1.FileName
```

will be the file's filespec—including drive, path, filename, and extension.

✔ **Example 9** **U.S. Presidents** The following program displays the contents of a text file selected by the user with an Open dialog box:

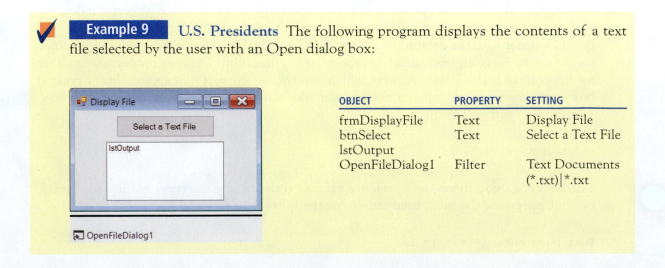

OBJECT	PROPERTY	SETTING
frmDisplayFile	Text	Display File
btnSelect	Text	Select a Text File
lstOutput		
OpenFileDialog1	Filter	Text Documents (*.txt)|*.txt

```
Private Sub btnSelect_Click(...) Handles btnSelect.Click
  Dim textFile As String
  OpenFileDialog1.ShowDialog()  'Open dialog box appears and program
  '                              pauses until a selection is made
  textFile = OpenFileDialog1.FileName
  lstOutput.DataSource = IO.File.ReadAllLines(textFile)
  lstOutput.SelectedItem = Nothing
End Sub
```

[Run, and click on the button. (Assume that the user makes choices leading to the situation in Fig. 8.4.) Select the file USPres.txt, and click on the *Open* button in the dialog box.]

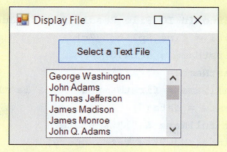

■ Excel and CSV Files

CSV files can be converted to Excel spreadsheets and vice versa. If you open the file in Excel and select comma when asked for the delimiter, Excel will create a spreadsheet with the proper number of lines and columns. Conversely, a spreadsheet you create or download from the Internet can be converted to a CSV file. After clicking on "Save As" from the Excel FILE menu, choose "CSV (Comma delimited)(*.csv)" in the "Save as type" dropdown box.

■ Comment

1. In Example 7, the array *states* could have been omitted and the first line of the query changed to

   ```
   Dim query = From line In IO.File.ReadAllLines("USStates.txt")
   ```

   However, with this change the text file would be read each time the user requested the name of a state. Ideally, a file should be read only once from a disk each time the program is run.

Practice Problems 8.1

1. Consider Example 7. Suppose the last line of the query were changed to

   ```
   Select name, abbr
   ```

   What change would have to be made to the following line?

   ```
   txtName.Text = query.First
   ```

2. The second clause of the query in Example 1 is

   ```
   Let age = CInt(line.Split(","c)(1))
   ```

   The program would produce the correct result even if the CInt function were omitted. Why is that so, and why should CInt be used in general?

3. Does the array `array1.Concat(array2).ToArray` contain the same set of values (disregarding order) as the array `array2.Concat(array1).ToArray`? Is the same true for Union, Intersect, and Except?

Exercises 1 through 10 refer to the file Justices.txt that contains data about the Supreme Court justices, past and present. Each record contains six fields—first name, last name, appointing president, home state, year appointed, and year they left the court. (For current justices, the last field is set to 0.) The first two lines of the file are as follows:

```
Samuel,Alito,George W. Bush,NJ,2006,0
Henry,Baldwin,Andrew Jackson,PA,1830,1844
```

In Exercises 1 through 6, determine the first two lines of the new file created by the code.

1.
```
Dim query = From line In IO.File.ReadAllLines("Justices.txt")
            Let data = line.Split(","c)
            Let firstName = data(0)
            Let lastName = data(1)
            Let fullName = firstName & " " & lastName
            Let state = data(3)
            Select fullName & "," & state
IO.File.WriteAllLines("NewFile.txt", query)
```

2.
```
Dim query = From line In IO.File.ReadAllLines("Justices.txt")
            Let data = line.Split(","c)
            Let firstName = data(0)
            Let lastName = data(1)
            Let fullName = (firstName & " " & lastName).ToUpper
            Let yrAppointed = CInt(data(4))
            Select fullName & " was appointed in " & yrAppointed & "."
IO.File.WriteAllLines("NewFile.txt", query)
```

3.
```
Dim query = From line In IO.File.ReadAllLines("Justices.txt")
            Let lastName = line.Split(","c)(1)
            Let pres = line.Split(","c)(2)
            Let presLastName = pres.Split(" "c).Last
            Let phrase = lastName & " was appointed by " & presLastName
            Select phrase
IO.File.WriteAllLines("NewFile.txt", query)
```

4.
```
'Note: Today.Year is the current year
Dim query = From line In IO.File.ReadAllLines("Justices.txt")
            Let lastName = line.Split(","c)(1)
            Let yrAppointed = CInt(line.Split(","c)(4))
            Let years = Today.Year - yrAppointed
            Let phrase = lastName & " appointed " & years & " years ago"
            Select phrase
IO.File.WriteAllLines("NewFile.txt", query)
```

5.
```
Dim query = From line In IO.File.ReadAllLines("Justices.txt")
            Let data = line.Split(","c)
            Let firstName = data(0)
            Let lastName = data(1)
            Let yrAppointed = CInt(data(4))
            Let newLine = lastName & "," & firstName & "," & yrAppointed
            Select newLine
IO.File.WriteAllLines("NewFile.txt", query)
```

6.
```
Dim query = From line In IO.File.ReadAllLines("Justices.txt")
            Let data = line.Split(","c)
            Let lastName = data(1)
            Let pres = data(2)
            Let state = data(3)
            Let presLastName = pres.Split(" "c).Last
            Let newLine = presLastName & "," & lastName & "," & state
            Select newLine
    IO.File.WriteAllLines("NewFile.txt", query)
```

In Exercises 7 through 10, describe the new file created by the code.

7.
```
Dim query = From line In IO.File.ReadAllLines("Justices.txt")
            Let data = line.Split(","c)
            Let firstName = data(0)
            Let lastName = data(1)
            Let yrAppointed = CInt(data(4))
            Let fullName = firstName & " " & lastName
            Let newLine = fullName & "," & yrAppointed
            Where lastName.StartsWith("B")
            Order By yrAppointed
            Select newLine
    IO.File.WriteAllLines("NewFile.txt", query)
```

8.
```
Dim query = From line In IO.File.ReadAllLines("Justices.txt")
            Let data = line.Split(","c)
            Let firstName = data(0)
            Let lastName = data(1)
            Let state = data(3)
            Let yrAppointed = CInt(data(4))
            Let fullName = firstName & " " & lastName
            Let newLine = state & "," & fullName
            Where (yrAppointed >= 1990) And (yrAppointed < 2000)
            Order By state
            Select newLine
    IO.File.WriteAllLines("NewFile.txt", query)
```

9.
```
Dim query = From line In IO.File.ReadAllLines("Justices.txt")
            Let data = line.Split(","c)
            Let firstName = data(0)
            Let lastName = data(1)
            Let pres = .data(2)
            Let newLine = firstName & "," & lastName & "," & pres
            Select newLine
    IO.File.WriteAllLines("NewFile.txt", query)
```

10.
```
Dim query = From line In IO.File.ReadAllLines("Justices.txt")
            Let data = line.Split(","c)
            Let firstName = data(0)
            Let lastName = data(1)
            Let yrAppointed = CInt(data(4))
            Let yrLeft = CInt(data(5))
```

```
                    Let fullName = firstName & " " & lastName
                    Let newLine = fullName & "," & yrAppointed
                    Where yrLeft = 0
                    Order By yrAppointed
                    Select newLine
        IO.File.WriteAllLines("NewFile.txt", query)
```

In Exercises 11 through 14, describe the new file created by the code. Assume the file NYTimes.txt contains the names of subscribers to the *New York Times* and the file WSJ.txt contains the names of the subscribers to the *Wall Street Journal*.

11.
```
Dim times() As String = IO.File.ReadAllLines("NYTimes.txt")
Dim wsj() As String = IO.File.ReadAllLines("WSJ.txt")
IO.File.WriteAllLines("NewFile.txt", times.Union(wsj))
```

12.
```
Dim times() As String = IO.File.ReadAllLines("NYTimes.txt")
Dim wsj() As String = IO.File.ReadAllLines("WSJ.txt")
IO.File.WriteAllLines("NewFile.txt", times.Intersect(wsj))
```

13.
```
Dim times() As String = IO.File.ReadAllLines("NYTimes.txt")
Dim wsj() As String = IO.File.ReadAllLines("WSJ.txt")
IO.File.WriteAllLines("NewFile.txt", times.Except(wsj))
```

14.
```
Dim times() As String = IO.File.ReadAllLines("NYTimes.txt")
Dim wsj() As String = IO.File.ReadAllLines("WSJ.txt")
Dim unionArray() As String = times.Union(wsj).ToArray
Dim intersectArray() As String = times.Intersect(wsj).ToArray
IO.File.WriteAllLines("NewFile.txt", unionArray.Except(intersectArray))
```

In Exercises 15 through 18, use the file USPres.txt that contains the names of all the presidents of the United States and the file VPres.txt that contains the names of all the vice-presidents.

15. U.S. Presidents   Write a program that creates a file containing the names of every president who also served as vice-president. The program also should display the number of those presidents in a message box.

16. U.S. Presidents   Write a program that creates a file containing the names of every person who served as either vice-president or president. The program also should display the number of those names in a message box.

17. U.S. Presidents   Write a program that creates a file containing the names of every person who served as either vice-president or president, but not both. The program also should display the number of those names in a message box.

18. U.S. Presidents   Write a program that creates a file containing the names of every president who did not also serve as vice-president. The program also should display the number of those presidents in a message box.

In Exercises 19 through 26 , write a program for the stated example or exercise from Section 7.3 without using a structure.

19. Section 7.3, Example 2

20. Section 7.3, Example 4

21. Section 7.3, Exercise 18

22. Section 7.3, Exercise 19

23. Section 7.3, Exercise 20

24. Section 7.3, Exercise 21

25. Section 7.3, Exercise 22

26. Section 7.3, Exercise 26

27. **Colors** At the beginning of 1990, a complete box of Crayola[1] crayons had 72 colors (in the file Pre1990.txt). During the 1990s, 8 colors were retired (in the file Retired.txt) and 56 new colors were added (in the file Added.txt). Write a program that creates a text file listing the post-1990s set of 120 colors in alphabetical order.

Exercises 28 through 34 should use the file Justices.txt discussed at the beginning of this exercise set.

28. **Supreme Court** Write a program to create a file in which each record consists of two fields—the full name of a Supreme Court justice, and the justice's state.

29. **Supreme Court** Write a program to create a file similar to Justices.txt, but with the state field deleted.

30. **Supreme Court** Write a program that displays the entire contents of the file Justices.txt in a DataGridView control. See Fig. 8.5.

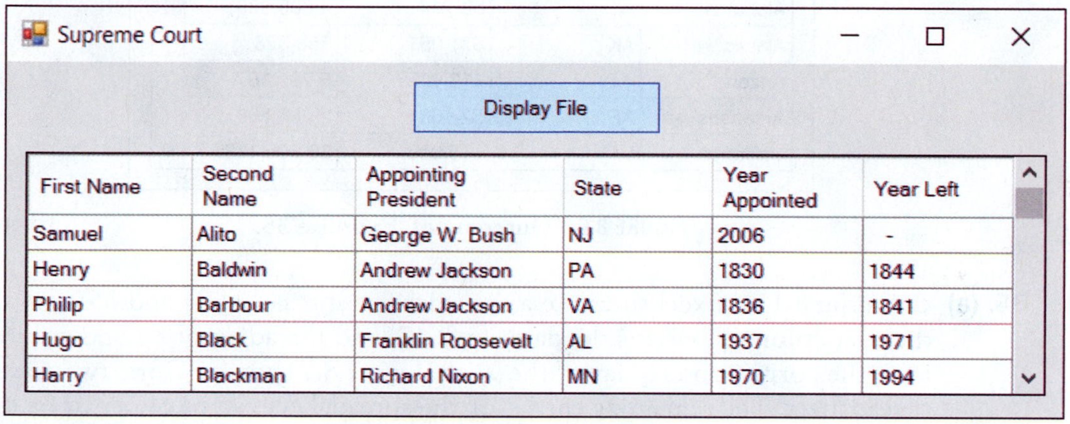

FIGURE 8.5 Outcome of Exercise 30.

31. **Supreme Court** The file USStates.txt contains information about each of the 50 states. Each record contains four fields—name, abbreviation, land area (in square miles), population in the year 2015. The records are ordered by the states' date of entry into the union. The first five lines of the file are

```
Delaware,DE,1954,941875
Pennsylvania,PA,44817,12856989
New Jersey,NJ,7417,8969545
Georgia,GA,57906,10206445
Connecticut,CT,4845,3620979
```

Write a program that creates a file consisting of the states that have not produced any Supreme Court justices.

32. **Supreme Court** The first Supreme Court justice was appointed in 1789. Write a program to create a file that lists the years from 1789 through 2015 in which no Supreme Court justices were appointed. The first four lines of the file will be 1792, 1794, 1795, and 1797.

33. **Supreme Court** Write a program to create a file that lists the states that have produced Supreme Court justices, along with the number of justices produced. The states should be in alphabetical order by their abbreviations. The first four lines of the file will be **AL,3; AZ,2; CA,5; CO,1**. *Hint:* Define a function named NumberOfJustices that accepts a state as input and returns the number of justices from that state.

---

[1]Crayola is a registered trademark of Binney & Smith.

34. Supreme Court Write a program to create a file that lists the presidents who have appointed Supreme Court justices, along with the number of justices appointed. The presidents should be in alphabetical order by their full names. The first two lines of the file will be **Abraham Lincoln,5; Andrew Jackson,5**.

35. U.S. States Consider the file USStates.txt described in Exercise 31. Write a program to display the entire contents of the file in a DataGridView control with the states in alphabetical order. See Fig. 8.6.

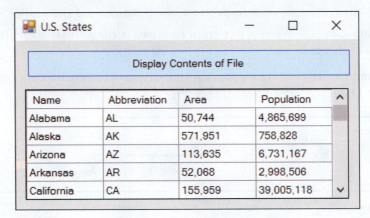

FIGURE 8.6 Outcome of Exercise 35.

36. (a) Calendar Use Excel to create a spreadsheet of 2 columns and 365 rows, where the first column contains the dates in 2017, and the adjacent second column contains the corresponding day of the week. Figure 8.7 shows the first two rows of the spreadsheet. The remaining entries of the spreadsheet can be obtained by selecting the cells in Fig. 8.7 and dragging them down until 365 rows have been created.

(b) Save the spreadsheet as a file of type CSV (Comma delimited)(*.csv) named **Calendar2017.csv** and then change its name to **Calendar2017.txt**.

(c) Use the text file in a program that requests a date in 2017 as input and then gives its day of the week. See Fig. 8.8.

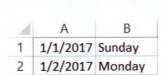

FIGURE 8.7 Spreadsheet for Exercise 36.

Source: Excel 2016, Windows 10, Microsoft Corporation.

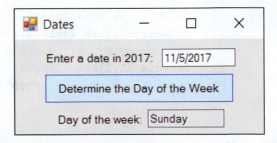

FIGURE 8.8 Possible outcome of Exercise 36.

Solutions to Practice Problems 8.1

1. The line would have to be changed to

```
txtName.Text = query.First.name
```

2. The ages of the presidents are all two-digit numbers and therefore will be ordered correctly when sorted as strings. In general, however, with arbitary ages, the query would not produce a correct result. For instance, a nine-year-old would be considered to be older than an eighty-year-old, and a centenarian would be considered to be younger than a nine-year-old.

3. The answer to the first question is "Yes". The same is true for Union and Intersect. However, the two arrays are different when Except is used. For instance, if the two arrays were reversed in the last event procedure of Example 5, then the contents of the file Except.txt would be the single word Delta.

8.2   StreamReaders, StreamWriters, and Structured Exception Handling

So far we have accessed the data in a text file by filling an array with the lines of the file and then accessing the array. However, sometimes we want to read or write a text file directly one line at a time without using arrays as intermediaries.

■ Reading a Text File with a StreamReader

Lines of a text file can be read in order and assigned to variables with the following steps:

VideoNote

StreamReaders
and
StreamWriters

1. Execute a statement of the form

```
Dim srVar As IO.StreamReader
```

A StreamReader is a class from the Input/Output namespace that can read a stream of characters coming from a disk. The Dim statement declares the variable *srVar* to be of type StreamReader.

2. Execute a statement of the form

```
srVar = IO.File.OpenText(filespec)
```

where *filespec* identifies the text file to be read. If *filespec* consists only of a filename (that is, if no path is given), Visual Basic will look for the file in the program's *bin\Debug* folder. This statement, which establishes a communications link between the computer and the disk drive for reading data from the disk, is said to **open a file for input**. Data then can be input from the specified file and assigned to variables in the program.

Just as with other variables, the declaration and assignment statements in Steps 1 and 2 can be combined into the single statement

```
Dim srVar As IO.StreamReader = IO.File.OpenText(filespec)
```

3. Read lines in order, one at a time, from the file with the ReadLine method. Each line is retrieved as a string. A statement of the form

```
strVar = srVar.ReadLine
```

causes the program to look in the file for the next unread line of data and assign it to the variable *strVar*.

The OpenText method sets a pointer to the first line in the specified file. Each time a ReadLine method is executed, the line pointed to is read, and the pointer is then moved to the next line. After all lines have been read from the file, the value of

```
srVar.EndOfStream
```

will be True. The EndOfStream property can be used in the condition of a Do loop to iterate through every line of a text file. Such a loop might begin with the statement **Do Until** *srVar*.**EndOfStream**.

4. After the desired lines have been read from the file, terminate the communications link set in Step 2 with the statement

```
srVar.Close()
```

Example 1   U.S. States The following program uses a StreamReader to carry out the same task as the program in Example 7 of the previous section. That is, it finds the name of the state whose abbreviation is given in a masked text box.

```vb
Private Sub btnFind_Click(...) Handles btnFind.Click
  Dim sr As IO.StreamReader = IO.File.OpenText("USStates.txt")
  Dim abbr As String = mtbAbbr.Text.ToUpper 'mask is LL
  Dim line As String
  Dim foundFlag As Boolean = False
  Do Until foundFlag Or sr.EndOfStream
    line = sr.ReadLine
    If line.Split(",")(1) = abbr Then
      txtName.Text = line.Split(",")(0)
      foundFlag = True
    End If
  Loop
  If Not foundFlag Then
    Dim str As String = " is not a valid state abbreviation."
    MessageBox.Show(mtbAbbr.Text.ToUpper & str, "Error")
    mtbAbbr.Clear()
    mtbAbbr.Focus()
  End If
  sr.Close()
End Sub
```

[Run, enter a state abbreviation into the masked text box, and click on the button.]

■ Creating a Text File with a StreamWriter

In Section 8.1 we created text files by copying the contents of arrays into the files with the WriteAllLines method. However, sometimes we want to write to a text file directly one line at a time without using an array. The following steps create a new text file and write data to it:

1. Choose a *filespec*.

2. Execute a statement of the form

   ```vb
   Dim swVar As IO.StreamWriter = IO.File.CreateText(filespec)
   ```

   where *swVar* is a variable name. This process is said to **open a file for output**. It establishes a communications link between the program and the disk drive for storing data onto the disk. It allows data to be output from the program and recorded in the specified file. If *filespec* consists only of a filename (that is, if no path is given), Visual Basic will place the file in the program's *bin\Debug* folder. **Caution:** If an existing file is opened for output, Visual Basic will replace the file with a new empty file.

3. Place data into the file with the WriteLine method. If *info* is a literal, variable, or expression of any data type, then the statement

swVar.WriteLine(info)

writes the information into a new line of the file.

4. After all the data have been recorded in the file, execute

swVar.Close()

This statement is very important because the WriteLine method actually places data into a temporary buffer, and the Close method transfers the data to the disk. Therefore, if you omit the statement *swVar*.Close(), some data might be lost. The statement also breaks the communications link with the file. Therefore its omission might prevent other procedures from using the file.

Example 2   **Computing Pioneers** The following program creates a text file consisting of several last names of computing pioneers and then displays the entire contents of the file in a list box:

```
Private Sub btnCreateFile_Click(...) Handles btnCreateFile.Click
  'Create the file Pioneers.txt
  Dim sw As IO.StreamWriter = IO.File.CreateText("Pioneers.txt")
  sw.WriteLine("Atanasoff")
  sw.WriteLine("Babbage")
  sw.WriteLine("Codd")
  sw.WriteLine("Dijkstra")
  sw.WriteLine("Eckert")
  sw.WriteLine("Faggin")
  sw.WriteLine("Gates")
  sw.WriteLine("Hollerith")
  sw.Close()    'If this line is omitted, the file will be empty.
  MessageBox.Show("Names recorded in file", "File Status")
End Sub

Private Sub btnDisplayFile_Click(...) Handles btnDisplayFile.Click
  'Display the contents of the file Pioneers.txt in a list box
  Dim sr As IO.StreamReader = IO.File.OpenText("Pioneers.txt")
  lstNames.Items.Clear()
  Do Until sr.EndOfStream
    lstNames.Items.Add(sr.ReadLine)
  Loop
  sr.Close()
End Sub
```

[Run, click on the first button, close the message dialog box, and then click on the second button.]

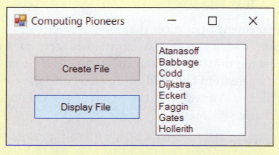

■ Adding Items to a Text File

Data can be added to the end of an existing text file with the following steps:

1. Execute the statement

   ```
   Dim swVar As IO.StreamWriter = IO.File.AppendText(filespec)
   ```

   where **swVar** is a variable name and *filespec* identifies the file. This process is said to **open a file for append**. It allows data to be output and recorded at the end of the specified file. If *filespec* consists only of a filename (that is, if no path is given), Visual Basic will look for the file in the program's *bin\Debug* folder.

2. Place data into the file with the WriteLine method.

3. After all the data have been recorded into the file, close the file with the statement

   ```
   swVar.Close()
   ```

The IO.File.AppendText option is used to add data to an existing file. However, it also can be used to create a new file. If the file does not exist, then the IO.File.AppendText option creates the file.

The three states "open for input", "open for output", and "open for append" are referred to as **modes**. A file should not be open in two modes at the same time. For instance, after a file has been opened for output and data have been written to it, the file should be closed before being opened for input. Had the statement **swVar.Close()** in Example 2 been omitted, then the program might crash when the second button is clicked on.

■ The Exists Function

An attempt to open a nonexistent file for input terminates the program with a FileNotFound-Exception message box, stating that the file could not be found. There is a function that tells us whether a certain file already exists. If the value of

```
IO.File.Exists(filespec)
```

is True, then the specified file exists. Therefore, prudence dictates that files be opened for input with code such as

```
Dim sr As IO.StreamReader
If IO.File.Exists(filespec) Then
  sr = IO.File.OpenText(filespec)
Else
  message = "Either no file has yet been created or the file "
  message &= filespec & " is not where expected."
  MessageBox.Show(message, "File Not Found")
End If
```

■ Altering Items in a Text File

There is one file-management operation that we have yet to discuss: changing or deleting an item of information from a text file. An individual item of a file cannot be changed or deleted directly. A new file must be created by reading each item from the original file and recording it, with the single item changed or deleted, into the new file. The old file is then erased, and the new file is renamed with the name of the original file. Regarding these last two tasks, the Visual Basic statement

```
IO.File.Delete(filespec)
```

removes the specified file from the disk, and the statement

`IO.File.Move(`*`oldfilespec,newfilespec`*`)`

changes the filespec of a file. *Note 1:* The IO.File.Delete and IO.File.Move methods cannot be used with open files; doing so generates an exception. *Note 2:* Nothing happens if the file referenced in an IO.File.Delete method doesn't exist. However, a nonexistent *oldfilespec* in an IO.File.Move method generates an exception.

■ System.IO Namespace

Creating a program that has extensive file handling can be simplified by placing the statement

`Imports System.IO`

at the top of the Code Editor, before the **Class** *frmName* statement. Then there is no need to insert the prefix "*IO.*" before the words StreamReader, StreamWriter, and File.

 Example 3   **File of Names** The following program manages Names.txt, a file of names. The Boolean function IsInFile returns the value True if the file Names.txt exists and the name entered in the text box is in the file.

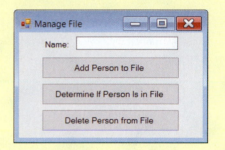

OBJECT	PROPERTY	SETTING
frmNames	Text	Manage File
lblName	Text	Name:
txtName		
btnAdd	Text	Add Person to File
btnDetermine	Text	Determine If Person Is in File
btnDelete	Text	Delete Person from File

```
Imports System.IO        'Appears at top of Code Editor

Private Sub btnAdd_Click(...) Handles btnAdd.Click
  'Add a person's name to the file
  Dim person As String = txtName.Text
  If person <> "" Then
    If IsInFile(person) Then
      MessageBox.Show(person & " is already in the file.", "Alert")
    Else
      Dim sw As StreamWriter = File.AppendText("Names.txt")
      sw.WriteLine(person)
      sw.Close()
      MessageBox.Show(person & " added to file.", "Name Added")
      txtName.Clear()
      txtName.Focus()
    End If
  Else
    MessageBox.Show("You must enter a name.", "Information Incomplete")
  End If
End Sub

Private Sub btnDetermine_Click(...) Handles btnDetermine.Click
  'Determine if a person is in the file
  Dim person As String = txtName.Text
  If person <> "" Then
```

```
      If IsInFile(person) Then
        MessageBox.Show(person & " is in the file.", "Yes")
      Else
        MessageBox.Show(person & " is not in the file.", "No")
      End If
    Else
      MessageBox.Show("You must enter a name.", "Information Incomplete")
    End If
    txtName.Clear()
    txtName.Focus()
  End Sub

  Private Sub btnDelete_Click(...) Handles btnDelete.Click
    'Remove the person in text box from the file
    Dim person As String = txtName.Text
    If person <> "" Then
      If IsInFile(person) Then
        Dim sr As StreamReader = File.OpenText("Names.txt")
        Dim sw As StreamWriter = File.CreateText("Temp.txt")
        Dim individual As String
        Do Until sr.EndOfStream
          individual = sr.ReadLine
          If individual <> person Then
            sw.WriteLine(individual)
          End If
        Loop
        sr.Close()
        sw.Close()
        File.Delete("Names.txt")
        File.Move("Temp.txt", "Names.txt")
        MessageBox.Show(person & " removed from file.", "Name Removed")
      Else
        MessageBox.Show(person & " is not in the file.", "Name Not Found")
      End If
    Else
      MessageBox.Show("You must enter a name.", "Information Incomplete")
    End If
    txtName.Clear()
    txtName.Focus()
  End Sub

  Function IsInFile(person As String) As Boolean
    If File.Exists("Names.txt") Then
      Dim sr As StreamReader = File.OpenText("Names.txt")
      Dim individual As String
      Do Until sr.EndOfStream
        individual = sr.ReadLine
        If individual = person Then
          sr.Close()
          Return True
        End If
      Loop
      sr.Close()
    End If
    Return False
  End Function
```

[Run, add some names, delete some names, and search for some names. After terminating the program, click on the *Refresh* button in the Solution Explorer window, click on the *View All Files* button, and look at Names.txt in the *bin\Debug* subfolder.]

■ Structured Exception Handling

VideoNote
Exception
Handling

There are two categories of problems that a program may encounter when it executes. The first is a *logic error*, which is caused by code that does not perform as intended. Common examples of logic errors are using the wrong formula and accessing the wrong property value. The second category is an *exception*, which typically occurs due to circumstances beyond the program's control. Two situations where exceptions occur are when invalid data are input and when a file cannot be accessed. (In Chapter 4, we showed a way to prevent invalid-data exceptions from occurring.) For example, if a user enters a word when the program prompts for a number, an exception is generated and the program terminates abruptly. In this situation, the programmer did not employ faulty logic or mistype. If the user had followed the directions, no problem would have occurred. Even though the user is at fault, however, it is still the programmer's responsibility to anticipate exceptions and to include code to work around their occurrence.

The Visual Studio environment contains powerful tools that programmers can use to find and correct bugs. These debugging tools are discussed extensively in Appendix D. This section describes techniques used to anticipate and deal with exceptions (in programming terms, this is called "handling exceptions").

An unexpected problem causes Visual Basic to raise an exception. If the programmer does not explicitly include exception-handling code in the program, then Visual Basic handles an exception with a default handler. This handler terminates execution, displays the exception's message in a window, and highlights the line of code where the exception occurred. Consider a program that contains the following code:

```
Dim taxCredit As Double

Private Sub btnCompute_Click(...) Handles btnCompute.Click
  Dim numDependents As Integer
  numDependents = CInt(InputBox("How many dependents?"))
  taxCredit = 1000 * numDependents
End Sub
```

A user with no dependents might leave the input dialog box blank and click on the OK button. If so, Visual Basic terminates the program and displays the box shown in Fig. 8.9 on the next page. (The problem was caused by the fact that the default value in an input dialog box, the empty string, cannot be converted to an integer. Text boxes also have the empty string as their default value.) Visual Basic also highlights the fourth line of code, since the exception was thrown while executing the CInt function. The program also would have crashed had the user typed in an answer like "TWO".

A more robust program explicitly handles the previous exception by protecting the code in a Try-Catch-Finally block. This allows the program to continue regardless of whether or not an exception was thrown. The computer tries to execute the code in the Try block. As soon as an exception occurs, execution jumps to the code in the Catch block. Regardless of

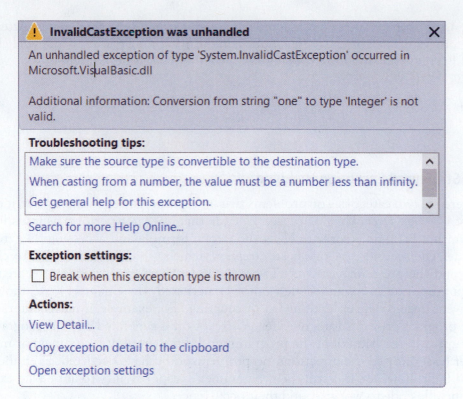

FIGURE 8.9 Exception handled by Visual Basic.

whether an exception occurred, the code in the Finally block is then executed. The following code is illustrative:

```
Dim taxCredit As Double

Private Sub btnCompute_Click(...) Handles btnCompute.Click
  Dim numDependents As Integer, message As String
  Try
    numDependents = CInt(InputBox("How many dependents?"))
  Catch
    message = "You did not answer the question with an " &
              "integer value. We will assume your answer is zero."
    MessageBox.Show(message, "Improper Response")
    numDependents = 0
  Finally
    taxCredit = 1000 * numDependents
  End Try
End Sub
```

This type of exception handling is known as **data validation**. It catches situations where invalid data cannot be converted to a particular type. An exception is thrown if the user enters data that cannot be converted to an integer using the CInt function. Table 8.1 lists several exceptions and descriptions of why they are thrown.

The Catch block above will be executed when *any* exception occurs. Visual Basic also allows Try-Catch-Finally blocks to have one or more specialized Catch clauses that handle only a specific type of exception. The general form of a specialized Catch clause is

```
Catch exc As ExceptionType
```

where the variable *exc* will be assigned the name of the exception. The code in this block will be executed only when the specified exception occurs.

TABLE 8.1	Some common exceptions.
Exception Name	**Description and Example**
ArgumentOutOfRangeException	An argument to a method or function is out of range. `str = "Goodbye".Substring(12,3)`

IndexOutOfRangeException	An array's subscript is out of range.
	 `Dim arr(3) As Integer`
	 `arr(5) = 2`

InvalidCastException	A value cannot be converted to another type. `Dim num As Integer = CInt("one")`

NullReferenceException	A method is called on a variable that is set to Nothing.
	 `Dim str As String, len As Integer`
	 `len = str.Length`

OverflowException	A number too big for the data type is assigned.
	 `Dim num As Integer = 2000000000`
	 `num = 2 * num`

IO.DirectoryNotFoundException	A file within a missing folder is accessed.
	 `Dim sr As IO.StreamReader =`
	 `IO.File.OpenText("C:\BadDir\File.txt")`

IO.FileNotFoundException	A missing file is accessed.
	 `Dim sr As IO.StreamReader =`
	 `IO.File.OpenText("Missing.txt")`

IO.IOException	Any file-handling exception, including those mentioned above. For instance, an attempt is made to delete or rename an open file, to change the name of a closed file to an already used name, or when a disk drive specified contains no disk. *Note:* If a series of IO exceptions is being tested with Catch clauses, this exception should be the last one tested. `IO.File.Move(filespec, AlreadyExistingName)`

The general form of a Try-Catch-Finally block is

```
Try
  normal code
Catch exc1 As FirstException
  exception-handling code for FirstException
Catch exc2 As SecondException
  exception-handling code for SecondException
  .
  .
Catch
  exception-handling code for any remaining exceptions
Finally
  clean-up code
End Try
```

The *normal code* is the code that you want to monitor for exceptions. If an exception occurs during execution of any of the statements in this section, Visual Basic transfers control to the code in one of the Catch blocks. As with a Select Case block, the Catch clauses are considered one at a time until the first matching exception is located. The last Catch clause in the preceding code functions like the Case Else clause. The *clean-up code* in the Finally block always executes last regardless of whether or not any *exception-handling code* has executed. In most situations, this code *cleans up* any resources such as files that were opened during the *normal code*. If clean-up is not necessary, then the Finally block can be omitted. However, to complete a Try block, a Catch block or a Finally block must appear.

In addition to data validation, a popular use of exception handling is to account for errors when accessing files. Visual Basic has the capability to access files stored on remote servers via the Internet. An exception is thrown if a desired file is missing (IO.FileNot-FoundException) or if the file cannot be read because the Internet connection between the computer and the server is broken (IO.IOException).

 Example 4 **Structured Exception Handling** The following program reads the first line from a file on a flash drive. The program expects the file to reside in the folder DataFiles. Note that the clean-up code, **sr.Close()**, in the Finally block is enclosed in a Try-Catch block of its own. This protects the Close method from any exceptions that might occur.

```
Private Sub btnDisplay_Click(...) Handles btnDisplay.Click
  Dim sr As IO.StreamReader
  Dim message As String
  Try
    sr = IO.File.OpenText("F:\DataFiles\USPres.txt")
    message = "The first president was " & sr.ReadLine & "."
    MessageBox.Show(message, "President")
  Catch exp As IO.FileNotFoundException
    message = "The file is not in the specified folder of the flash drive."
    MessageBox.Show(message, "Error")
  Catch exp As IO.IOException
    message = "Check to see if there is a flash drive in drive F:."
    MessageBox.Show(message, "Error")
  Finally
    Try
      sr.Close()
    Catch
      'Disregard any exceptions during the Close() method
    End Try
  End Try
End Sub
```

[Remove the flash drive from the F: drive, run the program, and then click on the button.]

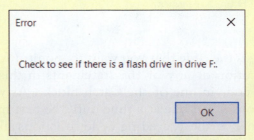

[Insert the flash drive containing the file USPres.txt (in the folder DataFiles) into the F: drive and then click on the button.]

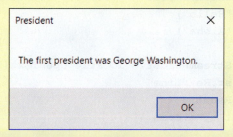

■ Comments

1. Any variable declared within a Try-Catch-Finally block has block scope. That is, it will not be available after the block terminates. Also, a variable declared in a Try block cannot be accessed in the corresponding Finally block.

2. Text files are also called *sequential files* because a SteamReader reads the records one at a time in sequence.

Practice Problems 8.2

1. Give three different ways to display the last record of the file USStates.txt in a message box.

2. Consider the following event procedure:

```
Private Sub btnCreate_Click(...) Handles btnCreate.Click
    Dim sw As IO.StreamWriter = IO.File.CreateText("ABC.txt")
    sw.WriteLine("abc")
End Sub
```

Describe the file ABC.txt after the button is clicked.

EXERCISES 8.2

In Exercises 1 through 10, determine the output displayed in the text box when the button is clicked.

```
1. Private Sub btnDisplay_Click(...) Handles btnDisplay.Click
    Dim salutation As String
    Dim sw As IO.StreamWriter = IO.File.CreateText("Greetings.txt")
    sw.WriteLine("Hello")
    sw.WriteLine("Aloha")
    sw.Close()
    Dim sr As IO.StreamReader = IO.File.OpenText("Greetings.txt")
    salutation = sr.ReadLine
    txtOutput.Text = salutation
    sr.Close()
End Sub
```

2.
```
Private Sub btnDisplay_Click(...) Handles btnDisplay.Click
    Dim salutation, welcome As String
    Dim sw As IO.StreamWriter = IO.File.CreateText("Greetings.txt")
    sw.WriteLine("Hello")
    sw.WriteLine("Aloha")
    sw.Close()
    Dim sr As IO.StreamReader = IO.File.OpenText("Greetings.txt")
    salutation = sr.ReadLine
    welcome = sr.ReadLine
    txtOutput.Text = welcome
    sr.Close()
End Sub
```

3.
```
Private Sub btnDisplay_Click(...) Handles btnDisplay.Click
    Dim salutation As String
    Dim sw As IO.StreamWriter = IO.File.CreateText("Greetings.txt")
    sw.WriteLine("Hello")
    sw.WriteLine("Aloha")
    sw.WriteLine("Bon Jour")
    sw.Close()
    Dim sr As IO.StreamReader = IO.File.OpenText("Greetings.txt")
    Do Until sr.EndOfStream
      salutation = sr.ReadLine
      txtOutput.Text = salutation
    Loop
    sr.Close()
End Sub
```

4. Assume that the contents of the file Greetings.txt are as shown in Figure 8.10.

```
Hello
Aloha
Bon Jour
```

FIGURE 8.10 Contents of the file Greetings.txt.

```
Private Sub btnDisplay_Click(...) Handles btnDisplay.Click
    Dim file, welcome As String
    file = "Greetings.txt"
    Dim sw As IO.StreamWriter = IO.File.AppendText(file)
    sw.WriteLine("Buenos Dias")
    sw.Close()
    Dim sr As IO.StreamReader = IO.File.OpenText(file)
    For i As Integer = 1 To 4
      welcome = sr.ReadLine
      txtOutput.Text = welcome
    Next
    sr.Close()
End Sub
```

5.
```vb
Private Sub btnDisplay_Click(...) Handles btnDisplay.Click
    Dim num As Integer
    'Assume that txtBox is empty
    Try
        num = CInt(txtBox.Text)
        txtOutput.Text = "Your number is " & num
    Catch
        txtOutput.Text = "You must enter a number."
    End Try
End Sub
```

6.
```vb
Private Sub btnDisplay_Click(...) Handles btnDisplay.Click
    Dim nafta() As String = {"Canada", "United States", "Mexico"}
    Try
        txtOutput.Text = "The third member of NAFTA is " & nafta(3)
    Catch exc As IndexOutOfRangeException
        txtOutput.Text = "Error occurred."
    End Try
End Sub
```

7.
```vb
Private Sub btnDisplay_Click(...) Handles btnDisplay.Click
    Try
        Dim usPop As Integer = 315000000    'Approx population of U.S.
        Dim worldPop As Integer
        worldPop = 21 * usPop
        txtOutput.Text = CStr(worldPop)
    Catch exc As ArgumentOutOfRangeException
        txtOutput.Text = "Oops"
    Catch exc As OverflowException
        txtOutput.Text = "Error occurred."
    End Try
End Sub
```

8.
```vb
Private Sub btnDisplay_Click(...) Handles btnDisplay.Click
    Dim flower As String = "Bougainvillea", lastLetter As String
    Try
        lastLetter = flower.Substring(14, 1)
        txtOutput.Text = lastLetter
    Catch exc As InvalidCastException
        txtOutput.Text = "Oops"
    Catch exc As ArgumentOutOfRangeException
        txtOutput.Text = "Error occurred."
    End Try
End Sub
```

9. Assume that the file Ages.txt is located in the *bin\Debug* subfolder of the folder *bin* and the first line of the file is "Twenty-one".
```vb
Private Sub btnDisplay_Click(...) Handles btnDisplay.Click
    Dim sr As IO.StreamReader
    Dim age As Integer
    Try
        sr = IO.File.OpenText("Ages.txt")     'FileNotFound if fails
        age = CInt(sr.ReadLine)                'InvalidCast if fails
```

```
      txtOutput.Text = "Age is " & age
    Catch exc As IO.FileNotFoundException
      txtOutput.Text = "File Ages.txt not found"
    Catch exc As InvalidCastException
      txtOutput.Text = "File Ages.txt contains an invalid age."
    Finally
      Try
        sr.Close() 'This code executes no matter what happens above.
      Catch
        'Disregard any exceptions thrown during the Close() method
      End Try
    End Try
  End Sub
```

10. Redo Exercise 9 with the assumption that the file Ages.txt is not located in the *bin\Debug* subfolder of the folder *bin*.

11. Assume that the contents of the file Greetings.txt are as shown in Figure 8.10 (on page 424). What is the effect of the following program?

```
Private Sub btnDisplay_Click(...) Handles btnDisplay.Click
  Dim g As String
  Dim sr As IO.StreamReader = IO.File.OpenText("Greetings.txt")
  Dim sw As IO.StreamWriter = IO.File.CreateText("Welcome.txt")
  Do Until sr.EndOfStream
    g = sr.ReadLine
    If (g <> "Aloha") Then
      sw.WriteLine(g)
    End If
  Loop
  sr.Close()
  sw.Close()
End Sub
```

12. Assume that the file Names.txt contains a list of names in alphabetical order. What is the effect of the Mystery function?

```
Private Sub btnFind_Click(...) Handles btnFind.Click
  MessageBox.Show(CStr(Mystery("Laura")))
End Sub

Function Mystery(name As String) As Boolean
  Dim sr As IO.StreamReader = IO.File.OpenText("Names.txt")
  Dim inputName As String
  Do Until sr.EndOfStream
    inputName = sr.ReadLine
    If inputName = name Then
      Return True
    ElseIf inputName > name Then
      Return False
    End If
  Loop
  Return False
End Function
```

In Exercises 13 through 18, identify any errors. Assume that the contents of the file Greetings.txt are as shown in Fig. 8.10.

13.
```
Private Sub btnDisplay_Click(...) Handles btnDisplay.Click
    Dim sw As IO.StreamWriter = IO.File.AppendText(Greetings.txt)
    sw.WriteLine("Guten Tag")
    sw.Close()
End Sub
```

14.
```
Private Sub btnDisplay_Click(...) Handles btnDisplay.Click
    Dim term As String
    Dim sw As IO.StreamWriter = IO.File.CreateText("Greetings.txt")
    term = sw.Readline
    txtOutput.Text = term
    sw.Close()
End Sub
```

15.
```
Private Sub btnDisplay_Click(...) Handles btnDisplay.Click
    'Copy the contents of the file Greetings.txt into the file NewGreet.txt
    Dim name, greeting As String
    Dim sr As IO.StreamReader = IO.File.OpenText("Greetings.txt")
    name = "NewGreet.txt"
    Dim sw As IO.StreamWriter = IO.File.CreateText("name")
    Do Until sr.EndOfStream
      greeting = sr.ReadLine
      sw.WriteLine(greeting)
    Loop
    sr.Close()
    sw.Close()
End Sub
```

16.
```
Private Sub btnDisplay_Click(...) Handles btnDisplay.Click
    Dim sw As IO.StreamReader = IO.File.CreateText("Greetings.txt")
    "Greetings.txt".Close()
End Sub
```

17.
```
Private Sub btnDisplay_Click(...) Handles btnDisplay.Click
    Try
      Dim age As Integer
      age = CInt(InputBox("Enter your age."))
    Catch
      MessageBox.Show("Invalid age.")
    End Try
    MessageBox.Show("You are " & age & " years old")
End Sub
```

18.
```
Private Sub btnDisplay_Click(...) Handles btnDisplay.Click
    Dim sw As IO.StreamWriter
    Try
      sw = IO.File.CreateFile("E:\Lakes.txt")
    Catch IO.IOException
      MessageBox.Show("Is there a CD in the F: drive?")
    End Try
    sw.Close()
End Sub
```

Exercises 19 through 25 are related and use the data in Table 8.2. The file created in Exercise 19 should be used in Exercises 20 through 25.

19. **Cowboys** Write a program to create the text file Cowboy.txt containing the information in Table 8.2.

TABLE 8.2	Prices paid by cowboys for certain items in the mid-1800s.
Colt Peacemaker	12.20
Holster	2.00
Levi Strauss jeans	1.35
Saddle	40.00
Stetson	10.00

20. **Cowboys** Suppose the price of saddles is reduced by 20%. Use the file Cowboy.txt to create a file, Cowboy2.txt, containing the new price list.

21. **Cowboys** Write a program to add the data Winchester Rifle, 20.50 to the end of the file Cowboy.txt.

22. **Cowboys** Suppose an order is placed for 3 Colt Peacemakers, 2 Holsters, 10 pairs of Levi Strauss jeans, 1 Saddle, and 4 Stetsons. Write a program to perform the following tasks:

   (a) Create the file Order.txt to hold the numbers 3, 2, 10, 1, and 4.
   (b) Use the files Cowboy.txt and Order.txt to display a sales receipt giving the quantity, name, and cost for each item ordered. See Fig. 8.11.
   (c) Compute the total cost of the items and display it at the end of the sales receipt.

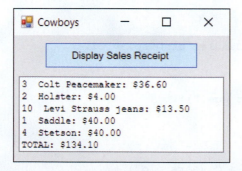

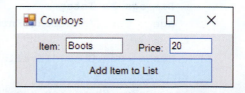

FIGURE 8.11   Outcome of Exercise 22.   FIGURE 8.12   Possible outcome of Exercise 23.

23. **Cowboys** Write a program to request an additional item and price from the user and then create a file called Cowboy2.txt containing the information in the file Cowboy.txt with the additional item (and price) inserted in its proper alphabetical sequence. See Fig. 8.12. Run the program for both of the following data items: Boots, 20.00 and Horse, 35.00.

24. Cowboys Write a program to allow additional items and prices to be input by the user and added to the end of the file Cowboy.txt. Include a method to terminate the process. See Fig. 8.13.

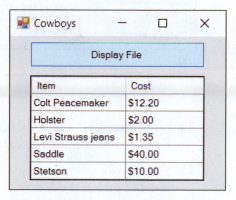

FIGURE 8.13 Outcome of Exercise 24.

FIGURE 8.14 Outcome of Exercise 25.

25. Cowboys Write a program using a StreamReader that displays the contents of the file Cowboy.txt in a DataGridView control. See Fig. 8.14.

26. Structured Exception Handling Visual Basic cannot delete a file that is open. Attempting to do so generates an exception. Write a short program that uses structured exception handling to handle such an exception.

In Exercises 27 through 32, write a program to carry out the task without using arrays or LINQ. Assume that the file Numbers.txt contains a list of integers.

27. Numbers Display the number of lines in the file Numbers.txt.

28. Numbers Display the largest number in the file Numbers.txt.

29. Numbers Display the smallest number in the file Numbers.txt.

30. Numbers Display the sum of the numbers in the file Numbers.txt.

31. Numbers Display the average of the numbers in the file Numbers.txt.

32. Numbers Display the last number in the file Numbers.txt.

Write the programs in Exercises 33 through 36 without using LINQ or the ReadAll-Lines statement. Use the file StatesBFNC.txt that contains the name, state bird, state flower, nickname, and capital of each state in the United States. The states are listed in alphabetical order. The first three lines of the file are

```
Alabama,Yellowhammer,Camellia,Cotton State,Montgomery
Alaska,Willow ptarmigan,Forget-me-not,The Last Frontier,Juneau
Arizona,Cactus wren,Saguaro cactus,Grand Canyon State,Phoenix
```

33. U.S. States Write a program using the file StatesBFNC.txt that fills a list box with the names of the states and then displays the state's bird, flower, nickname, and capital when the user clicks on a state in the list box. See Fig. 8.15 on the next page.

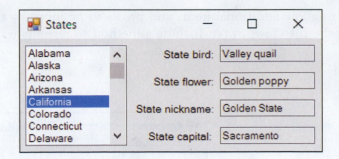

FIGURE 8.15 Possible outcome of Exercise 33.   **FIGURE 8.16** Outcome of Exercise 34.

34. **State Flowers**   Write a program using the file StatesBFNC.txt that displays the state flowers that contain the word *rose*. See Fig. 8.16.

35. **State Birds**   Write a program using the file StatesBFNC.txt that displays the state birds in a list box and the number of different state birds. Each bird should appear once in the list box and the birds should be in alphabetical order. See Fig. 8.17.

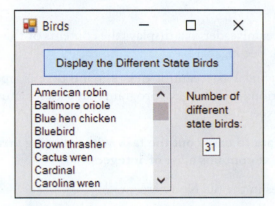

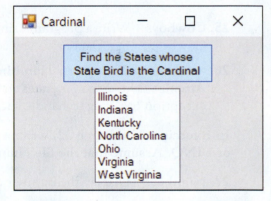

FIGURE 8.17 Outcome of Exercise 35.   **FIGURE 8.18** Outcome of Exercise 36.

36. **State Birds**   Write a program using the file StatesBFNC.txt that displays the names of the states whose state bird is the cardinal. See Fig. 8.18.

37. **Gettysburg Address**   The file Gettysburg.txt contains the entire Gettysburg Address as a single line. Write a program that displays the Gettysburg Address in a message box. See Fig. 8.19.

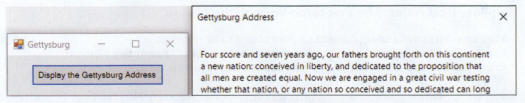

FIGURE 8.19 Outcome of Exercise 37.

38. Gettysburg Address The file Gettysburg.txt contains the entire Gettysburg Address as a single line. Write a program that analyzes the Gettysburg Address as shown in Fig. 8.20. *Hint:* Use the Split method to count the number of words. For the remaining analysis results, first convert the text to uppercase letters. The ANSI values of the uppercase letters will range from 65 to 90 (see Appendix A). Create an integer array of 26 elements and assign the number of times a letter occurs to the element numbered (Asc(letter) − 65).

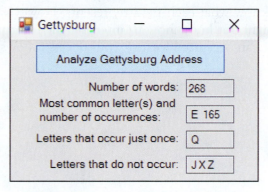

FIGURE 8.20 Outcome of Exercise 38.

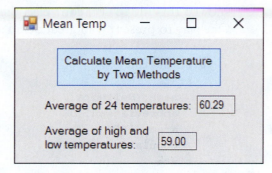

FIGURE 8.21 Outcome of Exercise 39.

39. Mean Temperature There are two commonly used methods for calculating the mean temperature for a day. One method is to calculate the average of 24 temperatures taken once each hour. The other method is to simply calculate the average of the high and low temperatures for the day. The file Temperatures.txt contains 24 temperatures taken once each hour. Write a program that uses the file to calculate the mean temperature with each method. See Fig. 8.21. The program should make just one pass through the file.

Solutions to Practice Problems 8.2

1. *First:*
```
Dim sr As IO.StreamReader = IO.File.OpenText("USStates.txt")
Dim temp As String = ""
Do Until sr.EndOfStream
  temp = sr.ReadLine
Loop
MessageBox.Show(temp)
sr.Close()
```

Second:
```
Dim states() As String = IO.File.ReadAllLines("USStates.txt")
MessageBox.Show(states.Last)
```

Third:
```
Dim states() As String = IO.File.ReadAllLines("USStates.txt")
MessageBox.Show(states(states.Count - 1))
```

2. The file ABC.txt will be present in the program's *bin\Debug* folder. However, the file will be empty. In order for the string *abc* to be placed in the file, the statement **sw.Close()** must be executed.

8.3 XML

As we have seen, CSV files are quite useful. However, the expansion of the Internet required a structured format for exchanging data. The World Wide Web Consortium recommended a format called XML (eXtensible Markup Language) to be that standard.

Consider the CSV file USStates.txt. The two lines of the file are

```
Delaware,DE,1954,941875
Pennsylvania,PA,44817,12856989
```

We are familiar with these records and know what each field represents. However, if we showed this file to someone else, they might not know how to interpret the information. One way to present it in great detail and in an organized format would be as follows:

```
U.S. States
  state
    name: Delaware
    abbreviation: DE
    area: 1954
    population: 941875
  state
    name: Pennsylvania
    abbreviation: PA
    area: 44817
    population: 12856989
```

■ Format of XML Files

The XML format for the state data, which has the look and feel of the presentation above, is as follows:

```
<?xml version='1.0'?>
<!-- This file contains data on two of the 50 U.S. states.-->
<us_states>
  <state>
    <name>Delaware</name>
    <abbreviation>DE</abbreviation>
    <area>1954</area>
    <population>941875</population>
  </state>
  <state>
    <name>Pennsylvania</name>
    <abbreviation>PA</abbreviation>
    <area>44817</area>
    <population>12856989</population>
  </state>
</us_states>
```

■ Comments on XML Format

1. Don't be concerned about the colorization. If the file is created in the Visual Basic IDE and given the extension *xml*, Visual Basic will automatically color it.

2. The first line identifies the format of the file.

3. The second line is a comment and is treated like any Visual Basic comment. It may appear anywhere in the file, is colored green, and will be totally ignored by any program accessing the file. Comments start with `<!--` and end with `-->`.

4. A line such as `<area>1954</area>` is called an **element** and the bracketed entities are called **tags**. Specifically, `<area>` is the **start tag** for the element and `</area>` is the **end tag**. The two tags are identical except for the presence of a forward slash (/) following the less-than sign in the end tag. The word inside the brackets, in this case *area*, is called the **name of the element**. The text surrounded by the two tags, in this case 1954, is called the **content** of the element.

5. Element names are case sensitive. For instance, the tag `<Area>` is different than the tag `<area>`. Also, start and end tags must have the same case.

6. Element names should convey the meaning of the content of the element. Element names cannot start with a number or punctuation character and can contain numbers and characters. However, they cannot contain spaces and cannot start with the letters *xml*.

7. In the XML file above, the content of the elements *name*, *abbreviation*, *area*, and *population* is text. However, the content of an element can be other elements. For instance, in the XML file above,

```
<state>
  <name>Delaware</name>
  <abbreviation>DE</abbreviation>
  <area>1954</area>
  <population>941875</population>
</state>
```

is such an element. Its start tag is `<state>` and its end tag is `</state>`. The elements that constitute its content are said to be its **children**. For instance, we say that *name* is a child of *state*. We also say that *state* is a **parent** of *name*, and that *name* and *abbreviation* are **siblings**.

8. The element *us_states* is called the **root element** of the file. An XML file can have only one root element.

■ LINQ to XML

LINQ can be used with XML files in much the same way as with CSV files—but with three differences:

1. Instead of being loaded into an array, the file is loaded into an XElement object with a statement of the form

    `Dim xmlElementName As XElement = XElement.Load(filespec)`

2. The From clause references the elements to be considered—namely, the children of each child of the root element. Children are referenced with the Descendants method.

3. Instead of using the Split method to extract the value of a field, queries use an expression of the form `<childName>.Value`.

 Example 1 **U.S. States** The file USStates.xml extends the records shown above to all 50 states. The following program uses the file to display the population densities of the states that begin with the word "*North*". The states are displayed in decreasing order of their densities.

```vb
Private Sub btnDisplay_Click(...) Handles btnDisplay.Click
  Dim stateData As XElement= XElement.Load("USStates.xml")
  Dim query = From st In stateData.Descendants("state")
              Let name = st.<name>.Value
              Let pop = CInt(st.<population>.Value)
              Let area = CInt(st.<area>.Value)
              Let density = pop / area
              Let formattedDensity = density.ToString("N")
              Order By density Descending
              Where name.StartsWith("North")
              Select name, formattedDensity
  dgvStates.DataSource = query.ToList
  dgvStates.CurrentCell = Nothing
  dgvStates.Columns("name").HeaderText = "State"
  dgvStates.Columns("formattedDensity").HeaderText = "Density"
End Sub
```

[Run, and click on the button.]

U.S. States	—	☐	✕

Display States		
State	Density	
North Carolina	205.78	
North Dakota	10.37	

Example 2   **U.S. States** The following rewrite of Example 7 in Section 8.1 uses an XML file rather than a CSV file. The variable *stateData* is given class scope so that the XML file will not be reread from disk each time a new state abbreviation is entered.

```vb
Dim stateData As XElement = XElement.Load("USStates.xml")

Private Sub btnFind_Click(...) Handles btnFind.Click
  Dim query = From st In stateData.Descendants("state")
              Let name = st.<name>.Value
              Let abbr = st.<abbreviation>.Value
              Where abbr = mtbAbbr.Text.ToUpper
              Select name
  If query.Count = 1 Then
    txtName.Text = query.First
  Else
    Dim str As String = " is not a valid state abbreviation."
    MessageBox.Show(mtbAbbr.Text.ToUpper & str, "Error")
    mtbAbbr.Clear()
    mtbAbbr.Focus()
  End If
End Sub
```

[Run, enter a state abbreviation into the masked text box, and click on the button.]

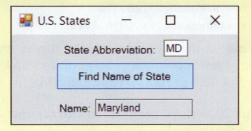

■ Comment

1. The content of an element can contain any characters except for "**<**" and "**&**". These characters must be replaced with "**<**" and "**&**", respectively. For instance, the following two lines might appear in XML files:

```
<college>William &amp; Mary</college>
<inequality>x &lt; 7</inequality>
```

Practice Problems 8.3

1. Suppose the query in Example 1 is replaced by

```
Dim query = From st In stateData.Descendants("state")
            Let name = st.<name>.Value
            Let pop = st.<population>.Value
            Order By pop Descending
            Select name, pop
```

Explain why this query will not display the states in descending order of their population.

2. Consider Example 2. Suppose the last line of the query is changed to

```
Select name, abbr
```

What change would have to be made to the following line?

```
txtName.Text = query.First
```

EXERCISES 8.3

In Exercises 1 through 6, determine if the name is a proper name for an element of an XML file.

1. 7up   2. vice president   3. _77   4. Fred   5. xmlTitle   6. ?mark

In Exercises 7 through 10, determine if the expression is a proper element.

7. \<begin\>Hello\</end\>   8. \<Team\>Oakland Raiders\</team\>
9. \<city\>New York\<city\>   10. \<first name\>John\</first name\>

11. **U.S. Presidents**   The first two lines of the file AgeAtInaug.txt are

```
George Washington,57
John Adams,61
```

where each record has two fields—name of president and his age when inaugurated. Create an XML file (with a text editor) containing these two records.

12. Supreme Court The first two lines of the file Justices.txt are

```
Samuel,Alito,George W. Bush,NJ,2006,0
Henry,Baldwin,Andrew Jackson,PA,1830,1844
```

where each record has six fields—first name, last name, appointing president, the state from which the justice was appointed, year appointed, and year they left the court. (For current justices, the last field is set to 0.) Create an XML file containing these two records.

In Exercises 13 through 20, write a program to extract and display the requested information from the file USStates.xml.

13. U.S. States The total population of the United States in the year 2015.

14. U.S. States The total area of the United States.

15. U.S. States The population density of the United States in the year 2015.

16. U.S. States The state (or states) with the longest name.

17. U.S. States The states with area greater than 100,000 square miles. Display both the name and area of each state, with the states in decreasing order by area. See Fig. 8.22.

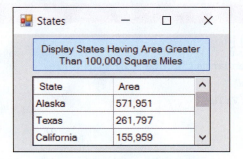

FIGURE 8.22 Outcome of Exercise 17.

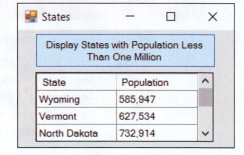

FIGURE 8.23 Outcome of Exercise 18.

18. U.S. States The states with population less than one million. Display both the name and population of each state, with the states in increasing order by population. See Fig. 8.23.

19. U.S. States The states whose names contain the most different vowels. See Fig. 8.24.

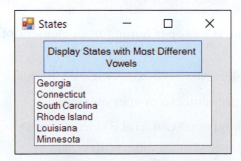

FIGURE 8.24 Outcome of Exercise 19.

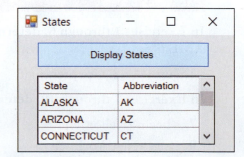

FIGURE 8.25 Outcome of Exercise 20.

20. U.S. States The states whose abbreviations are different than the first two letters of their names. Display both the name and abbreviation of each state in alphabetical order by the abbreviation. See Fig. 8.25.

The file Colleges.xml contains data on the colleges founded before 1800. The first thirteen lines of the file are shown in Fig. 8.26. Use this file in Exercises 21 through 24.

```
<?xml version='1.0'?>
<!-- This file contains data on the earliest U.S. colleges -->
<colleges>
  <college>
    <name>Harvard U.</name>
    <state>MA</state>
    <yearFounded>1636</yearFounded>
  </college>
  <college>
    <name>William & Mary</name>
    <state>VA</state>
    <yearFounded>1693</yearFounded>
  </college>
```

FIGURE 8.26 Beginning of the file Colleges.xml.

21. Colleges Write a program that displays the colleges alphabetically ordered (along with their year founded) that are in the state specified in a masked text box. See Fig. 8.27.

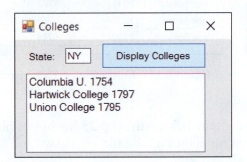

FIGURE 8.27 Possible outcome of Exercise 21.

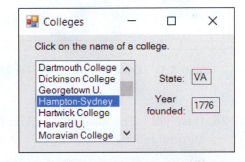

FIGURE 8.28 Possible outcome of Exercise 22.

22. Colleges Write a program that provides information about a college selected from a list box by the user. The colleges should be displayed in alphabetical order. See Fig. 8.28.

23. Colleges Write a program that fills a list box with the years before 1800 in which colleges were founded. When the user selects a year, the colleges founded that year should be displayed in another list box. See Fig. 8.29.

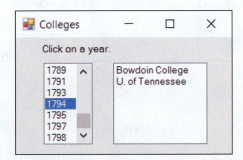

FIGURE 8.29 Possible outcome of Exercise 23.

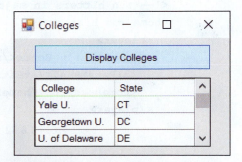

FIGURE 8.30 Outcome of Exercise 24.

24. Colleges Write a program that displays the colleges and their states in a DataGridView control where the colleges are alphabetically ordered by their state abbreviations and secondarily by the year they were founded. See Fig. 8.30.

25. U.S. Senate The CSV file Senate114.txt contains a record for each member of the 114th U.S. Senate. (The 114th U.S. Senate was installed in 2015.) Each record contains three fields—name, state, and party affiliation. Some records in the files are

```
John McCain,Arizona,R
Bernie Sanders,Vermont,I
Kirsten Gillibrand,New York,D
```

(a) Write a program that uses the file Senate114.txt and creates an XML file containing the same information.

(b) Write a program that uses the XML file from part (a) to display the names, states, and party affiliation of all the senators in a DataGridView ordered by their state. See Fig. 8.31. The two senators from each state should be ordered by their first names.

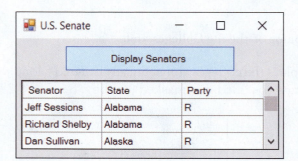

FIGURE 8.31 Outcome of Exercise 25(b).

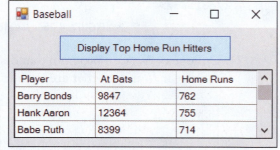

FIGURE 8.33 Outcome of Exercise 26(a).

26. Baseball The file Top25HR.xml contains statistics for the top 25 home-run hitters of all time in major league baseball. The first nine lines of the file are shown in Fig. 8.32.

(a) Write a program that displays the contents of this file in a DataGridView control in descending order by the number of home runs hit. See Fig. 8.33.

(b) Write a program that uses the file Top25HR.xml and creates a CSV file containing the same information.

```
<?xml version='1.0'?>
<!-- This file contains data on the all-time top 25 home -->
<!-- run hitters in major league baseball up through 2015. -->
<home_run_hitters>
   <player>
      <name>Barry Bonds</name>
      <atBats>9847</atBats>
      <homeRuns>762</homeRuns>
   </player>
```

FIGURE 8.32 Beginning of the file Top25HR.xml.

Solutions to Practice Problems 8.3

1. The problem is with the clause

```
Let pop = st.<population>.Value
```

Since there are no arithmetic operators or numeric conversion functions in the clause, local type inference will interpret *pop* to be a string variable. When the program is run, the first state listed will be Rhode Island, whose population is 998,000. The program will run as intended only if the clause is

```
Let pop = CDbl(st.<population>.Value)
```

2. The line would have to be changed to

```
txtName.Text = query.First.name
```

8.4 A Case Study: Recording Checks and Deposits

The purpose of this section is to take you through the design and implementation of a quality program for personal checkbook management. That a user-friendly checkbook management program can be written in less than four pages of code clearly shows Visual Basic's ability to improve the productivity of programmers. It is easy to imagine an entire finance program, similar to programs that have generated millions of dollars of sales, being written in only a few weeks by using Visual Basic!

■ Design of the Program

Though many commercial programs are available for personal financial management, they include so many bells and whistles that their original purposes—keeping track of transactions and reporting balances—have become obscured. The program in this section was designed specifically as a checkbook program. It keeps track of expenditures and deposits and produces a report. The program showcases many of the techniques and tools available in Visual Basic.

The general design goals for the program include the following abilities:

• Automatically enter the user's name on each check and deposit slip.
• Automatically provide the next consecutive check or deposit slip number. (The user can override this feature if necessary.)
• Automatically provide the date. (Again, this feature can be overridden.)
• For each check, record the payee, the amount, and optionally a memo.
• For each deposit slip, record the source, the amount, and optionally a memo.
• Display the current balance at all times.
• Produce a report detailing all transactions.

■ User Interface

With Visual Basic, we can place a replica of a check or deposit slip on the screen and let the user supply the information as if actually filling out a check or deposit slip. Figure 8.34 on the next page shows the form in its check mode. The DataGridView control at the bottom of the form will be used to display a report detailing all the transactions. The purposes of the four buttons and the text box above the DataGridView control are obvious.

The first time the program is run, the user is asked for his or her name, the starting balance, and the numbers of the first check and deposit slip. Suppose the user's name is David Schneider, the starting balance is $1000, and both the first check number and deposit slip number are 1. Figure 8.34 shows the form after the four pieces of information are entered. The upper part of the form looks like a check. The form has a color of light blue when in check mode. The Date box is automatically set to today's date but can be altered by the user. The user fills in the payee, amount, and optionally a memo. When the user clicks on the

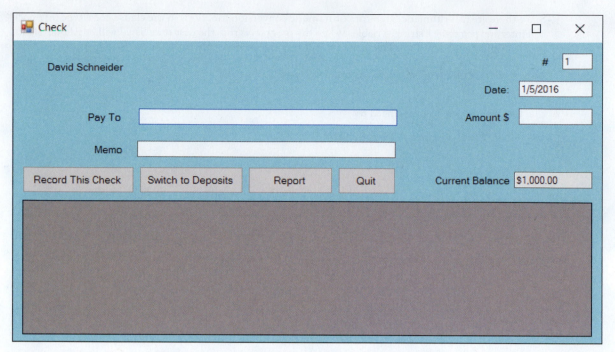

FIGURE 8.34 Template for entering a check.

Record This Check button, the information is written to a text file, the balance is updated, and check number 2 appears.

To record a deposit, the user clicks on the *Switch to Deposits* button. The form then appears as in Fig. 8.35. The form's title bar now reads Deposit Slip, the words Pay To change to Source, and the color of the form changes to light yellow. Also, in the buttons at the bottom of the slip, the words *Check* and *Deposit* are interchanged. A deposit is recorded in much the same way as a check. When the *Report* button is clicked on, a report similar to the one in Fig. 8.36 is displayed in the DataGridView control.

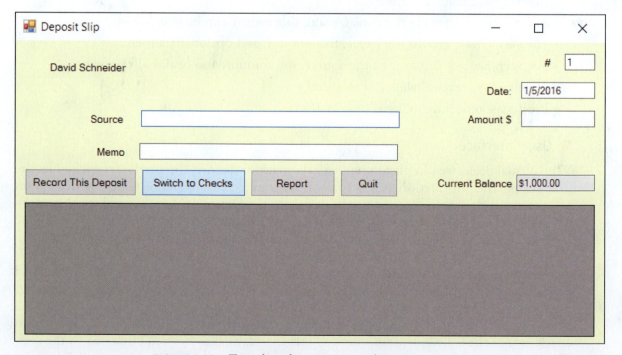

FIGURE 8.35 Template for entering a deposit.

Transaction Date	Description	Recipient or Source	Memo	Amount	Balance
6/2/2015	Check #1	Land's End	shirts	$75.95	$924.05
6/8/2015	Check #2	Whole Foods	groceries	$125.00	$799.05
7/22/2015	Deposit #1	Pearson	production costs	$245.00	$1,044.05
9/3/2015	Check #3	Politics & Prose	books	$79.05	$965.00
9/11/2015	Deposit #2	Staples	refund	$25.00	$990.00

FIGURE 8.36   Sample transaction report.

The common design for the check and deposit slip allows one set of controls to be used for both items. The text of the label lblName is set to the user's name, while the text of the label lblToFrom will change back and forth between Pay To and Source.

Table 8.3 lists the objects and their initial property settings. Because the program will always begin by displaying the next check, all the text for the labels and the BackColor property of the form could have been set at design time. We chose instead to leave these assignments to the SetupCheck method, which normally is used to switch from deposit entry to check entry but also can be called by the form's Load event procedure to prepare the initial mode (check or deposit) for the form.

The program uses CSV formatted text files named InitialInfo.txt and Transactions.txt. The file InitialInfo.txt consists of a single line with four comma-delimited pieces of information: the name to appear on the checks and deposit slips, the starting balance, the number of the first check, and the number of the first deposit slip. The file Transactions.txt contains a line for each transaction—that is, writing a check or making a deposit. Each transaction is recorded as a sequence of eight comma-delimited items: the type of transaction, the contents of txtToFrom, the current balance, the number of the last check, the number of the last deposit slip, the amount of money, the memo, and the date.

TABLE 8.3   **Objects and initial property settings for the checkbook management program.**

Object	Property	Setting
frmAccount		
lblName		
lblNum	Text	#
txtNum		
lblDate	Text	Date:
txtDate		
lblToFrom		
txtToFrom		
lblAmount	Text	Amount $
txtAmount		
lblMemo	Text	Memo
txtMemo		
btnRecord	Text	&Record This Check
btnMode	Text	&Switch to Deposits
btnReport	Text	Re&port
btnQuit	Text	&Quit
lblCurBal	Text	Current Balance
txtBalance	ReadOnly	True
dgvTransactions	RowHeaderVisible	False

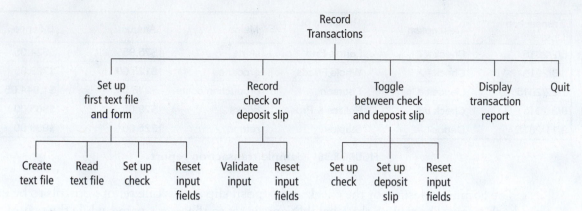

FIGURE 8.37 **Hierarchy chart for checkbook management program.**

■ Coding the Program

The second row of the hierarchy chart in Fig. 8.37 identifies the different events to which the program must respond. Table 8.4 lists the corresponding event procedures and the general procedures they call.

Let's examine each event procedure:

1. *frmAccount_Load* first calls the InitializeData Sub procedure to process the text file. This procedure first looks to see if the file InitialInfo.txt exists. If it does exist, the procedure uses it (along with possibly the last entry of Transactions.txt) to determine all information needed to proceed. If InitialInfo.txt does not exist, the Sub procedure prompts the user for the name to appear on the checks and deposit slips, the starting balance, and the numbers of the first check and deposit slip and then writes these items to the text file. The event procedure calls the SetupCheck Sub procedure next to set the transaction type to Check and sets the appropriate text and background color for a check. The event procedure then calls ResetInput, which initializes all the text boxes. The InitializeData Sub procedure employs structured exception handling to protect the code from invalid user input.

TABLE 8.4 **Tasks and their procedures.**

Task	Procedure
1. Set up first text file and form	frmAccount_Load
1.1 Create first text file	InitializeData
1.2 Read text files	InitializeData
1.3 Set up check	SetupCheck
1.4 Reset input fields	ResetInput
2. Record check or deposit slip	btnRecord_Click
2.1 Validate input	DataValid
2.2 Reset input fields	ResetInput
3. Toggle between check & deposit slip	btnMode_Click
3.1 Set up check	SetupCheck
3.2 Set up deposit slip	SetupDeposit
3.3 Reset input fields	ResetInput
4. Display transaction report	btnReport_Click
5. Quit	btnQuit_Click

2. **btnRecord_Click** first confirms that the required fields contain valid entries. This is accomplished by calling the function DataValid. If the value returned is True, then btnRecord_Click updates the current balance, opens the text file in append mode, writes eight pieces of data to the file, and then closes the file. When DataValid returns False, the function itself pops up a message box to tell the user where information is needed or invalid. The user must type in the information and then click on the *Record* button again. The DataValid function uses structured exception handling to ensure that the user's input is valid. If either the amount or number field is not a number, the InvalidCastException is thrown. The Catch block handles this exception by displaying an appropriate message asking the user to reenter the information.

3. **btnMode_Click** toggles back and forth from a check to a deposit slip. It calls SetupCheck, or its analog SetupDeposit, and then calls ResetInput.

4. **btnReport_Click** displays a complete history of all transactions, as shown in Fig. 8.36.

5. **btnQuit_Click** ends the program.

```vb
'Class-level named constants and variables
Const INIT_FILE As String = "InitialInfo.txt"
Const TRANS_FILE As String = "Transactions.txt"
'Variables used for each entry
Dim isCheck As Boolean
Dim nameOnChk As String    'name to appear on checks and deposit slips
Dim lastCkNum As Integer   'number of last check written
Dim lastDpNum As Integer   'number of last deposit slip written
Dim curBal As Decimal      'current balance in account

Private Sub frmAccount_Load(...) Handles MyBase.Load
  'Set the class-level variables.
  InitializeData()
  'Set the name and balance labels.
  lblName.Text = nameOnChk
  txtBalance.Text = curBal.ToString("C")
  'Set the date field to the current date.
  txtDate.Text = CStr(Today)
  SetupCheck()
  ResetInput()
End Sub


Private Sub InitializeData()
  If IO.File.Exists(INIT_FILE) Then
    Dim data() As String   'holds the data from a line of a file
    Dim initFileContents() As String = IO.File.ReadAllLines(INIT_FILE)
    'Split the single line of INIT_FILE using the delimiter.
    data = initFileContents.First.Split(","c)
    'Load the name to appear on checks, current balance, number of
    'last check written, and number of last deposit slip processed.
    nameOnChk = data(0)
    curBal = CDec(data(1))
    lastCkNum = CInt(data(2))
    lastDpNum = CInt(data(3))
    'Possibly update numeric values by looking at last record of TRANS_FILE
    If IO.File.Exists(TRANS_FILE) Then
      Dim transFileContents() As String = IO.File.ReadAllLines(TRANS_FILE)
      data = transFileContents.Last.Split(","c)
```

```vbnet
               curBal = CDec(data(2))
               lastCkNum = CInt(data(3))
               lastDpNum = CInt(data(4))
            End If
         Else
            'INIT_FILE does not exist, so get initial data from user
            Dim sw As IO.StreamWriter
            nameOnChk = InputBox("Name to appear on checks and deposit slips:")
            Try
               curBal = CDec(InputBox("Starting Balance:"))
               'Get numbers of last check and deposit slip
               lastCkNum = CInt(InputBox("Number of first check:")) - 1
               lastDpNum = CInt(InputBox("Number of first deposit slip:")) - 1
               'The single record in the text file records the name to
               'appear on checks plus the initial data for the account.
               Dim outputLine As String = nameOnChk & "," & curBal & "," &
                                   lastCkNum & "," & lastDpNum
               sw = IO.File.CreateText(INIT_FILE)
               sw.WriteLine(outputLine)
            Catch
               'If a number cannot be converted, then display message and quit.
               MessageBox.Show("Invalid number. Program terminating.", "Error")
               Me.Close()
            Finally
               'Close the writer no matter what happens above.
               sw.Close()
            End Try
         End If
   End Sub


   Private Sub btnRecord_Click(...) Handles btnRecord.Click
      'Store the input into the transactions file.
      Dim amt As Decimal
      Dim transType As String
      'Store only if all required fields are filled and valid
      If DataValid() Then
         amt = CDec(txtAmount.Text)
         'Adjust balance by amount depending on check or deposit slip mode
         If isCheck Then
            curBal -= amt
            lastCkNum = CInt(txtNum.Text)
            transType = "Check"
         Else
            curBal += amt
            lastDpNum = CInt(txtNum.Text)
            transType = "Deposit"
         End If
         txtBalance.Text = curBal.ToString("C")
         'String array contains information to be stored
         Dim transOutput() As String = {transType, txtToFrom.Text,
            CStr(curBal), CStr(lastCkNum), CStr(lastDpNum), CStr(amt),
            txtMemo.Text, txtDate.Text}
         Dim sw As IO.StreamWriter = IO.File.AppendText(TRANS_FILE)
         'Append the info to the text file, separated by the delimiter
```

```vb
      sw.WriteLine(Join(transOutput, ","c))
      sw.Close()
      'Reset input text boxes to blank for next entry
      ResetInput()
   End If
End Sub


Function DataValid() As Boolean
   'Return True if all data are valid, or display a message if not
   Dim errorMessage As String = ""
   'If one of the two essential pieces of information
   'is missing, assign its name to errorMessage.
   If txtToFrom.Text.Trim = "" Then
      If isCheck Then
         errorMessage = "Pay To"
      Else
         errorMessage = "Source"
      End If
      txtToFrom.Focus()
   ElseIf txtAmount.Text.Trim = "" Then
      errorMessage = "Amount"
      txtAmount.Focus()
   End If
   'If no errors yet, then check syntax of the two numerical fields
   If errorMessage = "" Then
      'Check syntax of the amount field (Double)
      Try
         If CDec(txtAmount.Text) <= 0 Then
            errorMessage = "The amount must be greater than zero."
            txtAmount.Focus()
         End If
      Catch exc As InvalidCastException
         errorMessage = "The amount " & txtAmount.Text & " is invalid."
         txtAmount.Focus()
      End Try
   Else
      errorMessage = "The '" & errorMessage & "' field must be filled."
   End If
   'Display error message if available
   If errorMessage = "" Then
      'All required data fields have been filled; recording can proceed
      Return True
   Else
      'Advise user of invalid data
      MessageBox.Show(errorMessage & " Please try again.")
      Return False
   End If
End Function


Private Sub btnMode_Click(...) Handles btnMode.Click
   'Toggle mode between Check and Deposit Slip
   If isCheck Then
      SetupDeposit()
```

```vbnet
      Else
         SetupCheck()
      End If
      'Set fields for next entry
      ResetInput()
   End Sub

   Sub SetupCheck()
      'Prepare form for the entry of a check
      isCheck = True
      Me.Text = "Check"   'set the title bar of the form
      lblToFrom.Text = "Pay To"
      btnRecord.Text = "&Record This Check"
      btnMode.Text = "&Switch to Deposits"
      Me.BackColor = Color.LightBlue
   End Sub

   Sub SetupDeposit()
      'Prepare form for the entry of a deposit
      isCheck = False
      Me.Text = "Deposit Slip"'set the title bar of the form
      lblToFrom.Text = "Source"
      btnRecord.Text = "&Record This Deposit"
      btnMode.Text = "&Switch to Checks"
      Me.BackColor = Color.LightYellow
   End Sub

   Sub ResetInput()
      'Reset all text entry fields except date
      txtToFrom.Clear()
      txtAmount.Clear()
      txtMemo.Clear()
      If isCheck Then
         'Make txtNum text box reflect next check number
         txtNum.Text = CStr(lastCkNum + 1)
      Else
         'Make txtNum text box reflect next deposit slip number
         txtNum.Text = CStr(lastDpNum + 1)
      End If
         'Set focus on To/From text box for the next entry
      txtToFrom.Focus()
   End Sub

   Private Sub btnReport_Click(...) Handles btnReport.Click
      If IO.File.Exists(TRANS_FILE) Then
         Dim transFileContents() As String = IO.File.ReadAllLines(TRANS_FILE)
         Dim query = From trans In transFileContents
                     Let data = trans.Split(","c)
                     Let transDate = CDate(data(7))
                     Let number = FormNumber(data(0), data(3), data(4))
                     Let toFrom = data(1)
                     Let Memo = data(6)
```

```vb
              Let Amount = (CDec(data(5))).ToString("C")
              Let Balance = (CDec(data(2))).ToString("C")
              Select transDate, number, toFrom, Memo, Amount, Balance
        dgvTransactions.DataSource = query.ToList
        dgvTransactions.CurrentCell = Nothing
        dgvTransactions.Columns("transDate").HeaderText = "Transaction Date"
        dgvTransactions.Columns("number").HeaderText = "Description"
        dgvTransactions.Columns("toFrom").HeaderText = "Recipient or Source"
    Else
        MessageBox.Show("There are no transactions to report.")
    End If
End Sub


Function FormNumber(type As String, checkNumber As String,
                    depositNumber As String) As String
    If type = "Check" Then
        Return "Check #" & checkNumber
    Else
        Return "Deposit #" & depositNumber
    End If
End Function


Private Sub btnQuit_Click(...) Handles btnQuit.Click
    Me.Close() 'exit program
End Sub
```

CHAPTER 8   SUMMARY

1. The *IO.File.WriteAllLines* method copies an array to a text file.

2. When data are stored in text files with the fields of each record separated by commas, LINQ can be used to sort, search, and reorganize the data with a little help from the Split method.

3. Arrays and queries can be combined with the set methods *Concat, Union, Intersect,* and *Except.*

4. When text files are opened, the program must specify whether they will be read using a *StreamReader* or written using a *StreamWriter.* Files used for input are specified with the IO.File.ReadText method. Output files can be created (IO.File.CreateText) or just added to (IO.File.AppendText). A line of data is written to a file with the WriteLine method and read from a file with the ReadLine method.

5. *Structured exception handling* can reduce the likelihood that a program will crash. If an exception occurs while the code in the Try block is executing, execution branches to the code in a Catch block that alerts the user of an error and provides a workaround. The Finally block contains code that executes regardless of whether an exception occurs.

6. *XML files* are text files of a special format that is popular for exchanging data over the Internet.

CHAPTER 8 PROGRAMMING PROJECTS

1. **Baseball** The file ALE.txt contains the information shown in Table 8.5. Write a program to use the file to produce a text file containing the information in Table 8.6 in which the baseball teams are in descending order by the percentage of games won.

TABLE 8.5	American League East games won and lost in 2015.	
Team	**Won**	**Lost**
Baltimore	81	81
Boston	78	84
New York	87	75
Tampa Bay	80	82
Toronto	93	69

TABLE 8.6	Final 2015 American League East standings.		
Team	**Won**	**Lost**	**Pct**
Toronto	93	69	0.574
New York	87	75	0.537
Baltimore	81	81	0.500
Tampa Bay	80	82	0.494
Boston	78	84	0.481

2. **U.S. Senate** The file Senate113.txt contains the members of the 113th U.S. Senate—that is, the Senate prior to the November 2014 election. Each record of the file consists of three fields—name, state, and party affiliation.[2] Some records in the file are as follows:

```
Richard Shelby,Alabama,R
Bernard Sanders,Vermont,I
Kristen Gillibrand,New York,D
```

The file RetiredSen.txt contains the records from the file Senate113.txt for senators who left the Senate after the November 2014 election due to retirement, defeat, death, or resignation. Some records in the file are as follows:

```
John Rockefeller,West Virginia,D
Tom Coburn,Oklahoma,R
Carl Levin,Michigan,D
```

The file NewSen.txt contains records for the senators who were newly elected in November 2014 or who were appointed to fill the seats of senators who left after the 2014 election. Some records in the file are as follows:

```
Shelly Capito,West Virginia,R
Steve Daines,Montana,R
Gary Peters,Michigan,D
```

(a) Write a program that uses the three files above to create the file Senate114.txt that contains records (each consisting of three fields) for the members of the 114th Senate where the members are ordered by state. Use this file in parts (b), (c), and (d).

---

[2]We refer to anyone who is neither a Republican nor a Democrat as Independent.

(b) Write a program that determines the number of senators of each party affiliation. See Fig. 8.38.

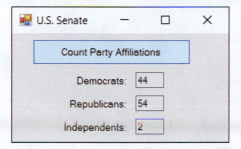

FIGURE 8.38   Outcome of Programming Project 2(b).

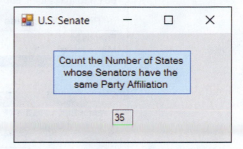

FIGURE 8.39   Outcome of Programming Project 2(c).

(c) Write a program that determines the number of states whose two senators have the same party affiliation. See Fig. 8.39. *Hint:* Use a procedure with the heading **Function SameParty(state As String) As Boolean**.

(d) Write a program that asks the user to select a state from a list box, and then displays the two senators from that state. See Fig. 8.40.

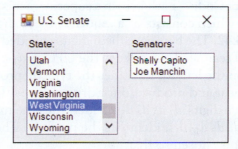

FIGURE 8.40   Possible outcome of Programming Project 2(d).

3. File of Names   The file Names.txt contains a list of names in alphabetical order. Write two programs that request a name from the user and insert the name into the list in its proper location. If it is already in the list, the name should not be inserted.

(a) Write the first program without using any arrays or LINQ; that is, use only a StreamReader and a StreamWriter.

(b) Write the second program using arrays and LINQ.

4. Telephone Directories   Write a program to create and maintain telephone directories. See Fig. 8.41 on the next page. Each telephone directory should be contained in a separate text file. In addition, a file named Directories.txt should hold the names of the telephone directories. At any time, names of all the telephone directories should be displayed in a list box. After a telephone directory is selected, it becomes the *current phone directory*. The following buttons should be available.

(a) Create a new telephone directory. (The filename should be provided by an input dialog box.)

(b) Add a listing (as given in text boxes) to the end of the current phone directory.

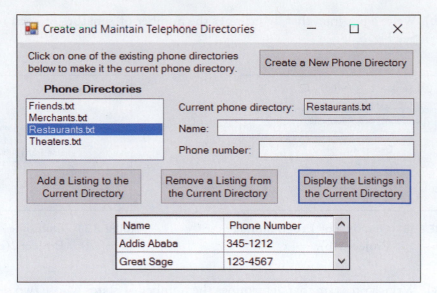

FIGURE 8.41   Possible outcome of Programming Project 4.

(c) Delete a name (as given in a text box) from the current phone directory.

(d) Display the names and phone numbers in the current phone directory. See Fig. 8.41.

5. **Universal Product Code**   Each item in a supermarket is identified by its Universal Product Code (UPC), which consists of a sequence of 12 digits appearing below a rectangle of bars. See Fig. 8.42. The bars have these digits encoded in them so that the UPC can be read by an optical scanner. Let's refer to the UPC as d_1-$d_2\ d_3\ d_4\ d_5\ d_6$-$d_7\ d_8\ d_9\ d_{10}\ d_{11}$-$d_{12}$. The single digit on the left, d_1, identifies the type of product (for instance, 0 for general groceries, 2 for meat and produce, 3 for drug and health products, and 5 for coupons). The first set of five digits, $d_2\ d_3\ d_4\ d_5\ d_6$, identifies the manufacturer, and the second set of five digits, $d_7\ d_8\ d_9\ d_{10}\ d_{11}$, identifies the product. The twelfth digit on the right, d_{12}, is a check digit. It is chosen so that

$$3 \cdot d_1 + d_2 + 3 \cdot d_3 + d_4 + 3 \cdot d_5 + d_6 + 3 \cdot d_7 + d_8 \\ + 3 \cdot d_9 + d_{10} + 3 \cdot d_{11} + d_{12}. \tag{*}$$

is a multiple of 10. For instance, for the UPC in Figure 8.42,

$$3 \cdot 0 + 7 + 3 \cdot 0 + 7 + 3 \cdot 3 + 4 + 3 \cdot 0 + 0 + 3 \cdot 0 + 0 \cdot 0 + 3 \cdot 3 + 4 = 40.$$

0   70734 00003   4

FIGURE 8.42   A Universal Product Code.

Since $40 = 4 \cdot 10$, 40 is a multiple of 10. In the event that the cashier has to enter the UPC manually and mistypes a digit, the above sum will not add up to a multiple of 10.

Write a program to simulate an automated check-out at a supermarket. A master file, called UPC.txt, should have a record for each item in the supermarket consisting of fields for the UPC, the name of the item, and the price of the item. For instance, the file might contain the following records:

```
037000004301,Jif Peanut Butter - 22 oz,2.29
070734000034,Celestial Seasonings Sleepytime Tea,2.59
099482403645,365 Soda Root Beer,.55
```

The program should allow the cashier to enter UPCs one at a time and should place the UPCs in a separate text file. Each UPC should be validated with the sum (*) as soon as it is entered and should be reentered if the sum is not a multiple of 10. After all items have been processed, the program should use the two text files to display (in a list box) a receipt similar to the one in Fig. 8.43.

```
22-oz Jif Peanut Butter: $2.29
Celestial Seasonings Sleepytime Tea: $2.59
365 Soda Root Beer: $.55
Total: $5.43
```

FIGURE 8.43   Possible output of Programming Project 5.

6. **Baseball**   The file Baseball.xml contains data about the performance of major league players in the 2015 regular season. (Only the top 141 hitters with at least 440 at bats are included in the file.) Figure 8.44 shows the beginning of the file. Write a program using the file Baseball.xml that requests a team as input from a list and displays the players from that team whose batting average was above the average of his teammates' batting averages that are listed in the file. The players should be sorted in decreasing order by their batting averages. The output should display each player's full name and batting average. See Fig. 8.45.

```
<?xml version='1.0'?>
<!-- This file contains data on major league baseball players.-->
<major_league_baseball>
  <player>
    <name>Miguel Cabrera</name>
    <team>Tigers</team>
    <atBats>429</atBats>
    <hits>145</hits>
  </player>
```

FIGURE 8.44   XML file for Programming Project 6.

FIGURE 8.45   Possible outcome of Programming Project 6.

9

Additional Controls and Objects

9.1   List Boxes and Combo Boxes

The **list box** and **combo box** controls allow the user to make selections by clicking on an item. Certain styles of combo boxes also allow for input by assisted typing.

■ A Review of List Box Features

A list box can be populated at design time with the String Collection Editor. Items are typed directly into the editor or copied (with Ctrl+C) from another application like Excel, Word, or Notepad and pasted (with Ctrl+V) into the editor. A list box can be populated at run time with the Items.Add method or by setting its DataSource property to an array or a query (converted to a list).

The items in a list box are indexed with zero-based numbering. That is, the items in a list box are identified as lstBox.Items(0), lstBox.Items(1), and so on. Table 9.1 summarizes the properties, methods, and events for list boxes that were presented in earlier chapters.

TABLE 9.1   Previously discussed properties, methods, and events.

lstBox.Items.Add(*value*)	Method: Insert the value into the list box.
lstBox.Items.Clear()	Method: Remove all items from the list box.
lstBox.Text	Property: The selected item as a string.
lstBox.Items.Count	Property: The number of items in the list box.
lstBox.Sorted	Property: If set to True, items will be displayed in ascending ANSI order.
lstBox.SelectedIndex	Property: The index of the selected item. If no item is selected, the value is −1.
lstBox.SelectedItem	Property: The currently selected item. It must be converted to a string before being displayed in a text or message box.
lstBox.Items(*n*)	Property: The item having index *n*. It must be converted to a string before being displayed in a text or message box.
lstBox.DataSource	Property: The source of data to populate the list box.
lstBox.SelectedIndexChanged	Event: Occurs when the value of the SelectedIndex property changes. It is the default event procedure.
lstBox.Click	Event: Occurs when the user clicks on the list box.
lstBox.DoubleClick	Event: Occurs when the user double-clicks on the list box.

Note: You can programmatically change the selected (that is highlighted) item by changing the SelectedIndex value in code: the corresponding item in the list box will appear highlighted.

 Example 1   **Create a File** The following program shows two ways to copy the contents of a list box into a text file. When the top button is clicked, the items in the list box populate an array that is then used to create a text file. When the bottom button is clicked, a StreamWriter is used to copy the contents of the list box directly into a text file. Notice that the StreamWriter does not have to convert the items in the list box to strings before copying them into the file.

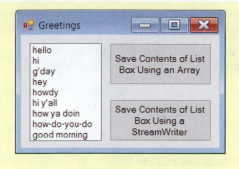

OBJECT	PROPERTY	SETTING
frmGreetings	Text	Greetings
lstBox	Items	(shown in screen capture)
btnArray	Text	Save Contents of List Box Using an Array
btnSW	Text	Save Contents of List Box Using a StreamWriter

```
Private Sub btnArray_Click(...) Handles btnArray.Click
  Dim ub As Integer = lstBox.Items.Count - 1   'upper bound of array
  Dim a(ub) As String
  For i As Integer = 0 To ub
    a(i) = CStr(lstBox.Items(i))
  Next
  IO.File.WriteAllLines("Greetings1.txt", a)
End Sub

Private Sub btnSW_Click(...) Handles btnSW.Click
  Dim sw As IO.StreamWriter = IO.File.CreateText("Greetings2.txt")
  For i As Integer = 0 To (lstBox.Items.Count - 1)
    sw.WriteLine(lstBox.Items(i))
  Next
  sw.Close()
End Sub
```

[Run, and click on each of the two buttons. Then end the program, click on the *Refresh* button in the Solution Explorer window, click on the *View All Files* button, and look at the new text files in the *bin\Debug* subfolder. Each text file will contain the contents of the list box.]

■ Some Additional Features of List Boxes

Table 9.2 shows some additional useful methods for list boxes.

TABLE 9.2 Some additional list box methods.

lstBox.Items.IndexOf(*value*)	Index of the first item to have the value.
lstBox.Items.RemoveAt(*n*)	Delete item having index *n*.
lstBox.Items.Remove(*strValue*)	Delete first occurrence of the string value.
lstBox.Items.Insert(*n*, *value*)	Insert the value as the item of index *n*.

Example 2   **Remove Duplicates** The following program removes all duplicates from a list box. The program looks at the first item in the list box and removes every matching item that follows it. The program then repeats the process with the next item remaining in the list box, and so on.

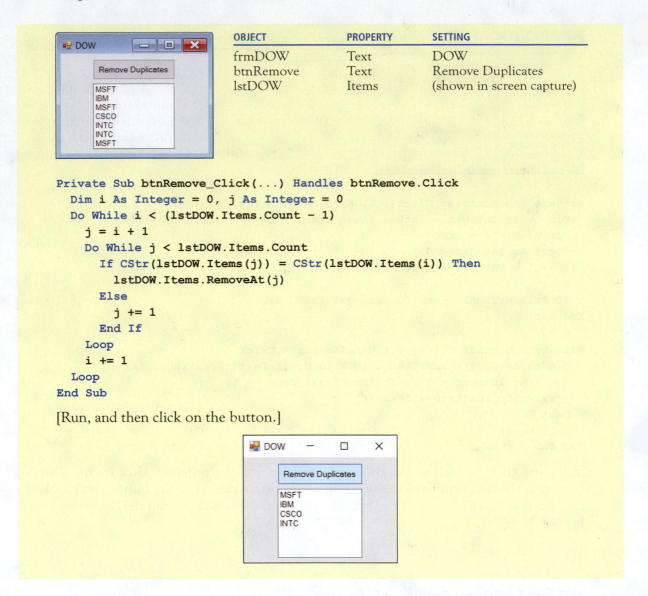

OBJECT	PROPERTY	SETTING
frmDOW	Text	DOW
btnRemove	Text	Remove Duplicates
lstDOW	Items	(shown in screen capture)

```
Private Sub btnRemove_Click(...) Handles btnRemove.Click
  Dim i As Integer = 0, j As Integer = 0
  Do While i < (lstDOW.Items.Count - 1)
    j = i + 1
    Do While j < lstDOW.Items.Count
      If CStr(lstDOW.Items(j)) = CStr(lstDOW.Items(i)) Then
        lstDOW.Items.RemoveAt(j)
      Else
        j += 1
      End If
    Loop
    i += 1
  Loop
End Sub
```

[Run, and then click on the button.]

■ The Combo Box Control

A combo box control can be thought of as a text box with a list box attached to it. Combo boxes have all the properties, methods, and events that list boxes have, plus a few more. The three different styles of combo box are shown in Fig. 9.1. (Each combo box's String

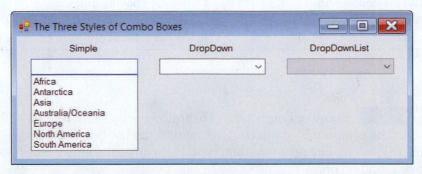

FIGURE 9.1 The three settings for the DropDownStyle property.

Collection Editor was used to populate the combo box with the names of the seven continents.) The style of a combo box control is specified by setting its DropDownStyle property to Simple, DropDown, or DropDownList. In a Simple style combo box the list box is always visible. With the other two styles, the list box appears only at run time when the user clicks on the down-arrow button. See Fig. 9.2. The standard prefix for the name of a combo box is *cbo*.

(a) DropDown   (b) DropDownList

FIGURE 9.2 **Combo boxes at run time after their down arrows are clicked.**

With a Simple or DropDown combo box, the user can fill the text box either by typing directly into it or by selecting an item from the list. With a DropDownList style combo box, the user can fill the text box only by selecting an item from the list. (DropDown is the default setting of a combo box's DropDownStyle property.) A list that has dropped down disappears when the user clicks on an item or presses the Enter key. With any of the three styles, the value of

cboBox.Text

is the contents of the text box at the top of the combo box. Just like list boxes, combo boxes can be populated with their String Collection Editor, the Items.Add method, and the DataSource property.

 Example 3 **Display a Full Name** The following program uses a Simple combo box to obtain a person's title for the first line of the address of a letter.

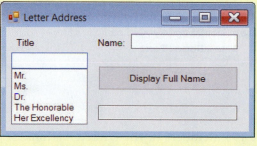

OBJECT	PROPERTY	SETTING
frmAddress	Text	Letter Address
lblTitle	Text	Title
cboTitle	Items	(shown in screen capture)
	DropDownStyle	Simple
lblName	Text	Name:
txtName		
btnDisplay	Text	Display Full Name
txtDisplay	ReadOnly	True

```
Private Sub btnDisplay_Click(...) Handles btnDisplay.Click
  txtDisplay.Text = cboTitle.Text & " " & txtName.Text
End Sub
```

[Run, select an item from the combo box, type a name into the Name text box, and click on the button.]

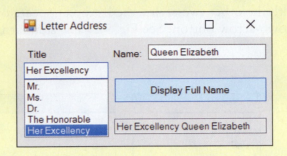

The same program with a DropDown style combo box produces the form shown in Fig. 9.3. The form will look about the same when a DropDownList style combo box is used.

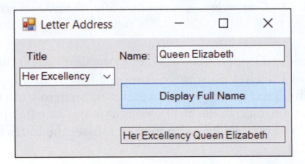

FIGURE 9.3 Example 3 with a DropDown style combo box.

✔ **Example 4** **Display a Full Name** The following variation of Example 3 uses the same form design and settings as Example 3 except that the combo box is not filled at design time:

```
Private Sub frmAddress_Load(...) Handles MyBase.Load
  Dim titles() As String = {"Mr.", "Ms.", "Dr.",
                          "The Honorable", "Her Excellency"}
  'Fill combo box with elements from array
  cboTitle.DataSource = titles
End Sub


Private Sub btnDisplay_Click(...) Handles btnDisplay.Click
  txtDisplay.Text = cboTitle.Text & " " & txtName.Text
End Sub
```

■ A Helpful Feature of Combo Boxes

The file Nations.txt contains the names of the 193 members of the United Nations. Suppose a Simple style combo box has been filled with the nations in alphabetical order. Figure 9.4(a) shows the combo box when the program starts. Each time a letter is typed into the text box at the top of the combo box the list scrolls in a helpful way. For instance, after the letter *N* is typed, the combo box appears as shown in Fig. 9.4(b). The combo box has scrolled down so that the first nation beginning with the letter *N* is at the top of the list. Similarly, typing additional letters causes the list to scroll down so that the first nation beginning with the typed letters is at the top of the list. See Fig. 9.4(c) and 9.4(d). [**Notes:** When the scroll box reaches the bottom of the scroll bar, no further scrolling will take place. Also, if the typed letters do not correspond to any nation, the list will return to the state in Fig. 9.4(a). Analogous results apply to DropDown style combo boxes.]

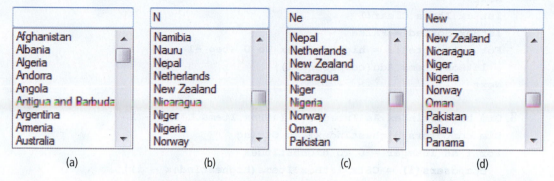

| (a) | (b) | (c) | (d) |

FIGURE 9.4 Successive combo box displays.

Practice Problems 9.1

1. Will the following two statements always have the same effect?

```
lstOxys.Items.RemoveAt(lstOxys.SelectedIndex)
lstOxys.Items.Remove(lstOxys.Text)
```

2. Based on your knowledge of the IndexOf method discussed in Section 3.2, what do you think is returned by `lstBox.Items.IndexOf(value)` if no item in the list box has the specified value?

EXERCISES 9.1

In Exercises 1 through 8, determine the effect of the code on the list box lstBox shown below. (Assume that the Sorted property is set to True.)

1. `lstBox.Items.Remove("Chopin")`

2. `lstBox.Items.RemoveAt(0)`

3. `lstBox.Items.RemoveAt(lstBox.SelectedIndex)`

4. `lstBox.Items.RemoveAt(lstBox.Items.Count - 1)`

5. `lstBox.Items.Add("Haydn")`

6.
```
Dim total As Integer = 0
For i As Integer = 0 To (lstBox.Items.Count - 1)
    If CStr(lstBox.Items(i)).Length = 6 Then
        total += 1
    End If
Next
txtOutput.Text = CStr(total)
```

7.
```
Dim highestIndex As Integer = lstBox.Items.Count - 1
Dim composers(highestIndex) As String
For i As Integer = 0 To highestIndex
  composers(i) = CStr(lstBox.Items(i))
Next
lstBox.Items.Clear()
lstBox.Sorted = False
For i As Integer = highestIndex To 0 Step -1
  lstBox.Items.Add(composers(i))
Next
```

8.
```
Dim highestIndex As Integer = lstBox.Items.Count - 1
Dim composers(highestIndex) As String
For i As Integer = 0 To highestIndex
  composers(i) = CStr(lstBox.Items(highestIndex - i))
Next
lstBox.Sorted = False
lstBox.DataSource = composers
```

In Exercises 9 through 16, assume that cboBox has DropDownStyle set to Simple, appears as shown below, and has its Sorted property set to True. Give a statement or statements that will carry out the stated task. (The statements should do the job even if additional items have been added to the list.)

9. Highlight the name Dante.

10. Highlight the third item of the list.

11. Delete the name Shakespeare.

12. Delete the name Goethe.

13. Delete the last name in the list.

14. Display every other item of the list in another list box.

15. Delete every item beginning with the letter M.

16. Determine if Cervantes is in the list.

17. **Sort a List**   Suppose all the items in lstBox are numbers. Write a program to display them in lstBox in increasing numerical order. **Note:** Setting `lstBox.Sorted = True` will not do the job.

18. **Remove Duplicates**   Rework the program in Example 2 using LINQ.

19. **Maintain a List**   Write a program that contains a list box (with Sorted = False), a label, and two buttons captioned *Add an Item* and *Delete an Item*. When the *Add an Item* button is clicked, the program should request an item with an input dialog box and then insert the item above the currently highlighted item. When the *Delete an Item* button is clicked, the program should remove the highlighted item from the list. At all times, the label should display the number of items in the list. See Fig. 9.5.

FIGURE 9.5   Possible outcome of Exercise 19.

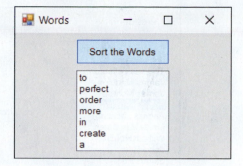

FIGURE 9.6   Outcome of Exercise 20.

20. **Sort a List**   Suppose all the items in lstBox are words. Write a program to display them in lstBox in reverse alphabetical order. In Fig. 9.6, the original words were the words in the phrase "in order to create a more perfect".

21. **Popular Names**   The file PopularNames.txt contains the 10 most popular names given to newborns in 2014. (**Source:** Social Security Administration). Write a program that uses a list box to sort the names into alphabetical order and then places the alphabetized list into a new ordered text file. See Fig. 9.7.

FIGURE 9.7   Outcome of Exercise 21.

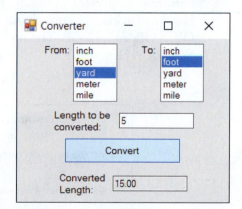

FIGURE 9.8   Possible output for Exercise 22.

22. **Convert Units**   Consider the Length Converter in Fig. 9.8. Write a program to carry out the conversion. (See the first programming project in Chapter 7 for a table of equivalent lengths.)

23. **U.S. Presidents**   The file AgesAtInauguaral.txt gives the ages at inauguration of the first 44 U.S. presidents. The first four lines of the file contain the data 57, 61, 57, 57; the ages of Washington, Adams, Jefferson, and Madison, respectively, at their inaugurations. The file USPres.txt contains the names of the first 44 U.S presidents in the order they were inaugurated. Write a program that places the names of the presidents into an unsorted list box and the ages at inauguration into an array. When the user clicks on the name of a president, his age at inauguration should be displayed in a text box. See Fig. 9.9 on the next page. (**Hint:** A president's index number in the list box will be the same as the index number of his age at inauguration in the array.)

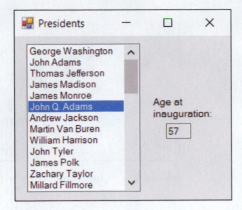

FIGURE 9.9 Possible output for Exercise 23.   **FIGURE 9.10** Possible outcome of Exercise 24.

24. **Monopoly**   Write a program to ask a person which Monopoly® space he or she has landed on and then display the result in a text box. The response should be obtained with a combo box listing the squares most commonly landed on: Park Place, Illinois Avenue, Go, B&O Railroad, and Free Parking. See Fig. 9.10.

25. **Describe Computer**   Write a program to question a person about his or her computer and then display a descriptive sentence in a text box. The form should contain combo boxes for brand, amount of memory, and screen size. The lists should contain the most common responses for each category. Some common computers are Compaq, Dell, Hewlett-Packard, Lenovo, and Apple. The most common amounts of memory are 4 GB, 8 GB, and 32 GB. The most common screen sizes are 17, 19, 21, 24, and 27 inches. See Fig. 9.11.

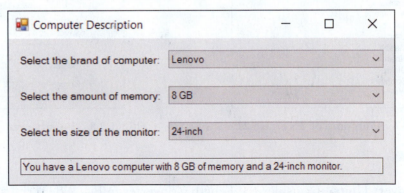

FIGURE 9.11 Possible outcome of Exercise 25.

Solutions to Practice Problems 9.1

1. Yes, if all the items in the list box are distinct. However, if an item is repeated and the second occurrence is selected, then the first statement will delete that item, whereas the second statement will delete the earlier occurrence of the item.

2. −1. Therefore, the IndexOf method can be used to determine if a value appears in a list box. Another method that will determine if a value is in a list box is the Contains method. The statement `lstBox.Items.Contains(value)` returns True if the value appears in the list box and False otherwise.

9.2 Eight Additional Controls and Objects

VideoNote
Timer,
Picturebox,
Menustrip,
and Scrollbar,
Controls

◼ The Timer Control

The **timer** control, which is not visible on the form during run time, raises an event after a specified amount of time has passed. (The timer control is found only in the *All Windows Forms* group of the Toolbox. When you double-click on the timer control in the Toolbox, it appears in the **component tray**, at the bottom of the Form Designer.) The length of time, measured in milliseconds, is set with the Interval property to be any integer from 1 to 2,147,483,647 (about 596 hours). The event that is raised each time Timer1.Interval milliseconds elapses is called Timer1.Tick. In order to begin timing, a timer must first be turned on by setting its Enabled property to True. A timer is turned off by setting its Enabled property to False. The standard prefix for the name of a timer control is *tmr*.

 Example 1 **Stopwatch** The following program creates a stopwatch that updates the time every tenth of a second.

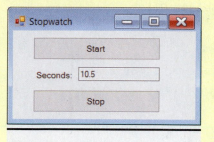

OBJECT	PROPERTY	SETTING
frmStopwatch	Text	Stopwatch
btnStart	Text	Start
lblSeconds	Text	Seconds:
txtSeconds	ReadOnly	True
btnStop	Text	Stop
tmrWatch	Interval	100

```
Private Sub btnStart_Click(...) Handles btnStart.Click
  txtSeconds.Text = "0"      'reset watch
  tmrWatch.Enabled = True
End Sub


Private Sub btnStop_Click(...) Handles btnStop.Click
  tmrWatch.Enabled = False
End Sub


Private Sub tmrWatch_Tick(...) Handles tmrWatch.Tick
  'Next line displays the time rounded to one decimal place
  txtSeconds.Text = (CDbl(txtSeconds.Text) + 0.1).ToString("N1")
End Sub
```

[Run, click on the Start button, wait 10.5 seconds, and click on the Stop button.]

■ The Random Class

Visual Basic has a useful object called a random number generator that is declared with a statement of the form

```
Dim randomNum As New Random
```

If *m* and *n* are whole numbers, with *m* < *n*, then the value of

```
randomNum.Next(m,n)
```

is a randomly selected whole number from *m* through *n*, including *m* but excluding *n*. The Next method of this built-in object allows us to produce some interesting applications.

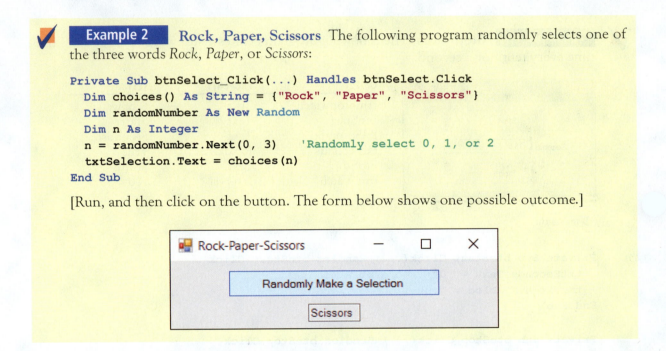

✔ **Example 2**   **Rock, Paper, Scissors** The following program randomly selects one of the three words *Rock*, *Paper*, or *Scissors*:

```
Private Sub btnSelect_Click(...) Handles btnSelect.Click
  Dim choices() As String = {"Rock", "Paper", "Scissors"}
  Dim randomNumber As New Random
  Dim n As Integer
  n = randomNumber.Next(0, 3)    'Randomly select 0, 1, or 2
  txtSelection.Text = choices(n)
End Sub
```

[Run, and then click on the button. The form below shows one possible outcome.]

The random number generator can be used to shuffle a deck of cards. Example 3 uses an efficient technique called the "inside-out algorithm" to shuffle a deck of cards. This algorithm takes the cards one at a time and then swaps the card randomly with one of the previously selected cards.

✔ **Example 3**   **Shuffle Cards** The following program creates a deck of 52 cards as an array, shuffles the elements of the array, and then displays the first five elements of the array:

```
Private Sub btnCreate_Click(...) Handles btnCreate.Click
  'Create a deck of cards in an array
  Dim deckOfCards(51) As String
  Dim suits() As String = {"Hearts", "Diamonds", "Clubs", "Spades"}
  'Populate each suit of the deck.
  For i As Integer = 0 To 3
    'Populate numbers 2 through 10.
```

```
      For j As Integer = 2 To 10
         deckOfCards(i * 13 + j) = j & " of " & suits(i)
      Next
      'Populate the honors cards.
      deckOfCards(i * 13 + 0) = "King of " & suits(i)
      deckOfCards(i * 13 + 1) = "Ace of " & suits(i)
      deckOfCards(i * 13 + 11) = "Jack of " & suits(i)
      deckOfCards(i * 13 + 12) = "Queen of " & suits(i)
   Next
   'inside-out algorithm
   Dim a(51) As String, k As Integer
   Dim randomNum As New Random()
   a(0) = deckOfCards(0)
   For i As Integer = 1 To 51
     k = randomNum.Next(0, i + 1)
     a(i) = a(k)
     a(k) = deckOfCards(i)
   Next
   'Display top five cards
   lstOutput.Items.Clear()
   For i As Integer = 0 To 4
     lstOutput.Items.Add(a(i))
   Next
End Sub
```

[Run, and then click on the button.]

■ The ToolTip Control

The Visual Basic IDE uses tooltips to identify buttons on the Toolbar and icons in the Toolbox. When we hover the mouse over one of these items, a small rectangular box appears after $1/2$ second and remains visible for 5 seconds. The ToolTip control allows us to create tooltips for the controls in our programs.

A ToolTip Walkthrough

1. Start a new program. (There is no need to give a name to the program.)

2. Double-click on the ToolTip control in the Toolbox. (The control will appear with the default name ToolTip1 in the component tray at the bottom of the Form Designer.)

3. Place controls on the form and enter code as shown in Example 4 on the next page. (The setting for the "ToolTip on ToolTip1" property of txtRate holds the information that will appear when the mouse hovers over the text box.)

Example 4 **Tooltip Assistance** In the following program, suppose the sales tax rate is 5%. The user might not know whether to enter 5 or .05 into the text box. A tooltip comes to the rescue.

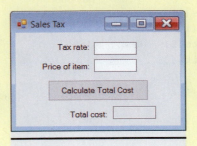

OBJECT	PROPERTY	SETTING
frmName	Text	Sales Tax
lblRate	Text	Tax rate:
txtRate	ToolTip on ToolTip1	Such as 5, 5.25, 5.5 . . .
lblPrice	Text	Price of item:
txtPrice		
btnCalculate	Text	Calculate Total Cost
lblTotalCost	Text	Total cost:
txtTotalCost	ReadOnly	True

```
Private Sub btnCalculate_Click(...) Handles btnCalculate.Click
  Dim taxRate As Decimal = CDec(txtRate.Text) / 100
  Dim price As Decimal = CDec(txtPrice.Text)
  Dim totalCost As Decimal = price + (taxRate * price)
  txtTotalCost.Text = totalCost.ToString("C")
End Sub
```

[Run, and hover the mouse over the first text box.]

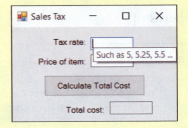

Normally, a control placed on a form does not have a "ToolTip on ToolTip1" property. That property appears in the Properties window only after a ToolTip control has been added to the component tray.

In the example above, we created a tooltip for only one of the text boxes. However, we could have specified a tooltip for the other controls.

By default, a tooltip appears $\frac{1}{2}$ second after the cursor hovers over a control and lasts for 5 seconds. These two durations can be altered with the ToolTip control's AutomaticDelay and AutoPopDelay properties. The numeric settings for these two properties are in milliseconds. Specifically, the AutomaticDelay setting determines the length of time required for a tooltip to appear, and the AutoPopDelay setting determines the length of time the tooltip remains visible while the cursor is stationary inside a control.

■ The Clipboard

The **Clipboard** object is used to copy or move information from one location to another. It is maintained by Windows and therefore even can be used to transfer information from one Windows application to another. It is actually a portion of memory that holds information and has no properties or events.

If *str* is a string, then the statement

```
Clipboard.SetText(str)
```

replaces any text currently in the Clipboard with the value of *str*. The statement

str = Clipboard.GetText

assigns the text in the Clipboard to the string variable *str*. The statement

Clipboard.Clear

deletes the contents of the Clipboard.

A portion of the text in a text box or combo box can be **selected** by dragging the mouse across it or by moving the cursor across it while holding down the Shift key. After you select text, you can place it into the Clipboard by pressing Ctrl+C. Also, if the cursor is in a text box and you press Ctrl+V, the contents of the Clipboard will be pasted over any selected portion of the text or at the cursor position if no text is selected. These tasks also can be carried out in code with the following statements:

txtBox.Copy()	Copies the selected text in txtBox into the Clipboard.
txtBox.Cut()	Cuts the selected text from txtBox and places it into the Clipboard.
txtBox.Paste()	Replaces the selected text in txtBox with the contents of the Clipboard. If no text is selected, the contents of the Clipboard are inserted at the cursor position. If the cursor is not in the txtBox, the contents of the Clipboard is concatenated to the end of the text in txtBox.

Note: If *strValue* is a string literal or variable, then **txtBox.Paste(*strValue*)** pastes the literal or the value of the variable into txtBox instead of the contents of the Clipboard.

■ The Picture Box Control

The **PictureBox** control is used primarily to hold pictures stored in graphics files such as bmp files created with Windows Paint, ico files of icons that come with Windows, or gif and jpeg images used on the World Wide Web. By convention, names of picture box controls have the prefix *pic*.

A picture can be placed in a picture box control with the Image property. If you double-click on the Image property during design time, an Open dialog box appears and assists you in selecting an appropriate file. However, prior to setting the Image property, you should set the SizeMode property. If the SizeMode property is set to AutoSize, the picture box control will be resized to fit the picture. If the SizeMode property is set to StretchImage, the picture will be resized to fit the picture box control. Therefore, with the StretchImage setting, pictures can be reduced (by placing them into a small picture box control) or enlarged (by placing them into a picture box control bigger than the picture). Figure 9.12 shows a picture created with Paint and reduced by StretchImage to fit the picture box.

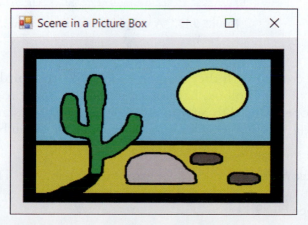

FIGURE 9.12   Picture box with desert scene.

A picture also can be assigned to a picture box control at run time. However, a statement such as

```
picBox.Image = filespec
```

will not do the job. Instead, we must create an Image object with a statement such as

```
picBox.Image = Image.FromFile(filespec)
```

The SizeMode property can be altered at run time with a statement such as

```
picBox.SizeMode = PictureBoxSizeMode.AutoSize
```

■ The MenuStrip Control

Visual Basic forms can have menu bars similar to those in most Windows applications. Figure 9.13 shows a typical menu bar, with the *Order* menu revealed. Here, the menu bar contains two menu items (*Order* and *Color*), referred to as **top-level** menu items. When the *Order* menu item is clicked, a drop-down list containing two second-level menu items (*Ascending* and *Descending*) appears. Although not visible here, the drop-down list under *Color* contains the two second-level menu items *Foreground* and *Background*. Each menu item is treated as a distinct control that responds to a Click event. The Click event is raised not only by the click of the mouse button, but also for top-level items by pressing Alt+*access*Key and for second-level items by just pressing the access key. The event procedure for the *Ascending* or *Descending* menu item also can be raised by pressing the shortcut key combination Ctrl+A or Ctrl+D. **Note:** Shortcut keys can be used at any time; whereas access keys can be used only when the command is visible and the access letter is underlined. Therefore, often the drop-down menu containing the command must be visible in order for an access key to be used.

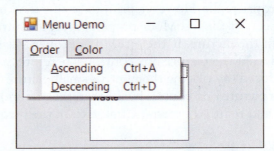

FIGURE 9.13 **A simple menu at run time.**

Menus are created with the MenuStrip control—the third control in the *Menus & Toolbars* group of the Toolbox. Each menu item has a Text property (what the user sees) and a Name property (used to refer to the item in code). The standard prefix for the name of a menu is *mnu*. The following walkthrough creates the menu bar in Fig. 9.13:

1. Start a new program.
2. Double-click on the MenuStrip control in the Toolbox. The control appears in the component tray, and a menu designer appears just below the title bar in the Form Designer. See Fig. 9.14.

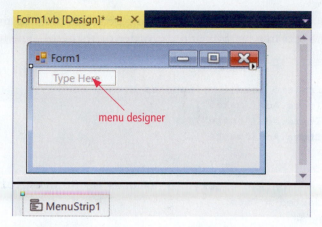

FIGURE 9.14 The MenuStrip control added to a form.

3. Click on the rectangle that says "Type Here", type in "&Order", and press the Enter key. (The ampersand specifies O as an access key for the menu item.) "Type Here" rectangles appear below and to the right of the *Order* menu item. The rectangle below the *Order* menu item is used to create a second-level item for the *Order* menu. The rectangle on the right is used to create a new first-level menu item.

4. Type "&Ascending" into the rectangle below the *Order* rectangle, and press the Enter key.

5. Click on the *Ascending* menu item to display its Properties window. In the Properties window, change the Name property of the menu item from AscendingToolStripMenuItem to mnuOrderAsc. Also, click on the down arrow at the right of the ShortcutKeys Settings box, click on the *Ctrl* check box under Modifiers, click on the down arrow button of the Key combo box, click on A in the drop-down list, and press the Enter key. ("Ctrl+A" will appear to the right of the word "Ascending".)

6. Type "&Descending" into the rectangle below the *Ascending* rectangle, press the Enter key, set the Name property of the *Descending* menu item to mnuOrderDesc, and set the ShortcutKeys property to Ctrl+D.

7. Click on the rectangle to the right of the *Order* rectangle and enter the text "&Color".

8. Type "&Foreground" into the rectangle below the *Color* rectangle, press the Enter key, and set its Name property to mnuColorFore.

9. Type "&Background" into the rectangle below the *Foreground* rectangle, press the Enter key, and set its Name property to mnuColorBack.

10. Click on the *Foreground* rectangle, and type "&Red" into the rectangle on its right. (We have just created a third-level menu item.) Set its Name property to mnuColorForeRed.

11. Type "&Blue" into the rectangle below the *Red* rectangle, and set its Name property to mnuColorForeBlue.

12. Click on the *Background* rectangle, type "&Yellow" into the rectangle on its right, and set its Name property to mnuColorBackYellow.

13. Type "&White" into the rectangle below the *Yellow* rectangle, and set its Name property to mnuColorBackWhite. Then set its Checked property to True. A check mark will appear to the left of the word "White".

14. Run the program; click on *Order* to see its menu items; click on *Color* and hover over the word *Foreground* to see its menu items. The menu items are useful only after we write code for their Click event procedures.

Example 5   **Use a Menu** The following program uses the menu just created to alter the color of the text in a list box and the order of its items. The form has the text "Menu Demo" in its title bar.

```
Private Sub frmDemo_Load(...) Handles MyBase.Load
  lstOutput.Items.Add("makes")
  lstOutput.Items.Add("haste")
  lstOutput.Items.Add("waste")
End Sub


Private Sub mnuOrderAsc_Click(...) Handles mnuOrderAsc.Click
  lstOutput.Sorted = True
End Sub


Private Sub mnuOrderDesc_Click(...) Handles mnuOrderDesc.Click
  'This code uses the fact that if a list is in ascending order,
  'then displaying it backward gives a descending list
  Dim temp(2) As String      'hold ascending array of items
  lstOutput.Sorted = True    'sort the items alphabetically
  For i As Integer = 0 To 2 'place sorted items into the array
    temp(i) = CStr(lstOutput.Items(i))
  Next
  lstOutput.Sorted = False  'turn off the Sorted property
  lstOutput.Items.Clear()
  For i As Integer = 2 To 0 Step -1
    lstOutput.Items.Add(temp(i))
  Next
End Sub


Private Sub mnuColorForeRed_Click(...) Handles mnuColorForeRed.Click
  lstOutput.ForeColor = Color.Red
End Sub


Private Sub mnuColorForeBlue_Click(...) Handles mnuColorForeBlue.Click
  lstOutput.ForeColor = Color.Blue
End Sub


Private Sub mnuColorBackYellow_Click(...) Handles _
          mnuColorBackYellow.Click
  'Make Yellow the background color of the list box, guarantee that a
  'check mark appears in front of the menu item Yellow and not in front
  'of the White menu item
  lstOutput.BackColor = Color.Yellow
  mnuColorBackYellow.Checked = True
  mnuColorBackWhite.Checked = False
End Sub


Private Sub mnuColorBackWhite_Click(...) Handles mnuColorBackWhite.Click
  lstOutput.BackColor = Color.White
  mnuColorBackYellow.Checked = False
  mnuColorBackWhite.Checked = True
End Sub
```

[Run, click on *Ascending* in the *Order* menu, click on the *Color* menu, hover over *Foreground,* and click on *Red.*]

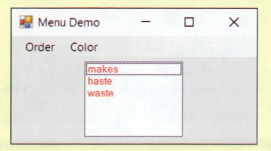

■ The Horizontal and Vertical Scroll Bar Controls

Figure 9.15 shows the two types of **scroll bars**. When the user clicks on one of the arrow buttons, the scroll box moves a small distance toward that arrow. When the user clicks between the scroll box and one of the arrow buttons, the scroll box moves a large distance toward that arrow. The user can also move the scroll box by dragging it. The main properties of a scroll bar control are Minimum, Maximum, Value, SmallChange, and LargeChange, which are set to integers. The standard prefix for the name of a scroll bar is *hsb* or *vsb*. At any time, hsbBar.Value is a number between hsbBar.Minimum and hsbBar.Maximum determined by the position of the left side of the scroll box. If the left side of the scroll box is halfway between the two arrows, then hsbBar.Value is a number halfway between hsbBar.Minimum and hsbBar.Maximum. If the scroll box is near the left arrow button, then hsbBar.Value is an appropriately proportioned value near hsbBar.Minimum. When the user clicks on an arrow button, hsbBar.Value changes by hsbBar.SmallChange and the scroll box moves accordingly. When the bar is clicked between the scroll box and an arrow, hsbBar.Value changes by hsbBar.LargeChange and the scroll box moves accordingly. When the scroll box is dragged, hsbBar.Value changes accordingly. The default values of Minimum, Maximum, Value, SmallChange, and LargeChange are 0, 100, 0, 1, and 10, respectively. However, these values are usually changed at design time. The width of the scroll box is equal to the value of LargeChange. Since hsbBar.Value is determined by the left side of the scroll box, the greatest value it can assume is (hsbBar.Maximum − hsbBar.LargeChange + 1). Vertical scroll bars behave similarly.

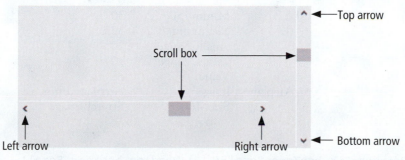

FIGURE 9.15 Horizontal and vertical scroll bars.

Note: The setting for the Minimum property must be less than the setting for the Maximum property. The Minimum property determines the values for the left and top arrows. The Maximum property determines the values for the right and bottom arrows.

The two controls are referred to as HScrollBar and VScrollBar in the Toolbox. Their default event, Scroll, is raised whenever the user clicks on any part of the scroll bar.

 Example 6 **Move a Picture** The following program uses scroll bars to move an airplane contained in a picture box around the form. The values picAirplane.Left and picAirplane.Top are the distances in pixels of the picture box from the left side and top of the form.

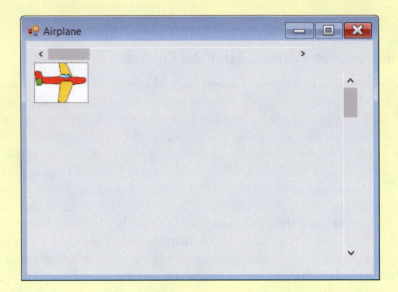

OBJECT	PROPERTY	SETTING
frmAirplane	Text	Airplane
hsbXPos	Minimum	0
	Maximum	300
	SmallChange	10
	LargeChange	50
	Value	0
vsbYPos	Minimum	30
	Maximum	300
	SmallChange	10
	LargeChange	50
	Value	30
picAirplane	Image	Airplane.bmp
	SizeMode	StretchImage

```
Private Sub hsbXpos_Scroll(...) Handles hsbXpos.Scroll
  picAirplane.Left = hsbXpos.Value
End Sub


Private Sub vsbYpos_Scroll(...) Handles vsbYpos.Scroll
  picAirplane.Top = vsbYpos.Value
End Sub
```

[Run, and move the scroll boxes on the scroll bars.]

Practice Problem 9.2

1. What is the effect of the following event procedure?

```
Private Sub btnDisplay_Click(...) Handles btnDisplay.Click
  Dim randomNum As New Random
  Dim contestant() As String = {"Mary", "Pat", "Linda",
                                "Barbara", "Maria"}
  Dim number As Integer, temp As String
  For i As Integer = 0 To 4
    number = randomNum.Next(i, 5)
    temp = contestant(i)
    contestant(i) = contestant(number)
    contestant(number) = temp
  Next
  lstOutput.Items.Clear()
  For i As Integer = 0 To 4
    lstOutput.Items.Add(contestant(i))
  Next
End Sub
```

EXERCISES 9.2

In Exercises 1 through 6, determine the effect of setting the property to the value shown.

1. Timer1.Interval = 5000

2. Timer1.Enabled = False

3. ToolTip1.AutomaticDelay = 1000

4. ToolTip1.AutoPopDelay = 4000

5. mnuOrderAsc.Checked = True

6. mnuOrderAsc.Checked = False

In Exercises 7 through 25, describe the effect of executing the statement(s).

7. ```
Timer1.Interval = CInt(intVar * 1000)
```

8. ```
Dim randomNum As New Random
txtBox.Text = CStr(randomNum.Next(1, 101))
```

9. ```
Dim randomNum As New Random
Dim number As Integer
'Assume the array states() contains the names of the 50 U.S. states
number = randomNum.Next(0, 50)
txtBox.Text = states(number)
```

10. ```
Dim randomNum As New Random
'95 characters can be produced by the computer keyboard
txtBox.Text = Chr(randomNum.Next(32, 127))
```

11. ```
Dim randomNum As New Random
Dim number As Integer, temp As String
'Assume the array states() contains the names of the 50 states
number = randomNum.Next(0, 50)
lstBox.Items.Add(states(number))
temp = states(number)
states(number) = states(49)
states(49) = temp
lstBox.Items.Add(states(randomNum.Next(0, 49)))
```

12. ```
Dim randomNum As New Random
Dim suit() As String = {"Hearts", "Clubs", "Diamonds", "Spades"}
Dim denomination() As String = {"2", "3", "4", "5", "6",
    "7", "8", "9", "10", "Jack", "Queen", "King", "Ace"}
txtBox.Text = denomination(randomNum.Next(0, 13)) & " of " &
              suit(randomNum.Next(0, 4))
```

13. ```
Clipboard.Clear
```

14. ```
Clipboard.SetText("Hello")
```

15. ```
Clipboard.SetText(txtBox.SelectedText)
```

16. ```
txtBox.Paste("Hello")
```

17. `txtBox.Copy()`   (Assume the text is "Hello" and "el" is selected.)

18. `txtBox.Cut()`   (Assume the text is "Hello" and "el" is selected.)

19. `txtBox.Paste()` (Assume the text is "Hello", "el" is selected, and the Clipboard contains "xx".)

20. ```
Dim strVar As String = "Happy"
Clipboard.SetText(strVar)
```

21. ```
Dim strVar As String
strVar = Clipboard.GetText
```

22. ```
PictureBox1.SizeMode = PictureBoxSizeMode.StretchImage
```

23. ```
PictureBox1.Image = Image.FromFile("Airplane.bmp")
```

24. ```
HScrollBar2.Value = CInt((HScrollBar2.Maximum + HScrollBar2.Minimum) / 2)
```

25. ```
VScrollBar2.SmallChange = VScrollBar2.LargeChange
```

In Exercises 26 through 44, write one or more lines of code to carry out the task.

26. Specify that Timer1 raise an event every half second.

27. Specify that Timer1 cease to raise the Tick event.

28. The array *names* contains twenty names. Display a randomly selected name in txtBox.

29. Display in txtBox a randomly selected number from 1 to 12.

30. Display in txtBox a letter randomly selected from the alphabet.

31. The file Towns.txt contains the names of cities. Display a randomly selected city in txtBox.

32. Display in txtBox the sum of the faces after tossing a pair of dice.

33. Suppose the array *rivers* contains the names of rivers. Randomly select two different rivers from the array and display them in lstBox.

34. Replace the selected portion of txtBox with the contents of the Clipboard.

35. Clear the contents of the Clipboard.

36. Place the word "Rosebud" into the Clipboard.

37. Copy the selected text in txtBox into the Clipboard.

38. Delete the selected portion of txtBox.

39. Assign the contents of the Clipboard to the integer variable *amount*.

40. Replace the contents of txtBox with the contents of the Clipboard.

41. Remove the check mark in front of the menu item named mnuOrderDesc.

42. Change the text for mnuOrderDesc to "Decreasing Order".

43. Move the scroll box of VScrollBar2 as high as possible.

44. Move the scroll box of HScrollBar2 one-third of the way from the left arrow to the right arrow.

Exercises 45 and 46 refer to Example 5.

45. Make a conjecture on the effect of the following statement and test your conjecture:

    ```
    mnuOrderAsc.Enabled = False
    ```

46. Make a conjecture on the effect of the following statement and test your conjecture:

    ```
    mnuOrderAsc.Visible = False
    ```

47. **Digital Clock** Write a program to create a decorative digital clock. The clock in the Digital Clock form in Fig. 9.16 is inserted in a picture box control containing the Trees. bmp picture. The values for hour, minute, and second can be obtained as Hour(Now), Minute(Now), and Second(Now).

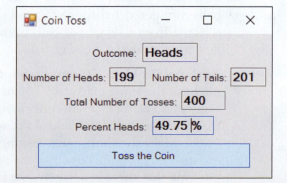

FIGURE 9.16 Possible outcome of Exercise 47.   **FIGURE 9.17** Possible outcome of Exercise 48.

48. **Coin Toss** Write a program using the form in Fig. 9.17 on the previous page. Each time the button is clicked, a Random object is used to simulate a coin toss and the values are updated. The figure shows the status after the button has been pressed 400 times. *Note:* You can produce tosses quickly by just holding down the Enter key. Although the percentage of heads initially will fluctuate considerably, it should stay close to 50% after many (say, 1000) tosses.

49. **Club Officers** The file Members.txt contains the names of the members of a large club. Write a program to randomly select people to serve as president, treasurer, and secretary. See Fig. 9.18. *Note:* A person cannot hold more than one office.

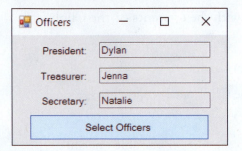

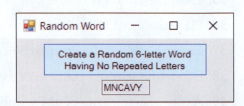

FIGURE 9.18 Possible outcome of Exercise 49.   **FIGURE 9.19** Possible outcome of Exercise 50.

50. **Random Word** Place the 26 uppercase letters into the array *alphabet*. Then use the inside-out algorithm from Example 3 to create a six-letter word containing no repeated letters. See Fig. 9.19.

51. **Moon Phases** The Ch09\Pictures folder contains files named Moon1.bmp, Moon2.bmp, . . . , Moon8.bmp, which show eight phases of the moon. Create a form consisting of a picture box control and a timer control. Every two seconds assign another file to the Image property of the picture box control to see the moon cycle through its phases every 16 seconds. One phase is shown in Fig. 9.20.

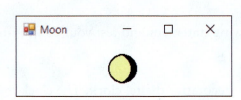

FIGURE 9.20 Outcome of Exercise 51.   **FIGURE 9.21** Possible outcome of Exercise 52.

52. **Powerball** In the Powerball lottery, five balls are randomly selected from a set of white balls numbered 1 through 69, and then a single ball, called the Powerball, is randomly selected from a set of red balls numbered 1 through 26. Write a program to produce a Powerball drawing. See Fig. 9.21.

53. **Birthday Problem** Given a random group of 23 people, how likely is it that two people have the same birthday? To answer this question, write a program that creates an array of 23 elements, randomly assigns to each subscripted variable one of the integers from 1 through 365, and checks to see if any of the subscripted variables have the same value. (Make the simplifying assumption that no birthdays occur on February 29.) Now expand the program to repeat the process 1000 times and determine the percentage of the time that there is a match. See Fig. 9.22.

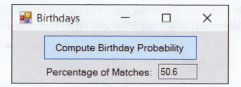

FIGURE 9.22 Possible outcome of Exercise 53.

FIGURE 9.23 Possible outcome of Exercise 54.

54. Carnival Game Consider a carnival game in which two cards are drawn at random from a deck of 52 cards. If either one or both of the cards is a diamond, you win one dollar. If neither card is a diamond, you lose one dollar. Simulate playing the game 1000 times and determine how much money you win or lose. See Fig. 9.23.

55. Tooltip Assistance Write a program containing text boxes named txtName and txtZipCode. The tooltip "Enter your full name." or "Enter your 9-digit zip code." should appear when the mouse hovers over the corresponding text box. See Fig. 9.24.

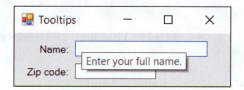

FIGURE 9.24 Outcome of Exercise 55.

FIGURE 9.25 Possible outcome of Exercise 56.

56. Tooltip Assistance Write a program containing a list box. The tooltip "Double-click on an item to delete it." should appear when the mouse hovers over the list box. See Fig. 9.25.

57. Display a Picture Write a program to display a picture (contained in a .bmp file) in a picture box. The .bmp file should be selected with an OpenFileDialog control.

58. Use a Menu Write a program with a single text box and a menu having the single top-level item *Edit* and the three second-level items *Copy*, *Paste*, and *Cut*. *Copy* should place a copy of the selected portion of the text box into the Clipboard, *Paste* should duplicate the contents of the Clipboard at the cursor position, and *Cut* should delete a selected portion of the text box and place it in the Clipboard. See Fig. 9.26.

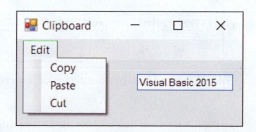

FIGURE 9.26 Possible outcome of Exercise 58.

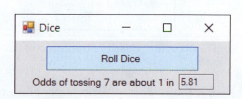

FIGURE 9.27 Possible outcome of Exercise 59.

59. Roll Dice Write a program that repeatedly rolls a pair of dice and tallies the number of rolls and the number of those rolls that total seven. The program should stop when 1000 sevens have been rolled, and then report the approximate odds of rolling a seven. (The approximate odds will be "1 in " followed by the result of dividing the number of rolls by the number of rolls that came up seven.) See Fig. 9.27.

60. Convert Temperatures   Write a program to synchronize the two thermometers shown in the Temperatures form in Fig. 9.28. When the scroll box of either thermometer is moved, the other thermometer should move to the corresponding temperature, and the two temperatures displayed above the thermometers should be updated. **Note:** F = (9/5)C + 32.

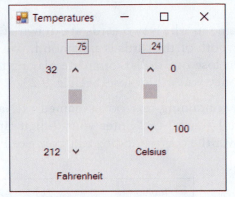

FIGURE 9.28   Possible outcome of Exercise 60.

FIGURE 9.29   Outcome of Exercise 61.

61. Times Square Ball   Create a form with a vertical scroll bar and a timer control. When the program is run, the scroll box should be at the top of the scroll bar. Each second the scroll box should descend one-tenth of the way down. When the scroll box reaches the bottom after 10 seconds, a message box displaying HAPPY NEW YEAR should appear. See Fig. 9.29.

62. Roll Dice   The folder Ch09\Pictures contains picture files named Die1.jpg, Die2.jpg, ..., Die6.jpg containing the six faces of a die. Write a program that randomly tosses a pair of dice and shows the dice and their sum. See Fig. 9.30.

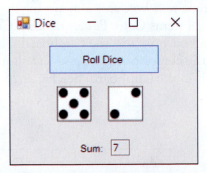

FIGURE 9.30   Possible outcome of Exercise 62.

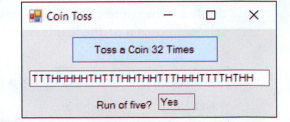

FIGURE 9.31   Possible outcome of Exercise 63.

63. Coin Toss   Write a program to display the result of tossing a coin 32 times and then determine if there is a run of five consecutive heads or a run of five consecutive tails. See Fig. 9.31. (**Note:** When you toss a coin 2^r times, you are more likely than not to have a run of r heads or r tails.)

Solution to Practice Problem 9.2

1. The event procedure places the names of the contestants in a list box in a random order.

9.3   Multiple-Form Programs

A Visual Basic program can contain more than one form. Additional forms are added from the Menu bar's Project menu by clicking on *Add Windows Form*, which brings up an Add New Item dialog box with "Windows Form" highlighted. To add the new form, optionally type in a name and press the *Add* button. The new form has a default name such as Form1 or Form2. The name of each form in the program appears in the Solution Explorer window. See Fig. 9.32. When you double-click on the name of a form, its Form Designer appears in the Document window. In practice, forms are given descriptive names. However, we will initially use the default names.

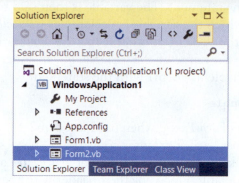

FIGURE 9.32   Solution Explorer window after a second form is added.

The most common use of an additional form is as a customized input dialog box (Fig. 9.33) or a customized message dialog box (Fig. 9.34). The form in Fig. 9.33 could appear to limit access to the rest of the program only to a user who enters a registered user name and password. In Fig. 9.34 the output of the Weekly Payroll case study from Chapter 5 is displayed in a second form instead of in a list box.

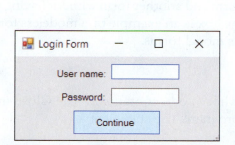

FIGURE 9.33   Customized input dialog box.

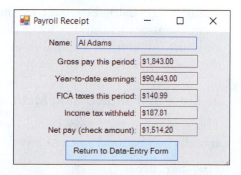

FIGURE 9.34   Customized message dialog box.

■ Startup Form

When a program starts running, only one form (called the **startup form**) will be loaded. By default, the first form created is the startup form. The following steps change the startup form.

1. Right-click on the name of the program at the top of the Solution Explorer window and click on *Properties* in the context menu that appears. The program's Project Designer will appear.

2. Click the Application tab.

3. Select a form from the *Startup form* drop-down list.

4. Close the Project Designer by clicking the × symbol on its tab.

■ Scope of Variables, Constants, and Procedures

We have considered block, procedure, and class scope. A variable or constant declared inside a block (such as a Do loop or If block) can no longer be referred to when execution passes out of the block. If you declare a variable or constant inside a procedure but outside any block within that procedure, you can think of the variable as having block scope, where the block is the entire procedure. You declare a class-level variable or constant for a form by placing its Dim or Const statement outside any procedure. Class-level variables or constants can be referred to anywhere in the form's code.

If a program has more than one form, then you can extend the scope of a class-level variable to all the forms in the program by using the keyword Public in place of the keyword Dim in its declaration statement. The variable is then said to have **namespace scope**. Let's refer to the form in which the variable is declared as its *declaration form*. When such a variable is referred to in the code of another form, the declaration form's name (followed by a period) must precede the name of the variable. For instance, the variable *total* declared as a namespace scope variable in Form1 with the statement

```
Public total as Double
```

must be referred to as *Form1.total* when used in Form2.

The scope of a class-level constant is converted to namespace-level by preceding the keyword Const with the keyword Public. A general procedure and a Structure declaration have namespace scope by default. Preceding their header with the keyword Private will limit their access to their declaration form. Controls always have namespace scope. Just as with variables, the names of namespace-level constants, general procedures, and controls must be preceded by their declaration form's name (followed by a period) when referred to in another form's code.

■ Modality

A form can invoke another form as a modal or modeless form. A **modal** form must be closed before the user can continue working with the rest of the program. (Ordinary input and message dialog boxes are examples of modal forms.) With a **modeless** (or **nonmodal**) form, the user can shift the focus between the form and another form without having to first close the initial form. (Visual Basic's *Find* dialog box is an example of a modeless form.) In this book, new forms will always be invoked as modal forms.

■ Close and ShowDialog Methods

The statement **Me.Close()** closes the form whose code contains it. The Close method actually can be used to close any form in the program. The statement

```
frmOther.Close()
```

where *frmOther* is a form other than the form containing the statement, closes frmOther.
The statement

```
frmOther.ShowDialog()
```

displays the other form as a modal form and gives it the focus. [The statement **frmOther.Show()** displays the other form as a modeless form.]

■ The FormClosing Event Procedure

The Load event procedure occurs before a form is displayed for the first time or before it is displayed after having been closed. Analogous to the Load event is the FormClosing event that occurs before the form is closed. (A form is closed by the execution of a Close method, by the user's clicking on the form's *Close* button in the title bar, or by the user's pressing Alt+F4.)

■ Importing an Existing Form

You can add a form created in another program to the current program with the following steps:

1. Click on *Add Existing Item* in the Menu bar's Project menu.

2. Navigate to the program containing the form. The program will contain a file named *formName.vb*.

3. Double-click on *formName.vb*. That file will be copied into your program's Solution Explorer and you will have added its form to your program. **Note:** If the added form refers to a text file, the text file will have to be copied separately into your program's *bin\Debug* folder.

■ Deleting a Form from a Program

To remove a form from a program, right-click on its name in the Solution Explorer, and click on *Delete* in the context menu that appears. (An input dialog box will ask you to confirm the deletion.) If the deleted form was the startup form, you will have to select a new startup form.

 Example 1 **Income** The following program uses a second form as a dialog box to obtain and total the different sources of income. Initially, only frmIncome is visible. The user types in their name and then clicks on the button for assistance in totaling the different sources of income. Clicking on the button from frmIncome causes frmSources to appear and be active. The user fills in the three text boxes and then clicks on the button to have the amounts totaled and displayed in the "Total income" text box of frmIncome.

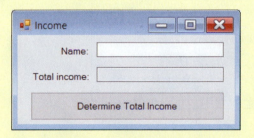

OBJECT	PROPERTY	SETTING
frmIncome	Text	Income
lblName	Text	Name:
txtName		
lblTotIncome	Text	Total income:
txtTotIncome	ReadOnly	True
btnDetermine	Text	Determine Total Income

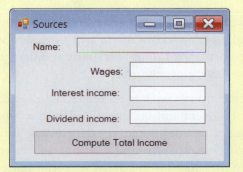

OBJECT	PROPERTY	SETTING
frmSources	Text	Sources
lblName	Text	Name:
txtName	ReadOnly	True
lblWages	Text	Wages:
txtWages		
lblIntIncome	Text	Interest income:
txtIntIncome		
lblDivIncome	Text	Dividend income:
txtDivIncome		
btnCompute	Text	Compute Total Income

```
'frmIncome's code (startup form)
Private Sub btnDetermine_Click(...) Handles btnDetermine.Click
  frmSources.txtName.Text = txtName.Text
  frmSources.ShowDialog()      'Show the second form and wait until it closes.
  '                      Then execute the rest of the code in this procedure.
  txtTotIncome.Text = (frmSources.sum).ToString("C")
End Sub


'frmSources's code
Public sum As Decimal      'holds the sum of the text boxes' values
Private Sub frmSources_Load(...) Handles MyBase.Load
  txtWages.Clear()
  txtIntIncome.Clear()
  txtDivIncome.Clear()
End Sub


Private Sub btnCompute_Click(...) Handles btnCompute.Click
  'Store the total into the namespace-level variable sum.
  sum = CDec(txtWages.Text) + CDec(txtIntIncome.Text) +
      CDec(txtDivIncome.Text)
  Me.Close()    'Close the form since it is not needed anymore.
End Sub
```

[Run, enter a name, click on the button, and fill in the sources of income.] **Note:** After the *Compute Total Income* button is clicked, frmSources will disappear and the sum of the three numbers will be displayed in the Income text box of frmIncome.

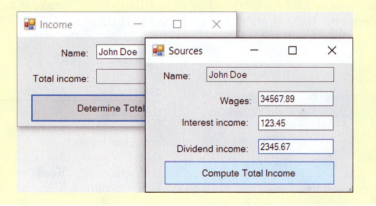

 Example 2 **Process an Order** The following program uses two forms. The startup form, frmOrder, processes an order after first requesting a user name and password with frmLogin. Even though frmOrder is the startup form, frmLogin is actually the first form seen by the user. It is invoked by frmOrder's Load event procedure.

The form frmLogin uses the text file MasterFile.txt to check for a registered user name and password. Each line of the text file consists of a user name concatenated with an underscore character and a password. The first three lines of the file contain the data dcook_idol08, JQPublic_vbguy21, and shawnj_dance09. After checking that the text boxes have been filled in, the program uses a query to determine if the user name and password combination is in the text file. The user gets three chances to enter an acceptable response. Code in a Form-Closing event procedure prevents the user from closing the login form without first giving a satisfactory user name and password.

OBJECT	PROPERTY	SETTING
frmLogin	Text	Login Form
lblUserName	Text	User name:
txtUserName		
lblPassword	Text	Password:
txtPassword		
btnContinue	Text	Continue

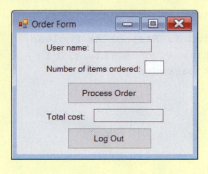

OBJECT	PROPERTY	SETTING
frmOrder	Text	Order Form
lblUserName	Text	User name:
txtUserName	ReadOnly	True
lblNumItems	Text	Number of items ordered:
txtNumItems		
btnProcess	Text	Process Order
lblTotalCost	Text	Total cost:
txtTotalCost	ReadOnly	True
btnLogOut	Text	Log Out

```vb
'frmOrder's code (startup form)
Private Sub frmOrder_Load(...) Handles MyBase.Load
  frmLogin.ShowDialog()
  txtUserName.Text = frmLogin.userName
End Sub


Private Sub btnProcess_Click(...) Handles btnProcess.Click
 Dim numItems As Integer
 Dim totalCost As Decimal
 numItems = CInt(txtNumItems.Text)
  'Cost per item: $20; shipping cost: $8
  totalCost = (numItems * 20) + 8
  txtTotalCost.Text = totalCost.ToString("C")
End Sub


Private Sub btnLogOut_Click(...) Handles btnLogOut.Click
  Me.Close()
End Sub

'frmLogin's code
Public userName As String
Dim numTries As Integer = 0, idVerified As Boolean = False

Private Sub btnContinue_Click(...) Handles btnContinue.Click
  If (txtUserName.Text = "") Or (txtPassword.Text = "") Then
    MessageBox.Show("You must enter both a user name and a password.")
  Else
    If Confirm(txtUserName.Text, txtPassword.Text) Then
      idVerified = True
```

```
        userName = txtUserName.Text
        Me.Close()
      Else
        MessageBox.Show("Improper user name or password.")
        txtUserName.Clear()
        txtPassword.Clear()
      End If
    End If
    numTries += 1
    If (numTries = 3) And (Not idVerified) Then
      MessageBox.Show("This program is being terminated.")
      frmOrder.Close()
      Me.Close()
    End If
End Sub

Function Confirm(userName As String, password As String) As Boolean
  Dim query = From line In IO.File.ReadAllLines("MasterFile.txt")
              Where line = userName & "_" & password
              Select line
  If query.Count = 1 Then
    Return True
  Else
    Return False
  End If
End Function

Private Sub frmLogin_FormClosing(...) Handles Me.FormClosing
  If Not idVerified Then
    MessageBox.Show("This program is being terminated.")
    frmOrder.Close()
  End If
End Sub
```

[Run, then enter a user name and password into the form.]

[Click on the button in the Login form. Then enter a quantity into the text box of the Order form below and click on the *Process Order* button.]

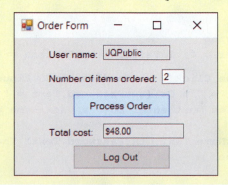

Example 3   **Weekly Payroll** We can easily modify the Weekly Payroll case study from Chapter 5 so that instead of the output being displayed in a list box, it is displayed in the form shown in Fig. 9.34 at the beginning of this section.

1. Start a new program with the name 9-3-3.
2. Delete Form1.vb from the Solution Explorer.
3. Add the existing form frmPayroll from the program 5-5 (Weekly Payroll) to the new program.
4. Change the startup form to frmPayroll.
5. Add a new form to the program and name it frmReceipt.
6. Design the form for frmReceipt as shown in Fig. 9.34 on page 479 with the settings in Fig. 9.35.

OBJECT	PROPERTY	SETTING
frmReceipt	Text	Payroll Receipt
lblName	Text	Name:
txtName		
lblGrossPay	Text	Gross pay this period:
txtGrossPay		
lblTotalPay	Text	Year-to-date earnings:
txtTotalPay		
lblFicaTax	Text	FICA taxes this period:
txtFicaTax		
lblFedTax	Text	Income tax withheld:
txtFedTax		
lblCheck	Text	Net pay (check amount):
txtCheck		
btnReturn	Text	Return to Data-Entry Form

FIGURE 9.35   Controls and settings for frmReceipt.

7. Add the code shown in Fig. 9.36 to frmReceipt.

```
Sub SetPayrollInfo(empName As String, pay As Decimal,
                   totalPay As Decimal, ficaTax As Decimal,
                   fedTax As Decimal, check As Decimal)
  txtName.Text = empName
  txtGrossPay.Text = pay.ToString("C")
  txtTotalPay.Text = totalPay.ToString("C")
  txtFicaTax.Text = ficaTax.ToString("C")
  txtFedTax.Text = fedTax.ToString("C")
  txtCheck.Text = check.ToString("C")
End Sub

Private Sub btnReturn_Click(...) Handles btnReturn.Click
  Me.Close()
End Sub
```

FIGURE 9.36   Code for frmReceipt.

8. In the btnDisplay_Click procedure of frmPayroll, replace the line

```
ShowPayroll(empName, pay, totalPay, ficaTax, fedTax, check) 'Task 6
```
with
```
frmReceipt.SetPayrollInfo(empName, pay, totalPay, ficaTax,
                          fedTax, check)         'Task 6
frmReceipt.ShowDialog()
```

Practice Problem 9.3

1. Rewrite the program in Example 2 without using the namespace-level variable *userName*.

EXERCISES 9.3

In Exercises 1 through 4, determine the output displayed when the button is clicked.

1.
```
'Form1's code (startup form)
Private Sub btnDisplay_Click(...) Handles btnDisplay.Click
  Form2.ShowDialog()
  txtOutput.Text = (Form2.totalCost).ToString("C")
End Sub

Function GetTotalCost(price As Decimal) As Decimal
  Return price + (Form2.SALES_TAX_RATE * price)
End Function

'Form2's code
Public Const SALES_TAX_RATE As Decimal = 0.06D
Public totalCost As Decimal
Private Sub Form2_Load(...) Handles Me.Load
  Dim price As String = InputBox("What is the price?")
  totalCost = Form1.GetTotalCost(CDec(price))
  Me.Close()
End Sub
```
(Assume that the response is 100.)

2.
```
'Form1's code (startup form)
Private Sub Form1_Load(...) Handles MyBase.Load
  Form2.ShowDialog()
  Dim name As String = Form2.txtName.Text
  Dim dob As Date = CDate(Form2.txtDateOfBirth.Text)
  Dim parsedName() As String = name.Split(" "c)
  Dim firstName = parsedName.First
  Dim message As String
  If dob.AddYears(21) <= Today Then
    message = ", you are at least 21 years old."
  Else
    message = ", you are not yet 21 years old."
  End If
  txtOutput.Text = firstName & message
End Sub
```

```
'Form2's code
Private Sub Form2_Load(...) Handles MyBase.Load
    txtName.Text = "John Doe"
    txtDateOfBirth.Text = "2/3/1989"
End Sub

Private Sub btnRecord_Click(...) Handles btnRecord.Click
    Me.Close()
End Sub
```

3.
```
'Form1's code (startup form)
Private Sub Form1_Load(...) Handles MyBase.Load
    Form2.ShowDialog()
    Dim name As String = Form2.fullName
    Dim lastName As String = Form2.GetLastName(name)
    txtOutput.Text = "Your last name begins with " &
                     lastName.Substring(0, 1) & "."
End Sub

'Form2's code
Public fullName As String

Private Sub btnDetermine_Click(...) Handles btnDetermine.Click
    fullName = "John Fitzgerald Kennedy"
    Me.Close()
End Sub

Function GetLastName(nom As String) As String
    Dim parsedName() As String = nom.Split(" "c)
    Return parsedName.Last
End Function
```

4.
```
'Form1's code (startup form)
Public average As Double

Private Sub Form1_Load(...) Handles MyBase.Load
    Form2.ShowDialog()
End Sub

Private Sub btnComputeAverage_Click(...) Handles btnComputeAverage.Click
    Dim num As Double
    Dim count As Integer = 0
    Dim sum As Double = 0
    num = CDbl(InputBox("Enter a nonnegative number"))
    Do While num <> -1
        count += 1
        sum += num
        num = CDbl(InputBox("Enter a number"))
    Loop
    average = sum / count
    Form3.ShowDialog()
    Me.Close()
End Sub

'Form2's code
Private Sub Form2_Load(...) Handles MyBase.Load
```

```
        Dim message As String = "The purpose of this program is to" &
            " calculate the average of a set of nonnegative numbers" &
            " input by the user. Enter the numbers one at a time" &
            " and enter -1 to signal the end of data entry."
        MessageBox.Show(message, "Instructions")
        Me.Close()
    End Sub

    'Form3's code
    Private Sub Form3_Load(...) Handles MyBase.Load
        txtAverage.Text = "The average is " & Form1.average & "."
    End Sub
```

(Assume the responses are 80, 100, and −1.)

5. **Movie Quotations**   Consider Example 2 of Section 6.1. Alter the program so that a second form appears (instead of a message box) when the button is clicked. The second form should allow the user to make a selection by clicking on one of three radio buttons with the captions *Movie 1*, *Movie 2*, and *Movie 3*.

6. **Parse a Name**   Consider the program in Example 8 from Section 7.1 that determines a person's first and last names. Alter the program so that the person's full name is typed into the startup form and a second form is used to display their first and last names.

7. **Compound Interest**   Consider Example 5 of Section 6.1. Alter the program so that a second form showing the balance after each year appears when the button is clicked on. See Fig. 9.37.

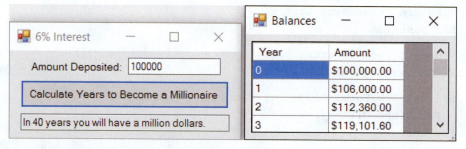

FIGURE 9.37   Possible outcome of Exercise 7.

8. **Analyze a Loan**   Consider the Analyze-a-Loan case study from Chapter 7. Alter the program so that the amortization table and the interest-rate-change table are each displayed in a separate form when requested. The program should have three forms, and the startup form should not contain a DataGridView control.

9. **Recording Checks and Deposits**   Consider the Recording Checks and Deposits case study from Chapter 8. Alter the program so that the list of transactions is displayed in a second form when requested.

10. **Student Grades**   Write a program that allows student grades on three exams to be entered one student at a time in frmStudent and then displays each student's average and the class average in frmGrades. Initially, frmGrades (the startup form) should look like Fig. 9.38 with the text box and DataGridView controls empty. The form frmStudent should initially look like Fig. 9.39 with the four text boxes empty. The Load event procedure of frmGrades should invoke frmStudent.

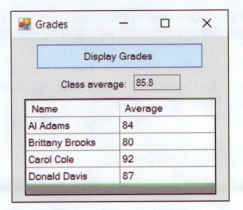

FIGURE 9.38   frmGrades.

FIGURE 9.39   frmStudent.

Each time a student's name and grades are recorded, the number in the title bar of frmStudent should increase by 1. The *Terminate* button should be clicked on after all students have been recorded. The data for the students should be stored in an array of structures with the structure having four members.

11. **Billing Information**   Write a program consisting of three forms that gathers customer billing information. The first form (the startup form) should initially look like Fig. 9.40, but with the text box and list box blank and no radio button selected. (The second and third forms should initially look like Figs. 9.41 and 9.43 with all text boxes blank.) After the user provides a name, selects a billing method, and clicks on the button in frmCustomer, either frmCustInfo or frmCardInfo should appear to obtain the necessary information.

FIGURE 9.40   frmCustomer.

FIGURE 9.41   frmCustInfo.

Let's first consider frmCustInfo, which appears when the *Bill Customer* radio button is selected. The Name read-only text box should be filled automatically with the name that was entered in frmCustomer. The user enters information into the other text boxes, selects a state from the sorted drop-down-list combo box, and clicks on the button to display the mailing address in the list box of frmCustomer as shown in Fig. 9.40. **Note:** The names of the states can be obtained from the file States.txt.

The form frmCardInfo, which appears when the *Bill Credit Card* radio button in frmCustomer has been selected, contains two text boxes, one simple combo box (for type of credit card) and two DropDownList style combo boxes. The Name text box is initially automatically filled with the name that was entered in frmCustomer. However, the name can be altered, if necessary, to look exactly like the name printed on the credit card. The list for the "Year" combo box should be filled by the Load event procedure and should contain the current year followed by the next five years. (**Note:** The current year is given by Today.Year.) After the user provides the requested data, the information is displayed in the list box of frmCustomer as shown in Fig. 9.42.

FIGURE 9.42 frmCustomer.

FIGURE 9.43 frmCardInfo.

12. **Dial a Telephone** Write a program containing the two forms shown in Fig. 9.44. Initially, the Number form appears. When the *Show Push Buttons* button is clicked, the Push Buttons form appears. The user enters a number by clicking on successive push buttons and then clicking on *Enter* to have the number transferred to the read-only text box at the bottom of the first form.

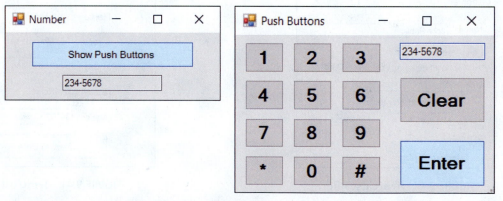

FIGURE 9.44 Possible outcome of Exercise 12.

Solution to Practice Problem 9.3

1. In frmLogin's code, delete the two lines

```
Public userName As String
```

and

```
userName = txtUserName.Text
```

In frmOrder's code, change the line

```
txt.UserName.Text = frmLogin.userName
```

to

```
txtUserName.Text = frmLogin.txtUserName.Text
```

9.4   Graphics

In this section, we draw bar charts and pie charts in a picture box, and illustrate one method for creating animation on a form.

VideoNote
Graphics

Caution: Since the programs in this section mix text and graphics, what you see on the monitor may vary with the monitor's DPI (dots per inch) resolution setting. To guarantee the intended outcomes, you should check that your monitor is set to display smaller DPI. For details, see the first item under "Configuring the Windows Environment" in Appendix B.

■ Graphics Objects

A statement of the form

```
Dim gr As Graphics = picBox.CreateGraphics
```

declares *gr* to be a Graphics object for the picture box picBox.

The unit of measurement used in graphics methods is the **pixel**. To get a feel for how big a pixel is, the title bar of a form is 30 pixels high, and the border of a form is four pixels thick. The setting for the Size property of a picture box is two numbers separated by a comma. The two numbers give the width and height of the picture box in pixels. You can alter these values to specify a precise size. Each point of a picture box is identified by a pair of coordinates

```
(x, y)
```

where *x* (between 0 and picBox.Width) is its distance in pixels from the left side of the picture box, and *y* (between 0 and picBox.Height) is its distance in pixels from the top of the picture box.

Text is placed in a picture box with a statement of the form

```
gr.DrawString(string, Me.Font, Brushes.Color, x, y)
```

where *string* is either a string variable or literal, Me.Font specifies that the Form's font be used to display the text, and the upper-left corner of the first character of the text has coordinates (*x, y*). The color of the text is determined by *Color*. IntelliSense will provide a list of about 140 possible colors after **"Brushes."** is typed. As an example, the statements

```
Dim gr As Graphics = picBox.CreateGraphics
Dim strVar As String = "Hello"
gr.DrawString(strVar, Me.Font, Brushes.Blue, 4, 30)
gr.DrawString("World", Me.Font, Brushes.Red, 35, 50)
```

produce the output shown in Fig. 9.45.

FIGURE 9.45   DrawString method.

■ Lines, Rectangles, Circles, and Sectors

Let *gr* be a Graphics object for picBox. Then the statement

```
gr.DrawLine(Pens.Color, x1, y1, x2, y2)
```

draws a straight line segment from the point with coordinates $(x1, y1)$ to the point with coordinates $(x2, y2)$. The color of the line is determined by *Color*. IntelliSense will provide an extensive list of possible colors after `"Pens."` is typed. For instance, the statement

```
gr.DrawLine(Pens.Blue, 50, 20, 120, 75)
```

draws a blue line from the point with the coordinates (50, 20) to the point with the coordinates (120, 75). See Fig. 9.46.

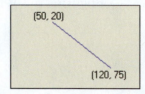

FIGURE 9.46 DrawLine method.

The statement

```
gr.FillRectangle(Brushes.Color, x, y, w, h)
```

draws a solid rectangle of width *w* and height *h* in the color specified and having the point with coordinates (x, y) as its upper-left vertex. The left side of the rectangle will be *x* pixels from the left side of the picture box and the top side of the rectangle will be *y* pixels from the top of the picture box. For instance, the statement

```
gr.FillRectangle(Brushes.Blue, 50, 20, 70, 55)
```

draws the rectangle shown in Fig. 9.47.

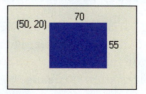

FIGURE 9.47 FillRectangle method.

The FillEllipse method draws a solid ellipse of a specified color, given the specifications of a circumscribed rectangle. The rectangle is specified by the coordinates of its upper-left point, its width, and its height. This method produces a circle when the width and height of the rectangle are the same. In particular, the statement

```
gr.FillEllipse(Brushes.Color, a - r, b - r, 2 * r, 2 * r)
```

draws a solid circle of the specified color with center (a, b) and radius *r*. For instance, the statement

```
gr.FillEllipse(Brushes.Blue, 80 - 40, 50 - 40, 2 * 40, 2 * 40)
```

draws a solid blue circle with center (80, 50) and radius 40. **Note:** If a rectangle were circumscribed about the circle, the rectangle would be a square with its upper-left vertex at (40, 10) and each side of length 80.

The FillPie method draws a solid sector of an ellipse in a color. The ellipse is specified by giving the coordinates, width, and height for the circumscribing rectangle, as in the Fill-Ellipse method. The sector is determined by a radius line and the angle swept out by the radius line. We are interested solely in the case where the ellipse is a circle. The shaded region in Fig. 9.48 is a typical sector (or pie-shaped region) of a circle. The sector is determined by the two angles θ_1 and θ_2. The start angle, θ_1, is the angle through which the horizontal radius line must be rotated clockwise to reach the starting radius line of the sector. Angle θ_2 is the number of degrees through which the starting radius line must sweep (clockwise) to reach the ending radius line of the sector. The angles θ_1 and θ_2 are referred to as the **start angle** and the **sweep angle**, respectively. Figure 9.49 shows the start and sweep angles for three sectors of a circle.

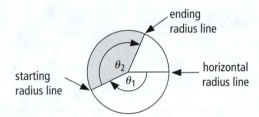

FIGURE 9.48   A typical sector of a circle.

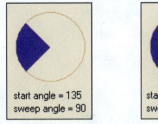

FIGURE 9.49   FillPie method.

In general, a statement of the form

```
gr.FillPie(Brushes.Color, a - r, b - r, 2 * r, 2 * r,
        startAngle,sweepAngle)
```

draws a sector of a circle of the specified color with center (a, b), radius r, and the given start and sweep angles. For instance, the middle image of Fig. 9.49 can be drawn with a statement such as

```
gr.FillPie(Brushes.Blue, 80 - 40, 80 - 40, 2 * 40, 2 * 40, 45, 180)
```

The Brushes, Pens, and Fonts appearing in the drawing statements so far are literals of objects. Variables also can be used to provide these values. For instance, the statement gr.FillRectangle(Brushes.Blue, 50, 20, 70, 55) can be replaced by the pair of statements

```
Dim br As Brush = Brushes.Blue
gr.FillRectangle(br, 50, 20, 70, 55)
```

The first statement declares *br* to be a variable of type Brush and assigns it the value Brushes.Blue.

Numeric variables used in the Draw and Fill statements discussed in this section cannot be of type Double. Therefore, we will give them Integer or Decimal data types.

■ Pie Charts

Consider the three pieces of data in Table 9.3. A pie chart can be used to graphically display the relative sizes of these numbers. The first step in creating a pie chart is to convert the numbers to percentages. Since the total expenditures are $419 billion, the federal outlay is 33/419 ≈ .08 or 8%. Similarly, the state and local expenditures are 49% and 43%. See Table 9.4. Our goal is to write a program to display the information in the pie chart of Fig. 9.50.

TABLE 9.3	Financing for public schools (in billions).
Federal	$33
State	$206
Local	$180

TABLE 9.4	Financing for public schools.
Federal	.08 or 8%
State	.49 or 49%
Local	.43 or 43%

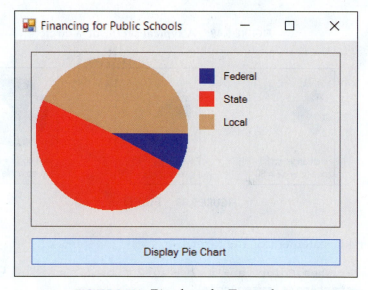

FIGURE 9.50 Pie chart for Example 1.

The blue sector in Fig. 9.50 has start angle 0 degrees and sweep angle .08 * 360 degrees. The red sector has start angle .08 * 360 and sweep angle .49 * 360. The tan sector has start angle .08 * 360 + .49 * 360 [or (.08 + .49) * 360 degrees] and sweep angle .43 * 360° degrees. Notice that each start angle is (sum of previous percentages) * 360. The sweep angle for each sector is the corresponding percentage times 360.

 Example 1 **School Financing** The following program creates the pie chart for the financing of public schools. (See Fig. 9.50.) The program is written so that it can be easily converted to handle a pie chart with up to six sectors. All that is required is to change the first two Dim statements and the Me. Text statement. The "Dim br() As Brush" line, which creates an array of brushes, has six brushes in order to accommodate additional sectors.

```vb
Private Sub btnDisplay_Click(...) Handles btnDisplay.Click
  Dim legend() As String = {"Federal", "State", "Local"}
  Dim quantity() As Decimal = {33, 206, 180}
  Dim percent(quantity.Count - 1) As Decimal
  Dim sumOfQuantities As Decimal = 0
  Dim sumOfSweepAngles As Decimal = 0
  Dim br() As Brush = {Brushes.Blue, Brushes.Red, Brushes.Tan,
          Brushes.Green, Brushes.Orange, Brushes.Gray}
  Dim gr As Graphics = picOutput.CreateGraphics
  'The picture box has width 312 and height 215
  Dim r As Integer = 100     'radius of circle
  Dim c As Integer = 105     'center of circle has coordinates (c, c)
  Me.Text = "Financing for Public Schools"
  'Sum the numbers for the quantities
  For i As Integer = 0 To (quantity.Count - 1)
    sumOfQuantities += quantity(i)
  Next
  'Convert the quantities to percents
  For i As Integer = 0 To quantity.Count - 1
    percent(i) = quantity(i) / sumOfQuantities
  Next
  'Display the pie chart and the legends
  For i As Integer = 0 To (quantity.Count - 1)
    gr.FillPie(br(i), c - r, c - r, 2 * r, 2 * r,
            sumOfSweepAngles, percent(i) * 360)
    sumOfSweepAngles += CDec(percent(i) * 360)
    'Display small colored square and legend
    gr.FillRectangle(br(i), 220, 20 + 30 * i, 20, 20)
    gr.DrawString(legend(i), Me.Font, Brushes.Black, 250, 22 + 30 * i)
  Next
End Sub
```

■ Bar Charts

Our goal here is to produce the bar chart of Fig. 9.51. The picture box for the chart has a width of 210 and height of 150 pixels. (Here, the BorderStyle property is set to FixedSingle for instructional reasons. In general, the bar chart will look better with the BorderStyle property of the picture box left at its default setting: None.)

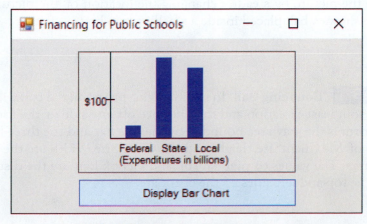

FIGURE 9.51 Bar chart for Example 2.

The three magnitudes for the graph are 33, 206, and 180. If we let a pixel correspond to one unit, then the largest rectangle will be 206 pixels high—a bit too large. With a pixel corresponding to 2 units, the largest rectangle will be 206/2 or 103 pixels high—a reasonable size. By setting the *x*-axis 110 pixels from the top of the picture box, the largest rectangle is accommodated comfortably. The top of the largest rectangle is 110 − 103 [that is, 110 − (206/2)] pixels from the top of the picture box. In general, a rectangle corresponding to the quantity *q* will be 110 − (*q*/2) pixels from the top of the picture box, and the height will be *q*/2 pixels.

Example 2   **School Financing**   The following program produces the bar chart of Fig. 9.51 on the previous page. Each rectangle is 20 pixels wide, and there are 20 pixels between rectangles.

```
Private Sub btnDisplay_Click(...) Handles btnDisplay.Click
  Dim quantity() As Decimal = {33, 206, 180}
  Dim gr As Graphics = picOutput.CreateGraphics
  'The picture box has width 210 and height 150
  gr.DrawLine(Pens.Black, 40, 110, 210, 110)   'x-axis
  gr.DrawLine(Pens.Black, 40, 110, 40, 0)       'y-axis
  gr.DrawLine(Pens.Black, 35, 60, 45, 60)        'tick mark; 60 = 110 - (100/2)
  gr.DrawString("$100", Me.Font, Brushes.Black, 5, 55)
  Me.Text = "Financing for Public Schools"
  For i As Integer = 0 To quantity.Count - 1
    gr.FillRectangle(Brushes.Blue, 60 + i * 40,
                  (110 - quantity(i) / 2), 20, quantity(i) / 2)
  Next
  gr.DrawString("Federal State Local", Me.Font,
          Brushes.Black, 50, 115)
  gr.DrawString("(Expenditures in billions)", Me.Font,
          Brushes.Black, 50, 130)
End Sub
```

■ Animation

One way to produce animation on a form is to place an image into a picture box and then move the picture by steadily changing the location of the picture box. The form in Example 3 shows a ball placed inside a small picture box.

Example 3   **Bouncing Ball**   In the following program, the ball will initially move diagonally in a southeast direction and then bounce off any side of the form it hits. The **client area** of a form is the gray area bounded by the title bar and the three borders of the form. The values of Me.ClientSize.Height and Me.ClientSize.Width are the height and width of the client area. The values of picBox.Top and picBox.Left are the distances of the picture box from the top and left sides of the client area.

The speed at which the ball moves is determined by the setting for the Interval property of Timer1. At each tick, the ball will move x pixels horizontally, where $x = 1$ or -1. When $x = 1$ the ball moves to the right, and when $x = -1$ the ball moves to the left. The value of x reverses when the ball strikes the right or left side of the form. The value of y determines the vertical motion of the ball in a similar manner:

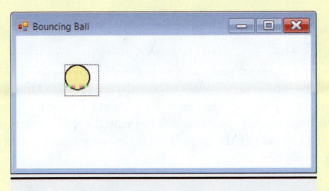

OBJECT	PROPERTY	SETTING
frmBall	Text	Bouncing Ball
	BackColor	White
picBall	Image	Moon5.bmp
Timer1	Interval	10

```
Dim x As Integer = 1
Dim y As Integer = 1

Private Sub frmBall_Load(...) Handles MyBase.Load
  Timer1.Enabled = True
End Sub

Private Sub Timer1_Tick(...) Handles Timer1.Tick
  If picBall.Left <= 0 Or
    picBall.Left >= (Me.ClientSize.Width - picBall.Width) Then
    x = -x
  End If
  picBall.Left += x
  If picBall.Top <= 0 Or
    picBall.Top >= (Me.ClientSize.Height - picBall.Height) Then
    y = -y
  End If
  picBall.Top += y
End Sub
```

■ Printing Text

A graphics object is used to print text. The following five steps send output to the printer.

1. Double-click on the PrintDocument control in the *All Windows Forms* or *Printing* group of the Toolbox. (The control will appear with the default name PrintDocument1 in a separate pane, called the **component tray**, at the bottom of the Form Designer.)

2. Double-click on PrintDocument1 to invoke its PrintPage event procedure. (The code for printing text will be placed in this event procedure.)

3. Place the statement

```
Dim gr As Graphics = e.Graphics
```

in the event procedure. (This statement declares *gr* as a graphics object capable of printing both text and graphics.)

4. Enter a statement of the form

```
gr.DrawString(str, font, Brushes.color, x, y)
```

for each line of text to be printed. Here *str* is a string; *font* specifies the font name, size, and style; *color* specifies the color of the text; and *x* and *y* are integers giving the location on the page of the beginning of the string. (The values of *x* and *y* are specified in points, where 100 points are about one inch.) Visual Basic indents all text by about 25 points from the left side of the page. The beginning of the string will be printed *x* + 25 points from the left side and *y* points from the top side of the page. Two different ways of specifying the font will be given in the example that follows.

5. Place the statement

```
PrintDocument1.Print()
```

in another event procedure, such as a button's Click event procedure. (This statement will cause all of the text specified in Step 4 to be printed.)

Some examples of DrawString statements are as follows. The statement

```
gr.DrawString("Hello World", Me.Font, Brushes.DarkBlue, 100, 150)
```

prints the words Hello World using the form's font in dark blue letters 1.25 inches from the left side of the page and 1.5 inches from the top of the page. The pair of statements

```
Dim font As New Font("Courier New", 12, FontStyle.Bold)
gr.DrawString("Hello World", font, Brushes.DarkBlue, 100, 150)
```

produce the same output using a 12-point bold Courier New font.

Visual Basic provides a control, called the **PrintPreviewDialog** control, which allows you to see how output will look before you send it to the printer. Just follow two steps:

1. Double-click on the PrintPreviewDialog control in the *All Windows Forms* or *Printing* group of the Toolbox. (The control will have the default name PrintPreviewDialog1 in the component **tray** at the bottom of the Form Designer.)

2. Place the pair of statements

```
PrintPreviewDialog1.Document = PrintDocument1
PrintPreviewDialog1.ShowDialog()
```

in another event procedure, such as a button's Click event procedure. These statements cause the text specified in the PrintDocument1_PrintPage event procedure to be displayed in a "Print preview" window when the event procedure is invoked. The preview window's toolbar contains a magnifying-glass button ( ) that allows you to zoom in on the text.

 Example 4   **Print a Table** The following program produces a two-column table of the top three all-time home-run hitters. Notice that the font is changed after the table's header is printed.

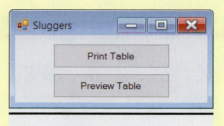

OBJECT	PROPERTY	SETTING
frmHR	Text	Sluggers
btnPrint	Text	Print Table
btnPreview	Text	Preview Table
PrintDocument1		
PrintPreviewDialog1		

```vb
Const ONE_INCH As Integer = 100      'number of points in an inch
Const LINE_HEIGHT As Integer = 25    'one-quarter of an inch

Private Sub btnPrint_Click(...) Handles btnPrint.Click
  PrintDocument1.Print()
End Sub

Private Sub btnPreview_Click(...) Handles btnPreview.Click
  PrintPreviewDialog1.Document = PrintDocument1
  PrintPreviewDialog1.ShowDialog()
End Sub

Private Sub PrintDocument1_PrintPage(...) Handles PrintDocument1.PrintPage
  Dim gr As Graphics = e.Graphics
  Dim x1 As Integer = ONE_INCH         'use one inch beyond left margin
  Dim x2 As Integer = 3 * ONE_INCH     'offset for second column
  Dim y As Integer = ONE_INCH          'use one inch top margin
  Dim font As New Font("Courier New", 10, FontStyle.Bold)
  gr.DrawString("PLAYER", font, Brushes.Blue, x1, y)
  gr.DrawString("HR", font, Brushes.Blue, x2, y)
  font = New Font("Courier New", 10, FontStyle.Regular)
  y += LINE_HEIGHT                         'move down one-quarter inch
  gr.DrawString("Barry Bonds", font, Brushes.Black, x1, y)
  gr.DrawString("762", font, Brushes.Black, x2, y)
  y += LINE_HEIGHT
  gr.DrawString("Hank Aaron", font, Brushes.Black, x1, y)
  gr.DrawString("755", font, Brushes.Black, x2, y)
  y += LINE_HEIGHT
  gr.DrawString("Babe Ruth", font, Brushes.Black, x1, y)
  gr.DrawString("714", font, Brushes.Black, x2, y)
End Sub
```

[Run, click on the *Preview Table* button, click the Zoom down arrow to the right of the magnifying glass, and select 100%. The following text appears in the preview window.]

PLAYER	HR
Barry Bonds	762
Hank Aaron	755
Babe Ruth	714

■ Printing Graphics

Graphics can be printed with a PrintDocument control in much the same way that text is printed.

Example 5 **Print a Bar Chart** The following program produces the same output as Example 2. However, the output is printed instead of being displayed in a picture box. The changes from Example 2 are as follows:

1. The code was moved from the btnDisplay_Click event procedure to the procedure PrintDocument1_PrintPage.
2. The source of the graphics object *gr* was changed from picOutput.CreateGraphics to e.Graphics.
3. The Me.Text statement was replaced with a DrawString statement.
4. The values of the *x*-coordinates were increased by 300 to approximately center the graph horizontally, and the values of the *y*-coordinates were increased by 200 to lower the graph from the top edge of the page.

OBJECT	PROPERTY	SETTING
frmBarChart	Text	Bar Chart
btnPrint	Text	Print Bar Chart
btnPreview	Text	Preview Bar Chart
PrintDocument1		
PrintPreviewDialog1		

```vb
Private Sub btnPrint_Click(...) Handles btnPrint.Click
  PrintDocument1.Print()
End Sub

Private Sub PrintDocument1_PrintPage(...) Handles PrintDocument1.PrintPage
  Dim quantity() As Decimal = {33, 207, 180}
  Dim gr As Graphics = e.Graphics
  gr.DrawLine(Pens.Black, 340, 310, 510, 310)    'x-axis
  gr.DrawLine(Pens.Black, 340, 310, 340, 200)    'y-axis
  gr.DrawLine(Pens.Black, 335, 260, 345, 260)    'tick mark
  gr.DrawString("$100", Me.Font, Brushes.Black, 305, 255)
  gr.DrawString("Financing for Public Schools", Me.Font,
           Brushes.Black, 300, 175)
  For i As Integer = 0 To (quantity.Count - 1)
    gr.FillRectangle(Brushes.Blue, 360 + i * 40,
             (310 - quantity(i) / 2), 20, quantity(i) / 2)
  Next
  gr.DrawString("Federal   State   Local", Me.Font,
           Brushes.Black, 350, 315)
  gr.DrawString("(Expenditures in billions)", Me.Font,
           Brushes.Black, 350, 330)
End Sub

Private Sub btnPreview_Click(...) Handles btnPreview.Click
  PrintPreviewDialog1.Document = PrintDocument1
  PrintPreviewDialog1.ShowDialog()
End Sub
```

■ Comments

1. A statement of the form

   ```
   Dim pn As Pen = Pens.Color
   ```

   declares *pn* to be a variable of type Pen and assigns it the value Pens.*Color*.

2. A statement of the form

   ```
   Dim fnt As Font = New Font(fontName, size)
   ```

   declares *fnt* to be a variable of type Font and assigns it the specified font and size. For instance, the statements

   ```
   Dim gr As Graphics = picBox.CreateGraphics
   Dim fnt As Font = New Font("Courier New", 10)
   gr.DrawString("Hello", fnt, Brushes.Blue, 4, 30)
   ```

   display the word Hello in 10-point Courier New font.

3. The statement

   ```
   picBox.Refresh()
   ```

   clears all graphics and text from the picture box.

Practice Problems 9.4

1. (True or False) The Draw and Fill methods discussed in this section use colored Brushes.

2. Write lines of code that place VB in large red Courier New letters in the upper-left corner of the form.

EXERCISES 9.4

In Exercises 1 through 4, write a program to draw the given figures in a picture box.

1. Draw a circle whose center is located at the center of a picture box.

2. Draw a circle whose leftmost point is at the center of a picture box.

3. Use the FillEllipse method to create an unfilled red circle of radius 20.

4. Draw a triangle with two sides of the same length.

In Exercises 5 through 18 display the graphics in a picture box.

In Exercises 5 through 8, write a program to create the flag of the designated country. Refer to Fig. 9.52. *Note:* The Swiss flag is square. For the other three flags, the width is 1.5 times the height.

Italy   Switzerland   Niger   Greenland

FIGURE 9.52   **Flags of four countries.**

Source: 9.52a - Anatoly Tiplyashin/Shutterstock; 9.52b -Eskemar/Shutterstock; 9.52c and d - Globe Turner/Shutterstock

5. Italy   6. Switzerland   7. Niger   8. Greenland

9. Write a program to draw displays such as the one in Fig. 9.53. Let the user specify the maximum number (in this display, 8).

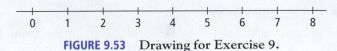

FIGURE 9.53 Drawing for Exercise 9.

10. Lines Write a program to draw displays such as the one in Fig. 9.54. Let the user specify the number of lines (in this display, 3).

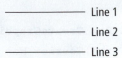

FIGURE 9.54 Drawing for Exercise 10.

11. Beverage Consumption Use the data in Table 9.5 to create a pie chart.

TABLE 9.5	United States recreational beverage consumption.
Soft Drinks	52.9%
Beer	14.7%
Bottled Water	11.1%
Other	21.3%

12. Minimum Wage Use the data in Table 9.6 to create a bar chart.

TABLE 9.6	United States minimum wage.
1959	1.00
1968	1.15
1978	2.65
1988	3.35
1998	5.15
2009	7.25

13. Smokers Write a program to create the line chart in Fig. 9.55. Use the data in Table 9.7.

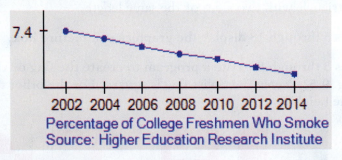

FIGURE 9.55 Line chart for Exercise 13.

Source: Data from The American Freshman by the Higher Education Research Institute.

TABLE 9.7	Percentage of college freshmen who smoke.						
	2002	2004	2006	2008	2010	2012	2014
Percent	7.4	6.4	5.3	4.4	3.7	2.6	1.7

Source: Data from The American Freshman by the Higher Education Research Institute.

14. College Enrollments   Write a program to create the line chart in Fig. 9.56. Use the data in Table 9.8

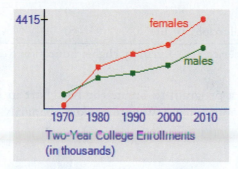

FIGURE 9.56   Line chart for Exercise 14.

TABLE 9.8	Two-year college enrollments (in thousands).				
	1970	**1980**	**1990**	**2000**	**2010**
Male	1375	2047	2233	2559	3265
Female	945	2479	3007	3390	4415

15. College Majors   Write a program to create the bar chart in Fig. 9.57.

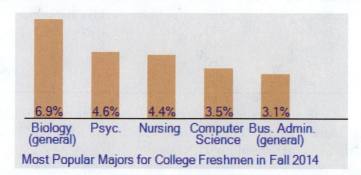

FIGURE 9.57   Bar chart for Exercise 15.

16. Life Goals   Write a program to create the bar chart in Fig. 9.58. Use the data in Table 9.9 on the next page.

FIGURE 9.58   Bar chart for Exercise 16.

TABLE 9.9	Freshman life goals (% of students committed to goal).			
	1978	1988	1998	2008
Be very well off financially	59	74	73	77
Develop a meaningful philosophy of life	60	43	44	51

Source: Data from The American Freshman by Higher Education Research Institute.

17. Languages Write a program to create the bar chart in Figure 9.59. Use the data in Table 9.10. **Note:** Mandarin and Wu are spoken primarily in China.

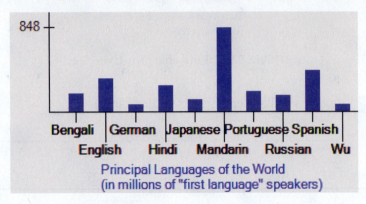

FIGURE 9.59 Bar chart for Exercise 17.

TABLE 9.10	Principal languages of the world.		
Bengali	183	Mandarin	848
English	335	Portuguese	203
German	78	Russian	167
Hindi	260	Spanish	414
Japanese	122	Wu	72

18. Budget Write a program that allows the user to display a budget as a pie chart. See Fig. 9.60. After the user enters numbers into the four text boxes and clicks on the button, the pie chart should be displayed.

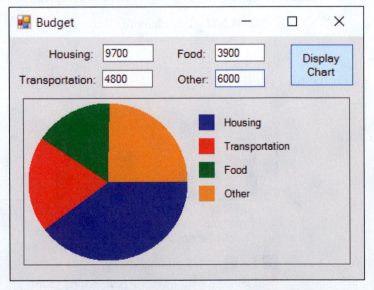

FIGURE 9.60 Possible outcome of Exercise 18.

19. Airplane   Write a program in which an airplane flies horizontally to the right across a form. See Fig. 9.61. After it flies off the form, the airplane should reappear on the left and fly horizontally across the form again. *Note:* Use the image Airplane.bmp found in the folder Ch09\Pictures.

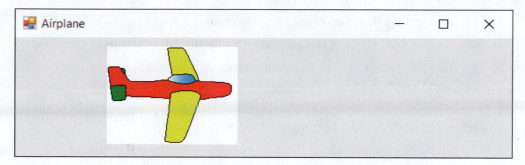

FIGURE 9.61   **Outcome of Exercise 19.**

20. Print a Table   Write a program to print the list of Internet lingo in Fig. 9.62.

```
PLS     Please                              % That uses
TAFN    That's all for now    Rank   Country   the Internet
HHOK    Ha, ha-only kidding   1      Norway    95.0%
FWIW    For what it's worth   2      USA       84.2%
IMHO    In my humble opinion  3      China     45.8%
```

FIGURE 9.62   **Output of Exercise 20.**   **FIGURE 9.63**   **Output of Exercise 21.**

21. Print a Table   Write a program to print the three countries ranked by the percentage of the population that uses the Internet. See Fig. 9.63.

22. School Financing   Rewrite the program in Example 1 so that the pie chart is printed instead of being displayed in a picture box. *Note:* You will most likely want to replace the variable c with the pair of variables cx and cy. Then the center of the circle will have coordinates (cx, cy).

23. Italian Flag   Refer to Exercise 5. Write a program to print the flag of Italy.

24. Niger Flag   Refer to Exercise 7. Write a program to print the flag of Niger.

Solutions to Practice Problems 9.4

1. False. Only the Fill methods and the DrawString method use colored Brushes. The DrawLine method uses colored Pens.

2. ```
Dim gr As Graphics = Me.CreateGraphics
Dim fnt As Font = New Font("Courier New", 20)
gr.DrawString("VB", fnt, Brushes.Red, 0, 0)
```

## CHAPTER 9   SUMMARY

1. *List boxes* provide easy access to lists of data. Items() holds the items stored in the list box. Each item is identified by an index number. The lists can be automatically sorted (Sorted property = True) and altered (Items.AddItem, Items.RemoveAt, and Items. Remove methods), the currently highlighted item identified (Text property), and the number of items determined (Items.Count property).
```

2. Simple and DropDown style *combo boxes* are enhanced text boxes. They allow the user to fill the text box by selecting an item from a list or by typing the item directly into the text box. The contents of the text box are assigned to the combo box's Text property. A DropDownList style combo box is essentially a list box that drops down instead of being permanently displayed.

3. The *timer control* raises an event repeatedly after a specified time interval.

4. An object of type *Random* can generate a randomly selected integer from a specified range.

5. The *ToolTip control* allows the program to display guidance when the mouse hovers over a control.

6. The *Clipboard* is filled with the SetText method or by pressing Ctrl+C, and its contents are copied with the GetText method or by pressing Ctrl+V.

7. The *picture box control*, which displays pictures, can expand to accommodate the size of a picture or have a picture alter its size to fit the control.

8. Menus, similar to the menus of the Visual Basic IDE itself, can be created with the *MenuStrip control*.

9. *Horizontal* and *vertical scroll bar controls* permit the user to select from among a range of integers by clicking or dragging with the mouse. The range is determined by the Minimum and Maximum properties. The Scroll event is raised by clicking on the scroll bar.

10. Additional forms can be added to a program to serve as customized dialog boxes. They are revealed with the *ShowDialog* method and removed with the *Close* method.

11. After a graphics object is produced with a *CreateGraphics* method, the *DrawString, DrawLine, FillRectangle, FillEllipse,* and *FillPie* methods can be used to display strings, lines, solid rectangles, solid ellipses, and solid sectors with colors supplied by Pen and Brush objects.

12. *Animation* can be produced by steadily moving a picture box containing an image.

13. The *PrintDocument control* is used to send output to the printer, and the *PrintPreviewDialog control* is used to preview the output.

CHAPTER 9 PROGRAMMING PROJECTS

1. **Membership List** Write a menu-driven program to manage a membership list. See Fig. 9.64. Assume that the names and phone numbers of all members are stored in alphabetical order (by last name, then by first name) in the text file MemberPhones.txt.

FIGURE 9.64 Possible outcome of Programming Project 1.

Each record consists of two fields—a name field and a phone number field. The names should appear in a list box when the form is loaded. When a name is highlighted, both the name and phone number of the person should appear in the text boxes at the bottom of the form. To delete a person, highlight his or her name and click on the *Delete* menu item. To change either a person's name or phone number, make the corrections in the text boxes and click on the menu item *Modify*. To add a new member, type the person's name and phone number into the text boxes and click on the menu item *Add*. When the *Exit* menu item is clicked, the new membership list should be written to the file and the program should terminate.

2. **Voting Machine**   The members of a club bring a computer to their annual meeting to use in the election of a new president. Write a program to handle the election. See Fig. 9.65. When the program is first run, the label at the top of the page should read as follows: Click "Nominate Candidate" to enter a candidate, or "Start Voting" to end nominations and start the voting. The program should add each candidate to a list box as he or she is nominated. After the nomination process is complete, club members should be able to approach the computer one at a time and double-click on the candidate of their choice. When the *Tally Votes* button is clicked on, a second list box, showing the number of votes received by each candidate, should appear along side the first list box. Also, the name(s) of the candidate(s) with the highest number of votes should be displayed in a message box.

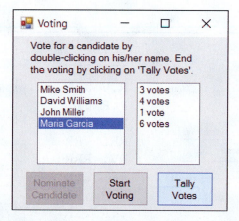

FIGURE 9.65   Possible outcome of Programming Project 2.

3. **Inventory Control**   Write a menu-driven multiform inventory program for a bookstore with data saved in a text file. Each record of the text file should consist of five fields—*title*, *author*, *category*, *wholesale price*, and *number in stock*. (The two categories are *fiction* and *nonfiction*.) At any time, the program should display the titles of the books in stock in a list box. The user should have the option of displaying either all titles or just those in one of the two categories. The user should be able to add a new book, delete a book, or alter any of the fields of a book in stock. The adding and editing processes use the second form, frmDetails. See Fig. 9.66 on the next page. At any time, the user should be able to calculate the total value of all books, or the total value of the books in either category. The menu item *File* contains the two second-level menu items *Save* and *Exit*. The menu items *Display* and *Values* each contain the three second-level menu items *All*, *Fiction*, and *Nonfiction*. (**Hint:** Store the data about the books in an array of structures.)

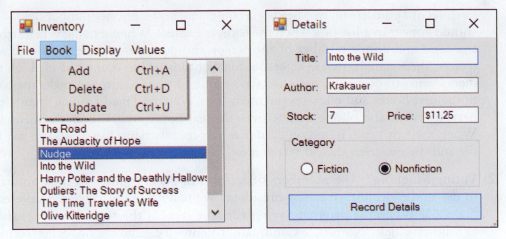

FIGURE 9.66 The two forms for Programming Project 3.

4. **Airplane Seating Chart** An airplane has 15 rows (numbered 1 through 15), with six seats (labeled *A, B, C, D, E,* and *F*) in each row. Write a multiform program that keeps track of the seats that have been reserved and the type of meal requested by each passenger. The seating chart should be displayed in a list box with a line for each row. See Fig. 9.67(a). When the ticket agent clicks on the desired row in the list box, the row

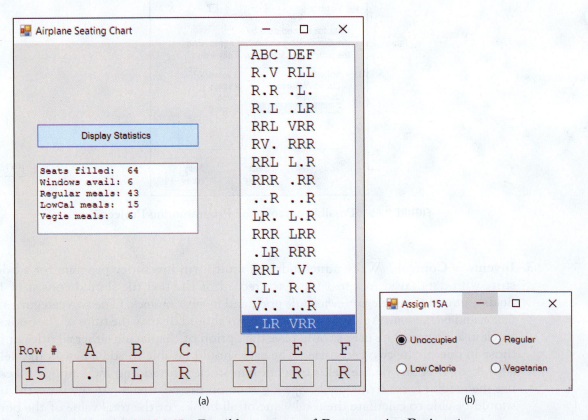

FIGURE 9.67 Possible outcome of Programming Project 4.

number and the status of the seats in the row should be displayed in seven read-only text boxes at the bottom of the form. When the agent clicks on one of the text boxes, a second form containing four option buttons labeled *Unoccupied*, *Regular*, *Low Calorie*, and *Vegetarian* should appear. See Fig. 9.67(b). Clicking on a radio button should close the second form and update both the text box and the row for that seat in the list box. Unoccupied seats are denoted with a period, and occupied seats are denoted with the first letter of their meal type. At any time, the agent should be able to request the number of seats filled, the number of window seats vacant, and the numbers of each type of meal ordered.

5. **The Underdog and the World Series**   What is the probability that the underdog will win the World Series of Baseball? What is the average number of games for a World Series? Write an animated program to answer these questions. For instance, suppose that the underdog is expected to win 40% of the time. We say that the probability of the underdog's winning a game is 40%. (In order for a team to be the underdog, the probability that the team wins a game must be less than 50%.) Figure 9.68 shows that the probability of a 40% underdog's winning the World Series is about 29%, and that such a series would last an average of about 5.70 games. The program should simulate the playing of 10,000 World Series where the underdog has the probability of winning that was entered into the first text box. The values of the horizontal scroll bars should extend from 0 to 10,000 and should be calculated after each series so that the scroll boxes steadily move across the bars. **Note:** In order to spare Visual Basic from being overwhelmed with changing the values in the twelve text boxes to the right of the scroll bars too often, just change the values after every ten series. Also, every time the values are changed, execute a Refresh method for each of these text boxes.

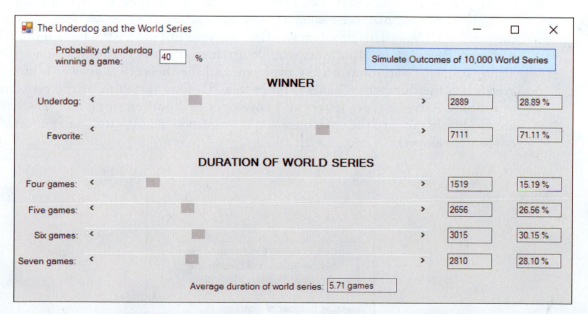

FIGURE 9.68   **Possible outcome of Programming Project 5.**

6. Business Travel Expenses Write a program to print a business travel expenses attachment for an income tax return. The program should request as input the name of the organization visited, the dates and location of the visit, and the expenses for meals and entertainment, airplane fare, lodging, and taxi fares. (Only 50% of the expenses for meals and entertainment are deductible.) Two outcomes are shown in Figure 9.69.

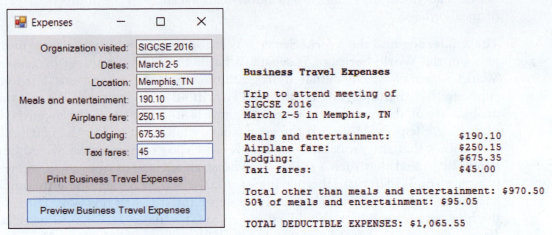

FIGURE 9.69 Possible outcomes of Programming Project 6.

7. Matching Cards Suppose two shuffled decks of cards are placed on a table, and then cards are drawn from the tops of the decks one at a time and compared. On average, how many matches do you think will occur? Write a program to carry out this process one million times and calculate the average number of matches that occur per deck of 52 cards. See Fig. 9.70. **Hint:** Make randomNum a class-level variable by placing **Dim randomNum As New Random** into the Declarations section of the program. (**Note:** This problem was first analyzed in 1708 by the French probabilist Pierre Remond de Montmort who determined that the theoretical answer is 1. There are many variations on the problem, and the theoretical answer is always 1 even when the number of items is other than 52. One variation of the problem is as follows: A typist types letters and envelopes to 20 different people. The letters are randomly put into the envelopes. On average, how many letters are put into the correct envelope?)

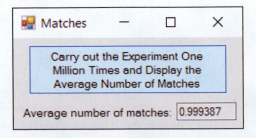

FIGURE 9.70 Possible outcome of Programming Project 7.

8. **Identify Country Flags**   Write a program that asks the user to identify flags. The text file FlagCountries.txt contains the names of the countries appearing in the list box in Fig. 9.71. The folder Ch09\Pictures\Flags contains files with names such as flagArgentina.jpg, flagCanada.jpg, and so on, where each file holds the picture of the flag of a country from the list box. After the program displays a randomly selected flag, the user should try to identify the flag by clicking on one of the countries in the list box. The messages "Correct!" or "Not Correct!" should be displayed depending on whether or not the user identified the flag correctly. (The user can guess as many times as he or she likes.) Clicking on the button displays another randomly selected flag that has not yet been displayed. After all the flags have been displayed, the user should be so informed the next time the button is clicked.

FIGURE 9.71   **Possible outcome of Programming Project 8.**

10

Databases

VideoNote

Introduction
to Databases

10.1   An Introduction to Databases

The management of databases is one of the most important uses of computers today. Airlines use databases to handle billions of passenger reservations per year. The 5,724 hospitals in the United States utilize databases to document the emergency department visits of over 136 million patients per year. Banks in the United States employ databases to monitor 1.6 billion credit cards. Although databases vary considerably in size and complexity, most of them adhere to the fundamental principles of design discussed in this chapter. That is, they are composed of a collection of related tables.

A **table** is a rectangular array of data. Table 10.1 provides information about large cities. Each column of the table is called a **field**. (The third column gives the 2014 population in millions and the fourth column the projected 2030 population in millions.) The names of the fields are *name*, *country*, *pop2014*, and *pop2030*. Each row, called a **record**, contains the same type of information as every other row. Also, the pieces of information in each row are related because they all apply to a specific city. Table 10.2, Countries, has three fields and ten records.

TABLE 10.1   Cities.

name	country	pop2014	pop2030
Buenos Aires	Argentina	15.0	17.0
Calcutta	India	14.8	19.1
Delhi	India	25.0	36.1
Dhaka	Bangladesh	17.0	27.4
Mexico City	Mexico	20.8	23.9
Mumbai	India	20.7	27.8
New York	USA	18.6	19.9
Sao Paulo	Brazil	20.8	23.4
Shanghai	China	23.0	30.8
Tokyo	Japan	37.8	37.2

Note: The population figures are for "urban agglomerations"—that is, contiguous densely populated urban areas.

TABLE 10.2   Countries.

name	pop2014	monetaryUnit
Argentina	41.8	peso
Bangladesh	166.3	taka
Brazil	202.7	real
China	1355.7	renminbi
India	1236.3	rupee
Indonesia	253.6	rupiah
Japan	127.1	yen
Mexico	119.7	peso
Pakistan	196.2	rupee
USA	318.9	dollar

Note: China's currency is also known as the "yuan" or the "yuan renminbi."

A **relational database** contains a collection of one or more (usually related) tables that has been created with **database-management** software. Microsoft Access is one of the best known database-management products. Some other prominent ones are Oracle, SQL Server, and MySQL. VB 2015 can interact with a database that has been created with any of these products.

The databases needed for the exercises in this textbook are contained in the materials downloaded from the companion website. They are in the folder Programs\Ch10\Databases. The database files were created with Microsoft Access and have the extension *accdb* (an abbreviation for ACCess DataBase). For instance, Megacities.accdb is the database file containing the two tables presented above. When the tables were created, each field was given a name and a data type. In the Cities table, the fields *pop2014* and *pop2030* were given data type Double and the other fields a data type compatible with the String data type.

■ The Data Source Configuration Wizard

Before a program can access a table in a database, a connection must be established. We will be using the Data Source Configuration Wizard to connect to databases in Visual Basic programs. The steps taken by the wizard vary slightly depending on the version of Visual Basic you are using and on whether you have previously used the wizard to connect to databases.

The Data Source Configuration Wizard requires your computer to have certain files that come with Microsoft Office. If you do not have Microsoft Office on your computer, you can download the necessary files for free from Microsoft. The details are presented at the end of Appendix B in the section "Install Office Data Connectivity Components".

■ Accessing a Database Table

The following steps provide one way to connect to the Megacities database and bind to the Cities table.

1. Start a new program.

2. Add a BindingSource control to the Form Designer.

   The BindingSource control can be found in the *All Windows Forms* or *Data* groups of the Toolbox. After you double-click on the control in the Toolbox, a control named BindingSource1 appears in the component tray at the bottom of the Form Designer.

3. Go to the Properties window for BindingSource1 and click on the down arrow at the right side of the DataSource property's Settings box.

   The panel in Fig. 10.1 appears.

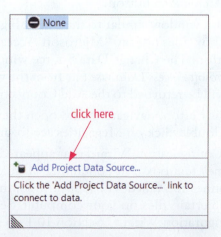

FIGURE 10.1   Panel produced by Step 3.

4. Click on *Add Project Data Source*.

The Data Source Configuration Wizard in Fig. 10.2 appears and asks you to "Choose a Data Source Type".

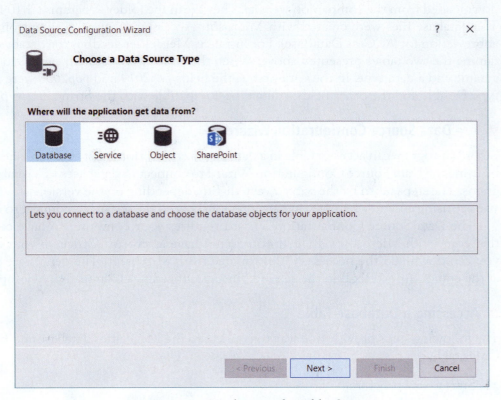

FIGURE 10.2 **Window produced by Step 4.**

5. Select the Database icon in the Data Source Configuration Wizard and click on the *Next* button. The Wizard now asks you to "Choose a Database Model". See Fig. 10.3.

6. Select the Dataset icon and click on the *Next* button.

The Wizard now asks you to "Choose Your Data Connection". See Fig. 10.4.

7. Click on the *New Connection* button.

An Add Connection window similar to the one in Fig. 10.5 on page 518 appears. If the (Data source) text box does not say "Microsoft Access Database File (OLE DB)", click on the *Change* button. The Change Data Source window in Fig. 10.6 on page 518 will appear. Select *Microsoft Access Database File* from the window's list box and click on the OK button. You will be returned to the Add Connection dialog box shown in Fig. 10.5.

8. Click on the *Browse* button, navigate to and open the Databases folder (a subfolder of Programs\Ch10), double-click on Megacities.accdb, and then click on the OK button.

The Data Source Configuration Wizard that appeared earlier should reappear with the "Database file name" text box now containing Megacities.accdb. If not, a message box stating that the connection failed will appear. If so, the failure might have been caused by the absence of certain files on your computer. See the second paragraph of "The Data Source Configuration Wizard" Section 10.1 on page 515.

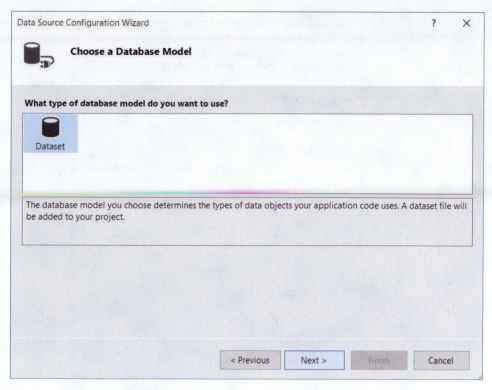

FIGURE 10.3   Window produced by Step 5.

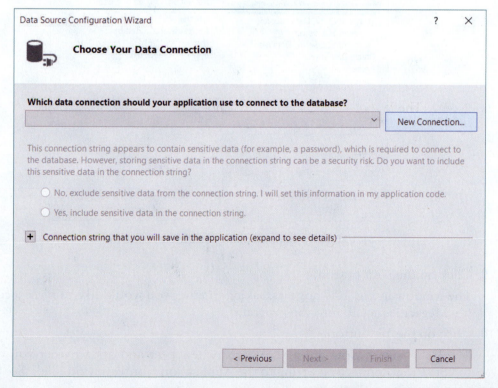

FIGURE 10.4   Dialog box produced by Step 6.

FIGURE 10.5 **First dialog box mentioned in Step 7.**

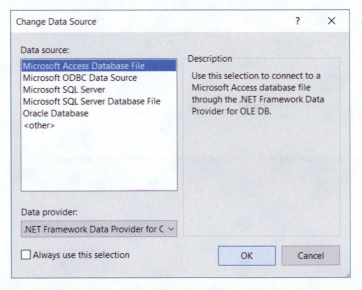

FIGURE 10.6 **Second dialog box mentioned in Step 7.**

9. Click on the *Next* button.

   The window in Fig. 10.7 appears, asking whether you would like to place a copy of the file Megacities.accdb into the program.

10. Click on the *Yes* button.

   The Data Source Configuration Wizard will appear and ask whether you would like to "Save the Connection String to the Application Configuration File". See Fig. 10.8.

11. Make sure that the *Yes, save the connection as:* check box is checked and then click on the *Next* button.

   The Data Source Configuration Wizard in Fig. 10.9 on page 520 will appear.

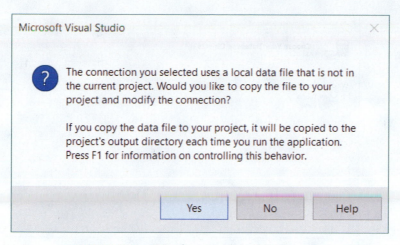

FIGURE 10.7 Window produced by Step 9.

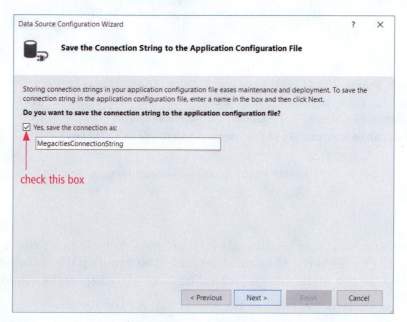

FIGURE 10.8 Window produced by Step 10.

12. Check the *Tables* check box and then click on the *Finish* button.

A DataSource property of BindingSource1 is now set to MegacitiesDataSet, and a MegacitiesDataSet icon has appeared in the component tray.

13. In the BindingSource1 Properties window, click on the down arrow at the right side of the DataMember property's Settings box.

A drop-down list containing the tables in the Megacities database will appear.

14. Click on *Cities* in the drop-down list.

A CitiesTableAdapter icon will appear in the component tray. Also, a Load event procedure containing one line of executable code is generated in the Code Editor. See Fig. 10.10 on the next page.

FIGURE 10.9 Dialog box produced by Step 11.

```
Private Sub Form1_Load(...) Handles MyBase.Load
  'TODO: This line of code loads data into the 'MegacitiesDataSet.Cities'
  'table. You can move, or remove it, as needed.
  Me.CitiesTableAdapter.Fill(Me.MegacitiesDataSet.Cities)
End Sub
```

FIGURE 10.10 Code generated by Step 14.

The Cities table can now be accessed by the program. You can easily view a list of the fields for both of the tables in the Megacities database. Just bring up the Solution Explorer window and double-click on the file MegacitiesDataSet.xsd to display the window in Fig. 10.11. **Note:** To close the window, click on the x symbol (✕) on its tab.

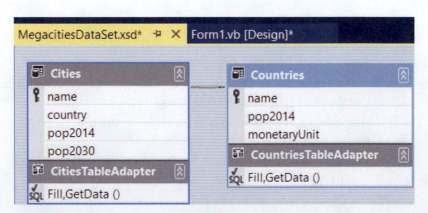

FIGURE 10.11 Tables and fields in the Megacities database.

■ Binding to Additional Tables

A program can access multiple tables through one database connection. The following steps bind the Countries table to the program created in the walkthrough above:

1. Add another BindingSource control to the Form Designer.
2. Set its DataSource property to MegacitiesDataSet.

   After you click on the down arrow, click on the right-pointing triangle to the left of Other Data Sources, click on the right-pointing triangle to the left of Project Data Sources, and then click on MegacitiesDataSet.

3. Set the DataMember property of the new BindingSource control to Countries.

   A CountriesTableAdapter icon will appear in the component tray, and another comment line and line of code will be added to the Load event procedure.

■ Browsing a Connected Database

After a database has been connected to a program, any table from the database can easily be displayed. The following steps display a table from the Megacities database.

1. Right-click on the name of the database (Megacities.accdb) in the Solution Explorer and click on *Open* in the context menu that appears.

   The Server Explorer window in Fig. 10.12 will appear in the location occupied by the Toolbox. With some versions of Visual Basic 2015, the window is titled "Database Explorer."

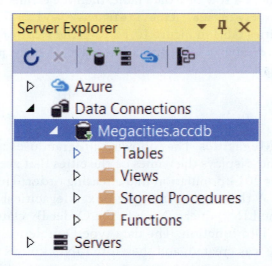

FIGURE 10.12 Database Explorer window.

2. Click on the right-pointing triangle to the left of the Tables folder.

   The folder will open and reveal the names of the two tables.

3. Right-click on Cities, and click on *Retrieve Data* in the context menu.

   The contents of the Cities table will be displayed in the tabbed window shown in Fig. 10.13.

4. Click on the x symbol (✕) on the window's tab to close the window.

■ Querying a Table with LINQ

Databases are usually quite large and so we rarely want to display an entire table. LINQ can be used to extract information from a data table using similar syntax as used to extract information from an array of records, a CSV text file, or an XML file.

VideoNote

Querying Tables

		name	country	pop2014	pop2030
▶		Buenos Aires	Argentina	15	17
		Calcutta	India	14.8	19.1
		Delhi	India	25	36.1
		Dhaka	Bangladesh	17	27.4
		Mexico City	Mexico	20.8	23.9
		Mumbai	India	20.7	27.8
		New York	USA	18.6	19.9
		Sao Paulo	Brazil	20.8	23.4
		Shanghai	China	23	30.8
		Tokyo	Japan	37.8	37.2
*		NULL	NULL	NULL	NULL

Cities: Query(C:\Dr...4\Megacities.accdb)

1 of 10

FIGURE 10.13 Contents of the Cities table.

A database table can be thought of as a sequence of rows with each row containing several fields. If *line* is a row of a data table, then the elements of the row are indentified by the names `line.fieldName`, `line.fieldName2`, and so on. For instance, if *city* is the first row of the Cities table in Figure 10.13, then the value of `city.name` is Buenos Aires, the value of `city.country` is Argentina, the value of `city.pop2014` is 15, and the value of `city.pop2030` is 17.

Example 1 **Megacities** The following program uses the Cities table of the Megacities database and displays the names of the cities that are located in India. The cities are sorted by their 2014 population in decreasing order. The program also displays the total population of those cities in a text box. MegacitiesDataSet.Cities serves as the data source for the LINQ query. **Note:** In the Order By clause of query1, there was no need to use the CDbl function. The data type Double was given to the *pop2014* field when the database was created, and therefore LINQ knows that `city.pop2014` has type Double.

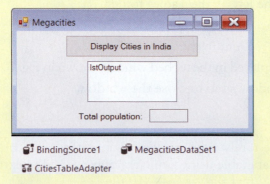

OBJECT	PROPERTY	SETTING
frmCities	Text	Megacities
btnDisplay	Text	Display Cities in India
lstOutput		
lblTotalPop	Text	Total population:
txtTotalPop	ReadOnly	True

```
Private Sub frmCities_Load(...) Handles MyBase.Load
  'Code generated automatically when DataMember was set to Cities
  Me.CitiesTableAdapter.Fill(Me.MegacitiesDataSet.Cities)
End Sub


Private Sub btnDisplay_Click(...) Handles btnDisplay.Click
  Dim query1 = From city In MegacitiesDataSet.Cities
               Where city.country = "India"
               Order By city.pop2014 Descending
               Select city.name
  lstOutput.DataSource = query1.ToList
  lstOutput.SelectedItem = Nothing
  Dim query2 = From city In MegacitiesDataSet.Cities
               Where city.country = "India"
               Select city.pop2014
  txtTotalPop.Text = CStr(query2.Sum)
End Sub
```

[Run, and click on the button.]

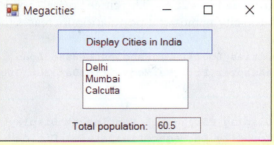

 Example 2   **Megacities** The following program searches the Countries table for a country requested by the user. Notice that the DataSource property displays "name", "pop2014", and "monetaryUnit" in the headers of the table, not "country.name", "country.pop2014", and "country.monetaryUnit". The variable *country* plays a supporting role similar to that of a looping variable in a For Each loop.

```
Private Sub frmCountries_Load(...) Handles MyBase.Load
  'Code generated automatically when DataMember was set to Cities
  Me.CountriesTableAdapter.Fill(Me.MegacitiesDataSet.Countries)
End Sub


Private Sub btnDisplay_Click(...) Handles btnDisplay.Click
  Dim query = From country In MegacitiesDataSet.Countries
              Where country.name = txtName.Text
              Select country.name, country.pop2014, country.monetaryUnit
  If query.Count = 1 Then
    dgvOutput.DataSource = query.ToList
    dgvOutput.CurrentCell = Nothing
  Else
    MessageBox.Show("Country is not in the table.", "Not Found")
  End If
End Sub
```

[Run, enter a country into the text box, and click on the button.]

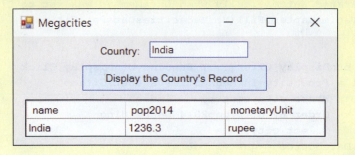

Example 3   **Megacities** The following program uses the Cities table of the Megacities database and displays the cities whose populations are predicted to increase by more than 7 million people from 2014 to 2030. The cities are ordered by their projected population increase, and both the city names and population increases (in millions) are displayed.

```
Private Sub frmCities_Load(...) Handles MyBase.Load
  Me.CitiesTableAdapter.Fill(Me.MegacitiesDataSet.Cities)
End Sub

Private Sub btnDisplay_Click(...) Handles btnDisplay.Click
  Dim query = From city In MegacitiesDataSet.Cities
              Let popIncrease = city.pop2030 - city.pop2014
              Let formattedIncr = popIncrease.ToString("N1")
              Where popIncrease > 1
              Order By popIncrease Descending
              Select city.name, formattedIncr
  dgvOutput.DataSource = query.ToList
  dgvOutput.CurrentCell = Nothing
  dgvOutput.Columns("name").HeaderText = "City"
  dgvOutput.Columns("formattedIncr").HeaderText = "Population Increase"
End Sub
```

[Run, and click on the button.]

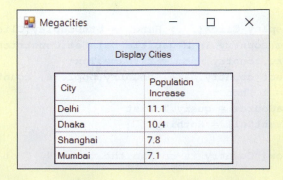

Example 4 **Megacities** The following program displays the cities from the Cities table in a list box sorted by their population in 2014. When the user clicks on one of the cities, its country, population in 2014, and population in 2030 are displayed in text boxes. In the second event procedure, a query is used to search for the desired record of the table. In this case, the query returns a sequence of one value. Since a sequence cannot be assigned to a text box, the First method is used to obtain the desired value. **Note:** Notice that the statement `lstCities.DataSource = query.ToList` in the Load event procedure is not followed by the statement `lstCities.SelectedItem = Nothing`. Had the SelectedItem statement been added, the initial display would show the data about Tokyo without revealing the city that the data referred to.

```
Private Sub frmCities_Load(...) Handles MyBase.Load
  Me.CitiesTableAdapter.Fill(Me.MegacitiesDataSet.Cities)
  Dim query = From city In MegacitiesDataSet.Cities
              Order By city.pop2014 Descending
              Select city.name
  lstCities.DataSource = query.ToList
End Sub


Private Sub lstCities_SelectedIndexChanged(...) Handles _
              lstCities.SelectedIndexChanged
  Dim query = From city In MegacitiesDataSet.Cities
              Where city.name = lstCities.Text
              Select city.country, city.pop2014, city.pop2030
  txtCountry.Text = query.First.country
  txtPop2014.Text = (query.First.pop2014).ToString("N1")
  txtPop2030.Text = (query.First.pop2030).ToString("N1")
End Sub
```

[Run, and click on one of the cities in the list box.]

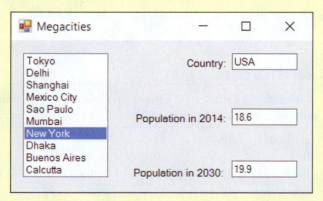

■ Primary and Foreign Keys

A well-designed table should have a field (or set of fields) that can be used to uniquely identify each record. Such a field (or set of fields) is called a **primary key**. For instance, in the Cities and Countries tables, each *name* field is a primary key. Databases of student enrollments in a college usually use a field of student ID numbers as the primary key. Student names would not be a good choice, because there could easily be two students having the same name.

When a table is created, a field can be specified as a primary key. If so, Visual Basic will insist that every record has an entry in the primary key and that the same entry does not appear in two different records. If the user tries to add a record with no data in the primary key, the error message "Index or primary key cannot contain a Null Value." will be generated. If the user tries to add a record with the same primary key data as another record, an error message will be displayed: "The changes you requested to the table were not successful because they would create duplicate values in the index, primary key, or relationship. Change the data in the field or fields that contain duplicate data, remove the index, or redefine the index to permit duplicate entries and try again."

When a database contains two or more tables, they are usually related. For instance, the two tables Cities and Countries are related by their fields that hold names of countries. Let's refer to these two fields as *Cities.country* and *Countries.name*. Notice that every entry in *Cities.country* appears uniquely in *Countries.name* and that *Countries.name* is a primary key of the Countries table. We say that *Cities.country* can serve as a **foreign key** of *Countries. name*. Foreign keys are usually specified when a database is first created. If so, Visual Basic will enforce the **Rule of Referential Integrity**—namely, that each value in the foreign key must also appear as a value in the primary-key field of the other table.

In the Megacities database, *Cities.name* and *Countries.name* have been specified as primary keys for their respective tables, and *Cities.country* has been specified as a foreign key of *Countries.name*. If the user tries to add to the Cities table a city whose country does not appear in the Countries table, an error message will be displayed: "You cannot add or change a record because a related record is required in table 'Countries'." The message will also be generated if the user tries to delete a country from the *Countries.name* field that appears in the *Cities.country* field.

■ The Join of Two Tables

A foreign key allows Visual Basic to link (or **join**) two tables from a relational database in a meaningful way. For instance, when the two tables Cities and Countries from the Megacities database are joined based on the foreign key *Cities.country* and ordered by city names, the result is Table 10.3. The record for each city is expanded to show its country's 2014 population and its monetary unit. This joined table is very handy if, say, we want to display a city's currency.

TABLE 10.3 A join of two tables.

Cities.name	Cities. country	Cities. pop2014	Cities. pop2030	Countries. name	Countries. pop2014	Countries. monetaryUnit
Buenos Aires	Argentina	15.0	17.0	Argentina	41.8	peso
Calcutta	India	14.8	19.1	India	1236.3	rupee
Delhi	India	25.0	36.1	India	1236.3	rupee
Dhaka	Bangladesh	17.0	27.4	Bangladesh	166.3	taka
Mexico City	Mexico	20.8	23.9	Mexico	119.7	peso
Mumbai	India	20.7	27.8	India	1236.3	rupee
New York	USA	18.6	19.9	USA	318.9	dollar
Sao Paulo	Brazil	20.8	23.4	Brazil	202.7	real
Shanghai	China	23.0	30.8	China	1355.7	renminbi
Tokyo	Japan	37.8	37.2	Japan	127.1	yen

The query that creates the join above begins as follows:

```
Dim query = From city In MegacitiesDataSet.Cities
            Join country In MegacitiesDataSet.Countries
            On city.country Equals country.name
```

The From clause is standard. The Join clause says that the Countries table should be joined with the Cities table. The On clause identifies the two fields whose values are matched in order to join the tables. The variables *city* and *country* in the first two clauses are looping variables and can have any names we choose. For instance, the query above could have been written

```
Dim query = From town In MegacitiesDataSet.Cities
            Join nation In MegacitiesDataSet.Countries
            On town.country Equals nation.name
```

 Example 5   **Megacities** The following program displays Table 10.3, the join of the two tables from the Megacities database:

```
Private Sub frmCities_Load(...) Handles MyBase.Load
  Me.CountriesTableAdapter.Fill(Me.MegacitiesDataSet.Countries)
  Me.CitiesTableAdapter.Fill(Me.MegacitiesDataSet.Cities)
End Sub


Private Sub btnDisplay_Click(...) Handles btnDisplay.Click
  Dim query = From city In MegacitiesDataSet.Cities
              Join country In MegacitiesDataSet.Countries
              On city.country Equals country.name
              Let cityName = city.name
              Let cityPop2014 = (city.pop2014).ToString("N1")
              Let cityPop2030 = (city.pop2030).ToString("N1")
              Let countryName = country.name
              Let countryPop2014 = (country.pop2014).ToString("N1")
              Select cityName, city.country, cityPop2014, cityPop2030,
                     countryName, countryPop2014, country.monetaryUnit
  dgvOutput.DataSource = query.ToList
  dgvOutput.CurrentCell = Nothing
End Sub
```

[Run, and click on the button.]

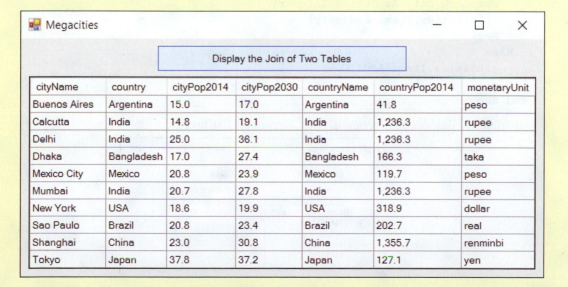

cityName	country	cityPop2014	cityPop2030	countryName	countryPop2014	monetaryUnit
Buenos Aires	Argentina	15.0	17.0	Argentina	41.8	peso
Calcutta	India	14.8	19.1	India	1,236.3	rupee
Delhi	India	25.0	36.1	India	1,236.3	rupee
Dhaka	Bangladesh	17.0	27.4	Bangladesh	166.3	taka
Mexico City	Mexico	20.8	23.9	Mexico	119.7	peso
Mumbai	India	20.7	27.8	India	1,236.3	rupee
New York	USA	18.6	19.9	USA	318.9	dollar
Sao Paulo	Brazil	20.8	23.4	Brazil	202.7	real
Shanghai	China	23.0	30.8	China	1,355.7	renminbi
Tokyo	Japan	37.8	37.2	Japan	127.1	yen

Example 6 **Megacities** The following program uses the join of the two tables in the Megacities database. When the form is loaded, the Currencies list box is filled with the monetary units from the Countries table in alphabetical order. When the user selects a currency, the cities that use that currency are displayed in the Cities list box in alphabetical order. **Note:** The Cities list box was filled with the Add method rather than the DataSource method, so that the word "NONE" could be displayed when no cities use the selected currency.

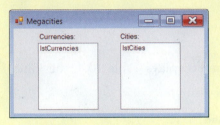

OBJECT	PROPERTY	SETTING
frmCities	Text	Megacities
lblCurrencies	Text	Currencies:
lstCurrencies		
lblCities	Text	Cities:
lstCities		

```
Private Sub frmCities_Load(...) Handles MyBase.Load
  Me.CountriesTableAdapter.Fill(Me.MegacitiesDataSet.Countries)
  Me.CitiesTableAdapter.Fill(Me.MegacitiesDataSet.Cities)
  Dim query = From country In MegacitiesDataSet.Countries
            Order By country.monetaryUnit Ascending
            Select country.monetaryUnit
            Distinct
  lstCurrencies.DataSource = query.ToList
End Sub


Private Sub lstCurrencies_SelectedIndexChanged(...) Handles _
                    lstCurrencies.SelectedIndexChanged
  Dim query = From city In MegacitiesDataSet.Cities
            Join country In MegacitiesDataSet.Countries
            On city.country Equals country.name
            Where country.monetaryUnit = lstCurrencies.Text
            Order By city.name Ascending
            Select city.name
  lstCities.Items.Clear()
  If query.Count > 0 Then
    For Each city As String In query
      lstCities.Items.Add(city)
    Next
  Else
    lstCities.Items.Add("NONE")
  End If
End Sub
```

[Run, and click on a currency in the Currencies list box.]

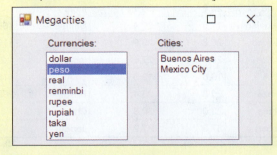

■ **Comments**

1. A database resides on a disk, and a DataSet resides in memory. A table adapter serves as a conduit to allow bidirectional data transfer between the two. A binding source is used to simplify attaching form controls to data sources.

2. The requirement that no record may have a null entry in a primary key and that entries for primary keys be unique is called the **Rule of Entity Integrity**.

3. The Join of two tables is a virtual construct. It exists only in memory.

Practice Problems 10.1

1. Consider the query in the Load event procedure of Example 6. What would happen if the LINQ operator Distinct were omitted?

2. Consider the query in Example 5. Why can't the Select clause be written as follows?

```
Select city.name, city.country, cityPop2014, cityPop2030,
       country.name, countryPop2014, country.monetaryUnit
```

EXERCISES 10.1

Figure 10.14 contains the outputs produced by the event procedures in Exercises 1 through 6.

cityName	monetaryUnit
Dhaka	taka
Buenos Aires	peso

(a)

cityName	country
Buenos Aires	Argentina
Tokyo	Japan

(b)

name	country
Calcutta	India
Dhaka	Bangladesh

(c)

name	monetaryUnit
Indonesia	rupiah
USA	dollar

(d)

name	country
Dhaka	Bangladesh
Sao Paulo	Brazil

(e)

name	monetaryUnit
Argentina	peso
Mexico	peso

(f)

FIGURE 10.14   Outputs for Exercises 1 through 6.

In Exercises 1 through 6, identify the DataGridView in Fig. 10.14 that is the output of the event procedure. Assume that each program has the same Load event procedure as Example 5.

```
1. Private Sub btnDisplay_Click(...) Handles btnDisplay.Click
     Dim query = From city In MegacitiesDataSet.Cities
                 Where city.country.StartsWith("B")
                 Select city.name, city.country
     dgvOutput.DataSource = query.ToList
     dgvOutput.CurrentCell = Nothing
   End Sub
```

2.
```
Private Sub btnDisplay_Click(...) Handles btnDisplay.Click
    Dim query = From city In MegacitiesDataSet.Cities
                Where city.pop2030 > 35
                Select city.name, city.country
    dgvOutput.DataSource = query.ToList
    dgvOutput.CurrentCell = Nothing
End Sub
```

3.
```
Private Sub btnDisplay_Click(...) Handles btnDisplay.Click
    Dim query = From country In MegacitiesDataSet.Countries
                Where (country.pop2014 > 250) And (country.pop2014 < 350)
                Select country.name, country.monetaryUnit
    dgvOutput.DataSource = query.ToList
    dgvOutput.CurrentCell = Nothing
Sub
```

4.
```
Private Sub btnDisplay_Click(...) Handles btnDisplay.Click
    Dim query = From country In MegacitiesDataSet.Countries
                Where country.monetaryUnit = "peso"
                Order By country.pop2014 Ascending
                Select country.name, country.monetaryUnit
    dgvOutput.DataSource = query.ToList
    dgvOutput.CurrentCell = Nothing
End Sub
```

5.
```
Private Sub btnDisplay_Click(...) Handles btnDisplay.Click
    Dim query = From city In MegacitiesDataSet.Cities
                Join country In MegacitiesDataSet.Countries
                On city.country Equals country.name
                Let cityName = city.name
                Where country.pop2014 < (5 * city.pop2014)
                Order By city.country Ascending
                Select cityName, city.country
    dgvOutput.DataSource = query.ToList
    dgvOutput.CurrentCell = Nothing
End Sub
```

6.
```
Private Sub btnDisplay_Click(...) Handles btnDisplay.Click
    Dim query = From city In MegacitiesDataSet.Cities
                Join country In MegacitiesDataSet.Countries
                On city.country Equals country.name
                Let cityName = city.name
                Where country.name.Length > 8
                Order By city.pop2014 Descending
                Select cityName, country.monetaryUnit
    dgvOutput.DataSource = query.ToList
    dgvOutput.CurrentCell = Nothing
End Sub
```

Exercises 7 through 16 require the Megacities database.

7. **Megacities**   Write a program that displays (in a DataGridView control) the names of all the cities, their countries, and the projected percentage growth of their populations from 2014 to 2030. Records should be sorted in descending order by their projected population growth. See Fig. 10.15.

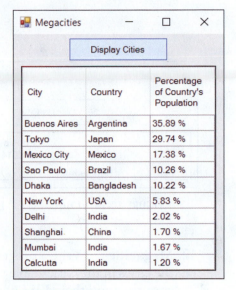

City	Country	Projected Population Growth
Dhaka	Bangladesh	61.18 %
Delhi	India	44.40 %
Mumbai	India	34.30 %
Shanghai	China	33.91 %
Calcutta	India	29.05 %
Mexico City	Mexico	14.90 %
Buenos Aires	Argentina	13.33 %
Sao Paulo	Brazil	12.50 %
New York	USA	6.99 %
Tokyo	Japan	-1.59 %

FIGURE 10.15   Outcome of Exercise 7.

City	Country	Percentage of Country's Population
Buenos Aires	Argentina	35.89 %
Tokyo	Japan	29.74 %
Mexico City	Mexico	17.38 %
Sao Paulo	Brazil	10.26 %
Dhaka	Bangladesh	10.22 %
New York	USA	5.83 %
Delhi	India	2.02 %
Shanghai	China	1.70 %
Mumbai	India	1.67 %
Calcutta	India	1.20 %

FIGURE 10.16   Outcome of Exercise 8.

8. **Megacities**   Write a program that displays (in a DataGridView control) the names of all the cities, their countries, and for each city the percentage of its country's population that lived in that city in 2014. Records should be sorted in descending order by the percentages. See Fig. 10.16.

9. **Megacities**   Write a program that displays (in a list box) the names of the cities in the Cities table whose populations are projected to exceed 20 million by the year 2030. The cities should be ordered by their projected population in descending order. See Fig. 10.17.

FIGURE 10.17   Outcome of Exercise 9.

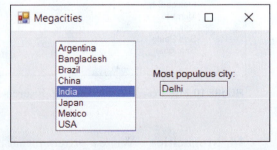

FIGURE 10.18   Possible outcome of Exercise 10.

10. **Megacities**   Write a program that shows (in a list box) the names of all the countries from the Cities table in alphabetical order. When the user clicks on one of the countries, the program should display (in a text box) the name of its most populous city in 2014. See Fig. 10.18.

11. **Megacities** Write a program to find and display (in a DataGridView control) the entire record for the city in the Cities table that will experience the greatest percentage growth from 2014 to 2030. See Fig. 10.19. **Note:** The percentage growth is (pop2030 – pop2014) / pop2014.

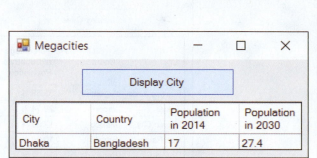

FIGURE 10.19 Outcome of Exercise 11.

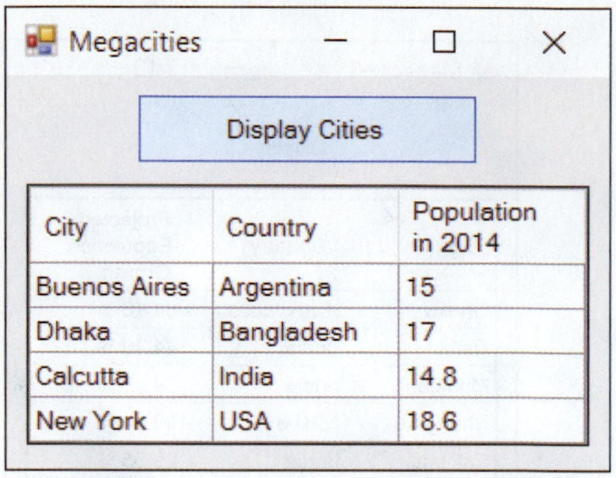

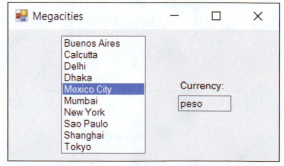

FIGURE 10.20 Outcome of Exercise 12.

12. **Megacities** Write a program that displays (in a DataGridView control) the names of the cities in the Cities table whose 2014 populations are between 13 and 19 million. The countries and their 2014 populations also should be displayed, and the records should be ordered alphabetically by the names of the countries. See Figure 10.20.

13. **Megacities** Write a program that displays the cities in a list box. When the user clicks on one of the cities, the program should display (in a text box) the percentage of its country's population that lived in that city in 2014. See Fig. 10.21.

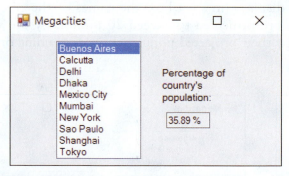

FIGURE 10.21 Possible outcome of Exercise 13.

FIGURE 10.22 Possible outcome of Exercise 14.

14. **Megacities** Write a program that displays the cities in a list box. When the user clicks on one of the cities, the program should display (in a text box) the city's currency. See Fig. 10.22.

15. **Megacities** Write a program that creates a CSV text file containing the contents of the Cities table. Run the program, and compare the size of the text file with the size of the file Megacities.accdb.

16. **Megacities** Write a program that creates an XML file containing the contents of the Cities table.

The database UN.accdb has the single table Nations that contains data for the 193 member countries of the United Nations. The fields for the table are *name*, *continent*, *population*, and *area*. (Population is given in millions and area in square miles.) Use the United Nations database in Exercises 17 through 19. Some records in the table are

Canada	North America	34.8	3855000
France	Europe	66.3	211209
New Zealand	Australia/Oceania	4.4	103738
Nigeria	Africa	177.2	356669
Pakistan	Asia	196.2	310403
Peru	South America	30.1	496226

17. **United Nations**   Write a program that displays the names of the continents from the Nations table in a list box. When the user clicks on a continent's name, the countries in that continent should be displayed in two other list boxes. One list box should display the countries in descending order by their population, and the other should display the countries in descending order by their area. See Fig. 10.23.

FIGURE 10.23   Possible outcome of Exercise 17.

18. **United Nations**   Write a program that displays the names of the continents from the Nations table in a list box. When the user clicks on a continent's name, the countries in that continent should be displayed (in a DataGridView) along with their population densities. The records should be in ascending order by their population densities. See Fig. 10.24.

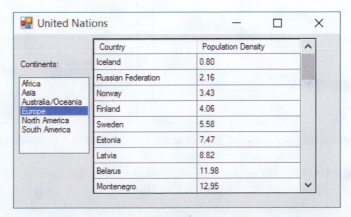

FIGURE 10.24   Possible outcome of Exercise 18.

19. **United Nations** Write a program to find and display (in a DataGridView control) two entire records, where the first record gives the data for the country with the largest population, and the second the data for the country with the smallest population. See Fig. 10.25.

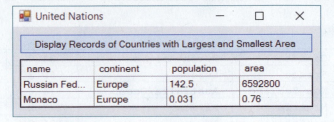

FIGURE 10.25 Outcome of Exercise 19.

The database Exchrate.accdb has the single table Rates that gives the exchange rates (in terms of American dollars) for 45 currencies of major countries in September 2015. Figure 10.26 shows the first eight records in the database in a DataGridView control. The USdollarRate column gives the number of units of the currency that are equal to one American dollar. For instance, one American dollar is equal to 687.853 Chilean pesos. Use the Exchrate database in Exercises 20 through 22.

country	monetary Unit	USdollar Rate
America	Dollar	1
Argentina	Peso	9.344
Australia	Dollar	1.404
Brazil	Real	3.876
Canada	Dollar	1.324
Chile	Peso	687.853
China	Yuan Renminbi	6.369
Colombia	Peso	3036.846

FIGURE 10.26 Exchange rates.

20. **Exchange Rates** Write a program that shows the names of the countries in a list box. When the user clicks on one of the names, the monetary unit and the exchange rate should be displayed. See Fig. 10.27.

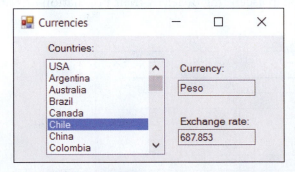

FIGURE 10.27 Possible outcome of Exercise 20. **FIGURE 10.28** Possible outcome of Exercise 21.

21. **Exchange Rates** Write a program that displays the names of the countries in a list box in ascending order determined by the number of units that can be purchased by one American dollar. When the user clicks on one of the names, the monetary unit and exchange rate should be displayed. See Fig. 10.28.

22. Exchange Rates   Write a program containing two list boxes as shown in Fig. 10.29. When the user selects two countries, enters an amount of money, and clicks on the button, the program should convert the amount from one currency to the other.

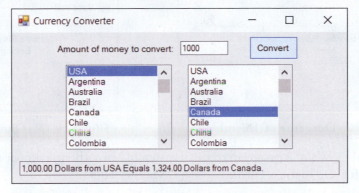

FIGURE 10.29   Possible outcome of Exercise 22.

The database Baseball.accdb has the two tables Players and Teams. The fields for the Players table are *name, team, atBats,* and *hits.* The fields for the Teams table are *name, location, league, stadium, atBats,* and *hits.* The database has been filled with information from the 2015 baseball season for the major league. The Players table lists the top 144 hitters with at least 440 at bats during the season. The Teams table lists all major-league teams. Use the Baseball database in Exercises 23 through 38. Here are three sample records from each table:

Players

Paul Goldschmidt	Diamondbacks	567	182
Nelson Cruz	Mariners	590	178
Carlos Beltran	Yankees	478	132

Teams

Cubs	Chicago	National	Wrigley Field	5491	1341
Nationals	Washington DC	National	National Park	5428	1363
Red Sox	Boston	American	Fenway Park	5640	1496

23. Baseball   Write a program that shows all the teams from the Teams table in a list box. When the user clicks on one of the teams, the program should display the team's home stadium in a text box. See Fig. 10.30.

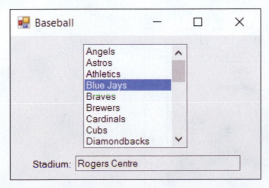

FIGURE 10.30   Possible outcome of Exercise 23.

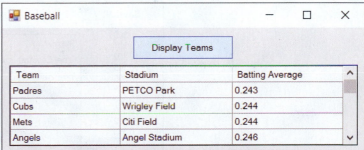

FIGURE 10.31   Outcome of Exercise 24.

24. Baseball   Write a program to display in a DataGridView control the names of all the teams, their home stadiums, and the teams' batting averages. Records should be sorted in ascending order by the batting averages. See Fig. 10.31.

25. **Baseball**   Write a program to display in a list box the player (or players) in the Players table with the most hits. See Fig. 10.32.

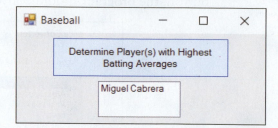

<table>
<tr><td>**FIGURE 10.32**   Outcome of Exercise 25.</td><td>**FIGURE 10.33**   Outcome of Exercise 26.</td></tr>
</table>

26. **Baseball**   Write a program to display in a list box the player (or players) in the Players table with the highest batting average. See Fig. 10.33.

27. **Baseball**   Write a program that shows all the teams from the Teams table in a list box. When the user clicks on one of the teams, the program should display in a DataGridView control the names of all the players in the Players table from that team, along with their batting averages. The players should be listed in descending order of their batting averages. See Fig. 10.34.

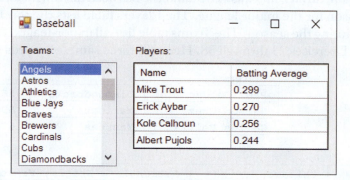

FIGURE 10.34   Possible outcome of Exercise 27.

28. **Baseball**   Write a program that shows all the players' batting averages above .300 in a list box. When the user clicks on one of the batting averages, the program should display in a DataGridView control the names of all the players in the Players table with that batting average, along with their teams. The players should be listed in alphabetical order by their last names. See Fig. 10.35.

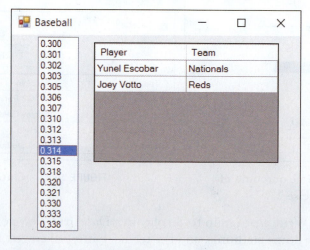

FIGURE 10.35   Possible outcome of Exercise 28.

29. Baseball Write a program that uses the Teams table to calculate the overall batting average for the players in the American League. See Fig. 10.36.

FIGURE 10.36 Outcome of Exercise 29.

FIGURE 10.37 Outcome of Exercise 30.

30. Baseball Write a program that uses the Teams table to calculate the total number of hits by teams in the National League. See Fig. 10.37.

31. Baseball Write a program to count the number of players in the Players table who play for a National League team. See Fig. 10.38.

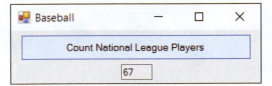

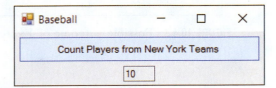

FIGURE 10.38 Outcome of Exercise 31.

FIGURE 10.39 Outcome of Exercise 32.

32. Baseball Write a program to count the number of players in the Players table who play for a New York team. See Fig. 10.39.

33. Baseball Write a program that contains two radio buttons captioned *American* and *National*. When the user clicks on one of them, the program should display in a Data-GridView control the names of all the teams in the Teams table from that league, along with their team batting averages. The teams should be listed in descending order of their batting averages. See Fig. 10.40.

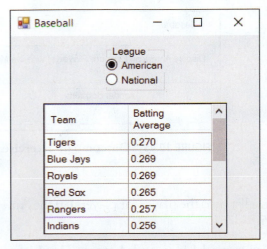

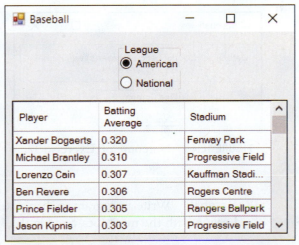

FIGURE 10.40 Possible outcome of Exercise 33.

FIGURE 10.41 Possible outcome of Exercise 34.

34. Baseball Write a program that contains two radio buttons captioned *American* and *National*. When the user clicks on one of the radio buttons, the program should display (in a DataGridView control) the names of all the players from the league who had more than 150 hits, along with their batting averages and home stadiums. The players should be listed in descending order of their batting averages. See Fig. 10.41.

35. Baseball Write a program that shows all the teams from the Teams table in a list box. When the user clicks on one of the teams, the program should display (in another list box) the names of all the players in the Players table from that team, whose batting average was greater than their teams' batting average. The players should be listed in descending order of their batting averages. See Fig. 10.42.

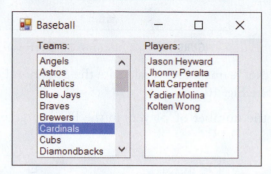

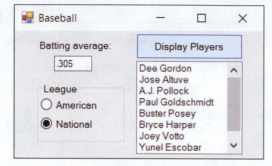

FIGURE 10.42 Possible outcome of Exercise 35.   **FIGURE 10.43** Possible outcome of Exercise 36.

36. Baseball Write a program that requests a batting average and a league (*American* or *National*) and then displays (in a list box) the names of all the players in the league whose batting average is greater than the given batting average. The players should be listed in descending order by the number of hits they had during the season. The program should not allow the given batting average to be greater than 1 or less than 0. See Fig. 10.43.

37. Baseball Write a program to display the player (or players) in the National League with the highest batting average. See Fig. 10.44.

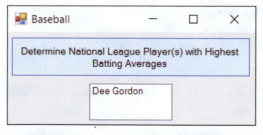

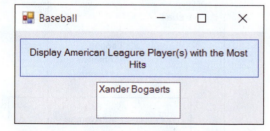

FIGURE 10.44 Outcome of Exercise 37.   **FIGURE 10.45** Outcome of Exercise 38.

38. Baseball Write a program to display (in a list box) the player (or players) in the American League with the most hits. See Fig. 10.45.

The database Movies.accdb has two tables named Lines and Actors. The Lines table contains famous lines from films that were spoken by the leading male actor. The first field of the table gives the famous line and the second field gives the film. Figure 10.46(a) shows the first three records of the Lines table. The Actors table contains some names of films and their leading male actors. Figure 10.46(b) shows the first three records of the Actors table. The *film* field in the Lines table is a foreign key to the *film* field in the Actors table. Use the Movies database in Exercises 39 through 44.

famousLine	film	film	maleLead
Rosebud.	Citizen Kane	On the Waterfront	Marlon Brando
We'll always have Paris.	Casablanca	Sudden Impact	Clint Eastwood
I coulda been a contender.	On the Waterfront	Taxi Driver	Robert De Niro
(a) Lines		**(b) Actors**	

FIGURE 10.46   Some records from the tables in the Movies database.

39. Movies   What is the primary key in the Actors table?

40. Movies   What is the primary key in the Lines table?

41. Movies   Write a program that fills a list box with the names of the films in the Lines table. When the user clicks on the name of a film, the lead male actor in that film should be displayed in a text box. See Fig. 10.47.

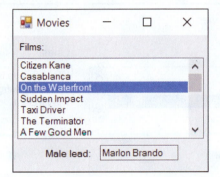

FIGURE 10.47   Possible outcome of Exercise 41.

42. Movies   Write a program that displays a DataGridView control containing all the famous lines from the Lines table along with the actors who spoke them and the films. See Fig. 10.48. **Note:** Set the AutoSizeColumnMode property of the DataGridView control to AllCells.

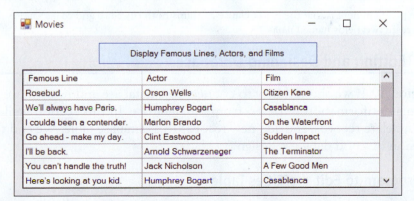

FIGURE 10.48   Outcome of Exercise 42.

43. Movies   Write a program that displays the names of the actors from the Actors table in a list box. When the user clicks on an actor's name, the famous lines from the Lines table that he spoke should be displayed in a second list box. See Fig. 10.49 on the next page.

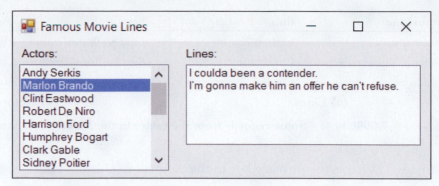

FIGURE 10.49 Possible outcome of Exercise 43.

44. Movies Write a program that displays the names of the films from the Actors table in a list box. When the user clicks on a film's name, the famous lines from the Lines table that were spoken in that film should be displayed in a second list box. See Fig. 10.50.

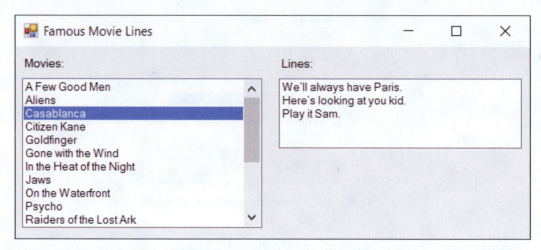

FIGURE 10.50 Possible outcome of Exercise 44.

Solutions to Practice Problems 10.1

1. In the absence of the Distinct operator, both "peso" and "rupee" would appear twice in the list box.

2. The problem here is that the Select clause contains both *city.name* and *country.name*. The query would try to create two fields named *name*.

10.2 Editing and Designing Databases

VideoNote

Editing
Databases

In Section 10.1, we showed how to connect to a database and how to use LINQ queries to manipulate information retrieved from the database. In this section we learn how to alter records, delete records, and add new records to a database table. We end the section with a discussion of good database design.

■ A Program to Edit the Cities Table

We begin by examining a program that edits the Cities table of the Megacities database; then we show how to create the program. The program, named 10-2-1, is in the folder Programs\ Ch10 that can be downloaded from the companion website for this book.

Figure 10.51 shows the form for the program. All of the controls on the form are familiar except for the navigation toolbar docked at the top of the form. Figure 10.52 shows the toolbar and identifies its components.

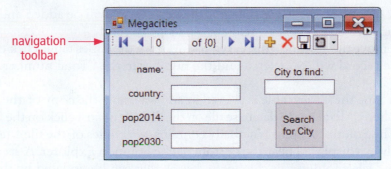

FIGURE 10.51 Form for the editing program.

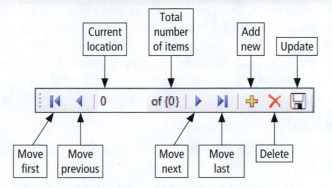

FIGURE 10.52 Navigation toolbar.

Figure 10.53 shows the form just after the program is run. The contents of the first record are shown in the four text boxes arranged vertically on the left side of the form. The *Move first* and *Move previous* buttons are disabled, since there are no records preceding the first record. When you click on the *Move next* button, the second record appears. In general, the four *Move* buttons allow you to navigate to any record of the Cities table. The first record of the table is said to have location 1, the second record location 2, and so on. If you place a number from 1 through 10 in the navigation toolbar's "Current location" box and then press the Enter key, the record having that location number will be displayed. For instance, if you enter 7 into the "Current location" box, the information for New York will be displayed. Another way to obtain a specific record is to type the name of a city into the text box labeled City to find: and then click on the *Search for City* button.

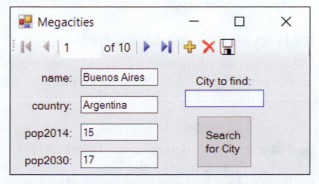

FIGURE 10.53 Table-editing program at startup.

To alter the data in the currently displayed record, just change the value in one or more of the text boxes and then click on one of the *Move* buttons.

To add a new record to the Cities table, click on the *Add new* button (✚). The text boxes for the four fields will become blank. After you type in the data for the new record, and click on one of the *Move* buttons, the new record will be added and the number in the "Total number of items" box will change from 10 to 11.

To remove the currently displayed record from the Cities table, click on the *Delete* button (✗). The record will be deleted and the number in the "Total number of items" box will decrease by 1.

Each time the Cities table is altered in any way, only the copy of the table in memory is actually altered. To alter the database file on the disk, you must click on the *Update* button (🖫). **Note 1:** The Solution Explorer actually contains two copies of the file Megacities.accdb. One copy is always displayed near the bottom of the Solution Explorer. A second copy is located in the *bin\Debug* folder. It is this second copy that can be updated by the program. **Note 2:** If the changes you made violate the Rule of Referential Integrity (every value in the foreign key must also appear in the primary key of the other table), the program will crash when the database file is updated. **Note 3:** Changes that violate the Rule of Entity Integrity (no record may have a null entry in its primary key and entries for primary keys must be unique) cause the program to crash as soon as a *Move* button is pressed. Exercises 10 through 12 discuss techniques for addressing the issues in Notes 2 and 3.

The following walkthrough will better acquaint you with the operation of the program.

1. Open and run the program named 10-2-1.

2. Click on the *Move next* button in the navigation toolbar twice to reveal the third record, the one for Calcutta.

3. Type "New York" into the City to find: text box and then click on the *Search for City* button to display the record for New York.

4. Click on the *Add new* button in the navigation toolbar and then enter the following data into the vertical set of four empty text boxes for the fields: Los Angeles, USA, 12.8, 13.2.

5. Click on one of the *Move* buttons in the navigation toolbar. Notice that the "Total number of items" box now shows that there are 11 records.

6. Terminate and then rerun the program. Notice that the "Total number of items" box shows that there are 10 records. The Megacities database file in the *bin\Debug* folder was not updated because we did not click on the *Update* button before terminating the program.

7. Redo Steps 4 and 5, and then click on the *Update* button.

8. Terminate and then rerun the program. Notice that the "Total number of items" box shows that there are 11 records. The Megacities database file in the *bin\Debug* folder was updated.

9. Experiment further with the program to test its other features.

■ Designing the Form for the Table-Editing Program

The following steps create the navigation toolbar for program 10-2-1, create the four sets of labels and text boxes on the left side of the form, bind the text boxes to the navigation toolbar, and implement the search capability.

1. Start a new program and bind the Cities table as was done in Section 10.1.

2. Add a BindingNavigator control to the form designer. (This control can be found in the *All Windows Forms* or *Data* groups of the Toolbox.) After you double-click on the control in the Toolbox, a control named BindingNavigator1 appears in the component tray at the bottom of the Form Designer. Also, a navigation toolbar will appear anchored to the top of the form.

3. Go to the Properties window for BindingNavigator1, click on the down arrow at the right side of the BindingSource property's Settings box, and set the BindingSource property to BindingSource1.

4. Notice that the toolbar is missing the *Update* button. Click on the toolbar. The rightmost item on the toolbar (see Fig. 10.54) is used to add an update button to the navigation toolbar. Click on the small down arrow on the right side of the rightmost item and then click on *Button* in the drop-down list that appears. A button showing a mountain () appears.

FIGURE 10.54   Original navigation toolbar.

5. Open the Properties window for the mountain button, change its name from ToolStrip-Button1 to btnUpdate, and set its Text property to Update.

6. Click on the ellipsis at the right side of the Image property's Settings box, and then click on the *Import* button in the Select Resource dialog box that appears. (An Open dialog box appears.)

7. Browse to locate the folder Programs\Ch10, and double-click on the file Disk.bmp to place its picture in the Select Resource window.

8. Click on the *OK* button to change the image on btnUpdate to a diskette (🖫).

9. Display the Data Sources window. If the window or its tab is not visible, click on *Data Sources* in the Toolbar's *View/Other Windows* menu.

10. Double-click on *Cities* in the Data Sources window to obtain the display in Fig. 10.55.

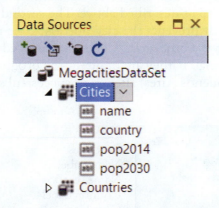

FIGURE 10.55   Data Sources window.

11. Click on *name* and drag it onto the form. Both a label and text box for the field *name* appear on the form. The label will be named NameLabel and the text box will be named NameTextBox.

12. Repeat Step 11 for each of the other three fields. The left side of the form has now been created and the four text boxes have been bound to the Cities table.

13. Create the remaining controls in Figure 10.51 in the usual way.

■ Writing the Table-Editing Program

We have seen that each record of the Cities table is given a location number from 1 through 10 by the navigation toolbar. For programming purposes, each record has an **index number** that ranges from 0 through 9. That is, the record for Buenos Aires has index number 0, the record for Calcutta has index number 1, and so on. BindingSource controls have a Position property and a Find method that return index numbers.

Assume the program is running. Let's refer to the record whose fields are displayed as the **current record**. At any time, the value of

```
BindingSource1.Position
```

is the index of the current record. Pay particular attention to the fact that the Position property gives the index, not the location!

If *n* is a nonnegative integer, then the statement

```
BindingSource1.Position = n
```

makes the record of index *n* the current record.

If *strVar* is a string variable whose value is a city in the Cities table, then the value of

```
BindingSource1.Find("name", strVar)
```

is the index of the record for that city. If the value of *strVar* is not a city in the table, then the Find method returns the value 0.

 Example 1   **Megacities** The following program edits the Cities table. Assume that the Cities table has been bound, and the navigation toolbar, text boxes, and *Search for City* button have been created as described above. The second statement inside the Load event procedure is optional. It prevents the city Buenos Aires from being highlighted when the program is first run. In the btnSearch_Click event procedure, the two statements that refer to *currentCity* are optional. If they are omitted, the program will display the record for the first city (in this case Buenos Aires) after an unsuccessful search. The remaining statements are self-explanatory.

OBJECT	PROPERTY	SETTING
frmCities	Text	Megacities
NameLabel	Text	name:
NameTextBox		
CountryLabel	Text	country:
CountryTextBox		
Pop2014Label	Text	pop2014:
Pop2014TextBox		
Pop2030Label	Text	pop2030:
Pop2030TextBox		
lblCity	Text	City to find:
txtCity		
btnSearch	Text	Search for City

```
Private Sub frmCities_Load(...) Handles MyBase.Load
  Me.CitiesTableAdapter.Fill(Me.MegacitiesDataSet.Cities)
  NameTextBox.SelectionStart = 0
End Sub


Private Sub btnUpdate_Click(...) Handles btnUpdate.Click
  'These two lines update the database file in the bin\Debug folder.
  BindingSource1.EndEdit()
  CitiesTableAdapter.Update(MegacitiesDataSet.Cities)
End Sub
```

```
Private Sub btnSearch_Click(...) Handles btnSearch.Click
  Dim currentCity As String = NameTextBox.Text
  If txtCity.Text <> "" Then
    BindingSource1.Position = BindingSource1.Find("name", txtCity.Text)
    If NameTextBox.Text <> txtCity.Text Then
      MessageBox.Show("City not found.")
      BindingSource1.Position = BindingSource1.Find("name", currentCity)
    End If
  Else
    MessageBox.Show("You must enter the name of a city.")
  End If
End Sub
```

■ Principles of Database Design

Good relational database design is more of an art than a science. However, the designer should keep in mind certain fundamental guidelines.

- *Data should often be stored in their smallest parts.*

  For instance, city, state, and zip code are usually best stored in three fields. So doing will allow you to easily sort a mailing by zip code or target a mailing to the residents of a specific city.

- *Avoid redundancy.*

  The process of avoiding redundancy by splitting a table into two or more related tables is called **data normalization**. For instance, the excessive duplication in Table 10.4 can be avoided by replacing the table with the related Table 10.5(a) and Table 10.5(b).

TABLE 10.4   A table with redundant data.

Course	Section	Name	Time	Credits	Prerequisites
CS102	1001	Intro to Databases	MWF 8-9	3	CS101
CS102	1002	Intro to Databases	MWF 1-2	3	CS101
CS102	1003	Intro to Databases	MWF 2-3	3	CS101
CS102	1004	Intro to Databases	MWF 3-4	3	CS101
CS105	1001	Visual Basic	MWF 1-2	4	CS200

TABLE 10.5(a)

Course	Section	Time
CS102	1001	MWF 8-9
CS102	1002	MWF 1-2
CS102	1003	MWF 2-3
CS102	1004	MWF 3-4
CS105	1001	MWF 1-2

TABLE 10.5(b)

Course	Name	Credits	Prerequisites
CS102	Intro to Databases	3	CS101
CS105	Visual Basic	4	CS200

- *Avoid tables with intentionally blank entries.*

  Tables with entries that are intentionally left blank use space inefficiently. Table 10.6 on the next page, which serves as a directory of faculty and students, has an excessive number of blank entries. The table should be split into two tables, each dealing with just one of the groups.

| TABLE 10.6 | A table with an excessive number of blank entries. | | | | | | |

Name	ssn	Classification	Date Hired	Dept	Office Number	gpa	Credits Earned
Sarah Brown	816–34–9012	student				3.7	78
Pat Riley	409–22–1234	faculty	9/1/02	biology	Y–3014		
Joe Russo	690–32–1108	faculty	9/1/05	math	T–2008		
Juan Lopez	509–43–4110	student				3.2	42

- *Strive for table cohesion.*

  Each table should have a basic topic to which all the data in the table are connected.

- *Avoid fields whose values can be calculated from existing fields.*

  For instance, if a table has fields for both the population and area of countries, then there is no need to include a field for the population density.

■ Comments

1. Since the *name* field of the Cities table is the primary key, each record of the table must have a value assigned to its *name* field. However, the database does not require that values be assigned to the other three fields.

2. In Example 1, the four pairs of labels and text boxes on the left side of the form have the names given to them by Visual Basic when the fields were dragged from the Data Sources window to the Form Designer. You can change these names if you like. For instance, CountryTextBox can be changed to txtCountry. Also, the names of the controls BindingSource1 and BindingNavigator1 can be changed to more meaningful ones, such as CitiesBindingSource and CitiesBindingNavigator.

Practice Problems 10.2

1. Can a record for any city be added to the Cities table?
2. Can a record for any country be added to the Countries table?
3. Can any record in the Cities table be deleted?
4. Can any record in the Countries table be deleted?

EXERCISES 10.2

In Exercises 1 through 8, carry out the following tasks on the Cities table with the program from Example 1:

1. Change the name of the city Mumbai to Bombay.
2. Add the following record: Karachi, Pakistan, 16.1, 24.8.
3. Use the *Search for City* button to find the record for Mexico City.
4. Find the record for the city in position 8.
5. Delete the record for Delhi.
6. Add a record that will raise an exception when you try to update the database file.
7. Add a record that will raise an exception as soon as you move to another record.
8. Add a record with some empty fields.

9. Consider Example 1. Let *strVar* be a string variable. Give a condition that will be True if the value of *strVar* is not the name of a city in the Cities table.

10. Consider Example 1. If you violate the Rule of Referential Integrity, an exception is generated when you click on the *Update* button. Revise the btnUpdate_Click event procedure so that the program will not crash when the principle is violated. **Note:** The name of the exception is OleDB.OleDbException.

11. **Megacities** Modify Example 1 so that a Rule of Referential Integrity violation is caught as soon as an improper country is entered into the country text box.

12. **Megacities** Modify Example 1 so that a Rule of Entity Integrity violation is caught as soon as the user leaves an empty NameTextBox or a NameTextBox whose entry duplicates a city from another record.

Exercises 13 through 18 refer to the database Movies.accdb discussed in the exercises for Section 10.1.

13. **Movies** Write a program that can be used to make changes to the Lines table. (There is no need to include a Search capability.) See Fig. 10.56.

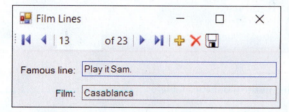

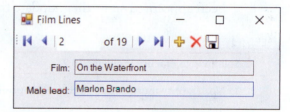

FIGURE 10.56 Possible outcome of Exercise 13. **FIGURE 10.57** Possible outcome of Exercise 14.

14. **Movies** Write a program that can be used to make changes to the Actors table. (There is no need to include a Search capability.) See Fig. 10.57.

15. **Movies** Use the program created in Exercise 13 to change the famous line "Here's looking at you kid." to the line "Play it, Sam." Both lines are from the same film.

16. **Movies** Use the program created in Exercise 14 to add the following record to the Actors table: Patton, George Scott.

17. **Movies** Why can't the following record be added to the Lines table: "Houston, we have a problem.", Apollo 13?

18. **Movies** Why can't the following record be deleted from the Actors table: Casablanca, Humphrey Bogart?

19. **Addresses** Eliminate the redundancy in Table 10.7.

TABLE 10.7 A table with redundancies.

name	address	city	state	stateCapital
R. Myers	3 Maple St.	Seattle	Washington	Olympia
T. Murphy	25 Main St.	Seattle	Washington	Olympia
L. Scott	14 Park Ave.	Baltimore	Maryland	Annapolis
B. Jones	106 5th St.	Seattle	Washington	Olympia
W. Smith	29 7th Ave.	Baltimore	Maryland	Annapolis
V. Miller	4 Flower Ave.	Chicago	Illinois	Springfield

20. **House of Representatives** Eliminate the redundancy in Table 10.8, a table of members of the U.S. House of Representatives. (**Note:** The value of *numColleges* is the number of colleges in the representative's state.)

TABLE 10.8 **A table with redundancies.**

name	state	party	statePop	numColleges
J. Conyers	Michigan	Democratic	10.2	97
S. Rigell	Virginia	Republican	7.8	83
D. Beyer	Virginia	Democratic	7.8	83
J. Sarbanes	Maryland	Democratic	5.8	97
S. Hoyer	Maryland	Democratic	5.8	97
R. Hurt	Virginia	Republican	7.8	83

21. **Supreme Court** The database Justices.accdb in the Programs\Ch10\Databases folder was current as of January 1, 2016. If some justices have retired and new justices have been appointed since then, update the database.

Solutions to Practice Problems 10.2

1. No. The city must be from a country appearing in the Countries table.

2. Yes.

3. Yes.

4. No. Only the records for Pakistan and Indonesia can be deleted.

CHAPTER 10 SUMMARY

1. A *table* is a group of data items arranged in a rectangular array, with each row containing the same categories of information. Each row is called a *record*. Each category (column) is called a *field*. A *database* is a collection of one or more tables that are usually related.

2. A *BindingSource control* can be used to bind a table of a database to a program.

3. *Server Explorer* can be used to view the table from a database that has been connected to a program.

4. *LINQ* can be used to set criteria for information retrieval from a table.

5. A sequence of records resulting from the execution of a LINQ query can be displayed in a *DataGridView control*.

6. A *primary key* is a field or set of fields that uniquely identifies each record of a table. The *Rule of Entity Integrity* states that no record can have a null entry in a primary key and that entries for primary keys must be unique. A *foreign key* is a field or set of fields in one table that refers to a primary key in another table. The *Rule of Referential Integrity* states that each value in the foreign key must also appear in the primary key in the related table.

7. The *Join operator* links two tables based on matching field values.

8. A *navigation toolbar*, which has icons on its buttons similar to those on a DVD player, can be used to view records, alter records, delete records, and add new records to a database table. A *BindingNavigator control* binds the navigation toolbar to the table via a BindingSource control. Searching for records in the table can be facilitated with the *Position property* and the *Find methods* of the BindingSource control.

9. Adherence to fundamental design principles can help database designers create efficient databases.

CHAPTER 10 PROGRAMMING PROJECTS

1. Orders and Inventory Management The database Microland.accdb is maintained by the Microland Computer Warehouse, a mail-order computer-supply company. Tables 10.9 through 10.11 show parts of three tables in the database. The table Customers identifies each customer by an ID number and gives, in addition to the name and address, the total amount of purchases during the current year prior to today. The table Inventory identifies each product in stock by an ID number and gives, in addition to its description and price (per unit), the quantity in stock at the beginning of the day. The table Orders gives the orders received today. Suppose that it is now the end of the day. Write a program that uses the three tables to do the following two tasks.

(a) Display in a list box the items that are out of stock and those that must be reordered to satisfy today's orders. See Fig. 10.58(a) on the next page.

(b) Display in a list box bills for all customers who ordered during the day. Each bill should show the customer's name, address, items ordered (with costs), and total cost of the order. See Fig. 10.58(b) on the next page.

TABLE 10.9   First three records of the Customers table.

CustID	Name	Street	City	AmtPurchases
1	Michael Smith	2 Park St.	Dallas, TX 75201	234.50
2	Brittany Jones	5 2nd Ave.	Tampa, FL 33602	121.90
3	Warren Pease	7 Maple St.	Boston, MA 02101	387.20

TABLE 10.10   First three records of the Inventory table.

itemID	description	price	quantity
PL208	Visual Basic	89.50	12
SW109	MS Office Upgrade	195.95	2
HW913	Scanner	49.95	8

TABLE 10.11   First four records of the Orders table.

custID	itemID	quantity
3	SW109	1
1	PL208	3
1	HW913	2
2	PL208	1

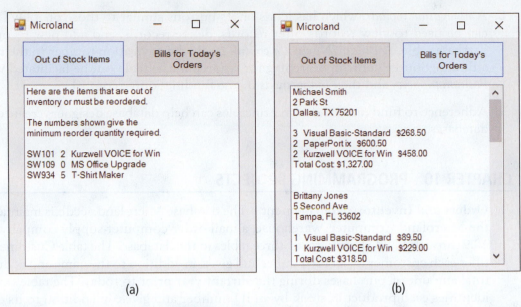

(a)   (b)

FIGURE 10.58   Possible outcome of Programming Project 1.

2. **Grade Book**   A teacher maintains a database containing two tables—Students and Grades. The Students table has three fields: *studentID*, *lastName*, and *firstName*. The Grades table has four fields: *studentID*, *firstExam*, *secondExam*, and *finalExam*. At the beginning of the semester, the Students table is filled in completely with a record for each student in a class, and the Grades table has a record for each student that contains only the student's ID number. (**Note:** The database is contained in the file Gradebook. accdb from the folder Ch10\Databases.) Write a program that allows the instructor to record and process the grades for the semester. The program should do the following:

(a) Use a navigation toolbar to fill the Grades table.

(b) After all grades have been entered, display a DataGridView control showing the name of each student and his or her semester average. The semester average should be calculated as (firstExam + secondExam + 2 · finalExam) / 4. See Fig. 10.59.

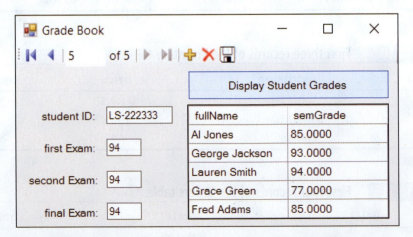

FIGURE 10.59   Possible outcome of Programming Project 2.

11

Object-Oriented Programming

11.1 Classes and Objects

noun: a word that refers to a place, a person, a thing, or an activity

verb: a word that describes an action or occurrence

adjective: a word that modifies a noun or a pronoun

"A good rule of thumb for object-oriented programming is that classes are the nouns in your analysis of the problem. The methods in your object correspond to verbs that the noun does. The properties are the adjectives that describe the noun."

Excerpt from Core Visual Basic, 5/e by Gary Cornell & David Jezak.
Published by Prentice Hall, © 1997.

Practical experience in the financial, scientific, engineering, and software design industries has revealed some difficulties with traditional program design methodologies. As programs grow in size and become more complex, and as the number of programmers working on the same project increases, the number of dependencies and interrelationships throughout the code increases exponentially. A small change made by one programmer in one place may have many effects, both intended and unintended, in many other places. The effects of this change may ripple throughout the entire program, requiring the rewriting of a great deal of code along the way.

A partial solution to this problem is "data hiding" where, within a unit, as much implementation detail as possible is hidden. Data hiding is an important principle underlying object-oriented programming. An object is an encapsulation of data and procedures that act on the data. A programmer using an object is concerned only with the tasks that the object can perform and the parameters used by these tasks. The details of the data structures and procedures are hidden within the object.

Two types of objects will be of concern to us: **control objects** and **code objects**. Examples of control objects are text boxes, list boxes, buttons, and all the other controls that can be created from the Toolbox. So far, most of our programs have contained a single class block beginning with a line such as "Public Class *frmName*" and ending with the line "End Class". A code object is a specific instance of a user-defined type, called a **class**, which is defined similarly to a structure, but in a separate class block of the form

VideoNote
Classes and
Objects

```
Class ClassName
    statements
End Class
```

Each class block is delineated in the Code Editor by an elongated left bracket appearing to the left of the block. Both control objects and class objects have properties, methods, and events. The main differences are that control objects are predefined and have physical manifestations, whereas the programmer must create the class blocks for code objects. In this section, when we use the word "object" without a qualifier, we mean "code object".

Whenever you double-click on the TextBox icon in the Toolbox, a new text box is created. Although each text box is a separate entity, they all have the same properties, methods, and events. Each text box is said to be an **instance** of the class TextBox. In some sense, the TextBox icon in the Toolbox is a template or blueprint for creating text boxes. When you look at the Properties window for a text box, the drop-down list box at the top of the window reads something like "TextBox1 System.Windows.Forms.TextBox". TextBox1 is the name of the control object and it is said to be an instance of the class "TextBox". You can't set properties or invoke methods of the TextBox class; you can only set properties or invoke methods of the specific text boxes that are instances of the class. The analogy is often made between a class and a cookie cutter. The cookie cutter is used to create cookies that you can eat, but you can't eat the cookie cutter.

Object-oriented programs are populated with objects that hold data, have properties, respond to methods, and raise events. (The generation of events will be discussed in the next section.) Five examples of objects are as follows:

1. In a professor's program to assign and display semester grades, a student object might hold a single student's name, social security number, midterm grade, and final exam grade. A CalcSemGrade method might calculate the student's semester grade. Events might be raised when improper data are passed to the object.

2. In a payroll program, an employee object might hold an employee's name, hourly wage, and hours worked. A CalculatePay method would tell the object to calculate the wages for the current pay period.

3. In a checking account program, a check register object might have methods that record and total the checks written during a certain month, a deposit slip object might record and total the deposits made during a certain month, and an account object might keep a running total of the balance in the account. The account object would raise an event to alert the bank when the balance got too low.

4. In a bookstore inventory program, a textbook object might hold the name, author, quantity in stock, and wholesale price of an individual textbook. A CalculateRetailPrice method might instruct the textbook object to calculate the selling price of the textbook. An event could be raised when the book went out of stock.

5. In a card game program, a card object might hold the denomination and suit of a specific card. An IdentifyCard method might return a string such as "Ace of Spades". A deck-of-cards object might consist of an array of card objects and a ShuffleDeck method that thoroughly shuffles the deck. A Shuffling event might indicate the progress of the shuffle.

An important object-oriented term is **class**. A class is a template from which objects are created. The class specifies the properties and methods that will be common to all objects that are instances of that class. Classes are formulated in class blocks. An object, which is an instance of a class, can be created in a program with a pair of statements of the form

```
Dim objectName As ClassName
objectName = New ClassName
```

The first of these two lines of code declares what type of object the variable will refer to. The actual object does not exist until it is created with the New keyword, as done in the second line. This is known as creating an **instance** of an object and is where an object is actually created from its class. After this second line of code executes, the object is then ready for use. The first line can appear either in the Declarations section of a class (to declare a class-level variable) or inside a procedure (to declare a local variable). The instantiation line can appear only in a procedure; however, any object variable can be instantiated when declared (as either class-level or local) by using the single line

```
Dim objectName As New ClassName
```

In a program, properties, methods, and events of the object are accessed with statements of the form shown in the following table:

TASK	STATEMENT
Assign a value to a property	`objectName.propertyName = value`
Assign the value of a property to a variable	`varName = objectName.propertyName`
Carry out a method	`objectName.methodName(arg1, ...)`
Raise an event	`RaiseEvent eventName`

The program in Example 1 uses a class named Student to calculate and display a student's semester grade. The information stored by an object of the type Student consists of a student's name, social security number, and grades on two exams (midterm and final). These data are stored in variables declared with the statements

```
Private m_name As String         'Name
Private m_ssn As String          'Social security number
Private m_midterm As Double      'Numerical grade on midterm exam
Private m_final As Double        'Numerical grade on final exam
```

The word "Private" guarantees that the variables cannot be accessed directly from outside the object. In object-oriented programming terminology, these variables are called **member variables** (or **instance variables**). We will follow the common convention of beginning the name of each member variable with the prefix "*m_*". Each of these variables is used to hold the value of a property. However, instead of being accessed directly, each member variable is accessed indirectly with a **property block**. For instance, the following property block consists of a Get property procedure to retrieve (or *read*) the value of the Name property and a Set property procedure to assign (or *write*) the value of the Name property:

```
Public Property Name() As String
  Get
    Return m_name
  End Get
  Set(value As String)
    m_name = value
  End Set
End Property
```

In a property block, additional code can be added after the Get and Set statements to validate the data before they are returned or stored. The word "Public" allows the property to be accessed from outside the code for the Student class block. For instance, the Name property can be accessed by code in the form's class block. On the other hand, since the member variables were declared as Private, they cannot be accessed directly from code in the form's block. They can be accessed only through Property procedures that allow values to be checked and perhaps modified. Also, a Property procedure is able to take other steps necessitated by a change in the value of a member variable.

A property block does not have to contain both Get and Set property procedures. For instance, the block

```
Public WriteOnly Property Midterm() As Double
  Set(value As Double)
    m_midterm = value
  End Set
End Property
```

specifies the Midterm property as "write-only". This property could be specified to be "read-only" with the block

```
Public ReadOnly Property Midterm() As Double
  Get
    Return m_midterm
  End Get
End Property
```

Methods are constructed with Sub or Function procedures. A Function procedure is used when the method returns a value; otherwise a Sub procedure will suffice. For instance, the method CalcSemGrade, which is used to calculate a student's semester grade, is created as follows:

```
Function CalcSemGrade() As String
  Dim grade As Double
  grade = (m_midterm + m_final) / 2
  grade = Math.Round(grade) 'round the grade.
  Select Case grade
    Case Is >= 90
      Return "A"
    Case Is >= 80
      Return "B"
    Case Is >= 70
      Return "C"
    Case Is >= 60
      Return "D"
    Case Else
      Return "F"
  End Select
End Function
```

An object of the type Student is declared in the form's code with a pair of statements such as

```
Dim pupil As Student    'Declare pupil as an object of type Student
pupil = New Student      'Create an instance of type Student
```

After these two statements are executed, properties and methods can be utilized with statements such as

```
pupil.Name = "Al Adams"               'Assign a value to m_name
txtBox.text = pupil.Name              'Display the student's name
lstBox.Items.Add(pupil.CalcSemGrade)  'Display semester grade
```

The first statement calls the Set property procedure for the Name property, the second statement calls the Get property procedure for the Name property, and the third statement calls the method CalcSemGrade.

 Example 1   **Semester Grade** The following program uses the class Student to calculate and display a student's semester grade. The structure Person in frmGrades is used by the btnDisplay_Click procedure to place information into the DataGridView control.

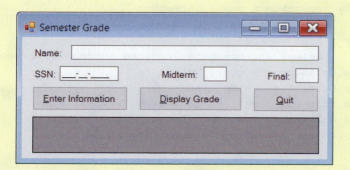

OBJECT	PROPERTY	SETTING
frmGrades	Text	Semester Grade
lblName	Text	Name:
txtName		
lblSSN	Text	SSN:
mtbSSN	Mask	000-00-0000
lblMidterm	Text	Midterm:
txtMidterm		
lblFinal	Text	Final:
txtFinal		
btnEnter	Text	&Enter Information
btnDisplay	Text	&Display Grade
btnQuit	Text	&Quit
dgvGrades	RowHeadersVisible	False

```
Public Class frmGrades
  Dim pupil As Student   'pupil is an object of class Student

  Structure Person   'for use in btnDisplay_Click
    Dim name As String
    Dim socSecNum As String
    Dim semGrade As String
  End Structure

  Private Sub btnEnter_Click(...) Handles btnEnter.Click
    pupil = New Student     'Create an instance of Student.
    'Read the values stored in the text boxes.
    pupil.Name = txtName.Text
    pupil.SocSecNum = mtbSSN.Text
    pupil.Midterm = CDbl(txtMidterm.Text)
    pupil.Final = CDbl(txtFinal.Text)
    'Clear text boxes
    txtName.Clear()
    mtbSSN.Clear()
    txtMidterm.Clear()
    txtFinal.Clear()
    'Notify user that grades for the student have been recorded.
    MessageBox.Show("Student Recorded.")
  End Sub

  Private Sub btnDisplay_Click(...) Handles btnDisplay.Click
    Dim persons(0) As Person
    persons(0).name = pupil.Name
    persons(0).socSecNum = pupil.SocSecNum
    persons(0).semGrade = pupil.CalcSemGrade
    Dim query = From someone In persons
                Select someone.name, someone.socSecNum, someone.semGrade
    dgvGrades.DataSource = query.ToList
    dgvGrades.CurrentCell = Nothing
    dgvGrades.Columns("name").HeaderText = "Student Name"
    dgvGrades.Columns("socSecNum").HeaderText = "SSN"
    dgvGrades.Columns("semGrade").HeaderText = "Grade"
  End Sub
```

```vb
      Private Sub btnQuit_Click(...) Handles btnQuit.Click
        Me.Close()
      End Sub
   End Class        'frmGrades

   Class Student
      Private m_name As String           'Name
      Private m_ssn As String            'Social security number
      Private m_midterm As Double        'Numerical grade on midterm exam
      Private m_final As Double          'Numerical grade on final exam

      Public Property Name() As String
        Get
          Return m_name
        End Get
        Set(value As String)
          m_name = value
        End Set
      End Property

      Public Property SocSecNum() As String
        Get
          Return m_ssn
        End Get
        Set(value As String)
          m_ssn = value
        End Set
      End Property

      Public WriteOnly Property Midterm() As Double
        Set(value As Double)
          m_midterm = value
        End Set
      End Property

      Public WriteOnly Property Final() As Double
        Set(value As Double)
          m_final = value
        End Set
      End Property

      Function CalcSemGrade() As String
        Dim grade As Double
        grade = (m_midterm + m_final) / 2
        grade = Math.Round(grade)   'Round the grade.
        Select Case grade
          Case Is >= 90
            Return "A"
          Case Is >= 80
            Return "B"
          Case Is >= 70
            Return "C"
          Case Is >= 60
            Return "D"
```

```
      Case Else
        Return "F"
      End Select
  End Function
End Class        'Student
```

[Run, enter the data for a student (such as "Al Adams", "123-45-6789", "82", "87"), click on the *Enter Information* button to send the data to the object, and click on the *Display Grade* button to display the student's name, social security number, and semester grade.]

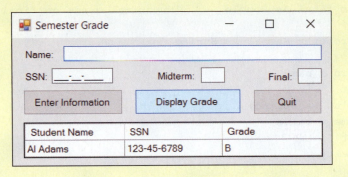

In summary, the following six steps are used to create a class:

1. Identify a *thing* in your program that is to become an object.

2. Determine the properties and methods that you would like the object to have. (As a rule of thumb, properties should access data, and methods should perform operations.)

3. A class will serve as a template for the object. The code for the class is placed in a class block of the form

```
Class ClassName
   statements
End Class
```

4. For each of the properties in Step 2, declare a private member variable with a statement of the form

```
Private variableName As DataType
```

Member variables can be preceded with the keyword "Public", which allows direct access to the member variables from the code in the form. However, this is considered poor programming practice. By using Set property procedures to update the data, we can enforce constraints and carry out validation.

5. For each of the member variables in Step 4, create a Property block with Get and/or Set procedures to retrieve and assign values of the variable. The general forms of the procedures are

```
Public Property PropertyName() As DataType
   Get
      (Possibly additional code)
    Return variableName
   End Get
   Set(value As DataType)
      (Possibly additional code)
    variableName = value
   End Set
End Property
```

In the Get or Set code, additional code can be added to prevent the object from storing or returning invalid or corrupted data. For example, an If block could be added to allow only valid social security numbers, alerting the user in the event of an invalid number.

6. For each method in Step 2, create a Sub procedure or Function procedure to carry out the task.

Example 2   **Semester Grade** The following modification of the program in Example 1 calculates semester grades for students who have registered on a "Pass/Fail" basis. We create a new class, named PFStudent, with the same member variables and property procedures as the class Student. The only change needed in the class block occurs in the CalcSemGrade method. The new code for this method is

```
Function CalcSemGrade() As String
  Dim grade As Double
  grade = (m_midterm + m_final) / 2
  grade = Math.Round(grade)   'Round the grade.
  If grade >= 60 Then
    Return "Pass"
  Else
    Return "Fail"
  End If
End Function
```

The only change needed in the form's code is to replace the two occurrences of *Student* with *PFStudent*. When the program is run with the same input as in Example 1, the output will be

```
Al Adams   123-45-6789   Pass
```

■ Object Constructors

A **constructor** is a special method named *New* that is executed when an object is instantiated. A constructor can take several different forms. The following constructor shows one way to pass data to an object.

```
Public Sub New()
  Assignment statement(s)
End Sub
```

When you don't create a constructor, Visual Basic creates a default constructor having no assignment statement, and that does not appear in the code for the class.

The graphical program in Example 3 illustrates the use of a constructor to specify the size and initial placement of a circle. This task involves pixels. To get a feel for how big a pixel is, the initial size of the form when you create a new project is 300 pixels by 300 pixels. Section 9.4 provides the details for displaying graphics inside a picture box control with the Graphics object gr = picBox.CreateGraphics. In Example 3, the statement

```
gr.DrawEllipse(Pens.Black, Xcoord, Ycoord, Diameter, Diameter)
```

draws a circle inside a picture box, where Xcoord and Ycoord are the distances (in pixels) of the circle from the left side and top of the picture box.

Example 3   **Moving Circle** The following program contains a Circle object. The object keeps track of the location and diameter of the circle. (The location is specified by two numbers, called the coordinates, giving the distance from the left side and top of the picture box. Distances and the diameter are measured in pixels.) A Show method displays the circle, and a Move method adds 20 pixels to each coordinate of the circle. Initially, the (unseen) circle is located at the upper-left corner of the picture box and has a diameter of 40. The form has a button captioned *Move and Show Circle* that invokes both methods. Notice that the Xcoord, Ycoord, and Diameter properties, rather than the member variables, appear in the methods.

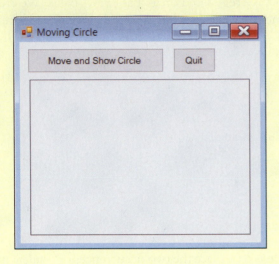

OBJECT	PROPERTY	SETTING
frmCircle	Text	Moving Circle
btnMove	Text	Move and Show Circle
btnQuit	Text	Quit
picCircle		

```
Public Class frmCircle
  Dim round As New Circle

  Private Sub btnMove_Click(...) Handles btnMove.Click
    round.Move(20)
    round.Show(picCircle.CreateGraphics)
  End Sub

  Private Sub btnQuit_Click(...) Handles btnQuit.Click
    Me.Close()
  End Sub
End Class        'frmCircle

Class Circle
  Private m_x As Integer    'dist from left side of picture box to circle
  Private m_y As Integer    'distance from top of picture box to the circle
  Private m_d As Integer    'diameter of circle

  Public Sub New()
    'Set the initial location of the circle to the upper-left
    'corner of the picture box, and set its diameter to 40.
    Xcoord = 0
    Ycoord = 0
    Diameter = 40
  End Sub
```

```vb
   Public Property Xcoord() As Integer
      Get
         Return m_x
      End Get
      Set(value As Integer)
         m_x = value
      End Set
   End Property


   Public Property Ycoord() As Integer
      Get
         Return m_y
      End Get
      Set(value As Integer)
         m_y = value
      End Set
   End Property


   Public Property Diameter() As Integer
      Get
         Return m_d
      End Get
      Set(value As Integer)
         m_d = value
      End Set
   End Property


   Sub Show(gr As Graphics)
      'Draw a circle with the given graphics context.
      gr.DrawEllipse(Pens.Black, Xcoord, Ycoord, Diameter, Diameter)
   End Sub


   Sub Move(distance As Integer)
      Xcoord += distance
      Ycoord += distance
   End Sub
End Class        'Circle
```

[Run, and click on the *Move* button ten times.]

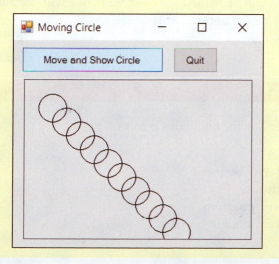

Constructors with Parameters

The constructor in Example 3 is called a **parameterless constructor**. The header of a **constructor with parameters** has the form

```
Public Sub New(parl As DataTypel, par2 As DataType2, ...)
```

After a constructor with parameters is defined, a statement of the form

```
objectName = New ClassName(argl, arg2, ...)
```

assigns the values of the arguments to the parameters after instantiating the object. These values can then be used by the assignment statements in the constructor.

For instance, in Example 3, the constructor can be written as

```
Public Sub New(x As Integer, y As Integer, d As Integer)
  'Set the initial location of the circle to x pixels from
  'the left side and y pixels from the top of the picture box.
  'Set the diameter to d pixels.
  Xcoord = x
  Ycoord = y
  Diameter = d
End Sub
```

and the instantiating statement can be changed to

```
Dim round As New Circle(0, 0, 40)
```

The use of parameters gives flexibility to programmers using the Circle class. They can determine where to place the first circle.

Auto-Implemented Properties

Some property blocks are very clear-cut in that they do not contain ReadOnly or WriteOnly keywords and have no additional code in their Get or Set blocks. Such property blocks can use the **auto-implemented properties** feature. This feature allows you to reduce a clear-cut property block to just its header, and to omit declaring a member variable for the property. Visual Basic automatically creates hidden Get and Set procedures and a hidden member variable. The name of the member variable is the property name preceded by an underscore character. For example, if you declare an auto-implemented property named SocSecNum, the member variable will be named _SocSecNum. We will use auto-implemented properties in the remainder of this chapter.

Practice Problems 11.1

1. Which of the following analogies is out of place?

   (a) class : object
   (b) sewing pattern : garment
   (c) blueprint : house
   (d) programmer : program
   (e) cookie cutter : cookie

2. In Example 1, suppose that the first five lines of the event procedure btnEnter_Click are replaced with

```
Private Sub btnEnter_Click(...) Handles btnEnter.Click
  Dim ssn As String = "123-45-6789"    'social security number
  'Create an instance of Student.
  pupil = New Student(ssn)
  pupil.Name = txtName.Text
```

Create a New procedure and revise the SocSecNum property block for the Student class to be consistent with the next to last line in the preceding code.

EXERCISES 11.1

Exercises 1 through 14 refer to the class Student from Example 1. When applicable, assume that _pupil_ is an instance of the class.

1. What will be the effect if the _Midterm_ property block is changed to the following?

```
Public WriteOnly Property Midterm() As Double
  Set(value As Double)
    Select Case value
      Case Is < 0
        m_midterm = 0
      Case Is > 100
        m_midterm = 100
      Case Else
        m_midterm = value
    End Select
  End Set
End Property
```

2. What will be the effect if the _Midterm_ property block is changed to the following?

```
Public WriteOnly Property Midterm() As Double
  Set(value As Double)
    m_midterm = value + 10
  End Set
End Property
```

3. Modify the class block for _Student_ so that the following statement will display the student's midterm grade:

```
MessageBox.Show(CStr(pupil.Midterm))
```

4. Modify the class block for _Student_ so that the student's semester average can be displayed with a statement of the form

```
MessageBox.Show(CStr(pupil.Average))
```

5. In the class block for Student, why can't the third line of the CalcSemGrade method be written as follows?

```
grade = (Midterm + Final) / 2
```

6. Write code for the class block that sets the two grades to 10 whenever an instance of the class is created.

7. What is the effect of adding the following code to the class block?

```
Public Sub New()
    SocSecNum = "999-99-9999"
End Sub
```

In Exercises 8 through 14, determine the errors in the given form code.

8.
```
Dim scholar As Student
Private Sub btnGo_Click(...) Handles btnGo.Click
    Dim firstName as String
    scholar.Name = "Warren"
    firstName = scholar.Name
End Sub
```

9.
```
Dim scholar As Student
Private Sub btnGo_Click(...) Handles btnGo.Click
    Dim nom as String
    scholar = Student
    scholar.Name = "Warren Peace"
    nom = scholar.Name
End Sub
```

10.
```
Dim scholar As Student
Private Sub btnGo_Click(...) Handles btnGo.Click
    Dim nom as String
    scholar = New Student
    m_name = "Warren Peace"
    nom = scholar.Name
End Sub
```

11.
```
Dim scholar As Student
Private Sub btnGo_Click(...) Handles btnGo.Click
    Dim nom As String
    scholar = New Student
    scholar.Name = "Warren Peace"
    nom = m_name
End Sub
```

12.
```
Dim scholar As Student
Private Sub btnGo_Click(...) Handles btnGo.Click
    Dim grade As String
    scholar = New Student
    scholar.CalcSemGrade = "A"
    grade = scholar.CalcSemGrade()
End Sub
```

13.
```
Dim pupil, scholar As Student
Private Sub btnGo_Click(...) Handles btnGo.Click
    scholar = New Student
    pupil = New Student
    scholar.Midterm = 89
    pupil.Midterm = scholar.Midterm
    lstGrades.Items.Add(pupil.Midterm)
End Sub
```

14.
```
Dim scholar As Student
scholar = New Student

Private Sub btnGo_Click(...) Handles btnGo.Click
  scholar.Name = "Manuel Transmission"
End Sub
```

15. In the following program, determine the output displayed in the list box when the button is clicked on:

```
Public Class frmCountry
  Dim nation As New Country("Canada", "Ottawa")

  Private Sub btnDisplay_Click(...) Handles btnDisplay.Click
    nation.Population = 31
    lstBox.Items.Add("Country: " & nation.Name)
    lstBox.Items.Add("Capital: " & nation.Capital)
    lstBox.Items.Add("Pop: " & nation.Population & " million")
  End Sub
End Class      'frmCountry

Class Country
  Private m_name As String
  Private m_capital As String
  Private m_population As Double

  Sub New(name As String, capital As String)
    m_name = name
    m_capital = capital
  End Sub

  Public ReadOnly Property Name() As String
    Get
      Return m_name
    End Get
  End Property

  Public ReadOnly Property Capital() As String
    Get
      Return m_capital
    End Get
  End Property

  Public Property Population() As Double
    Get
      Return m_population
    End Get
    Set(value As Double)
      m_population = value
    End Set
  End Property
End Class      'Country
```

Exercises 16 through 18 refer to the class *Circle*.

16. **Moving Circle** Enhance the program in Example 3 so that the Get and Set property procedures of the Xcoord and Ycoord properties are used by the form code.

17. **Moving Circle** Modify Example 3 so that the circle originally has its location at the lower-right corner of the picture box and moves diagonally toward the upper-left corner each time *btnMove* is clicked on.

18. **Moving Circle** Modify the form code of Example 3 so that each time *btnMove* is clicked on, the distance moved (in pixels) is a randomly selected number from 0 to 40.

19. **Geometry of a Square** Write the code for a class called Square. The class should have three properties—Length, Perimeter, and Area—with their obvious meanings. When a value is assigned to one of the properties, the values of the other two should be recalculated automatically. When the following form code is executed, the numbers 5 and 20 should be displayed in the text boxes:

```
Dim poly As Square

Private Sub btnGo_Click(...) Handles btnGo.Click
  poly = New Square
  poly.Area = 25
  txtLength.Text = CStr(poly.Length)
  txtPerimeter.Text = CStr(poly.Perimeter)
End Sub
```

20. **Geometry of a Square** Modify the class Square in the previous exercise so that all squares will have lengths between 1 and 10. For instance, the statement **poly.Area = 0.5** should result in a square of length 1, and the statement **poly.Area = 200** should result in a square with each side having length 10. See Fig. 11.1.

FIGURE 11.1 Outcome of Exercise 20.

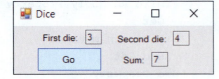

FIGURE 11.2 Possible outcome of Exercise 21.

21. **Dice** Write the code for a class called PairOfDice. A Random object should be used to obtain the value for each die. See Fig. 11.2. When the following form code is executed, three numbers (such as 3, 4, and 7) should be displayed in the text boxes:

```
Dim cubes As PairOfDice

Private Sub btnGo_Click(...) Handles btnGo.Click
  cubes = New PairOfDice
  cubes.Roll()
  txtOne.Text = CStr(cubes.Die1)
  txtTwo.Text = CStr(cubes.Die2)
  txtSum.Text = CStr(cubes.SumOfFaces)
End Sub
```

22. **Dice**   Write a program to roll a pair of dice 1000 times, and display the number of times that the sum of the two faces is 7. The program should use an instance of the class PairOfDice discussed in the previous exercise. See Fig. 11.3.

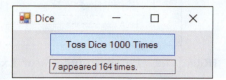

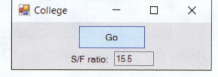

FIGURE 11.3   Possible outcome of Exercise 22.   **FIGURE 11.4**   Outcome of Exercise 23.

23. **Student–Faculty Ratio**   Write the code for a class called College. The class should have properties Name, NumStudents, and NumFaculty. See Fig. 11.4. The method SFRatio should compute the student–faculty ratio. When the following form code is executed, the number 15.5 should be displayed in the text box:

```
Dim school As College

Private Sub btnGo_Click(...) Handles btnGo.Click
  school = New College
  school.Name = "University of Maryland, College Park"
  school.NumStudents = 37272
  school.NumFaculty = 2409
  txtBox.Text = (school.SFRatio).ToString("N1")
End Sub
```

24. **Earnings**   Write a program that calculates an employee's pay for a week based on the hourly wage and the number of hours worked. See Fig. 11.5. All computations should be performed by an instance of the class Wages.

FIGURE 11.5   Possible outcome of Exercise 24.   **FIGURE 11.6**   Possible outcome of Exercise 25.

25. **Cash Register**   Write a program to implement the cash register in Fig. 11.6. The program should have a class called CashRegister that keeps track of the balance and allows deposits and withdrawals. The class should not permit a negative balance.

26. **Average**   Write a program that calculates the average of up to 50 numbers input by the user and stored in an array. See Fig. 11.7 on the next page. The program should use a class named Statistics and have an AddNumber method that stores numbers into an array one at a time. The class should have a Count property that keeps track of the number of numbers stored and a method called Average that returns the average of the numbers.

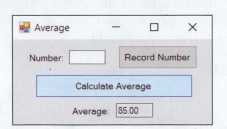

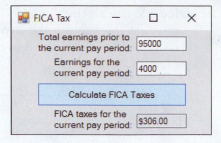

FIGURE 11.7 Possible outcome of Exercise 26. **FIGURE 11.8** Possible outcome of Exercise 27.

27. **FICA Tax** Write a program that calculates a single employee's FICA tax in 2015, with all computations performed by an instance of a class FICA. See Fig. 11.8. The FICA tax has two components—the Social Security Benefits tax, which in 2015 was 6.2% on the first $118,560 of earnings for the year, and the Medicare tax, which was 1.45% of earnings plus .9% of earnings above $200,000 (for unmarried employees).

28. **Add Fractions** Write a program that adds two fractions and displays their sum in reduced form. See Fig. 11.9. The program should use a Fraction class that stores the numerator and denominator of a fraction and has a Reduce method that divides each of the numerator and denominator by their greatest common divisor. Exercise 27 of Section 6.1 contains an algorithm for calculating the greatest common divisor of two numbers.

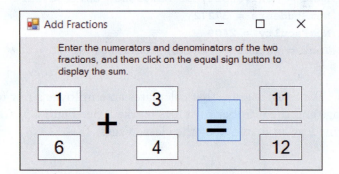

FIGURE 11.9 Possible outcome of Exercise 28.

29. **Mortgage** A mortgage is a long-term loan used to purchase a house. The house is used as collateral to guarantee the loan. The amount borrowed, called the *principal*, is paid in monthly payments, over a stated number of years called the *term* (usually 15, 25, or 30 years). The amount of the monthly payment depends on the principal, the interest rate, and the term of the mortgage.

If A dollars are borrowed at $r\%$ interest compounded monthly to purchase a house with monthly payments for n years, then the monthly payment is given by the formula

$$\text{monthly payment} = \frac{i}{1 - (1 + i)^{-12n}} \cdot A$$

where $i = \dfrac{r}{1200}$.

Write a program that calculates the monthly payment where the principal, interest rate, and term are input by the user. See Fig. 11.10. The program should use a class named *Mortgage* with instance variables for *principal*, *interest rate*, and *term*, and a method named *calculateMonthlyPayment*.

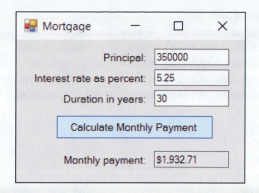

FIGURE 11.10   Possible outcome of Exercise 29.

Solutions to Practice Problems 11.1

1. (d) A programmer is not a template for creating a program.

2.
```
Public Sub New(ssn As String)
   'Assign the value of ssn to the member variable m_ssn.
   m_ssn = ssn
End Sub

Public ReadOnly Property SocSecNum() As String
   Get
      Return m_ssn
   End Get
End Property
```

Note: Since a student's social security number never changes, there is no need to have a Set property procedure for SocSecNum.

11.2   Working with Objects

"An object without an event is like a telephone without a ringer."

Anonymous

■ Arrays of Objects

The elements of an array can have any data type—including a class. The program in Example 1 uses an array of type Student.

VideoNote
Arrays of
Objects

 Example 1   **Semester Grades** In the following program, which uses the same form design as Example 1 of the previous section, the user enters four pieces of data about a student into text boxes. When the *Enter Information* button is clicked on, the data are used to create and initialize an appropriate object and the object is added to an array. When the *Display Grades* button is clicked on, the name, social security number, and semester grade for each student in the array are displayed in the grid.

```
Public Class frmGrades
  Dim students(50) As Student
  Dim lastStudentAdded As Integer = -1    'position in array of student
  '                                        most recently added
  Private Sub btnEnter_Click(...) Handles btnEnter.Click
```

```vb
      lastStudentAdded += 1
      students(lastStudentAdded) = New Student
      students(lastStudentAdded).Name = txtName.Text
      students(lastStudentAdded).SocSecNum = mtbSSN.Text
      students(lastStudentAdded).Midterm = CDbl(txtMidterm.Text)
      students(lastStudentAdded).Final = CDbl(txtFinal.Text)
      'Clear text boxes
      txtName.Clear()
      mtbSSN.Clear()
      txtMidterm.Clear()
      txtFinal.Clear()
      txtName.Focus()
      MessageBox.Show("Student Recorded.")
    End Sub


    Private Sub btnDisplay_Click(...) Handles btnDisplay.Click
      ReDim Preserve students(lastStudentAdded)
      Dim query = From pupil In students
                  Select pupil.Name, pupil.SocSecNum, pupil.CalcSemGrade
      dgvGrades.DataSource = query.ToList
      dgvGrades.CurrentCell = Nothing
      dgvGrades.Columns("Name").HeaderText = "Student Name"
      dgvGrades.Columns("SocSecNum").HeaderText = "SSN"
      dgvGrades.Columns("CalcSemGrade").HeaderText = "Grade"
      ReDim Preserve students(50)
      txtName.Focus()
    End Sub


    Private Sub btnQuit_Click(...) Handles btnQuit.Click
      Me.Close()
    End Sub
End Class        'frmGrades


Class Student
  Private m_midterm As Double
  Private m_final As Double

  Public Property Name() As String

  Public Property SocSecNum() As String

  Public WriteOnly Property Midterm() As Double
    Set(value As Double)
      m_midterm = value
    End Set
  End Property

  Public WriteOnly Property Final() As Double
    Set(value As Double)
      m_final = value
    End Set
  End Property

  Function CalcSemGrade() As String
    Dim grade As Double
```

```
    grade = (m_midterm + m_final) / 2
    grade = Math.Round(grade) 'Round the grade.
    Select Case grade
      Case Is >= 90
        Return "A"
      Case Is >= 80
        Return "B"
      Case Is >= 70
        Return "C"
      Case Is >= 60
        Return "D"
      Case Else
        Return "F"
    End Select
  End Function
End Class      'Student
```

[Run, type in data for Al Adams, click on the *Enter Information* button, repeat the process for Brittany Brown and Carol Cole, click on the *Display Grades* button, and then enter data for Daniel Doyle.]

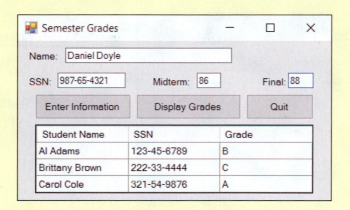

■ Events

In the previous section, we drew a parallel between classes and controls and showed how to define properties and methods for classes. Events can be defined by the programmer to communicate changes of properties, errors, and the progress of lengthy operations. Such events are called **defined events**. The statement for raising an event is located in the class block, and the event is dealt with in the form's code. Suppose that the event is named DefinedEvent and has the parameters *par1*, *par2*, and so on. In the class block, the statement

```
Public Event DefinedEvent(par1 As DataType1, par2 As DataType2, ...)
```

should be placed in the Declarations section, and the statement

```
RaiseEvent DefinedEvent(arg1, arg2, ...)
```

should be placed at the locations in the class block code at which the event should be raised. In the form's code, an instance of the class, call it *object1*, must be declared with a statement of the type

```
Dim WithEvents object1 As ClassName
```

or a statement of the type

```
Dim WithEvents object1 As New ClassName
```

in order to be able to respond to the event. That is, the keyword "WithEvents" must be inserted into the declaration statement. The header of an event procedure for *object1* will be

```
Private Sub object1_DefinedEvent(par1 As DataType1,
                par2 As DataType2,...) _
                Handles object1.DefinedEvent
```

 Example 2 Moving Circle Consider the Circle class defined in Example 3 of Section 11.1. In the following program, we add an event that is raised whenever the location of a circle changes. The event has parameters to pass the location and diameter of the circle. The form's code uses the event to determine if part (or all) of the drawn circle will fall outside the picture box. If so, the event procedure displays the message "Circle Off Screen" in a text box. Let's call the event PositionChanged.

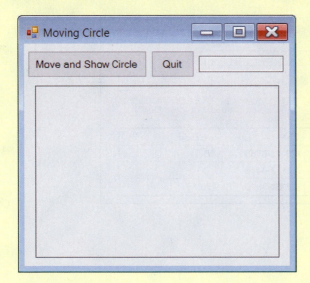

OBJECT	PROPERTY	SETTING
frmCircle	Text	Moving Circle
btnMove	Text	Move and Show Circle
btnQuit	Text	Quit
txtCaution	ReadOnly	True
picCircle		

```
Public Class frmCircle
  Dim WithEvents round As New Circle

  Private Sub btnMove_Click(...) Handles btnMove.Click
    round.Move(20)
    round.Show(picCircle.CreateGraphics).
  End Sub

  Private Sub btnQuit_Click(...) Handles btnQuit.Click
    Me.Close()
  End Sub

  Private Sub round_PositionChanged(x As Integer, y As Integer, d As Integer) _
        Handles round.PositionChanged
    'This event is raised when the location of the circle changes.
    'The code determines if part of the circle is off the screen.
```

```
      If (x + d > picCircle.Width) Or
         (y + d > picCircle.Height) Then
        txtCaution.Text = "Circle Off Screen"
      End If
    End Sub
End Class        'frmCircle

Class Circle
  Public Event PositionChanged(x As Integer, y As Integer, d As Integer)
  'Event is raised when the circle moves.

  Public Sub New()
    'Set the initial location of the circle to the upper-left
    'corner of the picture box, and set its diameter to 40.
    Xcoord = 0
    Ycoord = 0
    Diameter = 40
  End Sub

  Public Property Xcoord() As Integer

  Public Property Ycoord() As Integer

  Public Property Diameter() As Integer

  Sub Show(gr As Graphics)
    'Draw a circle with the given graphics context.
    gr.DrawEllipse(Pens.Black, Xcoord, Ycoord, Diameter, Diameter)
  End Sub

  Sub Move(distance As Integer)
    Xcoord += distance
    Ycoord += distance
    RaiseEvent PositionChanged(Xcoord, Ycoord, Diameter)
  End Sub
End Class        'Circle
```

[Run, and click on the *Move and Show Circle* button ten times.]

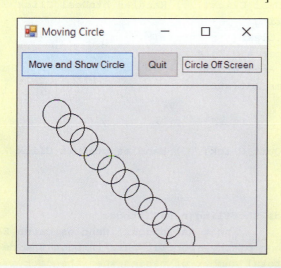

Note: As the last circle appears, the words "Circle Off Screen" are displayed in the text box.

■ Containment

We say that class A **contains** class B when a member variable of class A makes use of an object of type class B. In Example 3, the class DeckOfCards contains the class Card.

 Example 3 Poker The following program deals a five-card poker hand. The program has a DeckOfCards object containing an array of 52 Card objects. The Card object has two properties, Denomination and Suit, and one method, IdentifyCard. The IdentifyCard method returns a string such as "Ace of Spades". In the DeckOfCards object, the New event procedure assigns denominations and suits to the 52 cards. The method ReadCard(n) returns the string identifying the *n*th card of the deck. The method ShuffleDeck uses the Random class to mix up the cards while making 2000 passes through the deck. The event

```
Shuffling(n As Integer, nMax As Integer)
```

is raised during each shuffling pass through the deck, and its parameters communicate the number of the pass and the total number of passes, so that the program that uses it can keep track of the progress.

OBJECT	PROPERTY	SETTING
frmPoker	Text	Poker Hand
lstHand		
btnShuffle	Text	&Shuffle
btnDeal	Text	&Deal
btnQuit	Text	&Quit

```vb
Public Class frmPoker
  Dim WithEvents cards As New DeckOfCards

  Private Sub btnShuffle_Click(...) Handles btnShuffle.Click
    cards.ShuffleDeck
  End Sub

  Private Sub btnDeal_Click(...) Handles btnDeal.Click
    Dim str As String
    lstHand.Items.Clear()
    For i As Integer = 0 To 4
      str = cards.ReadCard(i)
      lstHand.Items.Add(str)
    Next
  End Sub

  Private Sub btnQuit_Click(...) Handles btnQuit.Click
    Me.Close()
  End Sub

  Private Sub cards_Shuffling(n As Integer,
                  nMax As Integer) Handles cards.Shuffling
    'n is the number of the specific pass through the deck (1, 2, 3...).
    'nMax is the total number of passes when the deck is shuffled.
    lstHand.Items.Clear()
    lstHand.Items.Add("Shuffling Pass: " & n & " out of " & nMax)
```

```
        For i As Integer = 1 To 1000000        'Slow down the shuffle.
        Next
      lstHand.Update()    'refresh contents of list box
    End Sub
  End Class          'frmPoker

Class Card
  Private m_denomination As Integer   'a number from 0 through 12
  Private m_suit As String            'Hearts, Clubs, Diamonds, Spades

  Public Property Denomination() As Integer
    Get
      Return m_denomination
    End Get
    Set(value As Integer)
      'Only store valid values.
      If (value >= 0) And (value <= 12) Then
        m_denomination = value
      End If
    End Set
  End Property

  Public Property Suit() As String
    Get
      Return m_suit
    End Get
    Set(value As String)
      'Only store valid values.
      If (value = "Hearts") Or (value = "Clubs") Or
         (value = "Diamonds") Or (value = "Spades") Then
        m_suit = value
      End If
    End Set
  End Property

  Function IdentifyCard() As String
    Dim denom As String = ""
    Select Case Denomination + 1
      Case 1
        denom = "Ace"
      Case Is <= 10
        denom = CStr(Denomination + 1)
      Case 11
        denom = "Jack"
      Case 12
        denom = "Queen"
      Case 13
        denom = "King"
    End Select
    Return denom & " of " & m_suit
  End Function
End Class          'Card

Class DeckOfCards
  Private m_deck(51) As Card 'class DeckOfCards contains class Card
  Public Event Shuffling(n As Integer, nMax As Integer)
```

```
    Public Sub New()
      'Make the first thirteen cards hearts, the
      'next thirteen cards diamonds, and so on.
      Dim suits() As String = {"Hearts", "Clubs", "Diamonds", "Spades"}
      For i As Integer = 0 To 3
        'Each pass corresponds to one of the four suits.
        For j As Integer = 0 To 12
          'Assign numbers from 0 through 12 to the
          'cards of each suit.
          m_deck(i * 13 + j) = New Card()
          m_deck(i * 13 + j).Suit = suits(i)
          m_deck(i * 13 + j).Denomination = j
        Next
      Next
    End Sub


    Function ReadCard(cardNum As Integer) As String
      Return m_deck(cardNum).IdentifyCard()
    End Function


    Sub Swap(i As Integer, j As Integer)
      'Swap the ith and jth cards in the deck.
      Dim tempCard As Card
      tempCard = m_deck(i)
      m_deck(i) = m_deck(j)
      m_deck(j) = tempCard
    End Sub


    Sub ShuffleDeck()
      'Do 2000 passes through the deck. On each pass,
      'swap each card with a randomly selected card.
      Dim index As Integer
      Dim randomNum As New Random()
      For i As Integer = 1 To 2000
        For k As Integer = 0 To 51
          index = randomNum.Next(0, 52) 'Randomly select a number
          '                               from 0 through 51 inclusive.
          Swap(k, index)
        Next
        RaiseEvent Shuffling(i, 2000)
      Next
    End Sub
  End Class        'DeckOfCards
```

[Run, click on the *Shuffle* button, and click on the *Deal* button after the shuffling is complete.]

Practice Problems 11.2

Consider the program in Example 1 **of** Section 11.1, **and suppose that mtbSSN is an ordinary (rather than a masked) text box.**

1. Alter the Set SocSecNum property procedure to raise the event ImproperSSN when the social security number does not have 11 characters. The event should pass the length of the social security number and the student's name to the form's code.

2. What statement must be placed in the Declarations section of the Student class?

3. Write an event procedure to handle the event ImproperSSN.

4. What statement in the form's code must be altered? What change must be made?

EXERCISES 11.2

1. **Semester Grades**   In Example 1 of this section, modify the event procedure btnDisplay_Click so that only the students who receive a grade of A are displayed.

   The file UnitedStates.txt provides data on the 50 states. (This file is used in Exercises 2 through 5.) Each record contains five pieces of information about a single state: name, abbreviation, date it entered the union, land area (in square miles), and population in the year 2015. The records are ordered by the date of entry into the union. The first three lines of the file are

   ```
   Delaware,DE,12/7/1787,1954,941875
   Pennsylvania,PA,12/12/1787,44817,12856989
   New Jersey,NJ,12/18/1787,7417,8969545
   ```

2. **U.S. States**   Create a class State with five properties to hold the information about a single state and a method that calculates the density (people per square mile) of the state.

3. **U.S. States**   Write a program that requests a state's name in an input dialog box and displays the state's name, abbreviation, density, and date of entrance into the union. See Fig. 11.11. The program should use an array of State objects.

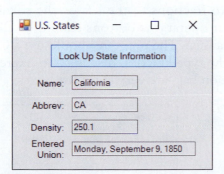

FIGURE 11.11   Possible outcome of Exercise 3.

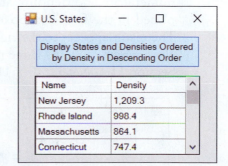

FIGURE 11.12   Outcome of Exercise 4.

4. **U.S. States**   Write a program that displays the names of the states and their densities in a DataGridView ordered by density. The program should use an array of State objects. See Fig. 11.12.

5. **U.S. States**   Write a program that reads the data from the file one line at a time into an array of State objects and raises an event whenever the population of a state exceeds ten million. States with a large population should have their names and populations displayed in a list box by the corresponding event procedure. See Fig. 11.13. (**Hint:** Create a class called UnitedStates that contains the array and defines a method Add that adds a new state to the array. The Add method should raise the event.)

FIGURE 11.13   Outcome of Exercise 5.

FIGURE 11.14   Possible outcome of Exercise 6.

6. **Dice**   Consider the class PairOfDice discussed in Exercise 21 of Section 11.1. Add the event SnakeEyes that is raised whenever two ones appear during a roll of the dice. Write a program that uses this event. See Fig. 11.14.

7. **Cash Register**   Consider the CashRegister class in Exercise 25 of Section 11.1. Add the event AttemptToOverdraw that is raised when the user tries to subtract more money than is in the cash register.

8. **Geometry of a Square**   Consider the class Square from Exercise 19 of Section 11.1. Add the event IllegalNumber that is raised when any of the properties is set to a negative number. Show the new class block and write an event procedure for the event that displays an error message.

9. **Add Fractions**   Consider the Fraction class in Exercise 28 of Section 11.1. Add the event ZeroDenominator that is raised whenever a denominator is set to 0. Write a program that uses the event.

10. **Fractions**   Write a program for the fraction calculator shown in Fig. 11.15. After the numerators and denominators of the two fractions to the left of the equal sign are placed in the four text boxes, one of four operations buttons should be clicked on. The result appears to the right of the equal sign. The program should use a Calculator class, which contains three members of the type Fraction discussed in Exercise 28 of Section 11.1. **Note:** In Fig. 11.15, the fraction bars are very short list boxes.

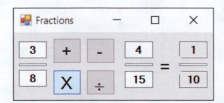

FIGURE 11.15   Possible outcome of Exercise 10.

FIGURE 11.16   Possible outcome of Exercise 11.

11. **Dice**   Write a program for a simple game in which each of two players rolls a pair of dice. The person with the highest tally wins. See Fig. 11.16. The program should use a class called HighRoller having two member variables of the type PairOfDice discussed in Exercise 21 of Section 11.1.

12. **Cash Register**   Write a program that takes orders at a fast-food restaurant. See Fig. 11.17. The restaurant has two menus—a regular menu and a kids menu. An item is ordered by highlighting it in one of the list boxes and then clicking on the >> or << button to place it in the order list box in the center of the form. As each item is ordered, a running total is displayed in the text box at the lower right part of the form. The program should use a Choices class, which contains a Food class. (The contents of each of the three list boxes should be treated as Choices objects.) Each Food object should hold the name and price of a single food item. The Choices class should have a ChoiceChanged event that can be used by the form code to update the cost of the order.

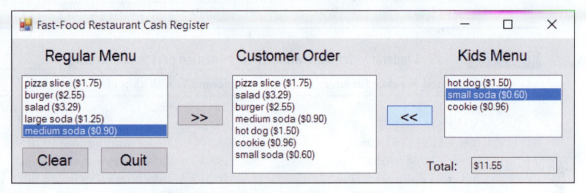

FIGURE 11.17   Possible outcome of Exercise 12.

13. **Weekly Paycheck**   Write a program to produce an employee's weekly paycheck receipt. The receipt should contain the employee's name, amount earned for the week, total amount earned for the year, FICA tax deduction, withholding tax deduction, and take-home amount. See Fig. 11.18. The program should use an Employee class and a Tax class. The Tax class must have properties for the amount earned for the week, the prior total amount earned for the year, the number of withholding allowances, and marital status. It should have methods for computing FICA and withholding taxes. The Employee class should store the employee's name, number of withholding allowances, marital status, hours worked this week, hourly salary, and previous amount earned for the year. The Employee class should use the Tax class to calculate the taxes to be deducted. The formula for calculating the FICA tax is given in Exercise 27 of Section 11.1. To compute the withholding tax, multiply the number of withholding allowances by $76.90, subtract the product from the amount earned, and use Table 11.1 or Table 11.2 on the next page.

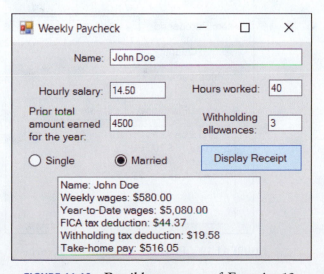

FIGURE 11.18   Possible outcome of Exercise 13.

TABLE 11.1	2015 federal income tax withheld for a single person paid weekly.
Adjusted Weekly Income	**Income Tax Withheld**
$0 to $44	$0
Over $44 to $222	10% of amount over $44
Over $222 to $764	$17.80 + 15% of amount over $222
Over $764 to $1,789	$99.10 + 25% of amount over $764
Over $1,789 to $3,685	$355.35 + 28% of amount over $1,789
Over $3,685 to $7,958	$886.23 + 33% of amount over $3,685
Over $7,958 to $7,990	$2,296.32 + 35% of amount over $7,958
Over $7,990	$2,307.52 + 39.6% of amount over $7,990

TABLE 11.2	2015 federal income tax withheld for a married person paid weekly.
Adjusted Weekly Income	**Income Tax Withheld**
$0 to $165	$0
Over $165 to $520	10% of amount over $165
Over $520 to $1,606	$35.50 + 15% of amount over $520
Over $1,606 to $3,073	$198.40 + 25% of amount over $1,606
Over $3,073 to $4,597	$565.15 + 28% of amount over $3,073
Over $4,597 to $8,079	$991.87 + 33% of amount over $4,597
Over $8,079 to $9,105	$2,140.32 + 35% of amount over $8,079
Over $9,105	$2,500.03 + 39.6% of amount over $9,105

14. Proceed to Checkout   Write a program that creates a checkout receipt for the items in the user's cart on a shopping website. The program should use a class named *Purchase* to hold the information about a single item purchased (that is, description, quantity, and price) and an array to hold a list of items of type *Purchase*. After the three text boxes in Fig. 11.19 are filled and the user clicks on the *Record* button, the data for the purchase should be placed into a single element of the array and the text boxes should be cleared. After all of the purchases have been entered, the *Create* button should be clicked on to display the receipt in a list box. The receipt shown in Fig. 11.19 resulted from the purchase of three shirts ($35 each), two ties ($15 each), and one coat ($100).

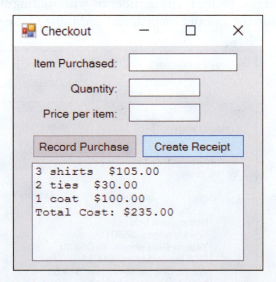

FIGURE 11.19   **Possible outcome of Exercise 14.**

```
1. Public Property SocSecNum() As String
     Get
       Return m_ssn
     End Get
     Set(value As String)
       If value.Length = 11 Then
         m_ssn = value
       Else
         RaiseEvent ImproperSSN(value.Length, m_name)
       End If
     End Set
   End Property
```

```
2. Public Event ImproperSSN(length As Integer, studentName As String)
```

```
3. Private Sub pupil_ImproperSSN(length As Integer,
               studentName As String) Handles pupil.ImproperSSN
     MessageBox.Show("The social security number entered for " &
           studentName & " consisted of " & length &
           " characters. Reenter the data for " & studentName & ".")
   End Sub
```

4. The statement

```
Dim pupil As Student
```

must be changed to

```
Dim WithEvents pupil As Student
```

11.3 Inheritance

VideoNote
Inheritance

The three relationships between classes are "use", "containment", and "inheritance". One class **uses** another class if it manipulates objects of that class. We say that class A **contains** class B when a member variable of class A makes use of an object of type class B. Section 11.2 presented examples of use and containment.

Inheritance is a process by which one class (the **child** or **derived** class) inherits the properties, methods, and events of another class (the **parent** or **base** class). The child has access to all of its parent's properties, methods and events as well as to all of its own. If the parent is itself a child, then it and its children have access to all of its parent's properties, methods, and events. Consider the classes shown in Fig. 11.20 on the next page. All three children inherit Property A and Sub B from their parent. Child2 and Child3 have an additional event and a property, respectively. GrandChild1 has access to Property A, Sub B, and Event C from its parent and adds Function E and Sub F. The collection of a parent class along with its descendants is called a **hierarchy**.

There are two main benefits gained by using inheritance: first, it allows two or more classes to share some common features yet differentiate themselves on others. Second, it supports code reusability by avoiding the extra effort required to maintain duplicate code in multiple classes. For these reasons, inheritance is one of the most powerful tools of object-oriented programming. Considerable work goes into planning and defining the member variables and methods of the parent class. The child classes are beneficiaries of this effort.

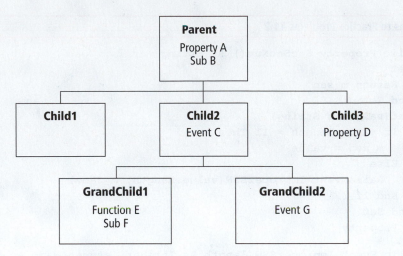

FIGURE 11.20 Example of inheritance hierarchy.

Just as structured programming requires the ability to break complex problems into simpler subproblems, object-oriented programming requires the skill to identify useful hierarchies of classes and derived classes. Software engineers are still working on the guidelines for when and how to establish hierarchies. One useful criterion is the **ISA test**: If one class *is a* more specific case of another class, the first class should be derived from the second class.

The Visual Basic keyword "Inherits" identifies the parent of a class. The code used to define the class Parent and its child class Child2 as illustrated in Fig. 11.20 is

```vb
Class Parent
  Public Property A
    'Property Get and Set blocks
  End Property

  Sub B()
    'Code for Sub procedure B
  End Sub
End Class

Class Child2
  Inherits Parent
  Event C()
End Class
```

As Child2 is itself a parent, its child GrandChild1 can be declared using a similar statement:

```vb
Class GrandChild1
  Inherits Child2
  Function E()
    'Code for function E
  End Function

  Sub F()
    'Code for Sub procedure F
  End Sub
End Class
```

Example 1   **Calculations** In the following program, the user is presented with a basic adding machine. The Calculator class implements the Multiply and Divide methods and inherits the FirstNumber and SecondNumber properties and the Add and Subtract methods from its AddingMachine parent. When the *Adding Machine* radio button is selected, the user may add or subtract two numbers using an AddingMachine object. When the *Calculator* radio button is selected, the user may add, subtract, multiply, or divide two numbers using a Calculator object. Notice that the multiply and divide buttons are hidden when the Adding Machine is selected, and how the Click event procedures for the *btnAdd* and *btnSubtract* buttons examine the state of the radio button to determine which machine to use.

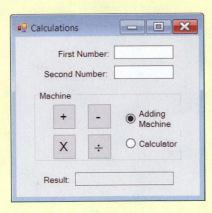

OBJECT	PROPERTY	SETTING
frmCalculate	Text	Calculations
lblNumber1	Text	First Number:
txtNumber1		
lblNumber2	Text	Second Number:
txtNumber2		
lblResult	Text	Result:
txtResult	ReadOnly	True
grpMachine	Text	Machine
radAddingMachine	Text	Adding Machine
	Checked	True
radCalculator	Text	Calculator
btnAdd	Text	+
btnSubtract	Text	−
btnMultiply	Text	×
btnDivide	Font	Symbol
	Text	(Cedilla)

```
Public Class frmCalculate
    'Create both machines.
    Dim adder As New AddingMachine
    Dim calc As New Calculator

    Private Sub radAddingMachine_CheckedChanged(...) Handles _
                    radAddingMachine.CheckedChanged
        'Hide the multiply and divide functionality.
        btnMultiply.Visible = False
        btnDivide.Visible = False
    End Sub

    Private Sub radCalculator_CheckedChanged(...) Handles _
                    radCalculator.CheckedChanged
        'Show the multiply and divide functionality.
        btnMultiply.Visible = True
        btnDivide.Visible = True
    End Sub

    Private Sub btnAdd_Click(...) Handles btnAdd.Click
        'Add two numbers.
        If radAddingMachine.Checked Then
            'If adding machine selected, use it to get the result.
```

```vbnet
        adder.FirstNumber = CDbl(txtNumber1.Text)
        adder.SecondNumber = CDbl(txtNumber2.Text)
        txtResult.Text = CStr(adder.Add)
      Else
        'If calculator selected, use it to get the result.
        calc.FirstNumber = CDbl(txtNumber1.Text)
        calc.SecondNumber = CDbl(txtNumber2.Text)
        txtResult.Text = CStr(calc.Add)
      End If
    End Sub


    Private Sub btnSubtract_Click(...) Handles btnSubtract.Click
      'Subtract two numbers.
      If radAddingMachine.Checked Then
        'If adding machine selected, use it to get the result.
        adder.FirstNumber = CDbl(txtNumber1.Text)
        adder.SecondNumber = CDbl(txtNumber2.Text)
        txtResult.Text = CStr(adder.Subtract)
      Else
        'If calculator selected, use it to get the result.
        calc.FirstNumber = CDbl(txtNumber1.Text)
        calc.SecondNumber = CDbl(txtNumber2.Text)
        txtResult.Text = CStr(calc.Subtract)
      End If
    End Sub


    Private Sub btnMultiply_Click(...) Handles btnMultiply.Click
      'Multiply two numbers.
      calc.FirstNumber = CDbl(txtNumber1.Text)
      calc.SecondNumber = CDbl(txtNumber2.Text)
      txtResult.Text = CStr(calc.Multiply)
    End Sub


    Private Sub btnDivide_Click(...) Handles btnDivide.Click
      'Divide two numbers.
      calc.FirstNumber = CDbl(txtNumber1.Text)
      calc.SecondNumber = CDbl(txtNumber2.Text)
      txtResult.Text = CStr(calc.Divide)
    End Sub
  End Class         'frmCalculate


Class AddingMachine
  Public Property FirstNumber() As Double
  Public Property SecondNumber() As Double

  Function Add() As Double
    Return FirstNumber + SecondNumber
  End Function

  Function Subtract() As Double
    Return FirstNumber — SecondNumber
  End Function
End Class        'AddingMachine
```

```
Class Calculator
  Inherits AddingMachine
  'Calculator inherits properties FirstNumber and SecondNumber
  'and functions Add() and Subtract().

  Function Multiply() As Double
    Return FirstNumber * SecondNumber
  End Function

  Function Divide() As Double
    Return FirstNumber / SecondNumber
  End Function
End Class       'Calculator
```

[Run, type in 12 and 3, and click on the + and − buttons. Click on the *Calculator* radio button, and click on the +, −, × , and ÷ buttons.]

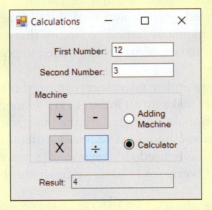

■ Polymorphism and Overriding

The set of properties, methods, and events for a class is called the class **interface**. In essence, the interface of a class defines how it should behave. The interfaces of the classes AddingMachine and Calculator used in Example 1 are shown in Table 11.3.

Consider the classes used in Examples 1 and 2 of Section 11.1. Both Student and PFStudent have the same interface, even though they carry out the task of calculating a semester grade differently. See Table 11.4 on the next page.

TABLE 11.3   Interfaces used in Example 1.

	AddingMachine	Calculator
Properties	FirstNumber	FirstNumber
	SecondNumber	SecondNumber
Methods	Add	Add
	Subtract	Subtract
		Multiply
		Divide
Events	(none)	(none)

TABLE 11.4	Interfaces used in Examples 1 and 2 in Section 11.1.	
	Student	**PFStudent**
Properties	Name	Name
	SocSecNum	SocSecNum
	Midterm	Midterm
	Final	Final
Methods	CalcSemGrade	CalcSemGrade
Events	(none)	(none)

If a programmer wants to write a program that manipulates objects from these two classes, they need only know how to use the interface. The programmer need not be concerned with what specific implementation of that interface is being used. The object will then behave according to its specific implementation.

The programmer need only be aware of the CalcSemGrade method and needn't be concerned about its implementation. The feature that two classes can have methods that are named the same and have essentially the same purpose, but different implementations, is called **polymorphism**.

A programmer may employ polymorphism in three easy steps. First, the properties, methods, and events that make up an interface are defined. Second, a parent class is created that performs the functionality dictated by the interface. Finally, a child class inherits the parent and overrides the methods that require a different implementation than the parent. The keyword **Overridable** is used to designate the parent's methods that can be overridden, and the keyword **Overrides** is used to designate the child's methods that are doing the overriding.

There are situations where a child class needs to access the parent class's implementation of a method that the child is overriding. Visual Basic provides the keyword **MyBase** to support this functionality.

Consider the code from Example 1 of Section 11.1. To employ polymorphism, the keyword "Overridable" is inserted into the header of the CalcSemGrade method in the Student class.

```
Overridable Function CalcSemGrade() As String
```

The PFStudent class inherits all of the properties and methods from its parent, overriding the CalcSemGrade method as follows:

```
Class PFStudent
  Inherits Student

  Overrides Function CalcSemGrade() As String
    'The student's grade for the semester
    If MyBase.CalcSemGrade = "F" Then
      Return "Fail"
    Else
      Return "Pass"
    End If
  End Function
End Class        'PFStudent
```

Example 2 **Semester Grades** In the following program, the user can enter student information and display the semester grades for the class. The PFStudent class inherits all of the properties from its parent Student, but overrides the CalcSemGrade method with its own implementation. The btnEnter_Click event procedure stores an element created by either class into the *students* array. However, the btnDisplay_Click event procedure does not need to know which elements are from which class, thus demonstrating polymorphism. **Note:** In the sixth line of the btn_Enter event procedure, the statement `pupil = New PFStudent` is valid, since, due to inheritance, every PFStudent *is a* Student.

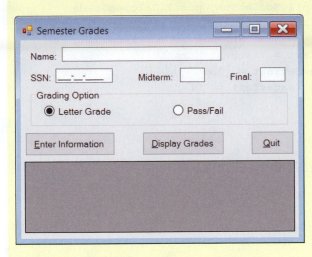

OBJECT	PROPERTY	SETTING
frmGrades	Text	Semester Grades
lblName	Text	Name:
txtName		
lblSSN	Text	SSN:
mtbSSN	Mask	000-00-0000
lblMidterm	Text	Midterm:
txtMidterm		
lblFinal	Text	Final:
txtFinal		
grpGradingOption	Text	Grading Option
radLetterGrade	Text	Letter Grade
	Checked	True
radPassFail	Text	Pass/Fail
btnEnter	Text	&Enter Information
btnDisplay	Text	&Display Grades
btnQuit	Text	&Quit
dgvGrades		

```
Public Class frmGrades
  Dim students(50) As Student          'stores the class
  Dim lastStudentAdded As Integer = -1   'last student added to students()

  Private Sub btnEnter_Click(...) Handles btnEnter.Click
    'Stores a student into the array.
    Dim pupil As Student
    'Create the appropriate object depending upon the radio button.
    If radPassFail.Checked Then
      pupil = New PFStudent
    Else
      pupil = New Student
    End If
    'Store the values in the text boxes into the object.
    pupil.Name = txtName.Text
    pupil.SocSecNum = mtbSSN.Text
    pupil.Midterm = CDbl(txtMidterm.Text)
    pupil.Final = CDbl(txtFinal.Text)
    'Add the student to the array.
    lastStudentAdded += 1
    students(lastStudentAdded) = pupil
    'Clear text boxes and list box.
    txtName.Clear()
    mtbSSN.Clear()
    txtMidterm.Clear()
```

```vb
      txtFinal.Clear()
      MessageBox.Show("Student #" & lastStudentAdded + 1 &
                      " recorded.")
      txtName.Focus()
    End Sub


    Private Sub btnDisplay_Click(...) Handles btnDisplay.Click
      ReDim Preserve students(lastStudentAdded)
      Dim query = From pupil In students
                  Select pupil.Name, pupil.SocSecNum, pupil.CalcSemGrade
      dgvGrades.DataSource = query.ToList
      dgvGrades.CurrentCell = Nothing
      dgvGrades.Columns("Name").HeaderText = "Student Name"
      dgvGrades.Columns("SocSecNum").HeaderText = "SSN"
      dgvGrades.Columns("CalcSemGrade").HeaderText = "Grade"
      ReDim Preserve students(50)
      txtName.focus()
    End Sub


    Private Sub btnQuit_Click(...) Handles btnQuit.Click
      'Quit the program
      Me.Close()
    End Sub
End Class          'frmGrades


Class Student
    'Member variables to hold the property values
    Private m_midterm As Double
    Private m_final As Double

    Public Property Name() As String

    Public Property SocSecNum() As String

    Public WriteOnly Property Midterm() As Double
      'The student's score on the midterm exam
      Set(value As Double)
        m_midterm = value
      End Set
    End Property


    Public WriteOnly Property Final() As Double
      'The student's score on the final exam
      Set(value As Double)
        m_final = value
      End Set
    End Property


    Overridable Function CalcSemGrade() As String
      'The student's grade for the semester
      Dim grade As Double
      'The grade is based upon average of the midterm and final exams.
      grade = (m_midterm + m_final) / 2
      grade = Math.Round(grade)   'Round the grade.
```

```vb
    Select Case grade
      Case Is >= 90
        Return "A"
      Case Is >= 80
        Return "B"
      Case Is >= 70
        Return "C"
      Case Is >= 60
        Return "D"
      Case Else
        Return "F"
    End Select
  End Function
End Class        'Student


Class PFStudent
  Inherits Student

  Overrides Function CalcSemGrade() As String
    'The student's grade for the semester
    If MyBase.CalcSemGrade = "F" Then
      Return "Fail"
    Else
      Return "Pass"
    End If
  End Function
End Class        'PFStudent
```

[Enter the data and click on the *Enter Information* button for three students. Then click on the *Display Grades* button, and finally enter the data for another student.]

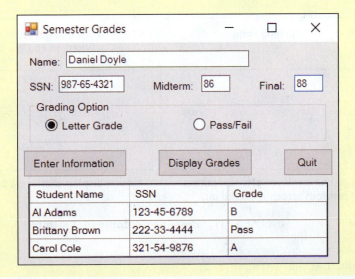

Example 2 employs inheritance and overriding to provide functionality to one child class. If a program contains two or more children of a class, however, the technique of overriding can lead to confusing programs. Visual Basic provides a cleaner design through the use of abstract classes.

■ Abstract Properties, Methods, and Classes

Sometimes you want to insist that each child of a class have a certain property or method that it must implement for its own use. Such a property or method is said to be **abstract** and is declared with the keyword **MustOverride**. An **abstract** property or method consists of just a header with no code following it. It has no corresponding **End Property**, **End Sub**, or **End Function** statement. Its class is called an **abstract base class** and must be declared with the keyword **MustInherit**. Abstract classes cannot be instantiated; only their children can be instantiated.

Example 3   **Rock, Paper, Scissors**   The following program allows you to play successive games of "Rock, Paper, Scissors" with a computer as your opponent. The program uses a class named *Contestant* having two child classes named *Human* and *Computer*. After you (the human) make your choice, the computer makes its choice at random. The *Contestant* class has an auto-implemented property named *Score* and an abstract method named *Choice* that is overridden in each child class as appropriate. Figure 11.21 shows the progression of the game. The names of the two read-only text boxes are *txtHumanScore* and *txtComputerScore*, and the name of the button is *btnPlay*. You make your choice in an input box and then the computer's choice (along with your choice and the outcome) is displayed in a message box. After the message box is exited, the new score is displayed and the game number on the *Play* button is increased. **Note:** *Rock* beats *Scissors* (*Rock* can break *Scissors*), *Scissors* beats *Paper* (*Scissors* can cut *Paper*), and *Paper* beats *Rock* (*Paper* can cover *Rock*.)

Opening Form

Input box displayed after *Play* button is clicked on and you type in your choice

Message box displayed after *OK* button in previous screen is clicked on.

Form displayed after *OK* button is clicked on.

FIGURE 11.21   Possible outcome of Example 3.

```
Public Class frmRockPaperScissors
   Dim gameNumber As Integer = 1
   Dim person As New Human
   Dim machine As New Computer

   Private Sub btnPlay_Click(...) Handles btnPlay.Click
      Dim humanChoice As String
      Dim computerChoice As String
```

```
        Dim result As String
        humanChoice = person.Choice()
        computerChoice = machine.Choice()
        Select Case humanChoice
          Case "Rock"
            Select Case computerChoice
              Case "Paper"
                machine.Score += 1
                result = "COMPUTER WINS"
              Case "Scissors"
                person.Score += 1
                result = "YOU WIN"
              Case "Rock"
                result = "TIE"
            End Select
          Case "Paper"
            Select Case computerChoice
              Case "Rock"
                person.Score += 1
                result = "YOU WIN"
              Case "Scissors"
                machine.Score += 1
                result = "COMPUTER WINS"
              Case "Paper"
                result = "TIE"
            End Select
          Case "Scissors"
            Select Case computerChoice
              Case "Rock"
                machine.Score += 1
                result = "COMPUTER WINS"
              Case "Paper"
                person.Score += 1
                result = "YOU WIN"
              Case "Scissors"
                result = "TIE"
            End Select
        End Select
        MessageBox.Show("YOUR CHOICE: " & humanChoice & " COMPUTER CHOICE: " &
                    computerChoice & " " & result, "RESULT")
        txtHumanScore.Text = CStr(person.Score)
        txtComputerScore.Text = CStr(machine.Score)
        gameNumber += 1
        btnPlay.Text = "Play Game #" & (gameNumber)
    End Sub
End Class      'frmRockPaperScissors


MustInherit Class Contestant

    Public Property Score As Integer

    MustOverride Function Choice() As String
End Class      'Contestant
```

```
Class Human
  Inherits Contestant

  Overrides Function Choice() As String
    Return InputBox("Enter your choice (Rock, Paper, or Scissors):")
  End Function
End Class    'Human

Class Computer
  Inherits Contestant

  Overrides Function Choice() As String
    Dim choices() As String = {"Rock", "Paper", "Scissors"}
    Dim randomNumber As New Random
    Return choices(randomNumber.Next(0, 3))
  End Function
End Class     'Computer
```

■ Comments

1. Visual Basic uses inheritance in every Windows application that is written. Examination of any program's code reveals that the form's class inherits from the .NET framework class System.Windows.Forms.Form.

2. In Example 2, the btnDisplay_Click event procedure does not need to know which elements of the Student array are instances of the Student class and which are instances of the PFStudent class. In some situations, however, the program may want to know this. Visual Basic provides the expression **TypeOf...Is** to test if an instance was created from a particular class (or from the class' parents, grandparents, etc.). For example, the following procedure counts the number of pass/fail students in the *students* array:

```
Sub CountPassFail()
  Dim query = From student In students
              Where TypeOf (student) Is PFStudent
              Select student
  Dim numPF = query.Count
  MessageBox.Show("There are " & numPF & " pass/fail students out of " &
                  lastStudentAdded + 1 & " students in the class.")
End Sub
```

3. Child classes do not have access to the parent's Private member variables.

Practice Problems 11.3

1. In the class AddingMachine of Example 1, the Add function could have been defined with

```
Function Add() As Double
  Return _FirstNumber + _SecondNumber
End Function
```

Explain why the Multiply function of the class Calculator cannot be defined with

```
Function Multiply() As Double
  Return _FirstNumber * _SecondNumber
End Function
```

2. Consider the hierarchy of classes shown below. What value is assigned to the variable *phrase* by the following two lines of code?

```
Dim mammal As New Mammals
Dim phrase As String = mammal.Msg


Class Animals
  Overridable Function Msg() As String
    Return "Can move"
  End Function
End Class


Class Vertebrates
  Inherits Animals

  Overrides Function Msg() As String
    Return MyBase.Msg & " " & "Has a backbone"
  End Function
End Class

Class Mammals
  Inherits Vertebrates

  Overrides Function Msg() As String
    Return MyBase.Msg & " " & "Nurtures young with mother's milk"
  End Function
End Class

Class Arthropods
  Inherits Animals

  Overrides Function Msg() As String
    Return MyBase.Msg & " " & "Has jointed limbs and no backbone"
  End Function
End Class
```

EXERCISES 11.3

In Exercises 1 through 4, identify the output of the code that uses the following two classes:

```
Class Square
  Overridable Function Result(num As Double) As Double
    Return num * num
  End Function
End Class

Class Cube
  Inherits Square

  Overrides Function Result(num As Double) As Double
    Return num * num * num
  End Function
End Class
```

1. ```
Dim sq As Square = New Square
txtOutput.Text = CStr(sq.Result(2))
```

2. ```
Dim cb As Cube = New Cube
txtOutput.Text = CStr(cb.Result(2))
```

3. ```
Dim m As Square = New Square
Dim n As Cube = New Cube
txtOutput.Text = CStr(m.Result(n.Result(2)))
```

4. ```
Dim m As Square = New Cube
txtOutput.Text = CStr(m.Result(2))
```

5. Consider the class hierarchy in the second practice problem. What value is assigned to the variable *phrase* by the following two lines of code?

```
Dim anthropod As New Arthropods
Dim phrase As String = anthropod.Msg
```

6. Consider the class hierarchy in the second practice problem. What value is assigned to the variable *phrase* by the following two lines of code?

```
Dim vertebrate As New Vertebrates
Dim phrase As String = vertebrate.Msg
```

In Exercises 7 through 16, identify the errors in the code.

7. ```
Class Hello
   Function Hi() As String
     Return "hi!"
   End Function
End Class

Class Greetings
  Overrides Hello
  Function GoodBye() As String
    Return "goodbye"
  End Function
End Class
```

8. ```
Class Hello
   Function Hi() As String
     Return "hi!"
   End Function
End Class

Class Greetings
  Inherits Hi()

  Function GoodBye() As String
    Return "goodbye"
  End Function
End Class
```

9.
```
Class Hello
   Function Hi() As String
      Return "hi!"
   End Function
End Class

Class Aussie
   Inherits Hello

   Function Hi() As String
      Return "G'day mate!"
   End Function
End Class
```

10.
```
Class Hello
   Function Hi() As String
      Return "hi!"
   End Function
End Class

Class WithIt
   Inherits Hello

   Overrides Function Hi() As String
      Return "Hey"
   End Function
End Class
```

11.
```
Class Hello
   Overridable Function Hi() As String
      Return "hi!"
   End Function
End Class

Class Cowboy
   Inherits Hello

   Function Hi() As String
      Return "howdy!"
   End Function
End Class
```

12.
```
Class Hello
   MustOverride Function Hi() As String
      Return "hi!"
   End Function
End Class

Class DragRacer
   Inherits Hello
```

```
      Overrides Function Hi() As String
        Return "Start your engines!"
      End Function
    End Class
```

13.
```
Class Hello
  MustInherit Function Hi() As String
End Class

Class Gentleman
  Inherits Hello

  Overrides Function Hi() As String
    Return "Good day"
  End Function
End Class
```

14.
```
Class Hello
  MustOverride Function Hi() As String
End Class

Class Euro
  Inherits Hello

  Overrides Function Hi() As String
    Return "Ciao"
  End Function
End Class
```

15.
```
MustOverride Class Hello
  MustOverride Function Hi() As String
End Class

Class Southerner
  Inherits Hello

  Overrides Function Hi() As String
    Return "Hi y'all"
  End Function
End Class
```

16.
```
MustInherit Class Hello
  MustOverride Function Hi() As String
End Class

Class NorthEasterner
  Inherits Hello

  Overrides Function Hi(name As String) As String
    Return "How ya doin', " & name
  End Function
End Class
```

17. Calculator Expand Example 1 to use a class ScientificCalculator that is derived from the class Calculator and has an exponentiation button in addition to the four arithmetic buttons.

18. Semester Grades Rewrite Example 2 so that the class Student has an abstract method CalcSemGrade and two derived classes called LGStudent (*LG* stands for "Letter Grade") and PFStudent.

19. Cash Register Consider the class CashRegister from Exercise 25 of Section 11.1. Create a derived class called FastTrackRegister that could be used at a toll booth to collect money from vehicles and keep track of the number of vehicles processed. Write a program using the class and having the form in Fig. 11.22. One dollar should be collected from each car and two dollars from each truck.

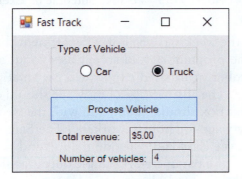

FIGURE 11.22 Possible outcome of Exercise 19.

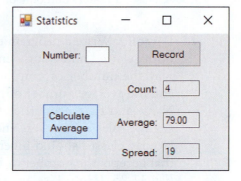

FIGURE 11.23 Possible outcome of Exercise 20.

20. Average Consider the class Statistics from Exercise 26 of Section 11.1. Create a derived class called CompleteStats that also provides a Spread function and an event called NewSpread. This event should be raised whenever the spread changes. (The *spread* is the difference between the highest and the lowest numbers.) Write a program that uses the classes to analyze up to 50 numbers input by the user. The program should display the number of numbers and the current spread at all times. When the *Calculate Average* button is clicked on, the program should display the average of the numbers. See Fig. 11.23.

21. Inventory Write a program that keeps track of a bookstore's inventory. The store orders both trade books and textbooks from publishers. The program should define an abstract class Book that contains the MustOverride property Price, and the ordinary properties Quantity, Name, and Cost. The Textbook and Tradebook classes should be derived from the class Book and should override property Price by adding a markup. (Assume that the markup is 40% for a trade book and 20% for a textbook.) The program should accept input from the user on book orders and display the following statistics: total number of books, number of textbooks, total cost of the orders, and total value of the inventory. (The value of the inventory is the amount of money that the bookstore can make if it sells all of the books in stock.) A sample output is shown in Fig. 11.24 on the next page.

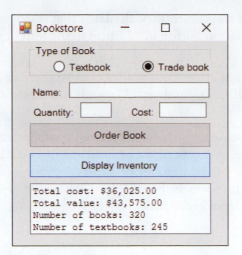

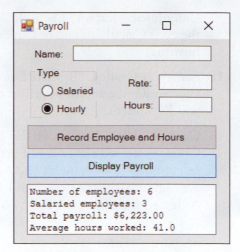

FIGURE 11.24 Possible outcome of Exercise 21.   **FIGURE 11.25** Possible outcome of Exercise 22.

22. **Payroll**   Write a program that records the weekly payroll of a department that hires both salaried and hourly employees. The program should accept user input and display the number of employees, the number of salaried employees, the total payroll, and the average number of hours worked. The abstract class Employee should contain Name and Rate properties. (The Rate text box should be filled in with the weekly salary for salaried workers and the hourly wage for hourly workers.) The Salaried and Hourly classes should inherit the Employee class and override the method GrossPay that accepts the number of hours worked as a parameter. A sample output is shown in Fig. 11.25. (**Hint:** Use an array of a structure that holds the employee object and the number of hours worked during the week.)

23. **Interest-Only Mortgage**   With an **interest-only mortgage**, the monthly payment for a certain number of years (usually, five or ten years) consists only of interest payments. At the end of the interest-only period, the amount owed is the original principal and the monthly payment is determined by the number of years remaining. We will assume that the interest rate for the second period is the same as the interest rate for the first period. (With some interest-only mortgages, the interest rate is reset to conform to prevailing interest rates at that time.)

   Create a class named *InterestOnlyMortgage* that is a subclass of the class *Mortgage* from Exercise 29 of Section 11.1. The class should inherit the instance variables from its parent class and have an additional instance variable named *numberOfInterestOnlyYears*, a method to calculate the monthly payment for the interest-only years, a method named *setTerm*, and a method named *getTerm*. Write a program that uses the class *InterestOnlyMortgage* to calculate the monthly payment where the principal, interest rate, term, and number of interest-only years are input by the user. The program should calculate the monthly payments for the early interest-only years and for the later principal plus interest years. See Fig. 11.26.

24. **Mortgage with Points**   Some loans carry **discount points**. Each discount point requires the borrower to pay up-front an additional amount of money equal to 1% of the stated loan amount. For instance, for a $200,000 mortgage with three discount points, the purchaser must pay $6000 immediately. Even though this payment has the effect of reducing the loan to $194,000, the monthly payment is calculated using a principal of $200,000. (However, the interest rate on the loan is reduced by about 0.25% for every point. Points also have an effect on the taxes a homeowner with a mortgage pays.

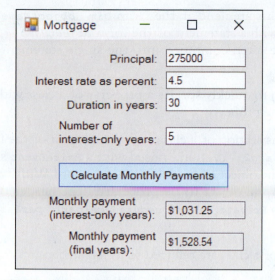

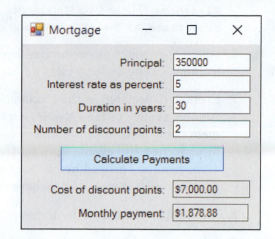

FIGURE 11.26 Possible outcome of Exercise 23.　　**FIGURE 11.27** Possible outcome of Exercise 24.

The up-front interest payment, that is, the $6000 to take advantage of the point offer, is tax-deductible. Mortgages with discount points are usually advantageous to people who intend to keep their house for more than seven years.)

Create a class named *MortgageWithPoints* that is a subclass of the class *Mortgage* from Exercise 29 of Section 11.1. The class should inherit the instance variables from its parent class, have an additional instance variable named *numberOfPoints*, and have an additional method to calculate the cost of the points. Write a program that uses the class *MortgageWithPoints* to calculate the monthly payment where the principal, interest rate, term, and number of discount points are input by the user. See Fig. 11.27.

Solutions to Practice Problems 11.3

1. While the derived class Calculator has access to the Properties and Methods of the base class AddingMachine, it does not have access to its Private member variables.

2. The string "Can move Has a backbone Nurtures young with mother's milk"

CHAPTER 11 SUMMARY

1. An *object* is an entity that stores data, has methods that manipulate the data, and can raise events. A *class* is a template from which objects are created. A *method* specifies the way in which an object's data are manipulated. An *event* is a message sent by an object to signal the occurrence of a condition.

2. Each class is defined in a separate block of code starting with Class *ClassName* and ending with End Class. Data are stored in member variables and accessed by procedures called properties.

3. A property routine contains a Get block to retrieve the value of a member variable or a Set block to assign a value to a member variable. These procedures can also be used to enforce constraints and carry out validation.

4. Visual Basic automatically invokes a New procedure when an object is created.

5. An object variable is declared with a statement of the form `Dim objectName As ClassName`, and the object is created with a statement of the form `objectName = New ClassName`. These two statements are often combined into the single statement `Dim objectName As New ClassName`.

6. *Auto-implemented properties* enable you to quickly specify a property of a class without having to write code to Get and Set the property.

7. Events are declared in the Declarations section of a class with a statement of the form `Public Event DefinedEvent(arg1, arg2, ...)` and raised with a `RaiseEvent` statement. The declaration statement for the object must include the keyword **WithEvents** in order for the events coming from the object to be processed. The header of an event-handling procedure has the form `Private Sub procedureName(par1, par2, ...) Handles objectName.DefinedEvent`.

8. The properties, methods, and events of a class are referred to as its *interface*.

9. *Inheritance*, which is implemented with the keyword *Inherits*, allows a new class (called the *derived* or *child* class) to be created from an existing class (called the *base* or *parent* class) and to gain access to its interface.

10. *Polymorphism* is the feature that two classes can have methods that are named the same and have essentially the same purpose, but different implementations.

11. The keywords *Overridable*, *Overrides*, *MustInherit*, and *MustOverride* allow derived classes to customize inherited properties and methods.

CHAPTER 11   PROGRAMMING PROJECTS

1. **Bank Account**   Write a program to maintain a person's savings and checking accounts. The program should keep track of and display the balances in both accounts, and maintain a list of transactions (deposits, withdrawals, fund transfers, and check clearings) separately for each account. The two lists of transactions should be stored in text files.

    Consider the form in Fig. 11.28. The two drop-down combo boxes should each contain the items Checking and Savings. Each of the four group boxes corresponds to a type of transaction. (When *Savings* is selected in the Account combo box, the Check group box should disappear.) The user makes a transaction by entering data into the text boxes of a group box and pressing the associated button. The items appearing in the DataGridView control should correspond to the type of account that has been selected. The caption of the second label in the Transfer group box should toggle between "to Checking" and "to Savings" depending on the item selected in the "Transfer from" combo box. If a transaction cannot be carried out, a message (such as "Insufficient funds") should be displayed. Two text files should be maintained (one for each type of account) and should be updated each time a transaction is carried out.

    The program should use two classes, Transaction and Account. The class Transaction should have properties for transaction name, amount, date, and whether it is a credit (deposit) or debit (withdrawal/check).

    The class Account, which will have both a checking account and a savings account as instances, should use an array of Transaction objects. In addition, it should have properties for name (Checking or Savings) and balance. It should have methods to carry out a transaction (if possible) and to load the set of transactions from a text file. The events InsufficientFunds and TransactionCommitted should be raised at appropriate times.

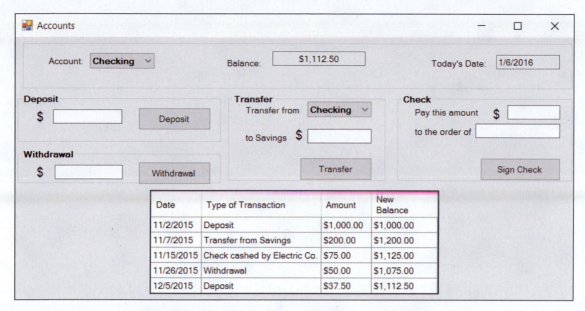

FIGURE 11.28 Possible outcome of Programming Project 1.

2. **Blackjack** Write a program for the game Blackjack. See Fig. 11.29. The program should use a DeckOfCards class similar to the one presented in Example 3 of Section 11.2.

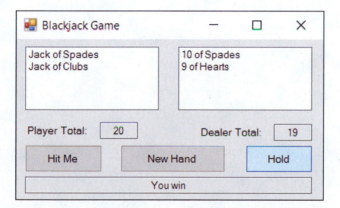

FIGURE 11.29 Possible outcome of Programming Project 2.

APPENDIX A

ANSI VALUES

ANSI Value	Character	ANSI Value	Character	ANSI Value	Character
000	(null)	046	.	092	\
001	□	047	/	093	]
002	□	048	0	094	^
003	□	049	1	095	_
004	□	050	2	096	`
005	□	051	3	097	a
006	□	052	4	098	b
007	□	053	5	099	c
008	□	054	6	100	d
009	(tab)	055	7	101	e
010	(line feed)	056	8	102	f
011	□	057	9	103	g
012	□	058	:	104	h
013	(carriage return)	059	;	105	i
014	□	060	<	106	j
015	□	061	=	107	k
016	□	062	>	108	l
017	□	063	?	109	m
018	□	064	@	110	n
019	□	065	A	111	o
020	□	066	B	112	p
021	□	067	C	113	q
022	□	068	D	114	r
023	□	069	E	115	s
024	□	070	F	116	t
025	□	071	G	117	u
026	□	072	H	118	v
027	□	073	I	119	w
028	□	074	J	120	x
029	□	075	K	121	y
030	□	076	L	122	z
031	□	077	M	123	{
032	(space)	078	N	124	|
033	!	079	O	125	}
034	"	080	P	126	~
035	#	081	Q	127	□
036	$	082	R	128	□
037	%	083	S	129	□
038	&	084	T	130	,
039	'	085	U	131	ƒ
040	(	086	V	132	"
041	)	087	W	133	…
042	*	088	X	134	†
043	+	089	Y	135	‡
044	,	090	Z	136	ˆ
045	–	091	[	137	‰

ANSI Value	Character	ANSI Value	Character	ANSI Value	Character
138	Š	189	1/2	240	ð
139	‹	190	3/4	241	ñ
140	Œ	191	¿	242	ò
141	□	192	À	243	ó
142	Ž	193	Á	244	ô
143	□	194	Â	245	õ
144	□	195	Ã	246	ö
145	'	196	Ä	247	÷
146	'	197	Å	248	ø
147	"	198	Æ	249	ù
148	"	199	Ç	250	ú
149	•	200	È	251	û
150	–	201	É	252	ü
151	—	202	Ê	253	‡
152	~	203	Ë	254	þ
153	™	204	Ì	255	ÿ
154	š	205	Í		
155	›	206	Î		
156	œ	207	Ï		
157	□	208	Ð		
158	ž	209	Ñ		
159	Ÿ	210	Ò		
160	(no-break space)	211	Ó		
161	¡	212	Ô		
162	¢	213	Õ		
163	£	214	Ö		
164	¤	215	×		
165	¥	216	Ø		
166	¦	217	Ù		
167	§	218	Ú		
168	¨	219	Û		
169	©	220	Ü		
170	ª	221	ý		
171	«	222	þ		
172	¬	223	ß		
173		224	à		
174	®	225	á		
175	¯	226	â		
176	°	227	ã		
177	±	228	ä		
178	²	229	å		
179	³	230	æ		
180	´	231	ç		
181	µ	232	è		
182	¶	233	é		
183	·	234	ê		
184	¸	235	ë		
185	¹	236	ì		
186	º	237	í		
187	»	238	î		
188	1/4	239	ï		

APPENDIX B
HOW TO

Launch and Exit Visual Basic

Note: Visual Basic is part of a suite of programs called Visual Studio, which also contains the C# (pronounced "C-sharp") programming language.

A. Start Visual Basic from Windows 10.

1. Click on the Windows Start button (▦).
2. Click on *All apps*.
3. Scroll down the long list of apps and click on 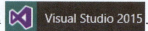.

B. Start Visual Basic from Windows 8.

1. Click on the Visual Studio tile on the Start Page.

or

1. Click on *Search* in the Charms bar.
2. Type "V" into the Search box in the upper-right part of the screen.
3. Click on the application containing the words "Visual Basic" or "Visual Studio" in the list on the left side of the screen.

C. Start Visual Basic from Windows 7.

1. Click the Windows *Start* button.
2. Hover over *All Programs*.
3. Click on Visual Studio 2015.

D. Exit Visual Basic.

1. Click on *Exit* in the File menu, or click on the red *Close* button located at the upper-right corner of the window. **Note:** If the current program has not been saved, Visual Basic will prompt you about saving it.

Manage Visual Basic Programs

A. Create a new program.

1. Click on *New/Project* in the File menu, or press Ctrl+Shift+N, or click on the *New Project* button (🗔) on the Toolbar. **Note:** If the current program has not been saved, Visual Basic will prompt you about saving it.
2. Check that Windows Forms Application is selected.
3. Optionally, type a name for the program into the *Name* text box.
4. Click on the OK button.

B. Run the current program.

1. Click on the *Start* button (▶) in the Toolbar, or press F5, or click on *Start Debugging* in the Debug menu.

C. End a program that is running.

    1. Click on the *Stop Debugging* button (■) in the Toolbar, or click on the form's *Close* button (✕), or press Alt+F4, or click on *Stop Debugging* in the Debug menu.

D. Save the current program.

    1. Click the *Save All* button ( ) on the Toolbar, or click on *Save All* in the File menu, or press Ctrl+Shift+S.

    2. If the program has not been saved previously, give it a name and then click on the *Save* button. **Important:** If the "Create directory for solution" check box is checked, then click on the check box to uncheck it. (You have to uncheck this check box only once; it will stay unchecked for all future programs.)

E. Close the current program.

    1. Click on *Close Solution* in the File menu.

F. Open a recently saved program.

    1. Hover the mouse over *Recent Projects and Solutions* in the File menu. (A numbered list of recent programs will appear on the right.)

    2. Click on a recent program, or if the program is preceded with a single digit, press the digit.

G. Open a saved program.

    1. Hover over (or click on) *Open* in the File menu and then click on *Project/Solution* in the context menu that drops down. **Note:** If the current program has not been saved, Visual Basic will prompt you about saving it.

    2. Navigate to the program's folder.

    3. Double-click on the folder, or highlight the folder and click on the *Open* button. (Several subfolders and files will be displayed.)

    4. Double-click on the file with extension *sln*.

    5. If neither the Form Designer nor the Code Editor for the program appears, double-click on *formName*.vb in the Solution Explorer window.

H. Change the name of a program.

    1. Open the program if it is not already open.

    2. The top two lines of the Solution Explorer window contain the current name of the program.

    3. For each of those lines, right-click on the name, click on *Rename* in the context menu that appears, and then enter the new name for the program.

    4. Right-click on the new name of the program in the second line, click on **Properties** in the context menu that appears, select *Application* on the large tab at the left side of the window that opens, change the contents of the "Assembly name:" text box to the new name of the program, and close the just-opened window.

    5. Save and close the program.

6. Navigate to the program's folder with File Explorer (or Windows Explorer), change the previous name of the folder to the new name.

7. (Optional Step) Open the folder's *bin\Debug* subfolder and delete all files that begin with the previous name of the program (except possibly for a txt file). Do the same with the *obj\Debug* subfolder.

I. Use the Solution Explorer window to view the Code Editor or the Form Designer.

Note: If the Solution Explorer window is not visible, click on *Solution Explorer* in the View menu.

1. In the Solution Explorer window, right-click on *fileName*.vb.
2. Click on either *View Code* or *View Designer*.

Text Manipulation

A. Select (or highlight) a block of text.

1. Move the cursor to the beginning or end of the text.
2. Hold down a Shift key, use the direction keys to highlight a block of text, and release the Shift key.

or

1. Move the mouse to the beginning or end of the text.
2. Hold down the left mouse button, drag the mouse to the other end of the text, and release the left mouse button.

Note 1: To deselect text, press the Esc key or click outside the text.

Note 2: To select a word, double-click on it. To select a line, move the mouse pointer just far enough to the left of the line so that the pointer changes to an arrow, and then single-click there.

B. Move text.

1. Select the text as a block, and drag it to the new location with the mouse.

C. Use the Clipboard to move or duplicate text.

1. Select the text as a block.
2. Press Ctrl+X to delete the block and place it into the Clipboard, or press Ctrl+C to place a copy of the block into the Clipboard.
3. Move the cursor to the location where you want to place the block.
4. Press Ctrl+V to place a copy of the text from the Clipboard at the cursor position.

D. Undo a change.

1. Click on *Undo* in the Edit menu or press Ctrl+Z to undo the last change made.

Note: An undone change can be redone by pressing Ctrl+Y.

E. Increase or decrease size of text in the Code Editor.

   1. Hold down the Ctrl key and move the mouse scroll wheel forward to increase the size of the text and backward to decrease the size.

Manage Visual Basic Controls

A. Resize a control.

   1. Select the control and drag one of its sizing handles. Or, select the control, hold down the Shift key, and press the arrow keys. Or, change the setting of the control's Size property. Or, use the *Make Same Size* option in the Format menu to give the control the same width and/or length as another control.

B. Move a control.

   1. Select the control and drag it to a new location. Or, select the control, hold down the Ctrl key, and press the arrow keys. Or, use the *Align* option in the Format menu to line up the control with another control.

C. Center a control in a form.

   1. Select the control.
   2. Use the *Center in Form* option of the Format menu.

D. Select multiple controls.

   1. Click on a control.
   2. Hold down the Ctrl key while clicking on additional controls.

   or

   1. Click on a place in the Form Designer outside the controls and start dragging. (A dotted rectangle will appear.)
   2. Drag the rectangle around a group of controls.
   3. Release the mouse button.

   Note: Multiple selected controls can be resized and moved as a group with the arrow keys as in parts A and B. Also, any property that is common to all of the controls in the group can be set simultaneously.

E. Create uniform spacing in a selected group of controls.

   6. Select *Make Equal* from the *Horizontal Spacing* or *Vertical Spacing* options of the Format menu.

   Note: After uniform spacing has been achieved, you can click on *Increase* or *Decrease* from the *Horizontal Spacing* or *Vertical Spacing* options of the Format menu to widen or narrow the spacing.

F. Let a label caption use more than one line.

   1. Change the label's AutoSize property setting to False and increase its height. (If the label is not wide enough to accommodate the entire caption on one line, part of the caption will wrap to additional lines. If the label height is too small, then part or all of these additional lines will not be visible.)

G. Let a text box display more than one line.

   1. Set the text box's MultiLine property to True. (If the text box is not wide enough to accommodate the text entered by the user, the text will wrap down to new lines. If the text box is not tall enough, some lines will not be displayed.)

H. Allow a particular button control to be activated by a press of the Enter key.

   1. Set the form's AcceptButton property to the particular button control.

I. Allow the pressing of Esc to activate a particular button control.

   1. Set the form's CancelButton property to the particular button control.

J. Have the form appear in the center of the screen when the program executes.

   1. Set the form's StartPosition property to CenterScreen.

K. Change the Name property of Form1 to frmElse.

   1. In the Solution Explorer window, right-click on the file Form1.vb.
   2. Click on *Rename* in the context menu that appears.
   3. Change the name of the file Form1.vb to frmElse.vb. (**Caution:** Retain the extension *vb*.)

L. Specify a custom background or foreground color for a control.

   1. In the Properties window, select the BackColor or ForeColor property.
   2. Click on the down arrow in the right part of the Settings box.
   3. Click on the Custom tab to display a grid of colors.
   4. Right-click on one of the sixteen white boxes at the bottom of the grid to display the Define Color dialog box. (The dialog box theoretically allows you to create over 16 million custom colors. The large variegated square is called the *color field* and the narrow rectangle the *color slider*.)
   5. To select a custom color, click on any point in the color field and then use the arrow head to move along the color slider. (At any time, the rectangle labeled "Color|Solid" displays the current color.)
   6. Click on the *Add Color* button.

M. Remove the blank column on the left side of a DataGridView control.

   1. Set the control's RowHeadersVisible property to False.

N. Guarantee that the grid to appear in a DataGridView control will fill the control horizontally.

   1. Set the AutoSizeColumnMode property to Fill.

O. Obtain a description of a property of a control.

   1. If the Description pane is not visible, right-click on the Properties window and then click on *Description* in the context menu that appears.
   2. Highlight the property in the Properties window. Its purpose will appear in the Description pane below.

P. Specify the control that will have the focus when the program executes.

   1. Set the control's TabIndex property to 0.

Q. Make the Properties window easier to use.

   1. Drag the Properties window title bar to the center of the screen. (Hold down the Ctrl key and double-click the title bar to return the Properties window to its original location.)

R. Lock and unlock the controls during design time.

   Note: When the controls are locked, they cannot be moved during the execution of the program.

   1. Right-click anywhere on the form and click on *Lock Controls* in the context menu that appears. (A small lock will appear in the upper-left corner of each control and you will not be able to move any of the controls.)
   2. Repeat Step 1 in order to unlock the controls.

S. Specify a button as the *accept button*.

   Note: The accept button is the button whose Click event is invoked whenever the Enter key is pressed.

   1. Click on the form to make it the selected object.
   2. Click on the AcceptButton property in the Properties window.
   3. Click on the down arrow in the right part of the Settings box.
   4. Click on the name of the desired button.

T. Specify a button as the *cancel button*.

   Note: The cancel button is the button whose Click event is invoked whenever the Esc key is pressed.

   1. Click on the form to make it the selected object.
   2. Click on the CancelButton property in the Properties window.
   3. Click on the down arrow in the right part of the Settings box.
   4. Click on the name of the desired button.

Working with Code

A. Rename all instances of a variable, control, Sub procedure, or Function.

   1. Select the name.
   2. Right-click on the name and click on *Rename* in the context menu that appears. (A Rename dialog box will appear.)
   3. Type the new name into the New Name text box.
   4. Click on the OK button to carry out the changes.

   Note: This process is known as *symbolic rename*. If the name of a variable having local (or block) scope is changed, the change will be limited to the procedure (or block) containing the variable.

B. Hide a long procedure.

   1. Scroll to the top of the procedure.
   2. Click on the box with a minus sign in it that is to the left of the header of the procedure. (Notice that the box now contains a plus sign and that the entire procedure is hidden on the one line. Click on the box again to show the procedure.)

C. Add a collapsible region.

   1. Type #Region *"regionName"* on the line before the code to be included in the region.

   2. Type #End Region on the line after the last line of code in the region.

   3. The region of code can then be collapsed by clicking on the minus box and restored by clicking on the plus box.

   Note: A region cannot be defined within an event, Function, or Sub procedure.

Setting Options

A. Turn off IntelliSense.

   1. Click on *Options* at the bottom of the Tools menu.

   2. In the left pane, expand "Text Editor".

   3. Expand the subheading "Basic".

   4. Click on the subtopic "General".

   5. Ensure that all the check boxes under the "Statement completion" heading are unchecked, and then click on OK.

B. Wrap words to the next line in the Code Editor rather than having a horizontal scroll bar.

   1. Follow Steps 1 through 4 of part A above.

   2. In the right pane, place a check mark in the check box labeled "Word wrap" and then click on OK.

C. Instruct the Code Editor to indent by two spaces.

   1. Follow Steps 1 through 3 of part A.

   2. Click on the subtopic "Tabs".

   3. In the right pane, change the number in the "Indent size:" text box to 2 and then click on OK.

Manage Text Files

Note: If the Solution Explorer window is not visible, click on *Solution Explorer* in the View menu. If the *bin* folder does not show in the Solution Explorer window, click on the *Show All Files* button in the Solution Explorer toolbar.

A. Display a text file associated with an open program.

   1. In the Solution Explorer window, open the *bin* folder by double-clicking on it.

   2. Open the *Debug* subfolder of the *bin* folder by double-clicking on it. (The text file should appear in a list of several files. If the file is not listed in the *Debug* subfolder, click the *Refresh* button in the Solution Explorer.)

   3. Double-click on the text file to open it. (The contents of the file will be displayed in a tabbed Text Editor in the Documents window, and the filename will appear in the tab.)

B. Save the file that is displayed in the Text Editor.

   1. Right-click on the tab and then click on *Save filename* in the context menu that appears. Or, press Ctrl+S. Or, click on *Save filename* in the File menu.

C. Close an open Text Editor.

   1. Click on the *Close* button (×) on the tab. Or, right-click on the tab containing the filename at the top of the Document window and click on *Close* in the context menu that appears. **Note:** If the text file has not been saved, Visual Basic will prompt you about saving it.

D. Import an existing text file into an open program.

   Note: This task is especially useful when importing a file from a "Text_Files_for_Exercises" folder.

   1. Click on the name of the program at the top of the Solution Explorer window.
   2. Click on *Add Existing Item* in the Project menu. (An "Add Existing Item" input dialog box will appear.)
   3. Navigate to the text file, and double-click on it. (A copy of the file will be placed into the Solution Explorer window.)
   4. Move the file into the *bin\Debug* folder.

E. Create a new text file in an open program.

   1. Click on the name of the program at the top of the Solution Explorer window.
   2. Click on *Add New Item* in the Project menu. (An "Add New Item" input dialog box will appear.)
   3. Select *Text File* in the middle pane of the input dialog box, and enter a base name for the file in the Name text box. (Visual Basic will automatically add the extension *txt* to the name.)
   4. Click on the *Add* button. (A tabbed Text Editor will appear in the Document window.)
   5. Type the contents of the file into the Text Editor.
   6. Right-click on the tab and click on *Save filename* in the context menu that appears.
   7. Right-click on the tab and click on *Close* in the context menu.

F. Modify the contents of an existing text file in an open program.

   1. In the Solution Explorer window, locate the text file in the *bin\Debug* folder.
   2. Double-click on the filename to display the contents of the file in a tabbed Text Editor.
   3. Alter the contents of the file using the Text Editor.
   4. Save the file and close the Text Editor.

G. Delete an existing text file from an open program.

   1. In the Solution Explorer window, locate the text file in the *bin\Debug* folder.
   2. Right-click on the filename and click on *Delete* in the context menu that appears.
   3. Click on the *OK* button in the message box that appears.

Configuring the Windows Environment

A. Determine and/or change the Windows DPI resolution for your monitor. (The DPI setting determines the size of text and other items on the screen.)

Windows 10

1. Right click on the Windows desktop to display a context menu.
2. Click on Display settings to invoke a "Customize your display" window.
3. Click on *Advanced display settings* at the bottom of the screen to invoke an ADVANCED DISPLAY SETTINGS window.
4. Click on *Advanced sizing of text and other items* near the bottom-left corner of the screen.
5. Click on <u>set a custom scaling level</u> in the first paragraph to invoke a "Custom sizing options" window.
6. All of the programs in this textbook were written with the setting "125%." With that setting, outputs should look like the screen captures in the textbook.
7. If you do not want to change the current setting, close all the windows you have opened.
8. Otherwise, select a different setting and click on the OK button. You will be instructed to restart your computer in order to allow the change to take place.

Windows 7 & 8

1. Right-click on the Windows desktop to display a context menu.
2. Click *Personalize* on the context menu to display the Personalization window.
3. Click on *Display* near the bottom of the left pane. Two or three radio buttons will appear. The first radio button will be labeled "Smaller–100%", the second radio button will be labeled "Medium–125%", and the currently selected setting will be selected. All of the programs in this textbook (except for a few programs in Section 9.4) were written with the setting "Medium–125%" and with that setting will have outputs exactly like the screen captures in the textbook. **Note:** Some versions of Windows 8 have a slider with Smaller on the left and Larger on the right instead of radio buttons.
4. If you do not want to change the current setting, close the window.
5. Otherwise, select a different setting and click on the *Apply* button. You will be instructed to log off your computer in order to allow the change to take effect.

B. Configure Windows to display filename extensions.

Windows 10

Windows 10 shows the full file name by default.

Windows 8

1. Click on *Search* in the Charms Bar.
2. Type "Folder" into the text box in the upper-right part of the screen.
3. Click on the command *Folder Options* at the top of the middle column on the screen.
4. Click on the View tab in the Folder Options dialog box. The dialog box in Fig. B.1 will appear.
5. If there is a check mark in the box next to "Hide extensions for known file types", click on the box to remove the check mark.
6. Click on the OK button to close the Folder Options dialog box.

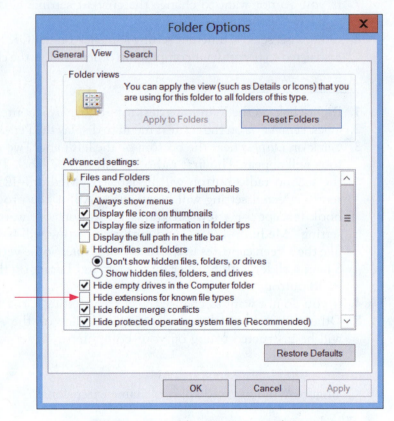

FIGURE B.1   **Folder Options window.**

Windows 7

1. Click on the Windows *Start* button.
2. Type "Folder Options" into the "Search programs and files" box. (A Control Panel box will appear.) Click on *Folder Options*. (A Folders Options dialog box will appear.)
3. Click on the View tab in the Folder Options dialog box. (The dialog box will be similar to Fig. B.1.)
4. If there is a check mark in the box next to "Hide extensions for known file types", click on the box to remove the check mark.
5. Click on the OK button to close the Folders Options dialog box.

Use a Printer

A. Obtain a printout of a program.

    1. Invoke the Code Editor.
    2. Click on *Print* in the File menu. Or, press Ctrl+P.
    3. Click on the OK button.

B. Print the contents of a DataGridView control.

    1. After a PrintDocument control has been added to the form, the following code prints the DataGridView control named dgvColleges when btnPrint is clicked:

```
Private Sub btnPrint_Click(...) Handles btnPrint.Click
   PrintDocument1.Print()
End Sub

Private Sub PrintDocument1_PrintPage(...) Handles _
                                   PrintDocument1.PrintPage
  Dim bm As Bitmap = New Bitmap(dgvColleges.Width,
                               dgvColleges.Height)
  dgvColleges.DrawToBitmap(bm, dgvColleges.DisplayRectangle)
  e.Graphics.DrawImageUnscaled(bm, New Point(75, 100))
End Sub
```

The argument `New Point(75, 100)` causes the table to be printed one inch from the left side and one inch from the top of the page. In general, `New Point(x, y)` causes the table to be printed about $(1/4 + x/100)$ inches from the left side and $y/100$ inches from the top of the page.

C. Print the contents of a list box.

    1. The code in part B above also can be used to print the contents of a list box. Just replace the name of the DataGridView control with the name of the list box.

Miscellaneous

A. Enlarge the Document window to fill the entire screen.

    1. Click on *Full Screen* in the View menu. (To return to the regular screen, click on the newly created *Full Screen* button at the right side of the Menu bar.)

B. Return the IDE to its original layout.

    1. Click on *Reset Window Layout* in the Window menu.

C. Store frequently used code for easy inclusion into other programs.

    1. Select the code as a block.
    2. Drag the block of code into the Toolbox. (You will now have the code in both the Code Editor and the Toolbox.)

Note: The block of code will be visible in the Toolbox whenever the Code Editor is open. At any time you can drag a copy of the code into the Code Editor.

D. Navigate folders and files

<u>Windows 10</u>

1. Right-click on the Windows *Start* button and click on *File Explorer* in the context menu that appears.

<u>Windows 8</u>

1. Click on *Search* in the Charms bar.
2. Type "Explorer" into the Search box in the upper-right part of the screen.
3. Click on "File Explorer" in the list on the left side of the screen.

<u>Windows 7</u>

1. Right-click on the Windows *Start* button and click on *Open Windows Explorer* in the context menu that appears.

E. Install Office Data Connectivity Components.

Note: This installation might be necessary for Chapter 10 (Databases) if Microsoft Office is not installed on your computer.

1. Go to the website http://www.microsoft.com/en-us/download/details. aspx?id=23734.
2. Download and install "2007 Office System Driver: Data Connectivity Components".
3. You might have to reboot your computer.

F. Debugging shortcut keys.

Debugging tasks can be initiated from the Debug menu, the Toolbar, or with keyboard shortcuts. We find the use of keyboard shortcuts to be the simplest method. However, the shortcuts used vary with the keyboard mapping setting on your computer. To enable the shortcuts specified in Appendix D, you should carry out the following steps:

1. Select *Options* from the Tools menu.
2. Click on *Keyboard* in the *Environment* list to invoke an *Options* dialog box.
3. Click on the down arrow at the right of the top drop-down list box and select *Visual Basic 6*.
4. Click on the OK button.

APPENDIX C

FILES AND FOLDERS

The following terms are used in this textbook.

Disk: A hard disk, a diskette, a USB flash drive, a CD, or a DVD. Each disk drive is identified by a letter followed by a colon and a backslash. The letter C is commonly used for the computer's primary hard drive.

Extension of a file name: One or more letters, preceded by a period, that identify the type of file. For example, files created with Word have the extension *doc* or *docx*. Two important extensions for Visual Basic files are *vb* and *sln*. **Important:** By default, Windows 7 and 8 show only the base names of files. You should configure Windows 7 and 8 to display the filename extensions for all known file types. The details are presented in Appendix B in part B of the "Configuring the Windows Environment" section.

File: Either a program file or a data file. Its name typically consists of letters, digits, and spaces. The name of the file is also called the *base name*. Some files appearing in this text books have the base names USPres, States, and Baseball.

Filename: The combination of the base name, the period, and the extension. The only characters that cannot be used in filenames are \, /, :, ?, ", and |. Filenames are not case sensitive. Some filenames appearing in this textbook are USPres.txt and Form1.vb.

File Explorer and **Windows Explorer:** Programs used to view, organize, and manage the folders and files on disks. The details for opening them are presented in the "Miscellaneous" section of Appendix B.

Filespec: An abbreviation of *file specification*, it is the combination of a drive letter followed by a colon, a path, and a filename. An example is C:\Programs\Ch07\Text_Files_for_Exercises\USPres.txt. In practice, you rarely have to type a filespec, since both Windows and Visual Basic provide Browse facilities that locate files and folders for you.

Folder: A container holding files and other folders. Folders also are known as *directories*. Each Visual Basic program is contained in a folder. As an example, the folder containing the program in Example 4 of Section 3.1 has the name 3–1–4.

Path: A sequence of folders, separated by backslashes (\), where each folder is a subfolder of the folder preceding it. Paths are used to identify the locations of folders and files. An example is Programs\Ch07\Text_Files_for_Exercises.

Root folder (also known as the **base folder**)**:** The highest folder on a disk. It contains all the other folders on the disk and can also contain files. The filespec of the root folder of your hard drive is most likely referenced as C:\.

Subfolder: A folder contained inside another folder.

APPENDIX D
VISUAL BASIC DEBUGGING TOOLS

Logic errors in programs are called **bugs**, and the process of finding and correcting them is called **debugging**. One method of discovering a logic error is by **desk checking**—that is, tracing the values of variables on paper by writing down their expected value after "mentally executing" each line in the program. Desk checking is rudimentary and highly impractical except for small programs.

Another method of debugging involves placing MessageBox.Show statements at strategic points in the program and displaying the values of selected variables or expressions until the error is detected. After correcting the error, you can remove the MessageBox.Show statements.

The Visual Basic debugger offers an alternative to desk checking and to inserting MessageBox.Show statements. It allows you to pause during the execution of your program in order to view and alter values of variables. These values can be accessed through the Immediate, Watch, and Locals windows.

Note: Debugging tasks can be initiated from the Debug menu, the Toolbar, or with keyboard shortcuts. We find the use of keyboard shortcuts to be the simplest method. However, the shortcuts used vary with the keyboard mapping setting on your computer. To enable the shortcuts specified in this appendix, you should carry out the following steps:

1. Select *Options* from the *Tools* menu.

2. Click on *Keyboard* in the *Environment* list to invoke an *Options* dialog box.

3. Click on the down arrow at the right of the top list box and select *Visual Basic 6*.

4. Click on the OK button.

There is a good chance that your computer currently has the "Visual Basic 6" keyboard mapping setting. If not, and you decide not to change the keyboard mapping setting, you can use the Debug menu or the Toolbar to initiate debugging tasks.

The Three Program Modes

At any time, a program is in one of three modes—**design mode**, **run mode**, or **debug mode**. (Debug mode is also known as **break mode**.) When the current mode is "run" or "debug", the words "Running" or "Debugging" are displayed (in parentheses) in the Visual Basic title bar. The absence of these words indicates that the current mode is "design".

Title bar, Menu bar, and Toolbar during design mode.

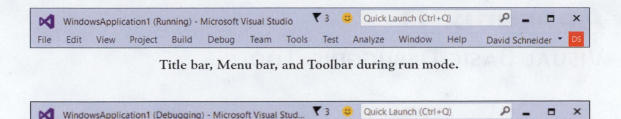

Title bar, Menu bar, and Toolbar during run mode.

Title bar, Menu bar, and Toolbar during debug mode.

With the program in design mode, you place controls on a form, set their initial properties, and write code. Run mode is initiated by pressing F5 or the *Start* button. Debug mode is invoked automatically when a runtime error occurs. Also, you can use Debug options to break programs at specified places. While the program is in debug mode, you can hover the cursor over any variable to obtain its current value. Also, you can use the debugging windows, such as the Immediate, Watch, and Locals windows, to examine values of expressions. When you enter debug mode, the *Start* button becomes a *Continue* button. You can click on it to continue with the execution of the program.

Stepping through a Program

The program can be executed one statement at a time, with each press of an appropriate function key executing a statement. This process is called **stepping**. After each step, values of variables, expressions, and conditions can be displayed in the debugging windows, and the values of variables can be changed.

When a procedure is called, the lines of the procedure can be executed one at a time, referred to as **stepping into** the procedure, or the entire procedure can be executed at once, referred to as **stepping over** a procedure. A step over a procedure is called a **procedure step**. In addition, you can execute the remainder of the current procedure at once, referred to as **stepping out** of the procedure. The three toolbar buttons shown in Fig. D.1 can be used for stepping.

FIGURE D.1   **The toolbar buttons used for Step Into, Step Over, and Step Out.**

Breakpoints

Visual Basic allows the programmer to specify certain lines as **breakpoints**. Then, when the program is run, execution will stop just before the first breakpoint line is executed, and a yellow arrow will point to the line. To specify (or unspecify) a line as a breakpoint, click on *Toggle Breakpoint* in the Debug menu.

When a breakpoint is reached, the program is in break mode. At that time you can view or alter the value of any variable with the Immediate, Watch, or Locals windows. Also, you can specify the next line to be executed when the program is continued by dragging the yellow arrow to that line. Then, you can either step through the program, or continue execution to the end of the program or to the next breakpoint.

Run to Cursor

You can have a program break at a specified line of the program by right-clicking on the line and clicking on *Run to Cursor* on the context menu that appears. When the program is run, execution will stop just before the line is executed and a yellow arrow will point to the line. You can then proceed as described in the second paragraph of the breakpoint section above.

Run to cursor	Press Ctrl+F10
Step Into	Press F11
Step Over	Press F10
Step Out	Press Ctrl+Shift+F11
Set a breakpoint	Move cursor to line, press F9
Remove a breakpoint	Move cursor to line containing breakpoint, press F9
Delete all breakpoints	Press Ctrl+Shift+F9
Continue execution of the program	Press F5

The Immediate Window

While in break mode, you can set the focus to the **Immediate window** by clicking on it (if visible), or by pressing Ctrl+Alt+I, or hovering the cursor over *Windows* in the Debug menu and clicking on *Immediate*. When you type a statement into the Immediate window and press the Enter key, the statement is executed at once. A statement of the form

```
? expression
```

displays the value of the expression on the next line of the Immediate window. (The question mark is shorthand for Debug.Print.) A statement of the form

```
var = value
```

assigns a value to a variable. In Fig. D.2, the variable *numVar* had the value 10 when the program was interrupted. **Note:** You can clear the contents of the Immediate window, or any of the other Debug windows, by pressing the right mouse button and clicking on "Clear All".

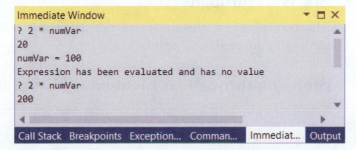

FIGURE D.2   **Three statements executed in the Immediate window.**

Watch Windows

A **Watch window**, which can be viewed only in break mode, permits you to view the values of variables and expressions. The Watch window in Fig. D.3 shows the values of one variable and two expressions. If you don't see a Watch window when you enter break mode, hover the cursor over *Windows* in the Debug menu, hover the cursor over *Watch*, and then click on one of four Watch windows.

Although you can type directly into the Watch window, the easiest way to add an expression to the window is to right-click on a variable in the Code Editor and then click on *Add Watch* in the context menu. You can then alter the expression in the Name column of the Watch window. To delete an expression from the Watch window, right-click on the expression and then click on *Delete Watch*. Also, you can directly change the value of any variable in the Watch window and have the values of the other expressions change accordingly.

Watch 1			▾ ▢ ✕
Name	Value	Type	
num	100	Integer	
5 * num	500	Integer	
num > 90	True	Boolean	

FIGURE D.3 A typical Watch window.

The Locals Window

While in break mode, you can open the Locals window from the Debug menu by positioning the cursor over *Windows* and then clicking on *Locals*. This window automatically displays the names, values, and types of all variables in scope. See Figure D.4. You can use the window to alter the values of variables at any time.

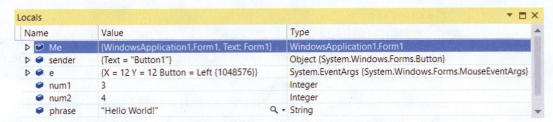

Locals			▾ ▢ ✕
Name	Value	Type	
▷ Me	{WindowsApplication1.Form1, Text: Form1}	WindowsApplication1.Form1	
▷ sender	{Text = "Button1"}	Object {System.Windows.Forms.Button}	
▷ e	{X = 12 Y = 12 Button = Left {1048576}}	System.EventArgs {System.Windows.Forms.MouseEventArgs}	
num1	3	Integer	
num2	4	Integer	
phrase	"Hello World!"	String	

FIGURE D.4 A typical Locals window.

Six Walkthroughs

The following walkthroughs use the debugging tools with the programming structures covered in Chapters 3, 4, 5, and 6.

Stepping through an Elementary Program: Chapter 3

The following walkthrough demonstrates several capabilities of the debugger:

1. Create a form with a button (btnPush) and a text box (txtBox).

2. Double-click on the button and enter the following event procedure:

```
Private Sub btnPush_Click(...) Handles btnPush.Click
    Dim num As Integer
    num = CInt(InputBox("Enter a number:"))
    num += 1
    num += 2
    txtBox.Text = CStr(num)
End Sub
```

3. Place the cursor on the header, press the right mouse button, and click on *Run to Cursor* in the context menu that appears. The program will execute, and the form will appear.

4. Click on the button. The Code Editor appears and a yellow arrow points to the header of the event procedure.

5. Press F11. The yellow arrow now points to the statement containing InputBox to indicate that it is to be executed next. (Pressing F11 is referred to as *stepping into*. You can also step to the next statement of a program with the *Step Into* option from the Debug menu or with the *Step Into* button in the Toolbar.)

6. Press F11. The statement containing InputBox is executed, and an input dialog box requesting a number appears. Respond to the request by typing 5 and clicking on the OK button.

7. Press F11 again to execute the statement `num += 1`.

8. Let the mouse hover over any occurrence of the variable *num* for a second or so. The current value of the variable will be displayed in a small box. See Fig. D.5.

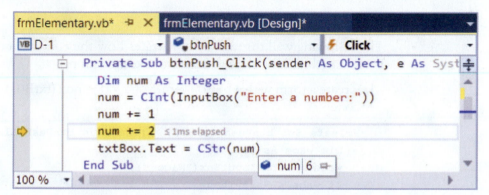

FIGURE D.5   **Obtaining the value of a variable.**

9. Click the Stop Debugging button on the Toolbar. (You also can stop debugging by clicking on *Stop Debugging* in the Debug menu.)

10. Move the cursor to the line

`num += 2`

and then press F9. A red dot appears on the gray border to the left of the line. This indicates that the line is a breakpoint. Pressing F9 is referred to as *toggling a breakpoint*.

11. Press F5 and click on the button. Respond to the request by entering 5 and clicking on OK. The program executes the first three lines inside the procedure and stops at the breakpoint. At this point, the breakpoint line has not yet executed.

12. Open the Immediate window. If necessary, clear the contents of the window by pressing the right mouse button and clicking on "Clear All". Type the statement

`? num`

into the Immediate window, and then press the Enter key to execute the statement. The appearance of "6" on the next line of the Immediate window confirms that the breakpoint line was not executed.

13. Move the cursor to the line `num += 1` in the Code Editor, click the right mouse button, and then click on "Set next Statement".

14. Press F11 to execute the selected line.

15. Return to the Immediate window by clicking on it. Type the statement "? num" and press the Enter key to confirm that the value of *num* is now 7. Then return to the Code Editor.

16. Move the cursor to the breakpoint line and press F9 to remove the red breakpoint circle.

17. Press F5 to execute the remaining lines of the program. Observe that the value displayed in the text box is 9.

Stepping through Programs Containing Selection Structures: Chapter 4

If Blocks

The following walkthrough demonstrates how the condition of an If statement is evaluated to determine whether to take an action:

1. Create a form with a button (btnPush), a text box (txtBox), and the following code:

```
Private Sub btnPush_Click(...) Handles btnPush.Click
   Dim wage As Double
   wage = CDbl(InputBox("Wage:"))
   If wage < 7.25 Then
     txtBox.Text = "Below minimum wage."
   Else
     txtBox.Text = "Wage Ok."
   End If
End Sub
```

2. Place the cursor on the line beginning "Private Sub", press the right mouse button, and click on "Run to Cursor". The program will execute and the form will appear.

3. Click on the button, and then press F11. The yellow arrow points to the statement containing InputBox.

4. Press F11 once to execute the statement containing InputBox. Type a wage of 6.25, and press the Enter key. The If statement is highlighted but has not been executed.

5. Press F11 once, and notice that the yellow arrow has jumped to the statement `txtBox.Text = "Below minimum wage."` Because the condition "wage < 7.25" is true, the action associated with Then was chosen.

6. Press F11 to execute the txtBox.Text statement. Notice that Else is skipped and the yellow arrow points to End If.

7. Press F11 again. We are through with the If block, and the statement following the If block, End Sub, is highlighted.

8. Click on the *Stop Debugging* button on the Toolbar.

9. If desired, try stepping through the program again with 7.75 entered as the wage. Since the condition "wage < 7.25" will be false, the Else action will be executed instead of the Then action.

Select Case Blocks

The following walkthrough illustrates how a Select Case block uses the selector to choose from among several actions.

1. Create a form with a button (btnPush) and a text box (txtBox). Double-click on the button and enter the following procedure:

```
Private Sub btnPush_Click(...) Handles btnPush.Click
    Dim age, price As Double
    age = CDbl(InputBox("Age:"))
    Select Case age
      Case Is < 12
        price = 0
      Case Is < 18
        price = 3.5
      Case Is >= 65
        price = 4
      Case Else
        price = 5.5
    End Select
    txtBox.Text = "Your ticket price is " & price.ToString("C")
End Sub
```

2. Place the cursor on the line beginning "age =", press the right mouse button, and click on "Run to Cursor". The program will execute and the form will appear.

3. Click on the button. The arrow will point to the statement beginning "age =".

4. Press F11 once to execute the statement beginning "age =". Type an age of 8, and press the Enter key. The arrow points to the Select Case statement, but the statement has not been executed.

5. Press F11 twice, and observe that the arrow points to the action associated with "Case Is < 12".

6. Press F11 once to execute the assignment statement. Notice that the arrow now points to End Select. This demonstrates that when more than one Case clause is true, only the first is acted upon.

7. Click on the *Stop Debugging* button on the Toolbar.

If desired, step through the program again, entering a different age and predicting which Case clause will be acted upon. (Some possible ages to try are 12, 14, 18, 33, and 67.)

Stepping through a Program Containing a General Procedure: Chapter 5

The following walkthrough uses the single-stepping feature of the debugger to trace the flow through a Sub procedure.

1. Create a form with a button (btnPush) and a text box (txtBox). Then enter the following two procedures:

```
Const INTEREST_RATE = 0.05 '5% interest

Private Sub btnPush_Click(...) Handles btnPush.Click
   Dim balance As Double
   balance = 1000 'principal
   balance = UpdateBalance(balance)
   txtBox.Text = "The new balance is " & balance.ToString("C")
End Sub

Function UpdateBalance(bal As Double) As Double
   'Calculate the new balance
   Dim interest As Double
   interest = INTEREST_RATE * bal
   bal += interest
   Return bal
End Function
```

2. Place the cursor on the header of the event procedure, press the right mouse button, and click on "Run to Cursor" in the context menu. The program will execute, and the form will appear.

3. Click on the button. In the Code Editor, a yellow arrow points to the header of the event procedure.

4. Press F11 once, and observe that the yellow arrow now points to the statement **balance = 1000**. This statement will be executed when F11 is next pressed.

5. Press F11 again. The statement **balance = 1000** was executed, and the yellow arrow now points to the statement calling the Function procedure UpdateBalance.

6. Press F11, and observe that the yellow arrow is now pointing to the header of the Function procedure.

7. Press F11 four times to execute the statements inside the Function procedure. The yellow arrow now points to the End Function statement. (Notice that the Dim and comment statements were skipped.)

8. Press F11, and notice that the yellow arrow has moved back to the event procedure and is pointing to the calling statement.

9. Press F11. Hover the cursor over the variable *balance* to verify that the Function procedure was executed.

10. Click on the *Stop Debugging* button on the Toolbar to end the program.

11. Repeat Steps 2 through 5, and then press F10 to *step over* the Function procedure. The Functions procedure has been executed in its entirety.

12. Press F5 to finish executing the event procedure.

13. End the program.

Displaying Values and Types of Variables in the Current Procedure: Chapter 5

The following walkthrough uses the Locals window to monitor the values of arguments and parameters during the execution of a program.

1. If you have not already done so, type the preceding program into the Code Editor.

2. Place the cursor on the header of the event procedure, press the right mouse button, and click on "Run to Cursor" in the context menu. The program will execute, and the form will appear.

3. Click on the button.

4. Click on the Debug menu, hover the cursor over *Windows*, and then click on *Locals*. Notice that the variable *balance* from the event procedure appears in the Locals window along with its current value. The other variables in the list (Me, sender, and e) needn't concern us.

5. Press F11 twice to point to the calling statement.

6. Press F11 to call the Function procedure UpdateBalance. Notice that the variables displayed in the Locals window are now those of the Function procedure.

7. Press F11 four times to execute the procedure.

8. Press F11 twice to return to the event procedure and execute the assignment statement. Notice that the value of the variable *balance* has received the value of the variable *bal*.

9. Close the Locals window.

10. End the program.

Stepping through a Program Containing a Do Loop: Chapter 6

The following walkthrough demonstrates the use of the Watch window to monitor the value of a condition in a Do loop that searches for a name:

1. Create a form with a list box (lstNames), a button (btnPush), and a text box (txtBox). Then double-click on the button and enter the following event procedure:

```
Private Sub btnPush_Click(...) Handles btnPush.Click
    'Look for a specific name
    Dim searchName As String, name = ""
    Dim i As Integer = 0
    Dim numNames As Integer = lstNames.Items.Count
    searchName = InputBox("Name:") 'name to search for in list
    Do While (name <> searchName) And (i < numNames)
        name = CStr(lstNames.Items(i))
        i += 1
```

```
      Loop
      If name = searchName Then
         txtBox.Text = name
      Else
         txtBox.Text = "Name not found"
      End If
   End Sub
```

2. Fill the list box's String Collection Editor with four lines containing the names Bert, Ernie, Grover, and Oscar.

3. Place the cursor on the line beginning "Private Sub", press the right mouse button, and click on "Run to Cursor". The program will execute, and the form will appear.

4. Click on the button. The yellow arrow points to the header of the event procedure.

5. Right-click on the variable *searchName*, and click on "Add Watch". The variable *searchName* has been added to a window titled Watch 1.

6. Repeat Step 5 for the variable *name*.

7. Drag the mouse across the words **name <> searchName** to highlight them. Then click the right mouse button, and click on "Add Watch". The Boolean expression has been added to the Watch window.

8. Press F11 five times to execute the statement containing InputBox. Enter the name "Ernie" in the input dialog box, and then click on the OK button.

9. Press F11 repeatedly until the entire event procedure has been executed. Pause after each keypress, and notice how the values of the expressions in the Watch window change.

10. Press the *Close* button on the form to terminate debugging.

Displaying Values in an Array Variable: Chapter 7

In the first walkthrough, we saw that during break mode the value of a simple variable appears when the mouse is hovered over the name of the variable. Figure D.6 shows that values of array variables also can be displayed. When the mouse is hovered over the array variable *teamNames*, the banner ▷ ● teamNames {Length=4} ⇨ appears below the array variable. When the mouse is hovered over the right-pointing triangle, Fig. D.6 results.

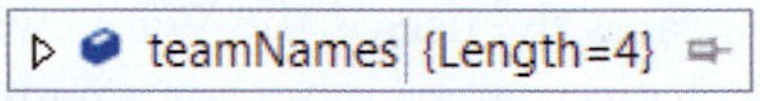

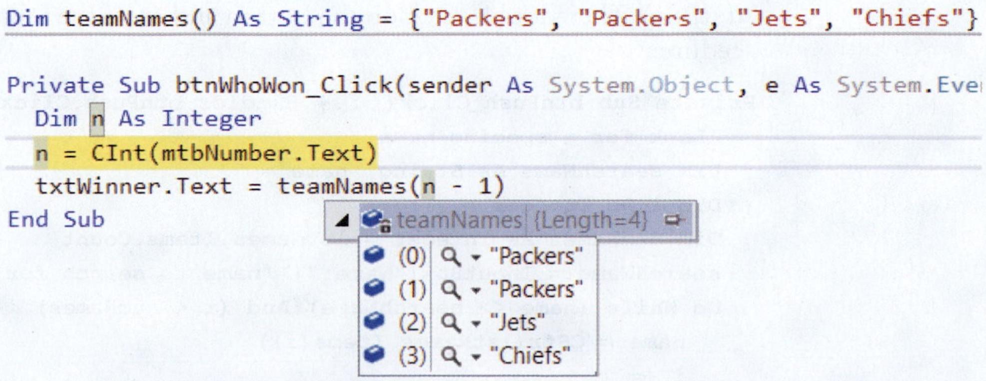

```
Dim teamNames() As String = {"Packers", "Packers", "Jets", "Chiefs"}

Private Sub btnWhoWon_Click(sender As System.Object, e As System.Eve
   Dim n As Integer
   n = CInt(mtbNumber.Text)
   txtWinner.Text = teamNames(n - 1)
End Sub
```

◢ ●₈ teamNames {Length=4} ⇨
   ● (0) 🔍 ▾ "Packers"
   ● (1) 🔍 ▾ "Packers"
   ● (2) 🔍 ▾ "Jets"
   ● (3) 🔍 ▾ "Chiefs"

FIGURE D.6   Obtaining the values of an array variable.

ANSWERS

This section contains the answers to all odd-numbered exercises from Chapters 2 through 7 and the answers to all short-answer odd-numbered exercises from the remaining chapters. The answers to all odd-numbered exercises from the book are contained in the Student Solutions Manual that can be downloaded from the companion website for the book.

CHAPTER 2

EXERCISES 2.2

1. While the mouse cursor is still hovering over the button that was just clicked, the button has a pale blue color. After the cursor leaves the button, the button has a dark blue border.

3. Click on the form to make it the selected object.
   Activate the Properties window.
   Select the Text property.
   Type "CHECKING ACCOUNT" and press the Enter key.

5. Double-click the TextBox icon in the Toolbox.
   Activate the Properties window.
   Select the BackColor property.
   Click on the down-arrow button to the right of the Settings box.
   Click on the Custom tab, and then click on the desired yellow in the palette.
   Click on the form to see the empty yellow text box.

7. Double-click on the Label icon in the Toolbox.
   Activate the Properties window, and select the AutoSize property.
   Set the AutoSize property to False.
   Select the Text property and type the requested sentence.
   Select the TextAlign property.
   Click on the down-arrow button to the right of the Settings box, and click on one of the center rectangles.
   Resize the label so that the sentence occupies three lines.

9. Double-click on the TextBox icon in the Toolbox.
   Activate the Properties window.
   Set the Name property to txtLanguage.
   Select the Text property and type "Visual Basic 2015".
   Select the Font property and click on the ellipsis to the right of the Settings box.
   Scroll up the Font box, and click on *Courier New* in the Font box.
   Click on the OK button.
   Widen the text box to accommodate its text.

11. Double-click on the Button icon in the Toolbox.
    Activate the Properties window, and select the BackColor property.
    Click on the down-arrow button to the right of the Settings box.
    Click on the Custom tab, and then click on the white square in upper-left corner of the palette.
    Select the Text property and type "PUSH".

Select the Font property, and click on the ellipsis.
Click on *Oblique* in the "Font style" list.
Click on 24 in the Size list.
Click in the OK button.
Resize the button.

13. Double-click on the Button icon in the Toolbox.
Activate the Properties window.
Select the Text property and type "PUS&H".
Click on the form to see the resulting button.

15. Double-click on the Label icon in the Toolbox.
Activate the Properties window.
Select the Name property and type "lblAKA".
Select the Text property and type "ALIAS".
Select the AutoSize property and set it to False.
Select the Font property and click on the ellipsis.
Click on *Oblique* in the "Font style" list.
Click on the OK button.
Select the TextAlign property, click on the down-arrow button to the right of the
Settings box, and click on one of the center rectangles.

17. Double-click on the Label icon in the Toolbox.
Activate the Properties window, and select the TextAlign property.
Click on the down-arrow button to the right of the Settings box, and click on one of
the rectangles on the right.
Select the AutoSize property and set it to False.
Select the Text property, type "VISUAL BASIC", and press Enter.
If the words "VISUAL BASIC" are on one line, resize the label until the words
occupy two lines.

19. Double-click on the Label icon in the Toolbox.
Activate the Properties window and set the Text property of the label to
PROGRAM.
Select the Font property, and click on the ellipsis to the right of its Settings box.
Click on *Oblique* in the "Font style" list and click on the *Underline* box.
Click on the OK button.

21. Double-click on the ListBox icon in the Toolbox.
Activate the Properties window, and select the BackColor property.
Click on the down-arrow button to the right of the Settings box.
Click on the Custom tab and click on the desired yellow square in the palette.
Click on the form.

23. In the Solution Explorer window, right-click on "Form1.vb" and select *Rename* from
the context menu that appears.
Change Form1.vb to frmYellow.vb, and click the *No* button in the box that appears.
Right-click on the form in the Form Designer, and click on Properties in the context menu.
Click on BackColor property in the Properties window.
Click on the down-arrow button in the right part of the Settings box, click on the
Custom tab, and click on a yellow square.

25. Begin a new program.
Change the text in the form's title bar to "Dynamic Duo".
Place two buttons on the form and position and resize as shown.

Enter "Batman" as the text of the first button, and enter "Robin" as the text of the second button.
Increase the font size for both buttons to 14.

27. Begin a new program.
Change the text in the form's title bar to "Fill in the Blank".
Place a label, a text box, and another label on the form at appropriate locations.
Change the Text setting of the first label to "I'm the king of the" and the Text setting of the second label to "A Quote by Leonardo DiCaprio".

29. Begin a new program.
Change the text in the form's title bar to "Uncle's Advice".
Place five labels and three buttons on the form at appropriate locations.
Change the Text setting of each label as indicated.
Change the settings of the buttons' Text properties to "1", "2", and "3".
Resize and position the labels and buttons.

33. 1   **35.** Each arrow key moves the text box in the indicated direction.

37. Pressing the right- and left-arrow keys widens and narrows the text boxes, buttons, and list boxes in the group of selected controls. The up- and down-arrow keys shorten and lengthen the buttons and list boxes in the group. The arrow keys have no effect on the labels, and only the left- and right-arrow keys affect the text boxes.

39. Drag a label and a list box onto the form.
Click on the label.
Hold down the Ctrl key and click on the list box. (You have now selected a group of two controls.)
In the Properties window, click on the symbol to the left of the Font property.
Click on the Size property, change the setting to 12, and press the Enter key.

(*Alternative:* Replace the last two lines with the following steps.)

In the Properties window, select the Font property.
Click on the ellipsis button to the right of the Settings box.
Click on 12 in the Size list and click on the OK button.

41. The label is positioned just to the left of the text box, and the middles of the two controls are aligned.

43. *Center* refers to the midpoint horizontally, whereas *middle* refers to the midpoint vertically.

45. First blue snap line: tops of the two controls are aligned
Purple snap line: middles of the two controls are aligned
Second blue snap line: bottoms of the two controls are aligned

47. The setting is cycling through the different available colors.

Exercises 2.3

1. The word Hello   **3.** The word Hello on an orange-colored background

5. The text box vanishes.   **7.** The word Hello in green letters

9. The word Hello on a gold background   **11.** Form1.Text should be Me.Text.

13. Red should be replaced with Color.Red.

15. Font.Size is a read-only property. The statement `txtOutput.Text = txtBox.Font.Size` is valid since it is reading the value of txtBox.Font.Size. However, `txtBox.Font.Size = 20` is not valid since it is setting the value of txtBox.Font.Size.

17. `lblTwo.Text = "E.T. phone home."`

19. `txtBox.ForeColor = Color.Red`
`txtBox.Text = "The stuff that dreams are made of."`

21. `txtBox.Enabled = False`   **23.** `lblTwo.Visible = False`

25. `btnOutcome.Enabled = True`   **27.** `txtBoxTwo.Focus()`

29. The Enter event occurs when a control gets the focus.

31.
```
Private Sub Label1_Click(...) Handles Label1.Click
    lstOutput.Items.Add("Click")
End Sub

Private Sub Label1_DoubleClick(...) Handles Label1.DoubleClick
    lstOutput.Items.Add("Double Click")
End Sub
```

Whenever the DoubleClick event is raised, the Click event is also raised.

33.
```
Private Sub btnLeft_Click(...) Handles btnLeft.Click
    txtBox.Text = "Left Justify"
    txtBox.TextAlign = HorizontalAlignment.Left
End Sub

Private Sub btnCenter_Click(...) Handles btnCenter.Click
    txtBox.Text = "Center"
    txtBox.TextAlign = HorizontalAlignment.Center
End Sub

Private Sub btnRight_Click(...) Handles btnRight.Click
    txtBox.Text = "Right Justify"
    txtBox.TextAlign = HorizontalAlignment.Right
End Sub
```

35.
```
Private Sub btnRed_Click(...) Handles btnRed.Click
    txtBox.BackColor = Color.Red
End Sub

Private Sub btnBlue_Click(...) Handles btnBlue.Click
    txtBox.BackColor = Color.Blue
End Sub

Private Sub btnWhite_Click(...) Handles btnWhite.Click
    txtBox.ForeColor = Color.White
End Sub

Private Sub btnYellow_Click(...) Handles btnYellow.Click
    txtBox.ForeColor = Color.Yellow
End Sub
```

37.
```
Private Sub txtLife_Enter(...) Handles txtLife.Enter
    txtQuote.Text = "I like life, it's something to do."
End Sub

Private Sub txtFuture_Enter(...) Handles txtFuture.Enter
    txtQuote.Text = "The future isn't what it used to be."
End Sub

Private Sub txtTruth_Enter(...) Handles txtTruth.Enter
    txtQuote.Text = "Tell the truth and run."
End Sub
```

39.
```
Private Sub btnOne_Click(...) Handles btnOne.Click
  btnOne.Visible = False
  btnTwo.Visible = True
  btnThree.Visible = True
  btnFour.Visible = True
End Sub

Private Sub btnTwo_Click(...) Handles btnTwo.Click
  btnOne.Visible = True
  btnTwo.Visible = False
  btnThree.Visible = True
  btnFour.Visible = True
End Sub

Private Sub btnThree_Click(...) Handles btnThree.Click
  btnOne.Visible = True
  btnTwo.Visible = True
  btnThree.Visible = False
  btnFour.Visible = True
End Sub

Private Sub btnFour_Click(...) Handles btnFour.Click
  btnOne.Visible = True
  btnTwo.Visible = True
  btnThree.Visible = True
  btnFour.Visible = False
End Sub
```

41.
```
Private Sub btnVanish_Click(...) Handles btnVanish.Click
  lblFace.Visible = False
End Sub

Private Sub btnReappear_Click(...) Handles btnReappear.Click
  lblFace.Visible = True
End Sub
```

43.
```
Private Sub btnAny_Click(...) Handles btnOne.Click, btnTwo.Click
  txtOutput.Text = "You just clicked on a button."
End Sub
```

CHAPTER 3

EXERCISES 3.1

1. 12   **3.** .125   **5.** 8   **7.** 2   **9.** 1   **11.** 3

13. Not valid   **15.** Valid   **17.** Not valid   **19.** 10   **21.** 16   **23.** 9

25.
```
Private Sub btnCompute_Click(...) Handles btnCompute.Click
  lstOutput.Items.Add((7 * 8) + 5)
End Sub
```

27.
```
Private Sub btnCompute_Click(...) Handles btnCompute.Click
  lstOutput.Items.Add(0.055 * 20)
End Sub
```

29.
```
Private Sub btnCompute_Click(...) Handles btnCompute.Click
  lstOutput.Items.Add(17 * (3 + 162))
End Sub
```

31.

	x	y
Private Sub btnEvaluate_Click(...) Handles btnEvaluate.Click		
Dim x, y As Double	0	0
x = 2	2	0
y = 3 * x	2	6
x = y + 5	11	6
lstResults.Items.Clear()	11	6
lstResults.Items.Add(x + 4)	11	6
y = y + 1	11	7
End Sub		

33. 6   **35.** 1   **37.** 1   **39.** 2
                    8   64   15
                    9

41. The third line should read `c = a + b`

43. The first assignment statement should not contain a comma. The second assignment statement should not contain a dollar sign.

45. 9W is not a valid variable name.

47. `Dim quantity As Integer = 12`

49. 10   **51.** 6   **53.** 3.128   **55.** −3   **57.** 0   **59.** 6

61. `cost += 5`   **63.** `cost /= 6`   **65.** `sum ^= 2`

67.
```
Private Sub btnCompute_Click(...) Handles btnCompute.Click
    Dim revenue, costs, profit As Decimal
    revenue = 98456
    costs = 45000
    profit = revenue - costs
    lstOutput.Items.Add(profit)
End Sub
```

69.
```
Private Sub btnCompute_Click(...) Handles btnCompute.Click
    Dim price, discountPercent, markdown As Decimal
    price = 19.95D
    discountPercent = 30
    markdown = (discountPercent / 100) * price
    price = price - markdown
    lstOutput.Items.Add(Math.Round(price, 2))
End Sub
```

71.
```
Private Sub btnCompute_Click(...) Handles btnCompute.Click
    Dim balance As Decimal
    balance = 100
    balance += 0.05D * balance
    balance += 0.05D * balance
    balance += 0.05D * balance
    lstOutput.Items.Add(Math.Round(balance, 2))
End Sub
```

73.
```
Private Sub btnCompute_Click(...) Handles btnCompute.Click
    Dim purchasePrice As Decimal = 215.50D
    Dim sellingPrice as Decimal = 644.99D
    Dim markup as Decimal = sellingPrice - purchasePrice
```

```
    Dim percentageMarkup as Decimal = 100 * (markup / purchasePrice)
    lstOutput.Items.Add(percentageMarkup)
End Sub
```

75.
```
Private Sub btnCompute_Click(...) Handles btnCompute.Click
    Dim acres, yieldPerAcre, corn As Double
    acres = 30
    yieldPerAcre = 18
    corn = yieldPerAcre * acres
    lstOutput.Items.Add(corn)
End Sub
```

77.
```
Private Sub btnCompute_Click(...) Handles btnCompute.Click
    Dim distance, elapsedTime, averageSpeed As Double
    distance = 233
    elapsedTime = 7 - 2
    averageSpeed = distance / elapsedTime
    lstOutput.Items.Add(averageSpeed)
End Sub
```

79.
```
Private Sub btnCompute_Click(...) Handles btnCompute.Click
    Dim waterPerPersonPerDay, people, days, waterUsed As Double
    waterPerPersonPerDay = 1600
    people = 315000000
    days = 365
    waterUsed = waterPerPersonPerDay * people * days
    lstOutput.Items.Add(waterUsed)
End Sub
```

81.
```
Private Sub btnCompute_Click(...) Handles btnCompute.Click
    Dim pizzarias, percent, restaurants As Double
    pizzarias = 70000
    percent = 0.12
    restaurants = pizzarias / percent
    lstOutput.Items.Add(Math.Round(restaurants))
End Sub
```

83.
```
Private Sub btnConvert_Click(...) Handles btnConvert.Click
    Dim conversionFactor As Double = 0.6214
    Dim kilometersPerHr, milesPerHr As Double
    kilometersPerHr = CDbl(txtSpeedKil.Text)
    milesPerHr = conversionFactor * kilometersPerHr
    txtSpeedMph.Text = milesPerHr.ToString("N")
End Sub
```

85.
```
Private Sub btnEstimate_Click(...) Handles btnEstimate.Click
    Dim cal As Double
    cal = (5280 ^ 3) * 48600
    lstCalories.Items.Add(cal)
End Sub
```

EXERCISES 3.2

1. Visual Basic   3. Ernie   5. flute   7. 123   9. Your age is 21.

11. A ROSE IS A ROSE IS A ROSE   13. 5.5   15. goodbye   17. WALLAWALLA

19. ABC
    2
    4
    55 mph
    STU

21. 12
    MUNICIPALITY
    city
    6

23. 8 (0 through 7)   25. True

27. The variable *phoneNumber* should be declared as type String, not Double.

29. "End" is a keyword and cannot be used as a variable name.

31. The IndexOf method cannot be applied to a number, only a string.

33. `2 ^ 3` is a Double value and therefore cannot be assigned to the Decimal variable *m*. Also, 4/2 is a Double value and cannot be assigned to an Integer variable.

35.
```
Private Sub btnDisplay_Click(...) Handles btnDisplay.Click
    Dim firstName, middleName, lastName As String, yearOfBirth As Integer
    firstName = "Thomas"
    middleName = "Alva"
    lastName = "Edison"
    yearOfBirth = 1847
    txtOutput.Text = firstName & " " & middleName & " " & lastName &
                     ", " & yearOfBirth
End Sub
```

37. `Dim str As String  'Place in the Declarations section.`

39.
```
Private Sub btnCompute_Click(...) Handles btnCompute.Click
    Dim distance As Double
    distance = CDbl(txtNumSec.Text) / 5
    distance = Math.Round(distance, 2)
    txtOutput.Text = "The distance of the storm is " & distance & " miles."
End Sub
```

41.
```
Private Sub btnCompute_Click(...) Handles btnCompute.Click
    Dim cycling, running, swimming, pounds As Double
    cycling = CDbl(txtCycle.Text)
    running = CDbl(txtRun.Text)
    swimming = CDbl(txtSwim.Text)
    pounds = (200 * cycling + 475 * running + 275 * swimming) / 3500
    pounds = Math.Round(pounds, 1)
    txtWtLoss.Text = pounds & " pounds were lost."
End Sub
```

43.
```
Private Sub btnAdd_Click(...) Handles btnAdd.Click
    Dim hr1, hr2, min1, min2, totalMinutes, totalHours As Integer
    hr1 = CInt(txtHours1.Text)
    hr2 = CInt(txtHours2.Text)
    min1 = CInt(txtMin1.Text)
    min2 = CInt(txtMin2.Text)
    totalMinutes = (min1 + min2) Mod 60
    totalHours = hr1 + hr2 + ((min1 + min2) \ 60)
    txtSum.Text = totalHours & " hours and " & totalMinutes & " minutes"
End Sub
```

45.
```
Private Sub btnCompute_Click(...) Handles btnCompute.Click
    Dim revenue, expenses, income As Decimal
    revenue = CDec(txtRevenue.Text)
    expenses = CDec(txtExpenses.Text)
    income = revenue - expenses
    txtNetIncome.Text = CStr(income)
End Sub
```

47.
```
Private Sub btnDisplay_Click(...) Handles btnDisplay.Click
    Dim speed, distance As Double
    distance = CDbl(txtDistanceSkidded.Text)
```

```
        speed = Math.Sqrt(24 * distance)
        speed = Math.Round(speed, 2)
        txtEstimatedSpeed.Text = speed & " mph"
    End Sub
```

49.
```
Dim number As Integer = 100  'in Declarations section

    Private Sub btnPressMe_Click(...) Handles btnPressMe.Click
      number = number - 1 'decrease number by 1
      txtOutput.Text = CStr(number)
    End Sub
```

51.
```
Dim sum As Double   'sum of the scores entered
Dim num As Integer 'number of scores entered

    Private Sub btnRecord_Click(...) Handles btnRecord.Click
      num += 1
      sum += CDbl(txtScore.Text)
      txtScore.Clear()
      txtScore.Focus()
    End Sub

    Private Sub btnCalculate_Click(...) Handles btnCalculate.Click
      txtAverage.Text = CStr(sum / num)
    End Sub
```

53.
```
    Private Sub btnCompute_Click(...) Handles btnCompute.Click
      Dim amount, percentage, tip As Decimal
      amount = CDec(txtAmount.Text)
      percentage = CDec(txtPercentage.Text)
      tip = amount * (percentage / 100)
      txtTip.Text = CStr(Math.Round(tip, 2))
    End Sub
```

55.
```
    Private Sub btnModifySentence_Click(...) Handles btnModifySentence.Click
      Dim sentence, oldWord, newWord As String
      Dim position As Integer
      sentence = txtSentence.Text
      oldWord = txtOriginalWord.Text
      newWord = txtReplacementWord.Text
      position = sentence.IndexOf(oldWord)
      txtOutput.Text = sentence.Substring(0, position) & newWord &
                       sentence.Substring(position + oldWord.Length)
    End Sub
```

57.
```
    Private Sub btnCompute_Click(...) Handles btnCompute.Click
      Dim num1, num2, sum As Double
      num1 = CDbl(txtFirstNum.Text)
      num2 = CDbl(txtSecondNum.Text)
      sum = num1 + num2
      txtSum.Text = CStr(sum)
    End Sub

    Private Sub txtEitherNum_TextChanged(...) Handles _
              txtFirstNum.TextChanged, txtSecondNum.TextChanged
      txtSum.Clear()
    End Sub
```

59.
```
    Private Sub btnCalculate_Click(...) Handles btnCalculate.Click
      Dim futureValue, interestRate, presentValue As Decimal
      Dim numYears As Integer
      futureValue = CDec(txtFutureValue.Text)
      interestRate = CDec(txtInterest.Text)
      numYears = CInt(txtYears.Text)
```

```
        presentValue = CDec(futureValue / (1 + interestRate / 100) ^ numYears)
        txtPresentValue.Text = CStr(Math.Round(presentValue, 2))
      End Sub
```

61.
```
Private Sub btnConvert_Click(...) Handles btnConvert.Click
  Dim feet, inches As Integer
  inches = CInt(txtInches.Text)
  feet = inches \ 12
  inches = inches Mod 12
  txtFeetAndInches.Text = feet & " feet and " & inches & " inches"
End Sub
```

EXERCISES 3.3

1. `1,235`   **3.** `1,234.0`   **5.** `0.0`   **7.** `-0.67`   **9.** `12,346.000`   **11.** `12`

13. `$12,346`   **15.** `($0.23)`   **17.** `$0.80`   **19.** `$0.08`   **21.** `100.00 %`

23. `66.67 %`   **25.** `Pay to France $27,267,622.00`

27. `25.6 % of the U.S. population 25+ years old are college graduates.`

29. `The likelihood of Heads is 50 %`   **31.** `10/23/2015`

33. `Thursday, November 24, 2016`   **35.** `10/2/2017`   **37.** `4/5/2019`   **39.** `29`

41. `5`   **43.** `1`   **45.** `2018`   **47.** `You might win 360 dollars.`

49. `Hello John Jones`   **51.** `$106.00`

53.
```
1234567890123456789012345678 90
Mountain    Place      Ht (ft)
K2          Kashmir    28,250
```
55.
```
12345678901234567890
Element Weight Percent
Oxygen  97.5   65.0 %
Carbon  27.0   18.0 %
```

57. The statement `n += 1` is not valid since the value of a constant cannot be changed.

59. The second line should use CDbl to convert the right-hand side to type Double.

61. (123456).ToString("N") is a string and therefore cannot be assigned to a numeric variable.

63. You must insert `.Show` after the word `MessageBox`.

65. `000`   **67.** `LLL000`   **69.** `0-00-000000-&`

71.
```
MessageBox.Show("First solve the problem. Then write the code.",
                "Good Advice")
```

73.
```
Private Sub btnDisplay_Click(...) Handles btnDisplay.Click
  Dim begOfYearCost, endOfYearCost As Decimal
  Dim percentIncrease As Decimal
  begOfYearCost = 200
  endOfYearCost = CDec(InputBox("Enter cost at the end of the year:"))
  percentIncrease = (endOfYearCost - begOfYearCost) / begOfYearCost
  txtOutput.Text = "The increase in cost for the year is " &
                  percentIncrease.ToString("P") & "."
End Sub
```

75.
```
Private Sub txtPhoneNumber_Enter(...) Handles txtPhoneNumber.Enter
  MessageBox.Show("Be sure to include the area code!", "Reminder")
End Sub
```

77.
```
Private Sub btnDisplay_Click(...) Handles btnDisplay.Click
  Dim firstDayOfYr, firstDayOfNextYr As Date
```

```
        Dim numDays As Double
        firstDayOfYr = CDate("1/1/" & mtbYear.Text)
        firstDayOfNextYr = firstDayOfYr.AddYears(1)
        numDays = DateDiff(DateInterval.Day, firstDayOfYr, firstDayOfNextYr)
        txtNumDays.Text = CStr(numDays)
    End Sub
```

79.
```
    Private Sub Determine_Click(...) Handles btnDetermine.Click
        Dim dt As Date = CDate(mtbDate.Text)
        Dim laterDate = dt.AddYears(10)
        Dim fullDate As String = laterDate.ToString("D")
        Dim position As Integer = fullDate.IndexOf(",")
        Dim dayOfWeek As String = fullDate.Substring(0, position)
        txtDayOfWeek.Text = dayOfWeek
    End Sub
```

81.
```
    Private Sub btnConvert_Click(...) Handles btnConvert.Click
        Dim dt As Date
        dt = CDate(txtUS.Text)
        txtEurope.Text = dt.Day & "/" & dt.Month & "/" & dt.Year
    End Sub
```

83.
```
    Private Sub Determine_Click(...) Handles btnDetermine.Click
        Dim month, yr As Integer 'month given as 1 through 12
        Dim dt, dt2 As Date
        Dim numDays As Double
        month = CInt(txtMonth.Text)
        yr = CInt(mtbYear.Text)
        dt = CDate(month & "/1/" & yr)
        dt2 = dt.AddMonths(1)
        numDays = DateDiff(DateInterval.Day, dt, dt2)
        txtNumDays.Text = CStr(numDays)
    End Sub
```

85.
```
    Private Sub btnCalculate_Click(...) Handles btnCalculate.Click
        Dim begSalary, salary As Decimal
        begSalary = CDec(txtBeginningSalary.Text)
        salary = begSalary + 0.1D * begSalary
        salary = salary - 0.1D * salary
        txtNewSalary.Text = salary.ToString("C")
        txtChange.Text = ((salary - begSalary) / begSalary).ToString("P")
    End Sub
```

87.
```
    Private Sub btnCalculate_Click(...) Handles btnCalculate.Click
        Dim distance As Double
        distance = CDbl(txtDistance.Text)
        txtFare.Text = (0.8 + 0.2 * (Int(4 * distance))).ToString("C")
    End Sub
```

CHAPTER 4

EXERCISES 4.1

1. `hi`   **3.** `The letter before G is F`

5. `"We're all in this alone." - Lily Tomlin`

7. True   **9.** True   **11.** True   **13.** True   **15.** False   **17.** False   **19.** True   **21.** True

23. False   **25.** False   **27.** False   **29.** True   **31.** Equivalent   **33.** Not equivalent

35. Equivalent   **37.** Not equivalent   **39.** `a <= b`   **41.** `(a >= b) Or (c = d)`

43. `(a = "") Or (a >= b) Or (a.Length >= 5)`

[In Exercises 45 and 47, execute a statement of the form `txtOutput.Text = CStr(Boolean expression)`.]

45. True   **47.** True   **49.** False   **51.** False   **53.** True   **55.** True   **57.** False   **59.** True

61.
```
Private Sub btnFind_Click(...) Handles btnFind.Click
    'Find the position of a letter in the alphabet
    Dim letter As String, position As Integer
    letter = txtLetter.Text.ToUpper
    position = Asc(letter) - 64
    txtPosition.Text = CStr(position)
End Sub
```

EXERCISES 4.2

1. `Less than ten.`   **3.** `Your change contains 3 dollars.`

5. `To be, or not to be.`   **7.** `Hi`   **9.** `You are old enough to vote in 7 days.`

11. Syntax error. Third line should be `If ((1 < num) And (num < 3)) Then`

13. Syntax error. Fourth line should be `If ((major = "Business") Or (major = "Computer Science")) Then`

15. `a = 5`

17.
```
message = "Is Alaska bigger than Texas and California combined?"
answer = InputBox(message)
If (answer.Substring(0, 1).ToUpper = "Y") Then
  txtOutput.Text = "Correct"
Else
  txtOutput.Text = "Wrong"
End If
```

19.
```
If IsNumeric(txtBox.Text) AndAlso (CDbl(txtBox.Text) < 0) Then
    MessageBox.Show("negative")
End If
```

21.
```
Private Sub btnCompute_Click(...) Handles btnCompute.Click
    Dim cost, tip As Decimal
    cost = CDec(txtAmount.Text)
    tip = cost * 0.18D
    If tip < 1 Then
        tip = 1
    End If
    txtOutput.Text = tip.ToString("C")
End Sub
```

23.
```
Private Sub btnCompute_Click(...) Handles btnCompute.Click
    Dim num, cost As Decimal
    num = CDec(txtNumber.Text)
    If num < 100 Then
        cost = 0.25D * num  '25 cents each
    Else
        cost = 0.2D * num   '20 cents each
    End If
    txtOutput.Text = cost.ToString("C")
End Sub
```

25.
```
Private Sub btnAskQuestion_Click(...) Handles btnAskQuestion.Click
    Dim name As String
    name = (txtAnswer.Text).ToUpper
    If name = "WILLARD SCOTT" Then
        txtOutput.Text = "Correct."
    Else
        txtOutput.Text = "Nice try."
    End If
End Sub
```

27.
```
Private Sub btnCompute_Click(...) Handles btnCompute.Click
    Dim s1, s2, s3 As Double '3 scores
    Dim avg As Double        'average of the two highest scores
    s1 = CDbl(txtScore1.Text)
    s2 = CDbl(txtScore2.Text)
    s3 = CDbl(txtScore3.Text)
    If (s1 <= s2) And (s1 <= s3) Then      's1 is smallest number
        avg = (s2 + s3) / 2
    ElseIf (s2 <= s1) And (s2 <= s3) Then  's2 is smallest number
        avg = (s1 + s3) / 2
    Else                                   's3 is smallest number
        avg = (s1 + s2) / 2
    End If
    txtAverage.Text = CStr(avg)
End Sub
```

29.
```
Private Sub btnCompute_Click(...) Handles btnCompute.Click
    Dim weight, cost, amount, change As Decimal
    weight = CDec(txtWeight.Text)
    amount = CDec(txtAmount.Text)
    cost = weight * 2.5D
    If (amount >= cost) Then
        change = amount - cost
        txtOutput.Text = "Your change is " & change.ToString("C") & "."
    Else
        txtOutput.Text = "I need " & (cost - amount).ToString("C") & " more."
    End If
End Sub
```

31.
```
Private Sub btnQuit_Click(...) Handles btnQuit.Click
    'Quit?
    Dim answer As String
    answer = InputBox("Do you really want to quit? (Y/N)")
    answer = answer.Substring(0, 1).ToUpper
    If (answer = "Y") Then
        Me.Close()
    End If
End Sub
```

33.
```
Dim numLines As Integer = 0  'in Declarations section
'numLines tells the number of lines that have been displayed.

Private Sub btnBogart_Click(...) Handles btnBogart.Click
  If numLines = 0 Then
    lstOutput.Items.Add("I came to Casablanca for the waters.")
    numLines += 1
  ElseIf numLines = 2 Then
    lstOutput.Items.Add("I was misinformed.")
    numLines += 1
  End If
End Sub

Private Sub btnRaines_Click(...) Handles btnRaines.Click
  If numLines = 1 Then
    lstOutput.Items.Add("But we're in the middle of the desert.")
    numLines += 1
  End If
End Sub
```

35.
```
Private Sub btnConvertToRegular_Click(...) Handles _
                              btnConvertToRegular.Click
  Dim partOfDay As String
  Dim time As String = mtbMilitary.Text
  Dim hours As Integer = CInt(time.Substring(0, 2))
  Dim minutes As String = time.Substring(2, 2)
  If hours >= 12 Then
    partOfDay = "pm"
  Else
    partOfDay = "am"
  End If
  If time = "0000" Then
    txtRegular.Text = "midnight"
  ElseIf time = "1200" Then
    txtRegular.Text = "noon"
  ElseIf hours = 0 Or hours = 12 Then
    txtRegular.Text = "12:" & minutes & " " & partOfDay
  Else
    txtRegular.Text = (hours Mod 12) & ":" & minutes & " " & partOfDay
  End If
End Sub
```

37.
```
Dim numGuesses As Integer = 0

Private Sub btnEvaluate_Click(...) Handles btnEvaluate.Click
  'Assume that the Text property of txtNumberOfGuesses
  'was set to 0 in the Form Designer.
  numGuesses += 1
  txtNumberOfGuesses.Text = CStr(numGuesses)

  Dim msg As String
  If txtAnswer.Text.ToUpper.IndexOf("COOLIDGE") <> -1 Then
    MessageBox.Show("Calvin Coolidge was born on July 4, 1872.",
                "Correct")

    Me.Close()
  ElseIf CInt(numGuesses) = 10 Then
    msg = "Calvin Coolidge was born on July 4, 1872."
    MessageBox.Show(msg, "You've Run Out of Guesses")
    Me.Close()
  Else
    If CInt(numGuesses) = 3 Then
      msg = "He once said, 'If you don't say anything," &
      " you won't be called upon to repeat it.'"
```

```vb
      ElseIf CInt(numGuesses) = 7 Then
        msg = "His nickname was 'Silent Cal.'"
      Else
        msg = "Sorry!"
      End If
      MessageBox.Show(msg, "Incorrect")
    End If
    txtAnswer.Clear()
    txtAnswer.Focus()
  End Sub
```

39.
```vb
Private Sub btnDetermine_Click(...) Handles btnDetermine.Click
    Dim dob As Date = CDate(txtDOB.Text)
    Dim numDays As Double
    Dim birthdayToUse As Date
    birthdayToUse = CDate(dob.Month & "/" & dob.Day & "/" & Today.Year)
    If birthdayToUse < Today Then
      birthdayToUse = birthdayToUse.AddYears(1)
    End If
    numDays = DateDiff(DateInterval.Day, Today, birthdayToUse)
    If numDays = 0 Then
      MessageBox.Show("HAPPY BIRTHDAY")
    End If
    txtNumDays.Text = CStr(numDays)
    txtToday.Text = CStr(Today)
  End Sub
```

41.
```vb
Private Sub Determine_Click(...) Handles btnDetermine.Click
    Dim dt, dt2 As Date
    Dim approximateAge As Double
    dt = CDate(mtbDate.Text)
    approximateAge = DateDiff(DateInterval.Year, dt, Today)
    dt2 = dt.AddYears(CInt(approximateAge))
    If Today < dt2 Then
      txtAge.Text = CStr(approximateAge - 1)
    Else
      txtAge.Text = CStr(approximateAge)
    End If
  End Sub
```

43.
```vb
Private Sub btnCompute_Click(...) Handles lblDetermine.Click
    Dim day As String
    Dim day1, day2 As Date
    Dim numDays As Double
    day = "1/1/" & txtYear.Text
    day1 = CDate(day)
    day2 = day1.AddYears(1)
    numDays = DateDiff(DateInterval.Day, day1, day2)
    If numDays = 366 Then
      txtLeapYear.Text = "YES"
    Else
      txtLeapYear.Text = "NO"
    End If
  End Sub
```

45.
```vb
Private Sub btnDetermine_Click(...) Handles btnDetermine.Click
    Dim gpa As Double = CDbl(txtGPA.Text)
    Dim honors As String = ""
    If gpa >= 3.9 Then
      honors = " summa cum laude."
    End If
```

```
        If (3.6 <= gpa) And (gpa < 3.9) Then
          honors = " magna cum laude."
        End If
        If (3.3 <= gpa) And (gpa < 3.6) Then
          honors = " cum laude."
        End If
        If (2 <= gpa) And (gpa < 3.3) Then
          honors = "."
        End If
        txtOutput.Text = "You graduated" & honors
      End Sub
```

47. ```
    Private Sub btnFind_Click(...) Handles btnFind.Click
        Dim largestNum As Double = CDbl(txtFirstNum.Text)
        If CDbl(txtSecondNum.Text) > largestNum Then
          largestNum = CDbl(txtSecondNum.Text)
        End If
        If CDbl(txtThirdNum.Text) > largestNum Then
          largestNum = CDbl(txtThirdNum.Text)
        End If
        txtLargestNum.Text = CStr(largestNum)
      End Sub
    ```

49. ```
    Private Sub btnCalculate_Click(...) Handles btnCalculate.Click
        'Buy two, get one free sale
        Dim cost1, cost2, cost3, minimumCost As Decimal
        cost1 = CDec(txtCostOfItem1.Text)
        cost2 = CDec(txtCostOfItem2.Text)
        cost3 = CDec(txtCostOfItem3.Text)
        minimumCost = cost1
        If cost2 < minimumCost Then
          minimumCost = cost2
        End If
        If cost3 < minimumCost Then
          minimumCost = cost3
        End If
        txtTotalCost.Text = (cost1 + cost2 + cost3 -
                            minimumCost).ToString("C")

      End Sub
    ```

51. ```
    Private Sub btnDetermine_Click(...) Handles btnDetermine.Click
        'Sort three numbers.
        Dim max, min As Double
        max = CDbl(txtNum1.Text)
        If CDbl(txtNum2.Text) > max Then
          max = CDbl(txtNum2.Text)
        End If
        If CDbl(txtNum3.Text) > max Then
          max = CDbl(txtNum3.Text)
        End If
        txtMax.Text = CStr(max)
        min = CDbl(txtNum1.Text)
        If CDbl(txtNum2.Text) < min Then
          min = CDbl(txtNum2.Text)
        End If
        If CDbl(txtNum3.Text) < min Then
          min = CDbl(txtNum3.Text)
        End If
        txtMin.Text = CStr(min)
        If (CDbl(txtNum1.Text) < max) AndAlso (CDbl(txtNum1.Text) > min) Then
          txtMiddle.Text = txtNum1.Text
        End If
    ```
    ```

```
      If (CDbl(txtNum2.Text) < max) AndAlso (CDbl(txtNum2.Text) > min) Then
        txtMiddle.Text = txtNum2.Text
      End If
      If (CDbl(txtNum3.Text) < max) AndAlso (CDbl(txtNum3.Text) > min) Then
        txtMiddle.Text = txtNum3.Text
      End If
    End Sub
```

EXERCISES 4.3

1. The price is $3.75
The price is $3.75

3. Mesozoic Era
Paleozoic Era
?

5. The equation has no real solutions.
The equation has two solutions.
The equation has exactly one solution.

7. Should have a Case clause before the 4th line.

9. `Case nom = "Bob"` should be `Case "Bob"`

11. Logic error: `>= "Peach"` should be `>= "PEACH"`.
Syntax error: `"ORANGE TO PEACH"` should be `"ORANGE" To "PEACH"`.

13. Valid   **15.** Invalid   **17.** Valid

19.
```
Select Case a
  Case 1
    txtOutput.Text = "one"
  Case Is > 5
    txtOutput.Text = "two"
End Select
```

21.
```
Select Case a
  Case 2
    txtOutput.Text = "maybe"
  Case Is > 5
    txtOutput.Text = "no"
End Select
```

23.
```
Private Sub btnDescribe_Click(...) Handles btnDescribe.Click
  Dim percent As Integer
  percent = CInt(txtPercent.Text)
  Select Case percent
    Case 0 To 30
      txtOutput.Text = "Clear"
    Case 31 To 70
      txtOutput.Text = "Partly cloudy"
    Case 71 To 99
      txtOutput.Text = "Cloudy"
    Case 100
      txtOutput.Text = "Overcast"
    Case Else
      txtOutput.Text = "Percentage must be between 0 and 100."
  End Select
End Sub
```

25.
```
Private Sub btnCompute_Click(...) Handles btnCompute.Click
  Dim shapeNum As Integer
  Dim radius, length, height, width As Double
  'Input choice of shape and its dimensions
  '1. Circle   2. Parallelogram   3. Kite
```

```
      shapeNum = CInt(mtbSelection.Text)      'mask is 0
      Select Case shapeNum
        Case 1
          radius = CDbl(InputBox("Input the radius of the circle: "))
          txtArea.Text = CStr(3.141593 * radius ^ 2)
        Case 2
          length = CDbl(InputBox("Input the length of the parallelogram: "))
          height = CDbl(InputBox("Input the height of the parallelogram: "))
          txtArea.Text = CStr(length * height)
        Case 3
          length = CDbl(InputBox("Input the length of the kite: "))
          width = CDbl(InputBox("Input the width of the kite: "))
          txtArea.Text = CStr((length * width) / 2)
        Case Else
          MessageBox.Show("Your choice is not valid.", "Try Again.")
          mtbSelection.Clear()
      End Select
      mtbSelection.Focus()
    End Sub
```

27.
```
    Private Sub btnAssign_Click(...) Handles btnAssign.Click
      Dim score As Integer, letterGrade As String
      score = CInt(txtNumericalGrade.Text)
      Select Case score
        Case 90 To 100
          letterGrade = "A"
        Case 80 To 89
          letterGrade = "B"
        Case 70 To 79
          letterGrade = "C"
        Case 60 To 69
          letterGrade = "D"
        Case 0 To 59
          letterGrade = "F"
        Case Else
          letterGrade = "Invalid"
      End Select
      txtOutput.Text = letterGrade
    End Sub
```

29.
```
    Private Sub btnDescribe_Click(...) Handles btnDetermine.Click
      Dim amountRecovered, payment As Decimal
      amountRecovered = CDec(txtAmount.Text)
      Select Case amountRecovered
        Case Is <= 75000
          payment = 0.1D * amountRecovered
        Case Is <= 100000
          payment = 7500 + 0.05D * (amountRecovered - 75000)
        Case Is > 100000
          payment = 8750 + 0.01D * (amountRecovered - 100000)
          If payment > 50000 Then
            payment = 50000
          End If
      End Select
      txtOutput.Text = payment.ToString("C")
    End Sub
```

31.
```
    Private Sub btnDetermine_Click(...) Handles btnDetermine.Click
      Dim tin As String = mtbTIN.Text
      Dim finalDigit As String = tin.Substring(3, 1)
```

```
        Dim suffix As String
        Select Case finalDigit
            Case "1"
                suffix = "st"
            Case "2"
                suffix = "nd"
            Case "3"
                suffix = "rd"
            Case Else
                suffix = "th"
        End Select
        txtYear.Text = "20" & tin.Substring(0, 2)
        txtWeek.Text = tin.Substring(2, 2) & suffix
    End Sub
```

33.
```
    Private Sub btnEvaluate_Click(...) Handles btnEvaluate.Click
        Dim amount, cost, costPerOzWithIncrease As Decimal
        Dim costPerOzWithDiscount As Decimal
        Dim betterOffer As String
        amount = 18
        cost = 9
        costPerOzWithIncrease = cost / (1.5D * amount)
        costPerOzWithDiscount = (0.65D * cost) / amount
        txt50percentMore.Text = costPerOzWithIncrease.ToString("C4")
        txt35percentDiscount.Text = costPerOzWithDiscount.ToString("C4")
        Select Case costPerOzWithIncrease - costPerOzWithDiscount
            Case Is > 0
                betterOffer = "35% discount"
            Case Is < 0
                betterOffer = "50% more"
            Case Else
                betterOffer = "same value"
        End Select
        txtBetterOffer.Text = betterOffer
    End Sub
```

35.
```
    Private Sub btnDisplay_Click(...) Handles btnDisplay.Click
        Dim pres, state, trivia, whichBush As String
        pres = txtLastName.Text
        Select Case pres.ToUpper
            Case "CARTER"
                state = "Georgia"
                trivia = "The only soft drink served in the Carter " &
                         "White House was Coca-Cola."
            Case "REAGAN"
                state = "California"
                trivia = "His secret service code name was Rawhide."
            Case "BUSH"
                state = "Texas"
                whichBush = InputBox("Are his middle initials HW or W?")
                Select Case whichBush.ToUpper
                    Case "HW"
                        trivia = "He celebrated his 85th birthday by parachuting " &
                                 "out of an airplane."
                    Case "W"
                        trivia = "He once owned the Texas Rangers baseball team."
                End Select
            Case "CLINTON"
                state = "Arkansas"
                trivia = "In college he did a good imitation of Elvis Presley."
```

```
        Case "OBAMA"
          state = "Illinois"
          trivia = "He was the eighth left-handed president."
        Case Else
          state = ""
          trivia = ""
      End Select
      If state <> "" Then
        lstOutput.Items.Clear()
        lstOutput.Items.Add("President " & pres & "'s" &
                            " home state was " & state & ".")
      lstOutput.Items.Add(trivia)
      End If
    End Sub
```

EXERCISES 4.4

1. The word "Income" becomes the caption embedded in the top of GroupBox1.

3. The CheckBox1 check box becomes (or remains) unchecked.

5. The radio button becomes (or remains) unselected.

7. The radio button's caption becomes "Clear <u>A</u>ll" when the Alt key is pressed.

9. `RadioButton1.Text = "Yes"`   **11.** `CheckBox1.Checked = True`

13. RadioButton2 is on and RadioButton1 is off.   **15.** Yes

17.
```
Private Sub CheckedChanged(...) Handles _
      radDeluxe.CheckedChanged, radSuper.CheckedChanged,
      chkUpgradedVideo.CheckedChanged, chkModem.CheckedChanged,
      chkMemory.CheckedChanged
    If radDeluxe.Checked Or radSuper.Checked Then
      Dim cost As Decimal = 0
      'Add amounts to the cost based upon selections.
      If radDeluxe.Checked Then
        cost += 1000
      Else    'Super model
        cost += 1500
      End If
      If chkUpgradedVideo.Checked Then
        cost += 200
      End If
      If chkModem.Checked Then
        cost += 30
      End If
      If chkMemory.Checked Then
        cost += 120
      End If
      txtTotalCost.Text = cost.ToString("C")
    Else
      MessageBox.Show("You must first select a model!")
    End If
  End Sub
```

19.
```
Private Sub btnVote_Click(...) Handles btnVote.Click
    If radCandidate1.Checked Then
      txtVote.Text = "You voted for Kennedy."
    ElseIf radCandidate2.Checked Then
      txtVote.Text = "You voted for Nixon."
```

```
      Else
         txtVote.Text = "You voted for neither."
      End If
   End Sub

   Private Sub btnClear_Click(...) Handles btnClear.Click
      radCandidate1.Checked = False
      radCandidate2.Checked = False
   End Sub
```

21.
```
   Private Sub btnRecord_Click(...) Handles btnRecord.Click
      Dim majorSelected As Boolean
      Dim yearSelected As Boolean
      If lstMajors.Text = "" Then
         majorSelected = False
      Else
         majorSelected = True
      End If
      If (radFrosh.Checked Or radSoph.Checked Or radJunior.Checked Or
                          radSenior.Checked) Then
         yearSelected = True
      Else
         yearSelected = False
      End If
      If majorSelected And yearSelected Then
         MessageBox.Show("Information Processed")
      ElseIf Not majorSelected Then
         If Not yearSelected Then
            MessageBox.Show("You must select a Major and a Year.")
         Else
            MessageBox.Show("You must select a Major.")
         End If
      Else
         MessageBox.Show("You must select a Year.")
      End If
   End Sub
```

23.
```
   Private Sub CheckedChanged(...) Handles _
               chkSenior.CheckedChanged, chkBlind.CheckedChanged,
               chkSpouse.CheckedChanged, chkSpouseBlind.CheckedChanged
      Dim count As Integer = 0
      If chkSenior.Checked Then
         count += 1
      End If
      If chkBlind.Checked Then
         count += 1
      End If
      If chkSpouse.Checked Then
         count += 1
      End If
      If chkSpouseBlind.Checked Then
         count += 1
      End If
      txtOutput.Text = CStr(count)
   End Sub
```

25.
```
   Private Sub btnCalculate_Click(...) Handles btnCalculate.Click
      Dim fee As Decimal = 0
      If radAdult.Checked Or radSenior.Checked Then
```

```
              Dim numExtras As Integer = 0
              If chkTennis.Checked Then
                numExtras += 1
              End If
              If chkLocker.Checked Then
                numExtras += 1
              End If
              If chkLaundry.Checked Then
                numExtras += 1
              End If
              If radAdult.Checked Then
                fee = 100 + (numExtras * 25)
              Else
                fee = 75 + (numExtras * 25)
              End If
              txtFee.Text = fee.ToString("C")
            Else
              MessageBox.Show("You must select a membership category.")
            End If
          End Sub
```

27.
```
    Private Sub btnCompute_Click () Handles btnCompute.Click
        Dim ageOnPlanet, ageInEarthDays, ageInEarthYears As Double
        Dim dt As Date = CDate(mtbDayOfBirth.Text)
        Dim nom As String
        Dim noResponse As Boolean = False
        txtToday.Text = Today.ToString("D")
        ageInEarthDays = DateDiff(DateInterval.Day, dt, Today)
        ageInEarthYears = ageInEarthDays / 365.26
        If radMercury.Checked Then
          ageOnPlanet = ageInEarthDays / 88
          nom = " Mercurian "
        ElseIf radVenus.Checked Then
          ageOnPlanet = ageInEarthDays / 224.7
          nom = " Venusian "
        ElseIf radEarth.Checked Then
          ageOnPlanet = ageInEarthYears
          nom = " Earth "
        ElseIf radMars.Checked Then
          ageOnPlanet = ageInEarthDays / 687
          nom = " Martian "
        ElseIf radJupiter.Checked Then
          ageOnPlanet = ageInEarthYears / 11.86
          nom = " Jovian "
        ElseIf radSaturn.Checked Then
          ageOnPlanet = ageInEarthYears / 29.46
          nom = " Saturian "
        ElseIf radUranus.Checked Then
          ageOnPlanet = ageInEarthYears / 84.07
          nom = " Uranian "
        ElseIf radNeptune.Checked Then
          ageOnPlanet = ageInEarthYears / 164.8
          nom = " Neptunian "
        Else
          noResponse = True
        End If
        If noResponse Then
          MessageBox.Show("You must select a planet.")
        Else
          txtAgeInDays.Text = ageOnPlanet.ToString("N1") & nom & "years"
        End If
    End Sub
```

29.
```
Private Sub btnCalculate_Click(...) Handles btnCalculate.Click
    'Compound interest
    Dim intRate As Decimal    'interest per period
    Dim n As Integer          'number of interest periods
    If (lstRates.SelectedIndex <> -1) AndAlso
       (lstCompounding.SelectedIndex <> -1) Then
      Select Case lstRates.Text
        Case "2%"
          intRate = 0.02D
        Case "2.5%"
          intRate = 0.025D
        Case "3%"
          intRate = 0.03D
        Case "3.5%"
          intRate = 0.035D
        Case "4%"
          intRate = 0.04D
      End Select
      Select Case lstCompounding.Text
        Case "annually"
          n = 1
        Case "semi-annually"
          n = 2
        Case "quarterly"
          n = 4
        Case "monthly"
          n = 12
        Case "weekly"
          n = 52
      End Select
      txtAmount.Text = (10000 * (1 + intRate / n) ^ (5 * n)).ToString("C")
    Else
      MessageBox.Show("You must select an item from each list box.")
    End If
End Sub
```

31.
```
Private Sub lstProperties_SelectedIndexChanged(...) Handles _
           lstProperties.SelectedIndexChanged
    'Railroad properties in Monopoly
    If lstProperties.Text = "Short Line" Then
      MessageBox.Show("Short Line is a bus company.", "Correct")
    Else
      MessageBox.Show("It is an actual railroad.", "Incorrect")
    End If
End Sub
```

CHAPTER 5

EXERCISES 5.1

1. 59   **3.** The population will double in 24 years.   **5.** 27 is an odd number.

7. Your state income tax is $150.00.   **9.** age before beauty

11. The function header should end with "As String", not "As Integer".

13.
```
Private Sub btnDetermine_Click(...) Handles btnDetermine.Click
    Dim radius, height As Double
    radius = CDbl(txtRadius.Text)
    height = CDbl(txtHeight.Text)
    txtAmount.Text = TinArea(radius, height) & " square centimeters"
End Sub
```

```
Function TinArea(radius As Double, ht As Double) As Double
  'Calculate surface area of a cylindrical can.
  Return 6.283 * (radius ^ 2 + radius * ht)
End Function
```

15.
```
Private Sub btnDetermine_Click(...) Handles btnDetermine.Click
  Dim speed As Double = CDbl(txtSpeed.Text)
  If Category(speed) = "" Then
    txtOutcome.Text = "Not a hurricane."
  Else
    txtOutcome.Text = "Category " & Category(speed) & " hurricane."
  End If
End Sub

Function Category(speed As Double) As String
  If speed < 74 Then
    Return ""
  ElseIf speed <= 95 Then
    Return "One"
  ElseIf speed <= 110 Then
    Return "Two"
  ElseIf speed <= 130 Then
    Return "Three"
  ElseIf speed <= 155 Then
    Return "Four"
  Else
    Return "Five"
  End If
End Function
```

17.
```
Private Sub btnDetermine_Click(...) Handles btnDetermine.Click
  Dim popcorn, butter, bucket, price As Decimal 'amount in dollars
  popcorn = CDec(txtPopcorn.Text)
  bucket = CDec(txtBucket.Text)
  butter = CDec(txtButter.Text)
  price = CDec(txtPrice.Text)
  txtProfit.Text = (Profit(popcorn, butter, bucket, price)).ToString("C")
End Sub

Function Profit(popcorn As Decimal, butter As Decimal,
               bucket As Decimal, price As Decimal) As Decimal
  'Calculate the profit on a bucket of popcorn
  Return price - (popcorn + butter + bucket)
End Function
```

19.
```
Private Sub btnCompute_Click(...) Handles btnCompute.Click
  Dim weight As Double
  weight = CDbl(txtWeight.Text)
  txtOutput.Text = (Cost(weight)).ToString("C")
End Sub

Function Ceil(x As Double) As Double
  Return -Int(-x)
End Function

Function Cost(weight As Double) As Double
  Return 0.05 + 0.1 * Ceil(weight - 1)
End Function
```

21.
```
Private Sub btnDetermine_Click(...) Handles btnDetermine.Click
  Dim x, y, z As Double
  x = CDbl(txtNum1.Text)
```

```vb
      y = CDbl(txtNum2.Text)
      z = CDbl(txtNum3.Text)
      txtMaximum.Text = CStr(Maximum(x, y, z))
    End Sub

    Function Maximum(x As Double, y As Double, z As Double) As Double
      Dim max As Double
      max = x
      If y > max Then
        max = y
      End If
      If z > max Then
        max = z
      End If
      Return max
    End Function
```

23.
```vb
    Private Sub btnAddressNGreet_Click(...) Handles btnAddressNGreet.Click
      Dim name As String
      name = txtName.Text
      lstOutput.Items.Add("The Honorable " & name)
      lstOutput.Items.Add("United States Senate")
      lstOutput.Items.Add("Washington, DC 20001")
      lstOutput.Items.Add("")
      lstOutput.Items.Add("Dear Senator " & LastName(name) & ",")
    End Sub

    Function LastName(name As String) As String
      Dim spacePos As Integer
      spacePos = name.IndexOf(" ")
      Return name.Substring(spacePos + 1)
    End Function
```

25.
```vb
    Private Sub btnDetermine_Click(...) Handles btnDetermine.Click
      If IsLeapYear(CInt(mtbYear.Text)) Then    'mask is 0000
        txtOutput.Text = mtbYear.Text & " is a leap year."
      Else
        txtOutput.Text = mtbYear.Text & " is not a leap year."
      End If
    End Sub

    Function IsLeapYear(yr As Integer) As Boolean
      Dim date1 As Date = CDate("#1/1/" & yr & "#")
      Dim date2 As Date = CDate("#1/1/" & (yr + 1) & "#")
      If DateDiff(DateInterval.Day, date1, date2) = 366 Then
        Return True
      Else
        Return False
      End If
    End Function
```

27.
```vb
    Private Sub btnCalculate_Click(...) Handles btnCalculate.Click
      'College tuition
      Dim resident As Boolean = False, undergraduate As Boolean = False
      Dim numCredits As Integer
      If IsNumeric(txtNumCredits.Text) Then
        numCredits = CInt(txtNumCredits.Text)
        If radYes.Checked Then
          resident = True
        End If
```

```
          If radUndergraduate.Checked Then
            undergraduate = True
          End If
          txtTuition.Text = (CalculateTuition(numCredits, resident,
                         undergraduate)).ToString("C")
       Else
          MessageBox.Show("You must enter the number of credits.",
                      "Missing Input")
       End If
   End Sub


   Function CalculateCostPerCredit(resident As Boolean,
                               undergraduate As Boolean) As Decimal
      If resident Then
        If undergraduate Then
          Return 90
        Else
          Return 110
        End If
      Else
        If undergraduate Then
          Return 150
        Else
          Return 180
        End If
      End If
   End Function


   Function CalculateTuition(numCredits As Integer, resident As Boolean,
                          undergraduate As Boolean) As Decimal
      Return numCredits * CalculateCostPerCredit(resident, undergraduate)
   End Function
```

29.
```
   Function Embed(strVar1 As String, strVar2 As String, n As Integer) As String
      If (n < 0) OrElse (n > strVar1.Length) Then
         MessageBox.Show("Task cannot be completed.")
         Exit Function
      End If
      Dim strVar3 As String = strVar1.Substring(0, n)
      Dim strVar4 As String = strVar1.Substring(n)
      Return strVar3 & strVar2 & strVar4
   End Function
```

EXERCISES 5.2

1. 88 keys on a piano

3. You look dashing in blue.

5. 1440 minutes in a day

7. Why do clocks run clockwise?

   Because they were invented in the northern
   hemisphere where sundials go clockwise.

9. It was the best of times.
   It was the worst of times.

11. divorced
    beheaded
    died
    divorced
    beheaded
    survived

13. 24 blackbirds
    baked in
    a pie.

15. `The first 6 letters are Visual.`   **17.** `Cost: $250.00`
`Shipping cost: $15.00`
`Total cost: $265.00`

19. `You passed with a grade of 92.`

21. There is a parameter in the Sub procedure, but no argument in the statement calling the Sub procedure.

23. Since "Handles" is a keyword, it cannot be used as the name of a Sub procedure.

25.
```
Private Sub btnDisplay_Click(...) Handles btnDisplay.Click
    Dim num As Integer = 7
    Lucky(num)
End Sub

Sub Lucky(num As Integer)
    txtOutput.Text = num & " is a lucky number."
End Sub
```

27.
```
Private Sub btnDisplay_Click(...) Handles btnDisplay.Click
    Tallest("redwood", 362)
    Tallest("pine", 223)
End Sub

Sub Tallest(tree As String, ht As Double)
    lstBox.Items.Add("The tallest " & tree &
                    " tree in the U.S. is " & ht & " feet.")
End Sub
```

29.
```
Private Sub btnDisplay_Click(...) Handles btnDisplay.Click
    DisplayHeader()
    Majors(0.146, "business")
    Majors(0.035, "computer science")
End Sub

Sub DisplayHeader()
    Dim phrase As String
    phrase = "Intended majors of freshmen in 2014:"
    lstOutput.Items.Add(phrase)
End Sub

Sub Majors(percentOfStudents As Double, field As String)
    'Display the information about the major
    lstOutput.Items.Add(field & ": " & percentOfStudents.ToString("P"))
End Sub
```

31.
```
Private Sub btnDisplay_Click(...) Handles btnDisplay.Click
    Dim num As Double
    lstOutput.Items.Clear()
    num = CDbl(txtBox.Text)
    Sum(num)
    Product(num)
End Sub

Sub Sum(num As Double)
    Dim phrase As String
    phrase = "Sum of favorite number with itself: "
    lstOutput.Items.Add(phrase & (num + num))
End Sub
```

```
        Sub Product(num As Double)
          Dim phrase As String
          phrase = "Product of favorite number with itself: "
          lstOutput.Items.Add(phrase & (num * num))
        End Sub
```

33.
```
    Private Sub btnDisplay_Click(...) Handles btnDisplay.Click
        ShowVerse("lamb", "baa")
        ShowVerse("duck", "quack")
        ShowVerse("firefly", "blink")
    End Sub

    Sub ShowVerse(animal As String, sound As String)
      'Display a verse from Old McDonald Had a Farm
      lstOutput.Items.Add("Old McDonald had a farm. Eyi eyi oh.")
      lstOutput.Items.Add("And on his farm he had a " & animal &
                      ". Eyi eyi oh.")
      lstOutput.Items.Add("With a " & sound & " " & sound & " here, and a " &
                      sound & " " & sound & " there.")
      lstOutput.Items.Add("Here a " & sound & ", there a " & sound &
                      ", everywhere a " & sound & " " & sound & ".")
      lstOutput.Items.Add("Old McDonald had a farm. Eyi eyi oh.")
      lstOutput.Items.Add("")
    End Sub
```

35.
```
    Private Sub btnDetermine_Click(...) Handles btnDetermine.Click
        Dim grade1 As Double = CDbl(txtGrade1.Text)
        Dim grade2 As Double = CDbl(txtGrade2.Text)
        Dim grade3 As Double = CDbl(txtGrade3.Text)
        DisplayHighestTwo(grade1, grade2, grade3)
    End Sub

    Sub DisplayHighestTwo(grade1 As Double, grade2 As Double,
                          grade3 As Double)
      Dim first, second As Double
      first = Max(grade1, grade2)
      If first = grade1 Then
        second = Max(grade2, grade3)
      Else
        second = Max(grade1, grade3)
      End If
      txtOutput.Text = "The highest two grades are " & first &
                      " and " & second & "."
    End Sub

    Function Max(num1 As Double, num2 As Double) As Double
      If num1 <= num2 Then
        Return num2
      Else
        Return num1
      End If
    End Function
```

37.
```
    Private Sub btnAlphabetize_Click(...) Handles btnAlphabetize.Click
        Dim word1 = txtWord1.Text
        Dim word2 = txtWord2.Text
        DisplayWords(word1, word2)
    End Sub
```

```
Sub DisplayWords(word1 As String, word2 As String)
   Dim first, second As String
   If word1 <= word2 Then
     first = word1
     second = word2
   Else
     first = word2
     second = word1
   End If
   lstOutput.Items.Add(first)
   lstOutput.Items.Add(second)
End Sub
```

39.
```
Sub ShowCentury(anyDate As Date)
   If anyDate >= Today Then
     MessageBox.Show("You did not enter a past date.")
     Exit Sub
   End If
   Select Case anyDate
     Case Is >= #1/1/2000#
       txtOutput.Text = "twenty-first century"
     Case Is >= #1/1/1900#
       txtOutput.Text = "twentieth century"
     Case Else
       txtOutput.Text = "prior to the twentieth century"
   End Select
End Sub
```

EXERCISES 5.3

1. Gabriel was born in the year 1980.

3. The state flower of Alaska is the Forget Me Not.

5. The first 3 letters of EDUCATION are EDU.

7. sum = 4
difference = 2

9.
```
Private Sub btnDisplay_Click(...) Handles btnDisplay.Click
   Dim firstName As String = "", lastName As String = ""
   Dim salary, newSalary As Decimal
   InputData(firstName, lastName, salary)
   newSalary = RaisedSalary(salary)
   DisplayOutput(firstName, lastName, newSalary)
End Sub

Sub InputData(ByRef firstName As String, ByRef lastName As String,
            ByRef salary As Decimal)
   firstName = txtFirstName.Text
   lastName = txtLastName.Text
   salary = CDec(txtCurrentSalary.Text)
End Sub

Function RaisedSalary(salary As Decimal) As Decimal
   If salary <= 40000 Then
     Return CDec(1.05 * salary)
   Else
     Return CDec(salary + 2000 + 0.02 * (salary - 40000))
   End If
End Function
```

```
Sub DisplayOutput(firstName As String, lastName As String,
                  newSalary As Decimal)
  txtOutput.Text = "New salary for " & firstName & " " & lastName &
                   " is " & newSalary.ToString("C") & "."
End Sub
```

11.
```
Private Sub btnCalculate_Click(...) Handles btnCalculate.Click
    Dim annualRateOfInterest, monthlyPayment, begBalance As Decimal
    Dim intForMonth, redOfPrincipal, endBalance As Decimal
    InputData(annualRateOfInterest, monthlyPayment, begBalance)
    Calculate(annualRateOfInterest, monthlyPayment, begBalance,
              intForMonth, redOfPrincipal, endBalance)
    DisplayData(intForMonth, redOfPrincipal, endBalance)
End Sub

Sub InputData(ByRef annualRateOfInterest As Decimal,
              ByRef monthlyPayment As Decimal,
              ByRef begBalance As Decimal)
  annualRateOfInterest = CDec(txtAnnualRateOfInterest.Text)
  monthlyPayment = CDec(txtMonthlyPayment.Text)
  begBalance = CDec(txtBegBalance.Text)
End Sub

Sub Calculate(annualRateOfInterest As Decimal, monthlyPayment As Decimal,
              begBalance As Decimal, ByRef intForMonth As Decimal,
              ByRef redOfPrincipal As Decimal, ByRef endBalance As Decimal)
  Dim monthlyRateOfInterest As Decimal = annualRateOfInterest / 12
  intForMonth = (monthlyRateOfInterest / 100) * begBalance
  redOfPrincipal = monthlyPayment - intForMonth
  endBalance = begBalance - redOfPrincipal
End Sub

Sub DisplayData(intForMonth As Decimal, redOfPrincipal As Decimal,
                endBalance As Decimal)
  txtIntForMonth.Text = intForMonth.ToString("C")
  txtRedOfPrincipal.Text = redOfPrincipal.ToString("C")
  txtEndBalance.Text = endBalance.ToString("C")
End Sub
```

13.
```
Private Sub btnDetermine_Click(...) Handles btnDetermine.Click
    Dim first As Double = CDbl(txtNum1.Text)
    Dim second As Double = CDbl(txtNum2.Text)
    Dim third As Double = CDbl(txtNum3.Text)
    Sort(first, second, third)
    txtMax.Text = CStr(first)
    txtMiddle.Text = CStr(second)
    txtMin.Text = CStr(third)
End Sub

Sub Sort(ByRef first As Double, ByRef second As Double,
         ByRef third As Double)
  Dim max As Double
  'Find greatest value
  max = first
  If second > max Then
    max = second
  End If
  If third > max Then
    max = third
  End If
  'Store maximum value in variable first
```

```
      If second = max Then
        Swap(first, second)
      ElseIf third = max Then
        Swap(first, third)
      End If
      'Order remaining two values
      If third > second Then
        Swap(second, third)
      End If
    End Sub

    Sub Swap(ByRef x As Double, ByRef y As Double)
      Dim temp As Double
      temp = x
      x = y
      y = temp
    End Sub
```

15.
```
    Private Sub btnCalculate_Click(...) Handles btnCalculate.Click
      Dim price, salesTaxRate, cost As Decimal
      price = 29.95D
      salesTaxRate = 0.05D
      cost = FindCost(price, salesTaxRate)
      txtResult.Text = cost.ToString("C")
    End Sub

    Function FindCost(price As Decimal, salesTaxRate As Decimal) As Decimal
      Return price * (1 + salesTaxRate)
    End Function
```

CHAPTER 6

EXERCISES 6.1

1. 18 **3.** 10 **5.** Maximum number: 7

7. Infinite loop. (To end the program, click on the *Stop Debugging* button on the Toolbar.)

9. Do and Loop are interchanged

11. `While num >= 7` **13.** `Until response <> "Y"` **15.** `Until name = ""`

17. `Until (a <= 1) Or (a >= 3)` **19.** `While n = 0`

21.
```
    Private Sub btnDisplay_Click(...) Handles btnDisplay.Click
      'Request and display three names.
      Dim name As String, num As Integer = 0
      Do While num < 3
        name = InputBox("Enter a name:")
        lstOutput.Items.Add(name)
        num += 1
      Loop
    End Sub
```

23.
```
    Private Sub btnDisplay_Click(...) Handles btnDisplay.Click
      Dim celsius As Double = 10
      lstOutput.Items.Add("Celsius    Fahrenheit")
      Do While celsius <= 40
        lstOutput.Items.Add("    " & celsius & "           " & _
                            Fahrenheit(celsius))
```

```
        celsius += 5
      Loop
    End Sub


    Function Fahrenheit(celsius As Double) As Double
      'Convert Celsius to Fahrenheit
      Return (9 / 5) * celsius + 32
    End Function
```

25.
```
    Private Sub btnCompute_Click(...) Handles btnCompute.Click
      Dim num, max, min As Double
      Dim count As Double = 0
      Dim prompt As String = "Enter a nonnegative number. " &
                             "Enter -1 to terminate entering numbers."
      num = CDbl(InputBox(prompt))
      max = num
      min = num
      Do While num >= 0
        count += 1
        num = CDbl(InputBox(prompt))
        If (num <> -1) Then
          If num < min Then
            min = num
          End If
          If num > max Then
            max = num
          End If
        End If
      Loop
      If count > 0 Then
        txtRange.Text = CStr(max - min)
      Else
        MessageBox.Show("No numbers were entered.")
      End If
    End Sub
```

27.
```
    Private Sub btnFind_Click(...) Handles btnFind.Click
      Dim m, n, t As Integer
      InputIntegers(m, n)
      Do While n <> 0
        t = n
        n = m Mod n      'remainder after m is divided by n
        m = t
      Loop
      txtOutput.Text = CStr(m)
    End Sub


    Sub InputIntegers(ByRef m As Integer, ByRef n As Integer)
      m = CInt(txtM.Text)
      n = CInt(txtN.Text)
    End Sub
```

29.
```
    Private Sub btnDetermine_Click(...) Handles btnDetermine.Click
      Dim dt As Date
      dt = CDate(txtMonth.Text & "/1/" & txtYear.Text)
      Do Until dt.ToString("D").StartsWith("Tuesday")
        dt = dt.AddDays(1)
      Loop
      txtDate.Text = dt.ToString("D")
    End Sub
```

31.
```
Private Sub btnCompute_Click(...) Handles btnCompute.Click
    Dim age As Integer = 1
    Do While (1980 + age) <> age ^ 2
        age += 1
    Loop
    txtOutput.Text = age & " years old"
End Sub
```

33.
```
Private Sub btnDetermine_Click(...) Handles btnDetermine.Click
    Dim amount As Double = 100
    Dim yrs As Integer = 0
    Do Until amount < 1
        amount = 0.5 * amount
        yrs += 28
    Loop
    txtOutput.Text = yrs & " years"
End Sub
```

35.
```
Private Sub btnDetermine_Click(...) Handles btnDetermine.Click
    Const INTEREST_PER_MONTH As Decimal = 0.005D
    Const MONTHLY_PAYMENT As Decimal = 290
    Dim loanAmount As Decimal = 15000
    Dim months As Integer = 0
    Dim balance As Decimal = loanAmount
    Do Until balance < loanAmount / 2
        balance = (1 + INTEREST_PER_MONTH) * balance - MONTHLY_PAYMENT
        months += 1
    Loop
    txtOutput.Text = months & " months"
End Sub
```

37.
```
Private Sub btnDetermine_Click(...) Handles btnDetermine.Click
    Dim months As Integer = 0
    Dim balance As Decimal = 10000
    Do Until balance < 600
        balance = (1.003D * balance) - 600
        months += 1
    Loop
    txtOutput.Text = months & " months; " & balance.ToString("C")
End Sub
```

39.
```
Private Sub btnCalculate_Click(...) Handles btnCalculate.Click
    'Determine the number of times a letter appears in a sentence.
    Dim letter As String = txtLetter.Text.ToUpper
    Dim sentence As String = txtSentence.Text.ToUpper
    Dim positionOfLetter As Integer
    Dim count As Integer = -1
    Do
        count += 1
        positionOfLetter = sentence.IndexOf(letter, positionOfLetter + 1)
    Loop Until positionOfLetter = -1
    txtNumberOfOccurrences.Text = CStr(count)
End Sub
```

41.
```
Private Sub btnDetermine_Click(...) Handles btnDetermine.Click
    'Determine when the population of India will exceed that of China.
    Dim chinaPop, indiaPop As Double, yr As Integer
    chinaPop = 1.37    '2016
    indiaPop = 1.31    '2016
    yr = 2016
```

```
        Do Until indiaPop > chinaPop
          yr += 1
          chinaPop *= 1.0066
          indiaPop *= 1.013
        Loop
        txtYear.Text = CStr(yr)
    End Sub
```

43.
```
Function Substitute(strVar As String, strVar1 As String,
                    strVar2 As String) As String
    Dim n As Integer
    Do Until strVar.IndexOf(strVar1) = -1
      n = strVar.IndexOf(strVar1)
      ListBox1.Items.Add(n)
      strVar = strVar.Remove(n, strVar1.Length)
      strVar = strVar.Insert(n, strVar2)
      ListBox1.Items.Add(strVar)
    Loop
    Return strVar
End Function
```

EXERCISES 6.2

1. Pass #1
   Pass #2
   Pass #3
   Pass #4

3. 2
4
6
8

5. 5
6
7

7. • • • • • • • • • •

9. 4

Who do we appreciate?

11. The loop is never executed since 25 is greater than 1 and the step is negative.

13. The For . . . Next loop will not execute since 20 is greater than 0. You must add **Step -1** to the end of the For statement.

15.
```
Private Sub btnDisplay_Click(...) Handles btnDisplay.Click
    For num As Integer = 1 To 9 Step 2
      lstBox.Items.Add(num)
    Next
End Sub
```

17.
```
Private Sub btnAnalyze_Click(...) Handles btnAnalyze.Click
    Const DECAY_RATE As Double = 0.12
    Dim grams As Double
    grams = 10
    For yearNum As Integer = 1 To 5
      grams = (1 - DECAY_RATE) * grams
    Next
    txtAmount.Text = grams.ToString("N") & " grams"
End Sub
```

19.
```
Private Sub btnFind_Click(...) Handles btnFind.Click
    Dim sum As Double = 0, num as Double = 0
    For i As Integer = 1 To 5
      num = CDbl(InputBox("Enter #" & i))
      sum += num
    Next
    txtAverage.Text = (sum / 5).ToString("N")
End Sub
```

21.
```
Private Sub btnCompute_Click(...) Handles btnCompute.Click
    Dim sum As Double = 0
```

```
         For denominator As Double = 1 To 100
            sum += 1 / denominator
         Next
         txtOutput.Text = sum.ToString("N5")
      End Sub
```

23.
```
      Private Sub btnAnalyze_Click(...) Handles btnAnalyze.Click
         Dim word As String = txtWord.Text
         Dim firstLetter, secondLetter As String
         Dim flag As Boolean = True
         For i As Integer = 0 To (word.Length - 2)
           firstLetter = word.Substring(i, 1)
           secondLetter = word.Substring(i +1, 1)
           If firstLetter > secondLetter Then
             txtOutput.Text = "No"
             Exit For
           End If
           If i = (word.Length - 2) Then
             txtOutput.Text = "Yes"
           End If
         Next
      End Sub
```

25.
```
      Private Sub btnCompute_Click(...) Handles btnCompute.Click
         Const PERCENT_RAISE As Double = 0.05D
         Dim name As String, age As Integer, salary As Decimal
         Dim earnings As Decimal = 0
         name = txtName.Text
         age = CInt(txtAge.Text)
         salary = CDec(txtSalary.Text)
         For i As Integer = age To 65
           earnings += salary
           salary = salary + (PERCENT_RAISE * salary)
         Next
         txtOutput.Text = name & " will earn about " &
                         earnings.ToString("C0") & "."
      End Sub
```

27.
```
      Private Sub btnComputeIdealWeights_Click(...) Handles _
                       btnComputeIdealWeights.Click
         Dim lower, upper As Integer
         lstWeightTable.Items.Clear()
         InputBounds(lower, upper)
         ShowWeights(lower, upper)
      End Sub

      Function IdealMan(height As Integer) As Double
        'Compute the ideal weight of a man given his height
        Return (4 * height) - 128
      End Function

      Function IdealWoman(height As Integer) As Double
        'Compute the ideal weight of a woman given her height
        Return (3.5 * height) - 108
      End Function

      Sub InputBounds(ByRef lower As Integer, ByRef upper As Integer)
        lower = CInt(InputBox("Enter lower bound on height in inches:"))
        upper = CInt(InputBox("Enter upper bound on height in inches:"))
      End Sub
```

```
Sub ShowWeights(lower As Integer, upper As Integer)
    lstWeightTable.Items.Add("          " & "WEIGHT  " & " " & "WEIGHT")
    lstWeightTable.Items.Add("HEIGHT" & "    " & "WOMEN   " & " " & "MEN")
    For height As Integer = lower To upper
        lstWeightTable.Items.Add(height & "        " &
                    (IdealWoman(height)).ToString("N1") &
                    "    " & (IdealMan(height)).ToString("N1"))
    Next
End Sub
```

29.
```
Private Sub btnAnalyzeOptions_Click(...) Handles btnAnalyzeOptions.Click
    'Compare salaries
    Dim opt1, opt2 As Decimal
    opt1 = Option1()
    opt2 = Option2()
    lstOutput.Items.Add("Option 1 = " & opt1.ToString("C"))
    lstOutput.Items.Add("Option 2 = " & opt2.ToString("C"))
    If opt1 > opt2 Then
        lstOutput.Items.Add("Option 1 pays better.")
    ElseIf opt1 = opt2 Then
        lstOutput.Items.Add("Options pay the same.")
    Else
        lstOutput.Items.Add("Option 2 pays better.")
    End If
End Sub

Function Option1() As Decimal
    'Compute total salary with a flat salary of $100/day
    Dim sum As Integer = 0
    For i As Integer = 1 To 10
        sum += 100
    Next
    Return sum
End Function

Function Option2() As Decimal
    'Compute total salary starting at $1 and doubling each day
    Dim sum As Integer = 0, daySalary As Integer = 1
    For i As Integer = 1 To 10
        sum += daySalary
        daySalary = 2 * daySalary
    Next
    Return sum
End Function
```

31.
```
Private Sub btnDisplay_Click(...) Handles btnDisplay.Click
    Dim balance As Decimal = 0
    Dim yr As Integer = 2016
    For i As Integer = 1 To 108
        balance = (1.0025D * balance) + 100
        If i Mod 12 = 0 Then
            lstOutput.Items.Add(yr & "   " & balance.ToString("C"))
            yr += 1
        End If
    Next
End Sub
```

33.
```
Private Sub btnCalculate_Click(...) Handles btnCalculate.Click
    txtNfactorial.Text = CStr(Factorial(CInt(txtN.Text)).ToString("N0"))
End Sub
```

```
      Function Factorial(n As Integer) As Double
        Dim product As Double = 1
        For i As Integer = 2 To n
          product *= i
        Next
        Return product
      End Function
```

35.
```
Private Sub btnRemove_Click(...) Handles btnRemove.Click
  Dim phoneNum As String
  Dim phoneNum2 As String = ""
  phoneNum = txtPhone.Text
  For i As Integer = 0 To (phoneNum.Length - 1)
    Dim character As String
    character = phoneNum.Substring(i, 1)
    If character <> "-" Then
      phoneNum2 &= character
    End If
  Next
  txtStrippedPhone.Text = phoneNum2
End Sub
```

37.
```
Private Sub btnDetermine_Click(...) Handles btnDetermine.Click
  Dim numberOfFridays As Integer
  Dim dt As Date
  For i As Integer = 2000 To 2999
    For j As Integer = 1 To 12
      dt = CDate(j & "/" & "13/" & i)
      If IsFriday(dt) Then
        numberOfFridays += 1
      End If
    Next
  Next
  txtNumberOfFridays.Text = CStr(numberOfFridays)
End Sub

Function IsFriday(x As Date) As Boolean
  Dim dt As String = x.ToString("D")
  If dt.StartsWith("Friday") Then
    Return True
  Else
    Return False
  End If
End Function
```

39.
```
Private Sub btnDisplay_Click(...) Handles btnDisplay.Click
  Dim price, quantity As Decimal
  lstOutput.Items.Clear()
  quantity = 80   'current crop of soybeans in millions of bushels
  lstOutput.Items.Add("YEAR" & "    " & "QUANTITY" & "     " & "PRICE")
  For yr As Integer = 2015 To 2024
    price = 20 - (0.1D * quantity)
    lstOutput.Items.Add(yr & "      " & quantity.ToString("N") &
                        "       " & price.ToString("C"))
    quantity = 5 * price - 10
  Next
End Sub
```

41.
```
Private Sub btnCompute_Click(...) Handles btnCompute.Click
  'Compare two salary options.
  Dim amount1 As Decimal = 0, amount2 As Decimal = 0
```

```
          Dim salaryPerPeriod1 As Decimal = 20000
          Dim salaryPerPeriod2 As Decimal = 10000
          'Option 1: each period is one year
          For i As Integer = 1 To 10
            amount1 += salaryPerPeriod1
            salaryPerPeriod1 += 1000
          Next
          txtOption1.Text = amount1.ToString("C0")
          'Option 2: each period is six months
          For i As Integer = 1 To 20
            amount2 += salaryPerPeriod2
            salaryPerPeriod2 += 250
          Next
          txtOption2.Text = amount2.ToString("C0")
        End Sub
```

43.
```
    Private Sub btnCount_Click(...) Handles btnCount.Click
          'Count the number of odometer readings containing the digit 1.
          Dim total As Integer = 0
          For i As Integer = 0 To 999999
            If CStr(i).IndexOf("1") <> -1 Then
              total += 1
            End If
          Next
          txtAnswer.Text = total.ToString("N0")
          'Note: The answer is 10^6 - 9^6, the total number of odometer readings
          'minus the number of odometer readings that do not contain the digit 1.
        End Sub
```

45.
```
    Private Sub btnCalculate_Click(...) Handles btnCalculate.Click
          'Calculate the likelihood of two people in a
          'group having the same birthday.
          Dim n As Integer = 365
          Dim product, prob As Double
          lstProbabilities.Items.Add("Number of People  Probability")
          For r As Integer = 20 To 30
            product = 1
            For i As Integer = 0 To (r - 1)
              product *= (n - i) / n
            Next
            prob = 1 - product
            lstProbabilities.Items.Add("           " & r & "                    " &
                                  prob.ToString("N3"))
          Next
        End Sub
```

EXERCISES 6.3

1. Mozart   **3.** Tchaikovsky   **5.** 3   **7.** 80   **9.** 70   **11.** 300

13.
```
    Private Sub btnCount_Click(...) Handles btnCount.Click
          Dim numWon As Integer = 0
          For i As Integer = 0 To (lstBox.Items.Count - 1)
            If CStr(lstBox.Items(i)) = "USC" Then
              numWon += 1
            End If
          Next
          txtOutput.Text = CStr(numWon)
        End Sub
```

15.
```
Private Sub btnCount_Click(...) Handles btnDetermine.Click
  Dim college As String = txtCollege.Text
  txtOutput.Clear()
  For i As Integer = 0 To (lstBox.Items.Count - 1)
    If CStr(lstBox.Items(i)) = college Then
      txtOutput.Text = "YES"
      Exit For
    End If
  Next
  If txtOutput.Text = "" Then
    txtOutput.Text = "NO"
  End If
End Sub
```

or

```
Private Sub btnCount_Click(...) Handles btnDetermine.Click
  Dim college As String = txtCollege.Text
  Dim i As Integer = 0
  Dim found As Boolean = False
  Do Until (found = True) Or (i = lstBox.Items.Count)
    If CStr(lstBox.Items(i)) = college Then
      found = True
    End If
    i += 1
  Loop
  If found Then
    txtOutput.Text = "YES"
  Else
    txtOutput.Text = "NO"
  End If
End Sub
```

17.
```
Private Sub btnReverse_Click(...) Handles btnReverse.Click
  Dim highestIndex As Integer = lstBox.Items.Count - 1
  For i As Integer = highestIndex To 0 Step -1
    lstBox2.Items.Add(lstBox.Items(i))
  Next
End Sub
```

19.
```
Private Sub btnAlphabetize_Click(...) Handles btnAlphabetize.Click
  lstBox2.Sorted = True
  Dim highestIndex As Integer = lstBox.Items.Count - 1
  For i As Integer = 0 To highestIndex
    lstBox2.Items.Add(lstBox.Items(i))
  Next
End Sub
```

21.
```
Private Sub btnDisplay_Click(...) Handles btnDisplay.Click
  Dim highestIndex As Integer = lstBox.Items.Count - 1
  Dim state As String
  For i As Integer = 0 To highestIndex
    state = CStr(lstBox.Items(i))
    If state.Length = 7 Then
      lstBox2.Items.Add(state)
    End If
  Next
End Sub
```

23.
```
Private Sub btnDetermine_Click(...) Handles btnDetermine.Click
    Dim highestIndex As Integer = (lstBox.Items.Count - 1)
    Dim state As String
    For i As Integer = 0 To highestIndex
      state = CStr(lstBox.Items(i))
      If state.StartsWith("New") Then
        txtOutput.Text = state
        Exit For
      End If
    Next
End Sub
```

25.
```
Private Sub btnDisplay_Click(...) Handles btnDisplay.Click
    Dim highestIndex As Integer = (lstBox.Items.Count - 1)
    Dim maxLength As Integer = 0
    Dim state As String
    For i As Integer = 0 To highestIndex
      state = CStr(lstBox.Items(i))
      If state.Length > maxLength Then
        maxLength = state.Length
      End If
    Next
    For i As Integer = 0 To highestIndex
      state = CStr(lstBox.Items(i))
      If state.Length = maxLength Then
        lstBox2.Items.Add(state)
      End If
    Next
End Sub
```

27.
```
Private Sub btnDetermine_Click(...) Handles btnDetermine.Click
    Dim highestIndex As Integer = (lstBox.Items.Count - 1)
    Dim state As String
    For i As Integer = 0 To highestIndex
      state = CStr(lstBox.Items(i))
      If NumberOfVowels(state) = 4 Then
        lstBox2.Items.Add(state)
      End If
    Next
End Sub

Function NumberOfVowels(word As String) As Integer
    Dim numVowels As Integer = 0
    word = word.ToUpper
    Dim letter As String
    Dim numLetters As Integer = word.Length
    For i As Integer = 0 To (numLetters - 1)
      letter = word.Substring(i, 1)
      If (letter = "A") Or (letter = "E") Or (letter = "I") Or
        (letter = "O") Or (letter = "U") Then
        numVowels += 1
      End If
    Next
    Return numVowels
End Function
```

29.
```
Private Sub btnDetermine_Click(...) Handles btnDetermine.Click
    Dim highestIndex As Integer = (lstBox.Items.Count - 1)
    Dim state As String
```

```vb
    Dim maxNumOfVowels = 0
    For i As Integer = 0 To highestIndex
      state = CStr(lstBox.Items(i))
      If NumberOfVowels(state) > maxNumOfVowels Then
        maxNumOfVowels = NumberOfVowels(state)
      End If
    Next
    txtOutput.Text = CStr(maxNumOfVowels)
  End Sub

  Function NumberOfVowels(word As String) As Integer
    Dim numVowels As Integer = 0
    word = word.ToUpper
    Dim letter As String
    Dim numLetters As Integer = word.Length
    For i As Integer = 0 To (numLetters - 1)
      letter = word.Substring(i, 1)
      If (letter = "A") Or (letter = "E") Or (letter = "I") Or
         (letter = "O") Or (letter = "U") Then
        numVowels += 1
      End If
    Next
    Return numVowels
  End Function
```

31.
```vb
Private Sub btnDisplay_Click(...) Handles btnDisplay.Click
  txtOutput.Text = CStr(lstBox.Items(0))
End Sub
```

33.
```vb
Private Sub btnDisplay_Click(...) Handles btnDisplay.Click
  txtOutput.Text = CStr(lstBox.Items(4))
End Sub
```

35.
```vb
Private Sub btnRecord_Click(...) Handles btnRecord.Click
  lstGrades.Items.Add(txtGrade.Text)
  txtGrade.Clear()
  txtGrade.Focus()
End Sub

Private Sub btnCalculate_Click(...) Handles btnCalculate.Click
  Dim sum As Double = 0
  Dim minGrade As Double = 100
  If lstGrades.Items.Count > 0 Then
    For i As Integer = 0 To (lstGrades.Items.Count - 1)
      sum += CDbl(lstGrades.Items(i))
      If CDbl(lstGrades.Items(i)) < minGrade Then
        minGrade = CDbl(lstGrades.Items(i))
      End If
    Next
  Else
    MessageBox.Show("You must first enter some grades.")
  End If
  txtAverage.Text = (sum / lstGrades.Items.Count).ToString("N")
  txtLowest.Text = CStr(minGrade)
End Sub
```

37.
```vb
Private Sub btnRecord_Click(...) Handles btnRecord.Click
  lstGrades.Items.Add(txtGrade.Text)
  txtGrade.Clear()
  txtGrade.Focus()
End Sub
```

```
       Private Sub btnCalculate_Click(...) Handles btnCalculate.Click
         Dim sum As Double = 0
         Dim maxGrade As Double = 0
         Dim minGrade As Double = 100
         If lstGrades.Items.Count > 0 Then
           For i As Integer = 0 To (lstGrades.Items.Count - 1)
             sum += CDbl(lstGrades.Items(i))
             If CDbl(lstGrades.Items(i)) > maxGrade Then
               maxGrade = CDbl(lstGrades.Items(i))
             End If
             If CDbl(lstGrades.Items(i)) < minGrade Then
               minGrade = CDbl(lstGrades.Items(i))
             End If
           Next
         Else
           MessageBox.Show("You must first enter some grades.")
         End If
         txtAverage.Text = (sum / lstGrades.Items.Count).ToString("N")
         txtRange.Text = CStr(maxGrade - minGrade)
       End Sub
```

```
39. Private Sub btnSearch_Click(...) Handles btnSearch.Click
       Dim letters As String = mtbFirstTwoLetters.Text.ToUpper
       Dim i As Integer = 49      'index of the state currently considered
       Do Until (CStr(lstStates.Items(i)).ToUpper <= letters) Or (i = 0)
         i = i - 1
       Loop
       If CStr(lstStates.Items(i + 1)).ToUpper.StartsWith(letters) Then
         txtOutput.Text = CStr(lstStates.Items(i + 1)) & " begins with " &
                       mtbFirstTwoLetters.Text & "."
       ElseIf CStr(lstStates.Items(0)).ToUpper.StartsWith(letters) Then
         txtOutput.Text = CStr(lstStates.Items(0)) & " begins with " &
                       mtbFirstTwoLetters.Text & "."
       Else
         txtOutput.Text = "No state begins with " &
                       mtbFirstTwoLetters.Text & "."
       End If
     End Sub
```

CHAPTER 7

EXERCISES 7.1

1. 101   **3.** Have a dessert spoon.   **5.** Yes   **7.** 12

9. You have a trio.   **11.** Your average is 80

13. The Artist won in 2012   **15.** one,two,three

17. 2 even numbers   **19.** Pearl Harbor: 1941

21. contains a 19th-century date   **23.** 6 words begin with a vowel

25. 4
6
2

27. a. Superior   (last name in alphabetical order)
b. Erie   (first name in alphabetical order)
c. Huron   (first name in the array)

   d. `Superior` (last name in the array)
   e. `5`   (number of names in the array)
   f. `Ontario` (second name in the array)
   g. `3`   (first array subscript whose element is Erie)

29. a. `6.7` (greatest population of a New England state)
   b. `0.6` (least population of a New England state)
   c. `3.6` (first population in the array)
   d. `1.3` (last population in the array)
   e. `6`   (number of numbers in the array)
   f. `1.1` (fourth population in the array)
   g. `3`   (first array subscript whose element is 1.1)

31. a. `lstOutput.Items.Add(states.First)`
   or `lstOutput.Items.Add(states(0))`
   b.
```
For i As Integer = 0 To 12
    lstOutput.Items.Add(states(i))
Next
```
   c. `lstOutput.Items.Add(states.Last)`
   or `lstOutput.Items.Add(states(49))`
   d. `lstOutput.Items.Add(CStr(Array.IndexOf(states, "Ohio") + 1))`
   e. `lstOutput.Items.Add(states(1))`
   f. `lstOutput.Items.Add(states(19))`
   g.
```
For i As Integer = (states.Count - 9) To (states.Count)
    lstOutput.Items.Add(states(i - 1))
Next
```

33.
```
Function Task(nums() As Integer) As Integer
    Dim sum As Integer = 0
    For Each num As Integer In nums
      sum += num
    Next
    Return sum
End Function
```

35.
```
Function Task(nums() As Integer) As Integer
    Dim maxEven As Integer = 0
    For Each num As Integer In nums
      If (num Mod 2 = 0) And (num > maxEven) Then
        maxEven = num
      End If
    Next
    Return maxEven
End Function
```

37.
```
Function Task(nums() As Integer) As Integer
    Dim twoDigits As Integer = 0
    For Each num As Integer In nums
      If (num > 9) And (num < 100) Then
        twoDigits += 1
      End If
    Next
    Return twoDigits
End Function
```

39. `nums(3)` should be changed to `nums()`

41. Logic error. The values of the array elements cannot be altered inside a For Each loop. The output will be 6.

43. `lstBox.Items.Add(line.Split(" "c).Count)`

45.
```
Private Sub btnDisplay_Click(...) Handles btnDisplay.Click
    Dim numStr() As String = IO.File.ReadAllLines("Numbers.txt")
    Dim nums(numStr.Count - 1) As Integer
    For i As Integer = 1 To (nums.Count - 1)
        nums(i) = CInt(numStr(i))
    Next
    lstOutput.Items.Add("Number of integers in the file: " & nums.Count)
    lstOutput.Items.Add("Sum of integers in the file: " & nums.Sum)
End Sub
```

47.
```
Private Sub btnDetermine_Click(...) Handles btnDetermine.Click
    Dim names() As String = IO.File.ReadAllLines("Names2.txt")
    Dim dups(names.Count - 1) As String
    Dim n As Integer = 0          'index for dups
    For i As Integer = 0 To names.Count - 2
        If (names(i + 1) = names(i)) And
                        (Array.IndexOf(dups, names(i)) = -1) Then
            dups(n) = names(i)
            n += 1
        End If
    Next
    If n = 0 Then
        lstOutput.Items.Add("No duplicates.")
    Else
        For i As Integer = 0 To (n - 1)
            lstOutput.Items.Add(dups(i))
        Next
    End If
End Sub
```

49.
```
Function Sum(nums() As Integer) As Integer
    Dim total As Integer = 0
    For i As Integer = 1 To (nums.Count - 1) Step 2
        total += nums(i)
    Next
    Return total
End Function
```

51.
```
Private Sub btnDisplay_Click(...) Handles btnDisplay.Click
    Dim lines() As String = IO.File.ReadAllLines("Sonnet.txt")
    Dim n = lines.Count - 1
    Dim numWords(n) As Integer
    For i As Integer = 0 To n
        numWords(i) = lines(i).Split(" "c).Count
    Next
    lstOutput.Items.Add("Average number of words per line: " &
                        (numWords.Average).ToString("N"))
    lstOutput.Items.Add("Total number of words: " & numWords.Sum)
End Sub
```

53.
```
Private Sub btnProcessEggs_Click(...) Handles btnProcessEggs.Click
    Dim heaviest, lightest, ounces As Double
    Dim jumbo, xLarge, large, med, small As Integer
    heaviest = 0     'can be any number lower than lightest egg
```

```
        lightest = 100   'can be any number greater than heaviest egg
        Dim strEggs() As String = IO.File.ReadAllLines("Eggs.txt")
        Dim eggs(strEggs.Count - 1) As Double
        For i As Integer = 0 To (eggs.Count - 1)
          eggs(i) = CDbl(strEggs(i))
        Next
        For i As Integer = 0 To (eggs.Count - 1)
          ounces = eggs(i)
          If ounces > heaviest Then
            heaviest = ounces
          End if
          If ounces < lightest Then
            lightest = ounces
          End If
          Select Case ounces
            Case Is < 1.5
              'too small & cannot be sold
            Case Is < 1.75
              small += 1
            Case Is < 2
              med += 1
            Case Is < 2.25
              large += 1
            Case Is < 2.5
              xLarge += 1
            Case Else
              jumbo += 1
          End Select
        Next
        lstOutput.Items.Clear()
        lstOutput.Items.Add(jumbo & " Jumbo eggs")
        lstOutput.Items.Add(xLarge & " Extra Large eggs")
        lstOutput.Items.Add(large & " Large eggs")
        lstOutput.Items.Add(med & " Medium eggs")
        lstOutput.Items.Add(small & " Small eggs")
        If lightest <> 100 Then
          lstOutput.Items.Add("Lightest egg: " & lightest & " ounces")
          lstOutput.Items.Add("Heaviest egg: " & heaviest & " ounces")
        Else
          lstOutput.Items.Add("File is empty")
        End If
      End Sub
```

55.
```
    Private Sub btnDisplay_Click(...) Handles btnDisplay.Click
        Dim strDigits() As String = IO.File.ReadAllLines("Digits.txt")
        Dim freq(9) As Integer
        For i As Integer = 0 To (strDigits.Count - 1)
          freq(CInt(strDigits(i))) += 1
        Next
        lstOutput.Items.Add("  Digit  Frequency")
        For i As Integer = 0 To 9
          lstOutput.Items.Add("      " & i & "            " & freq(i))
        Next
      End Sub
```

57.
```
  Dim colors() As String = IO.File.ReadAllLines("Colors.txt")

    Private Sub btnDisplay_Click(...) Handles btnDisplay.Click
        Dim letter As String = mtbLetter.Text.ToUpper      'mask is L
        lstColors.Items.Clear()
```

```
      For Each hue As String In colors
        If hue.StartsWith(letter) Then
          lstColors.Items.Add(hue)
        End If
      Next
    End Sub
```

59.
```
Dim colors() As String = IO.File.ReadAllLines("Colors.txt")

    Private Sub btnDisplay_Click(...) Handles btnDisplay.Click
      Dim letter As String = mtbLetter.Text.ToUpper      'mask is L
      lstColors.Items.Clear()
      For Each hue As String In SmallerArray(letter)
        lstColors.Items.Add(hue)
      Next
    End Sub

    Function SmallerArray(letter As String) As String()
      Dim smArray(colors.Count - 1) As String
      Dim counter As Integer = 0
      For Each hue As String In colors
        If hue.StartsWith(letter) Then
          smArray(counter) = hue
          counter += 1
        End If
      Next
      ReDim Preserve smArray(counter - 1)
      Return smArray
    End Function
```

61.
```
Private Sub btnDetermine_Click() Handles btnDetermine.Click
      Dim ages(43), numPres As Integer
      Dim temp() As String = IO.File.ReadAllLines("AgesAtInaugural.txt")
      For i As Integer = 0 To 43
        ages(i) = CInt(temp(i))
        If ages(i) < 50 Then
          numPres += 1
        End If
      Next
      txtNumber.Text = CStr(numPres)
    End Sub
```

63.
```
Dim grades(99) As Integer         'stores grades
    Dim numGrades As Integer          'number of grades stored

    Private Sub btnRecord_Click(...) Handles btnRecord.Click
      'Add a score to the array
      'If no more room, then display error message.
      If numGrades >= 100 Then
        MessageBox.Show("100 scores have been entered.", "No more room.")
      Else
        grades(numGrades) = CInt(txtScore.Text)
        numGrades += 1
        lstOutput.Items.Clear()
        txtScore.Clear()
        txtScore.Focus()
      End If
    End Sub

    Private Sub btnDisplay_Click(...) Handles btnDisplay.Click
      'Display average of grades and the number of above average grades
      Dim temp() As Integer = grades
      ReDim Preserve temp(numGrades - 1)
```

```
    lstOutput.Items.Clear()
    lstOutput.Items.Add("The average grade is " &
                        (temp.Average).ToString("N") & ".")
    lstOutput.Items.Add(NumAboveAverage(temp) &
                        " students scored above the average.")
End Sub

Function NumAboveAverage(temp() As Integer) As Integer
    'Count the number of scores above the average grade
    Dim avg As Double = temp.Average
    Dim num As Integer = 0
    For Each grade In temp
        If grade > avg Then
            num += 1
        End If
    Next
    Return num
End Function
```

65.
```
Private Sub btnDisplay_Click(...) Handles btnDisplay.Click
    If IsChainLink(txtSentence.Text) Then
        txtOutput.Text = "This sentence is a chain-link sentence."
    Else
        txtOutput.Text = "This sentence is not a chain-link sentence."
    End If
End Sub

Function IsChainLink(sentence As String) As Boolean
    sentence = sentence.Replace(",", "")    'Delete any commas.
    sentence = sentence.Replace(":", "")    'Delete any colons.
    sentence = sentence.Replace(";", "")    'Delete any semicolons.
    Dim word() As String = sentence.Split(" "c), ending As String = ""
    For i As Integer = 0 To (words.Count - 2)
        If (words(i).Length < 2) Or (words(i + 1).Length < 2) Then
            Return False      'if any word has is less than two letters
        End If
        ending = words(i).Substring(words(i).Length - 2).ToUpper
        If ending <> words(i + 1).Substring(0, 2).ToUpper Then
            Return False      'if ending does not match beginning of next word
        End If
    Next
    Return True   'If all words are OK, then it is a chain-link sentence.
End Function
```

67.
```
Dim mnths(11) As String
Dim dt As Date = #1/1/2017#
For i As Integer = 0 To 11
    Dim n As Integer
    n = dt.ToString("D").IndexOf(",")
    mnths(i) = dt.ToString("D").Substring(n + 2, 3)
    dt = dt.AddMonths(1)
Next
```

EXERCISES 7.2

1. 5
7

3. going
offer
can't

5. 6

7. 103

9. 8

11. 3 students have a grade of 100

13. 15
12

15. The average after dropping the lowest grade is 80

17. 37 is a prime number

19.
```
Private Sub btnDisplay_Click(...) Handles btnDisplay.Click
    Dim nums() As Integer = {3, 5, 8, 10, 21}
    Dim query = From num In nums
                Where num Mod 2 = 0
                Select num
    txtOutput.Text = query.count & " even numbers"
End Sub
```

21.
```
Private Sub btnDisplay_Click(...) Handles btnDisplay.Click
    Dim dates() As String = IO.File.ReadAllLines("Dates.txt")
    Dim query = From yr In dates
                Where (CInt(yr) >= 1800) And (CInt(yr) <= 1899)
                Select yr
    If query.Count > 0 Then
      txtOutput.Text = "contains a 19th century date"
    Else
      txtOutput.Text = "does not contain a 19th century date"
    End If
End Sub
```

23.
```
Private Sub btnDisplay_Click(...) Handles btnDisplay.Click
    Dim nums() As Integer = {2, 6, 4}
    Dim query = From num In nums
                Order By Array.IndexOf(nums, num) Descending
    For Each num As Integer In query
      lstOutput.Items.Add(num)
    Next
End Sub
```

25.
```
Private Sub btnDisplay_Click(...) Handles btnDisplay.Click
    Dim teams() As String = IO.File.ReadAllLines("SBWinners.txt")
    Dim query = From team In teams
                Order By team Ascending
                Distinct
    For Each team As String In query
      lstOutput.Items.Add(team)
    Next
End Sub
```

27.
```
Dim teamNames() As String = IO.File.ReadAllLines("SBWinners.txt")
    Private Sub btnDetermine_Click(...) Handles btnDetermine.Click
      'Display the number of Super Bowls won by the team in the text box
      Dim query = From team In teamNames
                  Where team.ToUpper = txtName.Text.ToUpper
                  Select team
      txtNumWon.Text = CStr(query.Count)
    End Sub
```

29.
```
Private Sub btnDetermine Click(...) Handles btnDetermine.Click
    Dim word1 As String = txtFirstWord.Text
    Dim word2 As String = txtSecondWord.Text
    If AreAnagrams(word1, word2) Then
      txtOutput.Text = "ARE ANAGRAMS"
    Else
      txtOutput.Text =  "NOT ANAGRAMS"
    End If
End Sub
```

```
Function AreAnagrams(word1 As String, word2 As String) As Boolean
  If word1.Length <> word2.Length Then
    Return False
  Else
    Dim n = word1.Length - 1
    Dim w1(n), w2(n) As String
    For i As Integer = 0 To n
      w1(i) = word1.Substring(i, 1)
      w2(i) = word2.Substring(i, 1)
    Next
    Dim query1 = From letter In w1
                 Order By letter
                 Select letter.ToUpper
    Dim query2 = From letter In w2
                 Order By letter
                 Select letter.ToUpper
    For i As Integer = 0 To n
      If query1.ToArray(i) <> query2.ToArray(i) Then
        Return False
      End If
    Next
    Return True
  End If
End Function
```

31.
```
Private Sub btnDisplay_Click(...) Handles btnDisplay.Click
  Dim grades(4) As Integer
  For i As Integer = 0 To 4
    grades(i) = CInt(InputBox("Enter grade #" & (i + 1), "Grades"))
  Next
  Dim query = From grade In grades
              Order By grade Descending
              Select grade
  grades = query.ToArray
  ReDim Preserve grades(2)      'lop off lowest two grades
  txtOutput.Text = CStr(grades.Average)
End Sub
```

33.
```
Private Sub btnDisplay_Click(...) Handles btnDisplay.Click
  Dim states() As String = IO.File.ReadAllLines("States.txt")
  ReDim Preserve states(12)
  Dim query = From state In states
              Order By state
              Select state
  For Each state As String In query
    lstOutput.Items.Add(state)
  Next
End Sub
```

35.
```
Dim nations() As String = IO.File.ReadAllLines("Nations.txt")

Private Sub frmNations_Load(...) Handles MyBase.Load
  lstNations.DataSource = nations
  lstNations.SelectedItem = Nothing
End Sub

Private Sub txtNations_TextChanged(...) Handles txtNation.TextChanged
  Dim query = From nation In nations
              Where nation.StartsWith(txtNation.Text)
              Select nation
  lstNations.DataSource = query.ToList
  lstNations.SelectedItem = Nothing
End Sub
```

```
Private Sub lstNations_Click(...) Handles lstNations.Click
    txtNation.Text = lstNations.Text
End Sub
```

37.
```
Private Sub btnSort_Click(...) Handles btnSort.Click
    'ListBox1.Sorted = True
    Dim n As Integer = lstOriginalList.Items.Count - 1
    Dim numbers(n) As Integer
    For i As Integer = 0 To n
        numbers(i) = CInt(lstOriginalList.Items(i))
    Next
    Array.Sort(numbers)
    For i = 0 To n
        lstSortedList.Items.Add(numbers(i))
    Next
End Sub
```

39.
```
Private Sub btnFind_Click(...) Handles btnDisplay.Click
    Dim states() As String = IO.File.ReadAllLines("StatesBFNC.txt")
    Dim data(3), line, flowers(49) As String
    For i As Integer = 0 To (states.Count - 1)
        line = states(i)
        data = line.Split(","c)
        flowers(i) = data(2)
    Next
    Dim query = From flr In flowers
                Order By flr.Length Ascending
                Select flr
                Distinct
    lstFlowers.DataSource = query.ToArray
    lstFlowers.SelectedIndex = -1
    txtNumber.Text = CStr(lstFlowers.Items.Count)
End Sub
```

EXERCISES 7.3

1. The area of a football field is 19200 square yards.

3. Duke was founded in NC in 1838.   **5.** heights are same
                                              170

7. Joe: 88   **9.** Mr. President lives in Washington, DC
    Moe: 90
    Roe: 95

11. In the event procedure, **peace** should be **prize.peace** and **yr** should be **prize.yr**.

13. The condition **(game1 > game2)** is not valid. Structures can be compared only one field at a time.

15. The cities in Texas, along with their populations. The cities are ordered by the sizes of their populations beginning with the most populous city.

17. The population growth of Phoenix from 2000 to 2010.

19.
```
Structure State
    Dim name As String
    Dim abbreviation As String
    Dim area As Double
    Dim pop As Double
End Structure
```

```
Dim states() As State

Private Sub frmStates_Load(...) Handles MyBase.Load
  Dim stateRecords() As String = IO.File.ReadAllLines("USStates.txt")
  Dim n As Integer = stateRecords.Count - 1
  ReDim states(n)
  Dim line As String
  Dim data() As String
  For i As Integer = 0 To n
    line = stateRecords(i)
    data = line.Split(","c)
    states(i).name = data(0)
    states(i).abbreviation = data(1)
    states(i).area = CDbl(data(2))
    states(i).pop = CDbl(data(3))
  Next
End Sub

Private Sub btnFind_Click(...) Handles btnFind.Click
  Dim stateAbbr As String = mtbAbbrev.Text.ToUpper
  Dim query = From state In states
              Where state.abbreviation = stateAbbr
              Select state.name, state.area
  txtOutput.Text = "The area of " & query.First.name & " is " &
                    (query.First.area).ToString("N0") & " sq. miles."
End Sub
```

21. (Begin with the code from Exercise 19 and replace the Click event procedure with the following event procedure.)

```
Private Sub btnDisplay_Click(...) Handles btnDisplay.Click
  Dim query = From state In states
              Let density = state.pop / state.area
              Let formattedDensity = density.ToString("N")
              Order By density Descending
              Select state.name, formattedDensity
  dgvOutput.DataSource = query.ToList
  dgvOutput.CurrentCell = Nothing
  dgvOutput.Columns("name").HeaderText = "State"
  dgvOutput.Columns("formattedDensity").HeaderText =
                    "People per Square Mile"
End Sub
```

23.
```
Structure Player
  Dim name As String
  Dim team As String
  Dim atBats As Integer
  Dim hits As Integer
End Structure

Dim players() As Player

Private Sub frmBaseball_Load(...) Handles MyBase.Load
  Dim playerStats() As String = IO.File.ReadAllLines("Baseball.txt")
  Dim n As Integer = playerStats.Count - 1
  ReDim players(n)
  Dim line As String
  Dim data() As String
  For i As Integer = 0 To n
    line = playerStats(i)
    data = line.Split(","c)
    players(i).name = data(0)
    players(i).team = data(1)
```

```
            players(i).atBats = CInt(data(2))
            players(i).hits = CInt(data(3))
    Next
    Dim query = From person In players
                Order By person.team Ascending
                Select person.team
                Distinct
    lstTeams.DataSource = query.ToList
End Sub


Private Sub lstTeams_SelectedIndexChanged(...) Handles _
                        lstTeams.SelectedIndexChanged
    Dim selectedTeam = lstTeams.Text
    Dim query = From person In players
                Where person.team = selectedTeam
                Order By person.hits Descending
                Select person.name, person.hits
    dgvOutput.DataSource = query.ToList
    dgvOutput.CurrentCell = Nothing
    dgvOutput.Columns("name").HeaderText = "Player"
    dgvOutput.Columns("hits").HeaderText = "Hits"
End Sub
```

25.
```
Structure Player
    Dim name As String
    Dim team As String
    Dim atBats As Integer
    Dim hits As Integer
End Structure

Dim players() As Player

Private Sub frmBaseball_Load(...) Handles MyBase.Load
    Dim playerStats() As String = IO.File.ReadAllLines("Baseball.txt")
    Dim n As Integer = playerStats.Count - 1
    ReDim players(n)
    Dim line As String
    Dim data() As String
    For i As Integer = 0 To n
        line = playerStats(i)
        data = line.Split(","c)
        players(i).name = data(0)
        players(i).team = data(1)
        players(i).atBats = CInt(data(2))
        players(i).hits = CInt(data(3))
    Next
End Sub


Private Sub btnDisplay_Click(...) Handles btnDisplay.Click
    Dim query = From person In players
                Let ave = person.hits / person.atBats
                Select ave
    Dim best As Double = query.Max
    txtBestAverage.Text = best.ToString("N3")
    Dim query2 = From person In players
                 Where person.hits / person.atBats = best
                 Select person.name, person.team
    dgvOutput.DataSource = query2.ToList
    dgvOutput.CurrentCell = Nothing
    dgvOutput.Columns("name").HeaderText = "Player"
    dgvOutput.Columns("team").HeaderText = "Team"
End Sub
```

27.
```
Structure Pioneer
    Dim name As String
    Dim accomplishment As String
End Structure

Dim pioneers() As Pioneer

Private Sub frmPioneers_Load() Handles MyBase.Load
    'Place the data for each college into the array schools.
    Dim people() = IO.File.ReadAllLines("Pioneers.txt")
    Dim n As Integer = people.Count - 1
    ReDim pioneers(n)
    Dim line As String      'holds data for a single college
    Dim data() As String
    For i As Integer = 0 To n
      line = people(i)
      data = line.Split(","c)
      pioneers(i).name = data(0)
      pioneers(i).accomplishment = data(1)
      lstPioneers.Items.Add(pioneers(i).name)
    Next
End Sub

Private Sub lstPioneers_SelectedIndexChanged() Handles _
            lstPioneers.SelectedIndexChanged
    txtAccomplishment.Text =
            pioneers(lstPioneers.SelectedIndex).accomplishment
End Sub
```

29.
```
Structure Justice
    Dim firstName As String
    Dim lastName As String
    Dim apptPres As String
    Dim state As String       'state abbreviation
    Dim yrAppointed As Integer
    Dim yrLeft As Integer
End Structure

Dim justices() As Justice

Private Sub frmJustices_Load(...) Handles MyBase.Load
    Dim justiceRecords() As String = IO.File.ReadAllLines("Justices.txt")
    Dim n As Integer = justiceRecords.Count - 1
    ReDim justices(n)
    Dim line As String
    Dim data() As String
    For i As Integer = 0 To n
      line = justiceRecords(i)
      data = line.Split(","c)
      justices(i).firstName = data(0)
      justices(i).lastName = data(1)
      justices(i).apptPres = data(2)
      justices(i).state = data(3)
      justices(i).yrAppointed = CInt(data(4))
      justices(i).yrLeft = CInt(data(5))
    Next
End Sub

Private Sub btnDisplay_Click(...) Handles btnDisplay.Click
    Dim query = From person In justices
                Where person.yrLeft = 0
                Order By person.yrAppointed
```

```
                    Select person.firstName & " " & person.lastName
            lstOutput.DataSource = query.ToList
            lstOutput.SelectedItem = Nothing
        End Sub
```

31. (Begin with the code from Exercise 29 and replace the Click event procedure with the following.)

```
        Private Sub btnDisplay_Click(...) Handles btnDisplay.Click
            Dim query = From person In justices
                        Where person.state = mtbState.Text
                        Let fullName = person.firstName & " " & person.lastName
                        Let yrs = YearsServed(person.yrAppointed, person.yrLeft)
                        Let presLastName = person.apptPres.Split(" "c).Last
                        Order By person.yrAppointed
                        Select fullName, presLastName, yrs
            If query.Count = 0 Then
              MessageBox.Show("No justices appointed from that state.", "NONE")
              mtbState.Focus()
            Else
              dgvOutput.DataSource = query.ToList
              dgvOutput.CurrentCell = Nothing
              dgvOutput.Columns("fullName").HeaderText = "Justice"
              dgvOutput.Columns("presLastName").HeaderText = "Appointing President"
              dgvOutput.Columns("yrs").HeaderText = "Years Served"
            End If
        End Sub

        Function YearsServed(enter As Integer, leave As Integer) As Integer
          If leave = 0 Then
            Return (Now.Year - enter)
          Else
            Return (leave - enter)
          End If
        End Function
```

33.
```
      Structure FamousPerson
          Dim name As String
          Dim sport As String
          Dim nickname As String
          Dim dateOfBirth As Date
      End Structure

      Dim famousPersons() As FamousPerson

      Private Sub frmFamous_Load(...) Handles MyBase.Load
          Dim people() As String = IO.File.ReadAllLines("SportsStars.txt")
          Dim n As Integer = people.Count - 1
          ReDim famousPersons(n)
          Dim line As String
          Dim data(3) As String
          For i As Integer = 0 To n
            line = people(i)
            data = line.Split(","c)
            famousPersons(i).name = data(0)
            famousPersons(i).dateOfBirth = CDate(data(3))
          Next
      End Sub

      Private Sub btnDisplay_Click(...) Handles btnDisplay.Click
          Dim query = From person In famousPersons
                      Where (person.dateOfBirth >= #1/1/1940#) And
                            (person.dateOfBirth < #1/1/1950#)
```

```
              Select person.name
        lstOutput.DataSource = query.ToList
        lstOutput.SelectedItem = Nothing
    End Sub
```

35.
```
    Structure Person
        Dim name As String
        Dim sport As String
        Dim nickname As String
        Dim dateOfBirth As Date
    End Structure

    Dim people() As Person

    Private Sub frmFamous_Load(...) Handles MyBase.Load
        'Place the data for each person into the array people.
        Dim group() As String = IO.File.ReadAllLines("SportsStars.txt")
        Dim n As Integer = group.Count - 1
        ReDim people(n)
        Dim data() As String
        For i As Integer = 0 To n
          data = group(i).Split(","c)
          people(i).name = data(0)
          people(i).nickname = data(2)
          people(i).dateOfBirth = CDate(data(3))
        Next
    End Sub


    Private Sub btnDisplay_Click(...) Handles btnDisplay.Click
        Dim query = From individual In people
                    Let dayOfBirth = DayOfWeek(individual.dateOfBirth)
                    Where individual.dateOfBirth.AddYears(50) <= Today And
                        individual.dateOfBirth.AddYears(60) > Today
                    Select individual.name, individual.nickname, dayOfBirth
        dgvOutput.DataSource = query.ToList
        dgvOutput.CurrentCell = Nothing
        dgvOutput.Columns("name").HeaderText = "Name"
        dgvOutput.Columns("nickname").HeaderText = "Nickname"
        dgvOutput.Columns("dayOfBirth").HeaderText = "Day of Birth"
    End Sub


    Function DayOfWeek(dt As Date) As String
        Dim d1 As String = dt.ToString("D")
        Dim d2() As String = d1.Split(","c)
        Return d2.First
    End Function
```

37.
```
    Structure Person
        Dim name As String
        Dim sport As String
        Dim nickname As String
        Dim dateOfBirth As Date
    End Structure

    Dim people() As Person

    Private Sub frmStars_Load(...) Handles MyBase.Load
        'Place the data for each person into the array people.
        Dim group() As String = IO.File.ReadAllLines("SportsStars.txt")
        Dim n As Integer = group.Count - 1
        ReDim people(n)
```

```
      Dim data() As String
      For i As Integer = 0 To n
        data = group(i).Split(","c)
        people(i).name = data(0)
        people(i).sport = data(1)
        people(i).nickname = data(2)
        people(i).dateOfBirth = CDate(data(3))
        lstStars.Items.Add(people(i).name)
      Next
    End Sub


    Private Sub lstStars_SelectedIndexChanged(...) Handles _
                        lstStars.SelectedIndexChanged
      Dim n As Integer
      n = lstStars.SelectedIndex
      txtSport.Text = CStr(people(n).sport)
      txtNickname.Text = CStr(people(n).nickname)
      txtBirthDate.Text = (people(n).dateOfBirth).ToString("D")
    End Sub
```

39.
```
    Structure Pictures
        Dim name As String
        Dim genre As String
    End Structure

    Dim films() As Pictures

    Private Sub frmOscars_Load(...) Handles MyBase.Load
      'Place the data for each picture into the array films.
      Dim flicks() As String = IO.File.ReadAllLines("Oscars.txt")
      Dim n As Integer = flicks.Count - 1
      ReDim films(n)
      Dim line As String 'holds data for a single film
      Dim data(1) As String
      For i As Integer = 0 To n
        line = flicks(i)
        data = line.Split(","c)
        films(i).name = data(0)
        films(i).genre = data(1)
      Next
      Dim query = From pic In films
                  Select pic.genre
                  Distinct
      For Each film As String In query
        lstGenre.Items.Add(film)
      Next
    End Sub

    Private Sub lstGenre_SelectedIndexChanged(...) Handles _
                        lstGenre.SelectedIndexChanged
      lstFilms.Items.Clear()
      Dim query = From pic In films
                  Where pic.genre = CStr(lstGenre.SelectedItem)
                  Select pic.name
      For Each film As String In query
        lstFilms.Items.Add(film)
      Next
    End Sub
```

41.
```
Structure Stock
    Dim company As String
    Dim symbol As String
    Dim exchange As String
    Dim industry As String
    Dim price2013 As Decimal      'price at end of 2013
    Dim price2014 As Decimal      'price at end of 2014
    Dim earningsPerShare As Decimal
    Dim dividend As Decimal
End Structure

Dim stocks(29) As Stock

Private Sub frmDOW_Load(...) Handles MyBase.Load
  Dim line As String
  Dim data(7) As String
  Dim securities() As String = IO.File.ReadAllLines("DOW2014.txt")
  For i As Integer = 0 To 29
    line = securities(i)
    data = line.Split(","c)
    stocks(i).company = data(0)
    stocks(i).symbol = data(1)
    stocks(i).exchange = data(2)
    stocks(i).industry = data(3)
    stocks(i).price2013 = CDec(data(4))
    stocks(i).price2014 = CDec(data(5))
    stocks(i).earningsPerShare = CDec(data(6))
    stocks(i).dividend = CDec(data(7))
    lstStocks.Items.Add(stocks(i).symbol)
  Next
End Sub

Private Sub lstStocks_SelectedIndexChanged(...) Handles _
                    lstStocks.SelectedIndexChanged
  Dim n As Integer
  n = lstStocks.SelectedIndex
  txtCompany.Text = stocks(n).company
  txtIndustry.Text = stocks(n).industry
  txtExchange.Text = stocks(n).exchange
  txtGrowth.Text = ((stocks(n).price2014 - stocks(n).price2013) /
                    stocks(n).price2013).ToString("P")
  txtPEratio.Text = (stocks(n).price2014 /
                    stocks(n).earningsPerShare).ToString("N")
End Sub
```

43.
```
Structure Stock
    Dim company As String
    Dim symbol As String
    Dim exchange As String
    Dim industry As String
    Dim price2013 As Decimal      'price at end of 2013
    Dim price2014 As Decimal      'price at end of 2014
    Dim earningsPerShare As Decimal
    Dim dividend As Decimal
End Structure

Dim stocks(29) As Stock
```

```
            Private Sub frmDOW_Load(...) Handles MyBase.Load
              Dim line As String
              Dim data(7) As String
              Dim securities() As String = IO.File.ReadAllLines("DOW2014.txt")
              For i As Integer = 0 To 29
                line = securities(i)
                data = line.Split(","c)
                stocks(i).company = data(0)
                stocks(i).symbol = data(1)
                stocks(i).exchange = data(2)
                stocks(i).industry = data(3)
                stocks(i).price2013 = CDec(data(4))
                stocks(i).price2014 = CDec(data(5))
                stocks(i).earningsPerShare = CDec(data(6))
                stocks(i).dividend = CDec(data(7))
              Next
            End Sub

            Private Sub btnDetermine_Click(...) Handles btnDetermine.Click
              Dim query = From equity In stocks
                          Let ratio = equity.dividend / equity.price2014
                          Order By ratio Descending
                          Let ratioPercent = ratio.ToString("P")
                          Select equity.company, equity.symbol, ratioPercent
              Dim queryAsArray() = query.ToArray
              ReDim Preserve queryAsArray(9)
              dgvStocks.DataSource = queryAsArray
              dgvStocks.Columns("company").HeaderText = "Company"
              dgvStocks.Columns("symbol").HeaderText = "Symbol"
              dgvStocks.Columns("ratioPercent").HeaderText = "Yield as of 12/31/2014"
              dgvStocks.CurrentCell = Nothing
            End Sub
```

45.
```
    Private Sub btnDisplay_Click(...) Handles btnDisplay.Click
      lstOutput.Items.Clear()
      For i As Integer = 0 To (club.Count - 1)
        lstOutput.Items.Add(club(i).name)
      Next
    End Sub
```

47.
```
    Private Sub btnDisplay_Click(...) Handles btnDisplay.Click
      'Displays the students who are enrolled in CMSC 100
      Dim subject = "CMSC 100"
      'Loop over all students in the club
      For i As Integer = 0 To (club.Count - 1)
        'Loop over all courses for that student
        For j As Integer = 0 To (club(i).courses.Count - 1)
          'If a course matches, display the student's name.
          If club(i).courses(j) = subject Then
            lstOutput.Items.Add(club(i).name)
          End If
        Next
      Next
    End Sub
```

EXERCISES 7.4

1. 1   **3.** 3   **5.** 55   **7.** 14   **9.** 2   **11.** 55

13.
```
Dim twice(2, 3) As Double
For r As Integer = 0 To 2
  For c As Integer = 0 To 3
    twice(r, c) = 2 * nums(r, c)
  Next
Next
```

15.
```
'Use a For Each loop
Dim total As Double = 0
For Each num As Double In nums
  If num Mod 2 = 0 Then
    total += num
  End If
Next
lstOutput.Items.Add(total)


'Use LINQ
Dim query = From num In nums.Cast(Of Double)()
            Where (num Mod 2 = 0)
            Select num
lstOutput.Items.Add(query.Sum)
```

17. 12

19.
```
Private Sub btnDisplay_Click(...) Handles btnDisplay.Click
  'Display a company's inventory from its two stores
  Dim inventory(,) As Integer = {{25, 64, 23}, {30, 82, 19}}
  Dim sales(,) As Integer = {{7, 45, 11}, {4, 24, 8}}
  Dim total(2) As Integer
  'Adjust the inventory values to reflect today's sales
  For store As Integer = 1 To 2
    For item As Integer = 1 To 3
      inventory(store - 1, item - 1) =
          inventory(store - 1, item - 1) - sales(store - 1, item - 1)
      'Accumulate the total inventory per store
      total(store) += inventory(store - 1, item - 1)
    Next
  Next
  'Display the store's inventory and totals
  lstOutput.Items.Add("    1    2    3    TOTAL")
  For store As Integer = 1 To 2
    lstOutput.Items.Add(store & "    " & inventory(store - 1, 0) &
                   "    " & inventory(store - 1, 1) & "    " &
                   inventory(store - 1, 2) & "    " & total(store))
  Next
End Sub
```

21.
```
Private Sub btnDisplay_Click(...) Handles btnDisplay.Click
  Dim ranking(2, 4) As String
  Dim disciplines(2) As String
  Dim table() As String = IO.File.ReadAllLines("Ranking.txt")
  Dim data() As String
  For field As Integer = 0 To 2
    data = table(field).Split(","c)
    disciplines(field) = data(0)
    For rank As Integer = 0 To 4
      ranking(field, rank) = data(rank + 1)
    Next
```

```
      Next
   Dim result As String = ""
   For category As Integer = 0 To 2
      For rank As Integer = 0 To 4
         If txtName.Text.ToUpper = ranking(category, rank).ToUpper Then
            'Append category name to result
            result &= disciplines(category) & "   "
         End If
      Next
   Next
   If result = "" Then
      txtOutput.Text = "None."
   Else
      txtOutput.Text = result
   End If
End Sub
```

23.
```
Private Sub btnDisplay_Click(...) Handles btnDisplay.Click
   'Load golf data, cumulate totals, and display results
   Dim scores(3, 3) As Integer
   Dim golfers(3) As String
   Dim table() As String = IO.File.ReadAllLines("Golf.txt")
   Dim data() As String
   Dim golferTotal(3) As Integer, roundTotal(3) As Integer
   For i As Integer = 0 To 3
      data = table(i).Split(","c)
      golfers(i) = data(0)
      For j = 0 To 3
         scores(i, j) = CInt(data(j + 1))
      Next
   Next
   For golfer As Integer = 0 To 3
      For round As Integer = 0 To 3
         golferTotal(golfer) += scores(golfer, round)
         roundTotal(round) += scores(golfer, round)
      Next
   Next
   'Display golfer's totals
   lstOutput.Items.Add("GOLFER TOTALS")
   For golfer As Integer = 0 To 3
      lstOutput.Items.Add(golfers(golfer) & ": " & golferTotal(golfer))
   Next
   lstOutput.Items.Add("")
   'Display average per round
   lstOutput.Items.Add("ROUND AVERAGE")
   For round As Integer = 0 To 3
      lstOutput.Items.Add(round + 1 & ": " &
                     (roundTotal(round)/4).ToString("N"))
   Next
End Sub
```

25.
```
Structure Month
   Dim name As String
   Dim avePrecip As Double
End Structure

Structure Year
   Dim name As Integer
   Dim totalPrecip As Double
End Structure
```

```vb
    Dim months(11) As Month
    Dim monthNames() As String = IO.File.ReadAllLines("Months.txt")
    Dim precipData(4, 12) As Double
    Dim years(4) As Year

    Private Sub frmRain_Load(...) Handles MyBase.Load
      Dim rowOfNums() As String = IO.File.ReadAllLines("Rain.txt ")
      For i As Integer = 0 To precipData.GetUpperBound(0)
        Dim line() As String = rowOfNums(i).Split(","c)
        For j As Integer = 0 To precipData.GetUpperBound(1)
          precipData(i, j) = CDbl(line(j))
        Next
      Next
    End Sub


    Private Sub btnDisplay_Click(...) Handles btnDisplay.Click
      For j As Integer = 0 To 11
        months(j).name = monthNames(j)
        Dim sum As Double = 0
        For i As Integer = 0 To 4
          sum += precipData(i, j)
        Next
        months(j).avePrecip = sum / 5
      Next
      Dim query = From mnth In months
                  Let ave = (mnth.avePrecip).ToString("N")
                  Select mnth.name, ave
      dgvOutputMonths.DataSource = query.ToList
      dgvOutputMonths.CurrentCell = Nothing
      dgvOutputMonths.Columns("name").HeaderText = "Month"
      dgvOutputMonths.Columns("ave").HeaderText = "Average Precipitation"
      For i As Integer = 0 To 4
        years(i).name = CInt(precipData(i, 12))
        Dim sum As Double = 0
        For j As Integer = 0 To 11
          sum += precipData(i, j)
        Next
        years(i).totalPrecip = sum
      Next
      Dim query2 = From yr In years
                   Let totPrec = (yr.totalPrecip).ToString("N")
                   Select yr.name, totPrec
      dgvOutputYrs.DataSource = query2.ToList
      dgvOutputYrs.CurrentCell = Nothing
      dgvOutputYrs.Columns("name").HeaderText = "Year"
      dgvOutputYrs.Columns("totPrec").HeaderText = "Total Precipitation " &
                  "for the Year"
    End Sub


27. Private Sub btnDisplay_Click(...) Handles btnDisplay.Click
      'Display the course and campus enrollments
      'Enrollment array named er
      Dim er(,) As Integer = {{5, 15, 22, 21, 12, 25, 16, 11, 17, 23},
                              {11, 23, 51, 25, 32, 35, 32, 52, 25, 21},
                              {2, 12, 32, 32, 25, 26, 29, 12, 15, 11}}
      'Define the arrays to accumulate the information
      Dim campusTotal(2), courseTotal(9) As Integer
      For campus As Integer = 0 To 2
        For course As Integer = 0 To 9
```

```
        campusTotal(campus) += er(campus, course)
        courseTotal(course) += er(campus, course)
      Next
    Next
    'Display the campus enrollment
    lstOutput.Items.Add("CAMPUS ENROLLMENT")
    For campus As Integer = 0 To 2
      lstOutput.Items.Add((campus + 1) & ": " & campusTotal(campus))
    Next
    'Display the course enrollment
    lstOutput.Items.Add("COURSE ENROLLMENT")
    For course As Integer = 0 To 9
      lstOutput.Items.Add((course + 1) & ": " & courseTotal(course))
    Next
  End Sub
```

29.
```
Private Sub btnDetermine_Click(...) Handles btnDetermine.Click
    Dim n As Integer = CInt(InputBox("How many elements are in each row" &
                            " and column of the array?"))
    Dim a(n - 1, n - 1) As Integer
    For i As Integer = 0 To n - 1
      For j As Integer = 0 To n - 1
        a(i, j) = CInt(InputBox("What is the entry in Row " &
                i + 1 & ", Column " & j + 1))
      Next
    Next
    If TestMagic(n, a) Then
      txtAnswer.Text = "Yes"
    Else
      txtAnswer.Text = "No"
    End If
  End Sub

Function TestMagic(n As Integer, a(,) As Integer) As Boolean
    Dim sum, total As Integer     'sum is the sum of numbers in first row
    'Find sum of numbers in first row
    For j As Integer = 0 To (n - 1)
      sum += a(0, j)
    Next
    'Test row totals
    For i As Integer = 1 To (n - 1)
      total = 0
      For j As Integer = 0 To (n - 1)
        total += a(i, j)
      Next
      If total <> sum Then
        Return False
      End If
    Next
    'Test column totals
    For j As Integer = 0 To (n - 1)
      total = 0
      For i As Integer = 0 To (n - 1)
        total += a(i, j)
      Next
      If total <> sum Then
        Return False
      End If
    Next
```

```
'Test first diagonal
total = 0
For i As Integer = 0 To (n - 1)
  total += a(i, i)
Next
If total <> sum Then
  Return False
End If
'Test second diagonal
total = 0
For i As Integer = 0 To (n - 1)
  total += a(i, n - i - 1)
Next
If total <> sum Then
  Return False
End If
Return True
End Function
```

CHAPTER 8

EXERCISES 8.1

1. `Samuel Alito,NJ`
`Henry Baldwin,PA`

3. `Alito was appointed by Bush`
`Baldwin was appointed by Jackson`

5. `Alito,Samuel,2006`
`Baldwin,Henry,1830`

7. The new file contains the full names of the justices whose last name begins with the letter *B* and the years they were appointed to the court. The justices are ordered by the year they were appointed.

9. The new file is the same as the original file except that the last three fields have been deleted from each record.

11. The new file contains the names of the people who subscribe to either the *New York Times* or the *Wall Street Journal*, or both.

13. The new file contains the names of the people who subscribe to the *New York Times* but not the *Wall Street Journal*.

EXERCISES 8.2

1. `Hello`   **3.** `Bon Jour`   **5.** `You must enter a number.`

7. `Error occurred.`   **9.** `File Ages.txt contains an invalid age.`

11. The file Welcome.txt is created and has the following lines:

`Hello`
`Bon Jour`

13. The filespec `Greetings.txt` should be delimited with quotation marks.

15. There should be no quotations around the variable *name* as the argument to the CreateText method.

17. The variable *age* is declared within the Try-Catch-Finally block. Therefore it has block-level scope and is not available below the line **End Try**.

EXERCISES 8.3

1. No   **3.** No   **5.** No   **7.** No   **9.** No

CHAPTER 9

EXERCISES 9.1

1. Chopin is deleted from the list.

3. The currently selected item in **lstBox**, Mozart, is deleted.

5. The item Haydn is inserted into **lstBox** between Chopin and Mozart.

7. The names in the list box will appear in descending alphabetical order.

9. `cboBox.Text = "Dante"`

11. `cboBox.Items.Remove("Shakespeare")`

13. `cboBox.Items.RemoveAt(cboBox.Items.Count - 1)`

EXERCISES 9.2

1. The Tick event will be triggered every 5 seconds (5000 milliseconds).

3. The tooltip will appear one second after the cursor is hovered over a control.

5. A check mark appears in front of the *mnuOrderAsc* menu item.

7. The Tick event will be triggered every *intVar* seconds.

9. The name of one of the U.S. states is selected at random and displayed in **txtBox.**

11. Two states are selected at random and displayed in the list box.

13. The contents of the Clipboard are deleted.

15. The text currently selected in **txtBox**, if any, is copied into the Clipboard.

17. The text "el" is copied into the Clipboard.

19. "Hxxlo" is displayed in **txtBox**.

21. The contents of the Clipboard are assigned to the variable *strVar*.

23. A picture of an airplane will be placed in the picture box.

25. Clicking on the arrow on either end of the scroll bar will move the button the same ("large") distance as clicking on the bar between the scroll box and an arrow.

45. The menu item *mnuOrderAsc* is grayed out and cannot be selected.

EXERCISES 9.3

1. $106.00   **3.** `Your last name begins with K.`

CHAPTER 10

EXERCISES 10.1

1. (e)

3. (d)

5. (b)

39. `film`

EXERCISES 10.2

7. Add a record to the Cities table whose name field is empty or contains the same name as an already existing record.

9. `BindingSource1.Find("name", strVar) = -1`

17. "Apollo 13" does not appear in the key field of the Actors table. Thus the Rule of Referential Integrity would be violated.

19. Replace the table with two tables. The first table should contain the fields *name*, *address*, and *city*. The second table should contain the fields *city*, *state*, and *stateCapital*.

CHAPTER 11

EXERCISES 11.1

1. Any negative grade will be recorded as 0 and any grade greater than 100 will be recorded as 100.

3. Remove the keyword `WriteOnly` from the `Midterm` property block and add the following Get property procedure to it:

```
Get
   Return m_midterm
End Get
```

5. The properties `Midterm` and `Final` are write-only.

7. The property `SocSecNum` is initialized to the value `999-99-9999`.

9. The keyword `New` is missing from the third line of the event procedure.

11. The statement `nom = m_name` is not valid. *m_name* would need to be Public and referred to by scholar.m_name.

13. The statement `pupil.Midterm = scholar.Midterm` and the statement `1stGrades.Items.Add(pupil.Midterm)` are not valid. The Midterm property is write-only; it can be set, but cannot return a value.

15. `Country: Canada`
`Capital: Ottawa`
`Pop: 31 million`

EXERCISES 11.3

1. 4

3. 64

5. Can move Has jointed limbs and no backbone

7. The keyword "Overrides" should be "Inherits".

9. The Hi function should be declared with the "Overridable" keyword in class Hello and with the "Overrides" keyword in class Aussie.

11. The Hi function should be declared with the "Overrides" keyword in class Cowboy.

13. The Hello class should be declared with the "MustInherit" keyword, and the function Hi should be declared with the "MustOverride" keyword.

15. The Hello class should be declared with the "MustInherit" keyword, not "MustOverride".

INDEX